THE
Deadliest Outlaws
THE KETCHUM GANG AND THE WILD BUNCH

SECOND EDITION

Jeffrey Burton

Number 8 in the A. C. Greene Series

U^NT PRESS

University of North Texas Press

Denton, Texas

10 9 8 7 6 5 4 3 2

Permissions:
University of North Texas Press
1155 Union Circle #311336
Denton, TX 76203-5017

The paper used in this book meets the minimum requirements of the American National Standard for Permanence of Paper for Printed Library Materials, z39.48.1984. Binding materials have been chosen for durability.

Library of Congress Cataloging-in-Publication Data

Burton, Jeffrey, 1936–
  The deadliest outlaws : the Ketchum gang and the Wild Bunch / Jeffrey Burton.—2nd ed.
  p. cm.—(A.C. Greene series ; no. 8)
  Includes bibliographical references and index.
  ISBN 978-1-57441-270-3 (cloth : alk. paper)
  ISBN 978-1-57441-474-5 (paper: alk. paper)
  ISBN 978-1-57441-356-4 (ebook)
  1. Ketchum, Black Jack, 1863–1901. 2. Outlaws—West (U.S.)—Biography. 3. Ketchum, Black Jack, 1863–1901—Friends and associates—Biography. 4. West (U.S.)—Biography. 5. Gangs—West (U.S.)—History—19th century. 6. Train robberies—West (U.S.)—History—19th century. 7. Frontier and pioneer life—West (U.S.) 8. West (U.S.)—History—1860–1890. I. Title. II. Series: A.C. Greene series ; 8.
  F595.K4B79 2009
  978'.020922—dc22
  [B]
                                                                                    2009009188

The Deadliest Outlaws: The Ketchum Gang and the Wild Bunch, Second Edition is Number 8 in the A. C. Greene Series.

Other works by Jeffrey Burton include: *Dynamite and Six-shooter* (1970), the forerunner of this volume; *Bureaucracy, Blood Money, and Black Jack's Gang* (1984); *Indian Territory and the United States, 1866–1906* (1995); *Constable Dodge and the Pantano Train Robbers* (2006); and *Western Story* (2008).

To truth-seekers and other romantics,
everywhere, this book is dedicated.

CONTENTS

LIST OF ILLUSTRATIONS

After Chapter 13

Maps

ৠ PREFACE ৢ

My first attempt at a narrative study of the life and criminal career of Thomas Edward Ketchum was published unobtrusively in Santa Fe at the end of 1970. It was not a finished piece of historical writing; I was all too well aware of important source materials that existed only in the original and were inaccessible to someone who, at that time, had visited the United States only once and whose direct experience of Texas was limited to a nocturnal journey across the Panhandle. Still, thanks to the intercession of friends and fortune, I had been able to draw together enough hitherto hidden data to justify publication.

With the march of time and technology, material that had been unobtainable in the 1960s became available during the following decades. Besides that, my own travels after 1970 put me on first-hand terms with research materials whose custodians could not always answer postal queries. Above all, new friends emerged with information I might never have found unaided even if I had known of its existence and whereabouts; without them, my hopes of repairing the deficiencies of the earlier book could not have been fulfilled.

Those who have read or referred to *Dynamite and Six-shooter* will recognize the titles of seventeen of the twenty-three chapters that comprise the present narrative. Passages of direct quotations in the earlier book also reappear, since, of course, they are just as relevant to the present volume as to its predecessor. Naturally, too, the construction of the new book has been guided by the same general lines as the older one. The most noticeable difference between the two works is that this one is more than double the length of its forebear. The text that was judged to be adequate in 1970 has nearly all gone, progressively superseded by a continuous and eventually comprehensive fusion of new writing and rewriting. Those considerations are more than enough to compel the relinquishment of the cover title upon which the idea of a biography of Tom Ketchum was founded almost forty years ago.

I owe much in both moral and material assistance to the generosity, enthusiasm, industry, and expertise of Karen Holliday Tanner and John D. Tanner, of Fallbrook, California. As correspondents, co-researchers, and hosts, over a period of nine years to date, they first persuaded me to undertake the labor of revision and then made the task vastly lighter and pleasanter. The endnotes will, in some part, attest to the value and extent of their contribution.

In the early 1970s, I received some prime information on the Ketchum family background from Sam Ketchum's great-grandson, Berry Spradley, then of Houston and Anton, Texas, and now of Spring, Texas. When, after an interval of thirty years, contact was re-established, he kindly provided me with an extensive summary of more than three decades of continuing research into the personal and genealogical history of the Ketchum family, along with many of the illustrations that enrich this narrative. Whether or not it is true that, wherever life takes us, most of us are never far from our origins, I believe this to be the most important and impressive single source of information on the Ketchum brothers and their kin.

Tom and Sam Ketchum were rarely mentioned in a long, though intermittent correspondence with Dan Buck, of Washington, D.C., but his lodestar research, with Anne Meadows, on those contemporaries of the Ketchums, Robert Leroy Parker and Harry Longabaugh, offered a copious draught of inspiration by example.

Others who helped me and whom it is now my pleasure to thank are Bob Alexander, Maypearl, Texas; Marinell Ash, from New Mexico but then (1983–4) living in Edinburgh, Scotland; Barbara Barton, Knickerbocker, Texas; Michael Bell, Rubery, Birmingham, England; Eric Bittner, Archivist, and predecessor, N.A.R.A., Denver, Colorado; John Boessenecker, San Francisco, California; Bill Doty, Archivist, N.A.R.A., Laguna Niguel, Californai; Donna B. Ernst, Ocean City, Connecticut and Lederach, Pennsylvania; Jo-Ann E. Palmer, Secretary, Sutton County Historical Society, Sonora, Texas; Chuck Parsons, Luling, Texas; Lawrence R. Reno, Denver, Colorado; Carol Roark, Manager, Texas/Dallas History, Public Library, Dallas, Texas, whose thoughtfulness enabled me to read a large section of a crucially important broadsheet source; David Smurthwaite, National Army Museum, Chelsea, London, England; Bob and Jan Wybrow, of Bickley, Kent, England; past and present staff members of the Arizona Historical Society, Tucson, and the Texas State Archives, Austin, and the far-sighted folk who created and have maintained the research facilities in the Public Libraries at Little Rock, Arkansas, and Denver, Colorado, University of New Mexico, Albuquerque, University of Texas at El Paso, and, above all, University of Arizona, Tucson; and my wife, Shirley, who cheerfully did most of the early typing, rescued the text of many faded documents by reproducing them as typescript, lent much time and effort to the checking and editing of the eventual manuscript, and finally retyped the whole thing onto a new computer system.

J.B.
21 June 2006

A Note to the Second Edition

At the very moment that the first edition of this book was coming off the press in England, late in April, 2007, its author set foot for the first time in San Angelo, Texas, having at last reached what many might regard as the logical point of entry for research on Sam and Tom Ketchum and their place in the history of West and Southwest Texas. Long before the end of a fruitful but woefully brief visit it began to look as though a second edition might be needed. That impression was resoundingly confirmed during a second visit just over a year later.

I had known for some years that a member of the Ketchum gang had dictated two sets of reminiscences on the incident-crammed decade that followed his bail-absconding departure from the United States early in 1901. I had not known that he had also gone on the record with recollections of his prior experiences as a posse-dodging and train-robbing fugitive. This is probably the most apposite as well as the handiest time and place to answer the hitherto unasked question: having subjected the memoirs of Dave Atkins to rigorous study, I have no doubt whatsoever of their authenticity.

Thus my first thanks go to Suzanne Campbell and her colleagues at the West Texas Collection, and Shannon Sturm, University Archivist, Porter Henderson Library, at Angelo State University, where I was a beneficiary of their enthusiasm, helpfulness, and knowledge. The bibliography and endnotes will give an idea of the extent and range of the debt this second edition owes to the holdings of the WTC.

In New Mexico, the tendency has always been to regard the story of Sam and Tom Ketchum as a New Mexico story, because that is where it ended. I have always seen it more as a Texas story, because that is where it started and where most of its future was shaped. I might, therefore, have overcompensated in the past by not giving quite enough attention to several aspects of the closing episodes of the Ketchums' story. I hope I have succeeded this time in righting any such imbalance. I am grateful for the advice and cheerful assistance of James Jeffrey and colleagues at the Public Library, Denver, Colorado, during my first visit to that city since 1972.

I am also more than glad to renew my acknowledgment of the peerless research facilities at the University of Arizona, Tucson.

Throughout the last year, John Tanner and Bob Alexander have continued to donate time from their own projects to assist mine with generous portions of information and encouragement. Nothing matters more than the friendship and goodwill of one's fellow toilers.

I thank Jo-Ann Palmer for further glimpses of the days that followed Will Carver's death in Sonora, Texas; Ross McSwain, of San Angelo, for his excellent company and for affording me an opportunity for a more extended view of the Arden, Sherwood, and Mertzon area than would otherwise have been possible; and Vernon, of Red Ball Taxis, for indulging my insistence on wandering around Christoval and what remains of old Knickerbocker.

Almost as I was drafting the foregoing lines, I found myself in the happy position of being able to express gratitude to Marilyn Foraker, of Lordsburg, New Mexico, and Jan Devereaux, of Maypearl, Texas, for allowing me the use of photographs that—only the day before yesterday, it seems—I could only have dreamed of ever seeing.

As always, it is to my wife, Shirley, that I am indebted for the patience, application, and technological dexterity needed to render this work presentable.

J.B.

9 November 2008

Acknowledgments from Dynamite and Six-Shooter

This book could not have been written without the generous assistance of many people who made available to the author much of the raw material from which this study of Tom Ketchum and his times has been fashioned. Writing is hard work that has to be borne alone; research, more often than not, is the sum of an author's indebtedness to others. This author can but hope that he has made good and conscientious use of all the help given to him.

A special word of thanks, first, to Phil Cooke, of Santa Fe, New Mexico. Over a period of several years he interviewed, read, transcribed—well, what I should say is that without his efforts and exhortations the book might not even have been started; more latterly, he and Mrs Cooke, Nena, even bestirred into useful activity a guest who, left to his own inclinations, might cheerfully have whiled away sun-laden hours with the dreams no stuff was ever made on.

Mrs Joyce Hines, of East Ham, London, deserves a particular word of praise for turning a manuscript that was written almost entirely in longhand into a neat final typescript.

I was fortunate enough to encounter, either in person or through correspondence, many other helpful and thoughtful people. Through them I obtained a great deal of information from both primary and secondary sources.

Rose Marie Alderete, Clerk of the Court, and Glenna Lawrence, Assistant, Supreme Court of New Mexico, Santa Fe; Mary Arnett, Librarian, The Light, San Antonio, Texas; Joseph "Mack" Axford, Tombstone, Arizona; J.E. Baker, Warden, and Tom J. Trujillo, Records Supervisor, State Penitentiary of New Mexico, Santa Fe; Larry Ball, of Boulder, Colorado; Xanthus "Kit" Carson, of Albuquerque, New Mexico; Mary G. Eckhoff, Assistant Director, Diplomatic, Legal, and Fiscal Records Division, National Archives, Washington, D.C.; Kay Evatz, University of Colorado Libraries, Western Historical Collection, Boulder, Colorado; Frank A. Eyman, Superintendent, Arizona State Prison, Florence, Arizona: Bill Farringdon, of Santa Fe, New Mexico; George Fitzpatrick, of Albuquerque; Jeanette Harris, Public Library, San Antonio, Texas; Susie Henderson, Museum Library, Santa Fe; Virginia P. Hoke, Southwest Reference Public Library, El Paso, Texas; Myra Ellen Jenkins, Archivist, State Archives of New Mexico, Santa Fe; the staff—I don't know any of their names—of the Photoduplication Service of the Library of Congress, Washington, D.C.; Lady Luck, of no fixed abode, who smiled from time to time, and not always to deceive; Louis E. Montgomery, Brady, Texas; Kathleen Pierson, State Historical Society of Colorado, Colorado State Museum, Denver; Colin Rickards, now usually in Toronto, Ontario, with whom I discussed the shape of the projected book on a number of occasions, and who offered much good advice; G. Martin Ruoss, Special Collections Librarian, Coronado Room, Zimmerman Library, Albuquerque; and Margaret Sparks, Research Librarian, Arizona Pioneers' Historical Society, Tucson, Arizona.

My grateful thanks to them all.

[10 May 1970]

Note for the Paperback Edition of
The Deadliest Outlaws

A stipulation that any textual changes introduced to the paperback reprint of a hard-cover book must not disturb the original pagination, permits little scope for revision. Fortunately for the purpose at hand, and except for two items to be summarized in this Note, not enough significant material has emerged since 2009 for the precondition to give cause for regret.

Nonetheless, a number of textual improvements can be accommodated within the existing pagination. The most substantial of these is the rewording of part of p. 83; the most important, the correction to the legend for Illustration #12, originally described as a photograph of William T. "Black Jack" Christian. The figure in that photo may well remain forever unknown; but, thanks to the persistence of Robert G. McCubbin, we may now say with almost absolute confidence that the subject, whether dead or alive, was *not* Black Jack Christian. We still await the discovery of an authenticated photograph of Christian.

Elsewhere, nearly a score of emendations have been brought to the main text, many of them on pp. 266–268, and the legend for Illustration #10 has been reworded. A dozen endnotes have been corrected or extended, and the same applies to a few Index entries and a couple of items in the Bibliography.

Several works relevant in greater or lesser degree to the subject of this book were published or awaiting publication while the first printing of this Second Edition was in the press. It would be remiss of me not to notice them now:

A short novel entitled *Black Jack Ketchum Before And After He Was Hung* (2009) is founded on the engaging premise that Tom Ketchum's execution ceremony was a hoax, devised and stage-managed to enable him to see out the balance of his natural life in Mexico. The book is of interest because its author, Beth Smith Aycock, is a grand-niece of Tom's brother, Berry Ketchum, and because, most unusually for a novel, it is illustrated by photographs, one of which shows Tom as a member of a trail-driving crew at Clayton, New Mexico.

The last two years have seen the publication of *The Sundance Kid*, by Donna B. Ernst (2009), and *The Bronco Bill Gang*, by Karen Holliday Tanner and the late (and greatly missed) John D. Tanner, Jr., (2011). These are authoritative studies of the lives and misdeeds of desperadoes who, on occasion, were not far from the center of the story of Tom Ketchum's gang.

Elzy Lay's fortunes were more closely bound up with those of the Ketchum gang. He is the subject of *The Educated Outlaw* (2009), a brief but informative family memoir by his grandson, Harvey Lay Murdock. Incongruously enough, Murdock's title echoes a phrase coined in the 1930s by Charles Kelly, whose knowledge of Elzy's home and educational background was very imperfect. The value of Murdock's book rests mainly on the facts he brings out about Lay's personal history following the conviction in New Mexico that ended his criminal career. As to the criminal episodes themselves, fuller and more accurate accounts are available elsewhere.

Then there are the works I had previously overlooked. By far the most impressive is *Riding the Outlaw Trail: In the Footsteps of Butch Cassidy and the Sundance Kid*, by Simon Casson and Richard Adamson (2004). Not only did Casson and Adamson accomplish the epic horseback ride from El Paso, Texas, to Climax, Saskatchewan, via Alma, Robbers' Roost, Brown's Park, Hole-in-the-Wall, and the Badlands, but, to quote Ranulph Fiennes's Foreword, did it "the hard way . . . at the height of a dry Western summer and without back-up." A fittingly remarkable book for a most remarkable feat.

In the spring of 2001 the centennial of Tom Ketchum's execution was celebrated in Clayton. One hundred copies of an unannotated sixty-page booklet by Shelley Jersig, bearing the functional title *Black Jack Ketchum*, were issued in conjunction with the macabre junket. Its early pages may be based partly upon family sources, but most of the other details will be recognizable to anyone familiar with previously published works on Ketchum. Much of the dialogue probably originated with the booklet.

Now to the two supplementary items that I could not insert into the main body of this work:

The first relates to one of two letters Tom Ketchum (now involuntarily left-handed) wrote to kinfolk after he had been sentenced to hang. He asked for $1,000 in the deluded belief, or under the pretense, that this sum was all he needed to remove himself from the shadow of the gallows. Even if his sisters or their husbands believed him, they did not produce the money.

There remains only the melancholy task of extending Endnote 10, Chapter 8 (p. 391):

Larry Link, the affable and personable owner of Steins Pass Ghost Town, New Mexico, was murdered there early on the morning of June 7, 2011. The crime is still unsolved. The Link family hope to reopen the Ghost Town soon.

We wish them well.

In the quiet interval between the initial publication of the Second Edition and the Publisher's decision to proceed with a paperback printing, several friends have helped me in their several ways: Bob Alexander (renewed encouragement and the inspiration of his own example); Dan Buck (much material on the Logan brothers); Bob Pugh, of Tucson, Arizona (books, information about books, and friendly guidance generally); and Berry Spradley (Ketchum family and other Southwest Texas memorabilia). My warmest thanks go out to them all.

[4 March 2012]

THE
Deadliest Outlaws

❴ 1 ❵

MEET THE GANG

The oral tradition of fable and ballad was fading in Tom Ketchum's own lifetime. He will never be one of those folklore villains whose violent and lawless ways have been burnished with an illusive romance. If he is remembered at all, it is mostly for the peculiar circumstances that attended the curtailment of his earthly career. Yet, as a man much noted in his day, who stood out above most others in his profession, he deserves more than passing mention. He and his companions were the boldest and deadliest outlaws ever to ride the Southwest.

Tom Ketchum and his older brother Sam were on the dodge in Texas, New Mexico, and Arizona for less than four years, and their career in serious outlawry lasted only from the spring of 1897 to the summer of 1899. When it ended, the gang had notched up seven killings—five of them murders in cold blood—and seven train holdups, five of which yielded a dividend. Their story did not end with the death of Sam and the capture of Tom, for their associates continued to ride, rob, and kill for several years more, usually in the company of some of the principal outlaws from the Northern Plains—Harvey Logan ("Kid Curry"), Robert Leroy Parker ("Butch Cassidy"), and Harry Longabaugh ("the Sundance Kid").

During most of its short but crowded life, the Ketchum gang had only four members: Tom and Sam Ketchum, Will Carver, and Dave Atkins. As long as this combination held together, Tom was leader, although, as he once stated, "everybody was consulted in most things." Cassidy's close ally William Ellsworth "Elzy" Lay, Bruce "Red" Weaver, and Edwin Cullen all rode briefly with the Ketchums. Also associated with the gang were Ben Kilpatrick, of Concho County, Texas, and his brothers George and Ed. Ben may have ridden alongside the Ketchums in 1898 before going north to join Logan, Cassidy, Longabaugh, and George Currie.

Tom's was always the gang's dominant personality, until the others found at last that they could stand no more of him and told him so. "Billy" Reno, a railroad detective who earned the right to judge the traits that made Tom Ketchum so dangerous a criminal, needed only five words: "a tiger in human form."

Dark skinned and black haired, he stood about an inch above six feet and weighed 180 to 190 pounds. "At close range," wrote the rancher Jack Culley, recalling his journey in the train which carried the convicted bandit to the penitentiary, "Tom Ketchum struck me as being one of the most powerful men I've ever seen, with corresponding activity. I had a feeling he could have taken the two sheriffs and everyone else on the coach and thrown us out onto the track . . . Every inch . . . seemed to me brawn and muscle." Leonard Alverson, who was wrongfully accused of taking part in one of the gang's holdups, also spoke of Tom's "wonderful physique."

Walter Hovey, whose connection with the Ketchum gang was similar to Alverson's, may have met Tom only twice, but remembered him as "a very fine looking specimen of a man."

Bob Lewis, who knew the Ketchums in both Texas and New Mexico, maintained that Tom was "a coward at heart." Lewis's neighbor William French condemned Tom and Sam even more damningly as "sneak-thieves and murderers . . . nothing but dirty thieves and murderers," whom the likes of Butch Cassidy "always despised;" but French affected an authority that he ought to have possessed but did not. He lived many years in New Mexico as manager of a ranch that ran cattle in two sections of the territory where the Ketchums were well known, yet never met either of them. Nor had he heard so much as a word about their background in Texas, the scene of their more successful criminal exploits.

Gerome Shield disagreed. Unlike French, he knew what he was talking about. He also knew Tom better than Lewis did. Shield had grown up alongside Tom in San Saba County, Texas, and, like him, moved to Tom Green County, where he served eight years as sheriff. He paid tribute to Tom's wonderful nerve," though he thought Sam "had better." On this question, the weight of informed testimony from elsewhere supports Shield against Lewis. Walter Hovey, for example, who went to prison on the Ketchums' account and hence had no reason to speak fawningly of them, described Tom as "utterly devoid of fear." A host of witnesses swore that he died game. The preponderance of evidence affirms that he lived game, too.

But Lewis's assessment of Tom as "the most cold-blooded individual I have ever met" has many an echo. John Loomis, a Concho County rancher well acquainted with the Ketchum family in Texas, characterized him as "undoubtedly one of the cruellest and most cold blooded killers in the whole history of the frontier." Joseph "Mack" Axford's succinct comment, "a very brutal man," derived from his talks with Dave Atkins, covers the whole range. But brutality need not imply cowardice. Ketchum was both brave and brutal.

He was devious and cunning, too; his instinct for concealment when in flight was as sharp as that of the wolverine. Loomis believed that, once Tom became an outlaw, he never slept in a house, but "lived in the wilds like a wolf." Though not much given to laughter, he sometimes showed a dry, sardonic twist of humor; while the childishness in him was as apt to manifest itself in a practical joke as in a swirl of rage.

Opinions differed over whether his features connoted the intelligence he undoubtedly possessed. "Tom Ketchum's face," commented Culley, "did not impress me as being that of a particularly intelligent man; it was the face essentially of a man of action. The small black eyes were the most notable feature of it, shining and piercing, and possessed of an extraordinary alertness, like that you see in the eyes of some wild animals. This feature it was doubtless that accounted for his ability to detect, and draw a bead on, an object simultaneously." According to one newspaper-man, they were "marvelous eyes . . . small, brown or greenish gray as his mood changed and indefinably swift and menacing." Another reporter noted that Ketchum had "an intelligent face and a pair of bright, piercing eyes." Gerrit Taft, a senior official of the Wells, Fargo express company, describing the outlaw for purposes of identification, drew attention to the "dark flashing eyes." Miguel Otero, the governor of New Mexico who declined to mitigate the death sentence pronounced upon Ketchum, likened them to "black coals of fire . . . piercing and radiant." Jack Potter, portraying Tom as "a big, handsome fellow with raven black hair and a swarthy complexion," confirmed that "his eyes were flashing black." Albert Thompson, who interviewed him when he was being held for trial, and again on the eve of his execution, observed that, when talking, Ketchum looked one straight in the face through eyes that were "dark, small, and piercing."

Behind those eyes lay a nimble mind, an uncertain temper, and a sullen and malevolent disposition. Tom's "natural capacity for leadership," which, Thompson declared, "was obvious upon a moment's acquaintance," holds much of the explana-tion for his success in crime before this quality was undermined by the destructive side of his character, until no one was willing to be led by him. A newspaper editor in San Angelo, Texas, perhaps quoting or paraphrasing Gerome Shield, commented with more than a hint of understatement that Tom "was known [as] a most overbear-ing man." John Wright, a significant but enigmatical figure at the outset of Ketchum's criminal history, told Loomis that "he had never seen a man with such an insane tem-per as Tom." "Human emotions seemed entirely foreign to his nature," observed one press correspondent; "An unloved leader, too heartless even for their [his fellow out-laws'] turbulent spirits," another declared; "Ignorant and brutish," was the dismis-sively terse verdict of a third. These were the pronouncements of newspaper reporters with nothing to draw upon beyond a single meeting with their subject, in his last hours or minutes of life, and a stock of hearsay, some of it created or elabo-rated by the newspapers themselves. Even so, they tallied with the views or judgments of people who had known Tom for years, before he became a hopeless and doomed convict. Most of the Western outlaws, like most of the criminals of any time or place, were quickly caught or killed because they liked or trusted too many people. Tom Ketchum was taken because he liked or trusted practically no one. Both his unbounded nerve and his bouts of wanton cruelty may be set down to his lack of regard for anything that breathed, not excluding himself.

In 1955, Elton Cunningham, a storekeeper in Alma and Mogollon, New Mexico, at the end of the nineteenth century, claimed that his friend Elzy Lay called Tom Ketchum (though not to his face) "the dirtiest bastard that ever lived." Cunningham, who apparently never met Tom or Sam, may or may not have been over-quoting Lay.

Whether or not Lay (or Cunningham) overdrew the picture, others did. Accusations that Tom Ketchum tortured animals, birds, and even insects were current in his own time and were repeated later, but they were always reported from hearsay, never from direct observation. They are not borne out by the direct recollections of people who had known him before he turned to crime. While we cannot be certain that they were untrue, a measure of skepticism would be in order. Such charges were conventionally leveled at individuals characterized in the public mind as villainy personified. After his capture in New Mexico, some of his old neighbors in Knickerbocker, Texas, who knew only too well just how dangerous an enemy he could be, still declared that Tom Ketchum was not nearly as bad as the more sensational newspapers portrayed him.

These unnamed people might have played down Tom's delinquencies to diminish their own culpability in cooperating with the gang; as Loomis recalled, "although the ranchmen in the region where they had their [Texas] hideout, feared them, they more or less protected them, and let them have horses. They realized that their own lives and property were at their mercy." Loomis did not add, but others did, that those who helped the gang were not always or solely motivated by fear; they were often paid for their trouble, and doubtless well paid. These standards applied in southwest and northeast New Mexico, as well as in their home territory of southwest Texas.[1]

Sam Ketchum, nearly ten years Tom's elder, and for that reason sometimes called "Dad" by his friends, was different in nearly every aspect of character. He was a big man, more than six feet tall but a shade shorter than his brother. He was fair skinned, with reddish-blond hair, blue eyes, and heavily freckled face and arms. "I picture him vividly," wrote Culley, "as the finest figure of a man in my recollection." Bob Lewis, whose loathing of Tom we have mentioned, said of his brother: "Sam Ketchum was a brave and courageous man and if his brother hadn't been such a bad influence he would have been all right." Tom Chaney (or Cheney), a Texas neighbor who confessedly knew outlaws "about as well as anyone not to have been one myself," had this to say: "Sam Ketchum was a mighty good man to die an outlaw. He was a very good friend of mine. He never would have been into anything, but got into trouble trying to save Tom." Axford also thought him "a fine man." Sam was always popular and his later career mystified many people who had known him on the range. Only Albert Thompson dissented; he called Sam "as irresponsible as his younger and more cunning relative." But Thompson never met Sam Ketchum, and it is not clear whether his opinion was guided by persons who had known Sam in Texas and disliked him for unstated reasons, or by his own imagination. Still, Sam's decision to take the left-hand trail cannot be attributed wholly to Tom's "bad influence." After Tom and several companions had murdered a rancher in Texas, Sam followed them west, presumably in order to avoid having to answer questions. To that extent, Tom Ketchum was the cause of his brother's outlawry. What was more significant, however, was that Sam was forty-two years old at this time, and he had nothing to show for a life which had been chiefly devoted to honest toil. This may go far towards explaining why, in the spring of 1896, he threw in with Tom. Thereafter, one thing followed another until soon there could be no turning back. Eventually he assumed leadership of the gang, only to demonstrate that there was little point in pulling a

successful outlaw coup unless the getaway could be handled as skillfully as the robbery itself.[2]

The third member of the gang, and the only one of the original four to venture
into the far more dangerous field of bank robbery, was Will Carver. Lighthaired and
fair-complexioned, but deeply sun-tanned, he was just below medium height for the
times—no more than five foot six or seven out of his boots—and rather stocky build,
weighing from 150 to 160 pounds.

The fullest description we have of him was published in the summer of 1899,
when his notoriety was at its peak:

> Age about 35; height 5 feet 8 inches; weight 170 pounds; medium dark complexion;
> full face, but not round; heavy dark brown mustache and dark beard, which shows red
> tint; square build; heavy body; broad across the eyes; eyelids open far back; when
> walking throws his body back with his feet forward; appearance of a cowboy gambler.

This is impressive as a summary of Carver's telltale characteristics, but less
secure on the closer details of his physical features. Two years later, when he was still
only thirty-two, his age was judged to be between thirty-five and forty. He was then
said to be only five foot six in height, and 150 pounds in weight, with brown hair
showing traces of dye. The reference to dye is significant; at different times he used
different tints, including red and black.

Leonard Alverson, who was well acquainted with the outlaws and their ways,
characterized Carver as "a nice fellow but very melancholy over the death of his wife."
Seaton Keith, a neighbor of the Ketchums in Texas, employed Carver and thought
him "a good, quiet, steady boy" who "seemed to go all to pieces" when his wife and
baby daughter died. Keith's friend and fellow-rancher John Loomis said much the
same: the outlaw "had a nice personality and everybody liked him" during his cowboy years; he was "devoted to his wife," and, after her death, he "fell to pieces," and
"got in with a wrong crowd." James H. Yardley, the long-serving foreman of Fayette
Tankersley's 7D outfit in Irion County, Texas, adjudged him "one of the best hands I
ever saw," and added: "We all liked him and was sorry to hear of his death . . . his
name got worse than his ways."

Thompson, who never met Carver but collected a miscellany of anecdotal material on the gang from first hand, depicted him in much harsher terms: "cold, fiendish,
calculating and a dead shot." There is plenty of corroboration for Thompson's last
assertion, but otherwise the judgment is a poor one. Whatever else he may have been,
William Carver was not "fiendish." Although cool-tempered and usually level-
headed, he seems not to have possessed the shrewdness of the "calculating" man.
Amiable on the surface, with a quick turn of wit, he was inwardly reticent—apparently unable or unwilling to enter into close friendships—rather than "cold."

Until the last weeks of his life, he avoided controversy and gunplay whenever he
could; up to then, he seemed to have nothing of the firebrand in him. But when he
was forced into a position when he really had to fight he was as game and deadly a
gunman as ever looked down the sights of a Winchester. Reported opinion is

unanimous in one respect: he was absolutely without fear. In the phrase of Tom Chaney, "he wasn't scared of the old Devil." An article in the *San Angelo Standard* sums him up best.

> Will Carver . . . was a plain, unassuming, quiet sort of desperado, of a very retiring disposition, and rather shunned than courted notoriety. He was adverse to society, and preferred to dwell in the solitudes of the great southwestern plains, with a few choice spirits . . .

That newspaper story was, in effect, Carver's obituary notice, and it was written because, a few months earlier, the bandit, throwing aside his customary reserve, had taken to deserting the "solitudes of the plains" for the hurly-burly of the red light districts, consequently to become either contemptuous of danger or merely careless in his movements. The death of Sam Ketchum, the capture of Elzy Lay and Tom Ketchum, his own narrow escapes, and his final flush of success with Cassidy and Longabaugh, loosened his grip on the realities of a life on the run. Finally, he began to hunt for trouble and to throw his reputation about, like a celebrity convinced of his own impregnability. Survival, for an outlaw, depended upon constant watchfulness. That is why few survived for long. Will Carver grew casual to the point of recklessness, and walked into trouble, with the usual result.[3]

Dave Atkins has always been the least known of the band, but he may have been the most interesting. His success in evading judicial retribution for twenty years after the downfall of the Ketchums and Carver is proof of his mastery of the three Rs of resilience, resourcefulness, and ruthlessness. He took part in at least three robberies before he broke with Tom Ketchum. In later years, his descent into crime was described with judicious economy by a former neighbor, Dave McCrohan. Atkins "killed a man, then deserted his family to escape punishment. This led him to train robbing, which was the most popular [form of] robbing during that age." He was five feet eleven inches in height, slimly-built, and weighed about one hundred and fifty pounds. His complexion was "very dark"—perhaps from an Indian strain which Joseph Axford, who met him in Arizona, mistakenly believed to be Comanche and an informant for the Wells, Fargo express company correctly thought to be Cherokee. His hair was brown and he sometimes wore a thin mustache. The description compiled by Pinkerton's National Detective Agency observed that he "drops his head when talking," and called attention to his "peculiar slouchy walk." Gerome Shield described him as "a fine shot and not afraid of man or devil." The memoirs he dictated barely a decade after the fall of the gang reveal a sharp but selective memory, a sense of the absurd, and a dry, sometimes mordant wit.[4]

Rather quaintly, the gang dubbed him "Tommy Atkins," the generic nickname of the British soldier. After his breach with Tom Ketchum, he tried briefly to go straight. Axford believed that "he had the quality to make it that way;" but Dave's difficulties were more complicated, and his personality more unstable, than Axford ever realized. Homesickness and domestic worries drove him to surrender in Montana, but once he was back in Texas he dared not face trial for the murder that had provided the original excuse for his outlawry. He fled to South Africa, and enlisted in the British Army, though not under the name of Atkins. For years after that he wandered from country to country, until at last he was caught, convicted, and imprisoned. His fate may have been the most wretched of all, for he passed the last thirty years of a long life in an asylum for the criminally insane.

Elzy Lay, previously Butch Cassidy's partner, and as such involved in armed robbery in Idaho and Utah, was with the gang for some three or four months. Many people, including Governor Otero, were genuinely impressed by his fortitude and gallantry. If others took a more critical view of his ability to charm authority, they have left no testimony to that effect. Almost alone of the truly notorious outlaws of the West, he was accorded sympathetic treatment. To his credit, he never reneged upon the trust placed in him.

Although, in the opinion William French attributed to Cassidy, Red Weaver lacked sand and was fit only to act as messenger, he probably assisted in at least one holdup. Loudmouthed and aggressive, he was also wilier than he appeared to be. He was arrested on three or four occasions, but never convicted; and at one stage may have played a double game without being detected. There was a retributive irony about the manner of his death.

All that needs to be said about Ed Cullen at this point is that he was a Texan, like the Ketchums, Carver, Atkins, and Weaver, and that his active career as a road-agent lasted for less than three hours.

Ben Kilpatrick worked on some of the same Texas ranches as the Ketchums and Carver. His acquaintance with them seems to have been intermittently renewed in New Mexico and further north, in such outlaw retreats as Hole-in-the-Wall and Brown's Hole. In time, his notoriety matched theirs, but his criminal career ran mainly parallel rather than in tandem with theirs, though he might have helped them in at least one of the Texas train robberies. His closest confederate in outlawry was Harvey Logan, perhaps the cleverest and certainly the most lethal of all the northern plains desperadoes.

Kilpatrick's attitude to the world beyond the narrow confines of his upbringing and early environment was often truculent or surly, while his demeanor and behavior were no strangers to boorish aggression. These displays concealed the intelligence he certainly possessed, but prison taught him to apply it to dissimulation. This helped to get him out of prison, but was not enough to save him from being fatally outwitted by an express messenger. Three of his brothers—George, Ed, and Felix—followed him into outlawry.[5]

One other man was involved with the Ketchum gang, though not quite part of it. Thomas Capehart was a cowboy and bronco-buster whose story has no beginning and no end, beyond the belief that he was born and died somewhere in Texas. The name appears to have been his real one, though it may have been derived from the Germanic Kephart and was sometimes misspelled that way. His identity had been obscured by persistent but wholly groundless assertions that his name was merely an alias for Harvey Logan, or, alternatively, for Harry Longabaugh.[6]

Unlike most, Capehart was, to some extent, pushed into crime. Along with Alverson, Hovey, and others, he was wrongly accused of one of the Ketchums' train holdups. When, eventually, he did turn outlaw, the Ketchum gang was already finished.

On May 8, 1897, the Ketchums' principal hometown newspaper, the *San Angelo Standard*, published the following item:

> A special from Clifton, Ariz., to the Albuquerque, N.M., Democrat, under date of April 29, says: Thomas Ketchum, alias Black Jack, was killed by a sheriff's posse at Charlie Williams['s] ranch 25 miles southwest of here, yesterday morning.

Brief as it was, the dispatch was at fault in three respects. First, the outlaw called Black Jack was killed eighteen miles east of Clifton, not twenty-five miles west of it. Second, the fatal bullet was fired not by a sheriff's posseman, but by a deputy U.S. marshal from New Mexico. Third, and more palpably, Thomas Ketchum was not only very much alive, but on the brink of a coup in crime that would outclass anything in that line attempted by his fallen precursor.

Tom Ketchum was not the real "Black Jack" and his gang was not the "Black Jack gang." But an unwitting fusion of identities, springing from a complexity of coincidence and controversy, and perhaps abetted by Tom himself even while the original bearer of the title still lived, established him immovably in the popular mind as the celebrated Black Jack. Almost forty years ago, the author predicted that Ketchum would be Black Jack "in scores of magazine articles as yet undreamed of." It still looks a good forecast.[7]

Because of the fallacious belief that he was "the original Black Jack," Ketchum has been connected with many crimes in New Mexico and Arizona, such as the robbery or attempted robbery of the bank at Nogales in 1896, which were the work of William Christian, the true Black Jack, or were assigned to "the Black Jack gang," when neither Christian nor Ketchum was to blame. Conversely, Ketchum's operations in Texas, where he was most successful, have been given scant attention or none.

It will be seen that some of the representatives of law and order were not outstanding for their integrity, their courage, or their sense of duty. The question of integrity was not paramount. People who have been robbed do not really care overmuch about the private character of a thief-catcher, as long as the thief is caught. Some of the officers who ought to have been keeping close tabs on the outlaw gangs of the Southwest did not even try very hard. Their failings placed a heavy burden upon the far fewer lawmen who strove to do all—or more than all—that duty required of them.

There were other handicaps. Successive United States marshals of New Mexico and Arizona, Democratic and Republican, were not making empty excuses when, every so often, they wrote to Washington to outline the difficulties of getting close to such outlaws as the Ketchums. The following, from William Griffith, marshal of Arizona, is typical of their letters:

> . . . [T]he country in which these parties operate is of great extent, parts of it very rough and mountainous and all of it very sparsely settled. The posse in search of them

must be in condition to travel fast and far at a moment's notice. This necessitates their being unencumbered with a pack train. They must, therefore, depend upon the country for food. The only places where this food can be obtained are at cattle ranches scattered throughout the country from 30 to 50 miles apart. Some of the owners are in sympathy with the outlaws and the news of a visit of a posse to their ranches could be scattered far and wide as fast as horseflesh could carry it. Even were the proprietors of all these ranches favorably disposed, they dare not sell or give aid to the posse. Did they do so their lives and property could pay the penalty as has happened in the past . . .

I would respectfully request . . . that the posse be allowed to purchase supplies in the field without being required to furnish receipts therefor.

I am liable to be called upon any moment to put a man in the field and am unwilling to do so unless allowed to exercise my discretion as to the method of supplying such men when on duty. I do not wish to uselessly jeopardize the lives of my men or the residents of the country in which they must operate, nor do I intend to put a force in the field unless there is a fair prospect of ridding the country of these outlaws . . . [8]

The rule that federal officers and possemen could claim expenses only on production of receipts and vouchers irritated and frustrated the marshals more than any other of the numerous obstacles to law enforcement.

Griffith's counterpart in New Mexico, Creighton Foraker, found the Department sympathetic, but powerless, when he tried to employ Will Loomis—chief deputy under the previous marshal—as an undercover agent. Foraker, a hefty man who could wield a hefty subjunctive, expressed his case thus:

I would have him authorized to render on oath an actual expenses account, to be approved by myself, and the U.S. Attorney and the judge, but not supported by vouchers, as he would as well take a brass band with him if he be required to advertise himself by procuring vouchers for expenses as a government officer. . . . That it is important to the government to suppress this gang I presume I need not argue. That my request to put a single man in the field is not unreasonable I will also not discuss . . .

Foraker's letter, dated October 9, 1897, was studied in Washington. In the end it was decided that Loomis could be so employed, but that he could not be given the power to make arrests. This was not quite what Foraker had wanted, but it was the best that could be done by officials who were bound by regulations laid down by Congress.[9]

Tom and Sam sometimes hid out on the ranch of their elder brother, Berry, or with their brother-in-law Bige Duncan, near San Angelo, Texas. Near the 7D ranch in Irion County, a little further to the west, they and the gang had a hideaway on what is known locally as Ketchum Mountain, or the Ketchum Hills. Here the "deep rough canyons and jutting cliffs . . . served as a protection as well as a lookout station." They were all well known at numerous ranch houses and horse camps throughout southwest Texas, in much of New Mexico, and in southeast Arizona. Bill Lutley, who ran a few cattle under the Bar Boot brand near Wildcat Canyon, the band's favorite retreat in Arizona, saw a great deal of the outlaws and kept his mouth shut. So did Ben Kemp, who ranched near the Black Range, in southwest New Mexico, where the bandits had a secluded hideout close to Wahoo Canyon. Lutley and Kemp were but two among many in Arizona and New Mexico.[10]

Always, though, there was the danger for the outlaws that someone might betray them, either deliberately or inadvertently. As Kemp commented when recalling one encounter in Wahoo Canyon, "Ketchum and his pal were friendly enough and laughed and joked with the cowboys, but it was easy to see they were continuously on the alert."[11] The capture of Elzy Lay was the eventual outcome of the gang's long-standing acquaintance with Virgil Hogue Lusk.

In all probability, the Ketchums first met Lusk when they were working as cowboys in the Pecos Valley. He ranched at Chimney Wells, some twenty-five miles east of the town of Eddy (later Carlsbad), New Mexico. It became their habit, in later years, to stop by at Lusk's place for a meal and a change of horses. They might trade horses with Lusk; or they might leave their worn-out mounts (usually stolen from one or other of the large cattle companies) somewhere in the vicinity of Lusk's range, intending to recover them the next time they passed through, perhaps several months later. This went on for two or three years until, in the end, Old Man Lusk decided that he had seen enough of it.[12] Lay might not have been captured if he had not put too much ground between himself and his rifle, but his initial mistake was to forget that Lusk might one day tire of being used by outlaws.

The cowboys, even more than the smaller ranchers, took sides with the outlaws. A minority were fugitives themselves. The general attitude was governed mainly by a deep prejudice against all lawmen and by the fact that almost all of the bandits of the Great Plains had punched cows at one time or another. J.S. "Rox" Grumbles, a pioneer cattleman in Lincoln County, New Mexico, vouchsafed to Jack Culley that "Tom Ketchum was the finest cowhand I ever knew."[13]

Nor should it be overlooked that some ranch women were more kindly disposed towards the outlaw than to the lawman. The outlaw, we are told, would usually offer to help with the dishes and would eschew rough language, whereas quite often the officer was a graceless, coarsely spoken fellow.

As a group, the Ketchum gang were anything but extrovert. "They are known to the officers as bushmen," said one report, "as they rarely go into a town, and spend all their time in the bush on ranches, where they are not likely to be found."[14] They were fond of gambling but, for a while at least, they kept away from liquor. Their abstinence, although amounting to no more than common sense, is testimony to the authority or persuasiveness of Tom Ketchum, who rarely drank anything stronger than coffee: after the others had got rid of Tom, they hastened their own downfall by hitting the bottle hard and behaving ineptly in other ways.

In two years and three months the gang stole well over $130,000; perhaps as much as $180,000. The comments of Jack Potter, coming from a man who knew the outlaws, are oddly wayward. "I figure," he wrote, "that every member of the Black

Jack [Ketchum] gang was a cowboy and [they] blundered by not having a yegg or dynamite man."[15]

In the first place, dynamite (or "giant powder") was readily obtainable; quite often a cowboy might become familiar with its use in the course of his duties on the range. Nor was any extraordinary skill required to blow up an iron safe. Whenever the gang forced their way into an express car, the safe was cracked without undue difficulty. If the first detonation did not finish the job, there was always enough "giant" in reserve for a second attempt, and for a third if necessary.

We come now to the hard questions.

First, how much actual cash did they get and what did they do with it? In one holdup, only, were there as many as five men to share the takings. In one instance, circumstances arranged matters in such a way that nearly all the swag fell to one man. His windfall amounted to nearly $60,000, and he endeavored to put it to good use. After the other robberies, the spoils would have been pooled, each man taking a one-fourth cut. Will Carver, the only man to take part in all five of the Ketchum gang's successful holdups, "earned" something between $45,000 and $50,000, minus most of his notional share on the occasion mentioned above. That would have left him with at least $25,000 net, to which must be added more than $10,000 known to have been his portion of the take from a bank robbery committed after the dissolution of the Ketchum gang. Tom Ketchum's share, from four robberies committed within a period of just fifteen months, could not have been much less. These were vast sums for men who pursued "a solitary outdoor life."[16]

There were deductibles. Some of the gang's looted currency and coin was spoilt by explosion or fire. Torn or singed bills or blackened coins could be safely negotiated only through an intermediary and at a discount. But how much damage, how much discount, and how much overall depreciation? Again, questions without answers. Even if we allow for the imponderable by halving the gang's gross receipts— and that would probably be too drastic a provision—each member of the gang ends up with far more money than he seems to have known how to spend.

Some of the money may have been impounded by people living in, or near, such Texas communities as Knickerbocker and Christoval who had undertaken to hold it in safekeeping for the gang. We may be sure that the outlaws disbursed a wide range of bribes, presents, and gratuities, in return for protection, shelter, and information. Several residents of San Angelo and district were suspected locally of earning commission "banked" with them by members of the gang. The man nearest the focus of the rumors was Berry Ketchum. Jack Huchinson, who had grown up alongside the Ketchum family in San Saba County, Texas, and later saw plenty of Sam and Tom in the Deming neighborhood of southern New Mexico, waited until he was ninety-nine before revealing what he knew, or believed:

"Berry Ketchum held the sack. He stayed in Tom Green County. He held the sack for 'em, you know . . . When they'd make a big haul, why they'd send him the money, see . . . He knew all about it all right, see, but he didn't say nothin'. Berry was a pretty good cowman and a good neighbor . . . he had a good name."[17]

We shall see that Tom himself, embittered at his helplessness in captivity, would accuse Berry of enriching himself from the thieving of the younger brothers.

But there is an inherent difficulty in proving such assumptions, or allegations, let alone putting a price on them. It would be a mistake alike to place blind belief in them or to ascribe them piously to empty gossip-mongering or mischief-making.

While the outlaws were habitual gamblers, it would be unrealistic to suppose that they were consistent and heavy losers; in any case, very often their opponents were each other, or cowboys with hardly a couple of dollars to rub together. Tom Ketchum aside, most of them are known, or may be assumed, to have spent money on booze, harlots, fashionable city clothing and footwear, and whatever other urban amenities suited their ideas of high living. But these splashes were rare, and the cumulative cost would have made shallow inroads into pockets as deep as theirs. The purchase of one or two items of jewelry for themselves or their friends seems to have marked the limit of their indulgence. As to their workaday personal expenditure, we know only that they usually paid for such items as their clothing, supplies, guns, and ammunition. Most of the money stolen by the gang simply cannot be accounted for.

Since, however, the four principals made no discernible effort to use their stealings to buy themselves out of crime, we are left with the toughest questions of all: why did they embark upon train robbery; and, having made more money out of it than they could use, keep on going back for more?

When Ed Cullen was killed while holding up a train in December, 1897, he became the fifth such fatality in the United States within two years. But it was not only the risk of meeting a defender's well-placed bullet that made train robbery so perilous a calling. As Clark Secrest has explained:

> Railroads were not small local businesses, as were banks. When the outlaws began assaulting trains, they were assaulting some of America's largest corporations, with enormous resources, powerful political connections, and influences extending from coast to coast.[18]

If the Ketchum-Carver-Atkins group ever considered this factor, its implications deterred them no more than Cullen's fate. Such warnings may even have acted more as a spur than as a rein.

Their motives and stimuli seem mainly negative. In part, they may have been in the game for the thrills and the sense of adventure it provided; but the intensity of their professional dedication points to further explanations. Their unrelenting pursuit of the railroads for money far in excess of their needs or ambitions seems manic and nihilistic. Most likely it did not spring directly from any condition as trite as the countryman's hatred for the power of the large moneyed interests. It looks more as if the outlaws were driven by sheer destructiveness. Such a mentality could have been engendered by a rage against the failure of their own lives, or against things and people in general. Annie Weldy Byler, looking back from some sixty years' hindsight, saw them as "[J]ust like boys . . . who are allowed to skip school, to go and come and do as they please."

[T]hey started out by taking things that did not belong to them and by destroying what they wanted to. The habit grew . . . [19]

Annie Byler was speaking of the mid-1890s, when the school attendance—or absenteeism—of the two principals, Tom and Sam Ketchum, was twenty to thirty years in the past, and not a subject of which she could have had direct knowledge. But her blunt recognition of the gang's destructive inclinations is eyewitness confirmation of characteristics that the record can only imply.

Since these men had little regard for the lives of others, it is not strange that they should have none for the property or everyday rights of others. Knights of the road they were not; ruffians of the road would be nearer the mark. Their story is one of violence and ultimate futility, with few softening lines of sentiment or humor. But it is a story that sheds light upon a facet of their times. Whatever their objectives and motivations, in their day these men were the most daring of their kind, and the most feared; the individual must judge how much of what they did was worse than what could be done against them in the name of the people.

2

"I COULD KILL A BUZZARD A-FLYING"

If the early direction of a life is resolved by the character-shaping coalescence of ancestry, environment, and upbringing, its ultimate course must still depend upon choice, subject only to the random interference of mere chance. The actions of maturity are not ruled by the lottery of heredity and childhood. Somewhere a choice has to be made and, like all who reach their middle years, Sam and Tom Ketchum made theirs. A study of what is known of their formative influences furnishes some insight into the character of these men without explaining what it was that led them, in their prime years, to stake their lives on their six-shooters.

They came of old Anglo-American stock. The first of the line is believed to have been Edward Ketcham, from Cambridge, England, who brought his wife, the former Mary Hall, and their four children to Ipswich, Massachusetts, circa 1630. It is definitely known that an Edward Ketchum, who was born in 1758 and lived in North Carolina, where he married Mary Reasor in 1791, was a direct ancestor of the outlaw brothers.

By the middle of the 19th century the Ketcham/Ketchum family tree had sprouted branches in New England, Virginia, Illinois, Tennessee, and several other southern and mid-western states. Their story is essentially a reflection in miniature of the great theme of settlement and migration.[1]

Peter Reasor Ketchum, grandfather of the future outlaws, was born in Virginia about 1800. He was living in Alabama when his son Green Berry Ketchum was born on November 10, 1820, the first of eight children. In 1825 he took his family to Christian County, Illinois, where Green Berry married Temperance Katherine Wydick, a native of Kentucky, on January 27, 1842. Tempa, as she was called, was the daughter of German immigrants, not quite eighteen years old. A story survives that, as a young girl, the only English word she knew was "cornbread." It is unlikely to have been literally true, and may have been more in the nature of a family joke.

The first of the clan to penetrate the frontier country of Texas was Jacob Ketchum, a brother of Peter. Others were close behind. Peter Ketchum's second son, James, a twenty-four year old native of Illinois, reached Guadalupe County, east of

San Antonio, in 1846 with his twenty-two year old wife Mary Ellen., originally from Kentucky, and their baby daughter Elizabeth. A second child, George W., was born a few months later; he was followed by three more girls and another boy.

In 1848 several further wagonloads of Ketchums settled in Caldwell County, just to the northeast of Guadalupe County. Besides Peter, senior, there were Green Berry and Temperance with their baby daughter, another Elizabeth, as well as most of Peter's other children—Peter, Jr., Lavinia, Chester Van Buren, Margaret, and John N. Almost at once sixteen-year old Lavinia left the family home to move to Fannin County as the bride of Reuben C. Smith.[2]

By the time Green and Tempa Ketchum cast their eyes on the fine grazing lands near the historic but long deserted Spanish mission of San Saba, 150 miles to the north, they had added two sons to their household. These were Green Berry, junior, but always called "Berry," born October 24, 1850, and Samuel Wesley, whose advent occurred on January 4, 1854.[3]

San Saba County covers nine hundred square miles of uplands and valleys near the geographical center of Texas. "The timbered uplands," wrote Commissioner of Statistics A.W. Speight, "are more or less undulating, and marked by narrow valleys along the streams. The bottoms and narrow uplands are more or less densely covered with mesquite, post-oak, cedar, elm, live-oak, wild china and hackberry, about tine tenths of the area being timbered. In the valleys bordering on streams the pecan and cottonwood attain a large size, but much of the timber [here] is scrubby and suitable chiefly for fuel and fencing."[4] Speight was writing in 1882, but, away from the farms and cattle ranges that had been established during the past twenty years, the face of the land had not changed much since the late 1850s. The main difference was the people: there were far more of them—5325 in 1880, compared with 1425 in 1870 and a few hundred in 1860.[5]

Richland Creek rises in western San Saba County. For six months of the year it is dry. When there is a flow, it runs nearly due east for thirty miles to empty into the San Saba River, a western tributary of the Colorado, at a point five miles west of San Saba town. There were almost no settlers along the creek when Green Ketchum and his brother James built their cabins to the north of the river, a few miles above the mouth of the creek, and began to establish themselves as cattlemen. Until the appearance of several white families at old San Saba during the first years of Texas statehood, the country had long known no human imprint save the marks of nomad Indians in passage. These Indians naturally viewed the intruders with resentment and tried to encourage them to leave, but the newcomers fought, stayed, prospered, and multiplied.[6]

In July 1860 the census taker for San Saba County, Assistant Marshal W.B. Coffee, noted that Green B. Ketchum, a stock raiser, owned personal estate to the value of $4534. There were four offspring, the youngest a girl six months old, Nancy B. Ketchum. The next house visited was that of John L. Harkey, a farmer, who had the same number of children as Green Ketchum but very little money. James Ketchum, another stock raiser, now had six children and was worth $3734. John Harkey's place was located directly between the ranches of the two Ketchums. Their other near neighbor, James C. Rogan, was a physician. Twelve-year old Elizabeth Ketchum and her brother Berry, who was nearly ten, had been enrolled at the Masonic school in San Saba town.[7]

Green and Tempa Ketchum's seventh and last child (two or three of the previous six died in infancy), was born on October 31, 1863. He was given the names Thomas Edward.[8]

Misfortune started to gather at the doors of the Ketchums before Tom was four years old.

In 1866 his uncle Peter R. Ketchum, Jr., was killed by Indians. More of the same followed just before Christmas of the following year. Green Ketchum's brothers James and John were returning from a cattle drive to New Mexico, their saddlebags loaded with money received from the sale of the herd in El Paso. Three cowboys were with them. Near the stage stand on the Concho River, about 60 miles west of Fort Concho, they were ambushed and killed by a band of Kickapoo Indians on December 21, 1867. Their bodies were buried near the site of Tankersley, a dozen miles southwest of the Fort.[9]

Mary Ketchum, her grown daughter, Elizabeth, and the oldest of the boys, George, were left to cope with the ranch and the other children. The widow met the situation by marrying J.L. Howard on March 12, 1868; her second daughter, Sarah, followed the same formula by marrying John N. Gauny (or Gauney) the same day. Gauny later served the community as district and county clerk.[10]

Tom was not quite five when the next blow fell. It was one that affected him far more directly, and perhaps profoundly: on October 28, 1868, his father died, and Berry, who had just turned eighteen, assumed a leading role in the management of the household.[11] If, as it appears, he did so with the active encouragement of their mother, there is no reason to suppose that she was motivated by any but practical considerations. Still, Tom, thirteen years Berry's junior, and even Sam, eight years older than Tom, may have felt somewhat put upon or left out.

By 1870 there were still only about ten families living along the creek. The census returns for that year give a fair indication of the difficulties experienced by the two Ketchum households: the personal estate of each was worth less than half of what it had been ten years before. Even so, they were very much better off than most of their neighbors. Green B. Ketchum, Jr., was now nineteen years old. Sam was sixteen, and Tom, six. Sheriff J. Frazer Brown, the enumerator, if he was not in a great hurry, must have been endowed with astonishingly weak powers of observation, for he classified young Tom Ketchum as "female."[12]

On September 7, 1871, Temperance Ketchum sold Berry a piece of land in Talladega County, Alabama, recently conveyed to her by one Andrew Cunningham, and part of a riverside tract five miles above San Saba town. Two years later she joined her husband in China Creek cemetery. Berry was now in sole charge and, as such, bore the bulk of the responsibility for the family's continued wellbeing.[13]

Central and western Texas could not yet count itself free of the threat of an Indian outbreak. On September 13, 1872, shortly before his mother's death, Sam had joined the Minutemen, a home defense force affiliated with the Texas Rangers. His service lasted only until November 15 of that year.[14]

For Tom Ketchum there were several years of schooling. The nature and scope of his formal education is worthy of more than idle interest, since in later years, after his half voluntary, half fortuitous association with the identity and inflated ill-fame of "Black Jack," stories crediting him with a college education were unblinkingly filed by newspaper correspondents. One imaginative gentleman of the press went so far as to designate Harvard as the alma mater of a "Black Jack" who was partly a creature of the press's own making.[15]

There were several privately-run educational foundations in the county—the San Saba High School; the San Saba Male and Female Institute; and the San Saba Academy.[16] These establishments advertised curricula that may have been more impressive in the promise than in the delivery; but the more imposing the pretensions, the readier the parents would be to credit the tutors' ability to impart a grounding in the three R's, or one or two of them, anyway. Moreover, as in schools everywhere at that time, there would have been pupils who aspired to a higher level of learning, and instructors capable of meeting their aptitudes and ambitions.

If Tom Ketchum was a college graduate, he would have attended some such institution as these. But he did not. The connection between Ketchum and any kind of college existed solely in the fantasies of penny-a-liners. Nor, apparently, did he or Sam follow Elizabeth and Berry into the Masonic school.

In 1899, Gerome W. "Rome" Shield, who had pursued a career opposite in character to Tom's, recalled having known him at school. At the time, Shield said nothing about the school itself; but in the light of his subsequent correspondence with Albert Thompson, and Thompson's reiterated assertion that Ketchum's educational attainments were "limited" and did not extend beyond reading, writing, and doing sums, we may be sure that Tom took his formal education from an ordinary "board school," supervised by the county government—either the one that was functioning successfully at Richland Springs in 1882, or a predecessor.

Shield was only about eighteen months older than Tom, but they could not have been schoolmates for more than a year or two before the Shield family moved to Coleman County in 1874. However, Rome and Tom would see plenty of each other in later years. Shield would be elected four times as sheriff of Tom Green County: a fine officer, an energetic and successful cattleman and entrepreneur, and a great humorist—and all this despite recurrent bouts of serious ill-health, some of which rumor attributed to over-subscription to the bottle.[17]

Although religion was not a softening influence in San Saba County, many of the people were fervent churchgoers. Perhaps they needed to be; but there were the social aspects to be considered, too. Baptists, Methodists, and members of the Church of Christ sect were the most plentiful groups. Green Berry Ketchum, Sr., had registered his family as members of the Cumberland Presbyterian Church, on Simpson Creek, south of San Saba town. Others of the family adhered to the Baptist faith. Tom Ketchum, in his later life, had no use for any form of religion, yet his almost total abstinence from strong drink and his reflections on the nature of Hell might have owed something to Sundays in the pew.[18]

There may have been only a handful of families living by Richland Creek in 1870, but they were large ones. Most numerous were the Harkeys, among whom was a four-year-old boy, Daniel Riley "Dee" Harkey, who in time would become a controversial figure in Carlsbad (originally Eddy), New Mexico, first as a peace officer and then, much later, as an author. Then there were the Halls, the Weavers, and the Browns. Finally there were the Duncans, headed by Alabama-born Abijah Elam Duncan, Sr., "an old Indian fighter," and his wife Mary. Their eldest son was named after his father but usually called "Bige." Richard H. "Dick" Duncan, their second son, became Tom Ketchum's closest boyhood friend. He was born in Leon County, Texas, on December 6, 1862, which made him ten months older than Tom.[19]

Some of the escapades of their adolescence were worse than pranks. In 1876 the two lads were taken to court for the theft of seventy-five cents' worth of property. The nature of the property and the disposition of the charge are unknown.[20] Another case against Tom was called on March 17, 1880, as number 29 on the docket. There is no note as to the charge or outcome. Many years afterwards it was said that, in his youth, he failed to attend court when summoned as a witness. If this be so, one charge against him could have been contempt.[21]

Berry and Tom are missing from the San Saba County census returns compiled early in June of that year. It is not known where they were, or whether they were together. Tom's failure to show up in court may have been the unpremeditated consequence of his absence; alternatively, the court summons may have been the cause of the absence. Probably the brothers had gone on a cattle drive or to a distant roundup. At all events, they were soon back in the county.

There may be a link between one or more of these cases and one recalled by Frank Shelton, a contemporary who became a sheriff in West Texas during the 1890s and hunted the Ketchum gang after one of their train robberies. Shelton's story is that Tom, as a boy, helped himself to a generous measure of revenge after receiving a whipping for stealing nuts from a neighbor's pecan grove. First, he took lessons in the use of dynamite from an Irish well-driller. Then he stole some dynamite and blew up the pecan grove. No documentary support has been found for this act of criminal vandalism, but Shelton was a generally dependable witness.[22]

Dick and Tom were in trouble for such offenses as "malicious mischief" and gambling. Some of their neighbors would have shrugged off the latter as the breach of a statute that could only be justified by an excess of morality. Many other citizens would have been less broad minded, especially when these charges were followed by graver ones, such as the theft of livestock.[23]

Tom himself is the sole available authority on what he described as his "first experience in shooting a man."

> [I]n Texas, when I was a boy I had it in for a fellow down there, and I decided to shoot him. My brother tried to persuade me to use juniper berries, which would not hurt him much. I used buckshot, though, and thought those would suit my purpose better, so I laid in wait for him in the brush, and as he passed I fired two shots at him. He did not die—got well—but it used him up for awhile.[24]

The brother is likely to have been Sam; nothing that is known about Tom's life from beginning to end suggest that he would ever willingly have confided in Berry on anything, least of all on a plan to ambush and kill a neighbor. Tom's admission, although as yet unsupported, looks and sounds authentic, at core. We know enough about Tom Ketchum to say that the plan, the act, and the casual and boastfully unrepentant style of his disclosure, are bang in character. It will be apparent that, already, those whom young Ketchum "had it in for" did not constitute a small and exclusive club. The day was not afar when he would "have it in" for most of his world.

In his book *Mean as Hell*, Dee Harkey states that the Duncan boys, Bige and Dick, were the first cousins of Berry, Sam, and Tom Ketchum (they were not); that the Duncans were thieves (they were, but so were many of their neighbors); and that they "got to be vicious criminals" (true only of Dick).[25]

Abijah Elam "Bige" Duncan, Jr., married Tom's sister Nancy Blake Ketchum on December 11, 1879.[26] He eventually became an honest and respected cattleman—though his friendship for Sam and Tom Ketchum remained staunch throughout the brothers' careers in outlawry. Dick was hanged at Eagle Pass in 1891 for one of the foulest crimes of murder in late 19th century Texas. There were at least two other Duncan brothers—James P., born about 1862, and George Taplin, commonly known as "Tap," born in 1849.[27] Both would enter the story of Sam and Tom Ketchum.

As the threat of Indian trouble receded, the settlers of San Saba County concentrated increasingly upon harassing each other. Horse-theft was commonplace; cattle rustling a habit. Many a rancher registered several brands and owned one which bore a distinct similarity to that of some neighbor.[28] There was ill-feeling between the big cattlemen and the small ranchers. All of them stood arrayed in angry opposition to the grangers who began to move into the rich valley lands during the late seventies. To the thieving was added, occasionally, violence. Successive editor-owners of the little local weekly, the *San Saba News*, usually refrained from covering the incidents in depth or detail. Sometimes the paper spoke for the cowmen, sometimes for the grangers. Bald summaries of County Court and District Court proceedings, together with accounts of such episodes as the editor deemed deserving of more than a passing word or two, afford no more than a glimpse into the extent of the thievery. One week, a man would be flatteringly portrayed as a worthy citizen; the next week, his arrest in an adjoining county while in charge of a band of stolen horses would be reported without comment.

In local elections held in the fall of 1882, 104 votes were cast in the Richland Springs precinct. The Richland Springs community now comprised "a post office, three stores, a school house, blacksmith shop and several residences." Though not much of a town yet, remarked the *News*, it has "fine possibilitys." One unnamed ranchman had owned only eleven cows and calves ten years before; now his herd numbered four or five hundred.[29]

In this period several other Ketchums moved into the county. Dr. Nicholas Ketchum, born in Tennessee in 1830, came in 1880. At first he boarded with his partner, the druggist, David Fentress, in San Saba town. His family soon followed and he set up store in San Saba town to sell cantaloupes and five-cent cigars, twenty-five dollar sewing machines and "Champion Lamps giving the light of sixty candles, and warranted not explosive." This "practical druggist" swore by chloroform as "the very best of remedies for screw worm." He was also one of the stoutest pillars of the Baptist church. Henry Ketchum, one of Nicholas's grown sons, also went into pharmacy. He lent his support to the Methodist church, joined a Prohibition Convention, and taught school "for the good people of Wallace Creek," fifteen miles from San Saba. Nicholas and Henry may have been an uncle and a cousin of Berry, Sam, and Tom, at several removes.[30]

As the mid-seventies approached, Berry and Sam Ketchum were a pair of stalwart young bachelor ranchmen; first-rate cowmen with a flourishing herd and excellent range, doubtless as honest as any of their neighbors and more honest than some. Both seemed headed for success.

But Sam was becoming restive. One of the factors that shaped Sam's state of mind before he turned outlaw was the course his life took after he had given up bachelorhood. On February 4, 1875, one month after his twenty-first birthday, and at San Saba town, he married Louisa J. Greenlee, who was not yet sixteen, having been born in Arkansas on May 5, 1859. Their son, William Berry Ketchum, was born on October 24, 1876. A daughter, Laura, came along about a year later.[31]

On February 19, 1878, Sam and Louisa sold a piece of land to Elenora Crenshaw. Whether or not this transaction was charged with any special significance, the marriage was foundering. By June, 1880, Sam was boarding with his newly married sister, Nancy, and her husband, Bige Duncan. The census enumerator classified him as a "laborer."[32]

Little is known or can be inferred of the relationship between the brothers at this time. Berry was to say that both Sam and Tom were "wild."[33] But Berry was master and Sam might have grown into his twenties feeling unsettled and perhaps slightly jealous. Tom, very much the junior, would have had little or no voice in the running of the place. It is a fair surmise that Sam, himself discontented, began more and more to side with his younger brother. Unlike Tom, he never actually quarreled with Berry. But the rapid collapse of his marriage, whatever the reasons for it, brought out the instability within him and made him more inclined than ever to take Tom's part and keep company with him.

The incident that either created or confirmed the breach between Berry and Tom sprang from the older's refusal to allow the younger to use his prized thoroughbreds for joyriding. Tom's defiance of the prohibition earned a strong admonition and a severe thrashing.

Tom took his aching hide and battered pride to Sam:

"Berry has sure given it to me, but I swear before I die I'll kill him for that."

"No you won't, Tom."

"Hear what I say Sam; I sure will."

The story comes from Thompson, and is unsourced, but the author believes it to be authentic, the dialogue included; among Thompson's informants were Gerome Shield and an unidentified local woman—possibly a sister of the Ketchum boys. One of these, or some other unnamed "resident of San Angelo," also told Thompson that "Berry feared violence from his brother Tom, and always distrusted him."

Independent corroboration is supplied by Loomis, who quotes Berry's remark to a mutual friend, John Wright, that "he fully expected" Tom to kill him sooner or later. And Berry was no fantasist.[34]

As Tom grew to young manhood, he steadily won notice for his skill as a marksman. Nearly twenty years later, when his notoriety had struck its peak, a correspondent in Austin wrote that Tom was "widely known in this section as a dead shot with rifle and pistol."[35] Tom himself did not dissent.

"I was counted as fine a shot as ever fired a gun," he once declared. "I could take a rifle and kill a buzzard or anything that was a-flying; take a tomato can and shoot it up into the air and then hit it again and again before it came down."[36]

In 1930 an unidentified female resident of South Texas looked back fifty years to recall how Tom, then in his teens, would order her to lob empty cans into the air for him to shoot at. Refusal was overcome by threats. He would hand the girl two or three cans, she would pitch them skywards, and he would rapid-fire at them.

In time, young Ketchum "got so he rarely missed them."

"Throw them higher, higher," he would command.

> I can see them now as Tom's bullets struck and turned them over and over, see him twirl his six-shooter about his finger and as it came round, shoot. None of the boys equaled him in marksmanship, though Sam and Will Carver were good shots . . . I guess Tom was quickest of them all.

Drawing on this and other information, Thompson reported that Tom "could shoot with almost equal accuracy with either hand, and hit an object when firing over his shoulder."[37]

Ketchum himself would not have argued with this. When Thompson asked the imprisoned and crippled desperado, shorn of his right forearm by a train conductor's buckshot, whether he could fire from his left hand, the reply was prompt and assured:

"Sneak in a forty-four to me and see,"[38]

Nor did he practice fancy shooting merely as an art form or a circus trick:

"No use wasting lead and firing twice when once will do. It's best to get 'em the first time and not take chances."[39]

Wise words from a man whose criminal career was predicated upon chance-taking until the night came when he tried one chance too many.

Besides devoting a lot of his time to the expenditure of powder and lead, the young Tom Ketchum got through a good deal of hard work and became a good cowhand.

Despite Tom's juvenile misdeeds, nothing exists to show that any of the Ketchums stole during the early 1880s, but others with homes near Richland Springs did. The local paper began 1882 with the following story:

> On last Monday night [January 2] when J.W. Mullins, Richard Duncan and Hugh Harkey were returning home from a party at Henry McDaniels' they saw a large drove of horses standing at the gate of Mrs. Duncan's pasture, which is just below the Concho crossing . . . These gentlemen decided to see what it meant and just before

they reached the horses they saw three men leave at rapid speed on horseback. They then decided to pen the horses and hold them till morning when it was found all were stolen from parties living in this county. The owners now have their stock, most of which were [*sic*] unbranded. Messrs. Mullins, Duncan and Harkey deserve much credit for securing these horses, . . . about twenty head. As yet there is no clue to the thieves.[40]

And that was the end of that. Attention now switched to the operations of a mysteriously elusive lone thief. Before the end of the month Israel Harkey and Sam Ketchum were innocent but perhaps reticent witnesses to another of his unexplained disappearances.

A suspicious looking man was seen by Mr. I.M. Harkey on last Tuesday [January 24] crossing the river about four miles above town [San Saba]. He was riding a large sorrel horse branded LHF, connected, and leading a roan horse. He asked Mr. Harkey for directions to some place on the Colorado. Mr. Harkey came on to town and notified the authorities. Messrs. Alex Doran and M.J. Murray went in pursuit, and soon lost his trail, but went to the place he said he was going to, and learned there that no such man had been seen. In about an hour after he was seen by Mr Harkey, Mr. Sam Ketchum saw a man riding a horse and leading one, that suited the description given by Mr Harkey, going into the Longley pasture. It is thought he is the same man who stole Messrs. Murray and Bagley's horses last week. Horse stealing is getting to be quite common in those parts, and it is thought one man is doing it. It is strange that he can't be caught.[41]

No doubt the neighbors did not have to read too closely between the lines to understand what had happened.

Such stories, with variations, were coming in from all over the county and the region beyond it. At a public meeting on March 4, 1882 some of the cattlemen formed the San Saba County Stock Association. Cattle rustling and horse-stealing continued apace. On December 15, 1883, the editor went as far as he dared toward naming some of the culprits:

We are sorry to say that there are one or two parties in the county who think their brands are "too well known" and that it is not good policy, more especially for small owners, to make their brands and range locations known through the papers . . .

From there he argued at length that the reverse was true, and practically accused the smaller ranchers of rustling.[42] In the same issue he commented approvingly of an article recently passed by the state legislature "for the benefit of the wild and woolly and hard to curry" who could not restrain themselves from "wilfully disturbing a congregation of worshippers." The benefits came in the form of a $25 fine and, at the discretion of the jury, up to thirty days in the county jail. Every now and then the editorial displeasure would be directed at the young fellows, mostly "from the western portion of the county," who came into town weekends and signaled their departure with a crackle of revolver fire, but nothing decisive seems to have been done about them.

If the published word of Dee Harkey can be trusted, it would have been in 1884 or the early part of 1885 that Sam and Tom Ketchum became known as rustlers; no support has been found for the allegation that the pair were indicted and fled the county. Joseph M. Harkey, the sheriff, sent his brother Dee and Jim Hall to bring them back. The brothers—wrote Dee—were traced in Cow Valley, in McCulloch County, some twenty miles west of Richland Springs. Harkey relates in his book that the Ketchums saw them coming and escaped on "race horses."[43]

Even if this is true, it is improbable that Berry Ketchum's decision to leave San Saba County was brought about solely by the dereliction of Sam and Tom (although the writer has been told, informally, that accusations of stock theft, accompanied by threats, had driven them all out).[44] The county was becoming thickly settled, with no elbow-room for a well-to-do rancher eager to expand his interests. The newcomers were mostly tillers of the soil, many of them from Germany, and their development of the plentiful arable land constricted the cattle ranges. Some of the Halls, the richest cattlemen in western San Saba County, had already left for New Mexico and California.[45]

Other San Saba ranchers had moved, or were preparing to move. They resettled themselves near Roswell, or elsewhere in New Mexico, or in Tom Green and neighboring Texas counties.

Much of the migration was by family groups, but plenty of single men took part in it. One of these was Sam Ketchum.

Sam's actions were not those of a hunted man, merely those of a restless man. In December, 1884, presumably to raise ready cash, Sam sold Berry his holdings north of the San Saba River.[46]

Berry then shifted his home and stock to Tom Green County. He would have been on familiar ground, having already ridden the trail routes to and beyond San Angelo; he may on occasion have camped or boarded nearby for weeks at a time, giving some kind of basis for the belief of some that his move can be dated to 1882 or even earlier.[47] His new ranch was several miles south and slightly west of the hamlet of Knickerbocker and near what became the eastern line of Irion County. It was no more than a hundred miles west of Richland Springs. Sam moved in the same direction at about the same time. He may, in fact, have accompanied Berry and continued with their unequal partnership, but it was not long before he set his own course. In June, 1885, became an employee of the giant Half Circle Six ranch, and remained on the payroll until about the close of the year. At thirty-one, the once promising young rancher had become a hired hand. Berry's new ranch was the place Tom called home for the next two or three years and which he and Sam would visit thereafter at intervals for almost as long as they remained free men.[48]

Their brother-in-law, Bige Duncan, followed them to Tom Green County a year or so afterwards. In December, 1885, Bige stood trial at San Saba for "theft of cattle" (a felony), was found guilty of the lesser charge of "illegal driving" (an equivocation enabling theft to be downgraded to a misdemeanor), and fined $100. He and Nancy did not stay in San Saba County for long after that.[49]

Berry was not the first Ketchum to settle in Tom Green County. A George Ketchum, namesake of the eldest son of their uncle James, and his wife Gresella, had arrived in the 1870s. Both were natives of Mexico and not discernibly connected in any way with the descendants of Peter Ketchum.[50] The presence of two unrelated Ketchum households in a lightly populated county is further evidence of the proliferation of the family name over the preceding two and a half centuries.

Elizabeth, older sister of Berry, Sam, and Tom, had married John Wesley Smith, from Alabama, about 1868. She did not leave San Saba for Tom Green until the mid-nineties, but at least one of the Smiths' sons, Pat, preceded them there by several years and became a kind of protégé of Sam's. Another son, Lee Wilson Smith, was to command some of Tom's last thoughts on earth, though it is not known why.[51]

Other neighbors and kinsfolk of the Ketchums quit San Saba County during the 1880s. Among them were several Kuykendalls; J.T. "Tol" Rutledge, who had been convicted of "illegal driving" along with Bige Duncan, and went on to serve as sheriff of Irion County; William H. Chaney (sometimes spelled Cheney), co-defendant with Tap Duncan on an assault and battery charge, subsequently reduced to one of simple assault), later an intimate of several of the Ketchum gang, and later still an informant for Pinkerton's National Detective Agency; Thomas Chaney, Bill's younger brother; and James York, who, in 1904, was fleetingly mistaken for the infamous Harvey Logan, alias Kid Curry. We have not heard the last of most of these people.[52]

Too much weight should not be attached to the thefts of Sam and Tom Ketchum in the early 1880s, if in fact they committed any. (Almost the only hostile witness was Harkey, who was writing sixty years after the alleged incidents he portrays, and whose assertions are frequently at fault.) If they did, a presentable defense is available. Aside from the argument that many small men become big by successful pilfering of one kind or another, there is abundant evidence that many of the San Saba ranchers were thieves one day and victims the next.

Sheriff Joe Harkey, too, was in trouble soon enough. Shortly after he was beaten for re-election in 1886 it was noticed that his accounts were defective. In December 1887 a grand jury found that Harkey had embezzled several hundred dollars, in which endeavors he was aided by the County Commissioners. The grand jurors' investigation was thorough and their report, caustic. Yet they were inhibited by personal or partisan considerations from issuing indictments. All they did was "call attention" to the malpractices they had so fiercely condemned.[53]

But San Saba County was to live through far worse. Fiscal misappropriation by grubby-paw officials was a minor impropriety compared with the murderous activities of the San Saba Mob, degenerate successor of one or another of the local Associations, which dealt in assassination and intimidation for some twelve or fifteen years from its inception in the early eighties.[54]

Whatever might be charged against Tom Ketchum, it cannot be said that he made San Saba County a better place simply by betaking himself elsewhere.

{ 3 }

VAGRANT YEARS

Among the pertinacious but unsubstantiated stories about Tom Ketchum is the one in which he is said to have gone to Arizona and gambled away an inheritance of $1500. One form of this yarn would have it that Ketchum hailed from New Jersey and came into the money upon the death of a relative there.[1] Since this is palpably absurd the rest of the tale scarcely commands heed. What may have happened with the Ketchums is that Sam and Tom arrived at some sort of a settlement with Berry. But this is no better than a reasoned conjecture, and it would be vain to attempt to fit it into a chronological framework. All we know is that the definitive break between Berry and Tom occurred in 1889, four years after their departure from San Saba County.

Probably, too, Sam and Tom spent most of that period in and around Tom Green County, with one or two sorties into New Mexico and possibly as far afield as Arizona and Colorado. But the tale that they operated a so-called "ranch"—in reality, a thieves' holdout—in Snake Valley, a tract of desert forty miles west of Milford, in southwestern Utah, during the late 1880s, can now be seen as a canard. A Sam Ketchum did own such a place in that location at that time, but he was not Sam Ketchum of Tom Green County, Texas, nor any known kinsman of his.[2]

Almost as dubious is a passage in the reminiscences of Thomas Edgar Crawford, where he describes his alleged experiences while traveling in the company of "a character by the name of Black Jack Ketchum." The period would be roughly 1886–7.

The gist of Crawford's yarn is that, at the time of their first meeting, Ketchum was living in a cabin "on the middle fork of the Purgatoire River," a tributary of the Arkansas. That, if true, would place Ketchum in Las Animas County, Colorado, twenty miles east of Trinidad.

The two men teamed up and rode down into the Pecos Valley. Afterwards, says Crawford, they visited such places as Taos, Cimarron Canyon, Ute Park, Santa Fe, and Wagon Mound, all in New Mexico. Moving west, they passed what would have been the fall of 1886 working for "the C—outfit" in northern Arizona. The following spring saw them at Holbrook, Arizona, where they were hired by the Hash Knife ("of which Burt Mossman was manager of the Aztec Cattle Company"). After quitting the Hash Knife, they meandered northward to the Snake River country of southern Idaho and finally to Jackson Hole, in western Wyoming, where Crawford's narrative parts company with Ketchum.

It will be found that Tom Ketchum came to know most of these places; he would be intimately connected with some of them. Nor need it be doubted that Crawford, too, visited them. But when? If Crawford worked at the Hash Knife under Mossman, he would not have been on the payroll any earlier than 1898, the year in which Mossman joined the Aztec company. It was also the year that marked the zenith of Ketchum's banditry.

Crawford comes across as a nondescript wanderer who strove to enliven a pedestrian tale by introducing a succession of characters whose outlawry was well known, and contriving authenticity by suggesting that he himself was an outlaw.[3] He could have learned of Ketchum's roamings from hearsay or from the printed word; they were widely written up and talked about after his arrest.

In the same bracket is the "recollection" of the ranchwoman Ann Bassett—the celebrated "Queen Ann" of Brown's Hole—that Tom went gunning for William G. Tittsworth after Tittsworth's killing of Charley Powers, a friend of Ketchum's. But that killing occurred in the early 1880s, when Tom was still in San Saba County, and Ann a girl of seven or eight.[4]

An unorganized county named after the Confederate general Tom Green had been created on March 13, 1874. It was a gargantuan tract of territory now occupied by no fewer than sixty-seven counties, of which the present-day Tom Green County is the southeasternmost. By 1880 the formation of new counties across the north and center of this land mass had reduced Tom Green County to about one-fifth of its original size. As the trickle of settlers thickened during the 1880s, eight more counties came into existence, beginning with Midland County in 1885. By 1890 all that remained of the 1874 creation was the area that now comprises the counties of Reagan, Sterling, and Tom Green. Sterling County was formed in 1891, when William N. Hiler was elected sheriff for the first of two consecutive two-year terms.[5]

Tom Green County, observed the state Commissioner of Agriculture in his *Report* for 1891–2, is "largely high undulating prairie, with an occasional prominent peak."[6] When the elements were benign, as they usually were, it was fine country for both cattle and sheep, with an ample supply of what mattered most: water, principally from the Concho River ("Main Concho")—a tributary of the Colorado—and its three constituents (the North, Middle, and South Concho), but supplemented by some half-dozen substantial creeks. Grape Creek, to the north of the county, passes near Water Valley to join the North Concho; Spring Creek begins near Sherwood, the village which gave sparsely-peopled Irion County its seat of local government, and (in those days) emptied itself in the South Concho, twenty miles to the east; Dove Creek flows by Knickerbocker and on to San Angelo, twenty miles to the northeast; the source of Pecan Creek lies further to the south and east of the county; and Lipan Creek, still further east, runs northward to the Main Concho. Kickapoo Creek is just east of the line separating Tom Green and Concho Counties.[7]

But when the conditions were not benign they could be cruel. Like many other parts of the West, Tom Green and its neighboring counties were from time to time subject to the excesses of drought and flood. There might be a dearth of water, or a glut of it, the former being the more usual.[7]

In the mid-1880s the population of Tom Green County was about four thousand, roughly half of it in San Angelo, the county seat and almost the most important shipment point in the Southwest for both cattle and wool. For some years, the sheep industry had been in the ascendant; but toward the mid-1880s one of the periodic changes in market conditions shifted the balance toward the cattle business. The Half Circle Six, situated on the headwaters of Dove Creek, and owned by mainly absentee interests in Wisconsin, had switched from sheep to cattle only a year or two before Sam Ketchum went on their payroll.[9]

All three of the Ketchum brothers worked hard; but only Berry, who beyond question had got off to a better (and luckier) start, improved his fortunes. John Loomis, who knew him "quite well," remembered him as "large, well built, with very dark hair and eyes." "He looked like a bandit himself," wrote Loomis, "but he was no train robber." He was a shrewd judge of cattle, horses, and men; but a story told against him some years later as "A Good One on Berry," offers both an illustration of his almost unnervingly manic sense of humor and evidence that he could be outthought and outsmarted.

> Pete King tells a pretty good joke on Berry Ketchum. It was in the 80's and Berry was running a cow outfit on the South Concho. They had a "green Reuben" in the outfit and Berry decided he would play a good one on Mr. Greener. It was a bitter cold night and it was arranged that Berry should have a fit and they would send Mr. Reuben to Angelo, 20 miles distant, for a doctor. One of the boys remarked as they were sitting around the fire, "Berry, have you quit having fits?" "No," replied Berry, "and I feel like one was coming now," and accordingly, he fell over and commenced gritting his teeth and foaming at the mouth. "Run for a doctor, Reuben," the boys all shouted, "run and get a horse and go to Angelo for a doctor." A bucket of water was setting by half full of ice. Reuben grabbed it and sloshed the whole business in Berry's face, remarking "this is the way we do for fits down in Van Zandt [County]." Berry came to at once and has never had another fit.[10]

The inspiration behind Berry's misfired jest may have been an extreme instance of what Loomis called his "rough sense of humor." A multitude of other references leave no doubt that Berry was a card. It was no joke for Berry, however, when a "vicious horse" he was saddling "seized Mr. K's head and crushed the bones between his teeth." But he was a rough man all around, as able to take hard knocks as to hand them out. As an unsigned press correspondent expressed it, "Berry Ketchum happened to a very serious accident."[11]

We have only one fragment of memorabilia to attach to Sam's early years in Tom Green County. At the age of ninety-six Elender Ervin recalled hearing him remark that "all he wanted was a horse branded SLS." The sense and context are irrecoverable at this remove; but, whether earnest or jocular, it may have embodied an allusion to S.L.S. Smith—one of San Angelo's leading pioneers and public figures, physician and surgeon, and a director of the Concho National Bank.[12]

As he moved through his early twenties, Tom Ketchum was increasingly at odds with Berry. The brothers had not been in Tom Green County for long before Tom was camping out in a hideout cave on Burk's Creek, three miles east of Knickerbocker and one mile south of Berry's house. When the weather was too chilly for life in the outdoors, he would sometimes choose to sleep in the bunkhouse with the hired hands rather than in the ranch house.[13]

Tom's deepening alienation from Berry was not accompanied by a general slump into moody introspection. Out on the range he was, and always remained, the rough-and-ready extrovert.

Sometimes he was too ready to be rough. Seaton Keith, who knew the Ketchums well, tells of a roundup along the lower reaches of the San Saba River, east of Keith's Lipan Springs headquarters, where Tom picked on one of Keith's hands, a short, stocky fellow named Springstun, but commonly called "Dogie."

One evening, while the boys were waiting for supper, Tom stole up behind Dogie, seized him by the back of the collar, announced that he was going to take him down to the river for a ducking, and proceeded to drag him towards the water's edge.

Ketchum may not have known that his intended victim "had been quite a wrestler." At the opportune moment, Dogie reached out, upended Tom, and hurled him to the ground where he lay "limp and gasping."

"Dogie, you have killed Tom," said one of the boys.

"No, I reckon not," Dogie replied carelessly. Sure enough, Tom was able to "laugh with the others at himself." But not until the next day.[14]

Keith himself was victim to another of Tom's pranks. Keith, the monocled Edinburgh-born scion of a distinguished Scottish family and reputedly the best whist player in San Angelo, lived on Lipan Creek, well over on the eastern side of Tom Green County. Like many of his neighbors, he grazed some of his herds in Kansas and the Indian Territory, and was often there to keep an eye on them. His foreman, Charlie Bean, was in charge of the Lipan Creek ranch when Keith was away.[15]

Seaton Keith lovingly cultivated melons which Tom and his friends were no less assiduous in stealing. Keith, a realistic and tolerant man, knew who the culprits were and that he could not prevent their thievery. He decided to appeal to their sense of reason and fair play. It was all right, he told them, to carry on stealing melons, so long as they did not take the biggest, which he was saving for seed. That night Ketchum came back and stole it.[16]

Keith, the soul of magnanimity, bore no rancor and actually sympathized with Tom in his later tribulations.[17] But, already, Ketchum's overgrown schoolboy antics were imbued with an element of spite that was not far removed from cruelty.

Texas was not a lawless state. On the contrary, it had an amplitude of laws, with John Sayles to compile and annotate them and an army of lawyers and judges to live off them.[18] But it also had a large number of citizens who felt that the laws did not, or should not, apply to them. Sometimes it was the laws that were bad, sometimes the people.

Among the most popular among young men determined to break one or two of the more trivial of them were the statutes intended to preserve the peace and decorum of the Sabbath. One Sunday near the turn of 1892–93 Tom Ketchum flaunted his independence of spirit by terrorizing a dog until it was driven to seek sanctuary in a local house of worship. The dog tore down the aisle, and Tom tore after it, turning the service into utter disorder. This display of hooliganism occasioned an appearance in county court and a fine.[19]

This incident has previously been ascribed to late 1888 or early 1889, because of two connected statements that Tom's old schoolfellow, Gerome "Rome" Shield, gave to a newspaper in 1899. Shield stated that Tom Ketchum was the first man he ever arrested. He also said (or was understood to have said) that he was first elected sheriff of Tom Green County in 1888. But Shield was not elected sheriff in 1888; he did not succeed J. Willis Johnson as sheriff and tax collector until his bond was approved on November 24, 1892, sixteen days after his election. He was thirty years old—not much more than eighteen months older than Tom Ketchum.[20]

Tom may have been doing more than hurrahing a church congregation; he may also have been taking a rise out of the new sheriff and tax-collector, merely because he was his old schoolmate Rome Shield. He may also have set out to embarrass and annoy Berry by sowing friction between him and the new sheriff. If so, it worked against him; Berry's relationship with Tom had always been uneven, and often strained, and Berry was not going to jeopardize his public respectability by an excess of filial loyalty.

A prime component in the cementing of Berry's respectability, and the precipitant of one of the worst of his quarrels with Tom, was his marriage, nearly four years previously. The oldest Ketchum brother, thirty-eight years old by then, had been revisiting San Saba County, the chief object of his interest being Barsha Ola ("Barshie") Shields, sixth and youngest daughter of John and Matilda Lyons Rutherford Shields. The family, who were not related to that of Gerome Shield, had first settled on Wallace Creek in 1876, but left briefly after a few years.[21] Emily Jane, the oldest daughter, married during the 1870s. The fourth daughter, Eula, had boarded in Wallace Creek as an invalid and died there late in 1880, aged eighteen, at about the time the rest of the family returned to that locality.[22] There, on August 25, 1885, the fifth daughter, Clara Louise, married Henry Ketchum, son of Nicholas.[23]

In May, 1889, Berry started out on another trip to San Saba. Before departing he had a few words for the scapegrace younger brother: in effect, "Be gone for good before I come back." On May 23, Barshie and Berry were wed in San Saba County. When Berry brought his twenty-three year old bride to the ranch near Knickerbocker, Tom had vanished. So had one of Berry's best horses.[24]

Berry may have given his brother the horse, and he may also have given him money to pay off whatever reversionary interest was Tom's due. Tom would be back, many times; but always on sufferance and through the good offices of Sam or other kin.

Berry, for his part, steadily throve. He raised and traded cattle and good-quality horses, usually buying or selling "a.p.t."—at private terms. Though he lived closer to Knickerbocker, he and many of his friends spent more of their free hours in the smaller town of Sherwood, where they would sometimes "match" their horses in two-horse races for a prize purse and side-stakes.[25] In the spring of 1892 Berry was offering to pay $100 for the arrest and conviction of any thief found in possession of any horse bearing his UK brand. "This reward," he declared, "stands good forever." Did he have brother Tom in mind?[26]

Berry was esteemed as a successful stockman and noted as a character; "Berry Ketchum, the original," the *San Angelo Standard* once called him.[27] Elsewhere, it quoted him as remarking, unfathomably, "I don't want your newspaper. I have just bought a hundred bushels of corn."[28] Later, he would enter the sheep business—like most of his contemporaries he was a pragmatist, not a sentimentalist; he went where the money was likely to be. Astonishment was general when one of Berry's neighbors, M.B. "Nub" Pulliam, a branded-in-the-hide cattleman if there ever was one, forswore all his oft-repeated vows and bought several thousand sheep. His friends laughed; but not too loud, because Nub did not take kindly to ridicule—and not too long, for he made money out of the sheep.[29] Berry's partner in the sheep-raising venture was George Hamilton, of Crockett County, alongside whom he had worked on cattle roundups in past years.[30]

Even before their departure from San Saba County, the three Ketchums would probably have traveled both the Goodnight-Loving trail and the old Butterfield stage road that met it at Horsehead Crossing, on the Pecos. During the four years that followed, Sam and Tom had worked with Berry on and off, hired out to various cattle outfits near San Angelo and the Devil's River country to the south, taken part in roundups in the vicinity of Eldorado and Ozona, and trailed cattle along the Yellow Houses route to the southernmost division of the XIT ranching corporation at Yellow House Canyon, or beyond to the Llano Estacado (Staked Plain) of New Mexico. At that time, before the construction of stockyards at Clayton in the summer of 1888, the nearest railroad shipment point was Springer on the Atchison, Topeka and Santa Fe. Among the more durable of the many personal associations the Ketchums formed, or renewed, were their old friendship with Will and Tom Chaney, and newer ones with Will Carver and Ben Kilpatrick.[31]

They had long been familiar with the cow country of much of Texas to the south and west of Abilene; Tom was employed for a while by the Quien Sabe, of Midland—one of the two vast ranches owned by Mayer and Solomon Halff.[32] Now, after Tom's break with Berry, the pair lit out for eastern New Mexico. Both were hired as cowhands and trail drivers by the LFD, a derivative of the original LIT outfit, with ranch headquarters near Tascosa, in the Texas Panhandle.

During that period, the LFD operation covered 7500 square miles of southeastern New Mexico between the Pecos, just east of Roswell, and the Texas line.[33] The Ketchum brothers' service there is remembered only by a story, perhaps true, which instances the boorishness that the boorishly inclined were apt to laugh off as "cowcamp humor."

The boors of the story were Sam and Tom Ketchum. During a halt on the drive northward they amused themselves by shooting up the dust around the feet of a tenderfoot whom the trail boss, Charlie Walker, had hired for the drive. Walker disturbed the entertainment by inviting the brothers to make him dance; if they dared to try, he added, "he would get them both." The brothers sheepishly put aside their pistols and did not bother the recruit again.[34]

In an epilogue supplied by William M. "Bob" Beverly, Walker later "ran them off" (dismissed them), but was "scared to death when he found out who they were." But, since Walker would have known perfectly well who they were, the most that can be said for Beverly's afternote is that Walker might have become apprehensive a few years later, when he heard what they had become.[35]

Tom may have spent some time in Arizona in the late 1880s or early 1890s. One source (besides the untrustworthy T.E. Crawford) places him with the Aztec Land and Cattle Company, known from its brand as the Hash Knife, whose headquarters were at Joseph, just west of Holbrook. With him was either Will Carver or Tom Hilliard, one of whose many aliases was "Tod Carver."[36] Also, Edward Wilson said in his reminiscences that, "[a]bout 1892" he punched cows with Tom in the Apache reservation." Wilson says of Tom that he "was of medium height, weighed about one hundred and eighty pounds and was of rather light complection [*sic*]." Wilson's description casts doubt on his statement: he got Ketchum's weight about right, but nothing else; Tom was well above medium height and of dark complexion.[37] Wilson's little memoir was penned more than thirty years after the events it touches upon. Since there are other reasons for believing that Wilson did know Tom in Arizona, it is likely that the passage of time eroded the clarity of his recall. At the end of such a long interval, a lapse of memory could have caused him to connect the name of one man with the appearance of another.

For something like ten years from about 1885, Sam and Tom worked steadily as cowpunchers and trail hands. If they had felt themselves drawn toward outlawry, or committed to it, they would surely have turned bandit during the late eighties. In this period the Burrow gang, the Cornett-Whitley band, and sundry others were responsible for a dozen holdups in Texas. There were numerous robberies in Arizona and the Indian Territory. Further north, so called "cowboy bandits" robbed the bank at Grover, Wyoming; a Northern Pacific train at Big Horn, Montana; the banks at La Junta and Telluride, Colorado; a Denver and Rio Grande Western train near Thompson Springs, Utah; and, in 1890, another Northern Pacific train just outside New Salem, North Dakota. A train was robbed near Tascosa at about the time the Ketchums were working for the LFD. Nearly a year later one was stopped three miles south of Trinidad, Colorado, and the fireman was shot through the head—"for being sassy," as the conductor once put it.[38]

That New Mexico, almost alone among the western states and territories, experienced no serious activity from outlaws during the late eighties and early nineties may be attributed, in part, to a law enacted on February 23, 1887, under which the death sentence was mandatory for anyone convicted of holding up a train.[39] This law was retained by successive Territorial Legislatures. It was still in force in 1899, when Tom Ketchum protested that he had never heard of it.

But, in 1889 and 1890, neither Tom nor Sam had any cause to step wary of this law or any other. During these years, and the next four or five, they worked hard and saved little.

With the construction of the Fort Worth and Denver railroad during the late eighties, Amarillo became the shipping center for most ranchers in the Panhandle of Texas, while Clayton, founded in March of 1888, similarly served the interests of the cattle and wool industries in eastern New Mexico. In the autumn of 1889, when Tom Ketchum first came up to Clayton with the trail herds, the town could offer three stores, two respectable hotels, one church, and a fair number of brothels, saloons, and gambling houses.[40]

Tom and Sam, both of them votaries of Faro and Poker, made Charlie Meredith's saloon their favourite haunt. One of the resident gamblers, Frank Martinez, was "agreeable to play with," in Tom's view, "though Sam could beat him anytime dealing Monte." Whereas Sam, in common with most trail hands, had a liking for hard drink, Tom rarely or never touched the bottle.[41]

There was no serious misbehavior from the brothers either in town or out on the range, but an incident described by James F. Hinkle, who met them on several occasions when he was wagon boss for the CA Bar outfit, provides another instance of Tom's boisterous and somewhat roguish sense of fun:

> Tom Ketchum got behind a pile of ties near the depot and with a beanshooter took it out on an engineer who was oiling his engine. He hit the engineer with buckshot while the trainman was stooping over and kept it up for a time. Finally, the engineer located the trouble, got out his gun, and Tom hit it for the back end of a saloon.[42]

As nearly as can be stated with chronological exactitude, Tom trailed cattle to Clayton with the S Cross in 1890 and the Carrizozo Cattle Company, the Bar W, in 1891. The year after that he drove through Clayton and on to Cold Springs, in what is now the Oklahoma Panhandle, with the G-G herd, owned by Frank Garst, one of a number of ranchers who leased pasture in the Cherokee Outlet.[43] All that survives of his personal life during those times is a story in the "persistent rumor" category which casts him in the role of household predator. Although the girl's husband soon heard about the liaison he stood quietly aside until she became pregnant. Then, since it was obvious to all that the credit for her condition belonged to Thomas Ketchum, the cuckold reacted sharply by persuading the courts to undo the parson's work. There are no further details, except that the girl lived "somewhere above Amarillo."[44]

These trail-driving jobs lasted for no more than a few weeks or months of each year, and Tom's rovings took him further west. Thompson says he worked for Head and Hearst's Diamond A and other outfits near Lordsburg and Deming "[a]t intervals between the years 1892–6," which is too imprecise to tell us much, but likely to be true as far as it goes.[45]

William G. Urton, as a stockholder in the Missouri-based Cass Land and Cattle Company, had established Roswell as a cattle-raising center in 1884, although at that time the nearest railheads were at Las Vegas, 150 miles to the north of the company's 7HL headquarters in the Cedar Canyon country, and El Paso, a similar distance southwest of Roswell. The outfit would have been well known to the Ketchums, and many other Southwest Texans, long before 1889, when the recently expanded company changed its brand and became "the Bar V outfit." So far as can be learned, however, the brothers did not become Bar V employees until 1892.[46]

Late that year, or early in the next, Tom took a winter break in Tom Green County, where, as we have related, Rome Shield saw him for the last time before they met in very different circumstances in 1899.[47]

Sam also moved back to Knickerbocker and spent most of the winter there. He and his old pal and brother-in-law Bige Duncan were in San Angelo on Thursday, December 1, 1892, perchance to study the saloons.[48]

Sam and Tom were Urton employees again for part of the following year. With them was their eighteen year old nephew Pat Smith, who had come from San Saba County the previous year to attend the Knickerbocker school. Sam, who visited Tom Green County far oftener and more openly than Tom, and stayed longer, left Knickerbocker for New Mexico on February 27, 1893, accompanied by young Smith.[49] Later that year, Tom, with or without the others, trailed a Bar V herd to Clayton. The time he is known to have spent on Eugene Manlove Rhodes's ranch in the Jornada del Muerto, north of Engle, New Mexico, seems to have been during the fall of 1893 or the following winter.[50]

Sam was back in Knickerbocker by summer's end, 1893. During the last week of September he, Berry, and a number of other Knickerbockerites, including O.L. Tweedy, part-owner of the town's principal general store, and John Ryburn, part-owner and resident foreman of the Half Circle Six, were in San Angelo for the fifth annual Concho Valley Fair. As always, the biggest crowd puller was the steer-roping contest, held on the fourth day, Friday, September 29, 1893. Sam was one of eight entrants. He "caught three times, [the] rope breaking each time, [but] was successful fourth time, and finished in 2:04." This was far from a contest winning performance. Ben Jones, or "the Uvalde guy" as the locals called him, collected first prize with a time of fifty-seven seconds. Among the other losers was Jack Miles, son of San Angelo pioneer Jonathan Miles. Jack, a couple of years earlier, was reckoned in Southwest Texas to be the world's champion roper.[51]

The following year found Tom in the employ of the VV ranch, a Lincoln County outfit. He was now nearly thirty-one years old and no better off than he had been five years earlier. This, he promised himself, would be his last season on the trail. An account of how Tom held himself to his vow comes from the exuberant pen of Jack Potter, another of the VV hands on that drive.

Jack was about a year younger than Ketchum. He was one of the fifteen children of the peripatetic gambler-turned-parson Andrew Jackson Potter, who had finally settled his family in Tom Green County in 1883, not long before the Ketchums' arrival. His credentials as a trail hand and stock-raiser were exemplary.[52]

One of Ketchum's peculiarities, wrote Potter, was his habit of administering self-punishment for his mistakes. Awaking one morning to find that his horse had strayed during the night because the stake rope had not been secured, Tom made amends by directing a stream of abuse at himself as he walked down to the roundup camp, a mile away, occasionally reinforcing the catechism by beating himself about the head with his six-shooter. He had far stronger cause for self chastisement a few weeks later.

For three seasons Tom had been lying adroitly and convincingly to a girl in Lincoln County. Each time he swore that he would save up his wages and marry her upon his return. At the outset of this particular drive, when "ranch folk for miles around" congregated at Fort Stanton to see off the outfit, Tom's girl "wept a little on his shoulder and told him that she would wait for him and that she could never love another." Tom rode away, assuring the other boys that this time he meant what he told her.

Some days later the herd reached Fort Sumner and Potter went for the mail which was awaiting collection from the post office. Ketchum was expecting a letter from the girl, and was mortified when there was none. He sat down gloomily and wrote her a long reproachful letter. When they got the cattle moving again Potter noticed that Ketchum was missing and turned back to look for him.

> I found him pulling his hair and cursing like a sailor. He began by swearing at the ugly weather and scarcity of water and then started out about his sweetheart, saying that if she "throwed him" he would go to the Hole-in-the-Wall country and hide from women and hate them for the rest of his life.

But less than a week later, when they camped on Perico creek, within sight of Clayton, Tom was in his best humor as he waited for the messenger boy to return with the mail. He grabbed the letters and feverishly sorted them through until he found the one addressed to him. He read it in silence, then took down his rope and strode away. Soon the sounds of "the most terrible cursing" arose from below the bank of the creek.

"There was old Ketchum," recalled Potter, "holding the letter in one hand and the doubled rope in the other. While beating himself over the head he was cursing himself for having confidence in women."

Someone tugged the rope away and asked him what the trouble was.

"Plenty," he replied, and gave the letter to Potter, who read it out to the men:

Tom Ketchum
Trail Driver
With John C. Bose

Sir:
Yours from Fort Sumner received. Had I not received this I would never have written to you. You will remember the day that I bid you farewell and wept a little and told you that I could love no other.

That was a little bait fixed up especially for your benefit. C.G. Slim was standing nearby looking on and you had no more than got out of sight when we went down to [Fort] Stanton and got married.

He is a fine man and how I admire him! I hope that you will realize that you taught me how to lie and you will feel that you are now getting the results.

Mrs. Cora Slim.

Tom immediately settled up with the trail boss and cut his two horses from the remuda. As he was packing his possessions onto one of the horses he was threatening some unseen or imaginary foe: "I dare you to make a move. You are liable to find your carcase stretched out on the prairie furnishing the coyotes a mess of carne."

In twenty minutes he was mounted and ready to leave.

"Adios boys," he said quietly, "I'm heading for the Hole-in-the-Wall in Wyoming."[53]

This anecdote may illustrate why Tom Ketchum became a misogynist—he may have been a misanthrope already—and it may even have helped him to decide that his future lay in outlawry. But he would not have devoted himself to lawlessness simply because he thought he had been jilted. The clue to what must be the real explanation for his career in crime lies in the violence of the fit that seized him after his comeuppance.

Ketchum's final choice, one must judge, was the natural product of his own unstable personality and improvident ways. These characteristics were manifest in his last years, with one difference: his spasms of unreasoning anger would be turned not against himself, as in the past, but against others. Yet, for all of this, it should not escape notice that there is no indication from either fact or folksay that he ever had anything further to do with women. This need not mean that he shunned them; it does suggest that such relationships as he may have enjoyed would have been, as someone once put it, "fleeting and sordid."[54] As such, they would escape the record and elude the rumor-monger.

At about this time, John Wright and his wife Wincie moved onto the Berry Ketchum ranch. The Wrights had come to Texas by covered wagon from the back country of North Carolina in the 1870s, and John had joined the Rangers. After sundry ramblings following John's discharge, the Wrights "took root" on the Loomis ranch in Concho County. For fifteen years their home was a small house on the creek. John "was a hound man and a great hunter." So was Berry.

That fall, soon after Wright left Loomis to live on Dove Creek, he and Berry went on a bear hunt in the breaks of the Rio Grande. Tom was invited to accompany them, along with two young nephews of the Ketchum brothers. Flashpoint came when one of the nephews unintentionally shot a hole into a mule deer skin that Tom intended to have tanned. Tom threatened to kill the boy and might have done so had not Berry disarmed him. In a gust of rage, Tom cursed his brother and threatened to kill him for whipping him when he was a boy and forcing him to do chores. Wright later told Loomis that he had never seen a man with so "insane" a temper as Tom's. Berry's comment was that he fully expected Tom to kill him one day.

A day or two later, Wright found fresh bear sign in a large canyon. His dogs routed out three bears, two of which escaped through the heavy brush. Tom shot the third, but it kept running until it reached a small cave. Tom, supposing the beast to be fatally wounded, bounded after it, and groped inside the cave for his trophy.

But the animal was only slightly wounded. It reacted with vigor when Tom seized its hind legs. The bear hunt turned briefly into a Ketchum hunt, with Tom in full flight and the bear only just to the rear. Tom kept yelling to Berry to kill the bear, but the spectacle was killing the older brother; he laid his gun down and laughed. There were a couple of bad moments for Tom when he tripped and fell, but the bear merely jumped over him and tore away into the brush. Tom's pride would have stood between himself and Berry's sense of fun, and he would not have thanked his brother for not helping him.[55]

Sam Ketchum, like Tom, quit as a trail-driver in 1894. He was in Tom Green County on October 2 when Pat Smith, then in the employ of the Half Circle 6, fell victim to the prairie-dog menace. Pat was riding "a bronch horse" at Monumental Well, in the "Sixes" pasture in Irion County, when the animal stepped in a dog hole. Smith was thrown under the falling horse, his neck was broken, and he died ten hours later. Ketchum family tradition describes him as a married man, though he was only twenty.[56]

Pat Smith's was not the only local fatality brought about by the burrowing proclivities of this species of vermin. Rome Shield was one of several who narrowly escaped death from the same cause.[57]

A few days after this accident, Berry, Sam, and their cousin Pete Ketchum joined the Democratic Club. A Democratic party organization was set up in the Knickerbocker schoolhouse on October 8, but the Ketchums took out their subscriptions in San Angelo after attending a meeting at the Court House.[58] Among the many who joined at about the same time were Rome Shield, who had no interest in party politics but every interest in re-election, which he could not hope to accomplish without the endorsement of the Democratic party; Richard Franklin Tankersley, a veteran rancher from Spring Creek, above Knickerbocker, for whom Sam and Tom had worked in the later 1880s; and Charles Collyns, one of the numerous English cattlemen in that section. Charlie Collyns had married a young Texas lady named Collins. He, his cousin Will, and Charley's father Bailyn M. Collyns, ranched on the North Concho and Grape Creek.[59]

Sam, unlike Tom, had a least a little money to show for his efforts. At the age of forty he desired neither ranch nor another shot at marriage, even if that had been a legal option.

Instead, he took a gaming concession in a San Angelo saloon, with Will Carver as his partner. Public information on this venture is non-existent: gaming in a public place, and encouraging others to do so, were misdemeanors under Texas law, punishable in county court by a fine of $25 and ten days in jail for each offense. But they were so widely practiced by citizens of all classes that, seethe as the righteous minority might, no sustained drive to suppress gambling would be mounted. Periodical acts of enforcement were selective and for demonstrative purposes. Those caught in the net would pay their fine and serve their time, but before 1900 their names would not appear in newsprint.[60]

The saloons reserved a rear or upstairs room for gaming—the "club room," or an annexe to it. The city marshal of San Angelo during the 1890s, the man who led the occasional raids on the gamblers, was James J. "Big Jim" Crenshaw, proprietor of the Legal Tender, one of San Angelo's leading saloons and places of male recreation.[61]

All that can be said of the Ketchum-Carver gambling venture is that it must have begun some time between late 1893 and early 1895 and that it could not have occupied anything like the whole of the intervening period.[62] It may have been shortlived; but, while it lasted, the partners, though hardly the cream of society, were still a long way from outlawry.

Sam passed the summer of 1895 working for local ranchers. The *San Angelo Standard* noticed in mid-August that he was back from Chicago.[63] Presumably he had been in charge of a shipment of beeves.

He was now forty-one years old and getting nowhere in the world while most of his lifelong friends and acquaintances were doing well, or well enough. Even those of modest means owned a home, owned or rented land, and owned the live and dead stock that would enable them to make a living from the land, and often a profit. He had nothing, apart from his clothes, weapons, and a horse and saddle or two.

We have not a scrap of information to show how Tom Ketchum occupied himself during the time between his abrupt disappearance from the VV camp on Perico creek and his return to Tom Green County some months later. Perhaps he did go to Hole-in-the-Wall to meet some old acquaintances and seek new ones. This area had been the lair of rustlers and outlaws for many years and if Tom never visited it before he must have heard it talked about. For want of evidence to the contrary, we must assume that he was not up to any serious mischief while he was in Wyoming.

There is no telling whether Tom Ketchum went back to Texas with any fixed plan in mind, but it is clear that he had forsworn any pretension to a sense of scruple. He was not long in finding adherents. One was David E. Atkins, a twenty year old farmhand and cowboy.[64] Another may have been George Upshaw, Jr., (always known as "Bud"), a young man with family connections in Tom Green, Concho, and Val Verde Counties.[65]

In the late fall of 1895 Tom, and others, became party to a sordid and criminal intrigue which ended in murder. Will Carver could not have been involved; he was in Indian Territory at the time. Sam Ketchum may or may not have been concerned in the affair; his reaction was such that in the long run the question of his complicity had very little bearing on his future one way or the other. From then onwards he and his brother were fugitives.

⁍ 4 ⁌

WILL, LAURA, AND BEN; THE
COURSE OF TRUE LOVE?

Tom Green and the counties surrounding it were big range country in the 1890s. The 23-acre section (13,720 acre) pasture, with nearly two thousand cattle which the Ellis Brothers of Schleicher County sold to Godfrey Miller for $20,000, was a pocket-handkerchief size compared with some of the other spreads. John Loomis, whose ranch headquarters were eight miles west of Paint Rock, Concho County, could offer to rent out "130,000 acres in a body," and men like Charles B. Metcalfe, of the XQZ, with enough of a home range near San Angelo to support several thousand head, could take up the lease. Loomis could also lease out the "pecan privilege"—the right to collect the product of every pecan tree in a twenty-seven mile belt alongside the Concho River.[1]

West of Loomis's headquarters were the holdings of J. Willis Johnson. With his Crows' Nest and Door Key ranches, located respectively to the east and south of San Angelo and embracing between them well over 100,000 acres, and with a variety of interests elsewhere, Johnson would become the county's leading landowner before the end of the decade. Unlike some of his neighbors, he had come to Tom Green County with nothing except native ability and industry. His fortune was founded in the purchase of a few cattle in 1881. Three years later, at about the time of Berry Ketchum's arrival from San Saba County, Johnson beat the incumbent, James D. Spears, in the shrieval elections and entered the first of his four consecutive terms of office.[2]

Among the other massive cattle operations in that sector of Texas were those of the previously mentioned Collynses, whose holdings included the DOK outfit, and Richard Franklin (usually called Frank) Tankersley, of Dove Creek and the Middle Concho; Funk Brothers, of Arden, on Rockey (or Rocky) Creek, with half a dozen brands; the Sawyer Cattle Company, or Bar S, whose headquarters were sixty miles from San Angelo, near the western boundary of Irion County; the Comer Brothers' 4 Cross Bar L, whose 200,000 acres included a fifty-mile stretch beside the Middle Concho; J. Blakely Taylor's 4 Cross D outfit, generally called "Dr. Taylor's ranch," which had several large pastures, the biggest being by Devil's River; and, greatest of all, the 300,000 acre domain of the Half Circle Six—"the Sixes," or "the Six"—with the main headquarters ranch at the head of Dove Creek as its radial point.[3]

Typically, the Sixes crew would leave its headquarters at the head of Dove Creek, near Knickerbocker, early in May, and head south through Schleicher County for the town of Sonora, seventy miles to the south. There, in the Devil's River country of western Sutton County and eastern Crockett County, at the southernmost limit of the Sixes range, they would begin the real work of the spring roundup. Robert A. Evans, a Schleicher County rancher who had been a Sixes cowboy in his youth, recalled that during the winter blizzards "cattle from the Plains and San Angelo country drifted southward to the Devil's and the Pecos Rivers, and to the Rio Grande," keeping the men in the saddle day and night.: "It was a hard, gruelling life, with the men usually dead for sleep." Yet, said Evans, some of the hands gambled after every long day's work was done.[4]

By the third week in June, or the beginning of the fourth, they might be back at Dove Creek, where the roundup would be completed. Many of the cowhands would take a day or two off for the Fourth of July, which Knickerbocker celebrated with unfailing fervor, copious speeches, overflowing refreshments, a picnic, and a dance.[5]

Fall roundup would begin before the middle of September. The crew might work the upper ranges first, and then move south to Sonora and beyond. Finally, in the first days of December, the hands would set out for the winter roundup, again working the range as far south as Devil's River. Most of them would be discharged, or leave of their own will, just before Christmas.[6]

Roundups on some of the ranches would recommence as early as February, but many cowhands would not be re-engaged until late April, May, or even early June. The Sixes, Tankersley's, Blake Taylor's, Garrett and Levy's, and other local ranches were a valuable source of temporary work for many in and around Knickerbocker who owned or leased smaller ranches—or tried to farm on land that often lacked running water and needed irrigation. Such, during the 1880s and early '90s, were Berry Ketchum, his brother-in-law Bige Duncan, Jr., and, for awhile, Sam and Tom.[7]

Bige and Nancy Duncan were well-established in Knickerbocker by 1890. Already they had at least four children; eventually, there would be seven, the sixth named Gus Thomas Duncan after Bige's great friend, business partner, and boon companion Gus Thomas, "one of the pioneers of Knickerbocker."

Gus Thomas—"the inimitable Gus"—had been the Sixes' foreman during the 1880s. As one of the most seasoned cowmen in the country, Thomas was appointed wagon boss for the Sixes at roundup time, years after he had left their full-time employment. Late in April of 1893 he was put in charge of the roundup for both the Sixes and Frank Tankersley. But he did not participate in that year's fall roundup. By then, he was concentrating on establishing himself as a successful cattleman and displaying himself as a pillar of moneyed staidness. "Gus Thomas looks quite dignified now riding over the Boulevards of our city in his new phaeton," observed "Zoe," Knickerbocker's current gossip writer.[8]

Gus and Bige were called, aptly, "the inseparables." Another title conferred jointly upon them was that of "the hot tamales," presumably in recognition of their well-publicized liking for the good fellowship offered by San Angelo's saloons and the uncomplicated fun provided by the "French high kickers" of the traveling "leg shows" at the Opera House.[9]

During the early 1890s Bige, Gus, and Bob Lowe, a friend who later owned a livery stable in San Angelo, worked on the Spring Creek ranch of Willis Johnson's Door Key outfit. The ranch straddled the boundaries of Tom Green and newly-formed Irion County, well to the west of San Angelo. From the fall of 1893 onwards, Bige and Gus appear to have been running the Spring Creek outfit with something close to a free hand. Tom Ketchum freely admitted that Nancy and Bige—unlike Berry—had always welcomed him. It is not surprising that Tom should introduce the Door Key brand to the Territory of New Mexico, with or without the consent or knowledge of the management.[10]

Knickerbocker's post office was an annexe to the general store owned and operated by two brothers, Joseph W. and Oliver Lord ("Ollie") Tweedy. In the late 1870s Joe Tweedy and three other enterprising young men from New York State owned the biggest sheep outfit in the region. One of the partners had given Knickerbocker its name. Ollie Tweedy came out from Plainfield, New Jersey, a couple of years later. Joe Tweedy made money out of wool (until the slump of 1885 destroyed the partnership), and then out of the store, but did not make many converts to the Republican party whose local organizer he was.[11]

Tweedy's was the biggest general store in Knickerbocker, but it had strong competition. One store became a serious rival of the Tweedy concern. Its owner was Thomas R. Hardin, originally from Mississippi, who arrived from Kosse, Limestone County, later in 1891, twenty-seven years old and determined to make good. A year earlier he had been struck down by a debilitating disease. He had made only a partial recovery; thereafter he could barely walk without the support of an improvised crutch—a hoe or axe handle. Despite being a semi-invalid, he was energetic and full of initiative. By the spring of 1892 his store was doing well. In May, 1893, he went to Clio, Texas, to marry Daisy Baze, a dozen years his junior.

Daisy belonged to one of the founding families of the the area south and west of San Angelo. The Bazes were connected to several other of the neighborhood's pioneer families—the Ryans, Atkinses, and Becks. Daisy was the daughter of Michael Polk Baze by his second wife, the former Virginia Ryan. In 1882, a year after Virginia's death in childbirth, Polk Baze had taken Sarah Josephine Atkins as his third wife. This marriage had ended in divorce on December 2, 1891, eighteen months before Daisy wed Tom Hardin. Daisy's half brother, Albert, and many other kinsfolk were still living in Knickerbocker when the young woman returned with her ambitious and already prosperous husband. Some of her relations disliked Hardin and disapproved of the marriage; we cannot be sure whether the dislike preceded the disapproval or was caused by it.[12]

Soon Hardin was holding office in the local Democratic party organization. He was, the *San Angelo Standard* would comment, "well thought of by nearly everybody."[13] That took proper, though tacit, account of the few who did not like him, whether for family reasons, or because they saw him as too thrustful, or both. One who came to hate him was Dave Atkins, a hot-tempered, over-bibulous, and altogether unstable young cowpuncher and farmhand, ten years younger than his sister, the former Josephine Atkins Baze, and soon to be a founder member of the Ketchum gang.

David Edward Atkins, called Edward by his mother, was born near San Angelo on May 8, 1874, fifth of the six children of Orrin and Martha Atkins. Orrin Harrison Atkins had come west from Ohio. The former Martha Mary Baker was a native of Georgia, half-Cherokee on her mother's side. Whether or not the mother was a full-blood—even in the 1840s there was a strong element of European stock among both the Western and the Eastern Cherokee—Martha's Indian blood showed; or, at least, she thought it did, and was touchy about it. She may have feared the force of local memory, in which the ravages of roving bands of Comanches and Kiowas were close to the surface of recall. The Atkinses' neighbors did not know about Martha's Indian ancestry; or, if they did, they were untroubled by it. At any rate, John Jefferson Atkins, the couple's first offspring, was described as the second white child born in Tom Green County, or the first Anglo child to have been born in the Lipan Springs area.[14]

Atkins, senior, was a hunter and trapper; the second of his three sons, Walter Edwin, grew up with the same skills or predilection. But Orrin died of pneumonia in 1877, at the age of thirty-six, when John was eleven; Walter, six; and Dave, three. Martha Atkins took her young family, including a baby girl, first to Ben Ficklin and then, after the great floods of 1882 destroyed much of the town, to Knickerbocker.[15]

At the age of fifteen Dave quit the family farm to find work as a cowboy. He was soon looking beyond Texas. In 1891, he went to New Mexico. Many young and not-so-young Texans were leaving for New Mexico—sometimes to stay, sometimes to look, sometimes just for a change. With Dave Atkins, the New Mexico trip was the first expression of a deep-rooted restlessness that hardened into wanderlust. By his own account, he returned to Texas after a few months, remained for a few months, and went back again in 1892. This is verified by "Otto," the Knickerbocker press correspondent, who reported on January 18, 1893, that "Dave Adkins [*sic*] has returned from a long absence in New Mexico."[16]

Shortly after his return to the Atkins farm, he was off again, trying to make a go of cultivating the soil of desert country in the far south of Texas, not far from Rio Grande City. After a year or so of that, he was back in Knickerbocker, where he met Sabe Banner. On Christmas Eve, 1894, they were married at Mason, Texas.

The household was soon augmented by a baby girl, whom they named Ruby. But Dave was not much of a husband and father. He not only lived and worked in and around Knickerbocker; he caroused there. It was then that he ran up against Tom Hardin. The immediate source of the trouble between them was a bill that Atkins ran up at the Hardin store and had settled only in part. Words were exchanged. Atkins was disorderly and Hardin restrained him. Dave believed, or alleged, that Tom had slipped up behind him in the dark and struck him with an axe handle. Hardin denied it. Rome Shield, the sheriff, seems in later years to have accepted Dave's word. Dave brooded, but, for the time being, did nothing.[17]

Although the sheepmen from New York had bestowed the name Knickerbocker upon the village on Dove Creek, they were far from the first settlers in the area. Frank

Tankersley had been running cattle near Spring and Dove Creeks for nearly a decade when Joe Tweedy and his friends rolled up with their woollies. Others were only a year or two ahead of or behind the New Yorkers. Among these were a couple from Little Spring, Washington County, Arkansas, Elliott Rucker Byler and Serena Patton Byler, with their son Jacob A. ("Jake"), and daughters Stacy, Lucinda, Samantha (called "Manty"), Mary, and Viana. Their year of arrival is variously put at 1875, 1876, and 1878. If the first is correct, Jake would have been about fifteen when the Bylers unloaded their wagons beside Dove Creek; Viana, the youngest child, born July 24, 1874, would not yet have been a year old. Still in Arkansas were the oldest children of the family, all four of them married women. The youngest of these was Fereby, who on September 5, 1875, at seventeen, married J. Henry Bullion, fourteen years her senior.[18]

At their third attempt at home-making in Texas, the Bylers had settled at a point sixteen miles southwest of Fort Concho, roughly halfway between the future villages of Knickerbocker and Sherwood. Since their farm was beside the water's edge, the soil was good and they did well. In 1881, they were joined by Fereby Bullion and her three offspring: Laura, born some twelve months after her mother's marriage; Mary Frances (known as Fannie Lee), born in 1878; and two-year-old Daniel. Her marriage to Henry Bullion was over. Henry was not dead and there was no divorce; the couple had simply broken up.[19]

Fereby Bullion may or may not have been a faithless wife. As mother and daughter she was defective. The Bylers did their best for their young grandchildren, but the youngsters' flirtatious and flighty mother was not a steadying influence.

She worked as a housekeeper for the Grinnell family, and moved into a house on their sheep ranch, but she paid far more attention to the men who paid attention to her than she gave her children.[20]

In March 1888, after the death of the estranged husband, Fereby married James William Scott. She went off with her new husband, leaving Laura, Fannie, and Daniel in the care of her parents. Fortunately for all, most of the Byler children had grown up and were leaving home. Jake, who had spent most of the intervening decade elsewhere in Texas or in New Mexico, returned to Knickerbocker in 1885 and married Annie Weldy a year later. Soon afterwards Lucinda became the wife of James C. Lambert, who had succeeded Gus Thomas as foreman of the Sixes. A little later, two of the Bylers' other daughters, Manty and Mary, married a pair of brothers, Alonzo A. "Lon" and Charles Allen, cowboys with small ranching interests of their own. By 1891 only Viana, the Bylers' youngest daughter, was living with her parents.[21]

Fereby's choice of J.W. Scott had been a bad one; the marriage soon collapsed. Hard on the heels of this rapid change of circumstances was a bout of sickness that brought her life to an end on April 21, 1891. Laura Bullion was now fourteen and a half—two years younger than her aunt Viana; Fannie, thirteen; and Daniel, about twelve.[22]

As Laura was quick to say after her own descent from grace, her grandparents were of "eminent respectability." E.R. Byler was described by the stoutly Democratic *San Angelo Standard* as the "father of Democracy in Knickerbocker." He organized the local party, latterly with much help from Tom Hardin; took the chair at impromptu citizens' meetings; stood for office as Justice of the Peace for Precinct No. 4, which included Knickerbocker; and served on the board of trustees for the Knickerbocker Public School.[23]

It was probably in 1891 that Will Carver entered Laura's life, though at that time the focus of his eyes and ambitions was her aunt, Viana, now seventeen.

At that time William Richard Carver was an honest cowhand; generally quiet, reserved, perhaps even shy, but with a host of friends. Though he was also a most deadly shot with both pistol and revolver, this was taken merely as evidence of ordinary attributes developed to an extraordinary degree. Such marksmanship as his was exceptional; but it was admired or envied by his friends, who saw no ill-portent in the amount of practice he must have put in to achieve it.[24]

Will's parents, George Alfred and Martha Jane Rigsby Carver, had left Missouri for Texas during the Civil War. They settled first in Comanche County, in the heart of the state, where their first child, Frances Emeline, was born on January 9, 1866. Their next move took them to Wilson County, southeast of San Antonio, where William Richard first saw the light of day on September 12, 1868. Among their neighbors were Richard T. Carver, Will's "Uncle Dick," and a family named Causey, apparently kin to Dick Carver's wife Margaret. In 1870, George Carver vanished; it was said that he had become embroiled in a bitter feud and was afraid for his life. On the mistaken presumption that he was dead, Martha married Walter Scott Causey in San Antonio on April 16, 1872. Soon the Causeys and the Richard Carvers pulled out for Bandera County, where they settled on or near Pipe Creek, a few miles east of the town of Bandera and seventy miles northwest of their last home.[25]

Frances and Will Carver got on well with their father-in-law and the new half-brothers and half-sisters that time brought along, but kept their own family name. Years afterwards, Will, in search of a fresh alias, chose a surname that resembled his stepfather's, and became, pro tempore, "Will Casey."

After his sister Fannie married Frank Walter Hill in Bandera County on November 8, 1880, Will turned increasingly to his Uncle Dick, who was now living in Uvalde County, to the southwest of Bandera and within striking distance of Eagle Pass and Del Rio. Before long, Will, possibly seventeen or eighteen by now, and Dick, nineteen years older, were employed on roundups in the Devil's River country between Juno and Comstock. It may have been around 1887 or 1888 that Will was hired by Edward R. Jackson's 09 outfit. Ed Jackson knew Carver well and liked and trusted him well enough to accept the appointment of executor after the outlaw's death in 1901.[26]

Another who hired Carver during this period and thought well of him was W.L. (Lee) Aldwell. Jackson and Aldwell were friends who, in time, pooled their resources and expertise and became partners. They had extensive cattle interests in both southwest Texas and the Indian Territory. Later, they invested heavily and successfully in sheep. Finally, in 1900, they were co-founders of the First National Bank of Sonora, with Aldwell as cashier. This was the bank that Carver and three companions were planning to rob when he was killed.[27]

According to research first presented by John Eaton, Carver was on the payroll of the Half Circle Six by June 1889, when Jim Lambert was foreman; he might well have been engaged a few weeks before that date. This would have been when he started to see something of Lambert's sister-in-law, Viana Elliott Byler, and her niece, Laura Bullion.[28]

Tom Ketchum was in Tom Green County when the 1889 spring roundup began. That, it seems, is when he and Will met for the first time. The story comes from John J. Arthur, a schoolmate of Laura Bullion and a son of Judge Stephen D. Arthur, owner of a half share in Knickerbocker's cotton gin.

As Arthur told it to Roy Holt, who, like himself, belonged to a family resident in Knickerbocker from its early days, Ketchum was the bully of the outfit. Being a "green hand," Carver was made "the butt of a lot of joshing" from the rest of the crew, and knew it, but did not react. When the punchers turned in for the night, Ketchum placed his roll next to Carver's and lay down, still wearing boots and spurs. Speaking loudly enough for his voice to be heard by everyone, Tom warned the newcomer that he was subject to fits and apt to attack and put spurs into the occupant of the bed next to his. Will drew his gun—very slowly—and retorted that he was sure to wake up shooting if disturbed in the night. That was the end of the practical joking. It was also the beginning of a kind of rough and ready friendship that was to be fatal for them both.[29]

By now Uncle Dick Carver had gone his own way. Dick's wife died in 1889 and Dick went to the Indian Territory and immediately remarried. A son, Scott Carver, was born in November 1890.[30] There is no proof that Will ever saw him again; but since he is known to have visited Indian Territory for months at a time at least twice in the 1890s, it is likely that he did.

In Bob Evans's recollection, Carver was popular with the rest of the men; he was "generous and easy-going," and a good hand, though inclined, as most were, "to let off steam once in a while at the saloon." Evans is also the source of the story of how Will befriended George Hamilton, who took a job with the Sixes despite being tubercular. Carver took it upon himself to break in the "salty buckers" in Hamilton's string that George could not have handled. Hamilton, who beat his illness and became a successful rancher, was among those who would identify Carver as he lay dead or dying in Sonora in 1901.[31]

Carver's employment with the Half Circle Six in Texas ceased in the summer of 1892. During the preceding year he had been much in the company of Viana and Laura, though it was the older girl, and not fifteen-year-old Laura, who was the focus of his eyes and ambitions. On February 9, 1892, without the blessing of Viana's parents, she and Will Carver were wed in San Angelo. Only a few weeks later, Carver's employment took him to the Indian Territory.[32]

That summer Laura Bullion's life was changed forever by two unrelated events, the second of which also marked the turning point for Will Carver.

In the spring of 1893 Laura's uncle Jim Lambert resigned as foreman of the Sixes to take up a similar position with Blake Taylor's 4XD outfit—"Dr. Taylor's ranch." Since Taylor's main range in southwest Texas was in the Devil's River country, the day soon came for Jim and Lucinda to vacate their house in Knickerbocker and move south. Lon Allen, who had married Lucinda's sister Samantha, went with the Lamberts. One consequence of this was that, thereafter, the Bullion children were continually in transit. Evidently Elliott and Serena Byler's married daughters had agreed to relieve their ageing parents of some of the burden of caring for—and keeping an eye on—the three teenage Bullions.[33]

Then, on July 22, 1892, after less than six months of marriage (her husband an absentee for perhaps three of them), and two days short of her eighteenth birthday, Viana Byler Carver died of "complications [during] pregnancy;" there was a stillborn child, "sex unknown." She was buried in Sherwood cemetery. The stone that her parents placed above Viana Carver's grave was inscribed "Viana E. Byler."[34]

All authorities agree that Carver was badly broken up by what had happened. Bob Evans and John Rae, another local rancher, well known in Irion, Tom Green, and Schleicher Counties, agree that he never punched cows in Texas thereafter. Frank Shelton, who a few years afterwards would be doing his best to arrest Carver for train robbery, was another who knew him well. He also knew, or said, more of the circumstances of Viana's death and its effect upon Carver.

Carver, opined Shelton, was "a pretty decent youngster" and a steady worker. He "thought the world of" the "nice girl" he married, but after "she died giving birth to their child" the young widower "went to pieces. Drinking and gambling led him to outlawry." The record supports Shelton.[35]

Four or five years later, Carver was still disconsolate, as Leonard Alverson noticed and mentioned in his reminiscences.[36] Was his melancholy deepened by a sense of remorse, even a consciousness of guilt? The question is unanswerable, but not unreasonable. Equally, he may have been upset by the Bylers' rejection of him, and resentful of being unjustly blamed for Viana's decease. He was true to her memory—in his fashion: after her death he used many women, but never loved one, though Laura Bullion was deceived, or deceived herself, into thinking otherwise.

In the light of Elliott Byler's place in the community and involvement in school affairs, it followed that, so long as Laura, Fannie, and Dan Bullion were living in Knickerbocker, their record of school attendance was good. In November, 1892, Fannie and Daniel, Grade 4 pupils, each scored 90 marks for attendance and attainment. Daniel repeated this performance in December; Fannie, though a year older, had suffered demotion to the third Grade. Here she remained until the beginning of March, when she was restored to Grade 4.[37]

Daniel had made the Fifth Grade by September, 1893, the opening of a new ten-month term. That is the last we hear of his education; he must have been a bright boy, but in the absence of family means, he may have reached the point where he had to make his own way. If he did carry on with school, it would have been elsewhere; he may have been packed off to the Lamberts or other relations. Fannie and Laura certainly spent the summer on Devil's River with the Lamberts or the Lon Allens. On September 6, 1893, a couple of days into the scholastic year, the sisters traveled up to Knickerbocker and enrolled for school.[38]

Where had Laura been between the second half of 1892 and the summer of 1893? The prosaic answer would place her with the Lamberts, or one of the Allen households, or possibly with the Jasper Pecks, who were also kin to the Bylers. This is reasonable surmise, but no evidence exists to sustain it. There is, however, another credible explanation, and one that has at least one piece of evidence to commend it. Laura's cousin, Bernice Byler Haag, states that, sometime between 1891 and 1893, and against the wishes of the Bylers, Laura left her guardians' household for San Antonio.[39]

Commenting on this, Carolyn Bullion McBryde suggests that Laura lived and worked as a prostitute in Fannie Porter's Sporting House. The supporting evidence is skimpy: Laura's statement to a St. Louis detective that she "had shifted for herself, dancing in Wyoming and Texas gambling halls;" and the location of the Porter palace of pleasure at the corner of Military Avenue and Delarosa Street, coupled with her use of the alias "Della Rose." Discussion of the second item will be postponed for a few moments. The first implies no more than that Laura engaged in prostitution in various places at various times.[40]

And there is the negative evidence. Laura was small, slight, sallow, listless in manner and limp of personality. Here is the first of two contemporary portraits of Laura at the age of twenty-five:

> Laura is a rather dull, spiritless country girl, a product of Arkansas, reared on a farm and possessing the meagre intelligence and education common to that type . . . She is about 5 feet 2 inches tall; [four feet eleven and a half inches by actual measurement] and weighs about 90 pounds, and her appearance indicates extreme frailty [was the reporter referring to her morals or to her physique?]. Her face is shallow and expressionless, with an entire absence of mobility save when her lips relax ever so slightly in a smile or laugh. Her eyes are bright enough, but without any life or expression in them even in moments of excitement . . . Her whole face is suggestive of dullness of intellect, which is accentuated by her drawling speech.

Still, the reporter conceded, "her voice is low and pleasant."[41]

The second description is even more hostile:

> "Della Rose," or Miss Bullion, is far from attractive. She has a pointed chin, high cheek bones, and small, white "dog" teeth, and when she closes her mouth it is with a resolution so emphatic that it seems that she will never open it again. By people of refinement and culture she would be considered repulsive. There is that something about her that smacks of the gutter. Her features are irregular, her hair is arranged with no regard for adornment, and she has a sallow complexion. . . . [T]he general appearance of the woman would indicate that she was accustomed only to rural life and habits.[42]

That closing line was not meant as a compliment; rather, it looks as if it were written with a sneer and meant to be read with one.

Some corrective is needed. Those lines were drafted and published when Laura was between interrogations at a police station, having been caught red-handed with a valise full of forged banknotes. Almost worse; she had been living as a concubine.

Her best may not have been very good; but, whatever it was, she could not be looking or feeling it. And the press had no interest in making her look good.

All appearances to the contrary, Laura in maturity may have been endowed with sufficient sexual magnetism to attract and hold Will Carver and, later, Ben Kilpatrick. She possessed not an atom of the lurid, bold, or brassy appeal that was the stock-in-trade of the strumpets who draped the furniture of high-price emporiums such as Fannie Porter's. If Laura worked as a prostitute in San Antonio, it was not at Madam Porter's or any of the "classier" parlors. Conversely, if she worked for Fannie, she would not have been on the sales staff; she might have been employed as a chambermaid or in some even more menial capacity. The one certainty is that she could not have lived in San Antonio for as long as a year without knowing the location of the more notorious brothels. But what she lacked at twenty-five she could not possibly have had at fifteen or sixteen.

If she went to San Antonio as early as 1891—she did not turn fifteen until October that year—it would have been just before her young aunt's marriage to Will Carver; it might even have been because of it. As she herself was once quoted:

> "[Y]ou-all know how it is in small country places—they [sic] ain't much for a girl to do, and when a girl ain't got no parents to look after her and tell her how to do right, she just naturally gets to running wild. I got brushed up a heap agin Bill Carver, and he sort o' took a shine to me."[43]

The imputation would have pained the honest and diligent Bylers, who had done their best for their aberrant granddaughter. Knickerbocker at large seems to have been more affronted by the rustic idiom the St. Louis journalists put in Laura's mouth.[44] Her language had always been "fairly accurate and grammatical," the villagers insisted. They may have had a point. Whether or not her speech was as colloquial as the papers rendered it, surviving letters from her are not only grammatical but well written.[45]

She was not only better educated but more intelligent than the city journalists believed, or said. While in police custody she lied like a trooper (or a trouper) for as long as she could. She may have been acting the part of an untutored yokel to pull the wool over her interrogators' eyes.

Carver would have known where she was in 1892, and could have joined her in San Antonio in the last months of that year or early the next. It is not too fanciful to consider that he may have set himself to burn away his grief in dissolute abandon. Laura could have been part of the picture.

An alternative accounting for Carver's movements following his wife's death has him going to the Indian Territory shortly afterwards to take charge of the Half Circle 6's herds that were fattening at pasture there.[46] Depending on whether he went to the Territory in 1892 or 1893, he could have stayed awhile in San Antonio either before his departure northwards or after his return.

From September of 1893 onwards, we have a clearer view of events. Laura was placed in the fifth school grade, alongside Daniel, both earning an average of above

90; Fannie returned at once to Devil's River, only to be brought back by Jasper Peck on October 4. This time her schooling was resumed. She earned a rating of 92 in the fourth grade, but Laura, in the fifth, scored 93.[47]

On Sunday, October 28, the Bullion girls and their friend Mattie Holiman passed the day "at the famous spring near the six ranch." With them were Lee Yerby, who likewise was still at school, and Alex Jones, a young man from Falls County who was taking a health cure—for Knickerbocker and nearby Christoval were already winning notice as health resorts. The two young men had sold some wool in San Angelo two or three days previously and, no doubt, were in high spirits. "Zoe," the Knickerbocker press correspondent, always on the lookout for any hint of romance—and, as usual, short of real news—wrote the picnic into his weekly newsletter to the *Standard*.[48]

The academic month that ended January 8, 1894, saw Laura in the sixth grade, along with Mattie Holiman, Mary and Basil Arthur, and others. She was awarded an average of 90; Fannie, still in the fourth, but improving, received 95. After that, we have no word of the sisters' academic progress. Half the reason for this is that C.M Cash, the principal, and his wife, who assisted him, moved swiftly on to an opportunity elsewhere. The other half is that Professor Cash and "Zoe" were one and the same man.[49]

Once the Cashes were gone, the *Standard* had to do without correspondence from Knickerbocker until "Plucky" took over in mid-May, to report, amid very little else, that "Jim Lambert and family" were expected to return to Knickerbocker shortly. They did, three months later. They moved into their old home and Jim bought a one-third interest in the Arthur and Holiman cotton gin.[50]

Laura and Fannie continued with their schooling. Laura spent at least part of the 1895 summer vacation in Water Valley, in the northwest of Tom Green County, and about midway between San Angelo and Sterling City. It is not known who gave her roof and board; not the Lamberts, Pecks, or Lon Allens, who were all at Taylor's Devil's River ranch, nor her aunt Mary and Mary's husband, Charlie Allen. Charlie, if he was not a rolling stone by inclination, was kept on the move anyway by his duties on various cattle ranges. In September, 1895, he was in Ozona.[51]

At any rate, "Plutus," successor to "Plucky," reported in his letter of September 26 that Laura had returned to Knickerbocker from Water Valley to attend school. By now she was almost nineteen. Jasper Peck's son Walter arrived from the Taylor ranch at the same time.

"Plutus" had plenty else to write about: Laura's aunt, Lucinda Lambert, had been in Dallas for eye treatment; Berry Ketchum's mother-in-law had come from San Saba to visit Barshie; and, on Friday, September 20, burglars had cut their way into Tom Hardin's store, extracted $150 worth of goods—ranging from shirts and pants to cigars and chewing gum—and set the place alight "to cover their tracks" (or for added malice). Luckily for Hardin, the fire was soon extinguished. As Annie Weldy Byler recalled: " . . . Mr. Burleson's [Hardin's] store was stripped of food, ammunition and tobacco. They [the thieves] had set a bunch of papers and trash on fire in an attempt to burn the store. The fire that they lighted was too near a big sack of rice; when the sack began to burn, the rice began to spill out on the fire and smothered out the flames." His loss had been heavier the previous November 28, when the store was burglarized for the first time.

Hearsay of local origin has pointed blame at Tom Ketchum; but, whatever suspicions may have been voiced informally, no public accusations, let alone official charges, appear to have been leveled at him during his lifetime. His later record does not amount to an atom of evidence. We may note the suspicions, but must allow him the benefit of the doubt.[52]

What, meanwhile, of Will Carver? Very little is known. Whether or not he kept company with Laura in San Antonio in late 1892, he was most likely back from the Indian Territory by the following spring or summer. Since Sam Ketchum was in Tom Green County for much of both 1893 and 1894, it would have been during that time that he and Sam were running together, drinking hard, gambling, and briefly operating an unlawful gaming concession in a San Angelo saloon. If no liaison between him and Laura Bullion had existed before, one began now. It may have been then that, from Sherwood, he wrote her a letter that she kept for years. Sherwood is but eight miles from Knickerbocker, but Carver would not have had the face to call on her at or anywhere near the Byler farm; hence the letter. The letter, commented a journalist who saw it long after it had been written, was "of a friendly character." That may be why she kept it.[53]

Sometime during 1895, Carver paid another visit to the Indian Territory. It is not known why he went or what he did there. But "Plutus," recording Will's return from the Territory to spend that year's Christmas holidays at Knickerbocker, wrote as if he had been absent for some while.[54]

Probably it was during this second trip to the Territory that Will wrote to Laura from Ponca City, a post office in a small tribal reservation just east of the former Cherokee Outlet in the far north of Oklahoma Territory. This communication was written in the same terms of affection as the one from Sherwood, and the young woman preserved it along with the other.[55]

Carver made his holiday a good one. In the last week of January, 1896, a party left the village "on a big hunt." Four of the bunch struck out for the Pecos; the other four—Lon Allen, Will Carver, Wickes Martin, and William Johnson—set off for "the head draws of [the] Main Concho."[56]

Others had more serious matters to attend to: Jim Lambert and Jasper Peck drove out to Ozona with a load of corn; Sheriff Rome Shield, his deputies Arthur West and Dick or Charlie Runyon, and Sheriff William N. ("Uncle Bill") Elliott of Irion County were prowling about on business they did not disclose but whose purpose will emerge shortly.[57]

Carver now vanishes from the record for almost a year; but negative inference provides a sure pointer to his general whereabouts during most of the remainder of 1896. He is known to have stayed in southeast Arizona before he turned outlaw in 1897, and must have been there for some months to have become as well acquainted as he undoubtedly was with parts of Cochise and Graham Counties and an adjacent slice of New Mexico. Such a span of time otherwise unaccounted for is not available to him in any year prior to 1896.

Thus it would have been in the late spring or early summer of 1896 that he was hired by Bob Johnson, the newly-appointed foreman of the Erie Cattle Company. Carver's range skills were obvious, and Johnson, as was well known, cared about nothing else. Not that Carver was on the dodge—yet; an oft-repeated tale that he had fled from Texas after being "forced" to kill a man in self-defense was not heard until long after his death, for the very sufficient reason that it was untrue.[58]

With no indictments or warrants along his back trail, Will could, and did, go by his real name. But Johnson's discretion suited Carver's reticence. Will's past life, if not blameless, had been as good as most and better than many; but he wanted to put it behind him. He was well on the way to making up his mind to look for opportunities in crime.

Carver would not simply have traveled to Cochise County and headed directly for the Erie roundup. Someone must have shown him the way. He would have heard something about the cattle industry of southwest New Mexico and southeast Arizona long before he left Texas, and would have learned more during a brief period of employment on T.N. Hawkins's Cross H outfit in southeastern New Mexico, probably in the late winter or early spring of 1896.[59]

His next stopping place is a quasi-certainty. His sister Fannie had moved west with her husband and four children in the mid-1880s. Their fifth child was born in the silver-mining town of Kingston, New Mexico, in June, 1887. By the end of 1890 the family were living a few miles east of Duncan, Arizona, at a point just inside southern Grant County (now Hidalgo County), New Mexico. They were to remain there until 1901. That would have been where Will Carver paused before pushing on into Cochise County. The Hills, or some of their neighbors, could have told him all he needed to know before seeking employment locally.[60]

During his time with the Erie crew, or soon after it, he got to know Texas Canyon (familiarly, and more usually, called "Tex Canyon") and those who frequented this secluded valley in the lower east slope of the Chiricahua Mountains, close to the border with Mexico.[61]

Those were lively days in that corner of the Southwest. During the late summer and through the fall of 1896 public interest was seized and held by the outlandish exploits of the High Five or Black Jack gang, composed of men who had all been employed in Cochise County as cowhands or bronco-tamers. At least one of these men—William Christian, variously alias Ed Williams and Frank Williams, but dubbed "Black Jack"—had worked for the Erie outfit at about the same time as Carver. Matters were made more interesting—and, eventually, confusing—by the arrival in southeast Arizona of Sam and Tom Ketchum towards the end of 1896. By now, both brothers had blood on their hands; but, as no warrants were out for them, they could alternately travel and loaf about Graham and Cochise Counties under their true names.[63]

In December Carver went back to southwest Texas, where he visited his mother and the rest of the Causey household in Bandera County. Within five months he would become one of the most hunted desperadoes in the United States.[63]

Laura Bullion, as far as anyone can say, had been living quietly with her kinsfolk in Tom Green and Sutton Counties throughout 1896. She emerges briefly into the light on December 12 when she helped represent Knickerbocker at "the grand supper and ball" in Sherwood. Her sister Fannie was in the party, along with James Garrett and his wife, presumably the responsible adults who had arranged the outing; Lottie Veck, who was in charge of the Mexican school at Knickerbocker and belonged to San Angelo's unofficial first family; Mattie Holiman; Sam Moore, at that time a trusted employee of the Bar S ranch, who over the next few years would give the neighborhood grounds for both outrage and hilarity; John and Basil Arthur; and two other young men named Elmer Johnson and Arthur McGuirt. Berry Ketchum, meanwhile, was selling a couple of hundred steers at $22.50 per head, and Bige Duncan was visiting his brothers and other kin in San Saba County.[64]

Private lives, except perhaps those of the rich or famous, were seldom a matter of public notice. Criminals and their consorts, if their relationship was in any sense binding, were especially circumspect. All that is known of the affair between Will Carver and Laura Bullion is that it continued, furtively and spasmodically, for four more years. A trip to Fort Worth, which Laura vainly hoped would make her the second Mrs. Carver, most likely did not take place until 1898.[65]

Laura maintained that she did not meet Ben Kilpatrick until 1901. She was probably not telling the truth, but it is also likely that she had known him only slightly before they were brought together by Bill Chaney, once of San Saba County, now of Christoval, and a mutual friend of Will, Laura, and Ben.[66] Ben is supposed to have worked on the Half Circle Six at sundry times in the 1880s and 90s, but not even his industrious biographer, Arthur Soule, has produced any proof that he was. It will be shown in due course that Kilpatrick could not have been well known in the Knickerbocker area, nor Carver in Kilpatrick's home neighborhood of the Hills, Concho County, about thirty miles east of San Angelo.[67]

In 1880 the Kilpatrick family consisted of George William Kilpatrick, forty-three years old, originally from Tennessee; his wife, born Mary C. Davis in South Carolina, 1849; and nine children, all born in Coleman County, Texas.[68]

William, the oldest child, was born in 1870. Daniel Boone, known always by his middle name or initials, was born early in 1873; Benjamin Arnold on January 5, 1874; George M., in February of 1876; Edward J., just under a year later; and Alice E. in May, 1878. A second daughter, Etta C., and another son, Felix C., were born in January 1882 and April 1884, respectively, and the ninth child, Ola, joined the household in October, 1886, about a year after the family's move to Concho County.[69]

The progeny, not exceptionally numerous for the time and place, turned out to be unusually vexatious for the forces of law and order. Ben, George, and Ed, became outlaws and Felix—said to have been the "meanest" of the lot—also turned to crime though not, apparently, to armed robbery.

The journalist and local historian, J. Marvin Hunter, stated that the Kilpatricks were "well thought of by their neighbors." That is not what the neighbors themselves said of most of the Kilpatricks, nor what the Kilpatricks ascribed to the neighbors. John Loomis, the New York-born cattle king who lived nearby, admitted that George, Sr., was "an honest, industrious citizen" and that Boone, too, was respected. But Ben,

Ed, and George, Jr., were "natural born criminals who started their careers as boys in their early teens by robbing sheep camps." Both Ed and young George were employed for a time on the Loomis ranch. Loomis spoke of them as "lesser criminals" who never realized their ambition to follow Ben into serious brigandage. If he had heard anything about their lives away from Texas he would have known otherwise. Ma Kilpatrick, to all intents and purposes the head of the house, never disapproved of their actions; on the contrary, she encouraged their criminality. Loomis characterized her as "a she-devil." His views on her and most of her brood were those generally held in the locality, and the Kilpatricks well knew it. Ma Kilpatrick, in turn, raged at the neighbors with an intense vehemence; to her, they were the "devils."[70]

Conscious as they were of their unpopularity, the Kilpatrick family habitually acted and reacted as though they were being persecuted by their neighbors. The truth may be on these simple lines: they were so widely suspected of thievery that they were held to blame even when they were innocent, leading the boys' mother to speak and act as though driven by a persecution mania.[71]

In the early 1890s the five older sons tilled the Kilpatrick farm and worked around the local ranches as cowpunchers and horse-breakers; but on which ranches, aside from Loomis's, and in which years, are missing details. Ben's biographer, Arthur Soule, quotes a statement that Ben—a boy of ten, but "big for his age,"—was employed as a helper in the roundup at Big Springs, Texas, as early as 1884, when he first met Harvey Logan—in later years, as "Kid Curry," the most wanted desperado in the United States. Working on the roundup as a ten year old? Not impossible; but an infusion of skepticism would not be out of order.[72]

Hunter portrayed Ben Kilpatrick as "a jolly, good-natured young man" who "made friends readily with those with whom he associated." Again, Hunter is at odds with the prevailing opinion and with the conclusions evident from the observable facts of Ben's career. His temperament was a combustible mixture of boisterousness and sullenness. He was intelligent and wrote fluently with fair spelling and a stylish hand; so much for the jest, popularized by the prolific author and non-historian James Horan, that Ben never ordered anything but beans from a menu because he could read no other words on the bill of fare. In Ben's instance, the triteism that he might have followed a worthier path in other surroundings may have merit. As it was, he was an often wily, sometimes careless, but always irrepressibly determined criminal.[73]

He stood just under six feet high in his stocking feet. That made him three to four inches taller than the average American male of his generation, but not so lofty as to justify the apparent distinction conferred on him by the nickname "the Tall Texan." The explanation may be that the phrase was first applied to him for comparative purposes, rather than in absolute terms. Ben may have been described as "the tall Texan" merely to distinguish him from companions who were neither tall nor Texan.[74] For a genuinely tall Texan of the 1890s, one need look no further beyond the law than L.L. Shield, brother of Sheriff Rome Shield. Lee Shield attained a height of six feet and seven inches. Rome himself, at six foot four, was no midget.[75]

Ben tried matrimony in 1892. On Christmas Day of that year, place unknown, he married Nancy Williams, from Mississippi, parentage also unknown. Their daughter, Abby Elmine, was born on October 14, 1893, and their son, Benjamin Franklin, on October 29, 1896, less than a year before the father's abrupt disappearance from Texas effectually ended the marriage.[76]

Ben and George became fugitives after an egregious exhibition of loutishness and stupidity turned a trivial and avoidable neighbors' dispute into a serious breach of the criminal code. With the neighborhood against them anyway, Ben and George may have felt in 1897 that they had no choice but to get out of Texas. Then, in November, 1898, Ed was charged with the theft of a horse from the Molloy ranch, near Eden. He posted bond, and was summoned to appear in court the following April. Whether through continuance, dismissal, or acquittal, the case was no curb on his liberty. He stayed in Texas—for the time being.[77]

In New Mexico and Arizona, Ben and George sought the company of outlaws, and soon rose to—or slid into—headline outlawry themselves.[78]

Four years had followed his initial flight from Texas when, in the mellow southern autumn of 1901, Ben's path met the no less tangled one of Laura Bullion. It would not be a lucky day for either of them. Yet it was the beginning of a love that was not always self-serving, even on Ben's side, and remained alight in a steady glow of constancy through years of separation and deprivation. Perhaps it was the long period of separation that kept them together.[79]

But in December, 1896 Ben's and George's flight from Texas and Will Carver's debut in train robbery lay just beyond the horizon. So, too, did the act that precipitated Dave Atkins into joining Carver and the Ketchums. Tom and Sam, on the other hand, were already, and irrevocably, travelers on the high road of crime.

Frank Shelton, a generally well informed witness, said long afterwards that Tom Ketchum put himself on the wrong side of the law in Tom Green County at about this time by robbing a store in Knickerbocker and stealing mavericks.[80] Probably Shelton had heard this and believed it. As we have noted, Tom may indeed have been under suspicion for any or all of these offenses; but if he was, the suspicion never hardened into formal accusation by a public authority.

That Tom Ketchum was in the Knickerbocker area during the last months of 1895 is a certainty. That he left after the commission of a serious criminal offense is an established fact. But his exit from Tom Green County was impelled by something far higher in the hierarchy of felonious crime than burglary and cattle stealing. The word was murder.

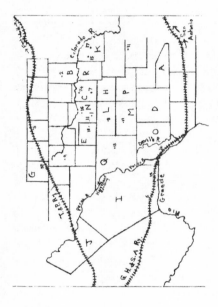

MAP 1. PART OF SOUTHWEST AND SOUTH-CENTRAL TEXAS
(CIRCA 1890)

The sketch map shows the county boundaries, towns or villages, rivers, and railroads most important to the narrative.

COUNTIES: A. BANDERA B. COLEMAN C. CONCHO D. EDWARDS
E. IRION F. KERR G. MARTIN H. MENARD I. PECOS J. REEVES
K. SAN SABA L. SCHLEICHER M. SUTTON N. TOM GREEN
O. VAL VERDE P. KIMBLE Q. CROCKETT R. McCULLOCH

Places: 1. Christoval 2. Coleman 3. Colorado City 4. Comstock 5. Del Rio
6. Dryden 7. Eden 8. Eldorado 9. Fredericksburg 10. Garden City
11. Knickerbocker 12. Lozier 13. Ozona 14. Paint Rock 15. Richland Springs 16. San Angelo 17. San Saba 18. Sherwood 19. Sonora 20. Stanton

Railroads: T & P Ry = Texas and Pacific Railway; G.H. & S.A. Ry = Galveston, Harrisburg & San Antonio Railway

Map 1

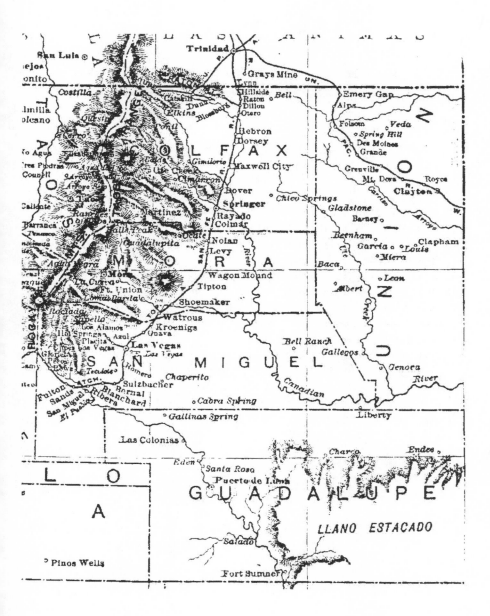

Map 2

{ 5 }

THREE MURDERS AND
A DEAD RINGER

"**John Wright gave me a brown horse** to do what I did, and then he came over and took it from me. It was Wright's intention to take Old Lady Powers and leave the country with her. That was his intention . . . Old Man Powers was killed . . . There were four or five implicated in it."[1]

In those laconic and impersonal terms, and with only minor variations in the reporting of his exact words, Tom Ketchum described the murder of Jasper N. "Jap" Powers, "one of the first crimes that I was ever implicated in." There must have been a great deal more to it than that. If, as he implied, he was hired to assassinate Powers, Tom would have wanted more from Wright than the gift or loan of a horse. Tom had never killed a man up to this time. It stands to reason that he would not have murdered Powers merely to indulge a whim or oblige a friend. Mrs. Sallie E. Powers may have connived at the murder, and Dave Atkins may have been as deeply involved in it as Tom himself. So, according to the authorities, was George W. "Bud" Upshaw, although Tom later maintained that Bud "knew nothing about it."[2]

John Loomis wrote that Berry Ketchum was one of the signatories to a letter from local cattlemen offering Powers the choice of leaving the neighborhood or being killed. Powers stayed put and died. Wright, Loomis continued, was one of those who found the body and was later blamed for the murder by Tom Ketchum's friends, although "everyone suspected" that Tom and one of his followers "had executed the man."

Loomis believed that Wright was in no way connected with the crime. We cannot be so certain. Loomis did not explain, or even mention, Wright's move from Berry Ketchum's ranch to become Powers's foreman.

He did not say what had become of Wright's wife Wincie. Large, strong of muscle, and fierce of aspect, she dipped snuff, chewed tobacco, stood no nonsense from liberty-takers, and was "quite a character herself." He made no reference to any liaison between John Wright and Mrs. Powers, or to rumors of one. Whether through forgetfulness, or out of discretion, he omitted Powers's name from his recollections, and did not so much as mention that the man had a wife.[3]

Loomis likened Wright to Daniel Boone. He saw him as a "throwback to the fron-tiersmen of the eastern forest country . . . quiet and kind, with an intense love of nature in the raw, a courageous fighter when necessity compelled." Though "entirely without book learning," Wright had "a natural refinement which must have been inherited." He would put his hand to whatever kind of labor was set before him, and, at relaxation in camp, could listen with enjoyment to the Loomises' readings from Trollope.[4]

Loomis seems to have idolized and idealized his employee and hunting compan-ion. Either he knew that Wright was incapable of involving himself in anything so low as the assassination of a defenseless and unsuspecting neighbor, or he refused to consider the possibility that he might have been.

It is on the record that Powers was believed to be a stock thief. Case No. 1064, State of Texas vs. J.N. Powers, theft of cattle, appeared in the District Court Docket for the December term of 1893. When court reconvened after Christmas that year a jury heard the case against him and returned a verdict of not guilty. The owner or owners of the allegedly stolen livestock cannot be identified. Nor is anything known of the nature of the evidence.[5]

The following summer Jasper Powers was summoned to County Court to answer a charge on some unspecified misdemeanor. All that is known about these proceedings is that the case was continued.[6]

Certainly rumor was current that Powers was badly crosswise with his neigh-bors. Another—which might be part of the same one—was that he had dishonored a gambling debt to Sam Ketchum and Will Carver. These tales are of local origin, which in itself offers no security for their authority.[7]

Powers was shot down in his pasture, ten or eleven miles southwest of Knickerbocker, Wednesday, December 11, 1895. At nine o'clock that morning, he left the house, as usual, to fetch his saddle horses from the pasture. He had walked six hundred yards towards the hobbled horses when two men stepped out of the woods to meet him. They had come to kill him, but evidently they had something to say to him first. The three sat on a log and talked. As they did so, at least one of them whit-tled at a piece of kindling. Doubtless the visitors reminded Powers of the ultimatum in the round-robin letter from the aggrieved cattlemen. One or two other men may have been hidden in the woods. Suddenly Powers started to his feet and took to his heels. Several men opened fire with rifles. Three bullets struck him in the back; a fourth, perhaps fired from close range, split his skull.[8]

Mrs. Powers deposed later that, a few minutes after her husband's departure, she heard two shots, "and looking out of the house saw two men riding away over the hill." She paid no more attention to the shots, "it being nothing unusual to hear shooting in the neighborhood."

Much later, however, she grew "uneasy at his continued absence" and reported it. By now the evening was too advanced for the search to get under way, but a party started out early next morning, the 12th, and soon recovered the body. W.F. Holt, the Justice of the Peace for the Knickerbocker precinct, presided over the inquest and Sheriff Shield left San Angelo at noon on Friday, the 13th, accompanied by County Justice John O'K. White, to take up the investigation. Powers had been killed so near the Irion County line that Sheriff Bill Elliott also interested himself in the case. "Plutus," who had nothing to say about Powers or his widow or his character and reputation, reported that Elliott was in Knickerbocker for several days of the following week, "getting witnesses in the Powers case."[9]

The next visible evidence of official activity also attracted the notice of Plutus. Sheriffs Shield and Elliott were in Knickerbocker on Sunday night, January 26, 1896, with Shield's deputies Arthur West and Dick Runyon. This was the latest of several such trips, but the first to elicit public comment. "[A]s usual," Plutus remarked tartly, "it proved a windy, if you will pardon the slang."[10]

Rome Shield may or may not have pardoned the slang, but he did not excuse the sarcasm.

> I want to state to those whom [sic] I know are always ready to say that an officer is not doing his duty, that my trip was not a windy, but that the object of my trip did not pan out what we thought it would. I will state for Plutus' benefit that I have no warrant for anybody in his neighborhood, nor have I any evidence that would warrant me to make an arrest, and that the "windy trip" he refers to was made for the purpose of finding something that would give some light on the subject, and lead in to the arrest of the guilty parties. I did everything that could have been done under the existing circumstances. It has also been rumored that some of the parties are hard men and that I am not anxious to tackle them. My wishes are no figure in the case, get me the evidence is all I ask of anybody, and I will do the rest. Thinking this explanation will dispel all doubts in the public mind as to the sincerity of my effort in doing my duty, I remain,
>
> Yours truly,
> G.W. SHIELD, Sheriff[11]

Editor Murphy, who as Democratic mayor of San Angelo was a political besides a personal friend of the sheriff, naturally printed the letter. Thereafter the contributions of Plutus were less frequent and more guarded.

Shield's visits to Knickerbocker could hardly not have been in connection with the Powers case. The reason for the failure of the expedition of January 26 may very well be the sudden and recent unavailability of the "hard men" associated with the case. Shield may not have had warrants, but he must have had information and ideas. Their nature may be inferred from Albert Thompson's summary of part of a letter Shield sent him in 1930: Tom Ketchum had been "seen in the recent company of Powers, and there had been hard words used. Ill feeling between the two was known to exist. Circumstances were strong against Ketchem [sic], and the authorities decided he should be taken into custody."[12]

On paper, it does not look much of a case. Probably, however, Shield came to know, or hear, far more than he was willing to disclose to Thompson.

A story believed locally was that Tom Ketchum and Dave Atkins were indicted, but that the bills of indictment were quashed in the summer, after suspicion had switched to the widow and her foreman.[13]

But Atkins was not indicted for the Powers murder, then or later. If Upshaw was innocent, as Ketchum maintained, his could have been a case of mistaken identity. Mistaken for Atkins? Possibly; but a conditional presupposition, a rumor, and a guess do not make a fact.

On May 16, 1896, a grand jury of the district court then in session at San Angelo found true bills against Tom Ketchum (No. 1198), J.E. Wright (1199), S.E. Powers (1200), and Bud Upshaw (1201), for the murder of J.N. Powers. Thirteen witnesses had been heard: George Upshaw [Sr.], T.O. and R.B. [Beth] Votaw, John Lopez, [Mrs.] Fannie Wilson, Miss I. [Belle] Votaw, John Onalas [Ornelas?], Jose Montez, Mrs. Wellborn [Wilburn/] Miss [Alice] Wellborn, J.H. Wellborn, Jake Byler, and Tom Harden [Hardin]. Owing, doubtless, to nothing more unusual than clerical haste and carelessness, the crime was misdated October 9, 1895, on all four indictments. No reference has been found to the preliminary examination (or defendants' waiver) that must have preceded the grand jury's deliberations.

By then, Upshaw, like Ketchum, had faded into the wide blue yonder. Only Wright and the Widow Powers were at home. Sheriff Shield issued a capias for Powers on the 23rd, he or Constable S.B. Runyon served it, and before the end of the day she was in the County Jail. A correspondent's description of her as "a woman of middle age, of average intelligence, with a number of friends from the locality in which she lived," suggests that she lacked both the appearance and the reputation of an adventuress. On the Wednesday she was allowed to go home under the remarkably light bond of $1,000.[14]

John and Wincie Wright had moved to the Click brothers' ranch near Oxford, in Llano County, where John was arrested on May 20. He was conveyed to San Angelo and, like Mrs. Powers, bailed out for $1,000. R.W. and G.W. Click stood surety for him. His case, and hers, were set for trial in December 1896.[15]

As Will Carver was still in the Indian Territory at the time of the murder, he could not have had anything to do with its commission. Nor is there much possibility of his being in the conspiracy that led to it. But he had guilty knowledge of the crime after the event; he heard that Tom Ketchum was under suspicion, and was able to warn him before the law could act. After a few hurried words with Sam outside the Ketchum ranch, Tom struck out westward for the Pecos that night.

At desolate and dangerous Horsehead Crossing, 160 miles west of San Angelo, he could have continued southwest towards Fort Davis, or headed upstream into New Mexico. Whichever path he chose, he sent a note for Sam to join him at a specified rendezvous.[16]

Carver and his friends started out from Knickerbocker on their "big hunt" later in the week that had begin with Shield's abortive trip of January 26. This suggests that Carver delivered his warning less than a week before his party set out for the Concho. Atkins, presumably, fled at the same time. Shield missed his men by a few hours.[17]

In warning Ketchum, Carver made himself an accessory after the fact. That was reason enough for him to turn his face towards the southwest. He was not to know that years would pass before Shield learned of his collusion in Tom's flight.

As far as can now be seen, Sam Ketchum was not accused of complicity in the murder, but he may have perceived that his close association with the fugitives might direct suspicion toward him; at the least, the officers might detain him for questioning about his brother's whereabouts. Wholly innocent or not, he set off to meet Tom, leading Prince, one of Tom's favorite horses.[18]

Due process of law engendered the usual paper storm. In May the State issued subpoenas for all the original thirteen witnesses except Mrs. Wilburn, Ornelas, and Montez. The defense wanted some of the same witnesses—and others. In September, Wright requested subpoenas for T.G. Evans (who could not be found), J.D. Wagner, Thomas Votaw, Mrs. Matilda Votaw, Miss Belle Votaw, Mrs. John Lopez, "and Buddie Upshaw"—his fellow indictee! On October 2, Wright applied for the service of a witness attachment upin his friend, the rancher John Loomis. Sallie Powers asked the court to subpoena George Upshaw (Sr.), his wife Delphia, Alice Wellborn [sic], and Ben Spater. The following month, her attorneys were granted subpoenas for Tom Hardin, John Ornelas, and Jose Montez. At the same time, witness attachments on the defense's behalf were served on Thomas, Matilda, and Beth [R.B.] Votaw, Mrs Fannie Wilson, and Mrs. John Lopez, all of whom had recently taken a change of air from Tom Green to the Irion-Schleicher County line and thence to Menard County. The testimony of J.H. Wilburn was sought by both sides. He was in Irion County and he, too, became the subject of a writ of attachment. At some stage the defense presented an application for the attachment of Jake Byler and Mrs. [Annie] Byler from Irion County, and another for subpoenas upon three Tom Green County residents: Bud Upshaw's parents (who were about to take their family to Val Verde County, if they had not already done so), and Alice Wilburn. The attachment upon Jake Byler was served on December 7, 1896.[19]

Nothing came of it all. Months and years went by. In December, 1897, the district attorney moved to dismiss the case against Wright, on the grounds that the evidence available was insufficient to sustain a conviction. Almost eighteen months later, he disposed of the Sallie Powers case in the same way.[20] The resolution of the charges against Tom Ketchum and Bud Upshaw was for the future.

Even if they had been hired to kill Powers, Tom Ketchum and his fellow bushwhackers probably had reasons of their own for wanting him out of the way. They would hardly have accepted a commission to murder their neighbor if they had been on good terms with him.

In the end, nobody stood trial for the murder. The affair was murky then; the mystery of its inner ramifications seems impenetrable now. Those few words of Ketchum, the recollections of Loomis and Shield, the surviving documents of the district court, and the scant press coverage, bring us about as close to the solution as we are likely to get. The affair, a correspondent declared in 1896, was "shrouded in deep mystery." It still is.[21]

In the spring of 1896 the two Ketchums were engaged as line riders on Wilson Waddingham's Bell ranch, in San Miguel County, New Mexico. They were based on the southern side of Waddingham's range, near the remnants of Fort Bascom, five miles north of the future site of Tucumcari. Near the end of May, shortly after the beginning of the roundup, they joined the Bell wagons, north of where they had been riding line.

The cowhands guessed they were outlaws because "they had a great number of gold and silver watches and many bunches of keys among their effects." How the brothers acquired these items is a mystery, unless they really had committed burglaries in Knickerbocker and elsewhere in Tom Green County during 1894–95: no record has been found of any holdup or significant case of burglary in which Tom or Sam could possibly have been implicated in the early months of 1896.[22] The one such case that is worth looking at went back to August 16, 1895.

Two men had robbed a post office and store at Valentine, Texas, of considerable merchandise and a sizable sum in cash, and killed the town's watchman in escaping. The Ketchums had been accused on the not altogether convincing basis that the Valentine bandits stole some candy from the store, and Tom liked candy.

Officially, the crime was never solved, though for a while it seemed to have been. Two cowpuncher brothers named S.L. (Lorenzo, familiarly known as Ranzy) and Tom Holland were arrested on circumstantial evidence and subjected to a lengthy journey through the State judicial system. Tom Holland's defense was an alibi, which secured his release more than a year after his arrest. Ranzy Holland was acquitted of murder but convicted of robbery, sent up for fifteen years, awarded a retrial in Maverick County, and finally declared not guilty in late November, 1899.

In the midst of all this, the authorities seem to have developed second thoughts about Tom Holland's alibi, and fresh suspicions about another former cowboy. The effect was that Tom Ketchum's name joined that of Tom Holland on bills of indictment for murder, robbery, and conspiracy to rob and murder. But by then, two and a half years had elapsed since the Valentine episode, and Tom Ketchum's name had been made notorious by the train robberies and murders he had committed elsewhere in Texas and in New Mexico during that time, and by the mistaken but widely touted belief that he was Black Jack. This, and his acquaintance with the Holland boys—he rode the same trails as they in Texas and New Mexico, and could not possibly have not known them pretty well—may have been sufficient recommendation for the grand jurors.

Whoever was guilty, Sam Ketchum could not have been; his arrival in San Angelo from Chicago almost coincided with the date of the robbery and killing, which occurred some 250 miles southwest of Angelo. As for Tom Ketchum, the crime would have been pinned on him in Texas before 1898 had any actual evidence been in existence. The likelihood is that he was in, or near, Tom Green County in August 1895 and throughout the last months of the year.[23]

Sam and Tom had been hired by the Bell as line riders in March or April of 1896. The actions that followed their abrupt departure in early June generated detailed descriptions:

> The first has a dark complexion, dark brown hair, brown mustache, about six feet tall, weight, 185 to 195 pounds, stoop shouldered, brown eyes, very quick tempered, heavily built, and carries a 45-70 Winchester rifle.

The second is of light complexion, sandy mustache, red face, hair inclined to be red, blue eyes. He is about six feet tall, weight about 170 pounds, carries himself very erect, wears about No. 9 boots. His name is supposed to be Welsch [a misrendering of Welch?] as he carries a fine gold watch with the name of Welsch engraved upon it.

Other sources say that the first man was passing as "Steve." He refused to give any surname, and the matter was not pressed. In the words of Jack Culley, the range manager, the Bell ranch was a good place to be in . . . if you were wanted by the sheriff . . . . We asked no questions, only if a man could work cattle."[24]

Except for the stooping at the shoulders—another description (but only one—Albert Thompson's) depicts Tom as standing as "straight as an Indian"—Steve's particulars match those of Tom Ketchum. No great importance should be attached to the advertised coloring of his hair and eyes as brown, instead of black. Other pen-pictures of Tom gave the coloring of his hair as dark brown, rather than black; while strongly brown eyes are easily mistaken for black, and vice versa.[25]

Moreover, wanted men—and sometimes, out of vanity, men who were not on any list of fugitives—often tinted their hair and retouched their complexion. The man's use of the name "Steve" is also suggestive; when captured, years later, Tom introduced himself as "Stevens" (or, as sometimes given, "Stephens").[26]

The details provided for "Welsch" correspond almost precisely with those known to belong to Sam Ketchum.

Cowboys in eastern New Mexico during the 1890s did not usually wear pistols while out on the range; Tom never went anywhere without his. During the short time he was with the Bell roundup crew, he gave some memorable displays of his dexterity with the six-shooter. Culley recalled many years later what he was told by the waddies who had watched the gunplay:

> The fellow was an expert juggler with his six-shooter. He could twirl the big .45 round and round on the trigger finger, cocking and firing it at each turn with astonishing speed and accuracy. And he seemed fond of exhibiting his prowess.[27]

Tom worked on the Bell roundup for less than two weeks. One day he quarreled with his wagon boss, Tom Kane, collected his pay from the ranch book-keeper, and pulled out.

Sam Ketchum was working for another of the Bell wagons, a few miles to the north. Tom rode up and Sam quit soon afterwards.

For a day or so, they camped in the willow brakes of La Cinta Creek, near the north fence of the Bell. On Monday, June 8, they killed a steer, "used what meat they desired," and started south toward the Bell headquarters. Overnight they stole some supplies from the ranch storehouse. Tom Kane, who was a deputy sheriff, set off after them.

The Ketchums continued southeast across the Bell pastures, roughly in the direction of their old line camp. Late in the afternoon of June 10 they reached the little settlement of Liberty, in the extreme southeast of San Miguel County, where there was a store and post office operated by Morris and Levi Herzstein. Morris had opened the store in 1888; his twenty-two year old brother was a more recent arrival from Germany.

Jack Potter's story is that the Ketchums, having bought a few groceries, camped outside the store until one of the Herzsteins, seeing the stormclouds mounting overhead, invited them to spend the night indoors.

Whether or not the Ketchums took a drenching that night, they certainly looted the store in the small hours of Thursday. They pocketed all the money, including $44.69 from the post office till, loaded their packhorse with blankets, clothing, and provisions to the value of a further $200, then made their way toward the Pecos. A few hours afterwards Levi gathered up a three-man unofficial posse and went out in pursuit. Levi, in contrast to many of those who were elected or appointed to serve as officers, really tried to overtake his quarry. It was his misfortune that he succeeded in catching up with the two thieves. His fate illustrates tellingly why most experienced lawmen put safety first.

About noon the Ketchums halted near Plaza Largo arroyo, in Guadalupe County (now in Quay County), roughly twenty-five miles south and slightly west of Liberty. They were just finishing their meal as Herzstein and three companions came pounding into view.

There are a number of versions of what happened in the next few seconds. Both Thompson and Titsworth say that the Ketchums, taken off their guard, made as if to surrender; then when Herzstein's party moved closer, they stepped behind their horses, drew their guns, and started shooting before the men in the posse could do anything about it. Culley asserts that the outlaws were crouched by their horses, ready to open fire, when the pursuers saw them. One contemporary newspaper report states impartially that "a fight ensued;"another has it that the robbers began to shoot "as soon as they saw the posse."

The fight, if it amounted to that, was swiftly over. When Tom and Sam stalked out into the open, Levi Herzstein and Merejildo Gallegos were dead or dying and Placido Gurule was trying hard to make it look as though he were in a similar condition.

The pursuing party managed to make one shot count, killing one of the thieves' horses. The horse of the fourth member of the impromptu posse was another casualty. Its rider, whose name is variously given as Atanacio Borque and Juan Apodaca, now fled as fast as his feet could carry him.

Potter relates that Tom, surveying their bloody handiwork, said to his brother:

"I believe that damn Mexican lying there is not dead. I thought I saw his muscle move. I had better give him a little more lead."

"Don't waste ammunition on a dead man," Sam is supposed to have replied. "He is no doubt eating chile in hades with his compadre."

Culley tells how one of them, standing over the prostrate Herzstein, emptied his pistol into the body, snarling "You son of a bitch! You son of a bitch!" each time he fired.

Half a mile from the scene of the shooting, Borque (or Apodaca) ran into Sam Goldsmith and Harry Edwards, who had heard the firing and were on their way there. Gurule, they found, was only slightly hurt; Herzstein's body bore eleven wounds. Before riding off to the south, the killers had cut out the brand mark of their dead horse and taken one of the posse's surviving horses in replacement. Presently they stole a pair of horses from the H ranch and turned east toward the Staked Plains.

Gurule had been saved by his own nerve and by the apparent logic of Sam Ketchum's argument. Although wounded, he was able to mount his horse and ride home unaided. Years later, to his own satisfaction at any rate, he identified Tom Ketchum as one of his assailants. Even in his old age, he "humorously delighted in telling of his experience." He told Fabiola Gilbert, a local ranchwoman, that Herzstein had fallen from his horse wounded, "and was shot through the heart while begging for mercy."[28]

Tom Kane kept on the trail, albeit at a carefully regulated pace. As Culley commented:

> Tom was nervy, all right, but experienced. Unlike poor little Herzstein, he was wise to the kind of fellow he was following. I shall never doubt that from the moment he left the ranch in pursuit he was quite determined to keep one good day behind . . . [29]

The outlaws had veered back, evidently determined to get down to the Pecos. At Fort Sumner, Kane was joined by Deputy U.S. Marshal John B. Legg and an officer named Mike McQuaid, who declared that the man "Steve" was one Red Black (or Red Buck?), whom he had once arrested in Colorado for rustling cattle. Fred Higgins, town marshal at Roswell, joined Legg in cutting sign both east and west of the Pecos after Kane and McQuaid had retired from the hunt.

Charles (originally Christopher) C. Perry, the sheriff of Chaves County, was in Santa Fe at this time. In fact, he had been there for nearly a month and was not thinking of going back to Roswell.

Before leaving his bailwick, "Charley" Perry had closed his account with the Bank of Roswell. Among the funds now reposing under his name in a bank at Santa Fe were the proceeds of the recent tax collection. Several weeks previously Perry's original bondsmen had withdrawn their support; so, on June 9, he filed a second bond, nominally representing the requisite sum of twenty-five thousand dollars but actually worth little more than a quarter of that amount. The irregularities would be uncovered when the County Commissioners met in July, and the law insisted that he make settlement with the County or Territory by the tenth of that month. Charley was not worried by the prospect of the first because he had no intention of complying with the second. In short, the sheriff was about to abscond.[30]

If the Ketchums had not stolen money which belonged to the United States Post Office, it is unlikely that Perry would have suffered his scheme to be disrupted by their actions. But he was also a deputy United States marshal; and, although he had put himself out of touch with the electors of Chaves County, he could be found with the utmost ease by U.S. Marshal Edward L. Hall, whose office was in Santa Fe. When the marshal placed a couple of blank warrants in his hands and told him to try and serve them on the robbers, Perry was forced to change his plans.

First, he called at the bank to pick up all the money he had placed on deposit a few weeks earlier. He then went directly to El Paso, Texas. Near the town of Pecos he met John Legg, who had trailed the killers onto Toyah Creek, a tributary of the Pecos River. Legg was now accompanied by two officers from Eddy, New Mexico: Cal Carpenter and Dee Harkey. For some days the posse drove around Reeves and Pecos counties in a couple of hired buggies, pausing here and there to wire optimistic reports to New Mexico. The Ketchums, meanwhile, had eluded their pursuers near Fort Davis and were escaping through the Davis Mountains and into the Big Bend country, south of Alpine.

On July 1 the posse heard that the police at Ojinaga, a town on the Chihuahua side of the Rio Grande, opposite Presidio, Texas, had arrested one Samuel Lockwood, believing him to be one of the fugitives. Legg sent a telegram from Ojinaga to notify Hall, and Perry offered to return to Santa Fe to obtain the necessary papers.[31]

But instead of going to Santa Fe, Charley headed east—all the way to South Africa. A few weeks after his exit the auditors, called in to examine the peculations of the departed sheriff, reported that he owed the territorial treasurer a sum "within a few shillings of $8,000." Six weeks later a late receipt of $357.35 left the taxpayers of Chaves County to survey a final audited deficit of $7639.02. The money was never collected.[32]

Nor were the rewards aggregating $2700, offered by Governor W.T. Thornton of New Mexico, Morris Herzstein, the United States Post Office, and A.J. Tisdale, manager of the Bell ranch, for the arrest and delivery of "Welsch" and "Steve." Legg took Morris Herzstein in the fruitless hope of identifying Lockwood, and that was the end of that. The murderers remained uncaught and, for awhile, unknown.[33]

Their identities did not stay secret for long. Those closest to the events, or to their instigators, were soon certain that Sam and Tom Ketchum were the guilty parties. Yet neither was ever indicted.

This is partly explicable by the paucity of witnesses in that sparsely populated locality. But what about the Bell cowboys, whose testimony could have provided strong circumstantial evidence against the miscreants? The oddest feature of the case, unremarked even after popular belief had assigned the crimes to Sam and Tom, is that not one of Waddingham's cowboys admitted to a prior acquaintance with them.

Yet this was country in which the brothers' faces had been familiar for the best part of a decade. If, after all, the Ketchums were not "Steve" and "Welch," it is barely conceivable that someone who had worked alongside the killers would not have made it known that Sam and Tom were innocent. If the muteness of the Bell hands was derived from reticence, rather than ignorance, it may have been the product of misplaced loyalty, aggravated by prejudice: Herzstein, they may have rationalized, was "only" a German immigrant, and Gallegos "only" a Hispanic.

Three years afterwards, the Santa Fe *New Mexican* press led, or reflected, conjecture that the territorial authorities might move to procure indictments against Tom Ketchum for the Liberty murders. Later, the paper seemed to want to associate Governor Otero with a forecast that indictment would follow as a matter of course. But Otero labored under no such assumption. Less than a week after the newspaper's prediction, he assured Governor Nathan Murphy of Arizona that if, through some fluke, Ketchum escaped conviction for the capital crime of armed assault upon a railroad train, he would not stand in the way of an extradition warrant. Whether or not indictments could have been sustained against him for burglary in San Miguel County, or murder in Guadalupe County, none were forthcoming.[34]

Still later, Tom himself professed to have been in Texas, recovering from injury, at the time of the killings. No one volunteered support for his statement. Nor can anything be said for his assertion that the killer of Herzstein and Gallegos was a man he had known for fifteen years, but would not name.[35]

During the first weeks after the murders, and in the face of the silence of people who may have known the culprits, the authorities had nothing to go on except for guesswork and the published particulars of the killers' appearance. Circulation of the descriptions, and speculation on the fugitives' place of origin and previous criminal history, foreshadowed the controversy that would arise from a jumble of diverse claims as to the identity of "Black Jack." In consequence, the operations and personnel of two separate bands of outlaws would become intertwined, and then interlocked, in popular press and official mind alike:

> . . . They are strangers in this territory, and at the Bell where they stopped for a short time, they showed a pocket-book full of finger rings and several watches, from which Marshal Hall is led to believe that they are train robbers, perhaps members of one of the gangs operating in the Indian Territory.[36]

Three to four months before the Liberty murders another pair of brothers had traversed eastern New Mexico, en route from the Indian Territory and North Texas, and bound for Cochise County, Arizona. Bob Christian, the elder, was of a similar complexion to Sam Ketchum, though much smaller and about fifteen years younger. Will Christian, like Tom Ketchum, was very dark of complexion, powerfully built, and about six foot tall. Tom's height was about the same as Christian's, his weight was rather less, and he was the senior by some eight years. The two men were altogether different in temperament and manner; but both were from Texas, both worked on the range when they worked at all, and both were criminals. At the time of the murders in Guadalupe County, the Christians were ranch hands in Cochise County; but their earlier career was akin to the one which Marshal Hall had incorrectly predicated for the killers of Herzstein and Gallegos.[37]

It is possible, though not likely, that the Bell cowboys were all strangers to the Ketchums, and that Tom and Sam, having learned this, took jobs on the ranch for that reason. Whatever the truth, they may not have intended to stay long. By now, both of them—Sam especially—would have stuck out as men too old and experienced for run-of-the-mill cowboy work. That alone might have created friction between them and any foreman with a care for his own authority. Tom's temper would have sparked the tinder before they had earned enough to pay for a stock of provisions. Thus the ransacking of the ranch storehouse and the Liberty post office-store would have been meant to compensate them for the time they did not put in at the Bell.

After Tom and Sam had lost the posses, south of Fort Davis, they also passed temporarily out of the reach of research. This may have been when they first went to ground in the Black Range, north of Kingston, southwest New Mexico, where their favored retreat has come to be called Outlaw Park Canyon. In prehistory a landslide had closed one end of the canyon, and it could be entered on horseback only through cracks at two concealed points at the base of its high walls. The provision of a cabin and corral made the canyon comfortable as well as secure. Its floor is flat, three hundred yards broad, and covered with grama grass. The place was known to the cowboys of the V+T and R-Bar-R outfits and to the smaller ranchers of the locality. The Ketchums could have heard about the canyon from Carver, who may have learned of it years earlier during a visit to his married sister when she was living near Kingston. Over the next three years the Ketchum gang made regular use of this fastness as a holdout and transit point. Later, other outlaws, such as Henry Hawkins and Ed Kilpatrick, did the same.[38]

They may also have spent several weeks of this period in the employ of John T. Muir, a Lordsburg rancher, and at the 76 ranch, twenty miles west of Deming. They were not only "excellent hands" but "rather popular with their associates." "Unquestionably," remarks Albert Thompson, "they were watching the movements of the Southern Pacific trains."[39]

Wherever they were, the brothers were using their own names again; they must have heard that they were not yet under suspicion for the recent burglaries and murders, and that, in official eyes, they had a clean bill of health for the Powers killing.

By the fall of 1896, they were in Cochise and Graham Counties, Arizona, still under their right names. They renewed contact with Will Carver; perhaps they met him at his sister's, east of Duncan, or if they looked him up on the Erie range during the fall roundup, she or her husband may first have posted them on his whereabouts.

Carver was not always where he could be found by the Ketchums. Sometimes he was with newly-made friends at the Tex ranch in Texas ("Tex") Canyon. Most of these men, maybe all of them, were part-time lawbreakers, but in Tex Canyon they had a first rate hideaway.[40]

Jess Benton, a cattleman who found the place by chance, decided he liked it, and eventually got it for himself, left a succinct description of its setting:

> . . . a wild and beautiful locality at the south end of the range, a wooded region with a pretty spring, and a chinked log house in a clearing, one of the first such log houses in Arizona . . . Right here were the ranch I wanted[41] . . .

Leonard Alverson and his partner, William Warderman (sometimes miswritten as Waterman), had moved into the house several years earlier, to be joined presently by one John Vinnedge (usually misspelled Vinnadge or Vintage), alias John Cush. Notwithstanding the prior arrival of Alverson and Warderman, the ranch was generally referred to as "Old Cushey's place." Actually, though, none of them enjoyed title. Either through carelessness, or to avoid property taxes, they had never filed ownership on their land. A Kansas-born cowpuncher named Walter Hoffman, whose real name was Walter C. Hovey, helped them in the roundup.

Hovey lived in Hunt Canyon, about seven miles away, and sometimes worked for the 7UP ranch, three miles from his home. He claimed that the pseudonym Hoffman had been "wished on him" by Charley Cook of the Three Bar Cattle Company in Sulphur Spring Valley. He, like Alverson, would later act as Tom Ketchum's barber. Two others who were always welcome at Cushey's were Tom Capehart and Henry Marshall. All were well known on the Erie, San Simon, and other local cow outfits.[42] Joseph "Mack" Axford, who worked with these last two during the winter of 1895–96, remembered Capehart as one of the finest "bronco stompers" on the range amd Marshall as "a fair to middling cowhand, more noted for his pleasant disposition and for being a steady worker." Capehart later impressed William French as one of the most capable hands he ever hired during his years as manager of the WS (though the Capehart who appears in French's writings looks like an amalgam of two, three, or even four different men).[43]

Though not yet well acquainted with Tom Ketchum, all six of these men— Alverson, Warderman, Vinnedge/Cush, Hovey, Capehart, and Marshall—would soon enough come to know him better than was good for any of them.

During the summer and autumn of 1896 everyone in the Southwest heard a great deal of the High Five gang, more popularly known as the Black Jack gang.

"Black Jack" was the nickname bestowed upon Will Christian soon after his appearance in Cochise County. With his brother, now riding as "Tom Anderson," and three other cowpunchers who had awarded themselves early retirement, he embarked on a series of robberies which, although feeble in terms of profit, sorely embarrassed two United States marshals, many of their deputies, half a dozen sheriffs, and several Post Office inspectors.

Some newspapers even blamed Black Jack and Anderson for the murders of Herzstein and Gallegos, furnishing details of the previous career of the alleged killers which corresponded so closely with what was recorded of the Christians that it is astonishing that throughout the gang's lifetime the two fugitives from Oklahoma were never identified by their real names, except by two or three informants, whose disclosures were ignored.[44]

Tom Ketchum later said that he met Black Jack once, and once only. He claimed that he rode into Black Jack's camp above Deming, was invited to join the gang, and rejected the offer. Whereupon, said Ketchum, the confrontation was brusquely brought to a finish by Black Jack's "threatening attitude."[45] Such an encounter could have occurred—in September, or towards the end of October, 1896—but the details as supplied by Ketchum need not be believed. It is likelier that Ketchum offered to join Black Jack, and was turned down.

Tom and Sam were in eastern Graham County at least as much as in Cochise County during these months. If it is true that a fellow customer in the Bucket of Blood saloon in Pearce—or the Brewery Gulch saloon in Bisbee—told Tom one day that he looked like Black Jack, it would have been at this time. Ketchum did not resemble Black Jack, except in being big, dark, and Texan; the man who passed the remark may not have known the real Black Jack at all—or may have been speaking in jest. Anyway, talk of the alleged likeness flew from Cochise County to Graham

County, where someone said something that became seed to the weed of misinformation: Black Jack was in Graham County and his name was Tom Ketchum.[46]

Word of this reached the ear of Ben R. Clark, deputy sheriff in the town of Clifton. Perhaps that is why he took a keen interest in the two Ketchum brothers, who moved in and out of his locality and were not gainfully employed. Graham County had, for many years, provided both shelter for itinerant thieves and fodder for resident ones. Perhaps he had been trying to keep tabs on the brothers from the first. The allegation that Tom was the elusive Black Jack would then have transformed a watching brief into a vision of kudos. At all events, Clark was convinced that Thomas E. Ketchum was always Black Jack.

In February of 1897, the sportive fates took a hand. The Ketchums slipped out of Graham County and into New Mexico. Coincidentally, and almost simultaneously, the original Black Jack and his pals crossed from New Mexico into the Solomonville-Clifton area of Graham County. Clark, and the rest of the sheriff's office in Graham County, was in ignorance of these comings and goings.

Black Jack and his partners did not stay put for long. They returned to New Mexico to plan a train robbery, then ducked back into Graham County after looting a couple of stores and the post office attached to one of them. Two of the gang, Black Jack and Sid Moore, allowed themselves no more than a day or two of rest. By the end of March they were headed northeast once more. On the night of April 3, 1897, Christian and Moore murdered George Smith, a rancher in the Magdalena country, who, they believed, had informed against them. The investigation led directly to Clifton.

Sid Moore, a ranch foreman turned rustler, was well known in Graham County and to Ben Clark. Black Jack was not, except in Clark's mind; he knew that Moore and the man called Black Jack were together. That, he believed, was the same as knowing Black Jack. So he told the officers from New Mexico that Smith's assassins were Sid Moore and one of the Ketchum boys. Which one? Well, Tom was the dark one; so it had to be him.[47]

Two weeks later a press dispatch from Albuquerque spread a report from George Smith's attorneys that the rancher's murderers were "Sid Moore and Tom Cox, two well-known rustlers." There was no Cox in the case; "Cox" is what happened to the name Ketchum when someone in the chain between Clark, the telegrapher, and an employee of the newspaper where the message found its outlet, misheard the first syllable and did not catch the second. Human fallibility needs no help from mendacity, but often gets it.[48]

On April 28, 1897, William Christian was killed in Cole Creek Canyon, eighteen miles east of Clifton. Ben Clark eagerly accepted (or directed) the word of a newcomer in town named James Speck, purportedly a brother-in-law of the dead man, that the slain outlaw was Tom Ketchum, alias Black Jack.[49]

It is not clear whether Speck claimed Black Jack as his brother-in-law and let Clark persuade him to say that his right name was Tom Ketchum, or whether he presented himself as a brother-in-law of Tom Ketchum and was coached by Clark into coupling Tom with the alias Black Jack. A material fact is that Tom and Sam Ketchum had no brother-in-law by the name of James Speck. Furthermore, other citizens recognized Black Jack; none said he was also Tom Ketchum. The whole scene looks like a charade concocted by Clark with Speck's ready cooperation.[50]

The muddle and controversy engendered by this blunder, or deception, was far-reaching and persistent; it is with us yet.[51] At first, it did Tom no harm; the signs are that it appealed to his warped sense of humor; that he reveled in it, exploited it for the sake of his own vanity, even played it up. In the end, it may have done for him.

By the second half of February, Tom Ketchum was on his way back to Texas. The pace of events suggests that he had already decided to hold up a train, and that Will Carver may have agreed to join him. We last saw Carver at his mother's and step-father's house on Pipe Creek. He and Tom now met by prearrangement.

If Sam was asked to be the third man in the plan, he declined. He made for Eugene Rhodes's ranch in the Jornada del Muerto; where, for what turned out to be the last time, he was employed in honest labor.[52] In the event, Tom and Will would not need him just then, for Dave Atkins was about to commit the murder that would make him irrevocably an outlaw. An alliance in armed robbery seemed the best option for all three of them.

While Ben Clark was endeavoring to bury Black Jack as Tom Ketchum, the real Tom Ketchum was three hundred miles away, preparing to break out into outlawry on a scale that would make the original Black Jack gang look like a bunch of scavengers. The situation was rich in humor. First of all, Tom Ketchum's crimes were being pinned upon Black Jack; and now Tom Ketchum had been appointed as tenant of Black Jack's grave. Time, with some help from Tom Ketchum himself, would see to it that the irony was redressed in full measure.

{ 6 }

EASY MONEY AND
HARD RIDING

Before he left Arizona late in 1896, Will Carver told Leonard Alverson that he was going to put a monument over the grave of his wife and did not know what he would do afterwards.[1] It would have chafed him that Viana's parents had already marked her resting place with a stone from which his family name was conspicuously absent. Perhaps, therefore, he really intended to plant his own token of remembrance at the graveside, though nothing survives to show that he did it. He also intended to visit his mother and her family in Bandera County, and did.[2]

But Carver's homeward journey was more than a sentimental one. Before he pulled out of the Chiricahuas, he struck a deal with Tom Ketchum. He would sit through the winter in Texas and wait for Tom to join him. When spring came they, with the help of one or two other fortune-hunters, would rob a train.

Through choice or circumstance, Sam Ketchum took no part in the episode that set the pattern for the remainder of all their lives. The two brothers left Arizona together in February 1897, but parted in southern New Mexico, where Sam remained for at least some of the spring and summer. Tom went on to his fateful meeting with Carver at some unknown point in southwest Texas.

Tom and Will may have drawn their inspiration from an event oft talked about in the bleak and lonesome sageland along the Rio Grande, beyond the great dip which is the eastern sweep of the Big Bend.

Four former cowboys, led by Jack Wellington, had stirred up much excitement by exacting a heavy toll from the Galveston, Harrisburg and San Antonio Railway (once an independent company, but now only the operating title of the Texas division of the Southern Pacific Railroad) at Samuels station, in western Val Verde County, on September 2, 1891. The victim was that perennial target of highwaymen, westbound train Number 20, and the incident noteworthy in its own context as marking the very first instance where train robbers opened an express safe by blasting it with dynamite. That was the through safe, which the messenger could not unlock because the combination was unknown to him. He had already opened the local safe, or way safe.[3]

Less well remembered by campfire raconteurs and would-be emulators was the robbers' undoing—but it has always been thus. They were caught seven weeks later through the skill and tenacity of the famous trailer, Joe Sitter. John Flynt (or Flint) evaded capture only by shooting himself. The others—Wellington, Tom Strouts (alias Fields), and Jim Lansford (or Langford)—were dealt with at Del Rio, Lansford turning State's evidence.[4]

Bud Newman, whose father John B. "Bee" Newman owned a ranch twenty miles north of Comstock, near the base of the Devil's River valley, was one local cowboy with ambitions to outshine the Samuels robbers. Gathering three kindred lights, professedly ordinary cowhands forced into crime by the prospect of a winter's unemployment, he held up No. 20 on Sunday night, December 20, 1896, near Comstock.[5]

The four wishful thinkers could not open the through safe and had to be satisfied with the contents of the way safe, said to have been one gold watch and seventy dollars in cash. Their failure to secure the intended prize excited much public derision; meager as their takings were, officials and onlookers laughingly depreciated them to zero. The whole masterful exploit seemed to have been fittingly sealed a few days later: Rangers swooped down on the Newman ranch and took away the four miscreants, all of whom, chortled one press correspondent, "wanted to confess at once" when presented with "circumstantial evidence of their guilt."[6]

Conviction of the men proved to be much harder to accomplish than their capture. Prosecution of the case was beset with troubles; in the end, only two of the four went to prison, and Bud Newman, the leader, was not one of them.[7] And, beneath the laughter, the Southern Pacific system and the Wells, Fargo Express Company were badly rattled by the ease with which the so called "Comstock Kids" had captured the train and kept it under control. They feared that more experienced and capable practitioners would soon seek to improve upon the performance of the Newman quartet. Worse; in March they were tipped off in vague, but insistent, terms that a gang in New Mexico was planning to hold up a train in southwest Texas. Lacking any information to the contrary, they wrongly assumed that the danger came from the original Black Jack or High Five gang.[8]

Tom Ketchum, for one, was not in the least deterred by the ill-success of Newman's gang; not much more than a year later he would even pay Bud Newman the compliment of springing one of his own enterprises upon Comstock station.

But for the scene of their first venture into train robbery, he and Carver had chosen Lozier, located on the creek of the same name just within the eastern boundary of Pecos County. (Later, that sector of Pecos County was detached to become Terrell County.) There was no community here; just a tiny depot and a telegraph office, then in charge of Miss Addie Upson. The station was on a dead-level stretch of track midway between Dryden and Langtry, two villages thirty miles apart, and much closer to the Rio Grande than to either of these places.[9]

Ketchum and Carver were thoroughly acquainted with the terrain and the scattered ranches. But two men might not be enough to get the job done; they needed at least one more.

Tom may have made one last effort to enlist Sam's support. He returned to San Angelo, perhaps knowing that he was no longer being sought for the Powers murder, but fearing that his name might have been coupled with the Liberty killings or with the crimes of the High Five gang further west. He wanted to get word to Sam, who was then said to be elsewhere in Texas, or was awaiting word from him.

When not keeping company with his horse in the wagon yard, Tom passed the hours gambling in the Club Room upstairs at the Legal Tender. One Sunday morning he encountered a teenage boy named Brook Campbell, who, with his father, was also camping in the wagon yard. Young Campbell, with nothing to look forward to except Sunday school at his mother's behest, was surprised but not thrilled out of his senses when Ketchum asked him to exercise his horse: the lad imagined that the horse would be "as wild as I thought he [Tom] must be." His alarm was misplaced; the horse was gentle, and the boy "sure enjoyed the ride." At the end of it, he entered the saloon and told Tom that the horse was outside. Ketchum left, petted the horse, and then turned to Brook: "C'mon, kid, let's see how many splitters [nickels and dimes] we can find." He led Brook up to the Club Room, "raked off a handful of nickels and dimes," and gave them to him. Brook was "tickled to death" and, after Sunday school, "rushed back to the wagon yard hoping to get to ride the horse again and earn some more 'splitters.'" The horse was there, and so was Tom; but something had changed his mood, and he was "pacing around very restlessly." He looked at the boy and spoke: "Kid, I think I'll exercise Streak this evening."

"He was soon off," Campbell recalled, "and I never saw him again." Evidently Ketchum had received bad news, or no news.[10]

Anyhow, Tom and Will would not be getting any help from Sam, and were still a man short. Their next approach may have been to Bud Upshaw, who was still in or near Tom Green County. Almost at this very juncture, however, events presented them with someone with far more pressing grounds for joining them in a rob-and-run venture.

On March 2, 1897, "Plutus" reported that "[a] Mr. Brown was in our city . . . We understand that he is figuring on opening a saloon here. We predict for him a failure on account of lack of patronage. A saloon is one of the luxuries that Knickerbocker can do without very well." And, it was true, Knickerbocker had been without a saloon for several years to no visible disadvantage. Nonetheless, W.K. Brown went ahead and opened a saloon. In the longer run, he did not justify Plutus's forecast of a financial failure; but did receive a short-term shock. His doors were hardly open when murder walked in.[11]

Dave Atkins and his friend, Sam Moore, were looking forward to going to a dance that Saturday night, March 20, 1897, in Knickerbocker's Mexican quarter. Sam Moore was a local cowboy and farmer. Like Atkins, he had been to New Mexico. "Plutus" had once called him one of Knickerbocker's "popular society gents;" but then Sam, unlike Atkins, was a single man. Unlike him also, he was a member in excellent standing of Knickerbocker's principal fraternity.[12]

Dave was unarmed when he and Moore entered Brown's saloon at five p.m. to prepare for the night's entertainment by taking a few drinks too many. Sam had a six-shooter and, quite properly, asked Brown to put it behind the bar. Two hours and half a dozen beers later, Moore asked for the return of his pistol, explaining that a friend wanted to borrow it. He did not say that the friend was his companion, Atkins.

Atkins and Moore went outside. Moore galloped up to Dee Kay's hotel, where he boarded. He borrowed Kay's Smith & Wesson double-action .38 and, finding only four cartidges, asked for more. When Kay expressed second thoughts about the loan of the pistol, Moore ignored them, hurried out, and rode away. A few minutes later several shots were fired at a distance of two or three hundred yards from the saloon. The two mischief-makers then returned to the saloon, where Brown "upbraided them for shooting, as it would bring his place into disrepute." When Moore denied having fired any shots, Atkins interjected, "You did shoot, Sam."

At this point, Tom Hardin the storekeeper came in. He ordered a bottle of beer, but at least half his object may have been to find out who had done the shooting. In view of earlier difficulties between Atkins and Hardin, it is also likely that at least half of the object of the shooting was to annoy Hardin and bring him out of doors.

Atkins and Moore were continuing their argument as to which of them had been shooting when Hardin broke in to observe that "it was a shame for people to hurrah the place by shooting and that one of the bullets had just missed his head." Moore replied that whoever blamed the shooting on him "was a liar, or words to that effect." Hardin's rejoinder was a further rebuke. Moore then owned up, but excused himself by saying that the shots had been fired to the west of Hardin's house, rather than over its roof, as Hardin maintained.

Atkins, his blood up, now took the lead. "Damn you, you struck me over the head with an axe handle once," he raged. Hardin's reply that he had done no such thing brought the customary retort: Atkins called Hardin a liar, with elaborations. Hardin's response was to place his right hand on the other man's shoulder, to restrain or remonstrate with him, at the same time telling him "not to abuse him that way." At that, Atkins, "quick as lightning," fired two shots from Moore's borrowed gun.

Hardin fell at the second shot, with a wound in the forehead and another just below the eye. He was reported to have lived about twenty minutes, but the doctor who examined the body found that death must have been instantaneous.

At this point, Atkins himself deserves a hearing. In his memoirs he explained that, "knowing that he [Hardin] was in the habit of carrying a pistol, and seeing him put his hand behind him," he believed that the storekeeper meant to shoot him and, therefore, made a point of getting his shot in first. Half-drunk and beside himself with fury as he was, he may have believed that Hardin was about to draw on him.

But why, if Hardin habitually packed a gun, would he leave it at home before going outside to challenge someone who was not only armed but shooting? Although the memoirs provide no answer, Atkins did not overlook the question when he had to stand before a court: his defense would be that Hardin *had* armed himself.

His efforts to set up a self-defense argument derived no support from the record of the inquest held on March 21. Even Sam Moore, having submitted his situation to sober reflection, was of no help to Dave; he had testified that he "did not see Hardin attempt to strike Atkins or draw a weapon of any kind." Through the years, however, partisans of Atkins not only reiterated and elaborated the self-defense plea but assembled a sort of moral case against Hardin. The details and their merits will be considered in their proper place; for the time being, and for some years to come, the only defense Atkins needed was a good horse, a few friends, and the wide open spaces.

Atkins and Moore "skipped immediately after the killing," and the saloon man, Brown, promptly headed for San Angelo to report the crime, arriving at 10:30 p.m. Sheriff Shield and two deputies, the brothers Silas ("Dick") and Charlie Runyon, accompanied Brown back to Knickerbocker. They arrested Moore for carrying a pistol and as an accessory to murder, but their "diligent search" failed to turn up any sign of Atkins. The *Standard* remarked; "Mr. Hardin was a first class citizen, a gentleman in every sense . . . this has been a dastardly murder, and we hope that the murderer will be speedily captured and Tom Green County treated to a genuine first class hanging."[13]

Nothing was heard of Atkins for a month, when word reached Shield that the killer had eaten dinner at a ranch at the mouth of Howard Creek in the lower Pecos country. Shield, and his deputy at Knickerbocker, Ben Cornelison, together with the local sheriff and his deputy, descended on the ranch "all . . . loaded for bear, bull elk, and alligator," only to learn that Atkins had never been there.[14]

Atkins had gone first to his brother Walter. The pair of them had then called upon their uncle, Virgil Ryan, who was not only a leading advocate and practitioner of irrigated farming but a well known horse breeder. Ryan lent Dave a fast horse. Then, said Dave, "I started the ride for my life."

His first thoughts were to head for Mexico, but a couple of narrow escapes soon changed his mind; Shield's posse came within a few hundred yards of him without spotting him, and then he almost ran into some Texas Rangers, who may or may not have been looking out for him. For two days he hid at or near the house of a friendly rancher, not far from Ozona. He then headed back for Knickerbocker and, on March 28, briefly returned home. He made temporary camp in a thicket in nearby Charlie Beck Hollow, before finding a safer billet on the Tweedy farm, six miles west of Knickerbocker. His cousin, Meritt Ryan, helped him butcher a calf.[15]

In the early hours of the morning of April 1 he awoke to find himself in the company of Tom Ketchum and another man. They were sitting on his bed.

This is the only instance in which Atkins's memoirs refer to Tom by name. The names of Sam Ketchum and Berry Ketchum do not appear at all, and that of Will Carver only once, towards the end, glancingly and distantly, as though he and Atkins had never known one another. He was Tom's unnamed companion that morning.

Atkins makes it sound as if the meeting was fortuitous, which it would not have been, but his subsequent narrative is credible as far as it goes. He related that they took him to their camp on Burk's Creek, where the three of them remained until May 5. His reminiscences give no account of their discussions, but his description of the outcome leaves no room for doubt about the subject.[16]

Since Berry Ketchum's house was only a mile away, it is hard to imagine that Tom would have set up camp so close to his brother's place if he feared to be seen by Berry. Did Berry have any idea—might he not have had a very good idea—of what was to happen next? This is a legitimate question to which no definitive answer can yet be given.

Train No. 20 was due to arrive at San Antonio from New Orleans, Houston, and Galveston, at 4:25 p.m. daily and depart westwards after twenty minutes' rest. If it kept time it would reach Lozier, 265 miles along the line, at 1:46 the next morning. Ketchum, Carver, and Atkins planned to intercept the train on the morning of Thursday, the 13th. They arrived at Lozier in good time, only to lose their nerve when the locomotive's headlight fixed them in its glare. They took refuge in a "big canyon" until about 6 p.m. and then "made another ride for the station."

Not long before what was to them the critical time on Friday, May 14, 1897, two men who were strangers to Telegraph Operator Upson approached her and, without showing any arms or making any threat, told her to make sure that the oncoming train stopped. Miss Addie replied that no special signal was needed; the train would stop anyway.[17]

That afternoon, No. 20 had pulled out of San Antonio a quarter of an hour late, but was running to time when it reached the little depot at Lozier for a few minutes' pause. As the train jerked out of Lozier station at 1:52, Conductor Jim Burns and Brakeman Allie Stevens caught a glimpse of two men, whom they supposed to be hoboes, running out from the depot building to swing onto the "blind" forward end of the baggage car. Upson also saw them and was sure they were robbers, not tramps. She began to tap out a warning for the operator at El Paso, but at that moment the third member of the gang snipped the wire at a point a mile or so west of Lozier. Their plan was to flee westwards after looting the train. With the wire down, it would be a while before a telegraphic warning could be sent out in that direction.

Just two minutes out of the station Ketchum and a companion scrambled across the tender and into the cab. A glance at the leveled pistols was all Engineer George Freese needed for confirmation of an abrupt command to bring the train to a standstill at the designated spot, where "[a] large bluff, about 50 feet high, stands along one side of the track." The third member of the gang was waiting on the hill, along with the dynamite. When he got down to the express car the other two were already beside it, holding Freese and the fireman, Will Bochat.

One of the enginemen started to bang on the door of express and baggage car no. 251 with a coal-pick, without evoking any response from Messenger William H. Joyce. While the trainman attacked the door, one of the gang "kept up a fusilade of shots along the side of the passenger coaches and shouted for the passengers to keep in their seats if they wanted to keep out of trouble."

Engineer Freese, his ribs sore from the sporadically repeated pressure of a Winchester muzzle, earnestly requested Joyce to open up. Joyce did so when a bullet crashed through, "striking a tin wash basin on the coal box by the stove." According to a story, untold at the time, which Joyce related with gusto many years after the event, the commotion aroused the messenger's bulldog, which "became very angry and very much excited and ran up and down the car floor growling and barking and bristles irritated to a standing point."

Ketchum brusquely ordered the messenger to chain the dog, and was clambering into the car when a voice from within cackled: "Say, who are you?"

"Hands up, hands up, or I'll fill you full of holes!" roared the bandit.

"That's only a parrot," said Joyce, indicating a cage in the corner of the car.

"Well, the damned thing scared me half to death," mumbled Ketchum.

After the question of Joyce's traveling livestock had been attended to, Ketchum began to interview him about the two safes aboard. A second bandit motioned Freese and Bochat to their engine. The third kept guard outside the express car.

Joyce explained why he could not unlock the larger safe; he had the key to the smaller safe, he added, but that one was empty. Ketchum had heard enough. He jogged the expressman's midriff with his rifle.

"I am a poor man and need money," he said, in a hollow tone that signified the closure of verbal negotiations. Instead of demanding the key, he and one of his companions lifted the small safe onto the larger one. He then produced some dynamite from the knapsack that Atkins or Carver handed to him, placed it against the smaller safe, and touched off the fuse. He and Joyce got out of the car just ahead of the explosion.

Two of the bandits climbed into the devastated car and extracted all the money from Joyce's "empty" way safe. Freese and Bochat were then taken back and directed to shift the wreckage from around the unopened through safe.

The freebooters had plenty to learn about the finer points of their new calling: three more charges were required before the large through safe surrendered. But, by 3:15 a.m., the bandits had three bulging sacks of loot to show for the work of one hour and twenty-three minutes. There would have been even more, had not "quite a quantity" of paper money been fragmented by the dynamite blasts. The bandits allowed these to remain in Messenger Joyce's care. All the usable American money, down to the smallest denomination, went into the three burlap bags.

Joyce also had "a lot of Mexican silver" in his care, which the robbers ignored; they could well afford to forgo it, even if they could have coped with the extra weight. They ordered the trainmen back to their places and admonished the engineer "to back the train out of bullet range." Four horses were tethered nearby. The bandits tied their booty onto one of these, then rode away to the north.

Eventually, an hour and forty minutes after the stoppage, the train resumed its journey; the express car was roofless, its floor and sides shattered, while the mail car—which the bandits had not entered, but which was carrying "quite a large amount of paper money"—was also badly damaged by the detonations and resultant fire.[18]

Addie Upson was already telegraphing the news back to San Antonio. In time the details got through to El Paso, the railroad's divisional headquarters, by "a round about route." All that was reported of the robbers' appearance was that two wore masks and the third, a false gray beard. They could not be overtaken, and would be hard to intercept in country they knew well. Lozier was then in Pecos County, and near its easternmost limits: the nearest sheriff, W.H. Jones of Val Verde County, was eighty miles to the rear even before the train carrying him and and his posse pulled out of Del Rio, the county seat. Jones was in time to pick up the trail during the day, but the bandits would have expected that and were too far ahead to care.[19]

Baggage car No. 251 and its attendant passenger coaches reappeared in San Antonio at 2 p.m. next day, as part of eastbound train no. 19. When the express drew into San Antonio, two hours late, the *Daily Light* reported that "hundreds of people flocked around it as if it was the much looked-for airship [a mysterious aerial phenomenon much reported in the skies of the American West and Southwest in the spring and early summer of that year]." The baggage car was booked for the repair shops at Houston. "[It] was a sight to behold," the *Light* reporter added, "and appeared as if it had gone through a well developed cyclone." Otherwise, the rolling stock was almost unmarked: only one passenger coach, no. 236, had been scored by a bullet.[20]

Immediately after the robbery, officials announced not only that a holdup had been expected for three months, but that the identities of the robbers were known. In the words of the *San Antonio Express:*

> Through an informer who was in the confidence of the robbers the officers were kept informed of their movements and plans up to a week ago. Since that time nothing has been heard from the informer and it is feared that the robbers discovered his treachery to them and have murdered him.[21]

This could have been a steer, planted by officers wanting it to be thought that their spies were everywhere. But, leaving out the surmise that the plotters had detected and killed the informer, it was more probably true. According to Atkins, he, Tom, and Carver had left their hideout near Knickerbocker on May 5—nine days before the holdup, and a day or two before the informant's reports ceased. Those nine days were as long as these men, knowing the terrain as well as they did, needed to travel by careful, easy, and unhurried stages from Knickerbocker to Lozier.[22]

Although the bandits enjoyed a long start on the law, Captain John Hughes and his Rangers, together with several sheriffs' posses and a number of deputy U.S. marshals, saw to it that the chase was hard and persistent. Ketchum and his partners, riding day and night, worked a double feint to get rid of the pursuit. First they headed for the Rio Grande; then, just short of the river, they turned north. They crossed the Pecos River at a point about fifty miles from Lozier, but had gone no more than ten miles along the east side of the stream when their overburdened pack horse gave out. Here they stopped to eat and to divide the money.

The exhausted horse was of no further use to them and had to be killed. Before decamping they cut out and destroyed the brand. A posse which came upon the place found only the mutilated carcase, three dollars in silver, and remnants of papers burned by the gang. Shortly after the shareout the men split up and "obliterated their respective trails." None of them rode on north into New Mexico; they simply took separate routes to the east, coming to a rendezvous at or near the Berry Ketchum ranch. In Atkins's words, "[I]t was a steady ride for four days back to Burk's Creek." On the night of May 18 "our old chum Little Bill Chaney" was there to greet them at Preacher Thicket. Atkins's reference to Chaney, later to be his mortal enemy, is tantamount to an admission that Berry Ketchum was fully posted. Chaney was associated with Berry for many years, often worked for him, and, four years earlier, had named his son after him.[23]

That same evening, May 18, John Hughes and his Rangers reached Ozona. They had trailed the Lozier robbers for eighty miles, but Hughes's duty was not yet done. He had to write out a report for Adjutant-General Woodford Mabry:

> . . . I think I have learned who the parties are. One of them has a brother near San Angelo but he will hardly stop there as he is wanted for murder in Tom Green County. His name is Tom Ketchum and is the same man who is reported to have been killed a short time ago near Clifton Ariz.[24]

Nine days passed before Hughes addressed his next report to Mabry. His letter of May 27 bore the heading of the Landon Hotel, San Angelo. He had just arrived from Sonora, where he had been working in conjunction with an Assistant Superintendent of Wells, Fargo. He had reversed his earlier opinion that the bandits would "hardly stop" in Tom Green County, and was not sanguine about the prospects of capturing them:

> I don't think there is any chance of catching them soon. I have no doubt but what they came to this county as they have lots of friends . . . [They] have probably left the county temporarily . . . I consider the leader of the Lozier robbers the hardest man to catch that we have had in Texas for many years.[25]

On June 2, with the trail dead, Hughes wrote from Company D headquarters at Ysleta that he would shortly be returning to San Angelo to confer with Richard C. "Dick" Ware, the one-time Ranger captain who was now U.S. Marshal for the Western District of Texas. The involvement and proximity of the two redoubtables did not frighten Ketchum and his partners out of their lair on Burk's Creek until July 1, when Chaney advised them to go to New Mexico. Probably they had always planned to go there, when the time was right.[26]

Their departure was not premature. They had been detected in Knickerbocker on June 18; or, anyway, that was the date on which their presence was reported to those who wanted them to be caught. Before any interested party could, or would, act on this intelligence, the three disappeared, traveling light. A last report reached San Antonio on July 7: the three had been seen two days previously, "sixty miles north of Langtry"—that is, near Ozona, where they had many friends.

The authorities really did know the names of two of the three robbers in advance of the crime, and had some reason to believe they knew the third. Information placed in the hands of Marshal Ware and various sheriffs later named the robbers as Tom Ketchum, Dave Atkins, and Bud Upshaw, three of the supposed or suspected principals in the murder of Jap Powers. Tom Ketchum's connections in New Mexico were known to the officers, for when the posses noted that the Lozier robbers had crossed the Pecos they guessed that the men were headed toward New Mexico, "where . . . they expect to be taken care of by friends in their old haunts."[27]

Who, then, was the informer? Again, the question is a good one lacking an answer. The only clue may be a false one: William Chaney did become an "informant" for the Pinkerton's National Detective Agency—but not, apparently, until 1901 or 1902.[28]

A larger and no less interesting question concerns the success of the Lozier adventure, from the viewpoint of the three participants. This time the right answer is available: Tom Ketchum and his mates could boast of a spectacular start in their new profession.

"[T]he daring and skill of the robbers have not been exceeded in the history of modern railroad robberies," a correspondent in San Antonio proclaimed in a wire to the West Coast, which had seen a good many train robberies from close up. A few of the likelier adjectives followed: "the methods were bold, unique and above all successful." Bold, certainly. Unique? Not by any stretch of the journalistic penchant for hyperbole. But successful far beyond even the least restrained of the early estimates.[29]

The booty was first reported as from five to seven or eight thousand dollars from the through safe, and two thousand from the way safe. This did not inhibit railroad officials in San Antonio from announcing a loss to the robbers of "not more than $300."[30] After the arrival of the breached express car at San Antonio, the *Light* reporter quoted a guess that the through safe had disgorged something close to $15,000.[31]

Despite that, a senior company representative tried to insist that hardly anything could have been lost to the robbers, because, as a consequence of heavy storms near El Paso and resultant washouts, all the heavy shipments had been diverted to a northerly route. This was such feeble stuff that even Wells, Fargo themselves did not persist with it. Instead, and without any great delay, they admitted a gross loss of $42,000.[32]

Joyce, the messenger, who lived in San Antonio, used his availability to tell the reporter that he himself had opened the way safe, which had contained no money. This was the sort of statement that Wells, Fargo expected from its messengers, but (or rather, *and*) it was most likely doubly untrue. But it did nothing to hide the fact that the bulk of the money was always in the through safe.[33]

Twenty-five years later Joyce, still a Wells, Fargo express messenger, said that the outlaws had taken about $6,000 from the through safe, the amount "consisting mostly of Mexican silver."[34] Old habits die hard; and Joyce, no doubt, was still a good company man in 1922. Six thousand dollars in anyone's money is just one-seventh of the sum Joyce's employers had immediately acknowledged as their loss. And, while several hundred dollars of Mexican money was removed from the safe, contemporary press accounts clearly state that the bandits had disdained to keep it.

The last and only authoritative word rests with Wells, Fargo. When, in due course, they adjusted their earlier figure of $42,000, it was to raise it to $48,980.[35]

Several reports placed Tom Ketchum, Carver, Atkins, and Bud Upshaw in that Territory during the summer of 1897. No report openly connected any of the quartet with the Lozier robbery or Powers murder, but a story in the *New Mexican* did so indirectly. It blamed a recent spate of murderous mischief in northern Grant County and western Socorro County on a new gang comprising "Tom Anderson, Dave

Atkins, Bud Upston and Tom Kitchum." All four, it added, were on the run from crimes recently committed in Texas.[36]

"Upston" and "Kitchum" were malformations caused by a printer's misreading of the names Upshaw and Ketchum in a handwritten letter or dispatch. "Tom Anderson" (Bob Christian) never kept company with the others, but a very superficial resemblance between his general description and Carver's may have led to a misallocation of identity. The absence of Carver's name indicates that, unlike the other three, he was not adversely known to the authorities in New Mexico, and, therefore, not yet wanted by the Texas authorities.

Confusion was compounded by the newspaper's qualifying reference to reports "some time ago . . . [that] Kitchum [*sic*] had been killed," which recalled Ben Clark's widely credited allegation that the man killed in Graham County, Arizona, on April 28, 1897, was "Thomas Ketchum, alias Black Jack."[37]

The fusion of Tom Ketchum and Black Jack into a single personality was becoming settled in the public mind. When it became known to all that Tom Ketchum was still demonstratively and menacingly alive, the impression was that Black Jack lived on in Ketchum's persona. Over the next two or three years, as if the ill-fame that was his by right were not enough, Tom appears to have helped the misconception along by perversely embracing the journalistically augmented ill-fame that was Black Jack's. The dissenting voices of those who had known Will Christian and the High Five were unheard or overborne. So was Tom's eventual repudiation of Black Jack's tawdry crown and overblown notoriety.

Atkins, Upshaw, Ketchum and the misnamed Carver were innocent of involvement in the troubles in Grant and Socorro Counties in the summer of 1897. At the time of the *New Mexican* report, mid-August, they were no longer even in the locality. All of them, except probably for Upshaw but with the recent addition of Sam Ketchum, were in Colfax County. Still, the story does justify the forecasts of the authorities in Texas that the Lozier robbers would take shelter in New Mexico, and does disclose that Tom, Atkins, and Upshaw were the three wanted in the Lone Star State.

A faint echo of the Lozier robbery sounded two years later. Deputy U.S. Marshal Fred Lancaster, with an eight-man posse, had stuck to the bandits' fading trail for four hundred miles, "riding hard day and night." A few days after he had given up the pursuit and returned to San Antonio, a letter came for him. It was purportedly from Wayne, in the Chickasaw Nation, and bore Tom Ketchum's signature:

> I saw you the other day near the Pecos. I advise you men who have families to quit chasing us fellows. If you was to come up with us some of you might get hurt. What does the Wells, Fargo Express company care for you all? Do you think they would care if you got killed? You know we help the poor and needy, and that Wells, Fargo can spare what we took.

The letter could have been written by Ketchum, but if it was sent from the Indian Territory, it could not have been mailed by him, and Lancaster would not have received it until weeks after Tom wrote it. Lancaster did not publicize the letter until August, 1899.[38]

Help for the poor and needy? Ketchum, Carver, and Atkins certainly paid those who provided them with shelter, provisions, and information about posses, and paid them well. Generosity was just another name for prudence. Still, it was not enough to inhibit some of their friends from helping themselves.

All the indications are that most of the stolen money stayed in Texas, either below ground in Tom Green County or deposited for safekeeping with such allies as Berry Ketchum. The intention of the thieves may have been to lie undercover for a while; to collect the money when they deemed they could comfortably get out with it to some distant place where they were unknown. But, as the weeks passed by, nothing was more natural than for them to reflect that what they had achieved so easily at Lozier they would have no difficulty in repeating elsewhere.

Sam Ketchum was still with Gene Rhodes when the Lozier trio crossed into New Mexico. One summer's day Tom turned up at the Rhodes ranch with an invitation for both of them to join him in a train robbery. Rhodes declined, adopting the unassailable moral argument that he was "flush just then." Sam decided that he could not afford to be so particular.

Sam Ketchum's outlawry, incomprehensible to those who knew him, has been ascribed to his loyalty to Tom. This, or something like it, may be part of the story. But after the murders of Herzstein and Gallegos there could be little peace or security for Sam Ketchum. When Tom asked him to make a fourth with Carver, Atkins, and himself, Sam probably did not make much of a debate out of it.[39]

In Colfax County the four first went to ground in the Taos Mountains in a secluded and heavily wooded spot called Turkey Creek Canyon (or simply Turkey Canyon), west and slightly north of Cimarron, wedged between Dean Canyon to the north and Cimarron Canyon to the south.

The gang's camp, in a glade near the northwest end of the canyon, could be reached by two trails, both of them narrow, tortuous and in places almost impassable. The westerly trail wound circuitously past a massive boulder. A rivulet tumbled across this boulder and on down to the canyon floor, its waters forming a clear pool some yards below a cave large enough to accommodate several men. The easterly entrance was a gash in the rock face, four miles from Cimarron.[40]

How or when the outlaws found this natural stronghold is unknown; the most plausible surmise is that Sam or Tom stumbled onto it or were told about it in the late 1880s, during the period they were, variously, employed on the cattle ranges above Springer, trailing a herd there, or wandering between jobs from one cow or sheep camp to the next. At some point in time they had thrown up a corral beside the cave, and laid logs among the rocks for further fortification.

This was their home base for the next six or seven weeks, with one short but all-important interval. Occasionally they would visit Cimarron, but they saw far more of Elizabethtown, twenty-four miles to the west by the stage route through Cimarron Canyon. The once thriving town of Elizabethtown, or "E-town," had very few residents in the 1890s but was frequented by a number of hard characters, some of them at outs with the law. One of these was "Charles Collins" (or "Collings"), a red-haired Texan in his twenties, then employed as superintendent of the Aztec mine, at Baldy, below the mountain of that name, four miles east of Elizabethtown. The occupations to which he was more accustomed were those of cowpuncher, bronc rider, and rustler. His right name was Bruce Weaver, but his complexion assured him of the cognomen "Red." "From all reports," says Thompson, "Collings was a good sport and an excellent Poker player." He appeared to gain the confidence of the Ketchum outfit so swiftly that he must, in reality, have been an old acquaintance of theirs. At any rate, their camping ground or meeting place in that locality was a cave at the base of Baldy Mountain.[41]

Every night for several weeks the Ketchum gang went down to Elizabethtown, always riding away at daybreak. Their hours were whiled away at the saloon owned by George W. Moore (whose father and uncle had founded the town and named it for his sister). On their first visit, as Moore told the story years later, they threw a hundred dollar bill on the counter and called upon him to serve drinks for the company. Upon Moore's admission that he was short of change, Tom Ketchum promised to change the bill for him "before morning" if he could let them have a room for Poker. Several of the saloon regulars accepted Tom's invitation to join "a nice honest game." To show his good faith, he stood the bill for refreshments. According to Moore, the men were strangers to all. Be that as it may, they built up so close a rapport that when Moore left for Idaho a few months afterwards—as Donna Ernst's research has shown—he located his ranch near the isolated store operated by Bige Duncan's brother Jim.

Then, one night late in August, the four card players failed to appear for their habitual bout of Poker. They were not seen again. Collins, too, dropped out of sight.[42]

William Burr Childers, United States Attorney for the Territory of New Mexico, later maintained that "Charles B. Collings, William Carver, Thomas Ketchum, Samuel Ketchum, 'Bob,' 'Jim,' 'John,' whose other and full names are unknown . . . with divers other persons . . . unknown" were parties to a conspiracy formed as early as April, 1897.[43] But at least two of those most prominently named in the New Mexico indictment were in Texas at that time, perfecting another conspiracy—the one that produced the Lozier robbery.

Childers's theory was that "the said conspirators, or some of them" laid their plans in April, May, and early June, 1897 at Baldy, and perfected them in the latter part of August in meetings at Baldy, Maxwell City, Teneja City, and Raton, all in Colfax County. At the beginning of September, in the attorney's submission, the conspirators gathered again at Baldy and, on the 3rd, they met at Des Moines station, sixty miles away to the northeast.[44]

Childers's findings, or deductions, are neither supported nor disputed by Atkins's graphic but characteristically spare account of how the gang passed the months of July and August. Since he did not want to mention Sam Ketchum, or identify anyone who had helped any of the gang, his narrative is silent on the journey from Burk's Creek to northeast New Mexico. It picks up at the point at which, having "rested" for three weeks, he and his comrades set off from the Cimarron-Elizabethtown area to "touch" [rob] the railroad between Denver and Fort Worth.

Their route was generally to the northeast, though more to the east than the north. It took the gang "over a rough country lined with trees," through "a deep rough canyon," down the eastern face of the mountain range, and on to the brakes of the South Canadian River close to the tracks of the Atchison, Topeka and Santa Fe Railroad, which connected Trinidad, Colorado, with East Las Vegas, New Mexico. They tore a gap into the railroad fence, about midway between Maxwell and Raton, followed the track north for a short distance, and broke through the fence on the eastern side of the line near Hebron.

That brought them into "a very rough washed-out country," and they "had to climb a mountain so steep it took [them] all day to reach the summit." Presumably they went over the mountain in order to avoid the even more rugged country to the north, or around Dwyer Mesa, to the east and south. The afternoon or evening found them north of the Mesa, in "a heavy timbered but level country, mostly firs and poplars."

At last they had a clear run. They rode thirty miles through the night until they reached the southern edge of "the Malpais Hills"—Atkins's term for the lava beds below Mount Capulin. Hereabouts, Atkins recalled, they "had a fight with a small band of Mexicans." (He did not say why.) They continued east and, probably on September 2, crossed the next set of railroad tracks and took shelter in the brush nearby.[45]

When the railroad connecting Fort Worth with Denver was completed in 1888, the spike sealing the link between the two sections was driven in at Folsom, sixty miles above Clayton, the cattle shipping point the Ketchums knew so well. Consolidation with other lines led to a new corporate title in 1890: the Union Pacific, Denver and Gulf Railroad. Generally it was known by its informal name, "the Gulf line."[46]

As darkness gathered on Friday, September 3, the four made camp near the Gulf trackside in Union County, below the village of Folsom, which lay ten miles below the Colorado border. Four to five miles along the upgrade southeast of Folsom stands Twin Mountain (or Twin Mountains), a conical mound formed from lava spewed out of the volcanic Mount Capulin. Here the railroad winds skein-like around an acute double curve, to emerge on the east side of the hill. The robbers' camp was three and a half miles southeast of Folsom by crow's flight but, because of the bends and twists in the track, the two points were twice that distance apart in rail miles.

The surrounding country was arid and mountainous, with no settlement of any consequence between Trinidad and Clayton, but the spot chosen for the looting of the train was a shallow cut which faded into a stretch of level ground to the southeast, just beyond the mountains and near the point where the track crossed the old wagon road.[47] Des Moines, the next station down the line, was another five miles to the southeast.

After nightfall two of the four men walked into Folsom to await the arrival of southbound train No. 1, the Texas Flyer, which had left Denver at 10 a.m. in the expectation of reaching Fort Worth at 5 p.m. next day. At about ten o'clock the train ground into Folsom station. A southbound freight train loaded with coal was standing on the sidetrack, waiting for the express to pass. Neither its crew, nor that of the passenger train, noticed anything untoward. The outlaws hauled themselves onto the blind baggage without being seen by anyone.

As the engine started to nose cautiously into the first sharp bend at Twin Mountain, the bandits descended into the cab. Engineer William Crofoot and Fireman Ed Cackley were quickly cowed by the cocked Winchesters and forced to halt the locomotive where the track straightened beyond the sweeping double bend, at the Des Moines crossing two miles down the line. They overshot the robbers' signal fire by thirty yards and were ordered to back the train to the spot first designated. Plainly visible to the engine crew, although not from the express car, were four horses, saddled and bridled.

The other two outlaws were already shooting over the passenger coaches, unnerving all the occupants except Conductor Frank E. Harrington, who fretted because he was unarmed, and the rear brakeman, Ernest Dixon. A passenger named Ike Mansker was one of the first to recognize the signs of an incipient holdup. He advised his fellow travelers to sit on the aisle of the coach to avoid being hit by flying glass if the bandits fired into the train.

As soon as the shooting had subsided, Harrington left his perch on the combination smoker and mail car and, lantern in hand, stepped down to warn the bandits against backing the cars any further, because the freight train was close behind the express. The robbers had no reason for taking the train further back, anyway. One of them roared at the conductor to put out his light, punctuating the command with a leaden warning of his own.

Dixon lit out for Folsom, thinking he had only a mile to run. The bandits' shouts and shots—he counted seven of the latter—soon turned him around and made him drop his lantern. When the guns were quiet, he rolled down the embankment and into a ditch. Then he retrieved his lantern and made his way towards the village.

Express Messenger Charles P. "Scotty" Drew, too, thought the train was where it was not. He believed they had reached Des Moines station, and opened the side door of his car. Before he realized anything was amiss he was covered by two guns. The two visitors climbed into the car and ordered him to open the way safe unless he would rather be killed.

"There's nothing in there you want," he replied.

"You lie, damn you!" snarled Sam Ketchum, as he clubbed Drew to the floor with the stock of his Winchester. Drew rose up only to be sent down again by a punch in the ribs.

One of the men repeated the threat to kill if the safe were not opened, but his companion knocked away the barrel of the gun as it was thrown down upon the dazed messenger. Drew, not caring to test their tempers further, now produced the keys and the bandits confiscated the money.

Next, they ordered him to unlock the through safe.

"I couldn't even if I would," he answered. It was true; the nearest person legally able to open the through safe was the express agent at Amarillo.

This time the outlaws offered neither violence nor demur. They must have expected the answer, and were prepared for it. They began forthwith to pack the outside of the safe with dynamite.

Two unsuccessful attempts were made to blow the safe before a third member of the gang lost patience.

"I'll bust her," he said, placing fourteen eight-ounce sticks of dynamite around the obstinate steel box. A quarter of beef was lifted onto the dynamite to keep the explosion down. Then a heavy trunk was placed across the beef just to make sure. The robbers touched off the fuse, then smartly vacated the car.

The blast wrecked the safe and much of the baggage. The bandits climbed in, emptied the safe, directed the engineer and fireman to stack up all the packages beside it and transfer them to sacks, helped themselves to whatever else they wanted from the car, ordered the engineer to pull out, and took their leave of the train after an hour and three quarters of undisputed possession.[48]

One yarn of local provenance has them cutting open a large leather valise belonging to a Mrs. T.E. Owens and extracting one of her dresses to wrap the loot in. But would the men have set out to rob the train without bags or sacks for the loot? Another neighborhood story that deserves no shrift holds that the bandits got $20,000 in gold and $10,000 in silver, besides the currency.[49]

A mile down the line an aroused Harrington ordered a halt and, after the wreckage of the express car had been tidied up a little, told the engine crew to back the train to the scene of the holdup, where the ground was examined for clues. No trace was found of the bandits or of the direction in which they had fled.

Also absent from the scene was Brakeman Dixon, who was running up the track to flag the oncoming coal train and report the robbery in Folsom. He got there at 12:10 a.m. and telegraphed the railroad offices. A few hours later he was telling his story to the newspapers in Trinidad. Soon some of the papers were telling stories of their own: there were eight robbers, not four, and the culprits were "the notorious Inman gang" from the Raton Mountains.

Eventually, No. 1 resumed its southward journey. When it reached Clarendon, Texas, the devastated express car was cut from the train and replaced by a Union Pacific freight car.[50]

A description of the robbers was soon racing through the wires. It was as good as darkness and confusion permitted, but too loose and vague to be helpful.

> One six feet tall, the other three were from five feet eight inches to five feet ten inches in height; all rode bay horses; one of the men had light complexion; all wore short stubby beards; all wore dark clothes; please advise the officers.[51]

At Trinidad, early next morning, railroad superintendent G.W. Webb's private dining car was hitched to a stock car and a passenger engine for a rapidly assembled posse of sixteen. Among them was a group of six, comprising most of the officers of Las Animas County, Colorado, including Undersheriff John Roosa, Deputy Sheriffs George Titsworth and Hugo Pfalmer, and Constable Wilson Elliott, most of whom will be heard from later. Luciano Gallegos, the sheriff of Union County, could not raise much of a posse, because the likeliest volunteers "were all on a cattle hunt." Only two men were with him to meet the Trinidad crowd at Des Moines and confer some kind of jurisdiction upon them.

The hunting party found a trail near the scene of the holdup and followed it west-wards into the mountains until it disappeared in thick grass. Soon afterwards they were caught in what George Titsworth called "the worst rain and electric storm I have ever witnessed." A rancher who had seen the suspects put the posse back on their track.

In the morning the posse proceeded to Johnson's Mesa, seven miles east of Raton. Here, after a short chase, they arrested four men and a boy—three brothers named Peenland, and two named Cowan—who may have been cattle rustlers, and were found in possession of a wagon full of what was thought to be stolen property. They were taken to Clayton, and exhibited to the returning crew of the robbed train, with negative results. The principal spokesman for the five kept insisting that they had not a cent between them. The three Peenlands, one of them no more than six-teen years old, were released on the 7th; the Cowans were held pending other charges.

The posse had strayed onto the wrong trail. Quite by chance, it seems, the five, while leading a band of horses towards Johnson's Mesa, had made camp at a spot pre-viously vacated by the robbers. Otherwise the evidence against them hardly amounted to a triumph for deductive reasoning: the removal of a saddle from the express car meant that the robbers had to be cowboys, and the Cowans and Peenlands were cowboys.[52]

The Ketchums, Carver, and Atkins assumed that the posses would take the prairie road, and at first eluded them by going into the hills further north. But the posse was closer than they could have expected. The outlaws were breakfasting at first light on the 6th when they saw "about 15 men coming up the draw." The gang circled the hill, took the next draw, and slipped around the opposite side. A ten mile ride across "a high rolling prairie" took them to "a gap between two big rough hills" with "small rough cedar hills" away to the south. At that point, Dwyer Mountain would have been three or four miles away on their right.

While three of them were eating their dinner, the fourth came in to report that he had seen a group of officers no more than three quarters of a mile distant. As Atkins recalled, they all saddled up and took "the roughest way we could, which was very rough cedar hills" to a stretch of rangeland beside the South Canadian. They crossed to the west bank near Hebron and "made good time" over the ten miles to the safety of the timbered foothills. That would probably have been late on the 6th or early next day, and would have put them well ahead of the fresh posse that left Raton on the morning of the 7th. After that, the gang completed their ride to Turkey Creek Canyon without incident and without leaving a trail.[53]

Here they divided the proceeds of their crime. These amounted to something between $2,000 and $3,500 in cash and a consignment of silver spoons—trifling remuneration compared with the sackfuls carried off from Lozier. They could not have failed to know that train robbery was a capital crime in New Mexico. The Folsom take was a poor return for a broken neck, but they must have expected to hit the express company far harder—and not to be caught.[54]

Northeastern New Mexico, which had not known any important case of armed robbery for a good fifteen years, was suddenly crowded with officers and detectives. The hunt was spearheaded not by Sheriff Gallegos, but by William Hiram Reno, chief of detectives for the Gulf railroad. Reno was still on the case long after the posses had dispersed.[55]

The four men dared not stay in the area for long. Any wandering cowboy or prospector might turn out to be a lawman seeking clues to the identities and whereabouts of the Folsom robbers. An immediate return to Texas was out of the question. When Carver suggested that they retreat to the Arizona-New Mexico border in southern Cochise County, where no one would be on the lookout for them, and hold up the Southern Pacific beneath Steins Mountain, there was discussion but no dissent. In Tom's words, this next venture "was planned in Colfax County, New Mexico, in the fall of 1897 by S.W. Ketchum (my brother), Will Carver, Dave Atkins and myself." The four began the long ride down to Cochise County in mid-September, after only a brief respite in Turkey Creek Canyon.[56]

Len Alverson, who lived in Texas Canyon, said that Will Carver led the party there in September, 1897. Atkins's narrative states in two places—both before and after mentioning the Folsom train robbery—that the gang remained in "the canyon" near Cimarron for six weeks. He could not have meant that they stayed in Turkey Canyon for six weeks before robbing the train, and another six weeks after it. He could only have meant that they were there for six weeks altogether. The outlaws were not seen in Baldy after mid-September, and were reported to have headed south not long after that.

Atkins goes on to say that they were on the road for three weeks before they reached southeastern Cochise County. His memoirs include a detailed description of a journey that would have taken about that long. Both his account and Alverson's show that they turned up in southern Cochise County in time for the height of the regular fall roundup. Their likely time of arrival would have been about one week into October—just a little later in the event than in Alverson's memory.[57]

Some of the money and at least one silver spoon stayed in the Cimarron-Baldy area, having passed into the possession of the man who called himself "Charles Collins." Soon the money and spoons were staking "Collins" at the Poker tables and saloon bars, and not everyone in the locality was uninterested in the source of the miner's new found prosperity. Erna Fergusson, in *Murder and Mystery in New Mexico*, relates amid a welter of confused chronology and identities that Collins "as good as admitted" he had been with the gang and was looking for someone to help him prove that two men could easily hold up a train at Twin Mountains.[58] Reno was already suspicious of him and his friends; he had traced them to Baldy, only to learn that all but Collins were heading southwest for some unknown destination. If Childers's information was correct, the gang was last seen in Baldy on September 15. Collins left some weeks later, taking the same direction as the others.[59]

"Jim," "Bob," "John," and the suspects whose names were not even partially known to the U.S. grand jury, were never identified. The name of Dave Atkins can be penciled in for one of these spectral personages; his own detailed admission, the public disclosures of William Reno, and Tom Ketchum's pre-execution statement are more than enough to constitute informal proof. Even if it did not exist, he can be put with certainty in the company of Tom and Carver so soon before the Colfax County interlude, and so soon after it, that he could hardly not have been with them between times.

Years later, Tom Ketchum would claim from a prison cell that, although he planned the Folsom robbery of 1897 and drew $500 as his share of the booty, he was in southern Colorado when it occurred. His tale was that he examined two banks at or near Alamosa, and the route of the local narrow-gauge railroad, as potential robbery sites, but rejected them all because the softness of the ground would make it too easy for the gang to be trailed after a holdup. Only after this tour of inspection, said Ketchum, did he head for Arizona.[60]

For added authentication, he explained that, although he planned all the robberies, he was so quick-tempered that Sam refused to let him take part in any.

This affectation of incompetence to facilitate a denial of guilt was not merely mendacious, but absurd. His evaluation of his own temperament was a just one, but neither his disposition nor Sam's recognition of it prevented him from taking the lead in four of the slickest pieces of train robbery ever seen in the West. The abject failure of his final attempt must have given him the idea of using temperamental instability as a plea for general innocence.

Nor could he have stayed in southern Colorado through the fall, and still managed to arrive in Arizona when he did, with the rest of the gang. Doubtless he did visit Alamosa to weigh up the prospects for a successful robbery in the area, but not in the fall of 1897.

Probably the strongest evidence against Ketchum's Alamosa story came out of his own mouth. Not long after his capture, when he was badly wounded and expecting a call from death, he admitted to George Titsworth that, on the occasion of the 1897 stoppage, he had boarded the locomotive and forced the engineer to halt the train.[61] The smooth attempt at evasion came when, aside from the loss of much of one arm, he had recovered, could not escape conviction in New Mexico on a capital charge, and had no hope of dodging the rope unless he could dissociate himself from all the other capital charges.

The four robbers may have acted wisely in quitting Colfax County, but within two or three months of their departure for southeast Arizona they were dealt so harsh an education in the risks of the game that they must have wished they had never heard of Steins Pass.

{ 7 }

CROSSED TRAILS

According to Leonard Alverson, none of the Ketchum gang, except Will Carver, had visited Texas Canyon before the September of 1897, when Carver led the party thither following the Folsom robbery.[1] Aside from the likelihood that they showed up early in October, rather than September, there is no cause to dispute this, even though Alverson, in general, may have understated his dealings with the outlaws. Tom and Sam had seen something of Cochise County during late 1896 and early 1897, but many with a far more thorough knowledge of the country would not have been able to locate the canyon. Atkins's detailed account of their long ride shows clearly that he had never been there before.

In the fall of 1897, Walter Hovey, alias Hoffman, was fresh from a killing. Walter, commonly described as a cowboy or "farm laborer," had fallen afoul of a ranchman named Joe Richards. Each threatened to kill the other, and one night someone tried to ambush Hovey near his home in Hunt Canyon. The conclusion followed swiftly. On the morning of Saturday, August 14, Hovey ran Richards to earth at the John Banke (or Bankey) ranch in Horseshoe Valley, in the Swisshelm Mountains, near Bisbee. Both men were armed. Hovey said afterwards that Richards reached for his gun with the words "God damn you, I'm going to kill you."

"But I got the drop first," added Walter, "and that's all there is to it."

The probate judge found that Richards had been the aggressor and discharged Hovey.[2]

As Hovey related it to a press correspondent in Tombstone, their difference arose because Richards had "wrongfully accused him of carrying tales with regard to cattle brands." A version of this side of the dispute which he gave to the euphoniously-titled *Bisbee Lyre* was more explicit with names and circumstances, but amounted to the same. As the *Lyre* judged it, the killing was "the result of tale bearing busy bodies who are supposed to be friends of both parties." The real reason, or a further one, may have been that Richards had spoken freely of Hovey's friendship with Black Jack Christian's old gang, the survivors of which were a migratory presence in upper Sonora and Chihuahua, southeastern Arizona, and southwestern New Mexico during the summer of 1897. U.S. Marshal Foraker claimed, perhaps extravagantly, that the Black Jack gang were "directly responsible" for the death of Richards.[3]

Foraker rightly discounted allegations that the Black Jack gang had committed the Folsom robbery, but he would have been surprised to hear that the authors of this latter crime were headed for the stretch of country where the Black Jack outlaws were then circulating. He did not know the names of the Folsom robbers; to his mind Tom Ketchum was long dead.[4] It was symptomatic of the hiatus between the law-enforcement agencies that Foraker had no knowledge of Tom Ketchum's feat in rising from the grave to lead the Lozier robbers.

The converse was true of the Texas officers. They may have laughed at the initial reports that Black Jack, the man slain in Cole Creek Canyon, was really Tom Ketchum. But they were slow to grasp that this mistaken belief persisted for months with many in New Mexico and Arizona.[5] By no means all the newspaper stories on the movements of outlaw bands were unfounded; the more inane were as likely to derive from a hasty official utterance as from journalistic licence. Cowpunchers, settlers, prospectors, or sheepherders would exchange news by word of mouth, but precious little trickled through to the officers in time for them to use it.

Official and journalistic disseminators of misinformation combined in the previously mentioned report in the *Santa Fe Daily New Mexican* of August 21, 1897, where Dud [Dave] Atkins, Bud Upston [Upshaw], and Tom Kitchum [Ketchum] were named along with Tom Anderson (Bob Christian, but identified here in mistake for either Carver or Sam Ketchum) as the authors of a complicated and bloody series of rangeland events in Socorro and western Grant Counties.[6]

But neither the Snaky Four nor the remnant of the High Five gang had any role in the tit-for-tat sequence of ambush and retaliation. All these incidents turned out to be part of a vendetta between rival cattlemen-cum-cattle rustlers. Nor could the outlaws have been involved even if they had wanted to be. At the time of the news story, the Ketchums, Carver, and Atkins were in Colfax County, while the High Five survivors were slipping back and forth across the boundaries between Arizona, New Mexico, and the Mexican states of Chihuahua and Sonora.[7]

A belated report from Duncan, Arizona, may have more substance. On October 18, "two white men passed through Duncan and remained here part of one night," displaying "a good supply of $20 bills," one of which stuck to the town. Deputy Sheriff J.T. Putman was asked to look out for the men, and Post Office Inspector George H. Waterbury to put afoot enquiries about the bill. Putman came up with nothing, Waterbury with the information that the bill was one of those stolen in the Folsom train robbery.[8] No doubt members of the gang, or friends of theirs, had ridden in for a visit to Will Carver's sister Fannie Hill.

During this period, Ben and George Kilpatrick left Concho County, Texas, under a small but deepening cloud. Whether or not they knew it at the time, their departure committed them to outlawry and eventual ignominy.

Their difficulties began at the turn of the year with "a dispute over an account" between Ben and a neighbor, Tom Benge. At first, it looked as though it might be resolved peaceably. Then, on the evening of Monday, January 4, Benge and another local man, Oliver C. Thornton, were at work "at the Sims pen" when Ben and George drove up with a load of wood.

They could have driven by. Instead, Ben addressed Benge and offered to "fight him a few jerks" if he would step out of the pen. Tom being ready to oblige, Thornton assumed the role of referee and "tapped off a ten minute fisticuff for them." The fight merely exacerbated the bad blood; it was quickly followed by "some very hard words" between Benge and George.[9]

All four men then went to Paint Rock, where Benge sought out Sheriff James E. Howze. As Benge and Howze stood talking outside G.W. Swofford's store, George Kilpatrick came up, wanting to know if Benge's knife "was in good shape." When Benge replied that it was, George drew his Colt's .45. The sheriff swiftly interposed himself between the pair, telling George not to shoot. An ugly situation had rapidly blown up out of next to nothing. It worsened considerably a moment later, when George cocked the gun and rammed it in Howze's belly with the uncompromising words: "If you don't get out of the way I'll shoot you." Benge, by now, had entered the store, either for safety's sake or to arm himself.[10]

With Benge out of the firing line, and perhaps also because the scene was attracting notice, young Kilpatrick allowed himself to be calmed down and taken under arrest to Howze's office. Next day the local J.P. fined Benge and the two Kilpatricks one dollar each for making an affray. George waived examination on three charges: aggravated assault, unlawfully carrying arms, and resisting an officer. He was released on a bond of $400 to await the action of the grand jury.[11]

Indictments were found on the first two charges and he was arrested at the end of March. Again he was bailed out. After the customary delays, November 1, 1897, was set as the date for his trial. When the first case against him was called he was not there to answer it; he and Ben had left Texas. Besides his home state, Ben left his wife Nancy and two infant children, one of them no more than twelve months old.[12]

The brothers had known the Ketchums and Carver; how well, and whether they knew Atkins at all, cannot be determined. When and where their acquaintanceship was renewed is also uncertain. But both Kilpatrick boys went to Hole-in-the-Wall, and perhaps to other northern outlaw strongholds, where they made friends with such notables as Butch Cassidy, George Currie, Harvey Logan, alias Kid Curry, his brother Loney, and Harry Longabaugh, the Sundance Kid.

Other old acquaintances of the "snaky four" who were on the move were Bige Duncan's younger brothers, Jim and Tap. They were employed as cowboys on the Diamond A ranch in southwest New Mexico during the early 1890s and followed the cattle trails and shipment routes northward. By about 1896 they had set up home in the hamlet of Three Creek, set amid hospitable, yet isolated, country in southwest Idaho, five miles north of the Nevada line. Tap's wife and infant son came up from Texas and the brothers settled on adjacent homesteads. Jim, who was now in his mid-thirties, married into a local family and opened a store.[13]

But peaceable Jim Duncan and his more volatile brother Tap did not cut themselves off from their Texas origins—and friends. Events would prove that the friends kept in touch with them. Tom and Sam Ketchum visited Idaho, and so did Dave

Atkins and Will Carver. Atkins's reminiscences do not mention the Duncans or Three Creek, but they do place him at or near Shoshone, no more than sixty or seventy miles to the north. It cannot be proved that the Ketchums stayed in or near Three Creek, but it would be strange if they did not.

Beyond all doubt Carver did put in an appearance at both Shoshone and Three Creek. He or the Ketchums introduced some of their non-Texan associates to the locality, or recommended it to them. They were Cassidy, Currie, Harvey Logan, Longabaugh, and William Ellsworth "Elzy" (or "Elza") Lay.[14]

But in the last months of 1897 this phase of the Ketchums' story lay in the near future.

Near the end of September, one James Roberts, a cattleman from Presidio County, in southwest Texas, reported in San Antonio that the three Lozier robbers had been seen near his ranch a few days earlier.[15] Throughout July and August all heavy shipments of money had been guarded along the route of the Southern Pacific between San Antonio and El Paso. After the warning from Roberts the precautions were tightened.[16] But, although three intending train robbers may have dropped in on the Roberts ranch, the Ketchum gang were far away, en route from Turkey Creek Canyon to Arizona.

Their three-week ride to the Arizona-New Mexico-Mexico borderlands can be viewed from the Atkins's own perspective. His recollections may be selective, but there is no shortage of descriptive detail.

He and his companions began by heading southeast across the South Canadian and into territory well known to all of them, the sparsely populated cattle country of eastern New Mexico. At Salado ("salty") Creek, a dozen miles northwest of Fort Sumner, they swung west and slightly south. Cimarron was now more than 150 miles behind them.[17]

The next stage of their journey took them through an almost wholly unpeopled tract of country. After pausing at a watering spot named Pinos Wells, ninety miles further along the road, they pushed on due west for another ninety and crossed the Rio Grande at La Joya, where, Atkins recalled, they "had a very nice time" even though the inhabitants did not understand English or "know straight up the kind of people we wanted to meet." Atkins, probably alone among the four, now found himself in new surroundings.

From La Joya, they passed through "rough gravelly hills" watered by the Rio Salado (unconnected except by name to the Salado Creek they had left far behind them) and entered a "deep canyon." When, after a leisurely two-day passage through the canyon, they emerged into the Plains of San Augustin, Atkins started to think that "we were at our road's end." But, after a couple of days of rest for the worn-out horses and antelope-hunting for the men, the westward ride was resumed. Atkins liked the "pretty" pine-covered Datil country and the "nice spring creeks full of mountain trout."

Soon enough, however, they were among people once more, and life was no longer idyllic. At Luna, on the San Francisco River, five miles short of the Arizona line, "we didn't know which side of our bread was buttered, or if we had any butter we didn't know it." There were about fifteen cowboys near the general store when the gang stopped beside the hitching post. Atkins dismounted to purchase tobacco and "a quart of Old Crow whiskey" but, when he turned to see whether he knew or was known to any of the crowd, the fifteen cowboys had turned into a single cloud of receding dust. Only the "lady [store] clerk" was left.

Atkins, all of a sudden conscious of the newcomers' bedraggled and hunted appearance, declared in his memoirs that he was surprised at the young lady's nerve in being able to "face the music" better than "fifteen of the worst men that had ever been in that part of New Mexico."

Atkins's tongue was wedged firmly in his cheek. In the first place, he did not know whether the Luna men mistook the four strangers for outlaws, possibly with designs on the store's cash and stock, or for officers hunting for outlaws (and for friends of outlaws). In the second place, he must have known when he told his story, and may have known even before he saw the town, that Luna was at the heart of an area much frequented by the old Black Jack or High Five gang. He and his companions would not have known that the reconstituted Black Jack gang, also four in number, had returned to that section of country and were getting ready to rob a train. Tom Ketchum's appearance in Luna that day might even have added support to rumors that Black Jack was still alive. The trails of the two gangs had crossed that summer, as will be explained; they would converge or intersect again and again.

The four were now in country which none of them had seen before. They needed directions for Bush Valley, "a little Mormon town about 18 [more like 13] miles [away]," and the girl in the store gave them, adding that when they got there they would be among a friendlier and more law-abiding set of folks. When they reached Bush Valley (now Alpine, Arizona), they noticed—or so Atkins commented—that each man had from seven to fifteen houses, and that each woman had a house to herself. Atkins the humorist reckoned that the Mormons were law-abiding people because they kept their women apart.

At Geronimo, sixty miles to the southwest, where they stopped "for a fresh supply of whiskey" (much of it for Atkins and little or none of it for Tom), they found an altogether different brand of people. "It seemed like all the men wanted to throw their hands up when we spoke to them," Atkins joked, "Even the [local] officers were standing ready to put their hands up at the word;" they had been robbed so often that they thought every stranger was a highwayman. But he and his comrades must have had a good idea all along that they would be in definitive outlaw country once they had reached this rugged land of cedar ridges, Spanish daggers, and "south side mesquite." And they felt at home there. Still, they did not loiter; everyone in town was greatly relieved when the gang "disappeared in the dark."

Their next stop was Fort Grant, almost due south, and they used about five days in covering the thirty-five miles between the two settlements. Atkins noted the progression of flats, hills, and valleys; the day might come when he would need to remember the lay of the land. Here they ran into their first unwelcome surprise: a bunch of officers—though not, as Atkins said, the very ones they had been dodging since the Lozier robbery five months previously. This posse probably believed, or hoped, that they had latched on to the old High Five or Black Jack gang; but the popular supposition that the Black Jack gang were the Folsom robbers made Atkins right, up to a point. Anyway, the posse was on their neck, and had to be thrown off.[18]

At the end of a forty-mile chase the fugitives were at the northern edge of the Sulphur Spring Valley, and, with their horses tiring, in awkward straits. Just in time, they lost themselves from the posse in a canyon on one of the ranches of the Chiricahua Cattle Company, probably on the northwest fringe of the Dos Cabezas Mountains. Atkins's comments were blunt, apposite, and topical:

> It seemed like the officers in New Mexico and Arizona couldn't trail an outlaw, only across the valleys. When they edged in towards the mountains, they would lose the trail if it was as big as a wagon road. It seemed strange but I guess it wasn't.[19]

The point had been seized upon in many a newspaper column and tested many an editor's penchant for satire, ridicule, and censure. Much of the criticism was justifiable. On the other hand, the customary reluctance of posses to follow criminals into mountainous country was, as Atkins remarked, not strange; it was human, and easily rationalized. It was a rule to which there were exceptions; but too many of the exceptions did not live to earn the plaudits of the press. The lawman who flouted the risks was apt to lose more than the trail; he might well lose his life, and no officer ever earned a second chance by getting killed. Such men as the Ketchums, Carver, and Atkins wrote the rule and wrote off the exceptions.[20]

Once they were sure that the posse had gone away, the gang rode south across the sage brush and mesquite flats past Willcox, brushing the western flank of the Chiricahuas, and veering southwest to the southerly foothills of the Swisshelms, where they halted at the 7 Up ranch, in Horseshoe Canyon. From here, if they wanted to, they could enjoy the view across Sulphur Spring Valley; "very pretty," said Atkins, who did. Finally, after following their southwesterly course for a further twelve miles, they "landed" at the headquarters of the Shattuck brothers' Erie Cattle Company, near Bisbee, at the lower end of the valley.

Atkins stated that they stayed at the Erie for about thirty days, but that is only half true. They stayed in touch with the Erie outfit for thirty days, or more, but did not stick to the Erie range.[21] It may be of some significance, or none, that one of the Ketchums' cousins was working as a cowboy for the San Simon Cattle Company.[22] The four men moved about, together or individually, but their rendezvous and home quarters were in Wildcat Canyon, adjoining Bill Lutley's Bar Boot ranch, a mile and a half north of Cushey's place.

The best description of this hideout is Len Alverson's:

> You could not have dragged them out of there with a locomotive to say nothing of with a posse of bar-room rounders. They would cross the San Simon and strike up what is still known as the Tom Ketchum Canyon.
>
> At the head of the Canyon the basin widens out into what was known as the Wild Cat. This was so called because some cow punchers once killed a beef and hung it in a tree. Every night something would come down and eat a piece. So the boys fixed a

loaded gun trap and the next morning they found a wild cat shot squarely between the eyes. Above the Wild Cat was a great bluff and many, many rocks, so wild and steep that no one could possibly climb from that side. Well, the outlaws would hobble their horses and leave them there, then climb up to the right and circle clear around the bluff over some almost impassable country and reach the top, almost over the Wild Cat. Here there were a series of little caves and great boulders dividing the top of the bluff up into rooms. One of these they called the kitchen and had their cook outfit there. Then there was the parlor and bedroom. They could go out on the bluff itself and with a glass see all over the country in all directions. They brought water up in 5 gallon cans from a spring about 3/4 of a mile away.

This hideout has been used by many outlaws, as it is very inaccessible . . . Now and then some of us cowpunchers would go in and bring out a maverick. But what few cattle were in there were wild. It was pretty near out of the world.[23]

Like many another outlaw holdout, Wildcat Canyon inspired fables of a hidden hoard. The gullible or greedy were invited to believe that one of the complex of caves, called Room Forty-four, was reserved for the storage of the gang's booty and that the treasure had never been removed. A mint of money awaited the happy finder![24]

This yarn does not go far towards explaining why Tom Ketchum's sense of penury became such that he felt driven to attempt the desperate measure of robbing a train all by himself. All the same, he seems to have been its originator. It was a hoax, devised with malice in mind, but the power of human credulity assured it of several takers.

Alverson recalled that Tom would help with a roundup "once in a great while— not often." The other three, more sociable and more industrious, regularly attended roundups; Carver, for example, went back to the Erie outfit. Individually they were affable, but reserved except when in the company of the few whom they felt they could trust. As Alverson put it, "all they wanted was to be left alone . . . if they got riled up they would not run from anybody but would strike and strike hard. They would not do to monkey with . . . "[25]

There was a cold, hard professionalism about them which was lacking in most of the other desperadoes who had frequented the region through the years. Their quiet ways, the suppressed violence in their demeanor, earned them their unflattering collective nickname of "the snaky four."

It was observed that each man was armed with a .30-40 Winchester carbine, 1895 model. These were the first such guns seen in Cochise County, just as they had been the first to be taken into Colfax County. The .30-40 cartridge comprised a steelnosed bullet detonated by smokeless powder, making this carbine a far deadlier weapon than the .30-30 Winchester then in general use as saddle-gun. Each of the four wore a Colt's .45 of the most recent pattern in the single action still preferred by most Westerners, twenty years after the double action revolver had first been manufactured in quantity. This uniformity of the caliber meant, of course, that all four outlaws would be dangerous as long as any one of them had a few cartridges. Well prepared as they were for a last ditch stand, they were continuously on their watch to obviate the need for it.[26]

Despite the unenviable characteristics they showed as a group, three of them stood highly with most of their fellows. Joseph "Mack" Axford, an Erie hand in 1897, met all four of them shortly after their arrival as a group in Cochise County and later struck up a friendship with Atkins, whose summation of his comrades mirrored the consensus: Sam Ketchum was "as fine a man as could be," Carver was a pretty good fellow, Tom Ketchum was just no good at all. But, as no one was willing to damn Tom to his face, he was a man without an obvious enemy. Alverson, who does not seem to have liked him much, made no remonstrance when the outlaw asked him to act as barber, as he had once asked Hovey.

> I do remember once when Tom came over to the ranch. He looked as if he had not been shaved for a month. He asked me to shave him and got out an old dull razor and a cake of laundry soap which he had wrapped in a silk handkerchief. I knew it was dull by the way he twisted his face. Every now and then he would say, "Let me have that thing a minute," and he would whet it on a silk handkerchief. When I got through he said, "You are a pretty good barber. I guess I will leave the razor with you to shave me again." I still have that razor . . . [27]

The Ketchum outfit were in Cochise County for no more than three or four weeks before they were temporarily evicted by a conspiracy of circumstances. In late October or early November they were nearly ready to start out to Steins Pass, fifty miles north of Texas Canyon, for a second joust with train No. 20. Then Dave Atkins got drunk at La Morita, a customs post and border resort in Sonora, eleven miles southeast of Bisbee, and told anyone who would listen all about himself, his partners, and their plans. Tom Ketchum was both disgusted and infuriated when he heard of Atkins's performance.[28]

At this time, too, further rumors that plans were ripening for a train robbery between San Antonio and El Paso had the effect of placing Rangers in each westbound express car. Guards employed by Wells, Fargo replaced the Rangers at El Paso to see the trains safely through New Mexico and Arizona.[29]

Tom Ketchum either learned that the trains were already being guarded or assumed, perhaps wrongly in the event, that word of Atkins's indiscretion would reach the authorities.

"It was then agreed that we should go across into Old Mexico for a while, which we did," he explained later. "Upon returning to Arizona we stashed away our grub in the Swisshelm Mountains, in a canyon about three hundred and fifty yards below what is known as the old High Line ranch, and about seventy-five or eighty-five yards below a box in the canyon."[30]

Rumors had been astir for weeks that the gang were bivouacked with the residue of the Black Jack outfit: "Tom Anderson" (Bob Christian); "Jesse Williams" (George Musgrave); "Theodore James" (Calvin Van Musgrave, George's older brother), and "Sid Moore" (Ef Hillman). In October two Texas Rangers, Robert C. Ross and John Watts, ascertained where the Musgrave brothers were holed up in northern Chihuahua state. On the fifteenth of the month, Ross wrote to Foraker, undertaking "to deliver the parties to . . . the Santa Fe jail" if the marshal would provide the rangers with extradition papers. Foraker at once asked him for further details.[31]

There were eight in the gang, Ross stated in his second letter, all "closely located" in Chihuahua. He had "reliable authority" that Tom Ketchum was also with the gang. His letter ended:

> One other man answers the description of Chas Perry the fugetive [sic] sheriff of
> Roswell, but I know Charley went to South Africa, but he may have returned, these
> parties were friends of his in days gone by. The papers are saying a great deal about the
> present whereabouts of this gang and the work must be done quickly.[32]

Rob Ross, in common with many of his calling, was unversed in the complexities of international law, or impatient of them. Almost the only way to restore an American renegade to his native climes—to their way of thinking—was to go to Mexico and fetch him out, papers or no papers. Kosterlitzky's rurales, and beyond them the whole structure of federal and state government in Mexico, were there to argue that it was better to have the extradition papers, unless it suited both parties to waive them.[33] Officialdom was there to see to it that the papers were granted only after protracted correspondence, if they were granted at all. No doubt Rob Ross and John Watts were aching to lay their hands on the outlaw, and Ross was anxious that the task should fall to no one but the Rangers; it made no difference— their elected or appointed overlords, mindful of earlier misunderstandings, had made it clear that the formalities must be observed. The outlaws did not have to be students of law to realize that they were safe in Mexico as long as they behaved themselves there.

The second letter ought to have made Foraker forsake his notion that Tom Ketchum was a mouldering corpse. He made no public disavowal, possibly because on October 16, only two or three days before he first heard from Ross, he had reiterated his credo that Ketchum had been killed in Arizona. "The original Black Jack," he averred, "is still at large with the gang."[34] Foraker, at this early stage of his marshalship an energetic and zealous officer, should have been disabused of these heresies long before. Perhaps he should not be reproached for not wanting to make himself look foolish by recanting immediately. Besides, he was more interested in bagging Christian and the younger Musgrave than in the question of whether Ketchum was a live outlaw or a dead one.

But he and Ross were beaten from the outset, and not solely by the system: a few days before Ross got in touch with the marshal, the Black Jack outlaws crossed into Arizona. As usual, they had outpaced those who informed against them.

The Ketchums, Carver, and Atkins probably did share camp with the Black Jack crowd in late 1897 or early 1898, but, through incompatibility of method or personality, there was no union of the two bands. A report that Charley Perry, the disappearing sheriff, was in camp with the outlaws, was groundless. Charley, as Ross rightly stated, had gone to South Africa, but he had gone with no thought of returning to the United States.

George Titsworth, at that time a deputy sheriff of Las Animas County, Colorado, later maintained that Tom Ketchum was the murderer of Angelo Carli, another deputy, who was shot and killed in Sopris, a mining village five miles southwest of Trinidad, the country seat. It was Titsworth's contention that witnesses, shown a photograph of Ketchum, identified him as the killer.[35]

The circumstances were these:

In the last days of October, 1897, three strangers appeared in the vicinity of Trinidad. They stole several horses and on Monday, November 1, committed some sort of robbery at Catskill. Three days later the Trinidad *Daily Advertiser* reported the shooting of Carli:

> Angelo Carli, proprietor of the Carli saloon and bakery at Sopris, was shot down in his place of business last night by two unknown men. About 9 o'clock the two strangers made their appearance at Carli's place of business and shook dice for the drinks. While [they were] engaged at this two Mexicans entered the saloon, one of them leaving a saddled horse tied outside. Upon their entrance the two strangers left. Soon after the Mexicans followed and found their horse gone. They spoke to Mr. Carli about the matter and went over to another saloon to make enquiries. While they were away the strangers passed the Carli place, one of them riding the missing horse. Mr. Carli, who is a deputy sheriff, stopped the pair and informed them that they were under arrest. They asked him for his authority and he replied that he would show it to them and turned and walked into his place of business, it is supposed to get his commission as a deputy. One of the men (the one who was on the ground) began shooting at him. Three shots were fired, one striking Mr. Carli in the hand and one entering his stomach.
>
> The authorities were at once notified and Sheriff [D.D.] Finch and Deputy Hightower were soon at the scene of the crime. Up to a later hour this morning no trace had been found of the would-be murderers or the stolen horse.[36]

Carli died in hospital that day. Titsworth and another deputy sheriff, Louis Kreeger, joined in the hunt, but accomplished only the routine roundup of bums, loafers, and drifters. One of the fugitives had lost his hat in the rush to get out of town. Otherwise there was no trace of the men who had been hovering around Catskill during the past few days.[37]

An account of the affair preserved in Titsworth's papers differs from that in the *Advertiser*. He wrote that the men were mounted when they first stopped at Carli's place, and that each was leading an unsaddled horse stolen from a Mexican rancher; the rancher followed them, entered the saloon as the dice were being rolled for the second round of drinks, and asked Carli to arrest the two strangers. The shooting occurred directly afterwards, and the men escaped through the crowd.

Titsworth also gave a description of each of the pair. Both were tall and clad in "cowboy outfits." The one who did the shooting, allegedly Tom Ketchum, had a black beard and mustache and wore a white hat, dark blue flannel shirt, and blue denims. The second man was clean-shaven and attired like his companion except that he wore light-colored corduroys and chaperajos. If the first man was Tom Ketchum, the other could have been Sam or Atkins. But those descriptions are vague enough to have fitted many others.[38]

No doubt those who subsequently identified Ketchum as the killer did so in good faith. But Carli was shot on Wednesday evening, November 3, 1897, when Ketchum was a long way south of Colorado.

No one was ever tried for the Carli murder, but no attempt seems to have been made to connect it with Ketchum in his lifetime, even when he was being held in Trinidad after his arrest in 1899. The Carli charge makes no better showing than Ketchum's own pretense to have been in Colorado at the time of the first Folsom holdup and for some weeks after it. Titsworth's allegations suggest an attempt to pin the crime on Ketchum on the strength of his eventual notoriety. Tom, most likely, was already prowling about along the United States-Mexico border on the day of the shooting.

Another incident in the Ketchum apocrypha took place in the same week as the murder of Carli.

On November 6, Bob Christian, George and Van Musgrave, and Sid Moore broke out of hiding to waylay a train at Grants, New Mexico. Richer by some $90,000, they may have buried some of their plunder in the Malpais country before pressing on through western New Mexico and eastern Arizona, finally to cross into Sonora state. Jubilant with success, they regaled their friends with stories of the holdup. These were picked up by the Ketchum gang, probably at second or third hand.[39]

Tom was impressed. In Cochise County he announced that he and his partners had pulled the Grants robbery. One of the bandits, while leaving the looted train, was widely (though incorrectly) said to have yelled out, "Tell them that Black Jack has come to life." Evidently this tale reached Tom's ears. His growing reputation as an outlaw, and his ability to recite purported details of the crime, made the boast believable to some.[40]

It may be that, in the fall of 1897, Tom Ketchum saw himself as natural heir to the title of "Black Jack" and all the concomitant prestige. If it is true that Tom was mistakenly or jocularly greeted as Black Jack in Bisbee or Pearce or somewhere else in Cochise County, it may also be true, as Lorenzo Walters wrote, that "after explanations had been offered and accepted," he announced that "from that day hence he would be known as Black Jack." Walters himself had no clear idea of where Christian's villainy ended and Ketchum's began; but in ascribing many of Christian's crimes to Ketchum he was only reproducing misinformation that had been widely peddled in the last two years of Ketchum's life. By then, the nickname had stuck to him like tar, and his final, frantic efforts to disown it were in vain.

Yet Ketchum was never "known as Black Jack" among those who rode with him or had been acquainted with Christian. Mack Axford, one of the few still living in 1970 who had first hand knowledge of both gangs, and one of those to whom Tom Ketchum "admitted" his part in the Grants robbery, said flatly: "Tom Ketchum was not Black Jack."[41] Nor, despite Axford's belief to the contrary, was he one of the Grants robbers. If he and his colleagues had gobbled up as much as ten thousand dollars, let alone ninety thousand, they would have shelved their scheme to rob the Southern Pacific at Steins Pass.

In fact, three of the Grants robbers were jailed in Fronteras for disturbing the peace on Thanksgiving Day, only to bribe their way to freedom within seventy-two hours of their arrest. Marshal Foraker, stung by this last manifestation of their flair for dodging justice, publicly inveighed against the international red tape that had thwarted his efforts to extradite the suspects at once.[42] Then he and Marshal Griffith, of Arizona, supported by officials of Wells, Fargo and the Southern Pacific, initiated the most vigorous campaign yet mounted against the outlaw bands of the Arizona-New Mexico border. Once again, guards were hired to accompany all express messengers on the S.P. route across New Mexico and Arizona. At the same time arrangements were made for a combined posse to assemble in Cochise County.[43]

The Ketchums, meanwhile, blithely concluded that this was the propitious moment for an assignment with train no. 20. Their decision to reinstate this item on their program was more than a blunder. It was ruinous for three of their friends in Tex Canyon, and fatal for a certain Ed Cullen.

⊰ 8 ⊱

THE STEINS PASS IMBROGLIO

A widely publicized statement by Tom Ketchum, in which Ed Cullen's surname was sometimes printed as "Bullin" or "Bullen," gave rise to a belief in some quarters that he was Ed Bullion, a brother of Laura. This theory ought not to have reached the printed page. Recent research has shown that Laura Bullion's only brother was named Daniel, and that he was living in Brewster County, Texas in 1900, more than two years after Ed Cullen's premature demise, and in Lincoln County, New Mexico, when he registered for military service in 1917.[1]

This much is known. Edwin H. Cullen's parents, Theodore J. and Nancy Cullen, had been neighbors of Sam and Tom Ketchum in San Saba County, where Ed was born on December 4, 1872. By 1880, the family had moved to Bandera County, close to the farm on which Will and Frances Carver were living with their mother and step-father. The Cullen household then comprised Theodore, (51); Nancy (36): James O. (9): Edwin H. (6); Lucy (5): Nellie (4); and Callie (2).[2]

We next hear of Ed in Colorado City, Mitchell County. In the 1890s, this town was a trail head and a shipping point for livestock. Perhaps Cullen, in his late teens or early twenties, drove cattle thither. He may have called himself John A. Hespatch, or been associated with someone of that name. Nothing more is known of his time there.[3]

Like Will Carver, Ed went to Cochise County in the mid 1890s and worked for the San Simon and Erie outfits. He became noted as a cowcamp cook and, like many of that avocation, an individualist. He also became the subject of the sort of camp-fire tales that were told for effect rather than for belief.

Thus: While working for the San Simon Cattle Company he had been awarded the nickname of "Shoot 'em up Dick" in recognition of his feat in being bested by one of the Chinamen who were frequently the butt of revelers and who seldom dared retaliate. When a Chinese restaurant owner pressed Cullen to pay his bill, the San Simon cook solemnly assured the man that he was "Shoot 'em up Dick," and would brook no further argument. Thereupon the Chinese grabbed a six-shooter, intimated he was "Shoot 'em up Sam," and positively insisted upon payment.[4]

This reverse, we are further advised, did not turn Ed Cullen into a timid character. Somewhat later, when in the employ of the Erie, he tersely educated one of the Eastern owners into the democracy of the range.

One morning the man brusquely demanded a pail of water from Cullen, whom he unthinkingly addressed as "servant."

"You get it yourself, you bald-headed son of a bitch," retorted Cullen, and the deflated magnate meekly did as he was bidden.

That anecdote, too, was good for a guffaw, but not much of it could have been true. The owners of the Erie were the brothers Enoch and Jonas Shattuck and, excepting their indisputably Pennsylvanian origin, everything that is known about them is the refutation of everything in the story. This much can be said for both tales: they delineate young Cullen as his contemporaries saw him—as a cowcamp "card," whose involvement in such situations would have been in character.[5]

In November of 1897, Cullen was out of work and not eager for more. His well-nursed ambitions to join the High Five outfit were unrealized; either he had failed to get in touch with its surviving members, or they had turned him away. But he probably had known all the Ketchum gang in Texas, and was on friendly terms with them. Here, he thought, was the key to his future.

At the end of the month, he told Sam Hayhurst of his decision. Hayhurst vainly urged the malcontent to "steer clear of that outfit." He refused to let the obdurate Cullen ride away on an Erie horse, but said he could take one of two flea-bitten grays which had strayed across from the Mexican side of the Line. Cullen roped one of the grays, and set out from Hayhurst's camp, south of Bisbee, for Texas Canyon. On his way there, he met Dave Atkins.

"I'm a loser [loner?]," Dave told him, "but there's a gang of three men in the mountains you could get with that might suit you better than throwing in with me."

Ed replied that just the two of them "would make a gang big enough." Whereupon, Atkins recalled, he "took him to his nest" and provided him with a good horse. Actually, although Dave did not admit it, the Erie Cattle Company was the provider, unknowingly, and Atkins merely its unofficial agent. Atkins, of course, had a standing arrangement with the Ketchums and Carver.[6]

It was about this time that Jess Benton, out on a cattle buying trip, happened upon the canyon:

> Smoke was coming out of the house, so I rode up to it. I were surprised to find eight outlaws there in a bunch, all from Texas, and I knew two of them, but the others I did not know. They were all wanted men and tough hombres. Some of them took part in the famous Steins Pass train robbery. I had been among outlaws on occasion all my life and knew how to handle them. Keep your mouth shut, attend to your business, and leave other fellers alone, and you will get by . . . William Downing [later imprisoned for his part in the Cochise train robbery of 1899] was there. I knew him well in Pearce. A man named Cush was the owner. I bought a few cattle off him, and then I said, "you want to sell this place?" "Not for sale," he said. I knew why. It were an ideal outlaw hideaway . . . I didn't push him. I decided just to bide my time and wait, and maybe my time would come . . . [7]

There is no suggestion that Benton did anything to help matters shape into what he wanted. Someone, though, was very talkative. In the first week of December, Foraker and Griffith were apprised that a train would be held up within the next ten days, at a point near the Arizona-New Mexico line.

Foraker immediately traveled to Deming to organize a posse. It was arranged that the posses of Foraker, Griffith, and the Wells, Fargo Company would meet at Bowie, Arizona, because "it would be a hard ride from any other point to get into the mountains where the robbers were supposed to be located, and furthermore there was no other place to unload the horses." Epes Randolph, divisional superintendent of the Southern Pacific, was "on the alert" from the outset; he "furnished transportation and kept the wires hot, and in every way assisted Marshal Griffith in his work." Foraker was the beneficiary of similar cooperation from railroad officials in New Mexico.[8]

Foraker's party of four, with the carload of horses, arrived in Bowie on the night of December 7, some hours ahead of the other two posses. Next day the combined force of fourteen—soon augmented to sixteen—made camp about seven miles east of Bowie. Foraker and Griffith stayed near Bowie station. The following morning, Thursday, December 9, the united posse was divided into two groups, each to search a section of the mountainous country along the southern stretch of the territorial line. In the evening the men returned to camp to "keep watch on the movements of the gang." Shortly after nightfall they noticed what appeared to be a signal, as though from a torch, in the mountains twenty miles to the west. Fifteen minutes later, an answering light rose from the south. The signals—if they were that, for their significance was never fully explained—were repeated at similar intervals until eleven o'clock. By then the Ketchum gang had played out their hand.[9]

Steins Pass was the name given in 1888 to a Southern Pacific station with a few adjoining dwellings, nineteen miles west of Lordsburg, New Mexico, and three and a half miles from the Arizona line. The general store founded by William Charles in 1880 is still trading; otherwise, nothing is left but the railroad tracks and the ruins of a few buildings. Steins Mountain (not to be confused with Steins Peak) is two miles to the northwest, at the southern extremity of the northern Peloncillo range.[10]

Steins Pass was a misnomer for the railroad depot and hamlet: the mountain pass to which the name rightly belongs is overlooked by Steins Peak, nine miles northwest of the site of the station. This pass runs into Doubtful Canyon, the rocky route across the territorial boundary preferred by the unlawfully inclined. In 1905 the boom town that had lately sprung up around the station and the S.P.'s rock crushing plant was more accurately renamed Steins.[11]

The little settlement had already received three personal calls from road agents. On February 22, 1888, Dick or Tom Johnson (whose real name may have been James Craven), and Dick Hart (a man with no discernible history), robbed the westbound train three miles west of the depot. They and a confederate, Larry Sheehan, were killed in Mexico after being on the run for three weeks.[12] Almost exactly seven years later, two novice bandits tried to repeat the operation, but their incompetence and loss of nerve combined to produce failure.[13] Last, and of recent memory, was the visit of the Christian brothers, George Musgrave, and Bob Hayes, on November 16, 1896.

These predators had done no worse than pilfer a few dollars from the store, express agent, and section boss.[14] They had told the postmaster, Emma Rodgers, that they would never rob a woman; but their show of magnanimity may have been motivated less by gallantry than by the expectation of a negligible haul from the till. Public relations exercises sometimes come cheap.

Emma Rodgers was absent on the evening of December 9, 1897, but the staff at Steins Pass station knew each other well and readily deputized for one another. Francisca Charles, the storeowner's wife, was present and either she or the station and express agent, Charles E. St. John, would have filled in for her, just as Rodgers would sometimes stand in for St. John as agent and telegraph operator. On this particular evening, St. John was acting postmaster. Also on the scene were St. John's wife, Daisey, the section boss, James McMullen, and a section hand of shifting identities whose name appears variously as Foley and Frank Cody.[15]

Dave Atkins and Ed Cullen presented themselves at Steins Pass station a few minutes after six o'clock that evening. The Ketchums and Carver rode in with them but, for the time being, remained offstage. As the train was not due until 8:35 there was no call for haste. Atkins and Cullen chatted awhile with Charles and Daisey St. John in or near the store-post office, a short distance south of the tracks. Here, before or after Mrs. St. John had served supper for all hands, the pistols were produced, St. John and McMullen robbed of their cash, and the post office till ransacked. The two ruffians may also have emptied the cash drawer of the Charles store; whether they did or not, they affected no qualms about robbing a woman.

Atkins, who described the proceedings with much gusto and more than a hint of caricature, averred that at some stage "an Irishman" (McMullen? Foley?) professed himself to be a man of much property and asked for time to make his will. Time was granted, said Atkins, and the will was made, "but not in my favor." Atkins may not have been the only off-center humorist on show.

At about 8 p.m. the pair took St. John to the depot, a few steps to the north, and entered the railroad and express office, where Sam Ketchum joined them in hunting for money and finding very little. In speaking of this, Atkins declared that neither he nor Cullen had the money to pay for their "very good supper" of milk, fruit, and cold bread; well, that was all right—the lady could be paid out of the Wells, Fargo drawer. And, said Atkins, so she was; but the better evidence is that the bandits kept whatever they took, such as it was.

Tom Ketchum and Will Carver, meanwhile, were cutting the telegraph wire. Tom appropriated the operator's Winchester .44 but scorned to accept a share of the paltry sum collected by his comrades. He and Carver then took the horses a mile and a half or two miles further west and built a bonfire on either side of the track, right below Steins Mountain.

The three bandits at the depot waited till the headlight of westbound train no. 20 swung into sight before they summoned St. John to the station platform and told him to turn on the red light. Then they bade goodbye to the St. John couple and Mrs. Charles, and prepared to meet the train. "We had it [the station] under martial law," Atkins reminisced. The train would prove to be more resistant.[16]

Inside the express car, besides Messenger Charles J. Adair, were two guards: C.H. Jennings, a thirty-one year old native of Brooklyn, N.Y., ("a little bit of a fellow, [who] used to work in Las Vegas for the Wells-Fargo company [and] is well known in New Mexico") and Eugene Thacker—son of John N. Thacker, who was in charge of the Wells, Fargo party then encamped in the San Simon Valley. As the train toiled up the long slow grade toward Steins station the three were eating supper. Young Thacker, out on his first trip, was being joshed about the hazards of the road. They all kept their shotguns close to hand, should the joke turn into reality. Everyone was mindful of the holdups in the past and acutely conscious of the warnings that another was expected; without the warnings, Jennings and Thacker would not have been aboard. Yet such tip-offs were often false alarms. Thus, when the attack came, its swiftness caught them by surprise.

When the train halted at the station, Conductor Russell and the brakeman ran into the agent's office for their orders, not expecting to have to take them from a bunch of robbers.

The command was succinct: "Get your hands up and keep quiet."

In a few moments they were free to do as they liked, for the three outlaws had mounted the engine and were getting acquainted with Engineer W.T. (Tom) North and his fireman, Robert W. Anderson. Again, no words were wasted. The locomotive men were curtly told to go ahead as far as the bonfires.

Three shots were fired near the mail and express cars as the bandits moved to the engine, but the nerves of the passengers were calmed when the train pulled out without delay; the shots could have been taken as the passing salute of local pranksters or inebriates. The guards must have been similarly reassured, if Adair spoke for all of them in an interview he gave at Los Angeles the following night. Only when the train pulled up between the two bonfires, said Adair, did he and the guards guess that the train was in the hands of robbers. Their impression was speedily confirmed by a tattoo of shots. They doused the lights, armed themselves, threw the doors wide open, and waited. None of the large complement of passengers lifted a hand to help them.

North was hustled out of the locomotive and ordered to uncouple the express car, which the gang intended to take a short distance up the line before breaching the express car and blowing the safe. As North started work on the couplings, one of the guards in the express car got off a shot through the open doorway. Other shots followed from both parties, the car door continually sliding shut and then open again as the expressmen kept up their side of the battle. The engineer's protests at "being between two fires, as it were" brought him no respite: a voice from the express car told him that "no parleying would be allowed." His efforts to induce the messenger and guards to direct their aim at the bandits' horses—starkly targeted against the firelight—went unheard or unheeded.

North not only failed to detach one of the two coupling chains, but also (though perhaps by accident) set the air brakes, immobilizing the train. Because they did not know how to remedy the fault caused by the expulsion of air, or were unwilling to waste time, the bandits decided to hold the entire train, with its passengers, and subdue the defenders there and then.

Their call for the messenger's appearance was met by a shotgun blast from the darkened car. The bandits, exposed to view by the flaring bonfires, bolted for cover. Four of them climbed onto the engine. Ed Cullen, more daring or more foolish than the rest, took up a position below the tender, by the near corner of the express car.

The fight lasted half an hour. At close quarters the shotguns of the defenders were more effective than the rifles of the bandits, and the Wells, Fargo men were better placed than their opponents; but this hardly blunts the force of what Adair and his companions demonstrated—that five professional criminals and accomplished marksmen could be held at bay and finally worsted by three determined novices.

Two of the outlaws were kneeling upon the tender, preparing the dynamite in between swapping shots with the men in the express car. Jennings spotted one of the gang, either Carver or Sam Ketchum, start to crawl under the train, and quickly sprayed the outlaw's rear with loose buckshot. This put an end to any plans to blast the guards out of the car.

At this stage the doors of the express car were being kept open, and a good many incoming bullets flew through them. Six bullets bored through the woodwork, and two narrowly missed the mail clerk, Frank Albright, though without rousing him into any sort of action, except the evasive kind. No one aboard was hit. But the four bandits who had been on the locomotive or under the express car were all wounded: Sam Ketchum's scalp was scored by two buckshot, and the other men suffered damage in various areas of the lower anatomy.

Years later, on two occasions and in two differing ways, Tom recalled a passage of conversation between Sam and another of the gang. At first, he did not connect the anecdote with the Steins or any other holdup.

"We got into a fight, Sam and Tommy [Dave] Atkins and me down in the territory, . . . and it was pretty hot for us. Tommy Atkins exclaimed all at once, 'Sam, I'm shot.' 'Where?' says Sam. 'In the leg,' says Tommy. 'Well, you white livered dude,' says Sam, 'go on shooting. I'm shot twice in the head.'"

Then, three hours before he was due to swing from the Clayton gallows, he included the story in his description of the Steins Pass affair, except that this time the exchange was between Sam and Carver and free of insults.[17]

By then, Tom had been found to have "a number of scars on [the] left leg above the knee."[18] If these were caused by shotgun pellets, they may have been a memento of this fight.

"There wasn't a word spoken by any of us in the car," Messenger Adair told a Los Angeles newspaperman some hours after the melee. He followed this statement with a testimonial to the junior member of the team:

"I tell you that kid, Thacker, stood up to it like a veteran," said Adair, cannily blending condign praise with judicious sycophancy. "He is a worthy son of his illustrious sire, John Thacker, who has grown gray in the service of Wells, Fargo."[19]

The passengers stayed put—all but Alexander F. Stoeger, a beer salesman from St. Louis, who ran some distance downtrack. There he lit a fire as a signal for the westbound Limited which followed no. 20, the Flyer. In the event, his initiative was unneeded; the stranded conductor and brakeman had already flagged the Limited from the station.[20]

By 9:15 Adair, Jennings, and Thacker had their shotguns loaded with the last of their ammunition. It seemed as though they would have to surrender, after all. Then, providentially, Ed Cullen reached into his belt for cartridges. As he did so he leaned forward, bringing his face close to the tip of Jennings's shotgun. Jennings promptly pulled the trigger and blew a hole in the bandit's forehead.

"Boys, I'm gone," cried Cullen, slumping back, "Boys, I'm dead." In a moment he was. Within a few moments, the boys were gone, too. They clambered down from the engine and scooted a hundred yards for their horses, all fresh mounts on unofficial loan from the Erie company. One of the gang paused long enough by Cullen to confirm Ed's own diagnosis. As the four were mounting up, Jennings gave them a parting shot from a Winchester rifle and thought he saw one of them fall, as if wounded. Most likely the shot was a miss; what he probably saw was an already-wounded bandit lurching as he mounted and being propped up by a companion. As one reporter put it, the man whose "posterior" had been peppered with loose buckshot "it is probable . . . will not be able to sit in a saddle for some time."

Soon the fleeing foursome were swallowed into the night.

Cullen's body was lifted onto the train and conveyed to San Simon, along with the abandoned box of dynamite and the loose sticks on the engine.[21]

Since the outlaws had cut the wire in one place only, and then on the east side of Steins station, the operator was able to send out a message to Bowie a minute or so after the seizure of the train. A courier rode out to inform the posse, eight of whom were back in camp. They boarded the special train laid on for Foraker and Griffith and were at Steins less than two hours after the defeat of the Ketchum gang.[22]

The special continued east with Cullen's body, which had already been identified from letters in the clothing. The following morning it turned up as the subject of an inquest at Lordsburg, New Mexico. A needless press argument then ensued over the identity of the fallen desperado. Foraker's announcement that the body was that of Edwin H. Cullen was met by misinformation from Colorado City that the right name of the dead man was John A. Hespatch. Voices in El Paso were insistent that the vanquished outlaw was actually Victor "Sandy" Collins, brother of the recent bride of a rich man in Chihuahua; the Hespatch connection, they alleged, was an invention of Collins's relatives. Whatever the truth about the use of the name Hespatch, Vic Collins was flesh and blood. He proved it by turning up alive and well two and a half years after the Steins Pass affair.[23]

The knowledge that, until lately, Cullen had been camp cook on the Erie, encouraged the mistaken idea that the assailants were all "cowboys organized for the purpose of this single crime." An appearance of substance was given to this theory by a local reporter who ascribed the jamming of the air brakes to the bandits' incompetence rather than to the engineer's opportunism or luck.[24]

Although the trail left by the disarrayed outlaws was easily discernible in the moonlight, the officers essayed no pursuit until daybreak. Their lack of any sense of urgency has a ready explanation. The posse, or some of its members, may already have formed a strong opinion as to where the chase would lead them.

That may not have been all. Certain of the possemen seem to have decided already that if they could not catch the actual robbers, they would rope in some of the unruly and intractable crowd who regularly consorted with the outlaws.

This attitude was justifiable to the extent that some of these men may have been accessory to the crime, before or after the fact, or both. If they were not, they might have committed other offenses, or might be thinking of doing so. It would do the officers no harm to shake down their camping place and pull them in for questioning. And if they could arrest more than four of them, then so much the better.

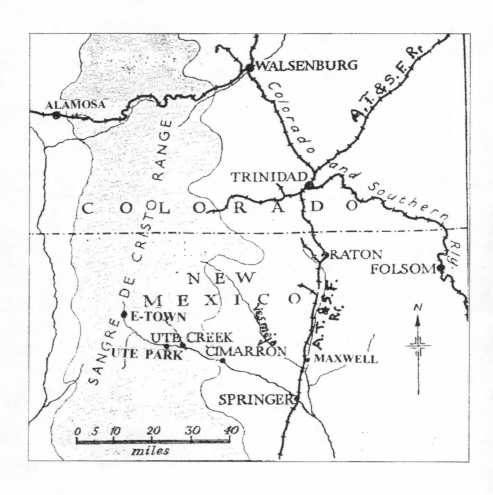

Map 3

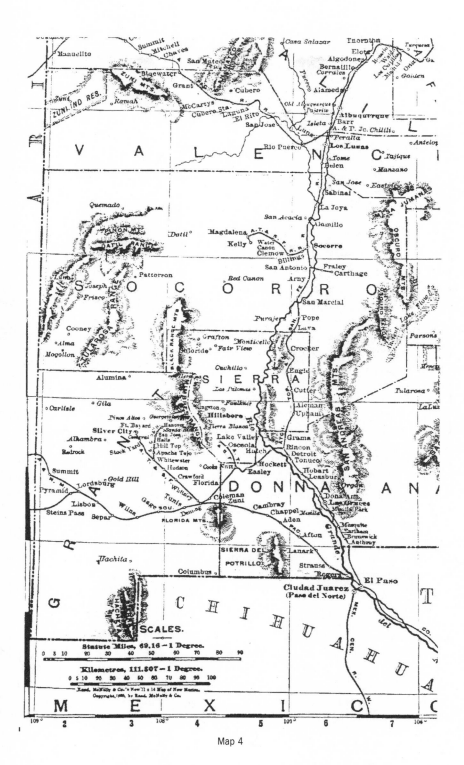

Map 4

FRAMED

Besides John N. Thacker, a detective of national note and second only to Chief of Detectives Jim Hume in the hierarchy of Wells, Fargo's force of investigators, the posse raised by Foraker, Griffith, and Wells, Fargo included nine men from Arizona and five from New Mexico. In the New Mexico squad were Cipriano Baca, Ben Williams, Tom McElroy, George Scarborough, and George's son Edgar. The Arizona nine were Jeff Milton, his nephew Jim Gamble, Sam Webb, Sam Finley, Charles Hood, Billy Hildreth, Severiano Bonito, Jesse [or Jesus?] Limon, and Lee Matney. Two others who cannot be named with certainty brought the number up to sixteen, plus Thacker and the two marshals. Only Milton, Baca, McElroy, and Finley held commissions as deputy U.S. marshals. Milton, Gamble, and Webb had been engaged by Wells, Fargo on December 6, when Milton was also sworn in as a deputy. All the rest were either put into the field by the express and railroad companies, or volunteered their services in the expectation of securing employment from them or the marshals. Presumably those who were not commissioned were sworn in as *posse comitatus*, doubtless without much formality. Some, or all, would have been drawn in by the lure of reward money. Others who were involved in the case later included Scott White, sheriff of Cochise County who was also a commissioned deputy marshal, and Dayton Graham, the Bisbee constable.[1]

Next to Thacker, Jeff Milton and George Scarborough were the most widely known. Milton was a thirty-six year old native of Florida, whose father, John Milton, a direct descendant of the poet whose name he bore, had served as a governor of the state.

By now Jefferson Davis Milton had been strenuously on the side of law enforcement in Texas and New Mexico for seventeen years, with only a few short breaks. For the last two years he had been a messenger for Wells, Fargo on the Nogales-Guaymas and Nogales-Benson routes, though in the spirit of enlightened self-interest the company would from time to time (though not as a matter of course) let him exchange routine express car duties for a spell of bandit chasing. His success as an officer sprang from a compound of courage, honesty, and shrewdness, firmly allied to skill with weapons.

Milton did not permit the finer meshwork of the law to interfere with his understanding of justice. Such an attitude runs dangerously close to arrogance. But if Milton's sense of honor was a little righteous or overbearing at times, he was respected even by most of those who had best cause to avoid him. In his old age, a conspiracy of longevity and vanity induced him to aggrandize his own standing by disparaging or demeaning some of those he had known and outlived. This did not escape the notice or censure of those of his contemporaries who were still alive.[2]

His close friend and associate George Scarborough was a man of curiously piebald reputation. He was born in Louisiana in 1859, one of a peripatetic family that finally settled in north-central Texas in 1874. Only ten years later, just past his twenty-fifth birthday, he was elected sheriff of Jones County. During his two terms in office, and later as a deputy United States marshal and state Ranger, his courage and integrity never failed the test; his professional standing and personal popularity were deservedly high. Then, in the middle of 1893, he moved to El Paso, and before long the skies darkened.[3]

In the summer of 1895, while moving among the complex underworld of El Paso, he employed the most questionable of means to lure Martin Mroz from the Mexican side of the Rio Grande into a fatal ambush. Mroz was a notorious thief and crook, but Scarborough's public character was gravely tarnished in the outcry that followed the affair. Nine months later he murdered Old John Selman, perhaps because he suspected that if he did not kill Selman, Old John—recently the murderer of the redoubtable and already legendary John Wesley Hardin—would kill him.[4]

Selman was a bad lot; but the manner of his removal made Scarborough unemployable in El Paso. At Milton's suggestion he moved to Deming, where he was engaged as detective for the Grant County Cattlemen's Association. His biographer, Robert DeArment, asserts plausibly but without documentation (though apparently on the basis of an assertion by Holmes Maddox, a cowboy who worked alongside Scarborough in the summer of 1897) that it was his undercover work that brought to light the Steins Pass robbery plot, and he who delivered the warning of what was afoot. But he had to wait until March 10, 1898, for a commission as field deputy under Foraker, and that expired on April 30 of the same year.[5]

No one was more thorough than Scarborough in hunting for bank and train robbers, or more contemptuous of adverse odds. Bellicose and fearless, he had come to relish trouble. For example, he wanted to kill Bob Johnson, foreman of the big Erie outfit, who not only employed fugitives from justice, but, in Scarborough's estimation, helped them evade officers searching for them.[6]

While his efficiency as a stock detective made him the hobgoblin of the rustlers, his methods and his manner were such that he was loathed by nearly everyone on the range other than the big cowmen. The truth may be that Scarborough, like many people who approach mid-career with a growing conviction that their merits and services have been ill-rewarded and insufficiently recognized, was in a rage against life. Someone had to pay for its unfairness.

These two, Milton and Scarborough, through their strategy of making the law work for them in thinning out the crop of thieves, smugglers, and abettors of outlawry, were the chief authors of the prelude to a judicial travesty.

Milton was at home in Nogales three days before the holdup. In response to a wire from Thacker or one of the marshals, he secured his deputy's commission from U.S. Commissioner Frank J. Duffy and set out with Webb and Gamble for Benson, the junction of the Southern Pacific and New Mexico & Arizona Railroads. They parried queries by explaining that they were going on a prospecting trip. From Benson, they went on to a point seven or eight miles from Bowie, where Foraker's men had unloaded the horses. Here, on the 8th, they met Baca, McElroy, Finley, and other members of the Foraker-Griffith-Thacker ensemble.

Milton and seven others were in camp when a rider from Bowie station galloped up with word that the express was being held up at Steins Pass. Men and horses piled into Foraker's special train, which reached Steins station about an hour and a half after the stoppage. If Milton's biographer, J. Evetts Haley, is correct, Jeff's group had already been joined by Scott White and "another young deputy named [Orville] Cooper."

The other eight men were still crossing the San Simon Valley on their way back to camp, reportedly after reconnoitering the Skeleton Canyon area. When they heard of the holdup, they set out for the scene, hoping to catch sight of the robbers or their sign in the bright moonlight. They and their comrades who had preceded them to Steins Pass were not disappointed; the tracks of the bandits' horses were plain to see. But, as we have seen, they elected not to take up the pursuit before daylight.[7]

As Milton told it to Haley, the consolidated forces of Griffith, Foraker, and Thacker were getting ready to move off from Steins Pass early on the Friday morning when a raven made its descent beside the tracks and proceeded to enjoy a portion of Ed Cullen's brain, which was splattered upon one of the ties.[8]

The combined posse followed the well-marked trail for a short distance south, when the decision was taken to split the posse into two groups which would take separate routes southward and meet again near Tex Canyon.

The bunch that included Finley, Baca, and George Scarborough stayed on the established trail from Steins Pass. The outlaws had taken the horse ridden by Cullen and the one on which they had intended to stow the loot. This satisfied the posse that they were after five riders with one extra horse.

The bandits were headed southwest. Presently, one of them veered away directly to the west; the posse let him go and trailed the other three to the Cienega ranch of the San Simon outfit, where the sign petered out. The three hands at the ranch were briefly under suspicion, until Scarborough, who had worked for the San Simon alongside the three whilst employed as an undercover range detective, spoke up for them. One of the three, Holmes Maddox, later corresponded with Albert Thompson on the subject of the case; later still, he wrote a laudatory article on Scarborough's career and character.

When, eventually, the bandit's tracks were found again, they were still leading southwards, along the western flank of the Chiricahuas.

In the afternoon the officers came upon two abandoned horses, one of them saddled. Nothing was more obvious than that there were only four bandits to be sought, but this scarcely weighed with the posse at all. Their course of future action was as clear as the tracks before their eyes: when they came to trail's end, they would gather in as many people as they found and let the courts iron out any differences. And they were at trails's end—Squaw Gap, beyond Squaw Mountain, fifty miles south and slightly west of Steins. The facts from all sources square with a statement in Atkins's memoirs that this was where the outlaws took the trail away from the posse. Tex Canyon was about ten miles to the south. The bandits turned north; the posses continued south; and Tex Canyon stayed where it was.

Milton and his party took the direct route "from the other side of the mountain[s]," guided only by assumption. Their rapid short cut from Steins Pass station to the lower slopes of the Chiricahuas by way of Skeleton Canyon saved them a good ten miles of the distance covered by the other half of the posse.[9]

Early on Sunday, December 12, the two sections of the posse were reunited near the extreme southeast corner of Cochise County. One clue had fallen into the hands of Scarborough or one of his companions in the seventy-five mile chase: a torn pair of overalls, discarded by one of the robbers.[10]

At about 10 a.m. the deputies rode up in a body to Vinnedge's Tex ranch, about sixty miles south and slightly west of Steins Pass station. Only Warderman and Hovey were there, so the posse waited all day and night. Alverson saw their horses near the mouth of Tex Canyon as he was riding up to the ranch on Monday morning. As he commented in his reminiscences, he could easily have turned back if he had any cause for apprehension. He merely rode on to the ranch house.

Towards noon, the posse moved in on the house. They encountered no resistance in arresting Alverson, Hovey, and Warderman as three of the Steins Pass robbers. Accounts differ over whether the three men were taken while inside the house or "in a wagon driving a span of mules:" the weight of evidence and probability favors the former. Whichever is correct, Hovey's statement that he was in bed when arrested is likely to have been true. Vinnedge, alias Cush, was not at home.

The three prisoners were in an awkward predicament at once, for the trail of the bandits had led directly into Tex Canyon. To make matters worse, the wagon contained more than one thousand rounds of ammunition. Even worse was the recent bullet wound in Hovey's leg. Worst of all, Scarborough was able to demonstrate that the rip in the cast-off overalls corresponded with the location of the bullet hole.[11]

In a little while, Finley and others intercepted Tom Capehart as he was making his way to the ranch. Thereupon, someone flourished the second item of evidence. This was a handkerchief mislaid at Steins Pass by Tom Ketchum, incriminatingly marked with the initials "T.K." The posse deduced that the handkerchief must belong to "Tom Kephart" and took him in charge. Capehart was, or recently had been, employed by the Diamond A, southwest of Deming.[12] According to Hovey's memoir of the case, Capehart had spent the previous night at the Tex ranch. Whether or not this was so, he was not at the house when the posse first went there.[13]

Presently Henry Marshall rode in. He was arrested for the holdup because he and Capehart were known to be partners. Both Capehart and Marshall had seen the saddled horses of the posse in time to have turned and ridden away without being noticed, had they any motive for flight. Moreover, four of the prisoners were quite unarmed, while the fifth had only a small revolver on his person. Real train robbers would have better prepared for unwelcome callers.[14]

While these scenes of mummery were being acted out, at least three of the four surviving robbers were tucked away in the Wildcat, a mile and a half away. They had been watching the posse, but could not tell what was happening. Then, during the afternoon, Milton and nine or ten others came down the canyon toward the hideout.[15]

The story Alverson got from Tom Ketchum two years later was that the gang "ranged themselves along the rim in such a position that they could have killed two or three of the posse with one shot if necessary," and would have opened fire if they had seen any prisoners. But Milton and his party, knowing nothing of the desperadoes concealed in the crags above, jogged on by without an uneasy thought. The gang waited until they were gone, then got their horses and left. A few minutes later the remainder of the posse, comprising Sam Finley, Sam Webb, and three or four others, passed through with the five prisoners lying handcuffed in a wagon.[16]

While Finley's detachment was taking the supposed robbers to San Simon, Milton and the rest searched for the Snaky Four, now increasingly spoken of as "Black Jack's gang." They learned of the hideout in the Wildcat and planned to storm it under cover of night. When the appointed hour came, Milton later related, only he and Scarborough would go. No blood was shed: the Ketchum gang had been gone for four or five days.

The gang had stored some blankets and provisions in a tree, but the officers found that these had been disturbed by a previous invader—a bear, drawn to the place by the scent of honey.[17]

Finley's party reached San Simon at about 8:30 in the morning of Tuesday, December 14, after an all-night journey. This confirms Hovey's statement, implicitly supported by Alverson, that the posse camped in the canyon overnight and did not arrest and remove the suspects until the following (Monday) afternoon. The officers had hoped to be in time for No. 19, the eastbound express, but missed it by a few minutes. Possemen and prisoners were exhausted, and so were the horses. All repaired to a local ranch for a few hours' rest and renewal.[18]

Griffith had agreed with Foraker that the prisoners should be sent from San Simon to Silver City, but in the circumstances he had them put on the next westbound train and packed off to Tucson, where he thought they would be safer. Jennings and the Thackers were in town when the party arrived on Wednesday morning. The elder Thacker was jubilant. "His face bears a look of satisfaction," observed the *Arizona Daily Star*, "One train robber beneath the roses, and five safely jailed."

An unnamed member of the escort party described the capture for the benefit of the *Star* readership. As for the prisoners: "They are all cow-boys, and known by the authorities of this territory, having worked in different localities" (as if that were enough to make them objects of suspicion). The official spokesman portrayed them, rather quaintly, as "all grown men, except one who is about twenty-six or twenty-seven years of age." Also present was the Tucson correspondent of the *San Francisco Chronicle*, who pictured the six as "large, muscular, reckless men, and . . . absolutely unconcerned."[19]

The *Star* informant and his fellow guards were under instructions not to divulge the prisoners' names to the press—a foolish restriction, since this information could be easily obtained from San Simon, but indicative of the deliberate isolation of the Texas Canyon crowd. Another ominous sign was that "for reasons best known to the marshal [Griffith]" they were held incommunicado. They sent for two friends whom they believed to be in Tucson—"parties . . . suspected of belonging to the Black Jack gang" burbled the *Chronicle* reporter—but were told that they had gone. If Hovey wrote the truth in 1934, this policy was pursued to the extent of keeping the prisoners not only away from reporters, but from each other.[20]

Despite all this, they were not yet so much perturbed as angry, if Len Alverson's memory did not mislead him:

> In order not to have any witnesses for the defense they had to implicate all of us. The only man of that posse I can speak a good word for is Jeff Milton. He acted like a man all the way through—he and [Frank] Cox the S.P. attorney. I have heard he did some big talking afterwards but I didn't pay any attention to it. I knew he was not that kind of a man and I told them if Jeff Milton had anything to say bad about me he would say it to my face . . .
>
> The thing was that they were as desperate as the outlaws, there had been innumerable hold ups and robberies and no one had been caught, so they had to make an example of some one.
>
> Well, they brought us to Tucson and I asked them to get me a lawyer so that I might get a writ of habeas corpus, because I thought I could prove my innocence and get out. But they said I would have to wait until we got to New Mexico where the crime was committed. Then I wanted to communicate with my friends, but they would not allow that. Even then none of the three of us (Alverson, Hovey, and Warderman) took matters too seriously, even joked about it, I remember Walter asked, as they took us from the jail in Tucson, "What do you suppose they are going to do with us?" and I said, "Hang us, I guess." "Well," he answered, "I hope they leave my legs untied because I would like to kick the block off one or two of them." Guess we laughed too soon.[21]

Hovey's recollections reflect anger and bitterness in even greater degree:

> After confiscating all of the firearms and ammunition at the ranch, the posse would walk one of us at a time down the canyon to hold a court of inquiry. They would yell and fire their six-shooters at our heads, vilifying and insulting us. They struck Tom Capehart in the face and over the head with a gun and jabbed him in the stomach with a cocked .45 Colt.[22]

He, too, spoke well of only one of the posse, but it was not Milton:

[B]ut . . . for . . . Cipriana [*sic*] Baca, we would have lost our lives then and there. "If any of these men are murdered I will kill the officer who fired the shot," he declared.[23]

Hovey admitted that, being confined to bed and unable to walk because of his wounded leg, he himself was not taken out for interrogation. All the same, he "didn't escape the grilling." Not surprisingly, the officers showed particular interest in his wound.[24]

Although they were in the custody of the federal authorities, the Tex Canyon people assumed, or were led to believe, that they would first be prosecuted by the Territory under the law which stipulated capital punishment for assault upon a railroad train. In this they were mistaken, or misinformed. The U.S. officials had no intention of yielding the men up to the Territory, not because they thought the death penalty incommensurately harsh, but because they believed that the men were likely to be acquitted by a Territorial court, even though the judge and district attorney would be the same as in a prosecution under federal auspices. The immediate issue for them was the question of whether the prisoners should be held in Arizona, where they had been taken, or in New Mexico, where the crime had occurred.[25]

Foraker rushed to Tucson on December 15 to demand custody of the five men. In his eagerness to secure it, he asked Washington for permission to invoke a procedure which he knew to be unusual, if not irregular:

> Laws say take before nearest [U.S.] commissioners for preliminary hearing. I think safer to take before U.S. judge. Please wire authority to do so, prisoners dangerous.[26]

It appears, though, that the proper course was adopted, for the men were committed at their hearing before U.S. Commissioner William H. Culver, and then taken before District Judge George R. Davis, who granted an order of removal.[27]

At Deming, where prisoners and escort changed trains for Silver City, a *Headlight* reporter tried to interview the suspects. He summed them up as "mild mannered bullwhackers [who] don't look as if they have sand enough to hold up a jack rabbit," even though Hovey had been fined for shooting up the town of Willcox that spring and had later killed Richards. Alverson, he observed, had been a friend of the outlaw Grant Wheeler, but had refused to join him in holding up a train at Willcox in 1895. Alverson and Warderman were now "believed to be doing well" as joint owners of "a little bunch of cattle in the Rucker district in Arizona." As for Capehart, he had earned "a good reputation" as a Diamond A. hand, and had many acquaintances in Deming; it was "a surprise to those who knew him" that he "should be implicated in such outlawry."

They declined to disclose their line of defense, and, beyond affirming their innocence, would say nothing except that the officers had forbidden them to speak to the press. Noting that the engineer and fireman had seen them at Tucson and identified them as the bandits, the reporter concluded that "these are undoubtedly the right fellows," despite their appearance and the unblemished character of all but Hovey.[28] The five alleged bandits were rehoused in the Silver City jail on Saturday, December 18. Alverson's comments, recorded forty years after the event, were acidic:

"Politics were rotten there [in New Mexico]," Alverson charged. "President McKinley had been asked to appoint some of them [sic—but Alverson may have added a term of opprobrium which the interviewer had thought it prudent to omit] to office, Frank W. Parker as Judge and W.B. Childers as U.S. District Attorney." One of these two men, he said, "was a drunken sot, in fact got to drinking so hard later that he went insane."[29]

While Alverson and his friends lay in jail at Silver City, the posse went after the Ketchum gang—their true quarry from the outset, whether or not they realized it. Finley soon rejoined Milton, and the search area was extended south into Mexico. Protocol was properly observed. At the custom house on the international border, the American officers were met by Colonel Emilio Kosterlitzky, of the Mexican federal rurales, and eighteen of his men. Kosterlitzky conducted the tour party to Dos Cabezas, 150 miles inside Sonora; from Dos Cabezas to Chuihuichopa, where they found the bandits' target shooting range but no bandits; and thence to Colonia Juarez, "200 miles south of El Paso [actually, 160 miles southwest of it], in the Sierra Madre mountains, state of Chihuahua." They then swept the same sector from east to west, covering almost the same ground as on their outward journey for no tangible yield except the continuity of cross-border goodwill.[30]

Finley and five companions returned to Tucson on the evening of January 15, 1898, after an almost unbroken absence of thirty-nine days. "[T]hey ascertained beyond any question of doubt," said the *Arizona Daily Star*, "that Black Jack is living and has a gang ranging from six to sixteen freebooters of the very worst character. Some of them are Indians and three of them Mexicans. They found the house he had built in the heart of the Sierra Madre which [has] strong fortifications and avenues of escape. They also found four other houses he had occupied . . . So they have all his retreats located."[31]

At one time or another they may have struck or crossed the trails of the Snaky Four, the surviving High Fives, and other law-dodgers from the United States. The Mexicans and Indians mentioned by Finley may have been collaborators or sympathizers of the outlaws rather than actual confederates. The most significant product of the six-week investigation was the palpable sense of certainty in the posse's pronouncement that Black Jack was still among the living. In truth, only the name lived on; but the process that would make it inseparable from that of Tom Ketchum was well under way.

Milton returned to his home in Nogales, but not for long. On February 6, according to Marshal Griffith, he went before Commissioner Duffy and swore out warrants for William Walters, alias Bronco Bill, William Johnson, and Daniel "Red" Pipkin.[32]

Although Griffith later professed to Attorney-General John Griggs that the three had "long been wanted by the U.S. authorities of New Mexico and Arizona," not a scrap of evidence exists to show that at that time any of the three had committed a federal offense of any sort. Months later they would venture into train robbery, but, as far as the record can show, they had made no plans in that direction when Milton applied for the warrants. Griffith, whose object was to justify Milton's expense claim (to the extent of vouchsafing that Milton had undercharged), advised Griggs that

Milton "had been informed that these parties were in hiding in the eastern part of this territory with other outlaws."[33] Yet Milton still had not confirmed the accuracy of his information when news came through of their holdup at Grants, New Mexico, on March 29.[34]

But Griffith's letter to Griggs was written on September 13, after Milton and George Scarborough had captured Walters and killed Johnson. Their notoriety, brief as it was, now belonged to history; but it could be used to justify expenditure predating it. The probable truth is that the writs procured by Milton in February were actually John Does—blank warrants. Thus armed, Milton and his chums could sally forth into the hills and pull in any known or suspected associate of outlaws. The policy that had been tried out so promisingly on the Tex Canyon crowd could be carried a stage further.[35]

It is certain that a group of officers, including Milton, Sam Webb, and George Scarborough, reappeared at Tex Canyon less than a week after Duffy issued the warrants. They had one genuine, if recalcitrant customer. John Vinnedge, alias Cush, de facto owner of the Tex ranch, had been absent when the posse called at his house after the Steins Pass affair, and had not shown up while they were waiting.

On or about February 12, Milton tried again, and again was too early or too late. Milton told Haley that Scarborough wanted to kill rather than arrest Vinnedge, in order to "get rid of a good nuisance." It may have been just as well for Vinnedge that Scarborough was not present a day or two later when Milton ran onto his quarry near the house and pulled down on him with his rifle.

In Milton's account, Scarborough was at the ranch house when the arrest was made, but proof exists that George was in Silver City on Sunday, February 13, and the arrest is likely to have happened that day or the next. Milton may have had Sam Webb for company, though he does not say so. Vinnedge was escorted to the handiest point on the Southern Pacific, ushered away to Tucson (not by Milton, who needed to be in Silver City), taken before Commissioner Culver shortly after arrival on the 16th, collected by Tom McElroy on Foraker's behalf early on the 19th, and put on the next train east.

After seeing off Vinnedge, Milton started for Silver City to join Scarborough in awaiting developments in the case against the rest of the alleged robber gang. He was in Steins Pass on the night of February 16–17 when a telegram came in with news of the sinking of the battleship *Maine* in Havana on the 15th. At the same time he learned that the wheels of justice were already in motion at Silver City.[36]

On Wednesday, the 16th, the grand jury for the Third Judicial District of New Mexico had presented a seven-count federal indictment against all six—Alverson, Hovey, Warderman, Capehart, Marshall, and Vinnedge (who was then in Tucson)—for attempting to rob the United States mail car (No. 1217), and another for "violating the postal laws" by robbing the postmaster, Charles E. St. John, "otherwise known as Charles E. Saint John" of "a large sum of money, to-wit nine dollars" (No. 1218).

Childers proceeded with the first indictment and the ritual of jury selection began. Parker set bond at ten thousand dollars for each man—five thousand dollars on each indictment. None of the defendants was able to take advantage of these deliberately rigorous terms. They lost very little liberty this way, as the selection of the petit jury was completed on the morning of the 25th, after several special venires.

Two more true bills were found that day. No. 1220, which named all six defendants as accessories after the fact of the attempt to rob Postal Clerk Albright, would become operative only if the prosecution failed with both 1217 and 1218. Lastly, No. 1221 averred that the six had conspired to the same end "with divers other parties to the grand jurors unknown." All the charges were brought under the Post Office act of June 8, 1872: specifically, sections 5472 (mail robbery), 5473 (attempted mail robbery), and 5534 (accessory after the fact).[37]

At Childers's side when the trial opened on the 25th was Assistant District Attorney George P. Money, with Frank Cox, of Phoenix, Arizona, the Southern Pacific's attorney, as Associate Counsel. No record of the testimony was taken by the stenographer. This was not through any turpitude on the part of that official; it was the consequence of a provision in federal law permitting a transcript to be made *if the trial judge so ordered*. It is not surprising that, with so broad an option open to him, the trial judge should exploit its generosity by rarely acknowledging any need to preserve the testimony.[38]

The purpose of this piece of misplaced parsimony was what it appeared to be: to save money for the U.S. government and, therefore, forestall complaints from those whose taxes kept it going. Its intellectual authority rested on three presumptions: no dutiful taxpayers would ever incur the wrath of the federal judicial system; federal prosecutors and judges were impartial and infallible; and juries, being composed of good citizens, would never err.

Any attempt to reconstruct the proceedings must depend on an outline drawn from such court records as were maintained and are extant; the competent but sketchy accounts supplied by a couple of newspaper correspondents; and the vivid, but imperfectly recalled and inherently biased, observations of two of the defendants, Alverson and Hovey, alias Hoffman.

James S. Fielder, the defense counsel, foresaw his opponent's strategy in the event of an acquittal and motioned the court to consolidate causes 1217 and 1218, as "the acts and transactions charged against these defendants [in No. 1217] constitute the same class of crimes in cause No. 1218." Parker denied the motion.[39]

Hovey wrote in 1934 that forty-two witnesses traveled from Arizona to testify for the defense, and that the prosecution called fifty-two. A correspondent who attended the first day's hearing reported, with greater fidelity, that more than fifty government witnesses had been subpoenaed. But not every subpoena brought a witness to court, and on March 3, a reporter put the number of witnesses at forty. Reference to the docket for that term of court discloses a total of thirty-two recipients of witness fees and, where applicable, travel expenses ("mileage fees"). Four of these thirty-two were not connected with the Steins Pass proceedings; they testified at another trial held during the term. If, therefore, forty witnesses were summoned, twelve would have been there on the defense's behalf.[40]

No governmental provision existed for witnesses required by the defense; defendants had to meet their witnesses' travel and subsistence expenses from their own funds, unless they could convince the government that they were too poor to pay. In this instance, the defendants apparently did not apply for "free service."

If the surviving records are accurate, twenty-eight witnesses testified for the prosecution; six of these were recalled to the stand. Subpoenas had been issued for a dozen others who could not be found or whose testimony, in the end, was not needed.[41]

Few of Fielder's witnesses can be identified; one, named by Hovey, was Scott White. But the testimony of several government witnesses may have been more beneficial to the defense than to the prosecution. Among these are likely to have been Bob Johnson, the liberal minded foreman of the Erie outfit, and Mr. and Mrs. Edward J. Roberts. Ed Roberts, a rancher from the San Simon Valley, had employed George Musgrave shortly before Musgrave joined the High Five gang, and remained on the friendliest of terms with him for long after that.[42]

Still, the preponderance of the juristic firepower was ranged against the defendants, for the other side had three resourceful and gifted attorneys against the no less talented Fielder's gallant lone hand.

Yet it was Childers who was soon floundering in an almost untenable situation. In a letter to the U.S. Attorney General, written a few weeks afterwards, he complained bitterly about the structure of the laws—forgetting, under the spur of expediency, that these were the laws he had ungrudgingly sworn to uphold.

> . . . the territorial laws applicable to summoning and empannelling [sic] juries cover United States cases in this Territory, and . . . the statute on that subject provides that the Territory shall have three challenges, the first named defendant five and each additional defendant two additional challenges, so that in this case the United States had three peremptory challenges and the defendants fifteen . . . [43]

Fielder made the most of these provisions. Two special venires had to be issued before the defense was satisfied with the jury, which, as finally constituted, consisted of five Anglos and seven Spanish-Americans.[44]

The first testimony was heard directly after the formation of the jury. W.T. North, the engineer, was altogether sure about it: Hovey and Alverson were two of the men who had boarded his engine. Robert W. Anderson, the fireman, "thought" he could identify Warderman as well. Albright, Jennings, and Gene Thacker could not identify any of the defendants. A post-mortem photograph of Ed Cullen was produced and verified. Various of the posse described how the trail of the bandits had been followed right into Texas Canyon, where the officers found "dynamite, fuses, ammunition and other articles such as would naturally be used in outlawry of the kind tried." Testimony was introduced to show that Cullen had been with the defendants just before the holdup.[45]

In his recollections of the Silver City trial, Hovey accused some of those who took the stand for the United States of bearing false witness: "[I]t hardly seems possible that these individuals have escaped the wrath or bullets of some honest man . . . [T]here are those who would not hesitate to swear away your life or liberty for a few dollars of renown." He was especially critical of the testimony of "Date Graham, a newly appointed town marshal from Bisbee, who had volunteered himself as an expert perjurer."[46]

Fielder called a few alibi witnesses and obtained evidence that Cullen "had stated that he was about to join the Black Jack gang of border bandits." One who may have testified to that effect—the absence of a transcript of the trial and the meagerness of the press coverage precludes certainty—may have been Bob Johnson (who, almost alone among the witnesses, relied upon horsepower for part of his trip to Silver City).[47]

The explanation as to how Walter Hovey came by the bullet hole in his leg was wonderfully improbable; but since Alverson and Hovey, in relating the circumstances, made admissions which were not in their own best interests, it may well have been something like the truth. Since the testimony is not on record, and none of their fellow-defendants or other persons connected with the trial is known to have reminisced about the case, we can only consider the explanations given many years afterwards by these two men. The individual must decide how much weight to place on the details where their two accounts diverge, and on the far greater extent to which they are in agreement.

Hovey said that he, Warderman, Alverson, and Vinnedge had intended for some while to round up stray stock in the Silver Creek area to prevent the animals from straying into Mexico. The lower end of the creek was only about six miles north of the international line and about twenty southwest of Tex Canyon—just a few hours' ride away. Vinnedge was unable to go when the others were ready, but the three of them set out on or about December 9 with three days provisions.

That evening, they saw three riders driving four pack animals. Their suspicions that these men were smugglers from Mexico were confirmed when the newcomers rode over to take supper with them, having satisfied themselves that Warderman, Alverson, and Hovey were not lawmen.

But, as the evening and their inebriation advanced, the trio from Tex Canyon decided to turn bandit. Their bid to relieve the smugglers of the whiskey failed; Hovey was wounded in the leg, and the smugglers got away with their contraband intact. Alverson and Warderman staunched their friend's wound, helped him to mount, and got him back to Tex ranch next morning. That afternoon they received a visit from James Hunsaker, a rancher from White River. Tom Capehart then rode up and stayed the night. Next morning they had more company: the sixteen men of the Bowie posse.[48]

Alverson's version was that he and his partners had held up a man near the border and robbed him of ten gallons of mescal. In the evening, while Hovey, in a drunken daze, was squatting beside the campfire, Alverson was lurching about in the brush nearby. Alverson, for some undisclosed reason, had drawn his pistol. When Alverson tripped up, the gun went off, "the ball ranging up through the calf of Walter's leg, coming out just below his boot top."[49]

The differences between the two accounts of the exact circumstances of Hovey's wounding are too great to be explained by the blurring of memories with the passing of time: at least one of the two men was lying. If both were lying, does that mean that the rest of the alibi was no less false? If one of the pair recounted the particulars truthfully, why did the other lie? One set of details was no more self-incriminating than the other. And was this single point of contradiction more important than the common factors of the two stories: the trip to the vicinity of the border, the highway robbery, and the drunkenness?

The fact that no Mexican travelers reported an assault by Americans near Silver Creek is nugatory; if the Mexicans were smugglers, the last thing they would want to do was advertise their presence to the Arizona authorities. Encounters like that with the Texas Canyon group were, to smugglers, just a hazard of the road.

Contrary to Alverson's assertion, a shot fired from an express car would not necessarily have ranged down through the leg of anyone who happened to be in the way. For a while, two of the gang had been lying underneath the express car, unseen by its occupants. As long as they were there, they could not have been hit at all. Although one was wounded in crawling away, he had been struck amidships and in the rear—not frontally and in the leg. Otherwise, aside from Cullen, who had done much of their shooting, the bandits were perched on the engine and tender. None of the assault party could have acquired an upward-ranging wound such as Walter's unless he had been kneeling or crouching in an absurd posture, leg extended and back turned toward the express car.

Childers maintained that "a complete case had been made out against at least five" of the six defendants. Fielder argued that the culprits were the Black Jack gang (like most people then, and many later, he could not distinguish the Black Jack or High Five gang from the Ketchum gang), that the explosives cached near the ranch were theirs, and that the defendants "dared not offend these outlaws and were of necessity aware of what was going on but could only remain quiet."[50]

The forensic battle was waged with great intensity on both sides of the case. At last, on Tuesday, March 8, the attorneys' work was done and Parker read out his instructions to the jury—four at the request of the prosecution, and two from the defense. A seventh instruction—asked for by the prosecution—was refused.

This was the most significant of the six that were given:

> [B]efore any of the defendants can be convicted, the fact of the presence at the place of the commission of the alleged crime and actual participation therein of one or more of the defendants must be shown beyond a reasonable doubt. But it is not necessary that you should find from the evidence that all of the defendants were so present and actually so participated in the commission of the crime if you believe, from the evidence, beyond a reasonable doubt . . . , that one or more of said defendants was so present and actually participated in the commission of the alleged crime, and other of the defendants though not so present and actually participating therein, advised, procured, aided and abetted in the commission thereof. And if you so believe . . . , then you should find all of said defendants, both those actually so present and participating and those not so present and participating . . . , guilty.[51]

That night, the jurors retired, stayed out long enough for a smoke, then confounded Childers's calculations by returning a verdict of not guilty.

Parker, beside himself with rage—or so Jeff Milton depicted him to Evetts Haley—assailed the jury with blame for the "worst disgrace in a courtroom" he had ever seen, and threatened never again to hold court in Silver City.[52] Such a public outburst seems an odd sort of display from a district judge in his own courtroom, whatever he may have said outside it.

The *Silver City Enterprise*, a Republican paper, after praising the efforts of the prosecuting attorneys, conceded that Fielder's "eloquent argument" and "dogged perseverance and marked legal ability" must have carried "great weight with the jury," but concluded that the verdict was "a great surprise." That verdict on the verdict could have been a sanitized epitome of the comments of Parker and Childers.

Childers was by no means through. The men went back to jail while the district attorney thought about what to do next. He represented his letter to the U.S. Attorney General, dated March 28, as a "special report and explanation of the case," but it is more than faintly redolent of self justification and raises doubts rather than settling them:

> ... I am fully satisfied that the jury in the case was tampered with, and that we will be able to discover before the next term of court how it was done and possibly have indictments found against the guilty parties.
>
> I am also fully satisfied that the next trial for robbery of the Post Office will result in a conviction of almost [all], if not all, of the defendants ...
>
> It is possible that they may be tried in the Territorial court for violation of the Territorial statute against train robbing, but I am very much afraid that the Territory will not be able to succeed in getting the witnesses necessary for a conviction. ...
>
> I desire if possible, to secure a conviction of these men as I am fully satisfied of their guilt, and if they were discharged it would have a very bad effect upon the element from which train robbers are recruited in this section of the country.[53]

The questions almost ask themselves.

First, the newspapers reported that the jury needed less than half an hour to reach its verdict. (Len Alverson said their deliberations occupied only eleven minutes.) Did the defense bribe all twelve of the jurors? And why was nothing more heard of Childers's expressed determination to take action against the alleged "guilty parties"?

Second, what made Childers feel so sure of reaping his convictions if the men were tried for the robbery of the post office? Although the emphasis placed upon the relevance of the various items of testimony would be different from before, the witnesses would be the same.

The district attorney's reluctance to make way for a prosecution by the Territory obviously owed nothing to logic and could not have been based on the reasons he advanced. It is manifest that a prosecution for attempted robbery of a passenger train would require exactly the same evidence and exactly the same witnesses as a prosecution for attempted robbery of the mail car attached to that train. And, under the provisions of territorial government, a trial in the territorial district court would be heard by the same judge (Parker) and prosecuted by the same attorney (himself) as one in the U.S. court for the same district.

If, as he pretended, his one concern was to see train robbers punished with a severity which would keep other men off the outlaw trail, Childers ought to have been delighted to yield to the Territory. Ten years' imprisonment was the heaviest sentence that could be imposed for armed interference with the United States mails. But under the Compiled Laws of 1897, Section 1151, which restated the law of February 23, 1887, the death penalty was mandatory for anyone convicted in a territorial court of "assault upon any railroad train, railroad cars, or railroad locomotive."[54]

The verdict of the Grant County jury gave the men no more freedom than the moments separating Parker's order for their release and their rearrest by Milton, as Foraker's deputy, to face trial for the robbery of acting postmaster Charles St. John (No. 1218).

Only for Henry Marshall did the clouds begin to lift. The following day, March 9, Parker responded favorably to a motion from Fielder. Marshall was released on his own recognizance and on a reduced bond of $2,000 in respect of Cause No. 1220, and a further $2,000 in respect of the more serious charge embodied in No. 1218. In return, Marshall undertook to present himself at federal court on September 5, 1898, the first day of the next judicial term.[55]

Meanwhile, at the beginning of June, a grand jury in Silver City at last indicted Warderman, Marshall, Hovey (as Hoffman), Alverson, and Vinnedge (as Cush) on the capital territorial charge of assault upon a railroad train. The case was at once continued to the next term.[56]

These were merely procedural formalities. Their emptiness exposed the real reason for the authorities' unwillingness to pursue the case through the territorial side of the court's jurisdiction. Grant County might indict, but it would not convict, defendants whom it had just acquitted of virtually the same offense. And, having declined to send them to prison, it would surely not dispatch them to the gallows on the basis of testimony it had already rejected. Childers and his associates had no intention of putting their witnesses before a Silver City jury for the second time. Instead, they would take their case to a different sort of town and put it before what was likely to be a different sort of jury.

On August 26, Parker ordered the transfer of the five remaining prisoners from Silver City to Las Cruces, the scheduled court town for the September term. In Las Cruces, wrote Hovey, "we were confined for months in a huge adobe dungeon with but one door and no window, filthy, unlit, verminous, mosquito-infested, and ridden with bedbugs and lice. For breakfast we would have *frijoles* and *tortillas* and sometimes later in the day we would have *tortillas* and *frijoles*. The sheriff who was also manager of this torture chamber, was none other than the notorious Pat Garrett."[57]

Taking Garrett as the basis for a comparison between "the nature of some mankind" and the wolf, Walter added that "the difference is that man conceals his true nature behind studied smiles and semi-civilized veneer."[58]

In fact, Hovey and his friends were not entombed in Las Cruces for months. Their second trial opened seventeen days after their introduction to their temporary quarters in Garrett's jail, and just one week after Henry Marshall rejoined them.[59]

As before, Childers was assisted by Money, with Cox as associate counsel, while Fielder handed the defendants' brief. The second trial attracted far less press interest than the first: not only was the Steins Pass affair no longer news, but any reporting of the testimony was likely to be a rehash of the coverage of the previous case—more or less the same witnesses, more or less repeating the evidence heard at Silver City.[60]

In the event, the U.S. sent for twenty-five witnesses, not quite as many as for the previous trial. Hovey, though tried as Hoffman, applied under his real name for "free process," on the grounds that he and his co-defendants were too poor to pay their witnesses' expenses.[61] Evidently it was not granted.

Somehow or other the necessary funds must have been raised, for Hovey stated in his recollections that all those who had testified for the defense at Silver City did so in the second trial.

Since Parker again saw fit not to require the stenographer to make a transcript, we have only a single press reporter and the vigorous but unsurprisingly one-sided recollections of Alverson and Hovey to add a little substance and color to the sparseness of such documents as were created.

A jury was empaneled with "[l]ittle difficulty" and the first witnesses were on the stand before midday on the 12th. By noon on Wednesday, the 14th, the prosecution in chief was closed.[62]

Fielder began the defense by trying to introduce testimony showing that "the famous Black Jack and his gang were know[n] to have been in that section of the country at the time of the holdup." Parker ruled the testimony out of order. A correspondent for the *Silver City Independent* doubted that, had such testimony been admitted, "it would have had much weight with the jury . . . in the face of the positive identification by Engineer North of . . . two [of the] defendants and the discovery of the others in their company at Vinnedge's ranch, together with the damaging evidence found there in the shape of guns, pistols, powder, fuse, cartridges, boot and overalls perforated by a bullet, etc."[63]

The defense, having been denied the right to put forward an alternative theory, had to place all its faith in an alibi argument and its ability to show that nothing in the so called "damaging evidence" was inherently incriminatory. These were the lines on which the defendants concluded their own case when they were called to the stand on the Saturday.[64]

The *Independent* reporter did not quite say that the jury's collective mind was made up before it had heard the case for the defense, but Alverson and Hovey were in no doubt about its partiality. Their comments on its members were derogatory in the extreme. Hovey said that he and his friends knew they were doomed "when we took one look at the jury of long-haired, seamy greasy faces."

> Most of the efforts of our attorney, Fielder [to remove unsuitable jurors], were overruled and it seemed that nothing could be done in our behalf. Jim Fielder had exhausted more than half of his challenges when he turned and whispered to me, "what is the use? Pat Garrett controls every Mexican in Dona Ana County."
>
> Not one of the jurors could speak or understand the English language, and most could neither read nor write. All testimony went through an interpreter and the answer to most questions asked of them was "Me no savvy."[65]

Alverson concurred. Sheriff Garrett "had the jury packed with some of his professional jurymen:"

> They were the most damnable looking lot of men you ever saw on a jury, a number of them the most ignorant kind of Mexicans, dirty and shod with pieces of leather and strings coming between the toes for shoes. Two were not even [American] citizens.[66]

Scanty as the records are, they undermine these aspersions. Not all of the jurors could have been ignorant of the English language, for three were bearers of unmistakably Anglo names. This circumstance suggests that the two defendants' imputations on the capacities of the other nine—who obviously were Spanish-American—should be viewed with reservations.

Nor should it be overlooked that six of the twelve who had voted for acquittal at Silver City were Spanish Americans, though Hovey's recollection weighted the ratio nine-three in favor of the Anglos. This detracts further from the contention of Alverson and Hovey that they could not get a fair hearing before a jury of Spanish-Americans—though, again, Silver City and Las Cruces were two very different towns.

But while all this proves that Alverson and Hovey overstated and overcolored their adversities, it does not show that their cries of innocence were an imposture. Their exaggerations could have been the product of bitterness, rather than mendacity.

"Never," wrote Hovey, "have I heard a more impassioned defense than our attorney made on our behalf, although most of the jurymen were looking out of the window. But to the final plea of the eloquent prosecutor, Childress [sic], they were all eagerness, nodding their heads and nudging one another."[67]

The trial ended on Tuesday, September 20, and the judge delivered his instructions, fourteen in all.

This time, though almost as an afterthought, Parker stated that "the case as to three of the defendants [Capehart, Marshall, and Vinnedge] relies on circumstantial evidence alone to establish their guilt . . . the prosecution must not only show that the alleged facts and circumstances are true, but all such facts and circumstances must not only be in harmony with the defendant['s] or defendants' guilt, but they must also be such facts and circumstances as are absolutely incompatible, upon any reasonable hypothesis, with the innocence of the accused, and incapable of explanation, upon any reasonable hypothesis, other than that of the guilt of the accused." Unexceptionable; but this important charge had been missing from his instructions at Silver City—and the men had still been acquitted.

He repeated the doctrine of guilt by association: if the jury believed any one defendant guilty of direct participation in the robbery, his guilt would belong equally to any "not actually present and participating in said robbery" who "did advise, procure, aid or abet the commission of said robbery."

In commenting on the defendants' alibi, Parker instructed the jury that, while this was "as proper and legitimate, if proved, as any other defense," they must bear in mind the instruction "concerning the legal consequence of advising, procuring, aiding or abetting the commission of the crime charged."[68]

At ten o'clock next morning, the verdict was read out. Warderman, "Hoffman," and Alverson were guilty; Capehart, Marshall, and Vinnedge, not guilty.[69]

The day passed, and on the following morning, September 22, Fielder went to court with a motion for a new trial, which Parker rejected. The honorable judge then pronounced sentence. Warderman, Hovey, and Alverson were to be confined at hard labor in the Territorial Penitentiary at Santa Fe for ten years, fined $500 each, and ordered to pay all the costs of their own prosecution ("seven thousand dollars," said Parker). They would "stand committed until such fine and costs are fully paid."[70]

The bite in Alverson's retrospective carries more force than Hovey's bile, despite their shared burden of contention:

> When the trial was over the Judge said, "Leonard Alverson, stand up. You are found guilty by twelve of your *superiors!*" . . . Cox, the Southern Pacific lawyer, though he was supposed to be against us, was so disgusted when he saw how they were railroading the case that he threw up the whole thing . . . [71]

Still the court was not finished with two of the men. A *nolle prosequi* was entered on Cause No. 1220 (accessories after the fact) for the three who had been convicted and Henry Marshall, but the indictment remained in force against Capehart and Vinnedge. The same course seems to have been adopted with No. 1221 (conspiracy to rob), except that the residual charge against Capehart and Vinnedge was redesignated Cause No. 1222 and then, through clerical incompetence or in the interests of some now impenetrable sleight of official jiggery-pokery, renumbered 1218.[72]

On September 27, 1898, Parker issued a writ to commit the three men to the penitentiary in the care of Marshal Foraker. Their ten-year term began when they arrived on the following day.[73]

"Ten years!" reflected Hovey, "It seemed impossible to grasp . . . I tried to think back in my life to recall [an] occurrence ten years in the past. I had run away from home eleven years before at the age of fourteen."[74]

Their appeal against Parker's refusal to allow a new trial was turned down, but Fielder and others continued to labor on their behalf. Nearly a year was to pass without any word from one of those best placed to speak for them, Sam Ketchum, and nearly two years more before Tom Ketchum amplified his brother's statement clearing the three men of participation in the holdup at Steins Pass station.[75]

Capehart and Vinnedge were kept in jail for a further five weeks. By now, Capehart's bond had been reduced to $1,000 and Vinnedge's to $500. On October 21 the brothers J.F. and J.A.Whitmire, of Grant County, agreed to bail them out. The two defendants put their signatures to the bond on November 2 and left Las Cruces.[76] They may have gone first to see their bondsmen, but before long they were back in Cochise County and among old and new friends.

A territorial charge was laid against Capehart, Marshall, and Vinnedge but dismissed early in December, 1898.[77] The federal government, too, gave up its pursuit of the two men. Tom Capehart, however, had already taken the lesson to heart. After his release he began to associate more closely with the outlaws, and soon became a professional bandit himself.

One other associate of the Ketchums was journeying through the courts during the greater part of 1898. This was Bruce Weaver, alias Charles Collins (or Collings—his signatures show that he used both forms), the Elizabethtown miner who had come by a wad of the money stolen from the train at Folsom.

Collins began to spend the money soon after the robbery, but some of the bills were torn and some of the coins defaced, attracting unfavorable notice. He, or someone else, inquired at a Trinidad bank as to whether damaged coins could be exchanged for undamaged ones. Eventually he sent the paper money to Washington for exchange, on the advice of Dr. J.J. Schuler (or Shuler), of Raton. Schuler, however, could not swallow the man's explanation that the notes had been chewed by rats. He reported his suspicions to William Reno, who got in touch with the Treasury. A check on the serial numbers of the damaged bills showed the money to be part of the Folsom loot.[78]

Collins was traced to Cochise County and arrested in Bisbee, partly on the strength of information obtained by Foraker's special officer, Will Loomis. He was returned to Springer on the last day of March. A week later the commissioner at Clayton bound him over to await the action of the U.S. grand jury for the Fourth Judicial District of New Mexico, sitting at Las Vegas.[79]

Four days after this, on April 11, the grand jury returned a true bill against "Charles B. Collings et al." This document, drafted by Assistant District Attorney George Money, comprised three counts. The burden of its allegations was that Collins had conspired with William Carver, Thomas Ketchum, Samuel Ketchum, "Bob," "John," "Jim," and "divers other persons . . . unknown" to "obstruct and retard the passage of a certain carriage, to-wit a certain railway car then and there carrying the mail of the United States;" and that, "to effect the object of said conspiracy," Collins and the others had made an armed assault on the engineer and fireman "then and there managing and running the locomotive engine of the railway train . . . upon the Union Pacific, Denver and Gulf Railway . . . , of which the said railway car . . . was a part . . . , and contained the said mail of the United States . . . and did compel the train to stop . . . "[80]

Collins did not find the $2,000 he needed to secure bail, but he did acquire excellent counsel in the person of Lewis C. Fort, who immediately set about giving Money a lesson in legal draftsmanship. Fort initially argued that the "multiplicity of counts" made it impossible for his client "to intelligently answer or plead to said indictment as a whole" and moved the court to order the plaintiff to specify which of the three counts it desired to proceed on. A few hours later, having had time to check the law and give some thought to it, he presented a five-point letter showing that the indictment was not merely defective but nonsensical.[81]

Only the third count made legal sense, said Fort, urging that the other two should be quashed. The court agreed; the defendant would be tried simply for obstructing and retarding the passage of the mail car on September 3, 1897.[82]

Collins was held for safekeeping in the Territorial Penitentiary pending trial. Unlike the Texas Canyon defendants, he was able to obtain "free service" for his witnesses; that is, the government agreed to pay their attendance and mileage fees. His witnesses were Mr. and Mrs. C.J. Galvin; Mrs. Ida Collins, presumably the defendant's wife; and several other residents of Baldy, including J.K. Lapsley, whose wife, Ashena, appeared for the prosecution.

Collins declared that Baldy was 150 miles from the scene of the robbery, though, in truth, the two points are not much more than half that distance apart. He maintained that the testimony of these witnesses would prove that he could not have been at the place of the robbery on the date of its commission.[83]

Among the government's witnesses were S. Marion Littrell, sheriff of Colfax County, and Wilson "Memphis" Elliott, itinerant younger brother of William Elliott, who, earlier in the decade, served two terms as sheriff of newly-formed Irion County, Texas. The younger Elliott, like his brother, knew all the Ketchum brothers well. He was also acquainted with Carver and Atkins. His familiarity with the men who had so quickly established themselves as the most dangerous criminal gang in the Southwest may explain his role in the case; but the paucity of newspaper coverage, and the federal trial judge's routine decision not to require the stenographer to record the testimony, makes it impossible to improve upon conjecture. A year later, Wilson Elliott did make himself a prominent figure in the campaign against the outlaws, though without attracting the heroic light he undoubtedly sought.[84]

Collins's trial opened at Las Vegas on November 23 and ended that day with his acquittal. He explained his possession of the stolen bills and one of the souvenir silver spoons by saying he had won them from Tom Ketchum in a Poker game at Trinidad. It was no truer than the one he had tried out on Dr. Schuler; for one thing, Ketchum could not have visited Trinidad at any time since the robbery.[85]

None of the train crew could identify the defendant. Nor could the express messenger or the mail clerk. The jury of twelve Spanish-Americans evidently found Collins a more persuasive witness than Schuler, and the alibi testimony too secure to be dislodged by Burr Childers's attempt to depict the robbery as the outcome of a conspiracy formed several months previously.[86]

On November 26, Collins was returned to the custody of the sheriff of Union County, where he was held on the territorial charge of train robbery until January 7, 1899, when a grand jury in Clayton found that he had no case to answer.[87]

William Reno, who had worked hard in gathering evidence against Collins and his associates, may have been disappointed by the failure of the prosecution, but he was not ready to give up. On January 28 he wrote to Secundino Romero, clerk of the U.S. court at Las Vegas, to prod him into returning the silver spoon that had been an important exhibit in the case. He also wanted Romero to send back "the original statement of Collings, telegrams and other papers, which I left there; as they are not held in evidence by the United States Court, of course, you would have no need of them there." The spoon, he emphasized, was "of great importance in this case, as I expect to convict Collings and his accomplices before I am through with them."[88]

As it turned out, the courts were through with Collins, even though Reno was not.

Collins, for his part, was not finished as a fringe character in the story of the Ketchum gang. After his release he made for southwestern New Mexico, where he reassumed his right name of Weaver and again fell in with the Ketchums and their comrades, old and new.

Alverson, Hovey, and Warderman served a little more than half of the terms to which they had been sentenced. In the spring of 1901, it was predicted that the three would shortly be released, but only after a change in the Administration and the passage of three more years was a presidential pardon forthcoming.

Hovey, unlike Alverson, said nothing of the Ketchums' presence in Tex Canyon just before the holdup or in the Wildcat at the time of the arrests. His silence indicates a closer association with the crime than he was willing to admit, but he made no secret of his dealings with outlaws during the prior weeks and months. "There were quite a few outlaws of varying degree in Cochise County . . . I believe most were my friends. I was anxious to have their goodwill because I wanted to stay in this country, and live. I never gave a posse a clue to their whereabouts and I gained the enmity of officers by my refusal . . . None of us was in any way connected with the Steins Pass train robbery and none of us that November [December] morning had any knowledge of the holdup until we were surrounded by a posse . . . "[89]

When Tom Ketchum confessed to the crime, a few hours before being led to the gallows, he told his attorneys where he had left various articles stolen from Steins.[90] Holmes Maddox, Scarborough's friend and fellow-worker on the San Simon, would have none of it. He contended that nothing could have been found at the location described by Ketchum, because nothing had been taken from the mail car or express car.[91]

But Maddox, and Albert Thompson, who quoted him and shared his view of the crime, overlooked the petty robberies at Steins that had preceded the arrival of the train. None of the newspapers had gone into much detail about these. Some of what is known was provided by Ketchum himself, in a press interview published in full by only a few of the larger papers. Obviously neither Maddox nor Thompson had seen this; they were familiar only with the short statement on the subject included in Ketchum's much more widely-publicized letter to President McKinley. Besides the small amounts of cash that were reported as stolen, the bandits may have purloined a miscellany of small items which the press—preoccupied with the battle for possession of the train—did not hear about or bother to mention. Tom admitted to having taken the agent's rifle, although he did not need it.

Jeff Milton's biographer, Evetts Haley, was another skeptic. He nominated Dave Adkins [sic] as leader of the gang, and identified the others, in addition to Cullen, as Warderman, Hovey, "and possibly Tom Capehart and an Erie hand named Alverson."[92] He does not say why he is so sure that Atkins was there and that Will Carver was not, or why he harbored doubts about Alverson's presence but none about the guilt of Warderman and Hovey. Haley's conclusions would not have displeased Milton's widow, but they do not satisfy the more exacting requirements of scrupulous and dispassionate historical inquiry.

Goldianne Thompson and her co-writers disagreed. Unlike Goldianne's father-in-law, they listened to Ketchum's attorney, John R. Guyer. Ketchum had given Guyer a "long article of facts" which, Guyer was certain, verified the confession. The lawyer had passed Ketchum's disclosures to his brother, George V. Guyer, a journalist, in order to publicize the injustice of the case and end the plight of Alverson, Hovey, and Warderman. Goldianne Thompson and her collaborators were convinced. They state flatly that Tom Ketchum and Will Carver received leg wounds during the Steins Pass holdup, name the man killed alongside them as Ed Cullin (not Bullin), and echo Tom's assertion that Alverson, Hovey, and Warderman "were as innocent as new-born babes."[93]

In 1910, Dave Atkins delivered his views on the case. Without naming any of those who took part in the robbery (except Cullen and himself), or any of the Texas Canyon people, he left no doubt about the identities of those who had *not* taken part. He was similarly mute on the identities of the officers, but more than forthcoming with his opinions of them:

> They wanted somebody for that robbery and the easiest men they could get was the ones they wanted. They sauntered around some squatters and arrested them . . . as they knew there would be no fight to make. Of course they could arrest these men and swear any kind of a lie on them and get their reward, and the gentlemen [in?] Santa Fe would be blessed with 4 or 5 more convicts of men that had never thought of doing as much as robbing a hen roost. Blood money is blood money and there are more men that is classed as good citizens after blood money than there is outlaws who would take it.[94]

Approbation of Atkins's fine lather of moral indignation must be tempered by recognition of his failure to do more for Alverson, Hovey, and Warderman than vouch for their innocence in his memoirs. Nor were the Tex Canyon fraternity quite as far above reproach as Atkins asserted.

Alverson, Hovey, and Warderman were not members of the assault party. That, in itself, does not make them blameless in the eyes of the law. For all of Alverson's and Hovey's denials in their later years, it is plain that the three men were accessory both before and after the fact; as much was implied in their defense at the trials. Did the Las Cruces jury believe that Hovey acquired his leg wound during the assault on the express car? If they did, their conviction of Warderman and Alverson was fully in order: the trial judge's instruction on the concept of guilt by association was unobjectionable.

If, however, as is plain from a reasoned consideration of the surviving evidence, Hovey's wound could not have been inflicted in the circumstances attendant upon the holdup, then the verdict was mistaken and possibly dishonest. But the jury could not be expected to know, as the defendants were bound to know, that the Ketchums, Carver, and Atkins had come away from Steins with lead in their hides.

Whether the condemned trio were in treaty with the bandits through inclination or out of prudence is of small account, for they were seen as having been arrested, charged, indicted, and convicted not as accessories but as robbers. The concept of an accomplice's incrimination through a guilty association with a principal (putatively the wounded Hovey) is not hard to understand once it has been explained, but it would have been *terra incognita* to most citizens pursuing the mostly humdrum ways of mostly ordinary lives.

In the public mind, once the men had been convicted, all three were train robbers in the general rather than in any narrow legalistic sense. Probably, however, most
people in that part of the United States would have taken a lenient view of the defendants' offstage or passive support for the actual robbers, had they known them to be
guilty of no worse. Punishment was their due; but not ten years' worth of hard labor,
plus a thumping fine. The fact that the law did not require more than one of the three
to be at the scene of the crime was not broadcast or widely understood.

It would be unfair to assert that all of those responsible for the ultimate conviction of these men knew them to be innocent of the principal charges, or that some
were not acting—however misguidedly—in pursuit of some notion of rough justice.
The conclusion, however, bears of no genuflection to charity. It is that the conviction
of Warderman, Hovey, and Alverson was callously engineered by men who, in the
main, neither knew nor cared whether the three were innocent or guilty, and had no
regard for the letter of the law, for justice as an abstract, or indeed for anything except
their own political future and personal wellbeing.

{ 10 }

DYNAMITE AND SIX-SHOOTER

Though the Snaky Four took cover in Mexico after their discomfiture at Steins Pass, they did not remain there for long. The posse that had joined forces with the rurales to hunt them through northern Sonora and Chihuahua returned to the United States in mid-January. The Ketchum gang may not have been far behind them. For the last six or eight weeks of the winter they loitered in and around Cochise County. They hid out mostly in the Swisshelm Mountains or in the Wildcat. Outwardly, at least, they were still welcome with the cowpunchers, prospectors, and small ranchers. The Milton-Scarborough expedition which hauled in John Vinnedge made them steer clear of Tex Canyon and the Wildcat for much of February, but never came close to rounding them up.

One man whom they regarded as a menace was John Slaughter, owner of the San Bernardino ranch and sometime sheriff. One day, while the gang were passing the time of day at a cabin near Mud Springs, in Sulphur Spring Valley, the conversation touched upon Slaughter. Tom Ketchum glared balefully.

"Let's go down and kill that little rat-headed son of a bitch," he proposed to the other three.

But before they had made up their minds how to do it, Slaughter drove up in his buggy. Seeing the four badmen lounging outside the house, he handed the reins to Mrs. Slaughter and ostentatiously rested his shotgun across his knees. As he passed by he looked them over, as if to dare them to make trouble. The outlaws said nothing until the rig was out of sight. Finally, one of them remarked drily: "Well, there he is, fellers; if you want him, go get him."

Tom Ketchum, it developed, did not want him all that badly, after all.[1]

Slaughter apart, those who really objected to the Ketchums were too afraid of them to turn informer; since, moreover, most of the local officers were cordially disliked or mistrusted, few people wanted dealings with the law anyway. Events after the Steins Pass holdup had afforded a vivid lesson of what was likely to happen in Cochise County when lawmen came looking for outlaws. The Ketchums, for their part, were wise enough after this not to imperil themselves by holding up another train in the neighborhood; to provoke a further incursion of deputies into eastern Cochise County might be to overstretch the tolerance of the inhabitants for the Ketchums and their like. Flat broke as they were—despite the massive haul at Lozier and the respectable returns from Folsom—and confirmed in their outlawry, only one course was open to them.

In contrast with Tom and Sam, Berry cut no caper and prospered. Toward the end of September, 1897, while his brothers, Carver, and Atkins were preparing to escape southwestwards across New Mexico to hole up in Wildcat Canyon, Berry was completing the purchase of Justice W.F. Holt's ranch near Knickerbocker.[2] As was usual with Berry, the deal was "a.p.t." More than four months had gone by since the Lozier robbery; surely enough of an interval to forestall rumors that he was financing his ranching interests with money stolen by Tom?

With the coming of spring in 1898, the four men laid plans for the future. The first item was the dissolution of the Snaky Four. Atkins could stand no more of Tom Ketchum's brutality and vicious temper. Tom still bore rancor towards Atkins because he had let liquor loosen his tongue while they were planning the Steins Pass robbery; moreover, he spoke of him as a coward.[3] Atkins was anything but a coward; but he may have lacked the depressive fatalism that steeled the others to fight against desperate odds. But, like Tom, he had a quick temper. At length, somewhere in Cochise County, there was a flare-up between the two men and Atkins left. Sam stuck loyally with his brother, perhaps in the belief that he could manage him and keep him out of worse trouble. Carver's concerns may have been more practical; despite the calamity at Steins Pass, the four of them had done well out of armed robbery, and the three could do as well or better in the months ahead. Their targets may already have been in their sights. If, with Atkins gone, they needed a fourth, they knew of several potential replacements.[4]

Although the breach seems to have been emphatic, it may not have been intended to be permanent. Can it be coincidence that all four of them turned were to turn up in Idaho—and, in all likelihood, in the same corner of Idaho—in the fall of the same year?

Leaving Atkins to set his own course, the Ketchum brothers and Will Carver pulled out of Arizona, crossed New Mexico, and rode down into Val Verde County, Texas. Three if not four of the places they visited en route may be plotted with fair certainty: Old Man Lusk's spread at Chimney Wells; the Berry Ketchum ranch on Dove Creek, with a possible side trip to see Bige and Nancy Duncan; and a cave on the Pecos ten miles south of Pandale, in northwest Val Verde County. Pandale itself is 35 miles south of Ozona. The boys were definitely back in home country.

Just before their departure from the Pandale vicinity, Tom, or someone with him more modest about his own notoriety than Tom's (and unable to spell Tom's family name correctly), scraped the name TOM KETCHAM in rough capitals on the wall of the cave, then added the date: 4.26.1898.[5] Once again the gang had plans for train no. 20 of the Southern Pacific—this time, as at Lozier, in its guise as the Galveston, Harrisburg and San Antonio Railway. In order to fulfill them, they had ridden five hundred miles to Comstock, where the Newman gang had robbed the train sixteen months previously.

Comstock is just thirty miles southeast of the Ketchums' hideout below Pandale. The locale was described vividly, though not without a hint of misplaced urban condescension, from the offices of the *San Antonio Daily Express*, just 180 miles to the east, as "the region of rocks, rattlesnakes and robbers, away out in the wild and wooly West, [which was] acquiring a reputation well sustained for train robbery and hold up of the train crews."[6]

Other reports noted that the atmosphere along that section of the Rio Grande was permeated with undertones of revolution. "Spanish sympathizers," who were numerous in the Texas border country during those days of high tension between Spain and America, were thought to be preparing to blow up the famous (and famously underused) High Bridge over the Pecos. A detachment of Rangers was being sent from Spofford Junction to guard the great bridge. That night they were aboard a special train traveling west three hours behind No. 20.[7]

The proceedings of late Thursday night, April 28, 1898, and the first hour of the following morning, were true in every detail to the well-tried formula which set out the so called "regulation style" for train robbers in the 1890s. From first to last, as the *El Paso Times* would remark, "[t]he robbers went about their work systematically, like old hands at the business."

No less faithful to its blueprint was the Wells, Fargo express company's display of its oft-practiced denial technique. Company spokesmen had been precipitated by the shock of the Lozier robbery into a rare fit of spontaneous candor; they had quickly admitted a loss of $42,000, and when they revised that figure, it was to substitute one nearly $8,000 higher. Such frankness was out of character for Wells, Fargo. Thereafter, older precedents would be honored.

No. 20 pulled out of Sunset depot in San Antonio at 4:50 that Thursday afternoon, five minutes late. When, nearly seven uneventful hours later, it reached Comstock at 11:30 p.m., two of the Ketchum gang boarded the blind end of the baggage and mail car, from the side of the track opposite the station buildings, and swung up onto the rear of the locomotive tender directly ahead of them.[8]

Their intention was to crawl over the coals as the train moved out, and then force the engine crew to halt just beyond the depot. But an unexpected delay compelled a partial change of plan; Engineer Walter Jordan kept the train lingering in the station so that he could oil the locomotive.

Patience is not a highwaymanly virtue. The two intruders sprang down and "paid their respects" to Jordan by telling him to "get out of the station at once." His request for more time to finish lubricating the engine was curtly refused. With the customary flourish of revolvers and profanities, the bandits ordered the train taken a mile ahead. Here, Jordan and his fireman were told to get down and unfasten the couplings which connected the express car with the passenger coaches. The uncoupling was not accomplished without noise and delay; if Postal Clerk C.F. Lippold, of San Antonio, and Express Messenger Richard H. Hayes, of El Paso, were not on the alert already, their notice was fully aroused before the operation was finished.

Further back in the train was Conductor James Burns, who had seen something of the Lozier robbers. This time he saw nothing. Perhaps he did not want to see anything. At any rate, he stayed with the passengers, as was his duty, and seems to have had nothing to say about the robbery afterwards, other than to report it to the telegrapher at Comstock.

Once the train had been divided, the bandits and their prisoners returned to the engine. The combination baggage and postal car and the express car were drawn two miles further west to a desolate place named Helmet, where two other bandits stepped out of the darkness. Postal clerk Lippold checked the time. It was ten minutes short of midnight. A minute or two later he was obeying a command shouted from outside to come down from his car.

All four of the bandits now approached the open door of the express car, prodding the engineer before them. All wore black masks and dark clothing. "One," the witnesses would report, "was quite a large man, who spoke with a German accent. Two were medium size and one a small man." The small man—Will Carver, presumably—"was supposed to be the leader." Dave Atkins was not among them; he had chosen to stay in Arizona. The fourth man cannot be identified. He might, therefore, have been Ben Kilpatrick, but no evidence has been found for or against.

If the robber quartet consisted of Tom and Sam Ketchum, Will Carver, and Ben Kilpatrick, an accurate outline description might be expected to depict them as three large men and one small. But the impact on the eye made by four figures walking about in uncertain light by the trackside, moving in or out of the night, is likely to differ markedly from that of the same four seen by daylight. As for the large man with the German accent, he would have been just as German as one of the Ketchum brothers speaking with an affected German accent. Other instances are known of Western train robbers disguising their voices by an alteration of pitch or by a change of accent or idiom. It may also be relevant that the Ketchums' mother was of German parentage.[9]

Messenger Dick Hayes later pictured himself as a figure of splendid defiance, frustrated first by a shotgun ("an old 10-bore Winchester") that hung fire when he had a clear bead on two of the robbers, and then by the concern for the safety of the engineer that kept him from taking on the desperadoes with his revolver. When two of the bandits climbed into the car and demanded money, he said there was none. To their retort that they would sooner have coin than his word, he credited himself with the sauce to reply: "I thought you got considerable money in your last haul. You should money have left." The allusion was to the Lozier robbery; the Germanic syntax, with the verb at the end, suggested a parody of the conversational style of the robber who was thought to be a German. "We got plenty," one of the bandits said, "but that's been spent."[10]

That was the end of the sparring. One of the robbers had a categorical demand; he wanted the keys to the way safe. Hayes, according to another of his stories to the press, denied having any key. When, stating the obvious, he declared that he could not open the combination and time locks of the through safe, one of the bandits was ready with a dry rejoinder: "We can open it." The messenger was ordered to clear away the express parcels that were heaped up near the through safe. Dynamite and fuse were then applied to it, the while Hayes vacillated from assurance that the safe was empty to entreaty for it not to be blown up.[11]

Everyone ducked away as the fuse was lit, and soon an almighty explosion rent the still night air, tearing "a hole as big as a barrel" through the roof as the way safe flew starwards, blasting an opening one foot in diameter in the top of the through safe, and splintering one side of the car "into kindling wood."[12]

The "shock of the explosion" extinguished the lamps in the mail car and set it aflame, but Lippold was able to put out the fire, and only a few pieces of mail were damaged by oil and water. The bandits ignored the mail car. They rummaged through the remnants of the express car, denuded the shelves of the riven safe, insisted on shaking hands with Messenger Hayes, then ordered the crew to reverse the engine and collect the abandoned passenger coaches with all the speed they could muster. After that they "walked round the engine and disappeared in the darkness." Soon they were seen and heard riding away; but before they passed out of view, they fired a parting volley toward the engine—in celebration, or to remind the crew of their instructions to start back for the coaches. When Jordan began to shunt the engine and money cars to Comstock, the fragile state of the wrecked express car kept his speed low. Altogether an hour and twenty or thirty minutes was lost before the reunited train began to limp towards El Paso.[13] It did not get there until 4 p.m.

Dispatches were humming over the wires from Comstock and beyond. Some were garbled, contradictory, or purposely untrue; none carried a comprehensive picture of the events. At 1:30 p.m., on the Friday, a reporter for the *San Antonio Daily Light* sought the latest intelligence from the local office of Wells, Fargo. The company spokesman was uninformative. Not only had he heard no details of the robbery; he dismissed the report that one had occurred. "I think it is a canard," he declared,[14] though he would not have thought anything of the kind. He was merely pushing discretion into disingenuousness.

San Francisco, corporate headquarters and terminal city for both Wells, Fargo and the Southern Pacific, had an interest in the Comstock affair. The bellowing headline in the *San Francisco Chronicle* would not have been to the liking of the executives of the two firms: BIG BOOTY FOR TEXANS. Nor would they have cared for the substance of the accompanying dispatch from El Paso, compiled soon after the belated arrival of the stricken train. "[A]ccording to the best accounts," ran the dispatch, the robbers "procured in the neighborhood of $20,000."[15]

The El Paso correspondent included all the evasions and prevarications that Wells, Fargo could manufacture from the resources available to its El Paso office. No booty had been obtained "except one small package of money destined for San Diego, Cal.," There had been nothing for the bandits because the company had "discontinued shipping by that route" several months previously, "on account of the frequency of hold-ups in the vicinity of Comstock." Messenger Hayes, of whom more would be heard later, was already filling the part allotted for him. He stoutly averred that the leader of the robbers, finding only one sealed package in the safe, had remarked that the messenger was right in saying there was no money to be had.[16]

The newspaper was rightly skeptical. It knew, as all but the stupidest of its readers would know, that Wells, Fargo did not put express cars on the railroad, install time-locked safes in them, maintain them, and employ armed men in the combined roles of clerk and guard to ride in them, for the joy of shipping nothing halfway across America.

Wells, Fargo did not underrate the value of obduracy in the conduct of human affairs. They may not have expected to be believed, but they understood that consistency in lying never betrayed any secret. Their faith in this credo was demonstrated when Gerrit A. Taft, superintendent of their divisional office at Houston, took charge of the public relations side of the investigation.

Taft got back from a trip to North Texas on April 29. He had already inquired into the extent of the company's loss, and was only too pleased to pass on the results to the reporter who greeted him on his return: the Comstock robbers had failed to secure a cent![17] All he had to do now was impart some pretense of plausibility to the conclusion he had formed before he began his investigation.

The following morning, April 30, Taft and his close friend, Fred Dodge, once of Tombstone but now attached to the Kansas City Office as one of the company's principal detectives, left for West Texas "to make a preliminary examination."[18]

No evidence survives of Dodge's involvement in the case. The memoirs he began late in life do not take his story beyond October, 1893, and it was not without cause that he prided himself on being known as "the man who could not be interviewed." All that is certain is that he did nothing to grab the attention of the newspapers.[19]

Overt attempts at pursuit were offered promptly but soon abandoned. First in the field was the Ranger force en route from Spofford Junction to the High Bridge on the night of the robbery. As their train came to the site of the holdup, they saw three horsemen beside the track. The train was stopped, the men retreated, and the Rangers advanced shooting. But by the time the Rangers' mounts were unloaded the suspects had all the start they needed; within a few seconds they were out of sight, and the Rangers had to wait until morning to begin looking for a trail.[20]

One was soon found, but it might as easily have been predicted. It led southward across the Rio Grande, a little way along the Mexican bank of the river, and then north again onto the Texas side. And there it gave out. Still, the renowned Captain John R. Hughes was coming from Valentine, with another force of Rangers; these men knew that section intimately and, said one prophet, would "make it hot for the robbers unless they have gone to Mexico."[21]

The robbers had not gone to Mexico, except momentarily, and their trail was too cold for Hughes and his cadre of local specialists. Nor were the clues thick on the ground for forensic investigation. The bandits had left two mementoes at the scene of the stickup: a mask made of an old coat lining with holes punched through for the eyes, nose, and mouth, and a paper with "Chris and Geo.,—San Angelo" printed on it.[22] Neither led the officers anywhere, although the missing surname could not have posed any problem: Chris and George Hagerstein, two of four brothers, owned the largest general store in San Angelo.

The open reference to San Angelo told the officers nothing that many of them would not have assumed anyway. Some may have suspected Bud Newman, of Carta Valley, who had planned and led the previous robbery at Comstock. But to most, the current exploit was stamped through and through with the authority of the Lozier looters. Besides, Newman was elsewhere; he and three friends had headed north and were soon to cross the Ketchums' home patch to attempt a train robbery at Coleman.[23]

By May 4, Gerrit Taft was back in Houston, where he favored the *Post* with his exposition of the evidence which purported to show that the stickup had been profitless:

> After the explosion, the leader climbed into the car again, and placing his hand in the hole in the safe's top, . . . remarked to his comrades that the old man [Messenger Hayes] was right—there was no money in sight. With a couple of shots, just to show they were around, and through with the job, the robbers rode away in the moonlight. Hayes had cleverly secreted all the money and valuables the small safe contained, thus keeping the bandits from getting a dollar.[24]

Not even Hayes himself had claimed to have hidden the contents of the small safe, but the question has no relevance anyway: their chief concern was with the large through safe, which Hayes could not have opened and whose contents he could not have known, much less hidden, unless he and employees senior to him were severely in breach of the company's strict rules on security. That was the safe the bandits had blown open and where one of them had delved for swag.

Taft tapered the edges of other parts of Hayes's original story, too; he had not liked the messenger's admission that the bandits had taken only one sealed packet— one stolen packet was one too many for the general superintendent's immovable contention that not a dollar had fallen into predatory hands. The same reasoning led him to ignore the "disclosure" by another official that the marauders had obtained only $4.80 in cash.

Taft also had an explanation for the failure of Hayes's shotgun to dislodge its load: "the shells were of the wrong gauge."[25]

Absurd as Taft's fabrications were, they served their object; only the highest officials of Wells, Fargo, and the outlaws themselves, knew how much was taken from the shambles of the express car. The correspondent who put the haul at $20,000 was only guessing; that much, or more, was often consigned over the Sunset route between Houston and San Francisco, but many runs would have been much lighter.

Whatever the gang gathered up from the express car, the mail car added no sweeteners, several of the early newspaper accounts to the contrary. In his *Annual Report* for 1898, the Postmaster General flatly stated that the robbers did not go into the car and took nothing from the clerk.[26]

No significance rides on the fact that the Ketchum robbed another train only two months after the Comstock episode. Less than five months separated their robberies at Lozier and Folsom in 1897, and the interval between the Folsom and Steins Pass holdups was barely more than three months. Yet they had tolled the S.P. system for almost fifty thousand dollars in the first, and gained a far from negligible $3,500 from their second attempt.

The mystery remains. If they had spent the stolen money, where and how did it all go? If on the other hand, they had managed to salt much of it away, who was looking after it, and what did they plan to do once they had stolen all they wanted? Their expenses—mostly bribes in one form or another—were high, but not so high as to account for the bulk of their spoils.

Wells, Fargo at once broadcast their belief that the Comstock and Lozier robberies were the work of the same hands. Already they had evidence connecting the Lozier and Folsom holdups. The Ketchums were the most wanted desperadoes; but not the most sought. Their elusiveness, or the hardness of their local reputation, together with the active or passive help given them by acquaintances of long standing, kept them clear of pursuit.

After their flight northwards through the Devil's River country of Val Verde County and on through Crockett County, the Ketchums and Carver were untroubled by any posse. Fresh horses were secured near Ozona, along with a saddle that was to turn up in New Mexico more than a year afterwards.[27]

A hundred miles north of Ozona, and nearly twice that distance from Comstock, lay the Berry Ketchum ranch, Bige Duncan's, and other places where as long as they did not move about too openly, and kept their eyes open, the outlaws could tarry safely, for all that Rome Shield and his deputies might want to put them out of circulation.

John Loomis has left an account of a meeting between Tom Ketchum and Rome Shield that did not quite happen. It probably belongs to this period of Ketchum's career. Loomis got the story from Shield, who had brought it back from a visit to Ketchum's jail cell in New Mexico.

The scene was "near the head of the Concho," in Tom Green County; the likely time, quite early in May of 1898, following the flight from Comstock and the temporary separation of the members of the gang. Tom had asked his sometime friend the sheriff whether he remembered being in the area with a squad of Rangers after a train robbery.

When Shield acknowledged that he did, Tom reminded him of the sudden shying of the posse's pack mule near a thicket of live oak. "Sure I remember," replied Shield; they had stopped, wondering what had upset the mule, and he had wanted to inspect the thicket, but the Ranger captain suggested the presence of hogs as the probable cause; "so we rode on." Ketchum interjected that it was "a damned good thing you didn't go back to investigate, for I was lying on the ground with four guns and plenty of ammunition." To Shield's rejoinder that he and the captain had enough men to charge the thicket and kill Ketchum, the outlaw retorted: "Well, just the same, it was a good thing for you and the Ranger that you didn't try it;" he had intended to shoot the captain through the middle of his body, and then, he assured the sheriff, "I would have killed you, too."[28]

It may have been during this late spring interlude that Will Carver and Laura Bullion went off to Fort Worth. Bullion herself is the sole authority for what little is known. She did not tie the visit to a date, but the verifiable details of Carver's criminal itinerary leave no space for this respite elsewhere in his timetable.

Laura said that Carver had admitted to having been in a train robbery, giving her to understand that he had left the gang—a statement which was not true and which she may or may not have believed. In her own words, as reported by a journalist intent on making her speech more picturesquely ungrammatical in print than in life: "I expected Bill was fixing to marry me, but nothing ever came of it. I knowed Bill had been train robbing, but he told me he'd reformed, and, as far as I know, he didn't do nothing in that line while I was with him. 'Course, he'd leave me and go away for days, but I never asked him no questions."[29]

By mid-June the reassembled gang were on the road again. Their departure may have been in accordance with a planned program, but it may also have been accelerated by the indiscretion of others.

Just before the second Comstock robbery, another bunch of criminals had quit Val Verde County. These men were Bud Newman, Pierce Keton (often misspelled Keaton or Keeton), and two brothers, Bill and Jeff Taylor. They had stopped at Sonora, in Sutton County, to buy dynamite, then headed northeast to Coleman, no more than sixty miles from San Angelo. There, on the night of Thursday, June 9, they held up a Santa Fe train, Newman greeting the engineer and fireman with a cheerful "Hello, boys!"

That was the end of the social side of the evening. A passenger, R.P. Buchanan, had a clear field of fire and used it to both good and ill effect. His shots wounded Newman and Keton, obliging them and the Taylors to decamp without a penny to show for overarching ambition. But Buchanan's deadliest shooting was reserved for the fireman, who died of an abdominal wound the following night. Colleagues of the victim criticized Buchanan for not getting close enough to the target area to distinguish friend from foe. In law, however, the robbers were the culpable parties.[30]

So ended one of the most misconceived and ill-executed attempts at armed robbery in the annals of outlawry. The several sequels are interesting, but have no bearing on the history of the Ketchum gang. Rumors charging the Ketchums with the affray, together with the direction of the pursuit, gave it a brief relevance. These circumstances might have been enough to hasten the Ketchum gang away from Tom Green County, had they not made plans to leave anyway.

If Sam and Tom asked Berry to hold on to most of their share of the Lozier, Folsom, and Comstock proceeds until they were ready to give up outlawry, they were deluding themselves, perhaps in more ways than one. But whatever the motivation, they had determined to rob another train before they left the state.

Andy Jones, owner of a ranch in Sterling County, furnished the gang with at least one horse, involuntarily or otherwise. Other ranchers nearby may have done the same. From the Sterling area they continued northwest to the tracks of the Texas and Pacific Railway, finally to make camp by Mustang Creek, four or five miles west of Stanton, and "one of the most desolate spots on the line."[31] Stanton, situated near the southeast corner of Martin County, of which it is the seat, is set amid flat, mainly bare country, twenty miles southwest of Big Spring. Fort Worth is nearly three hundred miles to the east; El Paso, about the same distance to the west.

William "Bob" Beverly, at that time a cowboy on the Quien Sabe ranch, near Midland, in later years shared his few remaining memories of the Stanton train robbery with the Texas field historian Hervey Chesley. Beverly, who had known the Ketchums, said that Tom boarded the engine at Stanton and held up the engineer at the Mustang Creek trestle; "another fellow," Beverly added, "had a horse there at the draw."[32] Otherwise Beverley could not supplement the rather sparse press coverage of a robbery whose success was only a little less impressive than the Lozier episode.

Train no. 3 of the Texas and Pacific Railway, the California Express, left Fort Worth early on the morning of Friday, July 1, 1898. It was running to time when it reached Stanton, a few minutes before ten p.m. Just outside Stanton an unmasked man, armed with a Winchester and a revolver, came down from the coal tender and joined Engineer Holmes and his fireman in the cab, where quickly and firmly he made his wishes known. Holmes, as ordered, brought the train to a standstill near a bonfire beside the track, four miles down the line, where two more armed men rushed up to the engine. A short distance ahead, a red light showed that the switch had been thrown. The mail clerk recorded the time of the stoppage: 10:05 p.m.[33]

Two of the men cut loose the express car while the third guarded the engine crew. Holmes was then told to go ahead, "on pain of death." Next, the express car was hauled down the spur track, three quarters of a mile beyond the stranded passenger coaches, where a fourth man waited with their horses and the explosives. Confronted by Messenger A.W. Moreland's insistence on keeping the door of the Pacific Express Company's car between the bandits and himself, the marauders settled the dispute by breaching the car with a charge of dynamite.

Moreland was taken to the locomotive and kept under guard alongside the engineer and fireman while two of the gang pillaged the express car. After the bandits had cleared out the contents of the way safe, they set about the through safe. Ten sticks of dynamite were placed on the strongbox, a wet bedquilt was laid on top of the dynamite, the way safe was lifted onto the quilt, the fuse was lit, and the men hurriedly quit the car to avoid being blown up with it.

This second explosion turned the car into a most spectacular wreck. Nearly all of it now littered the track and the surrounding prairie. The through safe had been blasted into fragments, its contents strewn about the remnants of the floor. A portion of one of the safes now lay eighty feet from the tracks.

Consequential damage was suffered by a consignment of melons, originally destined for a Fourth of July celebration. Since the fruit had been cracked open by the force of the detonation, three of the bandits—the fourth stayed out of sight—decided to enjoy some of it. As they sat at the railside, munching melon, one of the trainmen, chidingly or jokingly, told them that they ought to go to Cuba. "We're doing pretty well in this country," was the reply.[34]

Evidently the outlaws were well satisfied with the outcome, for when they rode away to the southwest a number of ten-dollar bills and some jewelry still lay amid the debris. The engine was reversed, the passenger coaches reattached, and the reassembled train was switched back to the main line. At Germania, the next station west, the first reports were telegraphed out.[35]

Officials of the Pacific Express Company maintained a stony silence on their cash loss. Hearsay could do no better than to place it somewhere between $1,000 and $50,000. A day or two later, a "thoroughly reliable source" anonymously credited the robbers with "something over $5,000" under shipment from a bank in Fort Worth to "another national bank in the west." Frank Shelton, sheriff of Martin County in 1898, supported this in a statement made in 1932; he identified the intended recipient as the Roswell National Bank. If that was true as far as it went, it would not have been the whole story; it would not have been the only money shipment in the safe.

Ten days after the stickup, a dispatch from Austin announced that it was "positively known that they secured over $30,000 in cash and express money aggregating over $50.000 from the safe." That looks suspiciously high; at the other end of the scale, and even less worthy of serious consideration, is a much later estimate, in which the Pacific's loss is put at only $500.[36]

Assistant Manager J.W. Everman of the T & P promptly offered $250 for the arrest and conviction of each robber. After a day or so, both Pacific Express and the State of Texas posted rewards also. Superintendent O.W. Case, of Pacific Express, telegraphed the state governor for Rangers to be put on the trail of the miscreants. The governor said the request "would receive attention."[37]

Posses went into the field from Martin, Midland, and Howard Counties, led by Sheriffs Frank Shelton, H.R. Wells, and James Baggott, who, in turn, were at first led by a team of bloodhounds. Sheriff John Y. Lovell, of Reeves County, far to the southwest, even started out in a special train loaded with deputies and horses.[38]

The outlaws' departure "at a rapid pace" was easily kept up for a while, as "the holdup occurred in an open prairie with no fences or other impediments to flight adjacent." Soon their trail swung southeast, towards Garden City. One confident report of a sighting was either a ludicrous mistake or a hoax. At about 1 p.m. on July 4, a party of four men was reported at or near Garden City, hardly twenty-five miles southeast of Stanton. "One of the robbers was on foot," was the message for the posses on their arrival five hours later, "one on a bicycle and two rode horses." The actual bandits, not a biker or a hiker among them, had passed Garden City early in the morning on July 2 and were seen later that day "going down the Concho river valley towards Sterling City and San Angelo."[39]

Shelton, Wells, and Baggott followed a well-marked trail: the horse of one of the bandits—Shelton said there were only three—had "a bad foot," which advertised the escape route for eighty-five miles. The bandits well knew it: as they neared San Angelo they covered their tracks by driving a herd of horses for ten or twelve miles. Even so, the posse unwittingly came close to their quarry. "I learned later," said Shelton, "that once when we stopped to debate which way to go, we were within three hundred yards of where they were hiding."[40]

On the 3rd or 4th of July, the three camped and ate dinner in a liveoak thicket on Fayette Tankersley's 7D ranch in Irion County. They were dividing the loot when a 7D line rider came up. He said later that they had a pile of silver about four feet high (surely an instance of hyperbole on the hoof), "besides more greenbacks than you ever saw in a bank." By then they had 7D horses; but, the rider carefully pointed out in speaking of the incident forty years afterwards, "They didn't steal them. They would catch and ride horses off the ranches but always managed to return them." (Always? Well, nearly always.)

The trio were not at all disconcerted by the arrival of the 7D man; they knew him, and he knew them. They may have expected him to turn up. Anyway, they gave him four $100 bills. He took them, but after submitting the question to judicious thought, gave them back. He did not want to make himself conspicuous by flashing century notes; and, if the desperadoes were so accommodating as to substitute bills of smaller denomination, he did not say so.

A few hours later, a posse reined in at the nearby Lone Joe line camp. When they left, a 7D rider called Mose went with them as guide. The party then rode directly, and erroneously, for the Concho country. After breaking camp, the bandits had split up, "each going his own way, but headed generally to the south."[41]

The three sheriffs, with two deputies, were soon in or near Knickerbocker. They nosed around Sherwood for a couple of days, making no arrests, but, opined the *Irion County Record*, "getting some valuable clues which will no doubt cause conviction of the robbers if caught."[42] Of course, the sheriffs had the most valuable clues of all almost as soon as the robbery was reported: they knew full well whom they wanted. Getting the evidence was not the problem; the whole of the difficulty lay in catching the men. And the men were not there; if their retreat had taken them to the Knickerbocker-Sherwood vicinity, they were not there for more than a few hours. Now they were on their way to New Mexico. A false echo of the robbery sounded faintly in "one little town" near Midland, when a bunch of "Schleicher County Boys En Route to Arizona . . . to look at the country" were mistaken for a combined party of arresting officers and arrested train robbers.[43]

Although Shelton stated in 1932 that there were only three robbers, whom he uncompromisingly named as Tom and Sam Ketchum and Will Carver, the contemporary reports point to four. Evidently one of the gang went off alone directly after the holdup and his trail was never picked up. That leads to two contingent possibilities. One is that Shelton suspected Dave Atkins, but, whether motivated by caution or sympathy, cut him out of his narrative because he knew that, in 1932, Atkins was alive, living in Texas, and in trouble on another charge. Alternatively, Shelton knew that the fourth man was someone else, whose name and participation he did not want to make public.

In this last connection, reference must be made to an incident related in the autobiography of Daniel Riley "Dee" Harkey, originally of San Saba County, who was a peace officer in Texas and later, for many years, in New Mexico. The notoriously inaccurate and self-flattering character of Dee Harkey's writings means that nothing he says should be accepted unless proved to be true; and the story in question is one on which no evidence can be located for or against. It is summarized here for as much as it may be worth.[44]

Harkey wrote that after "this outlaw" (name omitted or suppressed) robbed the train at Stanton, he stole a horse and saddle from H.D. Cowan, a prominent rancher in Pecos. Harkey went after him and eventually traced him in the Mogollons. A snow storm blew up—this would have had to be at least four or five months after the train robbery—and blanketed the fugitive's trail, enabling him to dismount, lie in wait, and get the drop on Harkey.

Finally, wrote Harkey, he persuaded the man not only to spare him but to surrender and return with him to Carlsbad, though Dee "did not have the nerve to put him in jail." The man was extradited to Texas and "sentenced for a long term in the penitentiary." After he had served about seven years, he was pardoned through the intervention of his friend, W.W. Camp, with help from Harkey.[45]

If anyone was sent to prison for the Stanton train robbery, evidence of his conviction would be a conspicuous entry in the public record. No such evidence has been found.

It is possible that the unnamed man pursued and brought back by Harkey was convicted in Texas for other offenses. Three of the Stanton robbers—Carver and the two Ketchums—were accounted for by other means. Dave Atkins was not in Texas at the time of the robbery; his restless feet were about to take him to Utah and beyond. Besides, he was not arrested in New Mexico or by Harkey. Bud Upshaw, another one-time companion of the Ketchums, was arrested seventeen months after the Stanton robbery; but not in New Mexico and not by Harkey. Furthermore, Upshaw was never publicly connected with the Stanton robbery, and, so far as can be ascertained, never stood trial for anything. Thus, while there may be something in Harkey's tale, the details remain elusive.[46] The only other possibility worth mentioning is that Ben Kilpatrick, rather than Atkins, might have been the fourth man at Stanton (and at Comstock); but there is nothing to speak for it other than past and future associations, Kilpatrick's status as a fugitive, the notoriety he later achieved, and the lack of any information on his whereabouts in the spring and early summer of 1898—in other words, no semblance of real evidence.

Not long after the Stanton robbery, there was another near-meeting between Shield and the Ketchums. On the next occasion, neither was looking for the other. The sheriff was taking his family back to San Angelo one Sunday after a few days at their ranch near Stiles, seventy miles west of town. He had no idea that the gang was holed up nearby and drove along the old stage road, just north of the Middle Concho, oblivious of the watching eyes. On the following Tuesday he received a note from Tom Ketchum. It went more or less like this: "Rome, you and your family passed within my firing range last Sunday afternoon. If you value your life or that of your family, do not pass this way again."

Shield's reaction was to raise a posse and ask the Irion County sheriff, Uncle Bill Elliott, to do the same. Tom's headstrong arrogance and aggressiveness could have been calamitous for the gang: they must have expected a posse, but were taken aback by the speed of its arrival. When the officers got to the wire-surrounded shin oak thicket where the gang had penned their horses, they found pack saddles, a stock of food, and a large sack of ammunition.[47]

On August 5, 1898, the young folk of Knickerbocker attended a "calico hop." Roxie Baze, Doda and Loyse Duncan, Mary Merrett, Mark Ryan, Jim Yerby, and many other former schoolmates of the Bullion girls were present, along with their kinsman (and Will Carver's friend) Jasper Peck; but Laura, Fannie, and Will were, for their different reasons, on the roll of the absent.[48]

A few days after the Ketchum gang crossed from Texas into New Mexico, a passage of robbery at arms transacted twelve hundred miles northwest of San Angelo provided the first tangible evidence of an understanding between the leading professional bandits of the southwest and those of the northwest. At one end of the chain were Tom and Sam Ketchum, Will Carver, and Dave Atkins. At the other end were several of the best known of the criminal habitués of Brown's Hole, where Utah, Colorado, and Wyoming all met, and Hole-in-the-Wall, in central Wyoming. In the middle—socially, not geographically—were Jim and Tap Duncan, once of San Saba County, Texas, but now residents of good standing in Owyhee County, Idaho, and innocent of everything but the crimes of some of their friends.

The origins of the connection between the two gangs have yet to be established; the best of the available guesses predicates an acquaintanceship between Harvey Logan and one or both of the Ketchums formed on the cattle ranges of Texas or New Mexico in the late 1880s or early 1890s. Logan was the only important member of the Hole-in-the-Wall outlaw fraternity to have worked as a cowboy in the Southwest. He may have run into the Duncans in Texas or New Mexico before he knew the Ketchums, or become friendly with Jim and Tap through prior acquaintance with Tom and Sam. Lastly, if it was not Logan who introduced the Ketchums to Hole-in-the-Wall in the early 1890s, that could have been where he and they met.

Here surmise ends: it is a fact that, by the summer of 1898, hardly a couple of years after the Duncans moved into Owyhee County, Three Creek and district became an outlaw holdout.

At 1:25 a.m. on Thursday, July 14, 1898, three men held up Southern Pacific train no. 1, eastbound, just outside Humboldt, Nevada. All was done to patent: two men boarded the engine; the train was halted at the point where a third man waited with the horses and dynamite; the messenger refused to let the bandits into his car, so they blew out the door and entered anyway; the safe and car were wrecked by another, and greater detonation; and the bandits were soon riding away with much more than Wells, Fargo's admitted loss of $450.[49]

The bandits fled north; had the posses been able to stick to the trail, they would have found themselves in southwest Idaho. But shortage of supplies, or stamina, soon compelled them to abandon the chase. Eventually the authorities arrested four men who were absolutely innocent of the Humboldt holdup, whatever they may have done elsewhere. Three were acquitted; the fourth was extradited to face charges in Arizona.[50]

Thanks to the series of wrong turns and blind alleys explored by the investigating and prosecuting officials, the identities of the actual culprits were never uncovered and their hideout in Owyhee County stayed free of suspicion.

In recent years, Donna Ernst has argued persuasively that the three Humboldt robbers were George Currie, Harvey Logan, and Harry Longabaugh, the Sundance

Kid. Mike Bell has presented convincing evidence that in 1900, before and after the bank robbery at Winnemucca, Nevada, members of the Wild Bunch again tucked themselves away in the Three Creek locality.[51] Finally, there is circumstantial evidence that the Ketchums visited Owyhee County in the fall of 1898. Carver may have gone there at about the same time, and Atkins definitely did, though they did not travel together or with the Ketchums.

Nothing is known of what the Ketchums and Carver did in the late summer of 1898. Whether they went first to Turkey Creek Canyon, or across southern New Mexico and into southeast Arizona, they probably did not travel as a group. Sam and Tom may have stuck together, while the younger man went his own way. The three had no conjoint plan, no need for one, and consequently no good reason for going about in a bunch. Their pockets were full, and their three contrasting temperaments did not belong together when there was no fortune to be sought.

Early in the fall of 1898, Tom and Sam Ketchum returned to Texas for a conference with Berry. It was later explained on Berry's behalf that he had given them money to buy a ranch in Idaho.[52] Very likely their discussions were on the subject of money, and Idaho may have been mentioned more than casually. But if Berry supplied his brothers with funds, he would not have raided his own exchequer. He would have been restoring to them money that was already theirs, if only because they had made it theirs by stealing it from the express companies. They could have asked him to take care of some of their swag, and they might have paid him handsomely to do so.

Berry, unlike his brothers, understood the uses of money. Late in July, 1898, for example, he moved his family onto the ranch he had just bought on western Independence Creek, in Pecos County. He retained the Knickerbocker ranch and henceforth shuttled cattle, staff, family, and himself between the two properties.[53]

After the visit to Berry's ranch, whether in Tom Green or Pecos County, Tom and Sam made their way to Lockhart, sixty miles northeast of San Antonio. From Lockhart, where they were not known, they traveled over the rails to Idaho.[54] If they took the best and usual route, they would have passed through Fort Worth, Raton, Pueblo, Denver, Cheyenne, and Salt Lake City. Their next, and last, rail stop could have been Twin Falls, Idaho. We have no evidence to place them in Owyhee County, beyond that of common sense: having made up their minds to travel that great distance, to country about which they knew nothing, they would go to people who had once been their neighbors and sidekicks. Only Jim and Tap Duncan fitted that bill, although both the Ketchums and the Duncans may well have known that Dave Atkins was living and working at Shoshone, within easy traveling distance.

The Ketchums, then, would have left the train at Twin Falls, bought or hired means of transportation (they would not have left their saddles in Texas) and ridden or driven to Three Creek.

A year or two later, Tom told his old friend Len Alverson—with a prison warder in attendance—that he went alone to Idaho, where he worked on a farm and met a girl who gave him a Bible. Some of the detail he supplied may have been untrue, but at its core is a consistency with references elsewhere to the Ketchum brothers' visit to

Idaho. Tom spoke of having made three trips between Arizona and Idaho in close succession. This story may have been devised to promote a crude alibi for the peak months of his career in crime, but it is possible that he did go to Idaho as many as three times over a longer period.[55]

Tom and Sam did not buy a ranch in Idaho in the fall of 1898, or, if they did, they did not live on it; they probably did not stay in the state for more than a few weeks. Once there, they might have ridden out to Brown's Hole, where they would have expected to see a friendly face or two. If they returned south by rail, they could have got out of the train at Raton or Springer, or gone on to Magdalena.

At about this time, Lawrence Rowell, manager of the Wells, Fargo express company, issued a proclamation from San Francisco, carrying descriptions of the Ketchums and their partners and placing a price on each of their heads. Thus their status as men living outside the law—as hunted criminals—was at last officially confirmed. The personal information on the wanted men had been compiled by Johnnie and Gene Thacker, and ranged in quality from the fairly full and authentic to the sketchy and misleading.

ONE THOUSAND DOLLARS REWARD FOR THE ARREST AND CONVICTION OF EACH OF THE FOLLOWING DESCRIBED PARTIES

Tom Ketchum, Alias Black Jack

Age about 35 years; height about 5 feet, 11 inches; very heavy set; large broad shoulders; weight 175 pounds; dark complexion; small black eyes; has been shot in one leg; has brother living in San Angelo, Texas; has a dimple in chin; has a large nose and regularly formed face.

Sam Ketchum

Age about 40 years; height 5 feet, 10 or 11 inches; very heavy set; large broad shoulders; weight 180 to 190 pounds; very red complexion; sandy; is known among the crooks as "Dad."

Will Carver

Age about 30 years; height about 5 feet, 8 inches; weight about 165 pounds; very dark complexion; might be taken for Spaniard; has one glass eye.

Dave Atkinson

Age about 28 years; height about 5 feet, 7 inches; weight about 150 to 160 pounds; very black, straight hair; might be taken for a Cherokee.

Red Pipkin or Dan Pipkin

Age about 28 years; height about 5 feet, 8 or 9 inches; weight about 160 pounds; red hair; freckled face and hands.

Jack Rollins
Known as the Black Man

Age 30 years; height 5 feet, 9 inches; weight 160 pounds; black straight hair; dark complexion; long sharp nose; prominent jaw; chews tobacco incessantly.

The above reward includes the standing reward of $300. In case any of the above-described parties are killed while resisting arrest, upon proper identification the reward will be paid the same as if the parties were convicted.

WRITE OR TELEGRAPH ANY INFORMATION TO

J.N. Thacker or to E.J. Thacker
Special Officer Special Officer
Wells, Fargo & Co. Wells, Fargo & Co.
San Francisco. Cal. Tucson, Ariz.

or to

L.F. Rowell, Manager, Wells, Fargo & Co.
San Francisco, California[56]

The $300 standing reward was the company's own; it was automatically payable upon the conviction (or death in resisting arrest) of anyone required by legally constituted authority to answer charges of stealing company property, or identified as suspects by the company itself. The "if . . . killed while resisting arrest" clause was, in practice if not in legal theory, generally recognized as a statement of "wanted, dead or alive." Those named in any such public notices were outlaws in official eyes as well as in popular understanding.

Neither Rollins nor Pipkin had any known involvement with the Ketchum gang but the reward notice did not actually state that they had. Rollins is a complete stranger to this narrative. Pipkin was a member of Bronco Bill's train robbing gang, which the younger Thacker had helped to hunt down in Arizona in the summer of 1898; but his connection with the Ketchums, if any, was tenuous.

If anything, Will Carver and Dave Atkins would have been reassured: the descriptions that the poster applied to them might just as well have been attached to such names as Michael Moe and James Noe. Carver's height may have been an inch or two overstated, and he weighed perhaps fifteen to twenty pounds less; but he was naturally of light complexion and, while he could speak some Spanish, it seems improbable that he would have been mistaken for a Spaniard even when he was using black dye as a disguise, as he often did. It would be enlightening to know who or what persuaded the compiler of these particulars—doubtless Thacker *fils*—that Will had a glass eye; he may have had a glassy stare on occasion, but both of his eyes were good. As for Atkins, the Thackers or their informants could not even fit him to his own name. Their remarks on his complexion accurately relay the impression that he might have had Indian ancestry; but the same was said of so many others in the

American West, and Atkins, at 5'10" and twenty-four, was so obviously taller and younger than the man billed as Atkinson, that the reward notice could not have cost him much worry.

The descriptions of Tom and Sam were a different matter, although both were an inch or two taller that the poster allowed, and Sam was four years older. The brothers were so widely known in the southwest that Wells, Fargo's operatives would have been under no difficulty in obtaining accurate details of their appearance. Tom's leg wound would have been the one sustained at Steins a year earlier.

When Dave Atkins's account of the Steins Pass episode reaches the point where the pursuing officers lost the trail below Squaw Mountain, it also loses the reader for seven months. Next to nothing would be known about this period in the gang's history if it were not for the publication in 1964 of Joseph "Mack" Axford's *Around Western Campfires*. Axford describes how the Snaky Four set up camp south of the 7 Up ranch at a time when he and his partner, Charlie Mowbry, were mining a copper claim in the nearby Swisshelms. The four regularly bought food and cartridges from the various local ranchers, who "tolerated" them, and from time to time dropped in on Axford and Mowbry for the same purpose.

One day Atkins showed up alone, explaining that he had broken with the Ketchums and Carver. He had decided to quit the bandit trail and travel north, where no one would be hunting him. For a week or ten days, while he was getting ready to go, he camped in the Swisshelms near Axford and Mowbry. Most evenings he would sit at their campfire and talk.

Atkins's disavowal of outlawry was not the product of a moral or spiritual conversion; he had left the gang because of "trouble he had with Tom Ketchum."

"What he told me about Tom Ketchum," Axford wrote in his old age, "convinced me that Tom was a cold-blooded murderer and a very brutal man." On the other hand, said Atkins, Sam Ketchum "was as fine a man as could be." Atkins also had "a good word" for Carver.

Atkins did not tell Axford, but implied in a short and enigmatical passage in his reminiscences, that his decision to pull out was also related in some way to the killing, on July 3, 1898, of the well-known Erie cowboy, gunslinger, and troublemaker Andy Darnell. Atkins, without naming him, called the man who killed Darnell "a little hyena." Here Atkins was a lone voice. Frank Johnson was well liked locally. He had killed Darnell in self-defense, and, in the opinion of most people, performed a public service in getting rid of him.

When the time came for Atkins to begin his journey, Axford rode alongside him for several miles. Later he received a letter from him, written in Idaho. He heard nothing more, but was sure that Atkins became a "good law-abiding citizen" because he "had the quality to make it that way."[57]

Atkins's own narrative resumes a few weeks later, after he had reached Utah. It is quite likely that he had traveled the whole distance on horseback; plenty of others had done the same. In Utah he took a job on a cattle ranch, and then accompanied the cattle by train to Pueblo, Colorado. From Pueblo he went by train to Denver, and from Denver to Shoshone, Idaho, where he was employed by a man named Rube

Brown. Here, he says, he was superintendent of the local Sunday school for six months, and looked after it "in a Christian like manner." So far, then, Mack Axford's expectations were being fulfilled. But the reminiscences are as silent on the wife and child in Texas as they are on the Ketchum brothers, who, perhaps not coincidentally, had arrived in Idaho at about the same time as he.[58]

If credence can be granted to an incident from the lively, urbane, but sometimes over-creative pen of William French, Tom and Sam must have returned to southwest New Mexico between mid-October and late November of 1898—roughly when Wells, Fargo were preparing to offer a reward for them—soon to hurry away north again, in this instance to Hole-in-the-Wall.

At the time of this occurrence, French, manager of the WS ranch at Alma, New Mexico, was on a kind of semi-vacation that took him to Ireland and the Near East. He had left Alma early in October, 1898, and returned sometime in the second half of December.

One day while he was away, French tells us, the brothers came in to the WS ranch, in western Socorro County, and asked for food and lodging. Sometime in the night they stole down to the stable and led out Rattler, French's favorite saddle horse. Next, their eyes fell covetously on a pair of horses in the pasture. These were French's buggy team. Major, the better of the two, was quickly secured; but his mate broke through the loop of the rope and would not be caught. Sam and Tom gave up trying and rode off northwards.

Major was ridden into the ground and was in such bad shape when found several days later that he had to be destroyed. Rattler, French's pet gray, was still in sound condition when, as French would have it, the Ketchums rode into Hole-in-the-Wall. No doubt the horses were stolen and overridden, as French related, but it is far from certain that the Ketchum brothers could have been the thieves. They may have been in Idaho or Wyoming when the animals were taken.[59]

Somewhere in the course of their travels in the north, one or more of the vacationers from Texas met two other notables, though perhaps not for the first time. One called "Butch," was Robert Leroy Parker, alias Cassidy. His personal and criminal history, from his birth in Utah in 1865, has been fully documented in several places, especially by Richard Patterson.[60] The other, usually addressed as "Elzy" or "Elza," was William Ellsworth Lay.

Elzy Lay was born in 1868 in Ohio, but taken to Coles County, Illinois, a few months later, and from Illinois to Union County, Iowa, before his fourth birthday.[61] There is nothing to give substance to the yarn that he had been through college, other than that he was intelligent and passably well-spoken. In the 1880s, he went to Colorado, got into some sort of trouble, and became a fugitive. Possibly he first met one or both of the Ketchums during these years of wandering the rangelands and holdouts of Wyoming, Colorado, and Utah. In 1896 he fell in with Cassidy, a bank robber and convicted rustler, just released from the Wyoming State Penitentiary, whom he had known on and off for six or seven years. The new criminal partnership of Cassidy and Lay pulled off robberies at Montpelier, Idaho, and Castle Gate, Utah. By the fall of 1898 they were ready to fade out for country where, for a while, they could pose as ordinary range hands—Cassidy as cowboy, Lay as bronco-buster.

Subsequent events indicate that they must have struck up an understanding with Carver and the Ketchums at this time; it was not random chance, but informed advice, that directed Cassidy and Lay to the Erie Land and Cattle Company in Cochise County. It was not usually easy for a ranch hand to find work during the winter months, but Cassidy and Lay would have known before leaving for Arizona that conditions at the Erie were far from the usual. The roundup then in progress would be its last. It would continue without a voluntary break until every head of cattle had been tallied and sold. This process was not expected to be completed before the end of 1899. When it was over, the Erie range would be sold and the company, dissolved.[62]

Cassidy showed up in Cochise County as "Jim Lowe" and Lay as "Will McGinnis" in November or early December, 1898. They were at once hired by Bob Johnson, the Erie superintendent. If French's story of the horse thefts and the chronological basis it imposes are accepted, the Ketchums could not have reached Hole-in-the-Wall many days before Cassidy and Lay departed. But Carver could have been there ahead of Tom and Sam, and may have been waiting for them. He, rather than they, was the likely source of the tip that persuaded Cassidy and Lay to apply for work on the Erie. But they had not been there for more than eight or ten weeks before more interesting work came their way.

William French had cut short his trip overseas. He had not crossed a continent and an ocean, with more land and water to come, merely out of a sentimental wish to see Ireland again and gawp at the sights of the Holy Land. Larcenous neighbors were steadily trimming the WS herds, unresisted by the foreman Clarence Tipton and his staff. His main reason for going to Jerusalem was the presence there of Harold Wilson, the owner of the WS. French badly needed to talk to Wilson to secure his backing for the drastic action he had in mind. French wanted the thieves curbed, and the stock rounded up, tallied, and driven northward to the railroad shipping point at Magdalena, taken by rail to Springer, and there unloaded and transferred to the northern pastures of the WS, by the Vermejo and Ponil.[63]

That was the plan discussed and formalized by the worried owner and his manager. French left Jerusalem before the middle of November, returned to Ireland for a few days, and was back in Alma by about Christmas time. In short order he had received Tipton's resignation and got rid of most of the other employees; persuaded Perry Tucker to leave the Erie and return to his old job as WS foreman; and, through Tucker, drafted a crew of men who could be relied upon to squelch the local rustlers.

Cassidy and Lay were among the first recruits. By February, 1899, they and three other Erie hands—Mack Axford, Jim James, and Clay McGonagill—had moved on to the WS, in response to a letter from Tucker. Tom Capehart and Bruce Weaver, free of their respective troubles in Las Cruces and Las Vegas, joined at about the same time.[64]

Carver and the Ketchums reappeared in the border southwest not long after Cassidy and Lay joined the WS. French was furious with the Ketchums for having stolen and maltreated two of his best horses, and neither they nor Carver were so tactless as to be seen near the WS ranch house. This did not prevent them from holding discussions with Cassidy, Lay, and Weaver.

Will Carver stood well with both Cassidy and Lay. But Cassidy's perspective on the Ketchums differed from Lay's. Butch had no use for either brother, and counseled his friend to have no dealings with them; Lay evidently thought well of Sam—most people did—and would have been prepared to work with Tom. Lay, against Cassidy's advice, agreed to join the Ketchums, Carver, and Weaver in robbing a train.[65]

By the spring of 1899, however, Tom Ketchum had about run his course as leader of a band of outlaws.

Friction had been mounting for some time, with the traits of meanness and surliness in Tom Ketchum's uneven temperament the prime source of it. Dave Atkins had left because of it.

Despite the tensions, the other three, mounted on horses stolen from the Erie, set out together across New Mexico.

This may have been the juncture at which Robert W. "Stuttering Bob" Lewis, foreman of the N-Bar-N in western Socorro County, who had known the Ketchums in San Saba County, was approached by Tom and two companions, all needing fresh horses. When Lewis replied that he had no horses to spare, Tom overbore him by threatening to take every horse in the corral unless Lewis cut three good mounts at once. The three men switched their saddles to the N-Bar-N horses, but did not let go of the animals on which they had arrived. As they were leaving, Tom pitched $320— or three twenty-dollar pieces?—at Lewis's feet. Lewis found his horses a few days later, not far from where the outlaws had abandoned them.[66] Evidently their plan had been to rest the horses they had "borrowed" in Arizona.

The three continued east, almost to the Texas line. Only two of them were to keep their appointment with Elzy Lay.

SEPARATE WAYS

On or about May 3, 1899, one of the three men was seen on the TX pastures, some thirty miles east of Roswell. His partners must have been close at hand for, barely a day later, three mounts were stolen from the nearby LFD horse camp, and the three Erie animals left in their place. Then, on May 6, the outlaws swapped the LFD horses for three from the—V (Bar V) ranch of the Cass Land and Cattle Company, north of Roswell. W.G. Urton, manager and part owner of the company and a former employer of the Ketchums, was particularly incensed because the thieves had killed one of his horses: when caught, it broke away with the rope and the outlaw, in a fit of irrational fury, had shot the animal. Sheriff Fred Higgins and his deputy, Will Rainbolt, were reported to have trailed the thieves closely; but they were never close enough to be seen by them.[1]

This is the last occasion on which the three outlaws were together. Very soon afterwards Tom Ketchum was either thrown out or deserted by the others. His sullen moods, charged with sudden paroxysms of savage rage, had become intolerable to them; even to Sam, who knew him best. Will Carver and Sam Ketchum were outlaws and desperadoes; if either of them were pressed to the point where he felt he had to kill a man, he would kill him and suffer few qualms or none. But neither would kill upon impulse, and neither was inclined to destructive tantrums. Dave Atkins had quit the gang because he could take no more of Tom Ketchum's brutal and quarrelsome nature. When Carver spoke to Axford some months afterwards, he explained his and Sam's decision to "divide blankets" with Tom in the same terms.[2]

After parting company with Tom Ketchum, Sam and Carver headed for Turkey Canyon to await the arrival of Elzy Lay. Every so often they would visit Cimarron or Elizabethtown to pick up a few supplies, take a few drinks, or play a few hands of Poker. James K. Hunt, the postmaster and principal merchant of Cimarron, first saw them in town during the latter part of May.[3]

It was probably during the first days of that month that Lay told William French he was leaving the WS, his pretext being that there were no more horses to be broken "and he did not much care for any other class of employment." Red Weaver quit at the same time. They traveled from Magdalena to Springer with a trainload of WS cattle for the new ranch on the Ponil. This was their last service for French, and it fitted in well with their plans.[4]

Weaver lazed about on the ranch for a while. Lay went directly back into Springer, stopping there until about the seventh of June, and then proceeding to Cimarron. According to George Crocker, foreman of the Red River Cattle Company, who had been raised in Cimarron and was then on a visit to his former home town, Lay put up at the St. James Hotel. Postmaster Hunt saw him shortly after he came into Cimarron and kept him in mind.

Red, meanwhile, had contracted smallpox. He was taken to Springer and placed in the ramshackle structure that served as the local pesthouse. Evidently he had fully recovered by the twelfth of June, for he and Lay were seen together in Cimarron on or about that day. Soon after this, Lay went to the house of Agapito Duran. He boarded there for a week or so. He dealt Monte at Charretta's saloon but otherwise appeared to be inactive. Occasionally Sam or Will would ride into town, but they and "McGinnis" affected not to know one another.[5]

The first time anyone in Cimarron ever saw "McGinnis" or "the Red man" in the company of the other two strangers was one day near the end of June, when Lay returned to Duran's place, bringing Carver with him. The gang must have met nearby a short time previously, most likely in Turkey Creek Canyon, Ponil Park, or Ute Park.[6]

Carver, giving his name as "G.W. Franks" and his address as "Simerone," wrote to James Correy, a storekeeper in Springer, ordering two forty-inch rifle scabbards and enclosing a five dollar bill in payment. He also wrote to Denver for certain other essentials: one .30-40 carbine and one thousand rounds of .30-40 smokeless ammunition. They were duly shipped to him by those dependable agents, Wells, Fargo and Company. The gun was for Lay. After a stay of four or five nights the two outlaws rode away from Duran's.[7]

From all that was officially disclosed, only two men in Cimarron seem to have been suspicious of or perturbed by the comings and goings of the strangers. One was James H. "Billy" Morgan, a freighter, on-and-off cowboy, once-upon-a-time Texas Ranger, and part-of-the-time private detective, who had recently been in the employ of the WS. He had known Ketchum and Carver, was aware of their association with Lay, and may have guessed the reason for it. The other was the watchful postmaster, Jim Hunt: he thought they meant to rob his store.[8]

But the two are unlikely to have been alone with their suspicions. Lay aside, the visitors were the men whose faces had been seen in the area over a period of some weeks prior to the train robbery of September 3, 1897. Those who recognized them, or thought they did, would not all have stayed silent about it.[9]

Ernest Ludlum, Hunt's nephew and assistant, recalled in later years that "old Sam Ketchum got very well tanked up one day" and "commenced getting tough with me and cussed me out" for not having a flannel shirt in his size. "Franks," as was his habit, was sitting outside on the sidewalk "with his hat pulled down almost over his eyes." In Ludlum's telling of the story, he got up and entered the store just as Sam was "acting ugly," and shut him up. By then, Ludlum wrote, "we knew who they were and

I have always respected Franks for what he had done for me," because Sam, "in a drunken stupor," might have taken it into his befuddled head to kill him.[10]

True? Partly true? We cannot be sure. But it is obvious that the plotters stayed too long in Cimarron and made themselves too noticeable for their own good.

In the meantime, officials in newly-formed Otero County had other, and lesser, outlaws to deal with. Three of them, led by Ernest Gentry, had robbed the pay-master's office of the Alamogordo Lumber Company on April 10.[11] Then a posse from Eddy County, headed by Sheriff Miles Cicero Stewart and including Constable Dee Harkey, caught up with another band of five men on May 1, in western Otero County, and captured four of them on the morning of the 2nd. By mischief or mis-chance, one was at first identified as Tom Ketchum. The four were Charles Ware; Dan Johnson, an uncle of the Musgrave boys; Sam Morrow, the one errant member of a well respected family; and, last and worst, James Knight (or Nite), alias Jim Jones, alias Jack Underwood, one of Bill Dalton's gang in the bank robbery at Longview, Texas, an old acquaintance of Will and Bob Christian in the Indian Nations, but now on the run from the Texas penitentiary. Hillary Loftis (or Loftus), alias Tom Ross, who in north Texas and the Nations had enjoyed the dubious benefit of having much the same circle of friends as Jim Knight, was the one that got away. Three of those taken by Stewart's posse—all but Knight—were on the loose again within a short time.[12]

Tom Ketchum himself was now more dangerous and more elusive than ever before. His statement, nearly two years later, that he was somewhere in the Sacramento Mountains during this time was, no doubt, a characteristic half truth: he might indeed have traversed the Tularosa country at least once in the spring of 1899, but he did not loiter there. If he was guilty of the next misdeed attributed to him—and such evidence as survives argues strongly that he was—he passed late spring and early summer in central Arizona.

The crime in question was an atrocious double murder in Yavapai County, Arizona, two hundred miles from any point where Ketchum is known to have been at any time previously, unless it is true that he had once worked on the Hash Knife ranch. The Hash Knife headquarters were near Holbrook, within eighty miles of the scene of the crime.[13]

R.M. "Mack" Rogers, a native of Arkansas, had lived in Texas for some years before joining relatives in the Verde Valley of central Arizona. In 1898 he went into partnership with Clinton D. Wingfield to purchase the old sutler's store at the former cavalry post called Camp Verde. Rogers was then a little over thirty, several years older than Clint Wingfield. Although good natured, and well-liked in and around Camp Verde, the two young merchants were said to be subject to fits of cyclonic rage and to have shown themselves to be grasping and unscrupulous in transactions further afield.

In the spring of 1899 Rogers made another enemy when he helped the author-ities to build up a case against Oscar Wade, an alleged horse-thief. After the jury had voted him free, Wade "made threats of getting even" with Rogers. Wade, who was well known in Camp Verde, did not try to carry out his declared intentions; and the question of whether he seriously meant to seek revenge was nullified by the intervention of someone else whose designs may have been similar.[14]

As twilight settled into nightfall on Sunday, July 2, 1899, Rogers and the clerk, Lou Turner, went out onto the porch to chat with the mail carrier and Captain John Boyd, a retired cavalry officer. Wingfield was in a bedroom, working on some papers. Somewhat after eight o'clock a man stepped up to the porch, walking so softly that the others saw him before they heard him. After the latecomer had seated himself in the porch he exchanged a few commonplace remarks with Boyd and the mail carrier. Rogers then got to his feet to close the store. He may or may not have asked the newcomer whether he wanted supplies; he seemed to have recognized the man, and saw that he was in trouble when the visitor ordered him to lead the way inside. As the storekeeper sprang through the doorway and ran for his six-shooter, the other man was no more than a pace or two behind.

"That won't do, Mack!" he called out. Rogers ran into a rear room, where a lighted candle was standing on the safe. He had no chance to escape or arm himself. The intruder's bullet, fired point blank at his head, broke his neck.

Wingfield started to his feet and hurried out to investigate. He might have asked himself whether the discharge could have come from a premature firecracker, and decided it was too loud and too near, before rushing for the front door. A moment later a revolver bullet tore through his stomach and smashed his spine, felling him as he crossed the threshold.

Without pausing to loot the place, the killer dashed out onto the porch as one of the onlookers started to lift Wingfield, declaring that he would "kill them all while he was at it" if they did not scatter. Boyd, a cripple, moved too slowly to satisfy the gunman, who sent a shot after him. The old man was wounded slightly in the leg, probably from a ricochet. Then the killer hastened on foot toward the stream, a mile away, stopping on the way only to eject the shells from his pistol and to reload.

One of the bystanders, Harvey Hance, mounted Clint Wingfield's "big fine sorrel" and rode to summon help from Prescott, forty-five miles distant. Sheriff John L. Munds, of Yavapai County, left at once with a deputy.

Wingfield lived for about two hours after he was shot. In that time he warned his twenty-two year old brother, Frank, not to go out after the killer. The death of Rogers had been instantaneous. Both were buried on the Fourth.[15]

Frank Wingfield ignored his dying brother's advice; if anything he was all too prominent in the manhunt, antagonizing possemen and settlers by his headstrong and domineering manner.

Although the search was lengthy and extensive, it was an ill-organized, harum-scarum effort during its first vital days. Almost at once the Camp Verde party ascertained that the killer was fleeing on an unshod horse, which he had tethered to a willow nearly a mile from the store. At first the trail was clear; then, at Mud Tanks Hill, east of the village, it was lost amidst the tracks of a herd of wild horses.

Sheriff Munds now arrived to take charge of the pursuit. He and the posse found what they thought was good sign and followed it north until, once again, it vanished.

But it led in the general direction of Charlie Bishop's cabin on the Mogollon Rim, and suspicion fastened on him.

Bishop had moved north from the Tonto Basin in 1887, after the death of his father, William Bishop, during the Graham-Tewksbury feud. More recently he had worked in western New Mexico. He was now living alone in a cabin on the Rim, between Camp Verde and Payson.

Charlie was innocent of the killings; but he did own the barefoot horse ridden by the murderer. Warned by instinct or information, he had kept well ahead of the posse and was not at home when the Munds posse rode up, though three hobbled horses were grazing in the meadow. Fresh impetus was given to the hunt by a report from two settlers that they had seen a rider, who may or may not have been Bishop. The unshod tracks were located and followed north of the cabin for five miles, where the trail ended with the discovery of the horse, unsaddled and placidly munching grass.[16]

Next day, the posse arrested Robert Lee Cutberth (or Cutbirth, or Cuthbert) and William H. Cameron. At the time, they were described as prospectors. Frank Wingfield, as quoted years afterwards, was blunter: "One was a horse thief and the other was no good."[17]

Another arrest followed in mid-July, when William Rose, a cowboy, was stopped between the Tonto Basin and Globe after being tailed for four days. He was taken "overland through the mountains" to Prescott, where he protested that he had heard nothing about the murders until several days after their occurrence. His only connection with the case appears to have been that he was a lone horseman who happened to have been noticed in the same general area as the scene of the crime.[18]

Cutberth and Cameron were thought to have more of a case to answer. It was one that, far from producing a solution, merely created a minor diversion. Even if both were thieves, or just unquantifiably "no good," neither was a murderer, nor wittingly an accomplice to murder. They were taken to Flagstaff, seat of Coconino County, and sent on to Prescott, where they were released on bond. Only after the withdrawal of all charges did they admit to having helped Bishop get away. Their explanation was simple: they were sure of his innocence. They might also have feared for his safety if he fell into the hands of the Camp Verde people, whose mood was ugly. As Elmer Jones remembered sixty-four years later, "I never saw a community more worked up. Had that murderer been caught he'd have swung from the tallest tree and no questions asked."[19] The unasked questions could have included one seeking to know the distinction between a proven killer and a mere suspect.

Bishop made his way to friends in the Payson vicinity. He stayed in hiding until the belief that the guilt lay elsewhere became both official and general.

Probably the man who abandoned the barefoot horse was the killer. When his trail showed again, he was riding a shod horse near Chevelon Canyon, twenty miles south of Winslow and sixty miles east of Camp Verde. He tried to conceal his route by covering the bed of each cooking fire with a large flat stone.[20]

The following anecdote, from Albert Thompson, has an authentic ring but, for want of corroboration, must be taken as standing somewhere betwixt hearsay and evidence.

A posse was formed at Camp Verde and the trail of the suspected assailant of Rogers and Wingate [*sic*] followed. The posse stumbled onto the camping place of the murderer. Here they found scrawled with a lead pencil: "Boys, I know you are after me. I'll be back in two or three hours and if not I'll be four miles north gathering bees." "How did you happen to write that, Tom?" asked District Attorney Leahy afterwards, in Clayton. "Oh, hell, I thought I'd like to have 'em know which way I'd gone so, when I left the place where I camped that night, I wrote a few lines on a cracker box for whoever might find it."[21]

Munds sent back most of the posse, including Frank Wingfield and his cousin, Ed. With a handful of riders he followed the suspect southeast, through Springerville, and across the New Mexico line before the trail disappeared near the Plains of San Augustin. There was little to guide them except a fair general description of the killer, his horse, his saddle, and reports that he was toting a Navajo blanket of a very distinctive and unusual design. They continued to look for a fresh lead in western New Mexico, enquiring after Bishop in the Luna Valley and the Upper Frisco Plaza, where he had formerly been employed. Towards the end of August, Munds was at a sheep ranch in Socorro County when he learned from a newspaper that Tom Ketchum had been arrested near Folsom.[22]

During these weeks a motley of discreditable (and mostly scurrilous) stories about Rogers and Clint Wingfield gave rise to, or were inspired by, all manner of surmise. Gossip dies hard, and the tales circulating in the valley were not stifled when, late in August, Sheriff Munds produced what he regarded as good evidence that the much-sought assassin was Thomas E. Ketchum.[23]

Whether Ketchum made the journey to Camp Verde especially to kill Rogers, whether he expected a friendly reception and started shooting only because Rogers tried to arm himself, or even whether two old enemies had been unexpectedly brought face to face by sheer coincidence, are unresolved questions. Nor, though robbery seems from most accounts not to have been attempted, is it certain that none was intended or, indeed, accomplished. If Ketchum had worked on the Hash Knife ranch, his shadow may have crossed that of Rogers; a meeting between the two might have produced a dispute. But a possibility dependent on a possibility does not amount to a plausibility. A competing possibility is that the secret underlying the bloody work of those few seconds is hidden in whatever past Mack Rogers left behind him in Texas. The simplest explanation is that, irrespective of whether he knew the storekeepers, the visitor intended only to buy or steal.[24]

As to the murder of Wingfield, the fact that he was ruthlessly shot down when unarmed—whereas the three bystanders, who could just as well have been killed too, and may indeed have been threatened with death, were in the end merely ordered to make themselves scarce—does not begin to prove that the murderer carried a grudge against him or even knew him. Wingfield had startled the intruder by bursting into the store from the side room; so he was shot, without any hesitation and probably without very much thought.

Two motives were open to the killer, though he may not have had time to for-
mulate either. One was that, for all he knew, Wingfield might have been armed; and
the safest way of settling that problem would be to kill him as soon as he showed.
The other was the need to eliminate a witness who was about to confront him in a
lighted room.

William Reno never doubted Tom Ketchum's guilt. In April, 1901, he gave the
Denver Republican a version of the affair which differed sharply from the one first
heard in Arizona and still generally accepted:

> "Tom" Ketchum came in and sat on the counter until it was time to close the place.
> When Rogers said to him "We'll have to close the place now," he replied "All right," and
> jumping down from the counter, shot and killed Winfield [*sic*], who was standing a
> few feet away, then shot down Rogers, Another man named Jones [John Boyd?], who
> put his head in to see what was going on, was shot and severely wounded. Then
> Ketchum robbed the store, mounted his horse, and rode away unmolested.[25]

Reno did not identify his sources. He would have heard something of the views
and findings of the officials most concerned with the case, but, like most people, was
not gifted with a perfect memory. All other accounts agree that Rogers and his killer
met on the porch, not at the counter.

In more recent years, the premise that Tom Ketchum was the author of the
Camp Verde killings has been disputed.[26] Yet, in the late summer and autumn of
1899, officials in Prescott and Phoenix were convinced that he was the man they
wanted. Their opinion was shared by the grand jury that indicted him.

Yet so tenaciously had the killings clung to the name of Charlie Bishop that it
was incorporated in the bill of indictment as Ketchum's alias.[27] Bishop's disappearance before Ketchum's name entered the case may have infected the minds of the
county attorney and grand jury with the belief that Bishop was merely an alias for
Ketchum. The history of the entanglement of identities seems to have been something like this:

For several weeks preceding the murders, a man had been camping near Johnny
Merritt's cabin, on the Rim above Payson. The stranger regularly went into Payson
for supplies, often purchasing ammunition. He was a fine shot with rifle and revolver,
using saplings for target practice. Bishop's place was nearby and he probably borrowed Charlie's unshod horse for the ride to Camp Verde. Since the animal was later
abandoned near Bishop's place, the killer is likely to have left his own horse either
there or at Merritt's. Apparently Frank Wingfield, and others, assumed at first that
Bishop was the mysterious marksman who subsequently traveled to Camp Verde and
killed the two storekeepers.[28]

Thus, when the news broke that Tom Ketchum was under arrest, and Munds
produced evidence that the notorious train robber was also the Camp Verde double
murderer, it was assumed that Bishop was merely one of Ketchum's aliases. The misconception persisted until the real Charlie Bishop came out of hiding.

Bishop might have let Ketchum borrow his horse, and he or Merritt may have hunted with him and let him graze his own horses on their pasture. One or both of them may have known Tom in the past. If so, they would have been aware of his criminality. These things taken together—and all of them are conjectural—fall far short of collusion in murder.[29]

When the hubbub died away, Bishop went back to his old home in Pleasant Valley, where he spent the rest of his life.[30]

It was through no lack of effort on their part that the Arizona courts were denied their right to decide whether or not Tom Ketchum was the guilty party. Ketchum's future was unaffected. An Arizona rope, after all, would not have differed overmuch from the one they were measuring him for in New Mexico.

{ 12 }

ANOTHER INCIDENT
AT TWIN MOUNTAINS

By the end of the first week of July, 1899, Sam Ketchum and party were almost ready to leave Cimarron. On Friday, the seventh, Sam and Carver bought supplies at Jim Hunt's store and stashed them away in Turkey Creek Canyon. Hunt, all eyes and ears, learned they had gone in the direction of Dean Canyon; in effect, the back door of their hideout. Lay and Weaver spent Friday night at Duran's and whiled away Saturday forenoon in the bar of "Lambert's saloon"—the name commonly given to the St. James Hotel. Early in the afternoon, Weaver settled up with Duran and rode off northeast. He had told Duran that he was going to pick up his "traps" from the WS ranch, but did not call there. Lay left at the same time, heading northwest for Ponil Park. This may have been a feint; he had plenty of time to change course and join the others in time for the planned robbery.

On Monday, July 10, the gang camped in the mountains, eighteen miles west of the railroad. Thomas Owen, of Folsom, writing many years later, identified the site as "the Daugherty Spring at the head of Dry Canyon about four miles from the XYZ ranch." He said that George McJunkin, a cowboy on the Owen family's Hereford Park ranch, came upon them and "decided that" one of them had to be "a boy raised in Johnson Park" who was able to tag McJunkin's horse as a six-year old because he "had known this particular horse from [when it was] a colt." In fact, none of the Ketchum gang had any family connection with the Johnson Park area.[1]

No sooner had the men left Cimarron than the cowboy-teamster-detective, James Morgan, reported his suspicions to Marshal Foraker (though not to Robert Campbell, the sheriff of Colfax County) and tried to get on the trail of the gang.[2] He was too slow: on the night of Tuesday, the 11th, train no. 1 of the Colorado and Southern Railway (the renamed and reorganized Union Pacific, Denver and Gulf Railroad) was held up and robbed by three or, more probably, four men. The robbery occurred at almost the same place as the one in September of 1897 and was accomplished in almost the same fashion. Among the passengers were two sheriffs: Fred Higgins of Chaves County and Saturnino Pinard of Union County. Frank E. Harrington was the conductor, as on the occasion of the previous stickup.

A good many railroad men were held up by robbers more than once. At the annual conventions they liked to fill the notebooks of the reporters with facetious and light-hearted recountals of their adventures with the bandits.[3] Harrington did not belong to this school of thought. It still rankled with him that he had been unable to intervene on the earlier occasion. The proceedings on the night of July 11, 1899 did nothing to make him a happier man.[4]

Train no. 1 steamed out of Denver at 11:20 that Tuesday morning, on time. At 10:10 p.m. two of the gang slipped aboard the blind baggage while the engine was being replenished at Folsom tank. Just as the locomotive was crossing the south switch, a little way beyond the station, Fireman Howard was distracted by the noise of a piece of coal rattling down from the tender. He threw a glance over his shoulder just as Elzy Lay stepped into the left hand side of the cab and pressed a six-shooter against him.

"Don't make any bad breaks," advised the outlaw. As the engineer, J.A. Tubbs, began to turn his head towards the disturbance he felt the barrel of a revolver touch his cheek. He took a quick look behind him and saw Sam Ketchum standing there.

Because "the engine was rocking some" and "the fellow was trying to steady himself," Tubbs at first took Sam to be "a drunken tramp who was trying to run a sandy." About the revolver he was under no misapprehension.

"Go ahead. I'll tell you where to stop," bellowed Sam, jabbing the gun into the engineers's ribs.

Five miles out of Folsom, as the train was gathering momentum for the grade at the great double-horseshoe bend through Twin Mountains, Sam spoke again:

"Stop where the last holdup was."

"I don't know where the last holdup was," Tubbs protested.

"There'll be a fire on the left hand side of the track," Sam replied, "Stop there."

Nearly two miles further along the track, as they entered the cut leading to the level ground beyond the curve, they saw the fire. Carver, lying behind a rock a dozen feet away from the fire, already had the train covered. Three horses were tied to a snow fence on the side of the track; nearby was a fourth horse, and probably a fourth man, Weaver. Less than a quarter of a mile away—in Harrington's judgment, the distance was only a hundred yards—was the scene of the first Folsom robbery.

"I intended to fall out the window after bringing the train to a standstill," Tubbs declared, later; but when the time came to jump, he concluded that it might be safer to stay where he was. Sam then motioned the two trainmen to step down ahead of him on the left hand side. Lay quickly crossed the cab and alighted from the right hand side.

By now Carver's voice and carbine were in action. "Come out of there, God damn you," he bawled at the unseen messenger. When there was no immediate response he fired a shot or two into the express car, yelling: "Open up! Come out of there!"

Sam marched Tubbs and Howard to the express car "to protect the robbers in case the messenger should do a little shooting." Just to make sure that he did not, the trainmen hollered out for him to hold his fire. It was well for the fireman that he did;

he was on his first run and the messenger, Hamel P. Scott, did not know him and was covering him with a shotgun.

Shots were ringing out from both sides of the train as Scott, having given up all idea of armed resistance, hurriedly unlocked the way safe and flung the railroad mail and most of the currency among the merchandise in the car: there was a far greater sum in the through safe, which he could not open. Then he unbarred the doors and got out.

One of the robbers took the messenger's place and ordered the bag containing the "giant" (dynamite) to be handed up to him. Lay, as Scott recalled it, "was helping to make us step around as they pleased" while the bandit in the car—probably Carver—was preparing the explosives.

When the train stopped Fred Higgins had asked Harrington to turn out all the lights in the coaches. Each of the sheriffs was wearing a pistol, and between them they had fourteen cartridges. They pointed out to the indignant conductor that a couple of six-shooters would be no match for an uncounted number of rifles. Their fellow passengers agreed; they had no wish to occupy the middle ground in a shooting match. Harrington, who was armed with nothing save anger and determination, at once proposed that they steal out of the coach, find the horses, and cut the hitching ropes.

The three men were still making their plans when the robbers touched off the fuse. The first detonation failed, but, with forty or fifty sticks of dynamite in reserve, the marauders were undismayed. They prepared for a second assault upon the through safe. A few seconds later a vast explosion cleft the big safe and heaved chunks of wreckage in all directions. When Harrington examined the express car, after the robbery, he saw that "the big safe had a hole in it about as big as a common soup bowl . . . it was blown down like someone had thrust a pile through it." The roof of the car, he observed, "was pulled back just like you peel a banana." Tubbs also had a good look. "Money and [railroad] mail was strewn all over the inside of the express car," he told a reporter two days later.

The outlaws removed every box and package from the safe and dumped them on the ground. They missed nothing except some loose bills. A consignment of pears was found amid the shambles and shared out between all hands, including the train men. Later, a carton of peaches was similarly doled out. Then, as Tubbs related it, one of the gang proffered a flask of whiskey and asked him to drink their health. This, said Tubbs, he declined to do; so they told him that it made no difference, and drank to themselves. "Those train robbers were not such bad fellows," Tubbs allowed, in describing his unwanted adventure a couple of days afterwards. All the same, he and his fellow employees were "a badly frightened crowd."

Carver, however, was irritated by the delay, and started to curse his companions, telling them they "didn't know enough to rob an ox train." Finally Tubbs, Howard, and Scott were escorted to the locomotive and ordered to pull out.

While the outlaws were looting the express car, Harrington and the two sheriffs crept nearer to the horses. They were still thirty yards short when the bandits started towards them. Fred Higgins made the most of his vantage point by taking careful note of everything the robbers did. In narrating his experiences to a newspaperman he seems to have remembered everything except the part played by Sheriff Pinard as a fellow-spectator:

"The robbers' horses were hitched near the track and with the conductor I crawled to the place and made as close an examination of the horses, saddles, etc., as the darkness would permit, and remained near the spot until the robbers returned. They seemed to have a great many packages and bundles and were some time getting them tied on their saddles. There were three horses and I think I recognized all three of the parties. I was armed only with a pistol and could not afford to fire in the open, exposing myself and the conductor to the guns of the gang. The passengers were badly frightened, and asked me not to shoot from the car, which would have been useless, as I could not see the robbers from that position."[5]

As the locomotive started to pull away, the bandits mounted and headed south into the darkness, marking their retreat with the customary six-shooter salvo. Higgins and his companions could choose between relief at being unnoticed by the gang and mortification at finding themselves in much the same situation as that in which they had hoped to place the outlaws. Fortunately for them, Tubbs soon stopped the train; the displaced roof of the express car was dragging and needed to be hacked away.[6]

Those "packages and bundles" carried away by the gang had contained a large sum of money—no less, probably, than the $70,000 reported to Governor Otero and at least $50,000, the figure mentioned in another generally well-informed compilation.[7]

News of the holdup reached Denver only narrowly ahead of announcements by the local express and railroad superintendents that no money had been taken. At Trinidad, on the morning of the 13th, Hamel Scott bustled in with an assertion that the road agents had not secured a cent of the company's cash. He could vouch for that; he had hidden the money from the way safe, which, moreover, "did not contain more than $100 in all." Company officials in Denver blandly explained that the messenger had concealed all the money before the robbers entered the car to blow the safe, and that nothing had been stolen except a saddle tree.

As an attempt at evasion this resembled and was as sublimely inept as the one fabricated after the Comstock robbery. Scott really had hidden the money from the small safe; the one blasted to pieces by the outlaws was the through safe, which could be unlocked only by certain station agents. Scott did not mention the through safe at all.

At first several of the Denver papers followed the official line, but the *Republican*, citing "[p]arties who claim to know," spoke of "a large amount of money in the express safe as well as valuable express matter." Within twenty-four hours, the Republican story was substantiated by Tubbs's description of the looting of the express car, and by the reports of the witnesses who had watched the bandits loading their packhorse with booty. Aside from all of which, the way safe money probably would not have escaped the attention of the robbers, anyway. Scott had thrown it among the boxes of fruit which the bandits later drew upon for refreshments.

Wells, Fargo doggedly maintained its pretense that it had lost nothing of value. When, on July 16, C.H. Young, the manager of the company's Denver office, repeated the corporate denial, with added detail for added emphasis, the *Rocky Mountain News* responded with renewed skepticism:

> Notwithstanding Mr. Young's statement, it is generally understood around the railroad offices that the thieves made more than good wages for their dangerous work, although the exact amount has been suppressed.[8]

The railroad's chief detective, William Reno, customarily stated that the amount of the money stolen by the bandits was "not known." In truth, he must have had a good idea of how much was taken.[9]

Reports of the affair were riddled with contradictory statements, as was usual after a highway robbery carried out after nightfall.

Most onlookers stated there were four of the robbers. Higgins, Pinard, and Harrington had seen only three horses and three bandits. Engineer Tubbs—unwilling to belittle the perils that had beset him—first swore that there were ten in the gang; some months later, he admitted in court that he had seen no more than three. Others said that one of the horses was carrying double as the men rode off. Someone else was reported as having noticed but two horses.

Juan C. Martinez, who lived near the scene of the holdup, soon came forward with the statement that at 6:00 a.m. on the day of the robbery he had seen three mounted men, one of them leading an extra horse, traveling east, towards the railroad. Three hours later, Martinez added, he had seen them camped on a hill half a mile from the tracks. At eleven o'clock, it developed, Juan Maria Apodaca, another local man, had ridden past the camp; he saw four horses, but only two men. He had stopped by to make enquiries about some strayed livestock of his own. Although, in due course, he was to identify Lay as one of this pair, it is much likelier that the two men were Carver and Weaver. The outlaws, at this time, had "one roan horse and three dark-colored horses."[10] Somewhere along their backtrail was a fifth horse, a gray.

Probably the first of the two men who were to board the locomotive at Folsom had been set down afoot before the party was encountered by Martinez. The second man must have left in mid-morning, meeting the other not far from Folsom station. Some hours later Carver had ridden down from camp leading two of the other horses, and had built the fire beside the tracks. The horses were tied to the fence alongside the railroad right-of-way. Weaver may have remained on the bank or at one end of the cut as a lookout. Later he would have gone down to join the others.

Although Harrington and other witnesses had seen only three horses, officers who examined the ground the following morning found the tracks of four; obviously, the fourth must have been by the fence at some stage. The heaviest articles extracted from the express car may have been placed on one saddle horse, which would at first have been used as a pack animal. That, at least, would explain the statement that one of the horses was carrying two men. Presumably it would not have had to do so beyond first light, when the men could pause to take stock of the packages and boxes and divide their weight more evenly between the four of them.

The four men rode directly west. They traveled in easy stages, knowing there was no east-west telegraphic or telephonic link between Folsom and Raton or Springer.

Shortly before nine o'clock on the night of the 12th, the four appeared at the horse camp of Roth's XL ranch, just east of Raton and less than thirty miles west of Twin Mountain. Here they stopped for "a bite to eat and some feed for their horses." Jack Stockbridge, the camp tender, "sized 'em up" as he prepared, and they consumed, a supper of beef, sourdough bread, and coffee. "Each one of them had a damn good horse and a good saddle, good outfit . . . and plenty of ammunition." One man had a long barreled .30-40 Winchester rifle; the rest of them, he thought, had .30-30s.

He was wrong: at least two of the three also had the .30-40. Probably these were of the carbine length preferred by most riders, and hence easily mistaken in indifferent light for the familiar .30-30 saddle gun.

After feeding them, Stockbridge invited them (or agreed to let them) sleep in the house. The four "took turn about watching," so that three at a time could sleep while the fourth kept guard. Jack did not sleep much. He had heard about the robbery—news of it had been telegraphed from Trinidad to Raton early that morning, and broadcast by word of mouth—and felt sure that his guests were the guilty parties. What ought he to do?

The visitors did not wait for the sun to rise. By four o'clock the obliging Stockbridge had served them a light breakfast and they were on their way.

As daylight came, Jack made up his mind. He told himself that the robbers "seemed like pretty nice fellows" and that he would help them all he could. Their departing tracks stood out clearly on the softened surface of ground watered by the recent rains. Stockbridge took good care of that problem by turning the twenty or thirty XL horses out of the corral and chasing them "around the ranch there" until they had destroyed the evidence of the bandits' coming and going.[11]

The outlaws stayed on course for the Ponil country. Just north of Springer, near the WS ranch, Weaver left the party. The other three went on to Turkey Creek Canyon, thirty miles further west. They still had four horses; but now these comprised a roan, two bays, and a gray.[12] The gang may have intended to hole up in the canyon for a day or two before riding down to Alma. None of them guessed that Morgan was already reporting to Foraker, or that he and Hunt had studied them over a period of several weeks and at once connected them with the train robbery.[13]

Foraker at once wired through a formal request to Washington for authority to send out a posse of five.[14] He then organized a posse without waiting for permission. This posse consisted in the first instance of only one man, Wilson "Memphis" Elliott. He was called a deputy United States marshal; but this was just a courtesy title, since he was only sworn in as a posseman, without being given a regular commission.[15]

The Colorado and Southern Railway reacted even more swiftly. Si Rainey, secretary to General Superintendent T.F. Dunaway, was awakened at 3 a.m. by a messenger with a telegram. William Reno was roused from his bed shortly afterwards, and at once made ready to go south. A force of twelve was mustered overnight in Walsenburg and Trinidad and taken to Folsom on a special train. Among the dozen were Sheriff Edward J. Farr, of Huerfano County, and Deputy Sheriff George

Titsworth, of Las Animas County. None of the party enjoyed any official standing in New Mexico; but the railway was looking after all expenses, which meant that Reno was in charge.[16]

Wells, Fargo were slower off the mark. Their Denver superintendent, C.H. Young, did not ask the C & S for a special train. He waited instead until 11:20, for the regular southbound express.[17] But he would not be heading the company's part in the investigation. That role would be assumed by John Thacker, who was being sent out from San Francisco.

A few days later Reno and several of his party were to join Foraker. Hardly less violent and dramatic than the battle that ensued when seven of the officers sprang a surprise upon the outlaws in Turkey Canyon was the barrage of accusation and recrimination afterwards hurled back and forth among the possemen themselves. Swept aside by the flood of sensation and controversy was the question of how the posse came to locate the gang that Sunday afternoon, July 16, 1899.

❄ 13 ❄

BULLETS IN TURKEY
CREEK CANYON

Posses led by Sheriff Saturnino Pinard and Special Officer Reno were in the saddle by mid-afternoon on the 12th. From the spot along the railroad right-of-way where the robbers had tethered their four horses, the posses followed the gang's westerly line of retreat. For a while the trail was blotted out because "there had been sheep all over the country," but when it reappeared it was still pointing "pretty due west." The posses had followed it for more than fifteen miles when, at 6 p.m., a driving rain extinguished all sign and forced them to seek shelter. Reno and the men with him passed the night in a ranch house.

There, or nearby, they learned that on Monday evening the gang had set up camp at Daugherty Spring. In the morning the officers inspected the campsite; then, having found "nothing of consequence," they moved on towards Johnson Mesa, a further ten miles west.

The downpour that had washed out the robbers' original trail now ensured that the softened ground would preserve the tracks they made on the morning after the rainfall. Farr and two other Colorado men—probably Reno and Titsworth—ran onto the tracks and were approaching Stockbridge's camp when the trail vanished under a chaos of XL hoofmarks.

Quite undeceived, the trio rode up to the corral and house. It was getting on for 9 a.m: nearly five hours after the robbers' departure.

Had Stockbridge seen any strangers lately?

He replied that he had not.

"Well," rejoined Farr, "We trailed some fellows, four men on horseback, to this place. So what happened to them?"

Stockbridge again denied having seen the men, or knowing anything about them: "I wasn't here all the time . . . They probably come by while I was in the pasture. I never paid no attention."

"Didn't you see any fresh tracks around here?" Farr persisted.

Stockbridge, who could not understand why officers from Colorado were in New Mexico investigating a crime that had taken place in New Mexico, professed not to have noticed anything of the sort and elaborated the excuse he had already given.

They declined his offer of coffee, and he declined their request to go with them: "I can't hardly get away. I've been trusted with these horses down there to take care of them and I don't want to get up and leave." Besides, he was convalescing after army service and could not ride far.

Eventually, the three left, having agreed among themselves to get someone from the Springer brothers' ranch instead. But they did not go on to the Springer ranch and thence to Turkey Canyon as Stockbridge always believed. For one thing, they could not have known that the gang had a hideout in Turkey Canyon; they may not have known where Turkey Canyon was, or even have heard of it. For another, and contrary to his supposition, they seem to have accepted Stockbridge's tale. All they did was rejoin the main party.

At around noon the combined posses split up into smaller groups to hunt for sign or information. They turned up neither. In the evening Reno returned to Folsom with Titsworth and a couple of other Colorado deputies. So did Pinard and his four possemen. Farr came in separately. Some of the other Colorado men went home.

An allegation that "information was furnished by an ex-member of the gang which was considered of sufficient importance to act upon" was then relayed by Associated Press. In fact the informant was Juan Martinez, one of the men who had seen the gang just prior to the robbery. He had taken his knowledge to Titsworth, who asked for and was given Reno's permission to "employ" the man.

In the morning, Reno and Farr left Folsom to pursue the investigation around Johnson Mesa from the greater comfort of a buggy, while Martinez guided Titsworth and another Colorado deputy, Hugo Pfalmer, to the place where the outlaws had camped on Tuesday morning. Titsworth picked up a torn envelope which, when pieced together, provided the clue that broke the case: the package bore a Springer postmark, about a fortnight old; was addressed to "G.W. Franks"; and had been collected from the Cimarron post office. Not for the last time in the case, the outlaws had misused fire—in this instance, by overlooking its virtues as a destructive agent.

When Reno and Farr returned to Folsom that night, having accomplished nothing, they took the obvious decision to head for Springer with all speed. This meant going northwest—to Trinidad, for a change of trains—to go southwest. Even so, the morning of Saturday, the 15th, found Reno, Farr, and Titsworth boarding the Santa Fe train that would set them down in Springer that afternoon.[1]

Foraker had arrived in Springer the previous day. With him was Wilson "Memphis" Elliott.[2]

Elliott was a Texas man who made his living from whatever form of law-enforcement work he could find, wherever he could find it; when he could not find it, he would take just about any kind of job that was going. In the mid-1880s he had kept a saloon in San Angelo. Since leaving the San Angelo area in 1888 he had been a railroad fireman in Mexico, cowboy and prospector in Arizona and New Mexico, constable, deputy sheriff, and building laborer in Colorado, and Wells, Fargo express guard on the Raton-Rincon run. Latterly he had worked on-and-off for Foraker and would still guard the occasional Wells, Fargo shipment, though without enthu-siasm; he thought the pay too low. We have seen that he was prominent in the arrest of the Peenland and Cowan brothers after the Folsom robbery of 1897. His former acquaintance with the Ketchums, and his work on the previous Folsom case, would have been his prime qualifications for the duties now delegated to him. Dedication to justice was not the mainspring to his keenness for the appointment. For him, as he readily admitted, the incentive was the standing reward of $1,000 per man that Wells, Fargo had placed on Tom and Sam Ketchum, Will Carver, Dave Atkins, "and two or three others" whose names he had forgotten.[3]

Early on the afternoon of July 15, Foraker and Elliott went to Cimarron. The marshal was expecting a report from his spy, Morgan.[4]

That same afternoon Reno, Farr, and Titsworth met John Thacker in Springer. Titsworth and Thacker stayed at Springer overnight; Reno and Farr, having made some inquiries in town, drove to Cimarron to interview Postmaster Jim Hunt that evening.[5]

Before the night was over, Foraker and Elliott learned the whereabouts of Ketchum, Carver, and Lay. Their informant was the versatile James H. ("Billy") Morgan, who had spent several hours "out in the mountains" on horseback.[6]

A version of the story given to the press told of an unnamed teamster coming in to report having encountered three riders with a packhorse two miles north of town near Dean Canyon. As Reno told the story to the *Denver Republican* nearly two years later, the horses were jaded and the men "tired and dejected." (Their dejection is understandable. They would have been mourning the great loss suffered by Wells, Fargo & Company.)

The nameless teamster could only have been Morgan. If the information was passed to him by "some movers" coming into Cimarron, as he would testify in court, or by "an outfit of freighters," in Elliott's words, their status as eyewitnesses would have compelled their appearance at Lay's subsequent trial. Since these personages were never so much as identified, they are likely to have been imaginary. Morgan was probably his own witness.[7]

Foraker may also have enjoyed the confidence of Bruce Weaver, whom he could have spoken to at Springer. Probably Weaver would not have deliberately set about betraying his partners. He could simply have mentioned that the men who had been with him in Cimarron village had a camp in an offshoot of Cimarron Canyon.[8]

One way or another, the officers were sure that the robbers, or some of them, were in Turkey Creek Canyon. On the Saturday night, Foraker raised a small posse. Its members assembled between seven and eight o'clock next morning, July 16. Besides Elliott and Morgan, the group comprised Farr, Reno, Henry M. Love, Perfecto Cordova, Santiago Serna (or Silva), and Frank H. Smith.

Serna and Cordova were local men, enrolled by Reno as special officers of the railroad. Frank Smith, a well-to-do young man with family connections in New York and Maryland, had been staying with his friends, the Chicago-based ranchers Garrett and McCormick. He could have had no real notion of the desperate charac-ter of the men he had volunteered to help run down. Love, originally from Illinois, was a cowboy in the employ of Charles Springer. He was also the local deputy sheriff, though in this case he was serving the interests of the federal government as a posseman under the direction of Foraker's representative, "Memph" Elliott. It was Love who would have joined Farr and Reno three days earlier had they gone on to Springer's ranch from the XL horse camp. He had been engaged in skinning the carcasses of cattle afflicted with blackleg, and the infected knife was still in his pocket when he joined the posse. Contrary to some reports, Thacker was not among the men who rode out with Wilson Elliott; he was not even in Cimarron when the posse was assembled, but in Springer.

Although Foraker had called at Elliott's home in Albuquerque, to enlist his help, Elliott was neither commissioned nor sworn in as a deputy U.S. marshal, though Foraker referred to him as such. The same degree of informality was extended to Morgan, Love, Cordova, Serna, and Smith. In a few of Foraker's words, they were simply "organized as a posse under authority from the Attorney General of the U.S." or "gathered together as a posse under his [Elliott's] direction."[9]

Reno and Farr were outside this arrangement, informal as it was; technically, therefore, they were without jurisdiction in New Mexico. Foraker's explanation at the time was that he had given Farr "discretionary powers." This was a bureaucrat's dream of an all-purpose phrase, capable of meaning both anything and nothing to anyone and everyone; if matters went awry, the wording would give infinite scope for argument and accusation, but none for definitive incrimination.[10]

Foraker's own authority was dubious. No writs had yet been issued in connection with Tuesday's holdup: all the marshal had was a warrant for Tom Ketchum, Samuel Ketchum, William Carver, and one other named person (whom he was reluctant to identify) for waylaying the mails near Folsom in 1897. That "one other" was the man formerly known as Charles Collins, or Collings, who, inconveniently for the credibility of Foraker's implied assumptions but conveniently for his current policy, had been acquitted of the crime. The marshal had no formal knowledge that Sam Ketchum was one of the parties in Turkey Canyon; none that "Franks" was Carver; none that any of them had committed train robbery on July 11, 1899; and no piece of paper identifying "McGinnis" with Elzy Lay, or directing him to arrest anyone bearing either name.[11]

At 9 a.m. on the 16th Elliott and Morgan, perhaps accompanied or followed by other members of the posse, headed for the bottom of Dean Canyon, near Nash's ranch, three miles north of Cimarron. Here, at the scene of the reported sighting, they found the expected fresh tracks of four horses. After following them for a couple of miles westwards into Dean Canyon, they started back to Cimarron to report to Foraker and were in town before noon. Elliott and Morgan, at least, ate dinner, though one of the posse—Cordova—had none. At one o'clock they were all in the saddle again.[12]

This time they headed west from the village, along the road beside the Cimarron River and through its canyon. Their plan, as Reno outlined it, was to intercept the presumed robbers before they could escape down Turkey Creek Canyon westwards over the mountains. Three and a half miles down the road they turned into the mouth of Turkey Canyon. One man, Serna, either dropped out along the way or was sent home. The others pressed on.

Once the hunt was under way, Farr and Reno behaved at times as though they were in charge of the expedition. In the haste and bustle of exigency, this may not have seemed to matter; afterwards, an issue was made out of it. The question is one of whether their arrogation of authority sprang from their over-assertiveness, Elliott's deficiencies as a leader, or a failure of organization by Foraker.

The posse followed the dry course of Turkey Creek for a little while, crossed to the north of the canyon, and rode along the ridge until they came across fresh tracks leading to the path through the canyon. Sometimes bunched in twos and threes, strung out in single file where the trail narrowed, dismounting to lead their horses over the steepest part of the incline, and with Elliott and Farr alternating in the lead, the posse advanced a further four miles into Turkey Canyon.

At a few minutes before a quarter past five in the evening the posse emerged from a patch of scrub oak to the crest of a steep hillock ("a right smart little hill," Elliott called it). Elliott, who was in front, turned in the saddle and motioned the rest of the party to dismount. He had seen smoke curling up from out of the brush on the high ground across the glade, eighty-five feet broad at its widest point, which separated the two rises. They were now about eight miles up the canyon, and ten or eleven from Cimarron as the crow flies.

Elliott's instructions were for the posse to open fire straight away if the suspects did not surrender at the first command. Farr also issued a directive, which Elliott and Morgan later denied having heard: "As soon as you see a man, shoot him down as quick as you can, as we have no chances to take if we kill them."

Just 240 yards lay between that campfire and the place where the posse had halted. The officers were as much forearmed by the carelessness of the bandits in leaving the approach to the camp unguarded as they had been forewarned by the rising smoke. Perhaps the outlaws were weary, and still drowsy from a few hours' sleep; perhaps overconfident. At any rate they had made another two amateurish blunders.

Reno, Farr, and Smith moved off to the left, keeping to the ridge; it was their purpose to gain a position from which they could look down upon the camp and enjoy a clear field of fire. Elliott and the others were to set up a crossfire by converging upon the camp from the lower ground, to their right; when they had reached the far side of the little valley they headed for a gulch that ran along the downward slope of the hill where the bandits were encamped. By following this gulch as it twisted up and around, Elliott and his men could creep upon the outlaws from behind.

But before any of the officers had reached their intended positions, Elzy Lay, disheveled and half-dressed, came into view. He was carrying a canteen but no rifle. As he made his way through the pines and brush to a pool in the rocks beside the dry creek, he was untroubled by any sense of alarm. Sam Ketchum and Will Carver were standing near the campfire, not far from the cave. Perfecto Cordova caught sight of them at about the same time as the other possemen noticed Lay.

Lay was about halfway between the camp and the creek when Reno urged his two companions to charge. They were more than one hundred yards from the outlaw, almost directly ahead of him but high above, and he did not see them. Farr and Reno may have ordered him to surrender; if they did, no more than a very few seconds were given him to think it over before they started shooting at him. Elliott, who was sixty-five yards from Lay and walking in roughly the same direction, also took aim at the outlaw and may or may not have shouted to him. The two sections of the posse were separated by something between fifty and seventy yards; Carver and Ketchum were less than thirty yards from Lay when the shooting started, but at this time were seen only by Cordova.

The first shot, Lay afterwards related, "just kind of dropped me, just the same as if I had been hit with a club." It was fired by Farr—"watch me knock him," the sheriff said to Reno, standing five feet to his right—and struck the outlaw in the left shoulder. An instant later a bullet from someone in Elliott's group (most likely Elliott himself) ripped into his back and would have knocked him down had he not been falling already.

"You made a good shot," Reno told Farr, perhaps not realizing that one of the Elliott party had made another at almost the same moment.

"I tried to move," Lay said later, "and I could not move. I felt just as if I had been cut in two from where the bullet struck me first; then the next sensation was just like my feet was turning back over my head. There were several shots fired . . . I think all the first volley was fired at me."

A man in a white shirt, believed to be Morgan, was heard to exclaim: "We've got one of the sons of bitches, anyway."

The outlaws' four horses were standing near the fallen man, and Elliott could make out the Bar V brand on one of them. He opened up on the horses and hit one.

Perfecto Cordova had joined the posse, in his own candid words, because "I thought we would not find anything." (Although he did not say so, the certainty that he would be paid for making the trip whether anything was found or not must have been another weighty consideration.) Perfecto found plenty. He saw the two men by the campfire; the smaller of them seemed to bear a resemblance to "McGinnis," whom he had seen in Cimarron more than once. Actually the two men were Ketchum and Carver. But before Cordova could make any movement of tongue or trigger, shooting broke out from others in the posse.

Sam Ketchum grabbed his rifle, fired a shot or two towards Farr, and shambled off in search of a suitably sturdy and well-sited pine. Carver at once tumbled onto his face, but in a moment he was on his feet again, now clasping his Winchester. He had not been hit; none of the shots had been directed at him or Ketchum anyway. But he had located Farr, Reno, and Smith, and did not lose another second in heading for a place where he would be safer from them than they would be from him.

Cordova, seeing Sam Ketchum running towards him, rushed back to where Elliott was standing.

"Look out! There's one of them right at you!" he yelled, "Look out, he'll shoot you!"

"Show me where he is at," Elliott rather naturally requested.

"I can't see him now," was the unhelpful reply.

"You ought to have shot when you did see him," Elliott chided.

"I didn't have time," Cordova argued.

Long before the finish of this unfruitful conversation, Sam Ketchum had stationed himself behind a tree less than forty yards from Elliott. Cordova had found a serviceable tree of his own a few moments after Sam reached his.

Both Elliott and Cordova caught glimpses of the top of Carver's head as he scurried, hatless, through the brush and up the slope. Though he was far away, they assumed that he was the man seen by Cordova less than a minute before. Elliott snapped a couple of shots at him, but it was a waste of good cartridges. Soon Carver was pouring lead at what little he could see of Farr, Reno, and Smith, who were nearly two hundred yards across the canyon from the rocky knoll where he had taken his stand. Elliott responded for the posse by shooting another of the outlaws' horses. That left them with two, including the one that had served them as packhorse.

Carver's opening shots flew too high to do more than curb the rasher impulses of Farr and Reno; he was placed just above the officers, and had not yet found the right trajectory. But a screen of bushes, and the almost smokeless powder of the .30-40 cartridge, made it impossible for the officers to locate him.

Far worse, from their standpoint, the tenderfoot, Smith, unthinkingly helped the outlaw to get a fix on their position, even though they had found good cover. While Smith was enthusiastically but fruitlessly throwing lead at his general notion of Carver's position, the smoke rising from his old-fashioned black powder cartridges was providing Carver with a target.

The sheriff and Smith had jumped behind one tree; it lacked the girth to conceal the persons of both men, and soon after Carver had started to direct his fire at them, down went Smith with a wound "through the fleshy part of the calf of the left leg."

The possemen either could not see Lay, or did not think of watching out for him after he had fallen. But, although hurt, bleeding, dazed, and shocked—and unarmed besides—he was not out of the fight. Within two or three minutes, the numbness in his legs and shoulder had started to ease away. Traveling mostly on all fours, he began to make his way back towards camp. He kept raising himself upright, but collapsed whenever he tried to walk. He got his rifle and crawled downcreek until he found satisfactory cover. Then, when he was fifty or sixty yards below Carver, he fainted. Perhaps ten minutes passed before he was conscious again. During that time Sam Ketchum was put out of action and Carver, for a while, had to take on the entire posse.

From his tree, no more than a hundred feet from Elliott's group, Sam had opened fire on Cordova, then turned his attention to Farr, who was about on a level with him and more than a hundred and fifty yards away. At one point, he raised his voice to invite the possemen to "come down here." Numerous shots were aimed at him by Elliott, Love, Cordova, and Morgan. Sam returned their fire until his active interest in the fight was ended by a bullet from Elliott which broke his left arm just below the shoulder. It had been a good shot, or a lucky one, for Elliott knew that the bullets from his .40-82 Marlin lacked the punch to penetrate the tree trunk which kept nearly all of Sam out of sight for nearly all of the time. The officer had borrowed

Morgan's gun, which fired a steel-nosed cartridge, and had reloaded it, before he realized that the outlaw was already finished.

About then, Carver widened his arc of fire to cover both flanks. Elliott's section were rather more than two hundred yards away, but clearly visible. Elliott later told Rome Shield that he avoided injury only "by keeping in constant motion, so as to afford no steady target." He and Morgan soon scrambled for safety behind a ledge of rocks and stones; they could not see the marksman, who was slightly above them, and hoped that he could not longer see them. Cordova and Love each stayed close to his own tree.[13]

This was the situation when Lay revived, twenty minutes after the opening shot of the engagement had laid him low. He quickly selected Sheriff Farr as his first mark.

Farr was peering around his tree in the hope of spotting Carver when a bullet from that quarter creased his right arm near the wrist. He drew back sharply. While wrapping the wound in a handkerchief he called across to ask Reno whether he had seen the man (Carver) who was shooting at them from across the canyon.

Angry because the sheriff had moved just as he was pulling the trigger for his first shot—which had been destined for the officer's protruding rear—Lay shifted aim to a point near the center of the tree trunk.

"You son of a bitch, I'll get you this time," he muttered, just before he "blew splinters clear through the officer." That pine trunk was about three feet in diameter; but Lay's bullet, from a range of roughly one hundred yards, struck it near its edge and tore through several inches of wood before entering the sheriff's body.[14]

Farr, a big, brawny man, fell across the prostrate Smith, gasping "I'm done for." The sheriff had been shot through the chest, near the heart, and died within five minutes, after whispering to Smith, "say goodbye to my wife and baby." Lay fainted again shortly afterwards, and took no further part in the fray; but that one shot was probably decisive in turning the fight against the possemen. Now it was they who were on the defensive. Carver, again unaided but occupying an excellent firing position, harassed and finally routed them.

First he silenced Reno, whose equanimity had already been ruffled by several bullets whistling only a few inches wide of him. Three or four slugs, by his reckoning, now whipped through his trousers and coat-tails, one of them inflicting a slight wound and "cutting two Winchester bullets [cartridges] in twain." This close call, coupled with the invisibility of his adversary, and following the shockingly efficient removal of Smith and Farr, convinced him that he was anything but master of the situation.[15]

With Farr dead, Smith wounded, and Reno quelled, Carver had been able to concentrate his fire on the four men, led by Elliott, who were spread below him on the other side. Although, as Reno would point out, the Elliott group "were better sheltered from the fire of the robbers" than were the three on the other side of the basin, their greater safety could not infuse them with greater valor. It depended on their remaining under cover—and Carver's shooting kept all their heads down. His most telling shot accounted for Henry Love: the bullet slammed against the cowboy-deputy's thigh, smashing the infected knife and driving the poisoned blades deep into the flesh and bone.

Smith, meanwhile, was groaning loudly, the pain from his wound greatly aggravated by the dead weight of the much bulkier form of the slain sheriff. Elliott and Morgan heard the groans, thought that the sufferer was Farr, and were not emboldened. The two shots that ended the fight were fired by Carver, at about six o'clock.

It had been a clear but cloudy afternoon. Early in the evening, a quarter of an hour or so after the last shots were heard, the rain began to come down. Keenly aware of their failure, and not daring to move or shoot, or even seek vocal contact with their unseen colleagues across the canyon, Elliott and his companions waited for nightfall. About all they could do in the meantime was to crouch under the rocky overhang and watch the rain soaking the ground beside them. Love's condition was deteriorating. He begged for a "little fire" to be built beside him, but the wetness of the ground and the steady rainfall prevented them from doing what would have been prohibitively dangerous anyway.

Reno waited in the falling darkness until his eyes could no longer make out the form of the bandits' gray horse seventy-five yards away or even distinguish the sights of the rifle he was holding. He had been waiting for one of the men to come for the horse, but evidently did not think of shooting it regardless.

By then, it was eight o'clock, and he was "apprehensive for Mr. Elliott and his men," having heard nothing from them for more than two hours. Nor did he know exactly where the robbers were, only that they were somewhere on the other side of the canyon. But at least he could now move with safety in his own immediate vicinity. He crossed the ten feet or so between his tree and the one behind which Farr and Smith had vainly sought safety, and dragged Farr's body from Smith's wounded and crippled leg. Now, as he laid his hand on the cold forehead of the dead sheriff, he understood how little protection a pine tree afforded against steel-nosed bullets from the .30-40 rifle. He asked Smith whether he wanted to go with him to summon help. Smith replied that he could not move, and urged Reno to go anyway. Reno then slipped away from the scene, leaving his rifle and pistol with the wounded man.

The posse's horses had been left more than two hundred yards down canyon. Reno could have no hope of finding his way back to Cimarron that night, with or without a horse, by attempting to retrace the route by which he had come. He would have to go over the mountain and descend to the road through Cimarron Canyon. Since the ridge (now known as Midnight Mesa) was almost impassable on horseback even in daylight, he faced a ten or eleven mile walk to Cimarron village.

Elzy Lay had recovered consciousness at dusk to see Carver standing over him. He struggled to his feet and went over with Carver to Sam Ketchum, who was lying among some rocks. Lay's wounds, fortunately for him, were "through and through," whereas the bullet that struck Sam was still in his arm. They had only two sound horses; one was dead, another too badly wounded for use. Two of the men would have to ride double, or one would have to walk.

As darkness settled they prepared to ride away; but Sam's broken arm prevented him from mounting. After he had failed several times to stay in the saddle he urged the others to go on without him, which they refused to do. At length, with Ketchum supported on his horse by Carver, the three men moved slowly out of Turkey Creek Canyon and continued west, towards Ute Park.

They had left a box containing thirty or forty sticks of dynamite, a saddle and bridle, a bloodied hat and slicker, a dead horse, another that was wounded (and had to be killed later by one of the posse), a large coffeepot, the tincans that had served them as cups, sundry provisions and cooking utensils,[16] and, more interestingly, but publicly undisclosed until Rome Shield repeated the account given him by his old friend "Memph" Elliott, "a grip which had been slit across the top, apparently because of a lack of time in which to open it." Twenty-three cartridge shells were scattered about the place recently vacated by Carver ("near a small bush").[17]

They had buried or hidden Sam's rifle and ammunition, doubtless because these were of no further use to him and he would be less conspicuous without them. Less explicably, they also buried the saddle tree taken from the express car.

The valise, it was surmised, "contained the money secured by the bandits in various holdups." This statement embodies two most unlikely assumptions—that it was the practice of the outlaws to hump their accumulated booty back and forth across the southwest, and that one traveler's grip would be big enough to accommodate the lot. Probably it would not have had the capacity to hold the whole of Tuesday night's loot; the fact that it had been ripped open may signify that the weight, or value, of whatever it did contain had been distributed between the three men, or between the saddlebags on the two horses.

Under those circumstances, and bearing in mind Sam's disablement and the outlaws' pressing need to make what little speed they could, the loss of two of their four horses would not have made any difference. Sam could not sit in the saddle without assistance and Carver could not have controlled a laden packhorse while looking after himself and his two wounded comrades.

Thus, when Ketchum, Carver, and Lay left Turkey Canyon, the bulk of their plunder did not go with them; they had only as much as they or their horses could easily carry.

It is most unlikely that they had hefted the booty all the way from Folsom to Turkey Canyon. Their slovenliness in letting themselves be caught off guard on the 16th, while (from their viewpoint) indefensible in any instance, suggests that they were no longer preoccupied with their swag; with $70,000 to look after, they would have taken better care to look after themselves. Besides, the conditions of their enforced departure—in gathering darkness, in haste, in the presence of several possemen who were unwounded and (for all that the fugitives knew) alert, and with Ketchum and Lay sorely hurt—would have given Carver no chance to secrete any large sum of money nearby. Nor would they have cached their loot before the posse's arrival: the Turkey Canyon hideout was their base camp; and, while they assumed—mistakenly—that they could slip away ahead of any oncoming posse, they would have expected the place to be found, and searched, sooner rather than later.

So, in all probability, the stolen treasure was never taken into Turkey Canyon. Ketchum, Carver, and Lay might have entrusted it to Weaver, on the understanding that he would convey it to Alma for division there. But, in the absence of severe duress, this would have been a large portion of trust for three men to place on the competence and goodwill of a fourth. Much the stronger possibility is that those three, with or without Weaver, committed the bulk of their haul—$58,000—to the soil at some point between Raton and Cimarron, most likely the mountainous country near the Vermejo River, a little way northwest of the new WS headquarters. They had ample time to choose a hiding place, having allowed themselves more than three full days for the ride from Folsom to Turkey Canyon—a distance that these men, with those horses, in that country, could quite comfortably have covered in a day and a bit.

The $58,000 would remain underground until such time as the men could return for it without exciting the interest of the authorities or arousing the avarice of their more rapacious friends. The remainder could have been stuffed into the grip, to be shared by the four of them—or three of them, if Weaver had already left with his cut—as a kind of interim dividend or living allowance. After the shoot-out in the canyon, the valise was slashed open and the money hurriedly split three ways, so that each man would have his share if the trio became separated.

At all events, dusk had not quite given way to darkness when the three of them left with their two horses, heard and perhaps dimly seen by members of the posse.

The pain was too much for Sam, and Lay was in no condition to help him much; so, just beyond the junction of Cimarron and Ute Creeks, with only three miles traveled, they decided to rest at a ranch cabin. The property was owned by Henry (né Henri) Lambert but occupied by Ed McBride, his wife, and their sons. McBride had been friendly towards the outlaws in the past and they believed they could trust him.

Sam told his companions that he could go no further. Carver, by now, was too anxious to keep ahead of the posses to argue with this. But Lay wanted to stay and fight. He began to pile sacks of flour against the windows. Finally Sam and Carver convinced him that it was of no use and prevailed upon him to leave.[18] Before they rode away, Sam gave Carver the more valuable of the two pocket timepieces he carried: "an octagon gold watch" whose chain was inlaid with oblong links of polished gold quartz, with "a big fob of gold quartz."[19] He also parted with his cash.

McBride, by his own story, came in later; he had been out hunting for strayed horses when the outlaws reached the ranch. Sam is alleged to have blamed his wound on a hunting accident (or, in a variant tale, on a mishap in a sawmill).[20] In reality, Sam had no reason to invent an explanation. The McBrides had heard nothing of the battle in the canyon, but that was immaterial. McBride knew what kind of men these three were, and what kind of trouble they were likely to get into; he may well have known the names of two of them.[21] Lay he would not have known.

More than two hours after the rain had set in on Sunday evening, Elliott and Morgan deemed it safe for them to walk over to where Farr, Reno, and Smith had last been heard from. Here the situation was even worse that they had feared. They found the dead Farr, the wounded Smith, and no Reno at all.

Smith explained that Reno had only just left, and that he had gone to Cimarron to report and to send for help, but the pair were disposed to make much more of the presence of the detective's guns and horses than the reason for the absence of the man himself. Elliott and Morgan knew that at least two of the presumed train robbers had escaped from the canyon (they expected to find the corpse of the one they had shot at the outset) and must have been conscious that not only their competence but their courage were open to question.

Reno's mission turned out to be far harder than he must have hoped. At midnight, or before, he lost his way and sought shelter from the unrelenting rain. At daybreak he found the road through Cimarron Canyon. It was not until 7 a.m. that he trudged into the village, exhausted and soaked to the skin. He called at the Hunt store, arranged for a doctor to be sent into Turkey Canyon, and made use of the only telephone in Cimarron to dictate telegrams to the telegraph operator at Springer, twenty-three miles away.[22]

Foraker then took the telephone and reported that everyone in the posse had been wounded. Later, less excusably, Elliott modified the marshal's error only to the extent of saying that he alone was unscathed, although he knew full well that Morgan and Cordova had also come out of the engagement without a scratch.[23]

Foraker then raised a search party and led it into the mountains. Later the marshal told the *Santa Fe Daily New Mexican* that he invited Reno to join him in the rescue mission, but that Reno declined because he wanted to go to the telegraph office in Springer. Whatever Reno said or did not say to Foraker, he did not leave for Springer until late that night.

From Springer the news was sent to Santa Fe and Denver, points beyond and points between. Reno had only an incomplete view of the battle, and some of what he had to say may have been progressively garbled or muddled in transmission and retransmission. More of the facts, garnished with a false accusation and a ludicrous instance of mistaken identity, would emerge with the return of the survivors.

Elliott and the remnants of his posse had camped by their horses and spent a miserable night in Turkey Canyon. Shortly after daybreak they set out for Cimarron, leaving Farr's body in the mountains. They went down canyon, returning along the route they had taken the previous afternoon. They hoped to meet someone going in to help them. With his thighbone shattered by the infected blades of the broken pocket knife, Henry Love was in a bad way and getting worse. His wound was so large that at first his companions accused the bandits of firing "explosive" (expanding) bullets.[24]

Elliott and Morgan entered Cimarron from the west soon after Foraker and his men had ridden out northwards. They secured help for Love and Smith, stopped in town just long enough to feed themselves, and started back with packhorses to collect the remains of Ed Farr and some of the things from the camp deserted by the outlaws. They were joined by the vigilant Jim Hunt; the Dean Canyon rancher, Bud Nash; and two other local men named William Bogan and Bill Lester.[25]

Foraker's party had approached Turkey Canyon from the Dean Canyon end, but did not enter it. Instead, they kept to the ridge that overlooked it. At last, after a ten mile ride, they struck the trail of some four or five horses, which the marshal decided to follow, without knowing whether he was on the track of robbers or possemen.

The tracks turned out to be those left earlier that morning by Elliott and his companions. When Foraker had finished trailing them into Cimarron he was told that Elliott and Morgan had been and gone. He at once turned back, taking a wagon for Farr's body.

At last, between three and four in the afternoon, the Elliott-Hunt group reached the scene of the affray. They "looked over the ground some," lashed the dead man to one packhorse and some of the bandits' discarded property to another, and started back. On their way in they met Foraker, transferred the body to the wagon, and presented him with the thirty or forty sticks of dynamite recovered from the robbers' camp.[26]

In Cimarron, some jackass assumed the body of the sheriff to be that of an outlaw "known by the names of William McGinnis and G.W. Franks." This misinformation, along with a description of the dead man—"a man 6 feet 2 inches high . . . about 200 pounds, light complexion"—was passed to Reno, who blundered badly by telephoning it through without first looking at the body. He may have assumed that the body was that of Sam Ketchum, whom the description could have fitted. Unfortunately for Reno, Si Rainey of the Colorado & Southern, whipped out the telegram a few days later as "proof" of the accuracy of their special officer's information. Evidently, Rainey was some way behind the news; the press had corrected the error twenty-four hours after its commission.[27]

Frank Smith provided a gleam of better news. After removal of the tourniquet from his knee the wound was bathed in a tin tub at Hunt's store. Once the bullet had been extracted he made a quick recovery.[28]

Both Reno and Foraker departed for Springer before the end of that long Monday, but for different purposes.

Re-enter, now, under false colors, Capt. Hon. William John French, manager of the WS outfit and future author of two volumes of ranching *Recollections*. The melodrama being played out so close to the WS pasture in Colfax County afforded an apt occasion for French, the narrator, to put French, the rancher, in the right place at the right time to make himself part of an anecdote connected with the sensational train robbery and mountain battle. He duly obliged with a rollicking account of how Billy Reno did not go to Springer. This is the ranchman's tale:

French had hired a rig in Springer, and was driving out to visit a Cimarron rancher, Joe Nash. He had put rather more than half of the outward journey behind him when his attention was seized "by a man coming along the prairie parallel to the road." French had just heard about the train robbery and had been greatly taken aback by the talk in Springer that one of the bandits was "Will McGinnis," whom he always regarded as "a paladin among cowpunchers." He did not at first connect this news with the stranger, "a small man, of what might be termed insignificant stature, with very fair hair and light eyebrows," who, as French represents him, was hatless and "gesticulating wildly" for French to stop and wait for him.

"For God's sake, take me into Springer," panted the apparition, adding that it was "an absolute necessity" for him to get to the telegraph office and railroad. After some demur, French agreed to turn back and Reno climbed into the buggy. After hearing the detective's description of the fight (which French's faulty memory misplaced in Cimarron Canyon when he came to write about this alleged encounter with Reno), the rancher

glanced at the torn coat-tail and made an uncharitable remark to the effect that if Reno had not run away from the bullet so swiftly he would be sitting less comfortably now. Reno, according to French, "didn't take [that] quite kindly."

That is French's story, and an adroitly inventive piece of comic writing it is, too. It is one of several episodes described by French that have no legitimate place in a work offered to the reading public as the *Recollections* of its author.[29]

Reno was indeed fair-complexioned and, at only a shade over five foot six, a little on the short side even for the late nineteenth century—as were, for example, Will Carver and Kid Curry. French may well have seen Reno, perhaps spoken to him, at some time; but their meeting, if there was one, could not have happened amid the surroundings or in the terms portrayed with such characterful vigor in *Some Recollections of a Western Ranchman.*

In the first place, no one in Reno's professional situation—let alone physical condition—would have contemplated setting out for Springer on foot. He would have traveled by Hankins's stage (there was a daily service in both directions between Elizabethtown and Springer); or hired or borrowed a vehicle; or, all else failing, gone on horseback.

Secondly, he was under no absolute need to get there, anyway; he had already spoken to the telegrapher by telephone, and the essence of Sunday's news was already in the hands of the law enforcement agencies, C.H. Young and John Thacker of the express company, and senior officials of the Colorado & Southern.[30] As a means of communication, this was unsatisfactory. Reno would have much preferred a direct link with the company headquarters in Denver. Still, sketchy as the picture was, it would have to suffice for the remainder of that morning: everyone who needed to know now knew there had been a desperate fight in the mountains; that Huerfano County, Colorado, no longer had a sheriff; and that other casualties had been incurred on both sides.

Thirdly, though Reno did want to go to Springer, he could not have begun the journey until Farr's body had been brought in and an inquest held. It was well into the evening of July 17 when the Elliott-Hunt party returned from Turkey Canyon with the dead man (which Reno himself reported over the telephone line to Springer), and well into the night when the coroner and his jury met for the inquest, at which Reno would have been one of the two principal witnesses, the wounded Frank Smith being the other.[31]

Lastly, Edward Farr was not only Reno's colleague, but his friend. Reno would have wished to accompany the body as far as Springer, where it would be put on the next northbound train for shipment via Trinidad to Farr's home town of Walsenburg, Colorado. That aside, Superintendent F.C. Webb, of the C &S, and others from Colorado whom Reno expected to meet in Springer, could not be there before nightfall. Reno would not have had to rush away from Cimarron that morning on their account.

In the event, the late hour at which the inquest was held meant that Farr's body could not begin its slow journey from Cimarron much before midnight, and did not reach Springer until 4:30 or 5:00 a.m. Reno is likely to have traveled with it; but even if he had gone on ahead, he could not have arrived more than a couple of hours earlier.

So much, till we meet him again, for William French, raconteur.

Webb had traveled down on a special train with David E. Farr, one of the dead man's brothers, who was a Bell ranch employee, and B.B. Sipe, coroner and undertaker at Trinidad and a friend of both the Farr family and the Colorado and Southern Railway. Before the train began its return trip, with Ed Farr's body in the baggage car, Reno asked Webb for the late sheriff's Winchester, vowing that "he would not give up the chase until he had succeeded in capturing the robbers who had killed his friend, and that furthermore he wanted to make the capture with his dead friend's gun."[32]

"Crayt" Foraker, for his part, was traveling over the rails of the A.T. & S.F. and Santa Fe-Pacific to his home and office in Albuquerque. Before leaving Springer, he expressed his well-founded belief that "one or more" of the fugitives "are wanted for other train robberies;" if this were so, he thought there was "a reward of $1500 on each." Sam Ketchum, he went on, was a suspect in both of the Folsom cases.

The marshal was not in a happy mood, and the burden on his mind was aggravated en route by his reading of freshly published Associated Press reports, which had credited Reno and Farr with leading the hunt for the Folsom robbers. During a halt at Las Vegas, sixty miles down the line, he was glad to be approached for another news interview. After pointing out that his man Elliott was officially in charge of the expedition—which, as matters shaped out, redounded to the glory of neither the deputy nor the marshal who had chosen him—Foraker as good as accused Reno of lying to the press, and categorically berated him for cowardice and desertion.[33]

Foraker also asserted that the outlaws had a forty-eight hour start on their pursuers.[34] It did not occur to him that the bandits' lead (probably more like thirty-six hours at that stage) would have been greater had not Reno, though a stranger in those parts, tramped eleven miles through the rain to seek help and raise the alarm—and less, had one of those self-vaunted frontiersmen, Elliott and Morgan, used his knowledge of the terrain to proper effect, instead of cowering all night under a rocky outcrop.

The manhunt intensified on the 18th. A force of sixteen men and horses from Huerfano County was unloaded at Maxwell City, the nearest station to the new WS ranch. David Farr added $400 to the rewards already advertised for the arrest and conviction of each of the three desperadoes. Thacker met Reno in Cimarron and organized a posse under the auspices of Wells, Fargo. Sheriff Campbell at last came briefly onstage, dispatching Alvin Ash and William Rogers as field representatives of Colfax County's law enforcement capability. Another of Campbell's deputies, Ed Coker, of Raton, hurried to Cimarron with Undersheriff Louis Kreeger and Deputy Sheriff Harry Lewis, of Las Animas County, Colorado. Elliott raised a posse of fifteen in the interests of the U.S. government and, after excavating the gang's cave and campsite in Turkey Canyon, cast for sign in the Ponil country immediately to the west. He found enough of a trail to track the outlaws as far as Ute Creek, but, seemingly, made no inquiries at the Lambert ranch.[35]

Altogether more than one hundred eager hunters were in the mountains, driven by the usual admixture of duty, indignation, bloodlust, and avarice. Many of them may have run into one another, but none had any bandit sighting to report. All were hampered by continuous rain, which not only brought discomfort but washed away all sign. In the face of such difficulties and discouragements, most of the posses swiftly melted away, without any of the publicity that had attended their arrival.

So far the hunt had turned up nothing except the articles the outlaws had jettisoned in Turkey Canyon, including the buried saddle tree (but not Sam's buried rifle; although they would have turned up Sam himself had they thought of looking for him at the Lambert ranch).

After the departure of Carver and Lay, Sam moved into the granary because, he said, he did not want to bring trouble to the house. The McBrides and their hired hand, Pearl (or Earl) Clause bandaged his wounds and gave him food and blankets. They also made up their minds to betray him; in truth, they could hardly risk doing anything else, though the allure of the reward money made it a desirable as well as a safe course.

Late on Tuesday the McBrides' older son, Jim, and Clause rode into Cimarron. They might have approached Foraker or Thacker, but neither was in town. Reno was, so they went straight to him.

Young McBride, Clause, and Van Allen, the stationkeeper at Ute Creek on the Cimarron-Elizabethtown stage line, were at once designated special officers of the railroad. Early on the Wednesday morning they guided Reno to the Ute Park ranch.

They knew that Ketchum was armed only with his revolver and was in a weakening condition, but no chances were to be taken. When they reached the ranch they devised a strategy whereby the outlaw could be disarmed. Clause and one of the young McBrides took a cup of coffee to the wounded man, and Clause asked Sam if he could borrow the revolver for a few moments to show the boy what a fine gun it was. Sam allowed him to do this. All at once Reno was at the open door ten feet away with Farr's rifle at the level.

In a moment the shed was full of armed men. The Springer correspondent declared that Sam "fought like a tiger" when the arrest party closed in, but here the reporter must have over-dramatized. The entrapped bandit, wounded and disarmed, would not have had the strength or the means to put up much resistance. Reno took possession of Ketchum's revolver, a set of loaded dice, a wild turkey bone, "which the bandits used to signal one another in the mountains," and his "special railway watch, seventeen jewels." The cylinder of the revolver, a stag handled Colt's .45, was smeared with blood.[36]

According to a memoir written by Mason Chase, Reno flew into a fury because the prisoner seemed disinclined to get up, and kicked and cursed him until restrained by Ed McBride.[37] But the statement should be viewed with reserve, partly because Chase was not present and partly because he lived locally and was on familiar terms with Lambert and the McBrides. On the whole, the citizenry of Cimarron and district did themselves little credit in the hunt for the Folsom robbers. Chase's account reads at this point almost as if the McBride crew's betrayal of Ketchum was done as an act of kindness. The truth is that the McBride people were motivated partly by a natural desire to keep out of trouble and partly by avarice. They believed that the safe delivery of Samuel Ketchum could be worth as much as $5,000 to them, and they wanted it. Reno made Jim McBride a specific offer of $500 on behalf of the C & S, and the railroad's check for that sum was soon in his hands.[38]

The McBrides had befriended the outlaws before the robbery; in easier circumstances they would have helped them afterwards, doubtless in the expectation of being well paid for their discretion. Wilson Elliott went so far as to charge that the combined "ranch house and country store" operated by "the scoundrel" McBride had been the headquarters of the gang before the robbery. Elliott may have exaggerated, but he was looking in the right direction.[39]

Ketchum was placed in a spring wagon and hauled into Cimarron. Two other Cimarronites, George Crocker and Ruth Crocker Crowder, the latter a child at the time, are the principal sources for what was said and done after Sam's arrival. Ruth said she had climbed over a wall to catch a view of the bad man and noticed that he was "holding his right arm with his left hand and clutching [clenching?] his teeth as though in pain." George was outside the St. James Hotel when the wagon drew up for a change of horses, and being in his thirties, saw and understood more then, and could say more about it later.

Sam—as George remembered it—admitted his identity when questioned by Jim Hunt, who probably would have known the answer long before putting the query. "I'm not a bad sort of fellow," Ketchum continued, adding that he hadn't done any great harm; then, pointing to Clause, who was standing nearby, "There's a meaner man than I am. If he hadn't worked it the way he did and got my gun, I'd have had his hide a-hanging on the fence."

Crocker also related that the captors were so eager to get to the hotel bar that they left Sam unattended, with one of their rifles lying within a few feet of him. He was about to move for the gun when Crocker spotted him and wrested it away. Ernest Ludlum, another eyewitness, mentioned no such incident, commenting only that "[a] more surly man was never seen than Sam after he was arrested."[40]

The newspapers confined themselves to the bald facts. Ketchum appeared before the Justice of the Peace, who bound him over for the murder of Farr; left Cimarron, with three guards, at eleven o'clock in the morning; and reached Springer at some time between 2:30 and four in the afternoon. This is enough to dispose of a local "tradition" that Ketchum was an overnight guest at the St. James Hotel.[41]

The senior McBride, "about 60 years old and pretty wiry," pretended in an interview with an Associated Press representative to have arrested Ketchum the previous night. The interview included McBride's version of the first of Sam's several brief statements on the fight and his attempt to escape.[42]

In this statement, as in those that followed, Ketchum maintained that, at his own insistence, his two companions had left him near the camp after failing to keep him in the saddle, and that he had made his way alone to the Ute Park cabin.

The contrary evidence is more convincing. Elliott said soon afterwards that the men had been trailed to Ute Creek, and therefore almost to the Lambert ranch. Carver subsequently told "Mack" Axford that all three had gone into the house. Sam had good reason to say otherwise. A disclosure by him that all had gone to the cabin might have given a clue to the direction subsequently taken by "Franks" and "McGinnis." McBride, of course, could not contradict Sam without incriminating himself and his household.[43]

When it was Lay's turn to speak he gave nothing away. At his trial he stated that he and "Franks" left Ketchum just where he had fallen, which was untrue. He also declined to say where they had eaten supper after escaping from the canyon. But throughout the trial he made it plain that he would not testify on anything not directly relating to the fight in the canyon; such answers as he did provide when questioned on other details were calculated to be of no use to the authorities.[44]

At Springer, John Thacker took one look at Sam. "That is he; we have him at last," he declared. If he gloated a little, he could be forgiven it.[45]

Sam was not the only member of the gang in custody at Springer that night. On July 17 one of the officers, probably Reno, had reported from Cimarron that among the robbers was "a man well known here, who was indicted for train robbery about the same place some time ago, and was acquitted at Las Vegas." He would say nothing more, but the stated circumstances fitted only one man. Two days later, Red Weaver was arrested at or near Raton, taken to Springer, and put under lock and key. When U.S. Commissioner Hugo Seaburg opened court on the morning of Thursday, July 20, Reno was on hand to swear out a complaint against "Bruce Wheeler [Weaver], alias G.W. Wheeler" for "unlawfully detaining by force and intimidation, obstructing and preventing from passage the United States mails, on or about the 11th day of July, near Folsom, N.M."[46]

News had come in of the death that morning of Henry Love. Contemporary accounts differ over whether his death occurred in Cimarron, Springer, or at the Chase ranch. The last was widely diffused by the A.P. reporter in Springer, but is contradicted by stronger evidence that he was taken to Cimarron. A previous report that Love was taken to Chase's after being brought out of the canyon is too insistent for disbelief, despite making no sense in the light of the reported facts. The posse might well have called at Chase's if they had come out of Turkey Canyon at the Dean Canyon end; but they had used the other exit. Yet Love was in urgent need of care, and the Chase ranch in Dean Canyon was much nearer than Cimarron approached from the southerly exit of Turkey Canyon and east along Cimarron Canyon. The obvious and likely explanation is that the posse took Love up canyon to the Chase place before doubling back down canyon, but that their errand of mercy went unreported. Love might have been taken from Cimarron to Springer on July 19 for more intensive medical treatment, had his condition permitted; but he could not be moved. His case was already hopeless, with gangrene and blackleg poisoning far advanced. He died in agony. Ludlum writes chillingly that "we could hear him screaming with pain all over the village."[47] Statements that his funeral was held at Springer are contradicted by press dispatches from Springer citing Cimarron as his burial place. Only with great difficulty, reported the *Denver Times*, were members of his family traced in Illinois and Kansas, and news of his death relayed to them.[48] His passing chalked up another red entry against the account of Samuel Wesley Ketchum, even though the fatal bullet was Carver's.

Foraker arrived in Springer from Santa Fe at about the time Sam Ketchum was answering a series of charges preferred by Reno. Two were for the territorial offenses of train robbery and murder. The others were for the federal side of the court's function. Ketchum, like Weaver, was charged with delaying the U.S. mails. Finally, he was accused of resisting federal officers in the performance of their duty. This last would have been a holding charge, for use if all other options failed.[49]

Ketchum waived his right to a preliminary examination on the specimen charge of interfering with the passage of the U.S. mails. His bond was set at $10,000. This amount, naturally, was not forthcoming; but had the territory proceeded at once with the murder charge, he could not have been bailed out anyway. Foraker, Thacker, and Wells, Fargo route agent W.F. Powars saw him onto a special train, accompanied by a press correspondent. The reporter, having observed that Ketchum "says a great deal in a kind of sarcastic way," jotted down what has become the most widely known of Sam's statements on the fight:

> They placed me on my horse twice, but I could not sit there. I was the first one shot. When I saw I could not ride I told the Kid to pull out and leave me. If they want my gun and ammunition it is hid up there in the rocks and they can have it if they find it. When they commenced firing I threw up my hands and then is when I was shot. If they had ordered us to throw up our hands we would have done so. After they had left me I was wet through. I could not cut kindling to build a fire and my matches were all damp and I could not light one after trying the whole box. Suppose they have me now. I am a brother of Tom Ketchum, the original "Black Jack."[50]

He then said, or was understood to say, that "his brother Tom, or 'Black Jack,' was killed over a year ago," and that "the name 'Black Jack' was given his brother about four years ago by one of the gang who has since been killed."[51]

Sam's terse lines are more vivid than truthful. The evidence that Sam was not the first one to be wounded, and that his hands were not upraised when he was shot, is plentiful and plain. As before, he gave the impression that he was by himself when he called at the Lambert ranch, when the better evidence says otherwise. But the real interest in the statement turns on the references to "the Kid" and "Black Jack."

Some commentators have conjectured, or even assumed, that "the Kid" who figured in Sam's statement was Harvey Logan, the redoubtable Kid Curry. Others have suggested that Sam was speaking of Harry Longabaugh, the Sundance Kid. Yet others have put forward the names of Tom Capehart and George Musgrave. Present needs will be served by a chain of simple assertions resting on evidence to be discussed later: neither Logan nor Longabaugh could have been in New Mexico in mid-July, 1899; consequently, if the identity of "G.W. Franks" were in doubt, Logan and Longabaugh would not have been available to dispel or foment it; and, self-evidently, the existence of positive evidence that "Franks" was Carver eliminates not only the Logan and Longabaugh theories, but all the others.[52]

There was an outlaw who may have been called "Kid Carver." This was Thomas Hilliard, alias "Tod Carver." Apparently he was unrelated to Will, and there seems to be no possibility of either man being mistaken for the other. Imprecise as were the official descriptions of "G.W. Franks" and "Tod Carver," they were too close to Will Carver and Tod Hilliard, respectively, for ambiguity, and too far apart from each other to be reconciled with any single unifying identity.[53]

So, Sam must have been referring to either Lay or Will Carver, both of whom were about fifteen years younger than himself. Since only Will Carver was physically able to lead the party out of the canyon, only he could have been "the kid" (rather than the journalist's "the Kid") to whom Ketchum was alluding. As far as is known, neither Sam Ketchum nor anyone else customarily called Carver "Kid." Sam's reason for doing so this time is obvious; it was an easy way of referring to a younger man without identifying him by name.

Though Ketchum made light of his wound—"Guess I can stand a little thing like that," he remarked dismissively to the doctor who was treating it—he may have been feverish. For that or some other reason, his speech may have been less fluent and coherent than the printed statement makes it look. Moreover, some of his words may have been paraphrased by a journalist who could barely tell the difference between Black Jack and Black Beauty. Thus his apparent declarations that Tom Ketchum was the "original Black Jack," and that "his brother Tom, or 'Black Jack' was killed over a year ago," may have been meant as a single connected assertion: he was the brother of Tom Ketchum; the original Black Jack was killed more than a year previously.

Alternatively, if Sam was quoted correctly, he had already formed a plan to mislead the officers into believing in Tom's death. With that in mind, he would have tried to get some running out of the erroneous news report of April, 1897, that Tom Ketchum was the true name of the Black Jack who had just been killed in Arizona; even the Ketchums' hometown paper, the *San Angelo Standard*, had printed the falsehood. Later Sam did say unequivocally that Tom was dead.[54] That was a hopeless lie; too many people who knew Tom had seen him more recently than 1897, and not all of them were going to keep quiet about it.

Similar ambiguities pervade Sam's supposed statement that "the name 'Black Jack' was given his brother about four years ago by one of the gang who has since been killed." The one member of the Ketchum gang to have been killed, up to that time, was Ed Cullen, but it strains belief that he, or anyone else, decided as early as 1895 that the nickname might suit Tom Ketchum. William Christian, however, had been decorated with the title more than three years before Sam's arrest. The name could have been thought up for Christian by either Code Young or Bob Hayes, members of the High Five or Black Jack gang who were killed before the end of 1896 (though there is no evidence that it was).

A statement attributed to Reno that Sam Ketchum "is the original 'Black Jack'" did nothing to promote clarity. Perhaps he was misquoted or misunderstood by the journalist who created the report.[55] If so, other officials were similarly misquoted or misunderstood. As one editor saw the controversy:

> Black Jack, the mysterious train robber, after dying upon the field of battle in New Mexico and Arizona, has finally surrendered himself in Colfax county. He says his

name is Sam Ketchum, brother of the notorious Jack, who he declares was killed more
than a year ago in the southern part of the territory, but some of the officers say it is
"Black Jack" himself. They identify him with all the positiveness with which he has
been identified numerous times heretofore, when laying [*sic*] a corpse before a coroner's jury. This does not prove that he should not be identified again, and the glory of
his capture be accredited to Colfax county.[56]

That editor was properly cynical, but, like many of his fellows, under-informed.
Once again, the words most grossly misinterpreted were those of Sam Ketchum.
All he said was that "Black Jack was killed over a year ago." He was speaking without footnotes, and did not stop to explain that some opinionated or misinformed
people had named the dead man as Tom Ketchum. The persistent misreporting of
the facts in northeastern New Mexico and southern Colorado was the consequence
of the apparent lack of any communication between officials in those areas with
those in southeast Arizona and southwest New Mexico, where the truth was known
to some.

Foraker, Thacker, and Powars escorted Sam to the territorial penitentiary at Santa
Fe, where he could be given proper medical treatment while the territorial and U.S.
authorities were reaching agreement as to which of them would try him. They arrived
in the evening and Ketchum was booked in as Number 129, a federal prisoner.[57]

Foraker and Reno evidently met in Springer before the marshal's departure with
Ketchum, for a day or so later the marshal complained in Santa Fe that, though he
had asked Reno not to wire the story of Sam's arrest until all the facts had been
learned, "the news was told at once anyway." If Foraker ever congratulated Reno on
his arrest of Ketchum,[58] he did so without eliciting a syllable of public notice. No
great percipience is needed to connect Foraker's displeasure to the fact that the arrest
was accomplished by Reno, rather than by someone from the marshal's office.

Reno's anger at the darts Foraker had previously hurled at him found an outlet
in an interview with the *Denver Republican*, much of which was also offered to the
rival *Rocky Mountain News* in the form of a written statement. The detective wisely
began by affecting not to believe that Foraker himself was their originator, thereby
throwing the onus upon Foraker to offer either a retraction or a rejoinder. But—
Reno's statement continued—if the marshal really had charged him with giving up
the fight at an early stage and deserting the posse, "he deliberately states what he
knows to be false or was misinformed."

Reno then proceeded to a description of the fight in the canyon. Next came a
retort that, despite Foraker's insistence to the contrary, Elliott was not in charge of
Farr or himself. After that, an avowal of harmony prior to the marshal's intervention:
"I did not know there was any dissension between our parties until my attention was
called to-day to that article attributed to Mr. Foraker."

Towards the end of his apologia, he reiterated its premise. His words, as the
News reported them, were these: "To say that I deserted in the fight is false." Readers
of the *Republican* were given more: "To say that I deserted the fight is a malicious
lie, and accuses Mr. Smith and poor Sheriff Farr, than whom a braver officer never

drew breath, of cowardice, and I say again no-one but a coward would make such a statement."[59]

Support for Reno was forthcoming in the same issue of both papers. His colleague Si Rainey spoke to the *News*. "[A] piece of base injustice to Reno," was his verdict on Foraker's intervention, "I have known him for a long time and I am sure he is of the stuff that would stand his ground. Besides he bears a scar to show that he was within reach of danger." The *Republican* printed a special from Trinidad, in which the surviving Farr brothers and Hugo Pfalmer angrily repudiated Foraker's attack upon Reno, stated that they could disprove the allegations, and observed that "Foraker did not get nearer the fight than Cimarron." Foraker neither reiterated nor withdrew, but renewed his accusations. The marshal might well have been irritated by what he could have seen as the meddling of interloping officials from Colorado. Their retort could have been that the refusal of the federal government to pay for more than five deputies, taken with the tepidity of the county's interest in the manhunt, justified and, indeed, necessitated intervention from outside. Neither Reno nor Foraker was a coward; in condemning each other as such, both had gone too far. The controversy would last for a further week; doubtless the ill-feeling outlived it.[60]

Meanwhile, Carver and Lay were getting away. Elliott was still in the field, along with Kreeger, Harry Lewis, Coker, and a few others; but the unending rain washed away all sign and with it, their chances. Elliott poked around the gang's former haunts at Baldy and had nothing to report except the dimness of the trail. Perhaps they were not altogether disappointed at the loss of an opportunity to try conclusions with one or more of the Winchesters that had destroyed the posse in Turkey Canyon.[61]

The fugitives had vanished. They would keep out of sight of all but a few friends for almost a month.

Red Weaver had already slipped out of the case. On the afternoon of July 20, on grounds and in a manner that were never disclosed or explained, Foraker procured Red's release. Weaver was freed on his own recognizance just before the southbound special train began the journey that would take Sam Ketchum to Santa Fe. He bought a ticket to Santa Fe, but shipped his saddle to Silver City, via Rincon and Deming.[62] Though he did not say so, his intention was to collect the saddle after his trip to Santa Fe, and then ride on to Alma to talk to Butch Cassidy, who was still employed on the WS's old ranch.

To a press correspondent who interviewed him in Springer just before his release, Weaver displayed a fine sense of outrage: "Just such arrests as this make train robbers. I have been arrested before for train robbery. Just because I came up here from Silver City with McGinnis is no evidence that I belong to this gang." The reporter, evidently knowing that Weaver had been discharged from the pesthouse some time before the robbery, was mystified by the whole affair:

> It is not known why Wheeler [*sic*] was released, for he was in continual company with McGinnis and Franks while they were at Springer and at Cimarron, after Wheeler was released from the pesthouse.[63]

That meeting at Springer between Foraker and Weaver may not have been their first since the robbery. If it was not, the warrantless "arrest" could have been prearranged to still conjecture as to why the officers were allowing Weaver to come and go as he pleased. Reno, who had obtained a writ for Red's arrest only a few hours before Foraker procured the man's release, said immediately after it that he did not believe Weaver to be guilty.[64] The whole sequence rings false.

If the authorities really believed that Weaver's contacts with the three principal suspects were incidental and innocent, they would have compelled him to testify for the Territory at Lay's trial for the murder of Farr. Since the prosecution needed to establish a connection between the robbery and the murder, testimony from Weaver on their movements and actions would have been of material help in securing that link.

Yet Weaver was not asked to testify. Why not? Surely because the officials knew that Red would not be able to cope well when Lay's attorneys set about him with questions about his own movements and actions between July 8 and July 11 and his precise whereabouts on the latter date. Weaver could not have told the truth without incriminating himself, and would not have been believed if he lied. Whichever he did, it was likely to antagonize jurors with no special affection for the railroads or for sheriffs from Colorado. Obviously, therefore, it was not in the Territory's interests that Weaver should be made to testify. But since, just as clearly, a summons to the stand would have been inimical to Red's own concerns, the territorial and federal authorities may have had the leverage to impose some kind of a deal on him.

If Weaver, like many another bandit, had traded a full confession for a promise of immunity from the courts, it is improbable that Foraker would have let him slope away so quickly. It is likelier that Red told a smooth story, gave a certain amount of general information, and perhaps even promised to keep in touch with the marshal's office. The purpose of Red's trip to Santa Fe was unstated, but he would have been there while Foraker, Thacker, and other officials were in attendance on Sam Ketchum. Whomever Weaver may have spoken to in Santa Fe, he disclosed nothing that might have led the officers to the WS and Butch Cassidy.

They might have wanted more than that. John Thacker, for all practical purposes Wells, Fargo's top detective, and Powars, the company's local route agent, were not hovering over Sam Ketchum's bedside to further their knowledge of medical science. They were hoping that Sam might say something to lead them not only to his principal confederates but, what mattered most, to the stolen money. If he remained incommunicative, they could try to make use of Red Weaver for the same ends.

They and Foraker may have figured that the bulk of the Folsom loot was unlikely to be in the saddlebags of the fleeing "Franks" and "McGinnis." Perhaps Weaver knew where it was. If he were allowed to go free, they might be able to track him to the hoard, or to someone with more precise knowledge than his. It would have been a good plan; the flaw was that Red and his friends were more cunning than the officers imagined.

While the tussle in Turkey Creek Canyon was a heavy tactical and moral defeat for the posse, it was in the longer term a kind of victory for them; there would be no Ketchum gang afterwards, whether led by Tom or Sam.

In a way, one man fashioned the course of events by having no part in them. If Tom Ketchum had been with the gang there might have been no incriminating envelope, no unguarded camp for a posse to surround at leisure, no battle in Turkey Canyon, and no Red Weaver.

Tom Ketchum at about twenty-five. *Courtesy Palomino Photo Collection.*

Samuel Wesley Ketchum (1854–99), aged about twenty.
Courtesy Palomino Photo Collection.

Temperance Katherine Wydick Ketchum
(1824–73). She and Green Berry Ketchum, Sr.,
(1820–68) were married on January 27, 1842.
Courtesy Berry Spradley.

Green Berry Ketchum (1850–1914), aged about thirty. *Courtesy Berry Spradley.*

Samuel Wesley Ketchum, aged about twenty-four. *Courtesy Berry Spradley.*

Louisa Greenlee Ketchum (1859–1943) (*at left*) in old age. *Courtesy Berry Spradley.*

Laura Ketchum (later Oliver, then Williams) (1879–1960), daughter of Sam and Louisa, in old age. *Courtesy Berry Spradley.*

Nicholas Ketchum (1829-1915),
a neighbor but no known blood relation of
the Green Berry Ketchum family. In 1885,
his son Henry married Clara Louise Shields,
whose sister Barsha Ola became the wife
of G.B. Ketchum, Jr., four years later.
Courtesy Berry Spradley.

William Richard Carver
(1868-1901), aged about fourteen. *Courtesy Causey family photo,
Donna B. Ernst Collection.*

William Carver, apparently between the ages of eighteen and twenty. The author found this photo on 24 May 2008, in the *Denver Republican* of 27 April 1901. Its earlier provenance has yet to be traced. *Courtesy Palomino Photo Collection.*

David Edward Atkins (1874–1964) (*left*) and unidentified friend or relative. *Courtesy Charles E. Avery.*

In 1967, the late Carl W. Breihan published this as a photo of William "Black Jack" Christian. The present writer accepted it as such until late in 2009, when Robert McCubbin of Santa Fe showed that the man in the photo, although unidentifiable, was almost certainly *not* Christian. *Courtesy Palomino Photo Collection.*

The caves in Cole Creek Canyon, near Clifton, Arizona, below which Christian was killed by an unaimed rifle shot from Deputy U.S. Marshal Fred Higgins, April 28, 1897. *Courtesy Palomino Photo Collection.*

Cave in Turkey Creek Canyon, near Cimarron, New Mexico, used as shelter by Will Carver during fight with posse on July 16, 1899. *Courtesy Donna B. Ernst.*

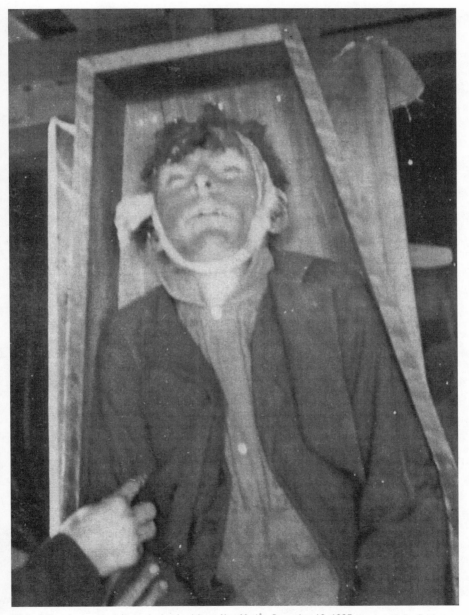

Edwin Cullen, deceased, photographed at Lordsburg, New Mexico, December 10, 1897. *Courtesy Marilyn Foraker.*

Steins Peak, New Mexico, seen from the east. *Courtesy Palomino Photo Collection.*

Steins Mountain, New Mexico, and the Southern Pacific track, seen from the east. *Courtesy Palomino Photo Collection.*

Two views of the former Charles store, Steins, New Mexico. In 1897 the building also accommodated the U.S. Post Office. *Courtesy Palomino Photo Collection.*

William Ellsworth "Elzy" Lay (1868–1934), alias William McGinnis, aged about twenty. *Courtesy Robert G. McCubbin Collection.*

William Kidder Meade (1851–1918), U.S. Marshal of New Mexico, 1885–89 and 1893–97, shown here in December, 1897, with canine friend, "Bob," during a visit to San Francisco. *Courtesy Palomino Photo Collection.*

Creighton Mays Foraker, (1861–1917), U.S. Marshal of New Mexico, 1897–1912 (*right*), and James J. ("Fighting Joe") Sheridan, his Chief Office Deputy from February, 1898, to November, 1900. Also present: "Bid the dog." *Courtesy Marilyn Foraker.*

William Hiram Reno (1862–1935), from a newspaper drawing of 1899, copied from a photograph. *Courtesy Donna B. Ernst.*

Edward J. Farr (1864–99), from a newspaper drawing of 1899, copied from a photograph. Farr arrived in Colorado from Kerrville, Texas, in 1881. *Courtesy Donna B. Ernst.*

Sam Ketchum, from a newspaper drawing, copied from a photograph taken just after his death on July 24, 1899. *Courtesy Palomino Photo Collection.*

Tom Ketchum, photographed in San Rafael Hospital, Trinidad, Colorado, August 21, 1899, by Deputy Sheriff George Titsworth, of Las Animas County. The man standing behind Ketchum is Harry Lewis, another local deputy sheriff. *Courtesy Palomino Photo Collection.*

Tom Ketchum posing with a revolver (unloaded), after removal of his beard. He was allowed to retain the small vanity of his large mustache. This is another of the four photographs taken by George Titsworth on August 21, 1899. *Courtesy Berry Spradley.*

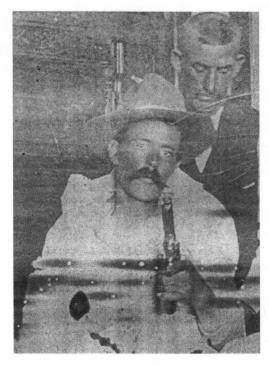

Tom Ketchum's buckshot-mangled right arm, photographed in the New Mexico Territorial Penitentiary by the visiting surgeon, Miguel Desmarias, shortly before amputation. *Courtesy Marilyn Foraker.*

Tom Ketchum's right arm, photographed by Dr. Desmarias, post-amputation, September 2, 1899. *Courtesy Marilyn Foraker.*

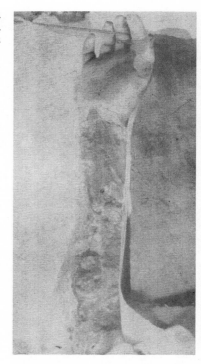

Elzy Lay, in custody, Carlsbad, New Mexico, probably August 17 or 18, 1899, before removal to Santa Fe via Trinidad, Colorado. *Courtesy Marilyn Foraker.*

Elzy Lay, as received by New Mexico Territorial Penitentiary under the name of William H. McGinnis, after his conviction on October 10, 1899, for second-degree murder and the subsequent rejection of his appeal. *Courtesy New Mexico Department of Corrections Glass Negative Collection, #13480.*

Elzy Lay, shown here in prison uniform and after the tonsorial attentions of the prison authorities, following his formal entry into the Territorial Penitentiary, May 4, 1900. *Courtesy New Mexico Department of Corrections Glass Negative Collection, #13486.*

Cicero Stewart, his wife Missouri, and their daughter and younger son, ca.1904. Courtesy Jan Devereaux and the Southeast New Mexico Historical Society, Carlsbad.

The photograph that is ubiquitous, yet indispensable: five of the most hunted criminals in America face the studio camera in Fort Worth, Texas, on November 21, 1900. *Left to right: standing,* Will Carver and Harvey "Kid Curry" Logan; *sitting,* Harry "Sundance Kid" Longabaugh, Ben Kilpatrick, and Robert "Butch Cassidy" Parker. *Courtesy Donna B. Ernst.*

Street scene and general view, Sonora, Texas, 1897. *Courtesy Sutton County (Texas) Historical Society.*

Interior of saloon, Sonora, Texas. *Courtesy Sutton County (Texas) Historical Society.*

The Owens bakery and store, Sonora, Texas. *Courtesy Sutton County (Texas) Historical Society.*

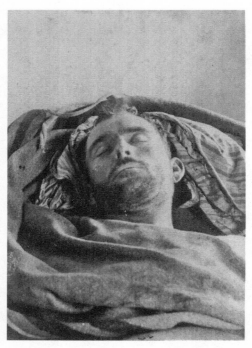

Will Carver, awaiting the undertaker, April 3, 1901. This is one of two photographs taken of Carver after his death from gunshot wounds sustained the previous evening. *Courtesy Sutton County (Texas) Historical Society.*

Will Carver's grave, Sonora, Texas. *Courtesy Sutton County (Texas) Historical Society.*

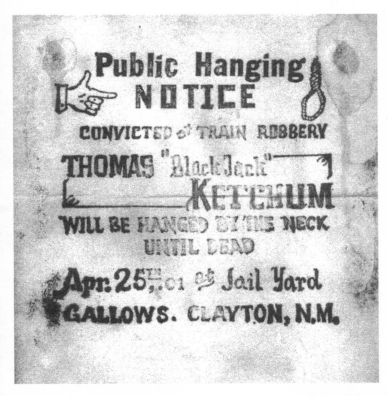

Public Hanging NOTICE

CONVICTED of TRAIN ROBBERY

THOMAS "Black Jack" KETCHUM

WILL BE HANGED BY THE NECK UNTIL DEAD

Apr. 25, 01 at Jail Yard

GALLOWS. CLAYTON, N.M.

Above: Poster announcing Tom Ketchum's forthcoming execution. The advertised date is a day ahead of the right one.

Right: Admission tickets were allocated before the date was reset. *Courtesy Berry Spradley.*

This Ticket Will Admit *A. W. Thompson* Within the enclosure as a witness to the execution of Thomas Ketchum, at Clayton March 22, 1901.

SHERIFF

APPROVED

DISTRICT ATTORNEY.

The Colorado & Southern Railway Company.

Railroad pass issued to Tom Ketchum for the journey that would take him from the Territorial Penitentiary to the Union County Jail, Clayton, New Mexico. *Courtesy Berry Spradley.*

Tom Ketchum, dressed for the occasion, stands in the corridor of the County Jail at Clayton, New Mexico, ready to meet the Press on the morning of April 26, 1901. *Courtesy Palomino Photo Collection.*

The yard, Clayton jail, 1:15 p.m; Tom Ketchum on the scaffold. *Courtesy Arizona Historical Society.*

Close-up of the same scene. *Courtesy Palomino Photo Collection.*

Approximately 1:18 p.m. One of the three photographs taken of the scene beneath the gallows directly after the execution. *Courtesy Palomino Photo Collection.*

Black Jack — After his execution.

Another of the three post-execution photographs. *Courtesy Arizona Historical Society.*

Berry and Barsha Ketchum (1865–1937), with Nora, the first of their three daughters. Nora was born on May 2, 1891 and was evidently about one year old when the picture was taken. *Courtesy Berry Spradley.*

Abijah Duncan, Jr., (1856–?) and Nancy Ketchum Duncan (1860–1937), and six of their seven children, about 1894. Nancy, Tom's favorite sister, and "Bige," a good friend of Sam in particular, had married on December 11, 1879. *Courtesy Berry Spradley.*

The Silver Dollar saloon, Agua Prieta, Sonora, Mexico, circa 1903/5. Agua Prieta and Douglas, Arizona, are separated by the international border and not much else. The saloon, or more probably the scene in front of it, is believed to have been of some significance to the life of Bige Duncan, but it is not known how or why. The man standing above the 'x', fourth from the left, cannot be identified. *Courtesy Berry Spradley.*

The Stag saloon, location unknown. This place, or someone shown standing in front of it, is also supposed to have been important to Bige Duncan, but, again, no explanation is available. *Courtesy Berry Spradley.*

John Wesley Smith (1847–1918) and Elizabeth Ketchum Smith (1848–1932), with six of their eventual eleven children, about 1883. Elizabeth, the elder of Tom's sisters, married John Smith in 1867. *Courtesy Berry Spradley.*

William Berry Ketchum, (1876–1951), son of Sam and Louisa, with his bride, the former Mattie Louise Hines (1886–1961). Their first child, Rosa Lee Ketchum, was born on October 17, 1907, a year or two after the apparent date of this photo.
Courtesy Berry Spradley.

First grave of Black Jack, before the body was removed to cemetery at Clayton, New Mexico.

Tom Ketchum's grave, outside Clayton, N.M., 1933. *Courtesy Philip St. George Cooke.*

Above: The courthouse and jail building at Clayton, 1969. *Courtesy Philip St. George Cooke.*
Below: Tom Ketchum's grave, 1969. *Courtesy Philip St. George Cooke.*

Daniel Moroni "Red" Pipkin (1876–1937), upon entering Arizona Territorial Prison, Yuma, October 20, 1900. *Courtesy Arizona State Prison.*

Grave of William "Bronco Bill" Walters (1869–1921), Hachita, N.M., Photograph taken in 2005. *Courtesy Palomino Photo Collection.*

Commemorative stone near grave of Samuel Wesley Ketchum. The corner of the Odd Fellows cemetery, where Sam was buried, was later overtaken by a road-widening program; so the grave itself now lies beneath the Albuquerque-Santa Fe highway. *Courtesy Berry Spradley.*

Commemorative stone on grave of Thomas Edward Ketchum. *Courtesy Berry Spradley.*

THOMAS EDWARD BLACK JACK KETCHUM
OCT 31, 1863 – APR 26, 1901
AND HOW HIS AUDIT
STANDS WHO KNOWS
SAVE HEAVEN

TOM AND BROTHER SAM CHOSE THE OUTLAW TRAIL AND PAID
THE ULTIMATE PRICE. SAM WAS SHOT BY A POSSE AND
IS BURIED IN SANTA FE. TOM WAS HUNG IN CLAYTON AND
IS BURIED HERE

Berry Spradley, c. 1982. Ernest Berry Spradley's mother, the former Wallene Ketchum (1919–2001), was the third daughter of William B. and Mattie Ketchum. Her brother, John Berry ("J.B.") Ketchum (1915–1973), married an Englishwoman during the Second World War. Their children were born in America but now live in England. *Courtesy Berry Spradley.*

{ 14 }

THE SIXTEENTH OF AUGUST

Sam Ketchum would have little information for the law, despite the pressing efforts of his official invigilators. Although much weakened by pain and the loss of blood, he "rested easily" the following afternoon, complaining only that his swollen arm "seemed to weigh about three hundred pounds." At one point he told Foraker that he was sure that "Bill McGinnis" was dead, "as his wound was dangerous and only his pluck kept him from dropping."[1] It is unlikely that Sam believed Lay's wounds to be mortal; his object may have been less to inform than to mislead.

In the cell next to is was an old acquaintance and fellow bandit, William Walters, commonly called "Bronco Bill," who had recovered from a severe wound suffered in the fight that ended with his capture and the death of his partner, Bill Johnson. Now, almost a year later, he still awaited trial. In a legal sense, their two cases were analogous: both Ketchum and Walters had committed train robbery, and both had been in battles in which pursuing possemen were killed.[2] In the medical sense, their cases were drastically different. Sam's wound, in itself, was less serious than Bronco Bill's: given prompt attention, he would have recuperated quite quickly. But gangrene had set in before he was captured. By the time he reached Santa Fe his condition was critical.

Foraker, Thacker, and Powars were at the penitentiary for most of July 21st. Before midday they were joined by Chief Justice William J. Mills, presiding judge of the fourth judicial district, Judge John R. McFie and District Clerk A.M. Bergere, both of the first district, and Governor Miguel A. Otero, for a thorough discussion of the Folsom case. Nothing emerged from the conference, apart from a vacuous announcement that "every effort [would] be exerted in bringing in the other two of the gang."[3]

Otherwise, Foraker assumed the role of spokesman for all. He grabbed the opportunity to renew his attack on Reno, charging him with premature disclosure of Ketchum's arrest and misrepresentation of the facts. When Reno's response to his earlier accusation was drawn to their notice, he, Thacker, and Powars at first "would express no opinion for publication on the merits of the case, but in private expressed themselves forcibly and freely."[4]

The case, Foraker maintained, was "entirely in [his] hands;" the only posse in the field was a force of ten men put into the field by himself and Wells, Fargo. Here, the marshal's self assurance had stolen a march on his information; while it was true that many who joined the hunt in its first days had now retired from the field, Reno was out again, this time with Kreeger, Titsworth, and David Farr.[5]

Foraker did not "think it possible" that the robbers had escaped from Turkey Canyon in daylight, even though one of the posse reported having seen them ride away. He denied the truthful claim, pressed oftenest and most forcibly by his chosen representative, Elliott, that two of the bandits' horses had been killed.[6]

Then, forgetting that he had just professed a judicious reticence about the controversy ignited by his allegations against Reno, he repeated them. He scored Reno for not seeking to make contact with Elliott after the fight, but offered no opinion on Elliott's failure to put himself in touch with Reno; an odd omission, especially in the light of the emphasis the marshal placed on Elliott's status as leader of the posse.

For interest superadded, Foraker complained about Reno's refusal to guide his search party to the scene of the action because, according to the marshal, he (Reno) wanted to go to Springer.[7]

We have already seen that Reno had no need to leave for Springer until late that night, and did not do so. The prosaic truth may have been that Reno, who had been on the mountain all night, was too tired to ride out with Foraker, who had been in bed all night.

Ketchum's trial, declared the *New Mexican*, would bring out the facts and "settle the dispute that has arisen between officer Reno and others."[8] This statement rested on the false assumption that the bandit would be put on trial, and the fallacious premise that the Foraker-Reno controversy could not be resolved by other means.

The territorial authorities, Sam knew, hoped to keep him alive only because they wanted him to stand trial for a capital offense. When he entered the penitentiary he evidently expected to survive his wound, and his opinion may have changed only in his last few hours.[9] He told both Reno and Foraker he had fired the shot that killed Ed Farr. Part of his motive may have been a desire to exonerate his companions; though his admission, if credited, would not help them evade a capital charge of train robbery. His other, and perhaps stronger reason, would have been to invite a trial for murder, instead of train robbery. A trial for train robbery was sure to end with his conviction and the death sentence. But if he were tried for murder, the circumstances of the Turkey Canyon affair were such that, given an adroit attorney and a fair hearing, he could come out of it with a conviction for murder in the second degree, or even manslaughter.

Whether Ketchum ever realized it or not, such considerations would soon be pointless. When, on Sunday, July 23, the prison surgeon, Miguel F. Desmarias, told him he would die unless the arm were amputated he refused to allow the operation and—if he accepted the doctor's prognosis—calmly awaited death. Desmarias tried to wring information on the Folsom robbery out of his patient, even spinning a yarn that "the other fellows" had been caught; therefore, argued the surgeon, Sam might just as well offer a full statement. "The other fellows will tell the story," Sam replied, with simple logic.[10]

But he did tell Desmarias that he and the rest of the Ketchum gang had attempted the train robbery at Steins Pass, and that the three men who had been imprisoned for the crime were innocent of it. He volunteered the same information to Ernest Hart, a convict nurse; to Robert Law, the cellhouse keeper at the penitentiary; and to Law's assistant, Antonio Borrego. Sam also retold his tale that his brother Tom had been dead for some months. This purported revelation, Sam explained, was intended for the consolation of his brother Berry—which suggests a glint of sardonic humor, given his knowledge of the true state of relations between Berry and Tom—rather than for the benefit of the officers, for whom he manifested "a violent hatred."[11]

In the small hours of the following morning, Bronco Bill Walters heard his neighbor walking about his cell. He heard nothing to indicate that the man was dying, but when the keeper entered the cell at 8 a.m. Sam Ketchum's life had run its course.[12]

Later that day H.O. Bursum, the superintendent of the penitentiary, wired Sheriff Shield that Sam had died of blood poisoning. Shield showed the telegram to Berry Ketchum, and the two men left San Angelo that night. They arrived at Santa Fe on Thursday, the 27th, and formally identified the body. Soon a confirmatory telegram was on its way from Berry to his wife.[13]

Shield listened to Memph Elliott's account of the Turkey Canyon shooting and looked in on another friend from the old days, Jim Hiler, "formerly a well known cattleman of Concho County," but now a resident of the New Mexico Territorial Penitentiary. Hiler had almost completed the sentence imposed on him for "killing a man several years ago, who alienated the affections of his wife."[14]

Berry declined to speak upon the subject of Sam's outlawry, although he found the face to assert that "he had neither seen nor heard from his brother for many years." After arranging with Undertaker Charles Wagner for the body to be interred in the Odd Fellows cemetery, Berry and Shield returned to San Angelo. The *New Mexican* reported that theirs had been a sad mission," and the scene beside Sam's corpse, a touching one. Still, their visit had not been impelled by sentiment alone; Shield, at least, was traveling at Wells, Fargo's expense.[15]

While Sam Ketchum's life was ebbing away in the territorial penitentiary, the search for Will Carver and Elzy Lay was quietly given up. The latest rumors put them on the road to Taos, but these produced neither results nor confirmation. Elliott seems to have abandoned the hunt even before his chief, Foraker, booked Sam Ketchum into the penitentiary. Reno, with Dave Farr, Kreeger, Titsworth, and Lewis, withdrew a day or two later. Their efforts, like Elliott's, ended on the slopes of Baldy Mountain.

After his return to Denver on July 24, Reno issued a description of the two wanted men:

McGinnis . . . is 33 years old, 5 feet 11 inches high, and weighs 175 pounds; medium complexion, brown moustache, large, gray, pop eyes. Franks is 35 years old, 5 feet 8 inches, stout build, and weighs about 170 pounds. When last seen he had a three months' growth of brown beard on his face. Slightly familiar with the Spanish [language]. Both men are from the Sulphur Spring valley, near the Mexican border.[16]

The particulars of "McGinnis," with his distinctive, slightly bulging eyeballs, are not only fuller but more accurate than those for "Franks," who was probably about twenty pounds lighter and an inch shorter than his description, as well as five years younger. Later, a more detailed set of particulars was issued for "Franks," but his weight and height were still overstated.[17]

Since Reno did not identify McGinnis as Lay, or Franks as Carver, the reward he advertised was for only $700 per man. Whether through the shortcomings of the published descriptions, the meagerness of the reward, or the slipperiness of the subjects, there were no early takers.

Reno's posse had accomplished one other important task in New Mexico. They went to the site of the killings in Turkey Creek Canyon, where Reno guided Dave Farr and the rest over the ground. Farr conducted what amounted to a one-man inquiry. He spoke to Smith, Elliott, Cordova, and Morgan, and on July 24 stated his conclusions in writing.

> I find that Mr. Reno stayed during the fight and fought as hard as any other man in the battle, and I find from the position of the train robbers and the position of the posse that Mr. Reno was placed in the hardest part of the fight with my brother and Mr. Smith . . . Mr. Reno was the first man after the fight to go to the assistance of the wounded men . . . Mr. Smith requested Mr. Reno to go and get help as soon as possible and Mr. Reno left his gun with Mr. Smith and started afoot for Cimarron as it was impossible for him to take his horse on account of the condition of the road and the darkness . . . This statement was made to me personally by Mr. Smith. I also saw the balance of the posse, who thoroughly confirmed Mr. Smith's statement regarding the actions of Mr. Reno during the fight . . . I have no hesitancy in saying that the reports regarding Mr. Reno are false and were published with the intention of doing him every injustice possible. I went to Springer and over to the ground . . . purely to ascertain whether my brother had been deserted by any one of the posse as reported in the newspapers. In justice to others who were in the fight . . . as nearly as I could ascertain, every man stood his ground bravely and did everything possible to capture the robbers . . . Yours truly
>
> D.E. FARR[18]

Thus Reno was vindicated in irrefutable terms. Farr could not have made it more obvious that the blame for the unseemly row belonged to Foraker, even without mentioning his name.

Regional self-regard may explain the failure of newspapers in New Mexico to publish a line on David Farr's findings. One must look further for an understanding of the hostility to Reno's name and reputation that persisted in northeast New Mexico long after the factual details of the Turkey Canyon fight had faded from local memory. We have already mentioned the derogatory tone that infuses William French's vivid account of a meeting with Reno that never happened. Mason Chase's version of the fight and subsequent arrest of Sam Ketchum, which we have also alighted on, is almost rabid in its denigration of Reno—and correspondingly fulsome in its commendation of the ambivalent "Billy" Morgan.

More surprising is the strain of malice in a transparently untrue anecdote retailed by Jim Hunt's nephew, Ernest Ludlum, whose reminiscences otherwise give the impression of a trustworthy witness and narrator. Ludlum first describes, quite accurately, how Reno arrived at the Hunt store at about seven o'clock on the morning after the fight, having walked all night and "got lost in the meantime." He then takes leave of factuality. Reno's derby hat, he remarks, was holed in a number of places; and, though "his swallow-tail coat was riddled on one side with bullet holes," his body was unscratched. The wiseacres of Cimarron, Ludlum would have us believe, "examined the coat," deduced that Reno would have been hit had he been wearing it in action, and concluded that he "had done his own shooting."[19]

Such taradiddle is deserving of the derision it seeks to excite. It requires no recapitulation of the facts; under the gentle pressure of a few seconds' thought, it refutes itself. Since Reno was unarmed when he left the canyon, he could not have stopped by the wayside to perforate his own habiliments with hot lead. He could not have done so before he quit the canyon without the action being noticed by Smith. If he had had the means and the intent to shoot holes through his garments after quitting the canyon, he would not have been so idiotic as to make a target out of his hat, because a hole in the hat would have to be matched by a hole in the head or a hair-raising description of a hair-parting near miss. Aside from which, neither Reno nor any contemporary reporter made any reference to the state of his hat.

Foraker's motive in attacking Reno is plain to see: the posse had suffered a bloody reverse, and someone was going to get the blame for it. Foraker knew who was principally at fault: he was. He ought to have chosen better material and better leadership for his posse, and given it clear instructions. As he could not possibly admit to such glaring culpability, the blame would have to be shunted along the line. Foraker was, on the whole, an energetic and capable officer. It should be stated in his defense that he was shackled by the regulations and policies that the Department of Justice was required to operate, and that he often complained about it. Even so, he cannot be said in this instance to have made the best of a bad job.

In Las Vegas, Santa Fe, and Albuquerque—far from the scene of the battle in the canyon—Foraker could deflect attention from his own mistakes by heaping odium on an outsider. Reno met that simple specification; therefore he could be charged with dereliction, never mind how unjustly but at all events loudly. Cries of cowardice and desertion would rally the emotional responses that inhibit scrutiny and thought.

Similar considerations may account for some of the animosity directed at Reno by residents of Colfax County. At its root may have been something close to a collective sense of guilt. Cimarron and district furnished only three members of the posse that engaged the robbers in Turkey Canyon. One of these, Morgan, had been living in the area for only eighteen months, and was on call as a semi-regular employee of the marshal's office, anyway. A second, Cordova, seems to have offered his services only because he wanted the fee. The third, Love, being a deputy sheriff, may have been genuinely public spirited, and was unlucky enough to have to pay for it with his life.

The robbery of 1897 was well remembered in Cimarron; the names of the main suspects were well known there, and their faces even more so. Sam Ketchum, for instance, was reported to have stayed at one of the town's three hotels just before the first Folsom robbery.[20] Many of the people of Cimarron must have known full well who and what their visitors were, but said and did nothing about it even after the second robbery. Only the storekeeper, Hunt, showed energy in keeping tabs on them and subsequently cooperating with the investigation. Like Foraker, but for different reasons, the citizenry of Cimarron wanted to evade the beam of adverse speculation. Foraker's allegations of Reno's defection provided the requisite diversion. All the law-abiding folk of Cimarron had to do was elaborate and distort them.

Cimarron, furthermore, was the kind of small, isolated place where railroad and express companies were unpopular, often because their shipping charges were held to be far too high. As an employee of the powerful Colorado and Southern Railway, Reno may have been taken as personifying its interests, and thus made the focus of the community's resentment of the company's policy.

There could have been a third factor. George Armstrong Custer's defeat and death at Little Big Horn had not slipped far away from public memory. Custer's subordinate, William Reno's distant kinsman Marcus Reno, was almost universally—though, as has been proved, unfairly—reviled for military turpitude, or worse.[21] Once Foraker's accusations against another Reno were in circulation, no great striving was needed to recast coincidence into an injurious association of ideas.

As Berry Ketchum and Gerome Shield rode the rails homeward through Trinidad and Fort Worth and on to San Angelo, much of the regional press was overtaken by a fit of irresponsibility of a different order. Stories were rife that the remnants of the "Black Jack Gang" were rampant in southwest Texas. Their ultimate source was a dispatch created by a nameless express company official in Fort Worth on July 27, the day on which Berry and Shield reached Santa Fe. The brunt of the allegations was that, on the preceding Sunday, July 23, the three unnamed desperadoes rode through San Angelo two or three times, "daring the authorities;" and that Shield had reacted by asking the attorney general of the state for a squad of rangers. The story, unchecked, embarked on a career of its own. One speciously circumstantial improvement, wired on July 28, put the trio near Knickerbocker, riding horses owned by a rancher from Sterling—that crossways for the gang on many of their journeyings between Texas and New Mexico. Some dispatches confidently identified Tom Ketchum as one of the three. One compiled in Austin, the state capital, foretold his capture; the rangers would have him next day.[22]

John "Pat" Murphy, the usually genial editor of the *San Angelo Standard*, reacted with fury when he saw the original Fort Worth telegram in the *Houston Post*. Doubtless he received every encouragement from a freshly returned and irate Gerome Shield. He reprinted the offending dispatch below a familiar quotation:

"SOMEONE HAS BLUNDERED"

Blunder? It was a fatuity. Let the editor speak:

> A statement more full of falsehood, and more utterly uncalled for, or with less foun-
> dation in fact, has never appeared in the public print of Texas. Not only is it untrue
> but it does injury in two ways: it reflects upon the officers of Tom Green county, and
> it casts a slur upon San Angelo's good name . . . Were an Eastern man to read that
> item, . . . he would come in fear and trembling . . . a "hog leg" in each coat pocket,
> wear a bowie knife in the waistband of his unmentionables, and come out prepared to
> kill or be killed . . . He would hardly believe his eyes when he saw two banks in a town
> of 5000 inhabitants carrying deposits to the amount of $1,000,000, and not having to
> be guarded by a whole regiment of soldiers . . . Out with such rot! . . . The telegraph
> editor of the Post must have been drunk when he allowed so obvious a lie to escape
> the devastating stroke of his blue pencil, and the Fort Worth reporter who sent it in
> and the express official who fathered it should draw off the addled batter that does
> them duty for brains, and fill the cavities in their skulls with brick dust. . . . The
> STANDARD files an emphatic protest [against] this method of manufacturing news
> at the expense of one of the most peaceful towns and best set[s] of officers in Texas.[23]

There was this much truth in the report: "Sheriff Shields [*sic*] did send in a telegram
to the state authorities requesting that rangers be sent to this section, but it was done
solely because . . . he desired their cooperation in looking after some train robbers
and cattle thieves who are known to infest some of the counties west of here."[24] The
miscreants were not identified; but, whoever they were, they had not trodden the
placid groves of Tom Green County.

That Tom Green County old boy, Will Carver, and the wounded Elzy Lay, might
have gone underground for all the authorities knew of their whereabouts. To this day no
firm evidence has emerged as to where they passed the three weeks that followed their
parting with Sam Ketchum on the night of July 16. One story has the outlaws hiding out
for several weeks on a ranch, a few miles south of Elizabethtown, where a local man with
some knowledge of medicine tended Lay's wounds. Another, maybe a variant of the
same one, was told in later years by Miguel Otero. In his memoirs, the ex-governor wrote
that Lay was hidden and looked after for four weeks by a Spanish-American couple, who
were well paid for their devotions. Carver, wrote Otero, went on alone to the Carlsbad
area while Lay's wounds were mending. Their rendezvous would be at or near the
Chimney Wells horse camp of V.H. Lusk in mid-August.[25]

The officers were looking elsewhere. In the absence of real information, they
were guided by the likeliest assumption, which was that their quarry had reached
Cochise County. This was reasonable, but wrong. Early in August, Jim Hunt, who was
becoming Reno's most willing assistant, accompanied the detective to Bowie,
Arizona, where they picked up a man thought to be "G.W. Franks." The journey was
a wasted one, but Hunt did not lose his appetite for detective work or for the concomitant publicity.[26]

At about this point, and in a manner yet to be fully determined, the problematic persona of Tom Capehart flits back into the picture. Even then, his place in it is as tentative as it is obscure. It depends largely upon the *Recollections* of William French, which sometimes offer more in the way of entertainment than enlightenment. Not to trifle with the truth, this younger son of lesser Anglo-Irish gentry sowed a fair crop of whoppers in his reminiscences of ranch life in New Mexico.

Tom Capehart appears in a dozen of French's pages, but we cannot be sure that French's Capehart is always the real Capehart. The suspicion arises that the Capehart who cuts so dashing a figure in the *Recollections* is a composite of the real Capehart, Will Carver, and the Sundance Kid, perhaps rounded off with a few furbelows from the honorable captain's imagination. The one certainty about French's Capehart is in the negative: he was not, in whole or in part, Harvey Logan, as some have asserted and others assumed.

Another part of the case for the reintroduction of Capehart at this juncture is negative, too. It rests on the impossibility of locating Capehart anywhere other than in northeastern and eastern New Mexico during July and the first half of August, 1899, which is where French says he was. But it is a fact that, sometime before the spring of 1900, Capehart joined a gang of outlaws in Arizona, whose membership included Will Carver and at least one of the Kilpatrick brothers.[27] Taking all in all, we can accept the core of French's testimony that Capehart and Lay were together after the Turkey Creek fight, despite the further difficulty that French wrongly identifies "Franks" as Capehart and mentions Carver nowhere at all.

It is likely, therefore, that Capehart was involved in the train robbing scheme from the beginning, though not as a participant. His role may have been to wait with a change of horses somewhere in the Ponil country, west of Turkey Creek. If we extend the credit we have allowed this segment of French's narrative, Capehart attended Lay during the wounded man's convalescence and accompanied him when the wound was sufficiently healed for travel.[28] This makes it easier to absorb Otero's story that Carver had gone ahead alone; it is hard to believe that the wounded man would have been left with no company other than that provided by the people who were harboring him.

The ride was a long one, which ended three hundred miles southeast of Taos, where rumor had last placed Carver and Lay. Given Lay's condition, they must have begun it a week or more before their presence was noted in southeast New Mexico, twenty-five miles east of the recently renamed town of Carlsbad (formerly Eddy).

But it was only the first stage of their journey. After a short stay in the Pecos country they intended to cross the territory and go to ground near Alma or in south-eastern Arizona. Capehart later told William French that his purpose had been to find employment on a local ranch until Lay was fully recovered. It was subsequently claimed in Carlsbad that Carver and Lay visited the town on four consecutive days during this time, allegedly to size up the possibilities of robbing the bank.[29] If this is true, the two are likelier to have been Carver and Capehart—since, in French's retelling of Capehart's story, Lay was resting. Either way, it is most improbable that they entertained serious thoughts of trying their hands at bank robbery just then.

Such an enterprise would have been quite as hazardous as a return to Colfax County for the Folsom loot. They might, however, have studied the bank and its surroundings for future reference.

At Chimney Wells, V.H. Lusk and his men were waiting for someone to claim the three Erie horses that had drifted down onto Lusk's range. Lusk knew, of course, which bunch of outlaws had turned the animals loose; it was the outfit who had stopped by his place a number of times in the last two or three years to swap their jaded mounts for horses they had left to fatten on his range, perhaps months earlier. Hence, he knew more or less whom to expect. By the summer of 1899, Lusk said, he was beginning to suspect that these men were horse thieves. He must have been strangely myopic before this, since the Ketchums had been widely known as cowpunchers in the Pecos Valley long before they became the most notorious professional robbers in the whole of the Southwest. But in the summer of 1899, a sudden and unforeseen change of circumstances told Lusk that the old laisser-faire understanding between himself and his freebooting visitors would have to end.[30]

Lusk seems to have been unsettled by a series of events that had begun with Cicero Stewart's capture of Knight, Ware, Morrow, and Dan Johnson in May, 1899, and the misidentification of Johnson as Black Jack. Enoch and Jonas Shattuck, owners of the Erie outfit of Sulphur Spring Valley, knew that three of their horses had been stolen by the so called "Black Jack gang." When they heard news of the arrests they asked Stewart by letter whether he had seen the Erie's Slash brand on any of the horses found in the possession of the four prisoners.

He had not; but a few days later another cowman, Tom White, told him that thieves had recently left three hard-ridden Slash-branded ponies at the horse-camp of his LFD outfit in exchange for three fresh mounts taken from there. When the three Erie animals drifted onto Lusk's range at Chimney Wells, Lusk either volunteered, or agreed, to send word to Stewart as soon as someone turned up to claim them. The probable alternative was to face prosecution for helping criminals to escape. It is also possible that, by this time, he was becoming tired of the periodical presence of the outlaws, anyway.[31]

None of this could have been suspected by Carver and Lay. On Tuesday evening, August 15, the two of them came up to the Lusk house from the east, riding two gaunt ponies and leading a third. Lusk, amenable as usual, gave them straight answers. Yes, the horses they wanted were on his range, although one of them, a gray, was running with Lusk's own remuda away on the salt-grass flat. He suggested they wait until morning before looking for the gray, and invited them to stay the night under his roof. They replied that they would rather sleep out, where there was better grazing for their ponies. Besides, they had lost a good many horses, and were anxious to start looking for those that were loose. Before the men went they told Lusk that, in the morning, they would be taking breakfast at his horse camp.

Lusk was worried lest something in his manner had put the outlaws on their guard. Reassured when he saw their campfire glowing through the dusk from a high hill to the north of the house, he mounted his best horse and rode to Carlsbad.

Cicero Stewart could not afford to use up time by raising a large posse. He enlisted the help of Rufus W. Thomas and John D. Cantrell, and got ready to leave at once.

Rufe Thomas, like Stewart, had known the Ketchums before they turned outlaw. He was also well acquainted with Will Carver. He had been raised on a cattle ranch in West Texas, and as a young man worked as a cowboy before finding his vocation. When he found it, he did well out of it. His calling was that of professional gambler, and he followed it successively in such towns as San Angelo, Sonora, and Roswell before moving to Eddy. Thomas was a small man, but, wrote his friend of long standing, John Loomis, "lithe and tough" and "an expert at handling a six-shooter . . . I doubt whether a cooler, braver man ever lived on the Texas frontier." When Stewart called at the gambling room he was then running in Carlsbad, Thomas at first declined to go with him. Stewart changed the gambler's mind by turning the request into something more like a challenge; Thomas, observed the sheriff, was "just like the rest of the citizens who refused to help in an emergency." Thomas, having no rifle with him, borrowed one from Silas T. Bitting's store, thinking little of a bystander's warning that the gun was liable to hang fire.

It was midnight when the three men began the twenty-mile ride to Lusk's horse camp, where they hoped to trap the fugitives. During the ride Thomas's horse missed its step and nearly threw him. Only later did he notice that his six-shooter was missing from its scabbard; it had been jerked free when his horse stumbled.

At about four o'clock in the morning they swung down from their exhausted mounts by Lusk's camp. John Lusk, the rancher's nineteen year old son, hobbled the horses of the posse in a dip, so that they would not be seen by the two incoming guests. He then cut the Erie gray from the herd and corraled the remainder. A tarpaulin was thrown over the saddles and equipment of the posse, who stationed themselves in a dry tank, encircled by barbed wire. Some two hundred yards from this tank was pitched a tent, which served as Lusk's camp headquarters. Daylight broke with no sign of the pair, and it began to look as if they were not going to put in an appearance.

Carver and Lay had rounded up two of the Erie horses and another, branded 8D Connected, which had been abandoned just over a year earlier, when the gang were fleeing across New Mexico after their raid on the Texas and Pacific. They were still determined to pick up the gray, and after a futile search Lay proposed that he and Carver take their breakfast by turns; while one man ate, the other would scour the prairie for the elusive pony, at the same time keeping watch for the approach of any unwanted stranger.

Mounted on the 8D horse and leading one of the Erie animals, Lay jogged down from the hill and into Lusk's camp. After dismounting, he surveyed the horizon through his field glasses, apparently uneasy because Carver had vanished from the skyline. Lusk, afraid that the newcomer might discover the posse before they were ready to act, then stepped up and with a good imitation of a hearty welcome, called the outlaw to go inside for breakfast. Lay tied the two horses to a wagon laden with barrels of water and followed Lusk into the tent. The wagon was a good deal closer to the tent than to the tank, but the horses were tethered on the side nearer to the officers.

Somewhere inside the tent Stewart had concealed a rifle. The stratagem was for Lusk to show himself at the entrance of the tent as soon as he had located the weapon; then, while the posse was charging across the open ground, the rancher was to seize the rifle and hold the men under guard. There were only two flaws in this plan: it was based on the assumption that the outlaws would ride into camp together, and it presupposed that Lusk would have no trouble in finding the gun. The second miscalculation would have been obviated if Stewart had shown the rancher where he had hidden the weapon, instead of merely telling him.

While Lay was gulping down his breakfast, Lusk shambled around the tent, hoping to chance upon the rifle. Thus preoccupied, he forgot about the prearranged signal and blundered into the opening of the tent. Immediately the posse scrambled over the barbed-wire fence and rushed toward the wagon. But their noisy struggles with the wire alarmed the horses, whose neighing added to the commotion. Lay rose in alarm, and glanced outside. At once he rounded upon Lusk.

"Did *you* do this?" he growled. But there was no time to settle the matter just then. In a desperate effort to get to his horses and rifle before the posse could reach them, he sprang through the opening and ran. Rufus Thomas almost beat him there but he ignored the posseman's leveled rifle and was deaf to his command to surrender. Drawing his pistol, he dodged under the wagon. Thomas twice squeezed the trigger of the borrowed rifle, but each time the gun misfired. With Stewart and Cantrell now joining the fight, Lay retreated toward the tent. He caught sight of Lusk, who, still unarmed, was trying to duck away from the line of fire. By now he had made up his mind about Lusk.

"You old son of a bitch, you're the cause of this!" he bawled. Lusk instinctively turned to run as the bandit took aim. The bullet plowed along the rancher's wrist and forearm but did not hamper his flight. Belatedly, Thomas remembered the advice shouted to him as he was riding out of town. At the third attempt, just as Lay was running behind the tent, he got off a shot from the rusty old weapon. Then Lay peered out and fired back. The gambler was knocked almost off his feet as the outlaw's second bullet scorched through his left arm and thudded beneath the shoulder blade.

Lay fired twice more, then ran back behind the tent. Stewart and Cantrell stayed where they were and kept shooting through the canvas. After about one minute of this, Stewart saw Lay standing by the corner of the tent. In another moment a bullet from either Stewart's or Thomas's rifle sent the outlaw tumbling face down into the grass.

Though stunned for an instant by the slug as it whipped past his forehead, Lay had worked out his next move before the possemen came up to him. First he made a studied pretense of examining his revolver, although he knew it to be empty. Then he raised his hands "in token of surrender" and started to get to his feet. Cantrell, nervous, suspicious, or angry, would have shot to kill, had not Stewart and Thomas restrained him: "He has shot Rufe, and I am going to kill the son of a bitch."

"He's wounded, I guess, he's fallen again," the sheriff remarked, as Lay allowed himself to keel over for a second time.

Stewart ordered the outlaw to rise and walk forward, and told Cantrell to "set his gun down against this stone here" before undertaking a search of the prisoner.

"Look here, Cis," said Cantrell, indicating a belt loaded with .30-40 cartridges which the bandit was wearing under what were described as his pantaloons. Cantrell had already taken possession of Lay's six-shooter. Stewart then came up, jerked open Lay's pants, and told his companion to unbuckle the cartridge belt.

As Cantrell walked away, carrying the belt and pistol, the sheriff dropped his eye off the prisoner. Immediately Lay's clenched left hand flew towards Stewart's jaw; his right darted for the officer's holstered revolver.

"Look out, he'll get your gun," yelled Cantrell.

Stewart was looking out. He partially deflected the blow with his arm and felled Lay with a single punch, only for the outlaw to jump up again and wrestle "like a wild man" against the clinches of Stewart and Cantrell until the sheriff drew his gun and administered "two severe cracks over the head" with it.

"By God, Cis, let's kill him," urged Cantrell.

"No, John, we won't kill him," replied Stewart, magisterially, "I suppose we ought to kill him, but he says he wants to give up and I won't kill him."

"No, don't kill me," Lay is alleged to have petitioned, "You can't blame a man for scuffling a little."

Cantrell got a rope and Stewart hogtied the glowering outlaw.

Lay's wounds had burst open in the tussle but he was less concerned by this than he was infuriated by the pistol-whipping.

"I may never get out of this," he told Stewart, "but if ever I do you had better leave New Mexico, for I'm coming after you."

Will Carver had seen the gray horse while Lay was riding into Lusk's camp. He roped the animal and left him hobbled on the prairie, returning to the crest of the hill after the posse had closed in on Lay. For a while he surveyed the scene through his field glasses, "but with no wild desire apparently to become a party" to the proceedings. When he saw Lay sprawled out on the ground, half or three quarters of a mile away, he at first thought him dead. He went back for the gray and was about to ride away when Stewart waved his hat. Carver returned the gesture and shouted "adios," perhaps to Stewart in derision, perhaps to Lay as a farewell.

Then he galloped out of sight of the glaring posse. As leader of a posse of two fit men, with a dangerous prisoner and two wounded men in his care, Stewart could have no thought of pursuit that morning. A hack was obtained for the wounded Lusk and Thomas, and they, the prisoner, the sheriff, and Cantrell were in Carlsbad by 9:30 a.m.

At ten o'clock that morning, Carver passed the Carlsbad schoolhouse, which was closed for vacation but open for a camp meeting. He was riding hard and could not fail to attract notice. He was next seen at Dagger Draw, twelve miles north of town. A couple of hours later he showed himself at Seven Rivers, twenty miles northwest of Carlsbad. It was supposed that when he reached the Rio Penasco, ten miles further north, he would head west for the mountainous country around Hope. That supposition was what he had counted on. At the Penasco, amid an empty landscape, he turned towards the Pecos River, four miles to the east. He crossed the river and, still unnoticed, started north along its eastern bank. Again he had slipped out of the noose.[32]

A few hours after the arrest of Lay, Capehart rode into Lusk's camp with provisions he had purchased for the ride to Arizona. John Lusk, in describing what had happened to the others, modified some of the details and omitted to mention that the sheriff had found the men only because the Lusks had told him where they were. As Capehart understood it, Lay would not have been captured had he not run out of ammunition. Without doubting anything he heard, he set out in the same general direction as Carver had first taken.[33]

Sheriff Stewart's prisoner was not loquacious. At different times he gave his name as John Thompson and Tom Johnson. His weapons and equipment were closely inspected. "The Winchester," observed one correspondent, "is a new gun, having seen little use:" the scabbard "was marked in plain gothic letters JO YOUNWA, the 'N' inverted and indistinct." The saddle was the one that the gang had obtained from Sam Murray, of Ozona, just after the Comstock robbery.[34]

Sheriff Stewart was more interested in the man's wounds. When he saw them he felt pretty sure he had "Will McGinnis." Louis O. Fullen, manager-editor of the *Carlsbad Argus*, thought so, too. "It was a very disastrous stop for Mr. Thompson," the paper commented, "The criminal traveling schedule has been revised lately and all the stopping places in Eddy county erased, but Señor Thompson had evidently not been supplied with a corrected edition and was traveling under the old schedule."[35]

When Rome Shield heard of the arrest he opined that McGinnis was "Dave Adkins [*sic*], another Tom Green county product . . . known to be a fine shot, and not afraid of man or devil."[36] Although a mistaken guess, it was not a bad one, for the two men were of similar height and build. But Shield's belief that Dave Atkins was still with the gang shows that, in some respects, the sheriff knew less than he thought he did. Atkins had been going his own way for more than a year.

Immediate confirmation of the suspicion that Stewart's once pugnacious but now reticent prisoner was "McGinnis" was precluded by startling developments elsewhere.

While Lay was making ready for his first night in a prison cell, Tom Ketchum was plodding along the Colorado and Southern right-of-way in the direction of Folsom.

For three months he had avoided all but the loneliest of trails, visiting no one except a few settlers whose homes were remote from any town or village and reading no newspapers. The killings at Camp Verde had aroused an energetic if ineffectual pursuit, but so far his name had not been publicly connected with the affair.

Plans for a second train holdup in northeastern New Mexico had been discussed before the quarrel which led to his banishment from the gang. Late in July he made up his mind to seek a reconciliation with his brother and Carver. He rode to Wagon Mound, thinking they might be in camp there.

The place was deserted; there was no one to tell him about the recent robbery at Folsom or the fight in Turkey Canyon. He decided to hold up the Atchison, Topeka and Santa Fe train near Wagon Mound. One night, the 10th or 11th of August, he walked up to the station. When the southbound express pulled in, he strolled casually alongside the coaches and towards the locomotive. As he passed the open door of the express car he glanced inside and at once recognized George Titsworth, who had been hired as a guard. Titsworth saw him and observed that his manner was "very unconcerned," but did not know him and suspected nothing. Desperate as he was, Tom had no intention of holding up a train which he knew to be guarded. He walked on past the blind baggage, past the engine, and into the darkness.

After this he did what must have seemed the easiest and most natural thing. He headed for Folsom, seventy miles further north and east. If he had heard about the holdup there, scarcely a month earlier, and about its aftermath, he might well have kept as much ground as he possibly could between Twin Mountains and himself.[37]

On Wednesday, August 16, Thomas Owen's brother Ben passed by him in the Dry Cimarron, two miles below Folsom. Ketchum was riding a fine horse and leading another, which carried a small pack. In the pack was his safe-blowing kit.

Tom, it was learned, went on to a cave about two miles south of Folsom, where he hid himself and his horses until darkness fell.[38] Then he rode back to the spot he had selected for the robbery, hitched the two horses, lit a fire, and started to walk towards Folsom.

Southbound train no. 1 chugged out of Folsom at about 10:20 that night, a few minutes late. Conductor Frank Harrington was about to be held up for the third time, but now he would not be taken unprepared. Since the second robbery he had never gone on duty without a double-barreled shotgun, which he had borrowed from a friend. He had resolved to do his best to ensure that any third similar occurrence would be some train robber's last exploit.[39]

In the express car was Messenger Charles P. "Scotty" Drew, whom Sam Ketchum had beaten up during the first robbery. Fred Bartlett was the mail clerk, Joseph H. Kirchgrabber the engineer, Tom Scanlon the fireman, and Robert B. Hawkins once again the brakeman.

They had proceeded just over a mile out of Folsom when Tom Ketchum slipped into the cab and nudged Kirchgrabber with the nozzle of his revolver. In compliance with the bandit's orders, Kirchgrabber stopped the train at a point some four miles south of Folsom. The wheels came to rest upon a curve in the track, and on a four-foot "fill" or embankment two miles short of the bonfire that marked Ketchum's camp.

Ketchum had cached a gunny sack containing a large stock of dynamite, caps, and fuses under a cattle guard, at a safe distance from his signal fire and almost at the site of the previous robberies. He intended to have the coaches uncoupled from the express car and locomotive; afterwards the engine could be run up to his camp and the express box blown without any risk of interference. When this was done, he reflected, he would get out of New Mexico and sail for South America, even if he found no more than five hundred dollars. It was learned, much later, that there was rather more—perhaps a great deal more—than five thousand dollars' worth of express matter in Drew's through safe that night.

From the beginning, the scheme would not unroll smoothly for Tom Ketchum. First of all, the engineer refused to get down from the locomotive.

"You son of a bitch, I'll kill you," snarled Ketchum, poking his unslung rifle into Kirchgrabber's armpit. "I'll shoot if you don't."

"Shoot away," was the stolid rejoinder.

Beaten for the moment, Ketchum turned upon the fireman, who stepped down without argument. With a rifle at his back, Scanlon raised his coalpick and banged on the door of the express car. Drew awoke with a start; he assumed—as he had assumed at the time of the first Folsom holdup—that the train had reached Des Moines station. He was halfway to the door when he was hailed by the fireman: "Hi, Scotty!"

He opened the door.

"Fall out of there goddamn quick," snapped Tom Ketchum, and Drew did exactly as he was told. He was then ordered to hold out a lantern while Scanlon tried to unfasten the drawheads of the couplings which attached the express car to the coal tender. Ketchum did not realize that the "Miller hook," the coupling device then in general use on the C&S, was certain to bind whenever a train was halted on a curve. It would then be almost impossible to separate the cars. Scanlon, however, set about the couplings as well as he knew how.

Every now and again, Drew would take a hurried look at the bandit. He could not but notice that Ketchum was "nursing" his gun "very tenderly."

Distracted for a moment when Bartlett, in the mail car directly behind the combination baggage and express car, craned forward to see what was going on, Ketchum shouted at him to "get back in there." To give point to his instructions, he threw a warning shot which glanced off a steel brace on the side of the car and through Bartlett's jaw, knocking out two double teeth, spinning him right around and felling him face downwards to the floor. Scanlon redoubled his efforts to break the couplings. Presently he said that he had unhooked the cars. Ketchum made the messenger and fireman walk ahead of him back to the engine. They all climbed into the cab and Kirchgrabber was ordered to pull ahead. He tried, but the train would not budge. Scanlon had succeeded only in cutting the air hose, thus sealing the brakes on all the coaches behind the express car. Ketchum guessed what had happened. By now he was past the stage where a railroad engineer could safely bandy words with him.

"If you won't come back there I'll kill you," he stormed, between curses. "I want you to cut the baggage car off."

Kirchgrabber, this time, went along quietly. He bent down over the couplings and strove to loosen them while Ketchum shuffled around impatiently, urging him to "hurry up." Drew, who was nearest to Ketchum, did not remember the exact texture of Ketchum's words; he could not forget the pain in his ribs or back as the bandit kept jabbing the Winchester into him to emphasize the orders and threats he was dishing out to Kirchgrabber.

"I'm going to shoot to kill now, pretty soon," he muttered at one point.

"Well now, partner, don't be in a hurry," said Kirchgrabber, whose memory for dialogue seems to have been stronger than Drew's, "We can't do these things all at once." But he sent the fireman back to the engine to fetch a jack bar or pinch bar— a rod about three feet in length, with which it might be just possible to prise the drawheads apart. Nearly twenty minutes had elapsed since the robber had first appeared in the locomotive cab, and Kirchgrabber knew that the man's temper was right on edge.

Frank Harrington, unlike Drew, guessed at once why the train had stopped. He and the brakeman, Hawkins, had got out of the train and gone up front to investigate. Discerning a group of men hovering about the express car, Harrington thought there were three or four robbers. Undeterred, he went back for his shotgun, unpacked it from his box, assembled it, and walked through the train to the combination mail car and smoker.

As he approached the end of the train, Harrington's resolve began to weaken. It stiffened again when he came to the mail car. There lay Bartlett, moaning that he was "bleeding to death." Harrington later described his reaction to Rome Shield: "When he saw the poor fellow bleeding, and, as he supposed, fatally wounded, his fighting spirit grew hot, and he . . . went out to kill somebody or be killed himself."

First, he left Bartlett in the care of the brakeman. Then, stealthily, he started to open the end door. The four men were standing below him, from ten to fifteen feet away. Just then, the moon escaped from a screen of cloud. Now he could recognize three of them: the fourth, the one with the rifle, was facing him but was partially blocked from view by the form of Charles Drew. Harrington's chance came when the messenger moved, as if to help Kirchgrabber, who was sweating over the stubborn couplings. Drew was still holding the lantern, and Harrington had a clear target. At once he threw the door wide open and fired from the hip. Ketchum looked up and, quick as light, switched his rifle from Drew towards the buttons glinting from Harrington's uniform. Eleven buckshot struck Ketchum just above the right elbow, an instant before the rifle bullet flicked Harrington's left sleeve.

"I wanted to hit the bandit in the heart," Harrington explained, afterwards, "but in the dim light I misjudged. It had to be done quickly. I knew that as soon as I opened the door my appearance would be noticed by the robber who faced me and I aimed the best I could." Or, as he more succinctly phrased it in the conversation reported by Shield, "Ketchum was the first man he saw who looked like a robber, and he let fly at him."[40]

Tom Ketchum said different things about it at different times. In his first public utterance on the subject he depicted his own ruthlessness in stark and un-selfconscious terms: "I saw him [Harrington] the second he pulled the trigger. Seventeen [*sic*] buckshot caught me in the right arm, which naturally dropped useless from my gun. I then fired, holding the gun like a revolver, with my left hand, but only wounded him slightly. If I had seen him a second before he fired, or he had hit me anywhere else, even in the heart, I would have killed Harrington. Twice I thought of killing the engineer, and now I am—sorry I didn't. Well, I guess this breaks up the old gang."[41] A later comment was more impersonal but only a degree less uncompromising: "His buckshot jiggled my aim. I'd have killed him if he'd waited a fraction of a second. I had a bead on his heart but he jiggled my aim." More than once he said that if he had not swung on Harrington as swiftly as he did, the buckshot load would have caught him in the chest rather than the right arm.[42]

Kirchgrabber and Scanlon fled in different directions. Drew stayed put, still hanging on to the lantern. Ketchum fell down the bank, then reeled across the front of the locomotive and away into the night. After he had crossed the tracks, he paused to take a couple of potshots at the glimmering flame of the lantern, each bullet puncturing the side of the mail car. Drew instantly turned out the lamp, but the danger had passed.

To resolve one inconsistency in his various statements: the weight of the evidence indicates that he had triggered his first shot as Harrington's buckshot tore into his right arm; only the later, futile shots would have had to be fired one-handed.[43]

With the bandit gone, Harrington's wound was dressed and the train resumed its run after a stoppage of thirty-five minutes; so the damage to the braking system must have been easily fixed. From the next station, and from various other points during the few hours that followed, word was sent out of what had happened, along with advice for officers to look out for a badly-wounded man near the scene of the holdup. A posse was rustled up in Denver, with William Reno in charge, and was soon headed south on the 3:20 train. The sheriff of Union County, with less than fifty miles to travel, could afford to make a later start.

Tom Ketchum had collapsed about a hundred yards north of the tracks. Some time in the night, he picked himself up and lurched towards his camp, where his two horses were staked out. But now he was assailed by the hopelessness that had swept over his brother just one month earlier.

"I tried a dozen times to mount my horse but was too weak to do it," he told Albert Thompson later. Exhausted and dizzy with pain, he sank down by the track to wait for the posse.

At eight o'clock next morning, the 17th, he saw a northbound freight train lumbering towards the place where he had attempted the robbery. He stuck his hat on the end of his rifle—or, perhaps, simply raised his left arm—and waved feebly. Perched on the roof of the cab was the front brakeman, John W. Mercer. He noticed the signal and the train ground to a standstill. Sheriff Saturnino Pinard, who had boarded the freight at Clayton, got out and followed the crew to the water hole, some three hundred yards away, beside which the outlaw was huddled, "his legs kind of cramped up, sitting on his feet."

Mercer and the engineer, Chris Waller, who were in the lead, halted some few paces from the wounded man. They eyed the rifle, which was "sticking out from beneath him."

"The distance is the same from here to there as it is from there to here," the outlaw called out. "You'll have to come down and get me." Then, almost casually, he lifted his canteen and took a sip of water. But as the men gingerly moved closer, he put aside the canteen and raised his six-shooter—smudged with blood, like his clothing and the patch of muddy ground on which he had lain.

"You wouldn't call a man out here to shoot him, would you?" quavered Waller.

"No, I guess not," replied Tom, after giving the question due thought, "I'll die anyway and the buzzards will eat me."

He let go of the pistol, only to reach for his rifle as the man edged still closer.

"Partner, don't do that," remonstrated Mercer, and Ketchum was persuaded. He allowed Mercer to pick up his rifle and six-shooter, but protested when the brakeman, searching for a second revolver, touched his wounded arm:

"I haven't any other . . . Don't do that, it hurts me."[44]

"How did you get that done?" Mercer asked, looking at the bloodied arm.

"Somebody shot me out of the baggage car last night when I was trying to hold up the train. I wish the son of a bitch had shot me through the head or heart and then this would have been over with. I hadn't done anything to him and I don't see what the son of a bitch wanted to shoot me for. If it hadn't been he shot my right arm off that I had my gun in, I'd have fixed the son of a bitch, all right."

Ketchum turned his eyes onto three other men who were walking toward him. Two of them were in uniform: they were the conductor, Clarke, and the rear brakeman, Robbins. The third man carried a rifle.

"Who is that son of a bitch with a gun there?" Ketchum wanted to know.

"It's the sheriff from Clayton," Waller replied.

"If I had that gun I could shoot the son of a bitch's heart out," Tom remarked, with a regretful glance towards the rifle he had just lost.[45]

"Yes," said Mercer, "but you haven't got your gun."

"I suppose I'm under arrest?" Tom asked Pinard.

"Yes, I'm the sheriff and you are my prisoner," responded Pinard. "Can you walk?"

"I wouldn't be here if I could," retorted Ketchum.

A wire stretcher was brought out.

"I'm so weak if I got on my feet I'd faint," Tom said to Clarke; but as they lifted him onto the stretcher he must have been feeling troubled for having let himself be taken without putting up a fight.

"If I could use my gun with my left hand, we'd have had a little fun," he declared, offering the best excuse he could think of. In other circumstances, he would have been happy to show that he could shoot from his left hand almost as well as from his right.

He was placed in the caboose and the freight trundled northwards. For awhile during the twenty-minute run the outlaw talked to Robbins, the brakeman. He gave his name as "George Stevens" (or perhaps he meant it to be taken for "Stephens") and said that he had "a brother and sister in the Panhandle country whom he would like to send word to, and if he did not die, why, he did not want them to know it." The holdup, he asserted, was his first attempt, "and a damned poor attempt I made."[46]

At Folsom the shattered arm was bandaged by Doctor Harry Lautmann (or Luteman), a railroad physician, and a posse from Colorado boarded the train. Superintendent Webb and Special Agent Reno were at the head of the party and were to take the outlaw into Trinidad. Present, too, were the town hotheads. When one of the Folsom men started to make some talk about getting a rope, a member of the posse, Harry D. Lewis, was quick to intervene.

"There will be nothing of that kind go on here," he told the ringleaders, "not so long as I have got these guns on me."[47]

For this he received scant thanks from Ketchum, who was not so ill as to miss an opportunity for a sly dig at the possemen. As the men were getting ready to leave on a hunt for his supposed confederates, Tom addressed Lewis.

"I wouldn't go if I were you, pal," he advised the officer, "I wouldn't go out with those fellows, pal, because them other fellows can shoot and you can't." But the posse left and spent two or three hours chasing nothing.[48]

Webb and Reno serenely took charge of the prisoner. The train carrying Ketchum and his escort "made all possible speed toward Trinidad."

Only one headline suited the events of August 16, 1899, and the *Denver Post* found it before the 17th was much older:

A BAD DAY FOR TRAIN ROBBERS

For Miles Cicero Stewart and William Hiram Reno, it had been a very good day.

Upon arrival at Trinidad the party from Folsom rushed to San Rafael Hospital, an institution run by the Sisters of Mercy, where the most notorious desperado in the Southwest modestly introduced himself by his impromptu alias of "George Stevens."[49]

15

DEAD TO RIGHTS

The removal of Thomas Edward Ketchum from Union County, New Mexico, to the most easily accessible hospital—which happened to be in Colorado—did not spring spontaneously from the exercise of plain common sense.

Sheriff Pinard had understood that the southbound special from Trinidad would be at his disposal; he would put himself and his prisoner aboard, and the train would continue south to Clayton. But when the northbound freight reached Folsom, soon after the special from Trinidad, Webb and Reno pounced on the wounded desperado. They exhibited a piece of paper which gave them authority to take the prisoner to Trinidad for interrogation. It also stated that a deputy U.S. marshal was on his way from Albuquerque to take official charge of the outlaw (though, in the event, the marshal had decided to send himself). This order was signed by Jeremiah Leahy, district attorney of Colfax and Union counties, and Chief Justice Mills, in his capacity as justice of the Fourth Judicial District. Pinard, disgusted by the palaver, had then led several newly-arrived Colorado deputies across country in search of the bandit's horses, dynamite, and presumed companions. Marshal Foraker was obliged to travel into Colorado to question a man who had been arrested in New Mexico. But at least the would-be train robber had been given the best chance to pull through and so become available for disposal by the courts.[1]

Ketchum still maintained that he was George Stevens, formerly a cowboy, more recently a miner; that his kinfolk lived in the Panhandle; that he was not a regular train robber; that he had resorted to crime this once only because he had been down on his luck. Now, however, he was insisting that he had made the attempt alone. Railroad officials commented that if all this were true, "he was not only nervy, but idiotic." The detectives stuck by their belief that there had been two other robbers, who had fled at the sound of the shots.[2] Foraker went one better. He told Washington that Ketchum had three assistants, and asked the Attorney General to let him employ six possemen for up to twenty days in order to catch them. In particular, he wanted to give the "tried and trusted" Wilson Elliott sixty days' paid employment.[3]

Ketchum was unmoved by the incredulity of those surrounding his bedside. "Did you ever hear of a man robbing a train alone?" he asked Webb. "I have. I'd have got away with that, partner, if we hadn't stopped on that curve." Ketchum had heard right; during the last ten years there had been four cases of an entire train being held up and successfully pillaged by one man acting alone. He may or may not have heard that three of the four solo artists were beginners in serious crime.[4]

At first, Tom seemed to be more worried about one of his horses than himself. Evidently anxious that the animal should not be left to starve, he gave the officers careful directions as to where he had picketed it. They tried to loosen his tongue further by telling him that he was near the point of death. Far from gratifying their hopes of a confession, Tom began to curse Kirchgrabber and Harrington, expatiating fervently upon what he ought to have done to them and what he would do yet if he should ever get the chance. (Twenty months later he was still damning them, and by then their names had been joined by others in his litany of unsettled grudges.) Conversely, he expressed regret at having shot Bartlett, now his fellow-patient in San Rafael Hospital: he had warned the mail clerk three times, he explained, and had fired only to frighten him away. This may well have been true, but Bartlett was not mollified, and in any case did not believe it: his feelings toward Tom Ketchum were much the same as those of Tom Ketchum toward Kirchgrabber and Harrington.[5]

For almost a week Ketchum would admit to no other name than that of "George Stevens" (rendered in some early reports as "Frank Stevens" or "Stephens"). But the officials guessed from the beginning that they had Tom Ketchum; and nothing would ever dissuade them from their belief that Tom Ketchum was the "Black Jack." who had made life so uncomfortable for postmasters and others during the fall of '96 and '97. It looked very much, too, as though they would soon be given the opportunity to pay for the outlaw's funeral, for his hold on life was precarious and he seemed determined to do nothing to improve his chances of recovery. Dr. John R. Espey, the Colorado and Southern's own surgeon, had advised him to agree to amputation of the mangled arm. Tom allowed the doctor to extract the buckshot but, like his brother before him, stolidly refused to undergo an operation. This did not prevent the appearance of a garish package of mendacity in which the bandit was portrayed as contemptuously declining an anesthetic and watching nonchalantly as Espey chopped off the putrefied member.[6]

Weak as he was, he was closely guarded. In the daytime he was under the eye of Harry Lewis; the night watch was assigned to George Titsworth. Ketchum talked a great deal to his keepers, and they to him. Once, apparently in jest, Lewis told him that there was eighty or eighty-five thousand dollars aboard the train he had failed to rob. It was no joke to Tom.

"If I hadn't bad luck, and got the money, they would never have seen my dust," he answered. He was probably wrong about that. If he had escaped from the scene, with or without booty, most likely he would have headed straight for Turkey Creek Canyon and into almost certain capture or death.

He wanted to know from Titsworth whether the charge of attempted train robbery would take precedence to that of the murder for which he was wanted in Texas.

It is not clear which of these two charges he feared the most, but, as Titsworth informed him, he would first be tried in the courts of the party by whom he was being detained—the United States government.[7]

On another occasion, Ketchum told Titsworth that the gold fountain pen found in his coat had been used to compile a history of outlawry; the manuscript, he assured the deputy, was three hundred pages long, and had been placed in safe hands in Texas. He also said that, notwithstanding his earlier denial, two other men really had been involved in the attempted robbery. When Titsworth asked him why he had not tried to rob a train on the Santa Fe line, Tom answered, "Why, I seen you there," and went on to describe how nearly they had met at Wagon Mound.[8]

Back in the Concho country, a young kinswoman of Tom Ketchum was attending a picnic when word came through that he had been wounded and captured. Dave McCrohan, who was there, recalled that the news "didn't seem to worry her." She did not leave the picnic ground, and stayed on for the dance that followed the picnic.[9]

Reno had only just returned from a futile trip to Solomonville, Arizona, where Deputy Sheriff Tol Bell was holding an uncommunicative stranger he had arrested at Fort Thomas. The man's appearance was similar in several respects to Reno's description of "G.W. Franks" (though conspicuously different in others), and he had declined to account for himself. Therefore Bell suspected him of being Franks and threw him into jail. On August 9, two weeks after his arrest, he was inspected by Reno and Jim Hunt, with results that were negative for everyone but himself.[10]

Now, barely a week after the Solomonville fiasco, it seemed that two of New Mexico's three most-wanted desperadoes were in the net. In the absence of proof, Foraker and Reno were anxious to go down to Carlsbad for a formal introduction to "McGinnis." As it was thought likely that Cicero Stewart might be able to identify "Stevens," Titsworth was shown how to operate a camera and was instructed to take photographs of the prisoner. On the morning of the 21st, "after considerable coaxing" by Titsworth, Ketchum agreed to face the camera. After Titsworth had taken his first picture, the outlaw's beard was shaved off; he had protested so vehemently when the razor was applied to his upper lip that he was permitted to keep the mustache. This touch of vanity may have expedited his identification. He would not pose for a second picture until someone handed him a revolver—after the cylinder had been emptied. Altogether, four pictures were taken.[11]

Some few hours afterwards Tom was told of the arrest of McGinnis, whereupon he "became very restless and ugly and begged the officer [Titsworth]) for a gun that he might kill himself." Later, thinking Titsworth asleep, he "removed the bandage from his arm, tied it around his neck, and, placing his foot in a loop at the end, tried to commit suicide by strangulation." Titsworth, through half-closed eyes, watched the macabre performance for a few moments before he jumped up to "put a stop to the game." The "game" had gone further than he thought, for Ketchum was already insensible; the movements detected by Titsworth were involuntary twitchings, induced by loss of consciousness.[12] Maybe the officer had dozed off for a minute or two, after all.

Copies of two of the photographs, showing the prisoner with and without beard, were sent to Rome Shield, who was "inclined" to accept them as a good likeness of

Ketchum, with the proviso that "the picture hardly indicates the prisoner to be as heavily built a man as Ketchum." But, commented the *San Angelo Standard*, "[I]t is almost impossible to positively identify a man from a photograph, especially after he has been pursued and pushed from pillar to post."[13] A day or two later, Shield received a detailed description of the prisoner from Gerrit Taft, assistant superintendent of Wells, Fargo:

> Height six feet, weight 190 pounds, dark complexion, long face, heavy chin, dark flashing eyes, black hair, very dark brown mustache and beard, now cut off, number of scars on left leg above the knee, two scars on muscle of right arm, about thirty-five years old, muscular build.[14]

Shield replied that he was almost convinced that the wounded bandit was Ketchum. He sent a telegram after Tom's brother Berry, who was traveling to Midland to attend a carnival, intimating that the prisoner was likely to die "at any time."[15]

Once inside the Eddy County Jail, Elzy Lay was civil but reticent. He would not give his real name or any details of his personal history, but did not mind being photographed. Editor Fullen, of the *Carlsbad Argus*, was not deceived by the prisoner's politeness and emotional restraint. "He is certainly a man of nerve and self-possession . . . wholly devoid of braggadocio, being a type of the cold, calculating criminal. Talks but little and is very guarded in what he says." He was, thought Fullen, "not bad looking, and dressed well, would easily pass for a quiet inoffensive citizen."[16]

Foraker and Reno, no longer openly warring with one another, arrived in Carlsbad on August 21 and 22, just after Stewart's return from the pursuit of Carver. With Reno were Jefferson D. Farr, who had been appointed to succeed his brother as sheriff of Huerfano County, and the omnipresent postmaster, Jim Hunt. Hunt walked into the jail and greeted the prisoner as "Mac" with a familiarity that caused him "to flush and choke very noticeably." But while the identification of "Thompson" as McGinnis was immediate, no one in authority identified McGinnis as Elzy Lay.

When Reno produced prints of the photographs taken in San Rafael Hospital, telling Stewart that he believed "George Stevens" to be Black Jack, the sheriff dissented vigorously. The face staring out of the snapshots did not belong to Black Jack; it was the familiar one of Tom Ketchum, whom Stewart had met on many a roundup in the Pecos Valley.[17]

Paradoxically enough, Stewart's opinion served as proof positive for Reno and Foraker; so far as they were concerned, Tom Ketchum and Black Jack were one and the same. The *Trinidad Chronicle-News* echoed their certainties.[18]

As Stewart wanted to see Ketchum in person, he would go with the officers who would be taking "McGinnis" to Santa Fe by way of Trinidad, where Ketchum was to be put aboard. Fayette Baird, a cowboy who had been Ketchum's "working partner" on the cattle ranges for a number of years, would also go along. That night, a crowd of over one hundred gathered to see them off. The prisoner marched to the depot "with his manacled hands in front of him with a confident poise, as if oblivious to the eager spectators."[19]

Lay was to be lodged in the Las Animas County Jail for a few hours until the time came for him and Ketchum to be put on the train for Santa Fe. A.F. Codington, one of Foraker's office deputies, joined the train en route. The party reached Trinidad at about six o'clock next morning, August 23. Lay was put safely under lock and key, and invited to sit for a photograph without the option of refusal. Stewart headed for the hospital.

"Hello, Tom!" he called, as he entered the room in which the outlaw was confined.

For the first time since his arrest, Ketchum was visibly agitated. He could only stammer out that he did not know the visitor, although he might have seen him somewhere before. When Stewart pressed him to think back to his days as a cowpuncher in the Pecos country, Ketchum shook his head, scowled morosely, and clammed up. Jim Hunt, who seemed to grow more and more knowledgeable with each passing day, was on hand to corroborate Stewart.[20]

Fullen of the *Argus* reckoned that Ketchum had $10,000 on his head, dead or alive, and forecast "some interesting scrapping to see who would get it." Unlike his friend and political ally Stewart, lawyer-editor Fullen was all at sea over the Black Jack question: "Sheriff [Frederick] Higgins, of Roswell, was paid $300 several months ago for having killed the same man in Arizona." Higgins's unaimed reflex shot had killed William Christian, the real Black Jack, and begun the process whereby Tom Ketchum was first turned into a second Black Jack and then assigned the crimes and inflated ill-fame of the original.[21]

Train no. 17, in which Ketchum and Lay were to be taken to Santa Fe, was due to leave Trinidad at 10:30 a.m. Everyone in town seemed to know this, and a throng of more than eight hundred was milling in the street and around the depot as the outlaws were driven to the A.T. & S.F. depot. Lay rode inside a closed carriage and was not bothered by the sightseers. Ketchum, reclining in an open spring wagon with a big white hat pulled down over his features, was almost drowned in a sea of bobbing faces. Badgered by the crowd because he kept his face hidden, "the star passenger" told Stewart that he undertook to remove the hat if the crowd would give him five dollars. Even this holdup failed, so the hat stayed where it was.

At the depot a reporter "endeavored to draw McGinnis into conversation but he politely declined to talk, other than to say that he was not wounded by the sheriff's posse near Carlsbad."

"They hit me a few licks on the head with their guns," he remarked, "but no damage was done except breaking the skin on my forehead."

By way of clarification he tilted the brim of his hat so that the spectators could stare at the large bump which darkened his brow.

"Several dimes and quarters were handed to him by those who sized him up," noted the *Chronicle-News* reporter, "McGinnis stood the searching gaze of the crowd without flinching in the least, but refused to be Kodaked."[22]

Ketchum was placed in a cot in the baggage car. He was feeling sick and "asked for a cantaloupe" just as the train was ready to pull out. Realizing the futility of denying his identity further, he talked quite freely but not always truthfully to Stewart, Foraker, and Reno during the journey. He spoke of the several phases of his life, touched upon various incidents in his outlaw career, told Foraker that he would not have essayed a holdup at Folsom had he known of the recent robbery, but dismissed their news of the capture and demise of his brother as an artifice to beguile him into divulging more than he wanted.[23]

At Raton, where the train paused at about 12:15 p.m., the *Gazette* reporter who looked in on him noted Ketchum's "very feeble" condition, and scoffed at the excuse he made for his failure:

> He did not know until told by the officers of the former Folsom holdup, nor of the death of his brother. When reminded that the newspapers were full of it, he said it was not his habit to read the papers. He said he would not have made the attempt if he had known the train had been held up so recently. He had sense enough to know that trainmen and passengers would be armed and on the alert for some time after a robbery. The incident shows that even bandits should read the papers.[24]

In a strange inversion of Sam's supposed admission that he was "a brother of Tom Ketchum, the original Black Jack," Tom said—or was understood to say—that Sam was the first Black Jack, though he himself was the current bearer of the name. Misquotation, misunderstanding, or misinformation, this suspect statement soon grew five legs and ran for a day: Black Jack, the *Albuquerque Journal-Democrat* confided, was a title that descended through mortality from each leader of the gang to his successor.[25]

For nothing like the first time, or the last, Tom "spoke slightingly of Berry Ketchum, his respectable brother," concluding with the request, "If I die here, don't let him have my body. Bury me with Sam. He was the best of the family."[26]

He attempted to mislead the officers by falsely confessing to the holdup of a Santa Fe train near Grants, and alleging that "'Billy' Carver, one of [his] most reckless retainers, was shot dead" by the defenders of the train. The *Rocky Mountain News*, perhaps gullible, perhaps just in too much of a hurry, fell for this and improved on it by proclaiming: "This is the first time the identity of the dead robber has been made public."[27]

But Ketchum had parceled four lies into one short sentence. In fact, he had not taken part in any of the three train holdups at Grants, New Mexico; nobody had been killed in any of them; Will Carver had not been killed anywhere; and the only member of the gang to be slain during an attempt at robbery was Ed Cullen, who was shot at Steins Pass. Sick as he was, his malevolent humor remained unsubdued. Tom would lie when he had nothing to gain from the exercise other than the hope of making officers and officials look and sound foolish. In the time left to him he would peddle many more sham revelations at their intended expense. The last laugh would be theirs.

At 7:15 p.m. the train reached Santa Fe. Ketchum and Lay were booked into the penitentiary as Numbers 130 and 131, U.S. prisoners. Before he was carried into the prison hospital, Ketchum urged Stewart to call on him later, vouching that, if in the meantime he had not died from blood poisoning, he would make an important disclosure. That night the outlaw's temperature was recorded as 103F, which seemed to suggest that his chances of pulling through were as poor as he thought they were. He appeared indifferent until he was handed a photograph of Sam, taken shortly after death. The sight of it destroyed his composure.

"When you're through with me," he said resignedly, "just plant me alongside Sam."[28]

Next day, Friday, the 25th, they were taken before U.S. Commissioner John P. Victory on the charge of interfering with the U.S. mails. The hearings were held at the penitentiary, and both men waived examination. They were bound over and, upon their inability to produce on the spot the ostensibly modest sum of $1,000 each for bail, formally committed to the penitentiary to await further proceedings.[29]

The sole purpose of the commissioner's hearing was to create a legal basis for the detention of the men while more serious charges were being prepared. The authorities in Arizona were already taking steps to have Ketchum extradited to face trial for the Camp Verde murders. His saddle—"high-forked, center-fire, full-stamped, with twenty-eight inch tapaderos and buckskin pockets"—his elaborately-woven Navajo blanket, and his own physical appearance matched the descriptions furnished by those who had encountered the killer as he fled across Arizona. An order of requisition was laid before Governor Otero on the 26th. Two days later he rejected it, on the grounds that the federal authorities were proceeding with their charge against Ketchum. Sheriff Munds, who was ferreting for clues in the Datil Mountain country of Socorro County, nevertheless made ready to go to Santa Fe.[30]

Meanwhile, on the evening of the 26th, Berry Ketchum turned up at the penitentiary with Jeff Minnis, also of San Angelo, another one-time friend of Tom's from his cowpunching days in New Mexico. Two weeks had passed since Tom's encounter with Harrington, and the shattered arm was "perfectly black from the elbow to the fingertips." Dr. Desmarias told Berry that amputation of the putrid limb might save its owner's life, as a similar operation might have extended Sam's, but Tom seemed as adamant as Sam; he would "die as he had lived, a whole man." He talked to Minnis at some length, but not, it would appear, directly to his brother.

Minis renewed acquaintance with Will Hall, formerly of Coleman, whose death sentence for murdering a man in Roswell was under appeal. Then he and Berry hotfooted it back to Midland "to take in the carnival, view the roping, see the balloon ascension and 'rubberneck' at the pretty lady, clad in pink tights, who showed her agility while the big bag soared heavenward, buck at the sure thing games, bet on the races, and see the wheels go round generally." A busted-out train robber with a blackened arm and a morose disposition could not compete with such exotica.[31]

An hour and a half before Berry and Minnis boarded the eastbound train on the evening of the 27th, two more visitors to Santa Fe had come in from the opposite direction.

"How are you getting along?" inquired Gerome Shield, as he and Bige Duncan greeted Tom Ketchum next day. This, Shield declared later, was his first meeting with Tom for six or seven years. He was not there merely out of curiosity or for old friendship's sake; as on his previous visit to the penitentiary, his expenses were being met by Wells, Fargo, and he would be in town for several days of inquiry and consultation.

"Very well, I'm sorry to say," was the cool reply. Tom was looking better that day, and confident of retaining his damaged arm.

Shield and Duncan had "a long talk" with the prisoner. Tom "talked freely about general subjects, but was very guarded concerning himself." When Shield asked him about the Lozier and Stanton robberies, "he merely laughed and refused to make definite answer." He admitted to having been in the San Angelo vicinity for several months in 1898, before leaving for Arizona in the fall. He declined to say anything at all about his actions since then, other than the botched holdup that had been his downfall. He vowed he "would never be hung . . . he would make a dash for liberty first and be shot down." Before the visit was over, though, he "broke down and cried like a child."

The sheriff looked in on Lay, saw that he was not Dave Atkins (as he had supposed), or anyone else known to him, and sent a brief telegram to his office:

SANTA FE, N.M., Aug. 28, 1899

J.M. MARTIN, San Angelo, Texas.

This is Tom Ketchum. Rode a brown Door Key horse. Mose Taylor saddle. Don't know McGinnis.

G.W. SHIELD[32]

Bige Duncan would at once have grasped the significance of the horse with the Door Key brand. When the contents of the telegram were broached, Willis Johnson, as owner of the brand, and Gus Thomas, as de facto co-manager with Duncan of the Door Key range, would have an opportunity to think about it during the seven days that would elapse before Shield was back in San Angelo. None of the three proffered any public statement on the matter, and the sheriff had nothing more to say about it. The provenance of the saddle confirmed the San Angelo connection, Mose Taylor being one of the town's two principal saddlers.[33] Presumably it, like the horse, had been stolen—or "stolen."

In Trinidad, where he and Duncan had to change trains, Shield offered to "bet a box of cigars with every officer in Las Animas County that the outlaw would not stretch hemp." Duncan "choked up several times" and "controlled his feelings and kept back the tears" only with difficulty. Shield, on the other hand, was most expansive.

"Tom Ketchum had great nerve, though I think his brother Sam had better," he declared. McGinnis, he opined, was "a 'ringer' . . . he may be a safe cracker or some general all-around crook." Bige managed to mumble that "the relatives were all broken up over the downfall of the boys."[34]

Scott White happened to be in Phoenix when news of the penitentiary visits came through, and was soon holding forth to a reporter for the *Herald*. His remarks were an admixture of the enlightening and the baffling:

> . . . Ketchum may be the original "Black Jack." but he was not the Arizona "Black Jack" who spread terror in his course . . . until two years ago, when . . . he was killed in the White Mountains and his body identified at Clifton. Ketchum appeared on the scene many years ago, and he may have assumed the name of "Black Jack," as many others have done since, but the Arizona "Black Jack" is dead.
>
> The Arizona outlaws known as "Black Jack's gang" was composed of cowpunchers who worked on the southwest ranges for many ears and were well known by many persons, including Mr. White. The leader took the name of "Black Jack," and his men were Code Young, Bob Hay[e]s and two men whose names are Anderson and Williams. The latter two are still at large . . . but Code Young, Bob Hays and "Black Jack" are dead.[35]

White was well posted on the old Black Jack or High Five gang, but his assertion that its members "had worked on the southwest ranges for many years" was as far from the truth as his statement that Ketchum "had appeared on the scene many years ago." The careers of the High Five on the Arizona rangelands lasted for only a few months before they took to banditry, while all the available evidence shows that Tom Ketchum did not go to southern Arizona until late in 1896 and was hardly on nodding terms with Cochise County before the following September. Most mystifying was the sheriff's apparent opinion that Ketchum "may be the original 'Black Jack.'" This view amounts to so grotesque a denial of the established facts that the suspicion must be that it was the reporter's rather than the sheriff's.

White was in no way implicated in the *Herald* writer's flippant payoff: "Ketchum may be the original 'Black Jack,' and if he is he should be punished for no other crime than filling the trail with bad men of his name and character." At the time, the punchline could have seemed as empty as it was frivolous, for Ketchum's refusal to submit to surgery assured him of death within a few days.

But within those few days the picture changed. Quite suddenly, Tom regained the will to live, perhaps because he could see some hope of escaping from the penitentiary. He told the doctors that he now wanted them to amputate, and Miguel Desmarias performed the operation on Saturday morning, September 2. Tom surprised the surgeon by refusing to take a drink after the sunderance of the rotting member. Desmarias, whose contract was with the territorial government, attached a photograph of the severed arm as a voucher to support the bill he presented to the federal authorities.[36]

The comments of Don Kedzie, the acerbic and to-hell-with-them-all editor of the Lordsburg, New Mexico, *Western Liberal*, were characteristically barbed and mordant: "If owing to alibi witnesses or crooked jurymen or Oliver Lee luck Ketchum and "Bronco Bill" should be turned loose both would have to practice shooting with the left hand before they could resume their original occupations." Walters, as Kedzie reminded his readers, was in scarcely better case than Tom, having lost "several inches of bone from the upper part of his right arm" after being shot by George Scarborough.[37]

Now that Tom Ketchum had been caught and crippled in the act of armed robbery, his hometown newspaper at last felt able to recognize him in print. On

September 6, "Woodyard Chipling," currently the Knickerbocker correspondent of the *San Angelo Standard*, whose talents as a columnist belied the fatuity of his pseudonym, came up with an idea:

> Several of our citizens, who know Tom Ketchum, take issue with the writer of a long article which appeared in a recent number of the *Houston Post*, purporting to be a history of his life as a bandit. They say the article in question is "way off" in most of its statements, and that it makes Tom Ketchum out a much worse man than he really was. Now, Mr. Editor, suppose you and Sheriff Shield put your heads together and write up the facts of the case. I am sure such a history, from an authentic source, would be of great interest to many of your readers. . . . [38]

Regrettably, but not unwisely, Pat Murphy and Sheriff Shield did not accept the invitation; they did not even acknowledge it. Any locally produced "history" of Ketchum's career would raise, if not answer, questions as to where, when, how, and above all, by whom he had been advised and succored. Names would be linked to accusations. Many of those names would have belonged to the neighbors and informants of "Woodyard Chipling." Most of all, there was the money angle. John Loomis wrote, "I have seen plenty of scorched folding money in circulation in San Angelo during Tom Ketchum's dynasty. We considered it rather a joke. Everybody had a good idea where it came from." But he wrote that nearly fifty years afterwards.[39] It would not have been much of a joke if it had been publicized while the stolen money, scorched or clean, was actually doing the rounds in Tom Green and adjacent counties.

Sheriff Munds added his name to Tom Ketchum's visitors' list on the day after the operation. When he left he was satisfied that he had at last found the slayer of Rogers and Wingfield; some time later he stated that Ketchum openly admitted having killed the two men. Then, on September 5, John Boyd—the witness with best cause to remember the killer—put the finger on Ketchum. Yavapai County, it seemed, could present an unassailable case against him; but Governor Otero was anxious to find a way to keep Yavapai County from getting him.[40]

Otero wanted to demonstrate that the territory was capable of dealing with its ruffians. People were saying that New Mexico was an outlaw paradise, utterly unfit for statehood; worse, they could count off a long list of cases in which the territory had failed to bring its desperadoes to account. Thomas Ketchum might be of help in mitigating these embarrassments.[41] First, though, "William H. McGinnis" had to be tried for the murder of Edward Farr. Chief Justice Mills and District Attorney Leahy would attend to that while Tom Ketchum was convalescing in the prison hospital.

16

POINTS OF LAW

District Attorney Leahy was assisted by Lewis C. Fort and Elisha V. Long in the preparation of the case against Lay for the murder of Edward Farr. Leahy and Fort were two of the ablest and most energetic prosecutors in the Territory. Moreover, they and Chief Justice Mills were of one mind: the mysterious prisoner was an outlaw, a pre-convicted train robber, and a salutary example was going to be made of him.[1]

No chances were to be taken. When rumor reached official ears that friends of the prisoner in El Paso were collecting money to bail him out, recourse was had to another section of the Post Office act of 1872. So, on September 15, Chief Deputy Marshal J.J. Sheridan presented additional charges of unlawfully detaining and attempting to rob the United States mail. Section 287 of the act might have been designed with a mind to flexibility.[2]

The purpose of this maneuver was wholly preemptive. Each charge would keep the defendant in custody pending an appearance before the U.S. commissioner, and after each hearing a further bond of $1,000 would be set. These were well-worn procedures, intended to ensure that the prisoner could not legally regain his liberty during the preparation of the substantive charges—in this instance, territorial charges of train robbery and murder.

As it happened, no one had much waiting to do before the grand jurors in Colfax and Union Counties indicted Lay on the territorial charges. On Sunday, September 16, Sheriff Harry Kinsell, of Santa Fe County, acting on behalf of his counterpart in Union County, served the defendant with a writ requiring his attendance at Clayton to answer the capital charge of train robbery. Then, on Tuesday, September 19, "William H. McGinnis," and "G.W. Franks, alias William Carver, whose full first name is to the Grand Jurors unknown," were indicted in Colfax County for the murder of Farr.[3]

The homicide case necessarily took precedence over the others. Lay would be taken to Raton and his trial there would start on Monday, October 2.[4] That left very little time for him to obtain witnesses or funds, or for his attorneys to prepare his defense.

Lay was represented by Edwin B. Franks and Andrieus A. Jones. If the record is any guide, very little play was made of the coincidence that the surname of one of the outlaws's attorneys was the same as Carver's alias.

One of the first actions of lawyer Franks was to send a telegram from Raton via Silver City to Elton A. Cunningham, a storekeeper and saloon owner of Mogollon, New Mexico, who had become well acquainted with Lay during the three or four months of the outlaw's employment on the Socorro County ranch of the WS. Cunningham was a frequent visitor to Alma and made friends with both Lay and Butch Cassidy in the early months of 1899, having no suspicion—so he would insist—of their prior involvement and continuing interest in the profession of armed robbery.[5]

The lawyer's telegram reached Cunningham on September 23, the day after its dispatch, and he took the first available stage from Mogollon to Silver City, ninety miles away. After the standard two-day rail journey from Silver City via Deming and Rincon, he arrived at Raton on September 27. He at once caught the eye of the *Raton Range*:

> E.A. Cunningham, of Mogollon, New Mexico, is in Raton, looking after the interests of his friend, William H. McGinnis, who is now on trial for his life.
>
> Mr. Cunningham says that McGinnis is well known and very popular with the cowboys and miners of the Mogollon district and that they all chipped in a few dollars each to help pay costs in his defense.[6]

Franks and Jones tried hard to secure a continuance. On September 29, Cunningham swore an affidavit claiming on behalf of McGinnis's friends that they would not be able to make up a fund for the defense until they had located William French and drawn the wages due to them. The Territory had no trouble in procuring three counter affidavits the same day. One of these was given by Wilson Elliott, who was "personally acquainted" with French. The other depositions were made by James Morgan and a man named W.G. Hughes, both of whom had worked for French in Colfax County. All stated that the WS cowboys were paid by the foreman of the ranch concerned, and not by French himself.[7]

In yet another sworn affidavit, dated September 29, Lay told the story of the Turkey Canyon fight in the words which, assertedly, the fugitive "G.W. Franks" would use were he to testify. Into this extraordinary document went an address for the missing witness: "In or near the town of Geronimo, Arizona Territory, to wit: at a place known as Freezeout Creek, on Nantac Mountain; the same being a distance of sixty miles north of said town of Geronimo."[8] It is possible that Carver was in the Gila Mountain country of Arizona: he had friends scattered all over the eastern half of that territory, from Flagstaff to the Mexican border, and his reputed whereabouts were within easy reach of his sister Fannie's home near the Arizona-New Mexico line east of Duncan. Lay's affidavit included a promise to procure Carver's attendance, or failing that, his deposition, if the trial were held over for the next term of court. The prosecution team countered with the observation that the Territory of New Mexico would very much like "G.W. Franks" to be in Raton for the current term.

After the rejection of these and all other moves by Lay's attorneys to gain a continuance, the trial opened on the date originally set. Not until the Wednesday was the jury of seven Anglos and five Spanish Americans empaneled from the seventy-five men examined by counsel.[9]

Mills had invited Governor Otero to attend the proceedings. Doubtless the judge was counting on the governor's bestowal of the seal of approbation, though he may have been extending a simple courtesy. Otero was present throughout. In due course of time he would castigate Mills for having grossly mishandled the trial and would turn out to be about the best friend Elzy Lay ever made.[10]

In his opening address, Leahy described the movements of McGinnis, Sam Ketchum, and G.W. Franks in Colfax and Union counties during the preceding summer. He dwelt lengthily upon the train robbery, contended that the first shots in the Turkey Canyon engagement had been fired by the defendant, and told the jury he expected them to return a verdict of guilty of murder in the first degree.

No sooner had the Territory's first witness, James Hunt, taken the oath than Ed Franks jumped up to state the defense's objection to the introduction of any testimony at all: there was no "legal indictment upon which to try the defendant," and "no issue joined between the Territory and the defendant; therefore no issue of fact to go before the jury."

"Is there no issue joined?" the court queried mildly, "Does the record show the defendant has pled not guilty?"

The clerk confirmed that the plea had been entered, the motion was formally turned down without discussion on the wording of the indictment, and the ruling of the court excepted to by Franks. Fort now got on with his examination of Hunt.

Almost at once he set the pattern for the first stage of the trial. Hunt testified that he had first seen McGinnis in Cimarron "about the 7th of June, - along the fore part of June," and was just going to respond to Fort's question as to how long the defendant had remained in the neighborhood, when Jones intervened:

"Judging from the statement made by counsel for the Territory, I presume we might as well object now to this line of testimony. I cannot imagine the purpose of it,—we desire to enter our objection to it, because it is irrelevant and immaterial and does not tend to prove any of the issues in this case."

"I will overrule your objection," replied the court. Jones and Franks reserved exception.[11]

Four of the Territory's witnesses were heard before court was adjourned at the close of the first day. Their testimony dealt mainly with the actions of the defendant and his three companions during the period just prior to the robbery.[12]

Numerous witnesses were calling on the next day, Thursday. All of them, like those who had gone before, offered evidence bearing in some way upon the defendant's participation in the train holdup. They included Conductor Harrington, Engineer Tubbs, and Express Messenger Scott.[13]

Scenes like the initial clash between counsel and judge were enacted, with variations, on more than a score of occasions during the first two days of the trial. Once, while Agapito Duran was on the stand, a long argument was waged between Jones on one side and Fort and Long on the other, with the court joining in, before the defense's motion was overruled. From beginning to end, very few of the defense's objections were sustained. Briefly stated, it was the contention of Leahy and his associates—and in this they were very largely upheld by the trial judge—that nearly everything Lay did, or was thought to have done, from the day he was first seen in Colfax County, to the moment he was put inside the Eddy County Jail, was related in some wise to the murder charge on which he was being tried.[14]

Franks and Jones would not fight on those terms. They intended to show that their client had not murdered Farr, or even shot at him, but that he would have been entitled to kill him to protect his own life; in their submission, all considerations save these were extraneous. A layman's view might be that the Territory was seeking to have the defendant informally convicted of train robbery in order to justify the indictment for murder in the first degree. But the wording of the statutes which defined the three degrees of murder left some scope for learned argument (statutes often do) on the interpretation of sundry provisions and their application to this particular case.[15]

The defendant's most valuable ally was the man seated next to Chief Justice Mills. In his reminiscences, written many years later with the help of his former secretary, Otero recorded some instructive comments on the trial:

> Public opinion was aroused to a high pitch against all persons connected with train robberies, and the courts were determined to stop this crime which gave New Mexico such a bad name for lawlessness, even though all points of law were not adhered to literally. Personally, I believe that all courts should be impartial and just at all times. Sometimes, however, popular clamor and political ambitions combine to banish the calm and careful consideration due to justice . . . I noticed that every ruling in the case went against the defendant . . . it seemed to me that he was convicted before he was tried . . . [16]

A recondite element was introduced with the testimony of William A. Chapman, superintendent of schools for Colfax County and surveyor by profession, who had been sent into Turkey Canyon to prepare a topographical map of the ground on which the fight had occurred. When Jones asked to see Chapman's memorandum book, the witness pointed out that it was "very hard for anyone to make out a surveyor's memoranda." Jones modestly allowed that he knew a little bit about surveying, himself, and maybe he could understand the notes. But in the end both sides of the courtroom seem to have been willing to accept that Chapman had drawn a pretty good map, and to let it go at that. (The court stenographer, plainly, knew less than nothing of the surveyor's craft: he consistently rendered the word "topography" as "typography.")[17]

After Chapman had stepped down, the Territory recalled H.P. Scott, the express messenger. The next witness, and the fifteenth, was W.H. Reno. He had told of his part in the investigation of the train robbery, and had described how the posse was assembled in Cimarron, when Fort concluded his examination:

"That is all for the present with this witness. I will recall him later."

Jones, to his subsequent regret, was satisfied with this.

"If he is to be recalled we will wait for cross examination until he is recalled," he told the court.[18]

The first testimony to be heard that dealt directly with the fight itself was Wilson Elliott's. Under examination by Fort, he gave a fairly clear and straightforward account of the events in Turkey Canyon. Andrieus Jones's cross examination was thorough, incisive, and sometimes sharpened by sarcasm.

Jones began by making Elliott recite the entire story of his variegated career over the past twelve years.

Q. And you did nothing in New Mexico as an occupation except to prospect prior to the time you came to Trinidad.

A. Most of the time I prospected. I ran a rock outfit down here on the road for awhile.

Q. When was that.

A. That was in 1892.

Q. What kind of rock outfit was that.

A. I had charge of an outfit that was getting out rock for the coke ovens.

Q. Where was that.

A. South of Cerrillos.

Q. How long were you engaged in that business.

A. I expect a month or so.

Q. Did you do any other work in New Mexico besides prospecting and that rock work.

A. No sir, not to amount to anything.

Q. Well, what was it if it did not amount to anything.

A. I prospected most of the times and worked in the mines a few days . . .

Q. What were you doing there [El Moro, Colorado].

A. Running an outfit, building some coke ovens.

Q. How long were you engaged in that job.

A. I don't remember, I think I moved to Trinidad in October 1893.

Q. Were you building those coke ovens all the time up to the time you moved to Trinidad.

A. I believe so, I don't remember.

Q. Did you do anything else at El Moro.

A. No sir.

Q. What business did you engage in after moving to Trinidad.

A. I was Constable of that Precinct in the town there . . .

Q. What did you do in Trinidad from 1893 to 1895.

A. I just rested around.

Q. That job of building coke ovens was a pretty hard one.

A. No, I did not work very hard.

Q. Well, it took you a good while to get rested.

A. I am not rested yet. I am tired now . . . [19]

And thus the interrogation was carried along for some little while. More recently, and for about a year, until June of 1899, witness had been employed by Wells, Fargo as an express guard; he had quit working regularly for the company because the pay was not high enough, but he still made the occasional run for them. When pressed, he admitted having known that, some time before the second Folsom robbery, the company had placed a standing reward of $1,000 each for "a man named Sam Ketchum, Tom Ketchum, William Carver, Dave Atkins and two or three others." As he understood it, the bounties would be paid whether the men were brought in dead or alive, although the company's offer was not worded quite in that fashion.

Elliott was forced to concede, under persistent questioning, that he had not received a commission from Foraker. Strictly speaking, then, Jones concluded, Elliott was not a deputy marshal at all—he had been merely a deputized posseman in charge of other deputized possemen. Apparently, Elliott was nettled by this disclosure; but the real damage was yet to come.

Jones now tackled the subject of the fight, and by the time he had finished with Elliott the witness had not only been shown up as untrustworthy, but now and again made to look foolish. He got more and more confused, contradicted himself at times, and had to admit more than once that he had forgotten his answer to this question or that one of a few minutes earlier. Fort's re-examination retrieved little or none of the lost ground, and Jones let the witness go.[20]

Perfecto Cordova was the next witness. Although he spoke and understood English well, he was served by an interpreter. This must have given him the opportunity to think twice before he answered any question. His performance was even more lamentable than Elliott's had been.

Cordova, when examined by Jerry Leahy, said that he thought McGinnis had been armed at the time he was shot, but was not more positive than this; he stated, however, that the defendant had certainly done some shooting in the later stages of the battle. In this he may have been lying, but he was not wrong; it was just as well for the outlaw that Perfecto's evidence was so patently at fault or equivocal in other respects.[21]

It was common knowledge in Cimarron that Cordova had told a number of people—Miguel Lopez, Patricio Montoya, a man named Strivens, and others—that the man called McGinnis had been shot down whilst unarmed. Edwin Franks, in cross examining the witness, reminded him of all this. Cordova wilted a little, but maintained that his words had been misunderstood. Nor would he knowingly change the sense of the story he had just given to Leahy, although Franks did manage to expose some of its inconsistencies. Moreover, since it had been established that the bullet which killed Farr had ranged upwards, Franks succeeded in weakening or muddling the Territory's case by drawing from Cordova the statement (undoubtedly incorrect) that the sheriff's position had been roughly level with or just above that occupied by Carver.[22]

Under re-examination, conducted by Fort, Cordova reiterated that the posse had been fired upon by all three of the fugitives. Jones, who put the witness through re-cross examination, seems to have been the first of the four lawyers to grasp what ought to have been clear all along: that the defendant had not been one of the two men whom Cordova had seen at the beginning of the fight. Fort realized what Jones was getting at, and asked leave of the court to have the witness explain further what he had seen of the movements of the man whom he "took to be McGinnis." Nothing was clarified by this, or needed to be; it must have been obvious by now that Cordova had been describing the actions of Carver, not those of the defendant.[23] Nearly forty years afterwards, Otero had this to say of Cordova's testimony:

> I do not pretend to know what changed Perfecto Cordova, but any person who heard his testimony could tell that he was following instructions. In fact, after the trial, he admitted to several that he had been mistaken about McGinnis firing his gun.[24]

In truth, Cordova had not been wrong about this; he just thought he had been wrong.

James Morgan had appeared on the stand, early in the trial, to describe how he had observed the movements of Ketchum, Carver, the man known as "Red" or "Wheeler" (Weaver), and the defendant, before the train robbery. Now, after the dismissal of Cordova, he was recalled to give testimony on the fight. His answers were far more helpful to the defense than to the prosecution: as nearly as he could tell, all the shots fired at the posse had come from Ketchum and Carver, or from the direction of the places from which these two were shooting. He was certain that McGinnis had not been carrying a rifle when the bullets started to fly.[25]

Morgan was followed by David E. Farr, who had gone into Turkey Canyon with Reno, George Titsworth, and others shortly after the fight. Dave Farr's testimony was mostly concerned with the firing positions taken by the three outlaws and with the nature of his brother's wounds. His findings tended to show that the defendant must have been the man who had shot Ed Farr; but such testimony as his, no matter how impartially and with what precision it was delivered, probably would have struck the jury much less forcibly than the testimony—and manner—of the eyewitnesses.[26]

M.C. (Cicero) Stewart was called next. He told the jury how the arrest of McGinnis had been accomplished. Then, during cross examination, he produced the clothing taken from the prisoner. The pants, the old grayish vest, the yellowish shirt which was really only an undershirt, were the garments which the outlaw had been wearing in Turkey Canyon. The vest and the bloodstained shirt, each with two bullet holes on the left hand side, were held up for the inspection of the jurors.[27]

"I believe the Territory will rest here," announced Fort, when Jones had concluded his cross examination.

This came as an utter surprise to Franks and Jones, who were most anxious to listen to Reno's version of the shooting. Jones protested that it was incumbent on the prosecution to examine Reno "as to the facts and circumstances occurring at the time of this homicide or alleged homicide." He had a fair point; Farr and Reno were so close to one another when the battle started that they could very nearly have shaken hands had they reached out.

"We do not desire to call Mr. Reno. We claim that we can call any witness we choose," Fort responded curtly.

Jones renewed his objections, contending that it was "a rule of law" that the prosecution produce all witnesses who were within its power; the record showed, he added, that Reno had "already been upon the stand as to a preliminary matter."

It was no good; his motion to have Reno put upon the stand was overruled.[28] The other material witness, Frank H. Smith, had returned to the East and had not been summoned back for the trial.

We have nothing to indicate just when or by whom it was decided that Reno should not be recalled. But no great percipience is required to understand why counsel for the Territory did not want him on the stand again. Some of his testimony was likely to diverge sharply from that rendered by the other material witnesses; from Cordova's above all. No one—apart from the absent Smith—had been so well placed to observe the actions of Farr and McGinnis.

But Leahy, Fort, and Long had a more particular reason for the suppression of Reno's testimony on the fight. Sam Ketchum had told both Reno and Foraker that he had fired the shot which killed Farr. Despite their other differences, the two men were at one in believing Sam.[29]

This statement, in itself, was not crucial to the success or failure of the case against McGinnis. Since it was not a dying declaration—indeed, Sam seems until his last day on earth to have expected to recover—any reference in court to his admission of culpability, whether from Reno or Foraker, would probably have been stricken from the record as hearsay. But, as an eyewitness, Reno stood in a very different light from Foraker; his testimony—certainly under cross examination—would both explain and support his belief that the fatal bullet came not from McGinnis, but from Ketchum.

Reno was more intelligent and articulate than either Elliott or Cordova; it would be unreasonable to doubt that his testimony would have been more coherent and credible than theirs. The prosecution case had already been hindered by Morgan's partial contradiction of Elliott and Cordova, and the unilaterally poor impression created by these two witnesses. Reno's testimony, if heard, may well have made the jurors more responsive to the argument that the defendant was unconscious when Farr was killed. That might easily have led to a conviction for nothing worse than third-degree murder, a term equivalent to culpable manslaughter. An acquittal, or a verdict of excusable homicide, which amounted to the same thing, would have been disastrous to the prisoner's interests, but neither was a realistic possibility.[30]

Edwin Franks chose not to make an opening statement for the defense. He was to call only two witnesses: Miguel Lopez, who had been subpoenaed to attend, and McGinnis himself. His intention was to use Lopez to complete the demolition of Elliott and Cordova, each of whom had already discredited himself, and the other, from the stand.

Several days previously, Lopez and the man Strivens had visited attorney Franks in his room at the Palace Hotel and had related the story of the fight as they had

heard it from Cordova. When he took the stand, though, Lopez was not too willing
to confirm the accuracy of what Franks had scribbled in his notebook during the
meeting at the hotel. Early in the examination the Territory was sustained in an
objection to the defense's impeaching its own witness. But Lopez did say that
Cordova had told him that he (Cordova) was not sure whether McGinnis was in
Turkey Canyon at the time of the fight, and that, even if defendant had been present,
Cordova did not know whether or not he was carrying a rifle. He recollected, too,
having been told by Cordova that Elliott and Farr, upon locating the outlaw camp,
had agreed to divide the posse into two sections—an assertion directly contrary to
Elliott's testimony, in which it was stated that Farr, Reno, and Smith had slipped away
unseen and unheard by the titular leader of the posse.[31]

Elliott's name was not brought into Fort's cross examination. Fort tried, but
failed, to persuade the witness that he could not remember what Cordova had said
about his doubts as to McGinnis's presence in Turkey Canyon and about his
inability to say truthfully whether or not the defendant could have been armed at
the time.[32]

The defendant then stood up to testify for himself, his manner so frank and fearless that Otero erroneously believed that he spoke the unalloyed truth. Indeed, he did
not tell many direct lies: as far as he could, he merely avoided mention of any facts
injurious to himself or to his associates in crime. Naturally, Edwin Franks's examination was not calculated to bring out any such facts.[33]

Towards the end of his evidence in chief, McGinnis paraded before the jury the
scars from his wounds, accompanying the demonstration with a brief descriptive
commentary.[34] Presently, after Long—who, thus far, had taken little visible part in
the proceedings—had risen to cross examine, there were theatricals of another kind.
It is plain that the authorities were still ignorant of the true identity of the defendant;
he was even accused of being Carver!

Q. What do you say your name is.
A. William McGinnis.

Q. Has that always been your name.
A. Yes sir.

Q. Ever go by the name of Carver.
A. No sir.

Q. Where were you born.
A. I was born in the East.

Q. Where.
A. In Illinois.

Q. What place in Illinois.

(WITNESS) Well, if the court please, I am here tried for murder. I understand
there is other charges against me, - for train robbery, - I have been put on trial
without any chance to get my witnesses.

(The court) Don't make any address to the jury, Mr. McGinnis, your lawyers will do that. What do you want to say? Don't you want to give an account of your life.

(WITNESS) What I mean to say is this, - I have got no way to protect myself and I positively refuse to answer any questions, except concerning this fight and I will not under any circumstances answer any.

(The Court) Very well.

Q. You put yourself in this attitude, do you, that you decline to answer any questions with relation to your past life.

A. I decline to answer any questions except concerning the fight.

Q. Do you decline to answer any questions which relate to your past life up to the time this occurrence happened? Answer Yes or No.

A. Yes, I decline to answer any except about this fight.

Q. Except on this particular occasion.

A. Yes sir.

Q. Where were you on the 11th day of July 1899.

A. I was at this camp on Turkey Creek.

Q. I don't believe you understand my question. I said the 11th of July.

(Mr Jones) If the court please, I submit that is not proper cross examination of this witness.

(The Court) Judge Long, the witness has declined to answer and I don't believe you ought to go into it.

(E.V. Long) Well, all right McGinnis . . . [35]

Most of the questions that were then asked of him about his companions he declined to answer. He denied having known that one of them was named Ketchum; this man was always called "Red," he declared, but sometimes was referred to as "the old man." Now Sam Ketchum had been of ruddy complexion and his hair had been reddish blond; but the nickname "Red" had already been assigned in evidence to its proper place: to the identity of the man whose real name was thought to be Wheeler—and he was nowhere near Turkey Canyon when the posse got there. It seems that the defendant seized upon a mild coincidence—the general similarity in stature and complexion of Ketchum and Weaver—to thicken the confusion. Anyway, Long designated Sam Ketchum as "Red" in his subsequent questions to the witness.[36]

McGinnis continued to insist that he had been shot first by someone in Farr's group, then, moments later, by someone in the Elliott party, and that he himself had been unarmed from start to finish. At no time did Long look like shaking him. His cross examination was aggressive, sometimes sly, but never shrewd.[37]

Fort then took the maladroit step of calling upon Elliott to make a rebuttal of the defendant's testimony. The credibility of Wilson Elliott, in the context of this case, is well conveyed in the closing exchanges of his cross examination by Jones:

Q. Didn't you state the first shot you fired was at the horses.

A. I perhaps did. I believe I shot the first shot at the horses. I don't know. I am not sure now. I don't know whether I fired the first shot at the horses or the first shot at this man up here.

Q. Well, didn't you so state in your previous examination, that the first shot you fired was at the horses.

A. I don't know whether I did or not.[38]

After the testimony, the closing speeches. Elisha Long, in his speech, made a flagrant attempt to browbeat the jury. The defendant, declared Long, had every opportunity to have a fair trial; if the jury were to make any mistake in bringing in a verdict which was not warranted by the evidence in the case (he meant any verdict that did not suit the prosecution), the court would set the verdict aside. The defense objected strongly to this, and Mills, perhaps embarrassed by the implications, commented:

"The court has a right to set aside such verdict, but I do not know whether such verdict would be set aside or not."

The defense were to find fault with this, too.[39]

Mills received from the prosecution twenty-five requests for instructions to the jury, but allowed only seven. The defense made fifteen requests, of which four were allowed. His own instructions were nineteen in number.

In essence, this was the proposition put to the jurors: if they accepted that Farr and his companions, whether a legally-constituted posse or not, had proper grounds for believing that McGinnis and the two men with him were in flight from the recent train robbery, and provided that the evidence showed that the suspects had been given a chance to surrender before any shots were fired at them, McGinnis should be found guilty of murder; and for this, in these circumstances, it did not have to be proved that he himself had fired the fatal shot. If, on these premises, the jury were not satisfied that the defendant, personally, had killed Farr, or were satisfied that one of the defendant's companions was the actual killer, the verdict would be returned as guilty of murder in the second degree. If, however, they believed that Farr was killed by the defendant himself, they would assess guilt in the first or the second degree, depending upon whether, in their view, the killing was part of a premeditated plan or common design, or whether it had been an act "perpetrated in the heat of passion." It was, of course, also open to the jury to find the defendant guilty of murder in the third degree or to acquit him. What Mills did not make plain to the jurors was the verdict they should find if they believed that Farr and those with him had fired on them without having first given them an opportunity to surrender.[40]

Before the trial, Mills had told a newspaperman in Raton that he expected the case to be over by Saturday night. On the Thursday, and again on the Friday, court had remained in session until eleven o'clock at night. It was now well into the evening of Saturday. He informed, or reminded, the jury that if they had not found a verdict by eight o'clock in the morning they would have to stay in the jury room for another twenty-four hours. A train for Las Vegas was due to pull out of Raton shortly after eight o'clock on Sunday morning, and Mills intended to be on that train. He would be back in Raton on Monday.[41]

As the jurors were about to retire to consider a verdict, counsel for the defense came forward to object and except, separately, "to each and every instruction given by the court upon its own motion or upon the request of the plaintiff, and also, . . . to the refusal of the court to give each and every instruction asked for by the defendant." Franks and Jones were given until Tuesday to file specific objections and exceptions.[42]

It took the jury about three hours to agree upon a verdict that McGinnis was guilty of murder in the second degree. This was punishable by imprisonment "for any period of time not less than three years." The defendant's attorneys then gave notice of a motion for a new trial.

On Tuesday, October 10, Mills overruled all the defense's objections and exceptions and denied the motion for a new trial. Then he passed sentence.

"It is therefore considered and adjudged by the court that the defendant, William H. McGinnis, be and hereby is sentenced to imprisonment for the full term of his natural life at the penitentiary situated at Santa Fe, Territory of New Mexico."[43]

So, on the 13th, the fallen "paladin" of the range again entered the gates of the penitentiary, this time as Prisoner Number 1348.[44] Mills had granted him leave to appeal to the Supreme Court, and the cause was heard in January 1900 before Justices Jonathan W. Crumpacker, John R. McFie, and Frank W. Parker.

Crumpacker began with a statement of what he called the "important facts in the case." Most of Crumpacker's "facts" on the shooting were items taken without reservation or qualification from Wilson Elliott's testimony. The trusting judge even repeated Elliott's assertion that the shooting had not lasted for more than ten minutes; Cordova and Morgan had testified (and, incidentally, Reno had stated outside the courtroom) that the fighting had gone on for about three quarters of an hour. No vital issue turned upon the disagreement over the duration of the shooting; the significant point is that Crumpacker let himself be guided solely by Elliott.

Appellant's argument that the killing of Farr could not have been "traceable directly to the conspiracy to rob the train" because the two events were separated by a period of five days and seventy miles was, remarked Crumpacker, "more ingenious than helpful in the case at bar." The judge commented at some length on such matters as how the basis for "common design" was constituted or could be constituted, and on the question of "mixed law and fact" through which it had to be determined whether the posse had been actuated by "good faith and honest purpose" and had "acted as reasonable men would have acted in like situation." His opinion ruled against the appellant on every issue, and—with McFie and Parker concurring—the sentence of the district court was affirmed.[45]

In an empirical sense, the verdict in the case against Lay, alias McGinnis, was the right one; he had killed Farr—although he must have been the only person in that courtroom who knew it—and undoubtedly the outlaws would have fought or run even if the posse had tried to take them alive, rather than dead. The sentence was much severer than the evidence, alone, would warrant: obviously Mills was influenced by factors that did not belong to the case at all. The judges of the Supreme

Court preferred the testimony most unfavorable to the defendant and stood by the doctrine that had governed Mills's conduct of the trial.

According to Charlie Siringo, the ex-cowboy author and detective, the outlaw's attorneys were paid out of the loot from the bank robbery at Winnemucca, Nevada. If this be true, they had to wait almost a year for their money.[46]

About the first news Lay heard when he entered the penitentiary as No. 1348 was that Tom Ketchum had already manifested unrest.

After his operation, Ketchum had swiftly regained his strength, and with it much of his old defiance. Despite the loss of the arm, and the vigilance enjoined upon the guards by Superintendent Bursum, he evolved and brought near to fruition an implausible yet ingenious scheme to escape from the prison hospital. His confederate was Prisoner No. 1208, George Attlebury, who was serving a three-year sentence for robbing a store in Colfax County and who was under treatment for "consumption." Their apparatus comprised one block of wood, one clockspring, and some tinfoil. The wood was painstakingly fashioned into a replica of a Colt's six-shooter and then encased in tinfoil; in uncertain light it would look most realistic to a guard if thrust suddenly into his face. The clockspring was cleverly improvised into a saw. In a field half a mile away a white pony was grazing, easily visible from the hospital and as elusive as a mirage to the imprisoned outlaws.

Ketchum and Attlebury planned to overpower their attendant and cut through the bars of the window. Next, they would waylay the watchman as he was making his rounds; they would hold him up with their wooden pistol, disarm him, and knock him senseless. If they got clear of the prison, Attlebury would catch the white pony, which would have to carry double until the men could find fresh horses.[47]

Ketchum, seriously handicapped and highly conspicuous as he was, could hardly have expected to get very far away. Yet, in the last days of September, his spirits were buoyant, his manner seasoned with bravado. He gained further stimulus from the visit of Cicero Stewart, who displayed an amazing lack of sagacity if he genuinely believed that the outlaw meant to make some important revelation to him. But Tom acted rather like the cheat who is so gratified by his own artfulness that he cannot resist letting his prospective victims into the secret.

In response to the sheriff's query, Ketchum jovially said: "I'm getting fat so that when they hang me they can eat me if they want to."

Then, adopting a confidential tone, he directed Stewart to the location of a certain juniper tree, in a box canyon in the Chiricahuas, forty miles northeast of Bisbee and a quarter of a mile from the Turkey Track horse camp. This juniper was fifty feet from the "large pile of ashes" which marked the camping place once used by the gang. Buried at its roots, he said, was the sum of $1,800 in gold. Stewart swallowed the whole story—or so Ketchum imagined—and hied him away to uncover the hoarded treasure.[48]

Prison secretary Billy Martin was more overtly perceptive. Sensing from Ketchum's jaunty banter—"pertness and gayety," the *New Mexican* called it—that the outlaw was planning to escape, he reported to Bursum on or about October 1. The dummy pistol was soon found in the hospital water-closet. An examination of

Ketchum's person brought forth the clockspring, wound around the outlaw's body and tucked into the bandage. The two convalescents were hustled away into cells. Ketchum "broke down with emotion" at the discovery of the scheme; but, only a short time later, his cellmate William Hall was surprised to see him dancing a jig.[49]

"I'll learn that fellow to punch cows with me and then come to Trinidad to identify me!" chortled Ketchum. "If he goes into that canyon, and the gang happens to be there, they'll fill his hide full of lead!"

For some days afterwards—as Livingston tells the story—Ketchum eagerly scanned the papers for news of Stewart's death. His disappointment owed nothing to any excess of caution on the part of the sheriff.

Stewart carried no writ outside New Mexico. He could have lobbed the problem into the lap of the Arizona authorities. Was he gullible enough—or greedy enough—to fall for Ketchum's tale? Or did he see straight through the scheme, and, like the conscientious and courageous officer he demonstrably was, make it his duty to shoulder part of the danger personally? Stewart had known Tom for years, and surely would have been familiar enough with his ways to distrust most of his words.

He went straight to Cochise County and consulted Steve Roup, a deputy sheriff from Bisbee—a game man and a proven fighter. The two officers then rode out to the canyon. They found everything as Ketchum described it, except the money.[50] Fortunately for them, there were no outlaws, either. But matters might easily have turned out as Ketchum had hoped. During that autumn Will Carver was roving about southeast Arizona and southwest New Mexico, together with Tom Capehart and others, including one or two of the Kilpatricks. Butch Cassidy, who had remained in Alma, and Red Weaver, who had rejoined him, were in touch with Carver and the rest.[51]

While it remains possible that Ketchum's object was merely to amuse himself by wasting official time and causing annoyance to Cicero Stewart, the sheriff did not doubt that the outlaw had planned to assassinate him by proxy.[52] A few weeks later, however, a visit to the prison by the mayor of Santa Fe, Dr. J.H. Sloan, gave Tom the occasion for a further piece of trickery, though one that was without sinister connotations. His meeting with Mayor Sloan also enabled him to practice his newly acquired ability to write and sketch left-handed.

Tom informed the mayor that $4,500 in Mexican gold lay buried on the 4 Cross L range, several miles west of Sherwood, Texas, and handed him a diagram on which the exact location of the supposed cache was clearly marked. Sloan took away Ketchum's map but, even if he believed the story, did not follow it up.

Others did. The tale, and the diagram, drifted back to "the goodly neighborhood of Sherwood" early in the New Year and stirred up the area "from center to circumference." Notable non-participants were the owners of the property. The 4 Cross L had changed hands in the late summer of 1898, shortly after the Stanton train robbery. E.C. (Cal) and J.D. (Ike) Sugg, who had purchased the 200,000 acre ranch from Comer Brothers, were so perturbed by the excavations that they threatened to sue the goldseekers for despoiling their pasture. The story quickly died. It is a safe bet that no one turned up anything but dirt and pebbles.[53]

We do not know whether reports of this pantomime penetrated the walls of the penitentiary, or whether Tom Ketchum would have been too preoccupied with his gathering predicament to savor the joke. For him there would be no further opportunity either to escape or to seek revenge, although, in a way, Governor Otero was zealous in his efforts to protect him from the Arizona courts. On November 9, 1899, United States District Attorney Childers acceded to the request of the Arizona authorities by waiving the federal charge against Ketchum "on the understanding that should he be acquitted or sentenced only to a term of years he should be brought back to be tried on the charges that the United States has brought against him."[54] This duly led to a second requisition from the governor of Arizona, and on the 11th Sheriff Munds reappeared in Santa Fe, flourishing the papers which wanted only the signature of Governor Otero to place Tom Ketchum at the disposal of Yavapai County. Governor Otero referred the application to his Solicitor General, Edward L. Bartlett, depending on him for a legally ironclad buffer against extradition. Bartlett answered the call:

> In the matter of the application . . . for extradition of Thomas Ketchum alias George Stephens, alias Charlie Bishop, . . . I have the honor to report:-
> That under the rules of practice adopted by the Inter-State conference . . . such requisitions <u>must</u> be by the District or prosecuting attorney, and all the regulations or requirements therein <u>must</u> appear by his certificate.
> The 8th Rule provides "that no requisition will be made for the extradition of any fugitive except in compliance with these rules." All of these requirements are mandatory and cannot be omitted with safety as habeous [*sic*] corpus proceedings would lie and would prevail.

Then Bartlett played his, and Otero's, master card. The submission from Arizona would have been impeccable but for one detail: it did not meet the stipulation of sub-rule H, in that there was "no reference <u>to the particular statute which defines and punishes the [crime alleged]</u>." The omission "in this particular case" was "very important," for it meant that the certificate from Arizona did not specify the nature of the punishment for murder in that territory.[55]

Otero had the surefire legal recipe he needed for the refusal of his signature, so Munds was again sent empty away. But in a letter to Governor N.O. Murphy, written three days later, Otero chose to overlook Bartlett's useful legalisms. He simply maintained that he had turned away the requisition because the crime charged against Ketchum in New Mexico carried the death penalty. This was true in practice, but would not have sufficed without the provision of which Bartlett had advised him.

Otero then showed Murphy that the governing factor in the case was not that Ketchum was accused of a capital crime, as such; it was that he was accused of the particular capital crime of armed assault on a railway train.

"Train robberies have been entirely too frequent in our territory to permit this one to go by un-noticed," he declaimed, "and I am determined that it must be stopped. Further, I am thoroughly satisfied that the courts and juries of our territory will uphold the law as set out in our Statutes." If, contrary to his expectation, the New Mexico courts failed in their duty, Otero would be happy to comply with any future request for extradition to Arizona.[56]

The following day he responded in similar vein to a telegram from the U.S. district attorney for Arizona, Robert E. Morrison. In closing, Otero mentioned that four indictments were pending against Ketchum in New Mexico, "so that I do not think you need have any fears that he will not receive full justice."[57]

Otero was unalterably determined that Tom Ketchum was to die by the rope and that the job was to be done in New Mexico. This, he hoped, would purge the territory both of highway robbers and its ill repute. More; it would proclaim that, at last, the celebrated "Black Jack" had been brought to the end which awaits all outlaws. There was said to be little chance of securing evidence to prove Ketchum guilty of the murders of Herzstein and Gallegos, which would otherwise have taken precedence. Hence the way was clear for him to be thrown before the bar of justice on the capital charge of assaulting a railroad train. Yet the Territory was in no hurry to take up the case. The prosecuting authorities of the Fourth Judicial District, which included Union County, left the early running to the federal side of the system.

As soon as the second requisition from Arizona had been turned down, therefore, the United States proceeded with its charges. Ketchum was taken to Las Vegas where, on November 15, he pleaded guilty to an indictment brought under R.S. 5473 (section 287 of the Post Office act of June 8, 1872), which covered any attempt to rob the mail "by assaulting the person having custody thereof, shooting at him or his horse, or threatening him with dangerous weapons," but without effecting robbery. The statute provided for a term of imprisonment at hard labor of "not less than two or more than ten years."[58]

Len Alverson alleged in his reminiscences that the federal officers had agreed to hoodwink Ketchum into entering a plea of guilty so as to facilitate conviction on the capital charge:

> They said, "Now, Tom, there is a federal charge against you which bears a maximum sentence of ten years. If you will plead guilty to that we will give you ten years. Meanwhile you can get your friends to working getting things fixed for the other charge and also toward getting a pardon." Well, he pleaded guilty but they sentenced him to only six months . . . [59]

Alverson could not have been right about the six-month sentence, because the statutory minimum sentence was one of two years. He may have been right about the negotiation of a guilty plea, though the *New Mexican* thought otherwise. In its view, Ketchum had acted "very cunningly" in entering an immediate plea of guilty. By taking this course, Ketchum prevented the prosecution from seeking the continuance that would create time for the Territory to bring its own case.

Cunning or not, the gambit failed. On November 18 the court simply announced that sentence in Case 648 would be deferred, and again remanded Ketchum to the custody of the U.S. marshal.[60]

Contrary to both a report in the *New Mexican* and a statement in a letter from U.S. District Attorney William Burr Childers to the Attorney General, the sentence was not "suspended," in the correct legal application of the term. Federal judges were categorically barred from suspending a sentence—a practice that allows a sentence to be waived and the convicted person to walk away unpunished. Despite the prohibition, federal judges had suspended sentence from time to time, and incurred Congressional wrath by doing it; but Justice McFie did not do so in this case. He merely postponed, or deferred, sentence.[61]

In theory, sentence could be deferred for almost two years, the duration of the statutory minimum prison term. In the interim, or until the moment he was convicted in territorial court, Ketchum would remain a prisoner of the United States. The federal authorities no longer needed the indictment in Case 626, relating to the first of the three Folsom holdups; Ketchum's guilty plea in Case 648 had given them an excuse to set it aside.

As Ketchum was driven to Las Vegas station after the trial, he was besieged by shoals of curiosity-seekers. His reactions were much the same as those he had evidenced in Trinidad.

"What in the hell is the idea of this crowd?" he demanded. Given the anticipated reply, he exclaimed: "To hell with them!" With that he drew his vest and shirt over his face. If the gathering would make up a purse of $25, he would let them see his face. The offer provoked "a lot of good-natured raillery;" but no hands shot moneywards.

Among the spectators was one who was more than a mere sightseer. He was Placido Gurule, who had so narrowly and so luckily survived the ambush in which Levi Herzstein and Merejildo Gallegos were killed in 1896. Gurule believed he recognized Ketchum, but never got the opportunity to say so in court.[62]

Nearly a year dragged by before Union County was ready to set in motion the legal machinery which, few doubted, would ceremoniously accomplish the removal of Tom Ketchum into the death cell. Public interest in him waned; it would not reawaken until he went on trial.

Still, although he was no longer news, his unearned and largely accidental acquisition of the euphonious title and overdrawn notoriety of Black Jack ensured that he remained an object of curiosity to strangers on prison visiting days. Mischievously, opportunistically, or just cynically, he tried to exploit his spurious fame. Outside his cell he placed a box, and beside it a notice reading "25 cents to see Black Jack." Upon payment of the quarter, he would pull back the shirt or jacket he was using to mask his features.[63]

His casting of himself as the attraction in a crude two-bit peepshow was, to say the least of it, a severe comedown for the man who had extracted almost fifty thousand dollars from the Wells, Fargo safe at Lozier. And before much longer, he may have regretted it, as he strenuously, truthfully, and for the most part vainly denied all legitimate connection with the name Black Jack.

At last, on the morning of Monday, September 3, 1900, Ketchum was escorted from the penitentiary by Deputy U.S. Marshal Frank W. Hall (a brother-in-law of Marshal Foraker), and Sheriff Harry C. Kinsell. At Trinidad, where they were to stay overnight, they were met by William Reno, who was in charge of arrangements for the second leg of the journey.[64]

Upon the morrow the town of Clayton turned out in force to gaze upon the doomed outlaw. The C & S special train bearing Ketchum, six guards, and a whole convention of railroad and express company men, arrived at Clayton depot at 12:30 p.m. Tom was in a reminiscent mood. This was very much the same town as the one he remembered so well from his trail-driving days. He spoke ruminatively of the places and people he had known—eight, ten years ago. The march ended at the Union County Jail. As Hall unlocked the shackles, Ketchum delivered himself of sentiments less amiable:

"Hall, you are the first man that ever put shackles on me. One of these days I'll do the same thing to you and I'll take you way off on the prairie and leave you."

Turning to survey the cells, Tom allowed that "these is right smart pleasant quarters;" but, he mused, "I'd a heap rather be out on the Perico eating dinner at the chuck wagon."[65]

Court was called to order at two o'clock. At 2:40 the outlaw, "looking rather nervous," was brought into the crammed courtroom to hear and answer to the three indictments. William J. Mills was presiding; the prosecution was being handled by Leahy and Fort. Before Leahy started to read the indictments, Ketchum asked and was granted leave to speak to Reno.[66]

The first indictment dealt with his felonious assault upon a railroad train. Perhaps contemptuous of the legal jargon, Ketchum "seemed impatient" and ran his eye over the faces of the spectators "as if seeking a friend somewhere." When Leahy had paused to clear his throat before turning to the second indictment, Ketchum rendered a plea of guilty. Mills refused to accept the plea; since the crime for which the indictment had been found was punishable by death, he told Ketchum, the only admissible plea was one of not guilty. The clerk was instructed accordingly.

To each of the other indictments, wherein he was charged with the wounding of Harrington and Bartlett, he pleaded not guilty. Since the defendant had neither counsel nor funds, the court appointed William B. Bunker to look after his interests.[67]

That night, Albert Thompson, formerly the editor of a local newspaper, "whose intimates called him 'Pin-Head' for some inexplicable reason," was permitted an unsupervised visit to Ketchum's cell. Most of the interviewing was done by the prisoner. He wanted to know whether the district attorney and judge would give him a square deal, and was assured that they would. But he should have had no fears on that score; his guilt was so palpable that legal finagling would have been pointless even if it had been possible.[68]

For much of Wednesday the outlaw was discussing his case with Bunker, a deputy remaining in close attendance throughout. Every now and again Ketchum wandered from the point, relating stories of diverse incidents in his past life. Bunker and his assistant, John R. Guyer, tried desperately to find some plausible defense for a man whose conviction was inevitable and who appeared supremely indifferent to his own case. Ketchum was somewhat surprised and hurt because no one had attempted to rescue him. "When a man is in, he ain't got no friends," he remarked to someone: but he had lost his friends while he was still out.[69]

Both parties were ready to go to trial on Thursday, September 6. The case was called at 2:30 p.m., and adjoined four hours later when twelve presumed peers of the accused had been selected. Bunker and Guyer then presented the court with a motion that the first indictment be quashed because the punishment was "unusual and excessive" for the crime of which Ketchum was accused and, as such, contrary to the provisions contained in Article 8 of the Constitution of the United States. "Cap" Fort disputed this, and Mills briskly set the motion aside. The court then rose.[70]

Ketchum appeared "very much bored" and "mean at times." "If I hang, my information hangs with me," he said grimly. His attitude showed that he "would like to make most any kind of a deal whereby he might escape the death penalty."[71]

Court resumed at nine o'clock the next morning for the taking of evidence. On almost every point, the testimony was straightforward and unequivocal. According to Albert Thompson's possibly over-adorned recollections of the case, one of the few incidents which stirred Ketchum out of his lethargy arose while Charlie Drew, the express messenger, was on the stand. The Thompson version amounted to this:

"You say the prisoner pounded on the door of your car and commanded you to open it?" asked Leahy, in Thompson's recreation of the scene.

"Yes, sir."

"Well, what did he say to you?" prompted the attorney.

"He said, pointing his gun at me, 'fall out of there damn quick.'"

"And what did you do?" Leahy pursued.

"I fell out of there damn quick. What would you have done, Mr. Leahy?" the witness flung back.

The district attorney, as Thompson wrote the script, did not duck the question.

"I would, too," he responded; then turning to the defendant, "Is that true, Tom?"

"You bet your god-damned life it's true," Ketchum declared, amid laughter, "and he didn't lose no time, either."[72]

Unfortunately, most of the lines in this vivid sketch are absent from the official transcript. This was the exchange, as the court stenographer recorded it:

A. (Drew) . . . He covered me with the gun and called out, - Come out of that door, or fall out of there, or words to that effect.

Q. (Leahy) And how close was he to you at this time when he pointed the gun in your direction.

A. Twelve to fifteen feet, I take it to be.

Q. What did you do.

A. I got out. There was nothing else to do.

Q. Did you get out or "fall out."

A. I did not fall out. I got out.[73]

There are times, alas, when fiction packs a stronger dramatic punch than documented fact. Still, it is a shame to toss away a good story without putting up a defense for it. It is not quite inconceivable that the passage was heard in court more or less as Thompson wrote, only for the trial judge to order the badinage to be shorn from the stenographic record.

Although Ketchum had not got his hands on a single dollar in his last holdup, Leahy questioned the witness closely as to how much money there had been in the express car at the time. Drew said that, as far as he could remember, there had been fifty dollars in the way safe; "the through safe contained valuables, paper and money, but I don't know what it contained, sir. I had no access to it." When asked to add to this statement, he admitted knowing that he had "more than five thousand dollars worth of stuff in the through safe," but emphasized that this was no more than a "rough estimate."[74]

Attorney Bunker found an awkward witness in Fred L. Bartlett. The mail clerk was as hostile as ever towards the man who had shot him. He had been disabled for life and was quite sure that his presence on the witness stand owed nothing to Ketchum's good intentions. It was going to take more than a clever lawyer to change his mind about this. Bunker tried:

Q. Could you get the motion of your head before the bullet struck you, after it
was fired.
A. It was quite evident I did.

Q. Do you know at what rate one of those bullets travels.
A. No sir. I never figured it out.

Q. Don't you know they travel 2400 feet a second.
A. It is possible.

Q. That would not give you much time to get your head out of the way.
A. The motion of putting the pistol [*sic*] forward might have given me warning.

Q. Did you see the pistol put forward to shoot.
A. I did.

Q. If that bullet had hit the iron plate on the door would it have hit you.
A. It would undoubtedly have hit me further back on the head.

Q. Do I understand you to say that if this bullet had have kept its course it would
have gone in rear of you.
A. No sir. If this bullet when it first struck the car had kept on its course it would
have hit me further back in the head or in the body.

Q. If you had your head in the car could you see the flash of the gun.
A. I said my head was out of the car leaning forward.

Further cross examination brought out an admission from Bartlett that the bullet, having been fired from below, must have ranged upward. Bunker then proceeded.

Q. Well, how do you explain to the jury that if the bullet had not struck the side of the car that it would have struck your body farther back or lower down.

A. It would have struck me about the back part of the head, I think.

Q. Then it would not have struck your body at all.

A. My head is part of my body.

Q. Didn't you swear that you had your head out of the car.

A. Yes sir, part of it.

Q. How much of your head was out of the car.

A. I never figured it out, but I had enough of it to see out.

Q. How far was the man who fired the shot from you.

A. Probably thirty or thirty-five feet.

Q. And you were in plain view, weren't you.

A. My head was.[75]

On the whole, the evidence left little room for argument. Frank Harrington and Joe Kirchgrabber, as well as Drew and Bartlett, gave details of the holdup. Chris Waller, John Mercer, Joseph Robbins, and F.F. Clarke related how Ketchum had surrendered and what he had said. Harry Lewis and George Titsworth testified on what he had told them afterwards.[76]

It was now for the defense to make what it could of a bad hand. Ketchum himself did not testify; if anything could have made a hopeless case worse, it would have been an appearance by him on the stand, his empty sleeve proclaiming his guilt. His most memorable contribution to the occasion was an exchange of jests with Harrington during a break in the formalities, when Tom told his vanquisher that, together, they could have robbed the United States treasury in Washington.[77]

Anything that Ketchum could have said from the stand would have been irrelevant to his defense, anyway. The only line available to his counsel was to advance an argument that the territorial court had forfeited jurisdiction. Their purpose was to show that the defendant had been placed in the custody of the United States shortly after his arrest by Pinard, that he had been brought to Clayton as a prisoner of the United States, and that he was still a prisoner of the United States.[78] They had three witnesses for the defense: F.W. Hall, Saturnino Pinard, and F.J. Dodge.

Fred Dodge, the veteran Wells, Fargo detective, was on the stand for only a couple of minutes. He told Bunker that he had come to Clayton the previous day with "Mr. [Si] Rainey, Division Superintendent of the railway company, Special Agent Reno, United States Deputy Marshal Hall, a man named Saxton, and a man named Kernochan." He added:

"There were two others. I don't know their names. I don't know the names of the train crew running the train. Neither do I know the name of the negro porter. I think that was all."

Q. Are you sure there was a negro porter on that train.

A. Yes sir. He got me a cup of coffee.

Q. An intimate friend of yours, was he.

A. He was a friend in need.

Q. I will ask you if the defendant was on that train.

A. Oh, yes, I forgot "Tom." He was there.

Q. You overlooked a very important personage.

A. That is right.[79]

This piece of frivolity concluded the testimony in the case.

As Bunker was taken ill, the task of making the closing speech for the defense fell to John Guyer. He did as well as he could, but the proposition was an impossibility. The jury needed little time to bring in a verdict of guilty.[80]

Messenger Drew, interviewed in Fort Worth on September 10, stated that Ketchum "seemed indifferent to his fate and sat through the proceedings as though nothing unusual was happening." Albert Thompson wrote much the same when he recorded his impressions thirty years later: "Ketchum evinced no emotion." A *New Mexican* reporter remarked, not without ambiguity, that the outlaw "was much affected by the verdict, but his great nerve kept him from making any demonstration."[81]

Guyer at once moved for a new trial. This request was considered on the following Monday and turned down. Next day, September 11, court assembled for the sentencing.[82]

"Have you anything to say why sentence should not be pronounced upon you?" asked Chief Justice Mills.

"Nothing at all," replied Ketchum.

The jury had fixed the penalty as death; the law gave it no alternative, anyway. It was then Mills's duty to set a date for the execution, and his privilege to advise the condemned man on how best to occupy himself in the meantime. (There was a convention, generally observed, that this privilege take the form of an expression of solicitude for the spiritual prospects of the condemned; it was almost as if a judge were both the servant of God and the instrument of Justice.) This is how Mills addressed himself to Ketchum:

> It is hereby ordered, considered and adjudged by the court that you, Thomas Ketchum, on the fifth day of October, A.D. 1900, between the hours of ten o'clock in the forenoon and four o'clock in the afternoon of said day, in an enclosure to be erected by the sheriff on the court house grounds in the town of Clayton, county seat of Union county, Territory of New Mexico, you be there hanged by the neck until you are dead by the sheriff of said county of Union, or such person as may be deputized by him . . . The court recommends to you that between now and the day of your said execution you prepare yourself by repentance for your past evil deeds to meet your God, and may God have mercy on your soul.

Ketchum smiled and gave his attention to his attorneys.

The judge granted Ketchum leave to appeal. This was tantamount to a stay of execution, as the Supreme Court was not due to meet until January, 1901.[83]

On Thursday, September 13, the rancher Jack Culley was waiting at Lamy, New Mexico, for the local train to Santa Fe when he saw Ketchum walking up and down the platform with Sheriff Pinard on one side of him and Deputy Gray on the other. When the train arrived Culley and others followed the trio into the smoker. Culley was surprised to see this dangerous and powerful man, still formidable despite the loss of his right arm, "entirely free, hand and foot." Speaking to Culley years later, Gray explained why he had been certain that Ketchum would not try to escape: "I know prisoners. I knew Tom was through."[84] What he meant was that he could see that Tom knew he was through.

That evening Pinard restored Ketchum to the care and protection of the territorial penitentiary until such time as he was required at Clayton to shake hands with the hangman.[85] Tom was now better able to compare notes with "Bronco Bill," who had held up a couple of trains in 1898 but had escaped the death penalty because he and Will Johnson had killed three members of the posse—and Bill had been convicted of second degree murder only; or with Elzy Lay, whose case had been broadly similar to that of "Bronco Bill;" or with Alverson, Hovey, and Warderman, who had been convicted in a federal court for a crime of which they were innocent and he was guilty.

His last journey to Santa Fe had been an uneventful one, but at Trinidad he was heard to deride any notion that he would swing.[86]

Hang a man for waylaying a railroad train? It was too ridiculous for words!

Map 5

Map 6

[17]

ATKINS SADDLES THE OCEAN

After the capture of Elzy Lay at Chimney Wlls, Tom Capehart rode hard across country until he reached the WS ranch in western Socorro County. At the horse camp, twenty miles from the ranch headquarters, he met Butch Cassidy, who was still in the employ of the WS. Red Weaver was also in the locality, having reappeared in Alma shortly after parting from Marshal Foraker.

For this phase of the story, we are entirely in the hands of William French, uncorroborated but uncontradicted. Since what he has to say is not inherently unlikely, we may reasonably accept it as true in outline.

French states that he left Cimarron to return to Alma several days after the Turkey Canyon affray. Some three or four weeks afterwards—not quite French's "more than a month later"—Cassidy and Capehart came to him with the news that "Mac" was a prisoner. Capehart gave French a quite extensive but purposely incomplete account of the capture, which the rancher related in his memoirs thirty years after hearing it. Whether errors in French's version came from failings of memory, or from misunderstanding or misstatement on Capehart's part, becomes unimportant once we have elected to believe that some such conversation did take place.

Tom had arrived late the previous night on a worn-out horse, the last of several he must have ridden in covering four hundred miles in three days; that is to say (although French did not), he must have reached Alma late on August 19. Cassidy and Capehart wanted French to go bond for "Mac" when his case came up for trial. French demurred. He thought, correctly, that a capital charge was not bailable in New Mexico. Moreover, he believed that Reno suspected him of complicity in his former employee's crimes. He told them that the best he could do was certify to the defendant's good conduct during his term of employment on the WS. Since Capehart was telling him no more than he thought necessary—for example, he did not explain how, when, or where "Mac" came by his wounds, not realizing that French already knew; and, rather than deny being the wanted "Franks," he said only that he was afraid of being taken for him—French concluded that Capehart "must be the man the authorities called Franks." The mistake was made easier and more understandable by the fact that, as far as can be judged from his *Recollections*, Will Carver was unknown to him in person and in name.[1]

Carver, as we have seen, had given Cicero Stewart's posse the slip. Stewart set out from Carlsbad at three in the afternoon of August 16 with J.J. Rascoe, Dee Harkey, D.D. Clark, and Harry Morrison. The posse had a clear trail to Carlsbad and onto the road to Seven Rivers. They continued into Seven Rivers, pressed on westward to Hope, thence to Weed, sixty miles west of Hope, and finally to Musgrave's Camp. This brought them to a point two hundred miles west of Chimney Wells, only two full days after their departure from Carlsbad. Fast time, indeed, but to no useful end; they had been following a hunch, not a trail, and the hunch turned out to be a bad one. It was obvious from the complete absence of sign and sightings that Carver could not have taken that route.

Three of the posse returned to Carlsbad on Sunday night, August 20. Stewart and Rascoe were twenty-four hours behind them, having paused to make further inquiries in the Seven Rivers vicinity. They concluded that Carver had duped them by making himself conspicuous on the road to Seven Rivers and then sliding away to the north-east when he was lost to sight. The search for him ended with the reasonable but untested assumption that he would continue northeast as far as the Panhandle of Texas, a destination that need take him no more than 150 miles from Carlsbad.[2]

Whether or not he did enter Texas, Carver was back in the southern border country of Arizona and New Mexico by fall. In the time left to him he neither forgot nor forgave Rufus Thomas's part in the arrest of Elzy Lay.[3]

Events eight hundred miles to the north brought a succession of new faces to the WS ranch and its locality. The Wilcox, Wyoming, train robbery of Friday, June 2, 1899, and subsequent murder of a pursuing sheriff, had stirred a hornets' nest. Directly after the robbery, the gang had split into two groups of three. One, comprising George Currie and the brothers Harvey and Loney Logan, had been chased northward. It was they who ambushed and fatally wounded Sheriff Josiah Hazen of Converse County on June 5. Their pursuers stuck to their trail tenaciously for almost three weeks. Harry Longabaugh, Bob Lee, and Ben Kilpatrick composed the second trio. They headed northwest, comparatively untroubled by posses. Members of the two groups were reunited in early July near the Montana—Idaho line or in Utah. The hunt for them continued, refreshed by the $3,000 offered for each robber scalp by the combined initiative of the United States Government, Union Pacific Railroad, and the Pacific Express Company.[4]

Two of the gang, Harvey Logan and Ben Kilpatrick, eventually found their way to Alma, by way of Nebraska, Kansas, Arkansas, and Texas, where they may have picked up Ben's brother George, or encouraged him to follow. That fall, Ben Kilpatrick joined the payroll of the WS as John Ward. He was called Big Johnny Ward, to differentiate him from another hand of the same name—apparently guiltless of criminal associations—who now became Little Johnny Ward. Logan and George Kilpatrick may have joined Carver in southeast Arizona, most likely in Graham County. They, Cassidy, Capehart, Ben Kilpatrick, Weaver, and one or two others, were in close touch.[5]

There were various rendezvous. One was in the Peloncillo Mountains, forty miles south of San Francisco ("Frisco"), New Mexico. The WS horse camp was another. A third, and more public, meeting place for them was the saloon attached to the Coats and Rowe store in Alma; Butch Cassidy took over the bartender's job in the late summer or fall. He may have had a financial stake in the venture and seems to have been able to combine this congenial post with ranch duties for what remained of the WS operation in Socorro County. Later in the year, he was joined by Harry Longabaugh, whom Elton Cunningham remembered as a "lunger . . . coughing and very bad . . . you could see he was short-breathed . . . a little bit and he coughed a good deal." Frank Gilpin, a boy of about twelve, took shooting lessons from the two men. Young Gilpin was left-handed, but switched his shooting hand from left to right by imitating the action of his mentors. Unfortunately, neither Cunningham nor Gilpin mentioned the name that Longabaugh was using at the time. In any event, he did not stay long. Before the end of the winter of 1899–1900, he returned to the North.[6]

The money stolen at Wilcox was said to have aggregated at least $30,000 in cash. Among the proceeds was $3,400 in bills, mostly hundreds and fifties, that were not quite right, in that they lacked the signatures of the president and cashier of the First National Bank of Portland, Oregon, to which they were being sent. During the later months of 1899 several of these entered circulation in southwest New Mexico. For a while they passed freely from hand to hand and no great notice was taken of them.[7]

Still buried in the mountains of Colfax County was the booty from the second Folsom robbery. The men planned to have the loot disinterred and distributed, but there were obvious difficulties. Carver could never again risk showing his face in the Cimarron area. Weaver, officially, had a clean bill of health in Colfax County, and probably would have liked to get his hands on the lot; but he, too, could hardly expect to be seen there without attracting the wrong sort of interest. So, for the time being, the cache remained undisturbed.

But the peace of southwestern New Mexico did not remain undisturbed. Las Cruces, where Alverson, Hovey, and Warderman had been convicted, had a bank owned by George D. Bowman & Son. Shortly after two o'clock on Monday afternoon, February 12, 1900, two horsemen turned into Main Street and rode slowly up to the bank. They were seen by "several parties at the Rio Grande Hotel," who attached no importance to them, "as there was nothing unusual in their appearance." The cream-colored horse ridden by one of the strangers attracted more notice than the two men. The men dismounted and entered. Cashier James G. Freeman and the woman bookkeeper were quickly covered by two six-shooters. Freeman dallied over opening the safe until one of the bandits snapped a pistol in his face a couple of times. The visitors cleared the safe of its contents, including, it was said, the payroll for the Torpedo mine, emptied the till, and left after counseling Freeman and his assistant not to make an outcry. Unconcerned bystanders watched them ride slowly out of town. Only when a citizen reacted to Freeman's bad news by firing his pistol into the air did the bandits break into a gallop. They took an easterly direction, towards the Organ Mountains. It was the first case of daylight bank robbery in the criminal history of New Mexico.[8]

Pat Garrett's posse started out twenty minutes after the robbery. They never made up the time. Instead, they arrested half a dozen men, none of whom had robbed the bank, though two—Will Craven and Print Rhode—might have been accessories. All were released almost at once, and three of them threatened to sue the county. But charges were later laid against Craven and Rhode.[9]

The posse also "arrested" three horses. One, a broken-down gray, Garrett tried to pass off as the cream horse: if the animal had looked to be cream-colored, he explained, it must have been because he had been ridden through a sand storm. The difference in movement, he said could be accounted for by the horse being "fagged out" and "only grass fed." No one was quite sure about the color of the horse ridden by the second man; so Sheriff Garrett produced two: a white-faced sorrel and a dun with black mane and tail. The horses, like the men, were released for want of evidence. Newspaper comment, as was the style of the times, began by making it "a pretty safe wager that these bank robbers will soon be rounded up unless they made [sic] a successful dash across the line into Mexico," and closed a few days later with the opinion that "the men and money are gone, likely not to return." The bank, meanwhile, soothingly "adjusted" its loss to a mere $1100, less than one third of the sum first reported.[10]

The two robbers did not make for the international line. Garrett's posse lost track of them somewhere north and west of the Organ Mountains. Garrett believed they changed mounts in the Organs country, the animals used for the ride-in and getaway being returned to their owners and the bandits fleeing on the horses they had left there earlier.

Both men were unknown to the townspeople who saw them. Tom Capehart might seem to have been a natural suspect, in the light of the bitterness he expressed at his brief but uncomfortable imprisonment at Las Cruces in connection with the Steins Pass charges. But it was merely incidental that George Bowman had been foreman of a Dona Ana County grand jury while Capehart was in the jail at Las Cruces; all the indictments against Capehart and the other Steins Pass defendants had been issued months earlier in Silver City under federal auspices.[11] Will Carver might have been another suspect; he was dangerously at large and available for such deviltry, and known to be friendly with Capehart.

Neither Capehart nor Carver had any but the most tenuous link with the affair. One of the robbers was William Wilson, whose origins are unknown beyond his own statement that they were in Texas. His partner in the bank robbery was Oscar Wilbur, who at different times claimed Texas and Ireland as his native home. It was assumed for official purposes that these were their real names. The fact that Tom Capehart sometimes used "Wilson" as an alias is no more than a mild coincidence. Another coincidence, or possibly more than that, was that the pair had planned the robbery in conjunction with James Brooks, whose wife, Lizzie, was a sister of Red Weaver. Brooks pulled out of the scheme after a dispute.[12]

Billy Wilson was known widely and unfavorably in Grant County, New Mexico, where he and Jim Brooks were co-suspects for a murder committed during a robbery in May, 1898. Wilson and Brooks were arrested and jailed for the crime, but, for want of evidence, never tried.[13]

After robbing the Las Cruces bank and shaking off the posses, Wilson and Wilbur escaped to El Paso and went on by train to San Antonio, where Wilbur had recently bought a house for his family. Their story might have ended happily but for Red Weaver's brother in law Jim Brooks. Soon after the bank robbery, he sent his wife from their home in Grant County to Cochise County by train. But when the time came for him to follow her, a few days later, he chose to save on the fare by going on horseback, and to save on the cost of a horse and saddle by stealing one of each. It was a false economy. The theft was quickly traced to him, and he to Arizona. Before long he was in Santa Fe to begin a five-year term for grand larceny.[14]

Perhaps in the unredeemed hope of securing light treatment, Brooks had pictured himself as rejecting an invitation to help in the robbery of the Las Cruces bank. His disclosure of the names of Wilson and Wilbur led speedily to their arrest in San Antonio. Wilbur owned up, testified for the Territory, and was released on January 7, 1901 after serving eight months of a five-year sentence. Billy Wilson also pleaded guilty but was put away for ten years.[15]

Dave Atkins may have had the qualities for good citizenship that Mack Axford ascribed to him, but they did not enable him to become a good citizen. After leaving for Idaho in 1898, he began promisingly enough by keeping out of crime's way and taking a chance on being able to square himself with the State of Texas over the Hardin case. He also missed his wife, and seems to have assumed that she missed him.[16] Like many chronic wanderers, Atkins often felt and responded to the tug of home ties; but, once home, could hardly wait to get away again.

His northern excursion lasted for twenty months. If, indeed, he did meet the Duncans, or the Ketchums, or Carver during his Idaho interlude, they could have advised him on the lie of the ground he was visiting and pass on to him the news from San Angelo. It is not known whether any word came to him from or about Mrs. Dave Atkins. In the late spring of or early summer of 1899 he moved from Idaho to Butte, Montana, where he worked as a laborer—making ties for the streetcar company, chopping wood, and finally in some unstated capacity for the Colorado Smelting Company in Butte. He had borrowed his mother's name and was living as "John Baker." He well knew that he was being hunted. Gerome Shield had not forgotten about the Hardin and Powers murder cases.

On September 13, 1899, Shield issued a writ of capias for Bud Upshaw. In November, Ranger John W. Matthews, Company D, Texas Rangers, traced Upshaw to Gila County, Arizona. On November 27, Shield applied to Governor Joseph Sayers for a writ of requisition, which Sayers approved on the 29th and which Shield then asked Matthews to serve. Bud's arrest in or near Globe followed on December 6. He was detained there until Deputy Marshal D.R. Hodges, as Shield's agent, arrived to collect him, and deposited him in the Tom Green County jail on December 18. On January 29, Bud was released on $2500 bail. His bondsmen were two young Concho County cattlemen, Bob and Will Jones, and Will Cheney, of Christoval, all of whom were well apprised of the character and reputation of Jap Powers—and Tom and Sam Ketchum, Will Carver, and Dave Atkins.[17]

At the same time, Lee Cutberth, or Cutbirth, or Cuthbert, who had been wrongly accused of being Tom Ketchum's accomplice in the Camp Verde murders, again fell under official suspicion. The cause of his current misfortune was his close physical resemblance to Atkins. On Monday, January 29, 1900, he was arrested at his home, south of Tempe, Arizona, at the request of Ranger Matthews. Cutberth admitted that he was a fugitive from a warrant issued in connection with a murder at Ysleta, but maintained that the charge was "imaginary." If he was quoted correctly, he did not even know that Ysleta was in Texas; he appeared to believe that it was in New Mexico. Above all, he was not Atkins.[18]

Cutberth's objections were no argument against the writ of requisition that Matthews presented at Phoenix a couple of days later. He was taken to El Paso, where he renewed his protestations in an interview for the *Daily Times*. He had worked on ranches all his life, and had gone to Arizona from Parker County, Texas; his mother was living in Hood County. He had never stopped in El Paso or been to New Mexico, except to travel through it. "I am a not bit worried by my arrest," he declared, "But I don't like being held here in jail."[19]

The reporter was unsympathetic. "He has not got a pleasing appearance, and talks in an independent kind of a style, like a person who had been in similar trouble before." The *Times* reckoned that El Paso had Atkins. It did not concern itself with the thought that arrest and prolonged detention were making Cutberth restive and that he had good cause for resentment.[20]

Ysleta, nine miles downriver from El Paso, and formerly seat of El Paso County, had nothing against Cutberth. Its only connection with his case, apart from its status as the headquarters of Company D of the Texas Rangers, seems to have been that "a woman . . . who knew the prisoner in former times" was living there. Whether her acquaintance was with Cutberth or with Atkins is not clear. All that is known is that Cuthbert was taken to Ysleta on February 6 and returned to El Paso on the 7th. His release was unnoticed but would have followed within a day or two.

A month after this story went into print Cutberth's point was made for him when the real Dave Atkins stepped into the light. He walked into the office of the sheriff of Jefferson County, in Butte, Montana, identified himself, stated where he was wanted by the law and for what, undertook to waive the formalities of extradition, explained that he was anxious to see his wife and child, and sat down to wait for Tom Green County to send for him.[21]

On Wednesday afternoon, March 7, Gerome Shield was seen in the express office at San Angelo, poring over a large map of the railroad system of the United States. His problem was twofold: he had never thought of going anywhere near Butte, and had no idea of how to get there; and he knew that he would not be back with Atkins in time to attend the forthcoming cattlemen's convention at Fort Worth.

Shield made unexpectedly good time. On the 12th, four days after the sheriff's departure, his deputy, Dick Runyon, received a telegram from Butte. Shield had Atkins in charge, and would leave next day.

Shield gave Atkins some news from home that had not reached him. His wife, Sabe, had moved to San Angelo, divorced him, and remarried. Her new husband was

Will Green, a dilettante actor and gadabout. Atkins, visibly distressed, said that if he had known that to be the state of affairs, he would never have surrendered.[22]

The sheriff was an affable man, and the rest of the long and wearing journey would not have passed in silence. One topic that may have arisen was the war being waged in South Africa between the imperial forces of Great Britain and the two "Boer republics" of Transvaal and the Orange Free State.

The war, as such, might have been of small concern to them; what would surely have commanded their interest was the number and range of acquaintances who had left or were about to leave the San Angelo neighborhood for South Africa—to tend mules and horses, to fight, or to look for money-making opportunities. They included R.E. Harris, once a Texas Ranger but more recently San Angelo's leading druggist; his older son, Felix; George Bent, whose sister was Mrs. Jim Landon, wife of the proprietor of the town's principal hotel; Jim Smith, nicknamed "Kid" and, even more familiarly, "Fatty," the hotel's "general factotum" and "ex-hero of the Cuban campaign;" and several of the best-known figures on the cattle ranges, Jack Miles and the brothers Jeff and Doc Moss.[23]

Shield and his prisoner arrived in San Angelo on the morning of the 18th. For the sheriff it had been a round trip of five thousand miles. When asked "how he liked the great Northwest," Rome replied that he "did not like it a little bit;" it was "sure enough winter up there, great snowclad mountains and big frozen rivers, and even yet the ice King rules supreme." For Atkins there was a visitor—the wife who had just divorced him; from William Reno, there were statements in the Denver press, naming Dave as one of the four principals in the first Folsom train robbery.[24]

Heinous as the murder of Hardin had been, Atkins was released amid public silence at the beginning of May 1900, on payment of a bond of $3,000. Thereafter, *State of Texas vs. Dave Atkins: Murder* sleepwalked its way through district court. No effort was made to advance charges against him in connection with the robbery at Lozier. He walked unfettered and unimpeded through seven months of continuance and adjournment.[25]

The war in South Africa, and San Angelo's contribution to the flow of men and material, were prominent in the news and talk of the town. As he pondered the future and what it might do to or for him, Atkins would have heard much more of the story of the father-and-son team of Bob and Felix Harris. They had left Texas to fight for the Afrikanders, only to experience a change of heart in mid-ocean and don the Queen's uniform instead.[26]

The Harrises had joined the Kaffrarian Rifles, one of the many irregular units created in the colony of Cape of Good Hope. Its name came from Kaffraria, the district surrounding the port of East London. Fittingly for an irregular outfit, it seems never to have made up its mind whether it was cavalry or mounted infantry. As such, it was characterized by the initiative, adaptability, and versatility that the military establishment detested but, in time, grudgingly accepted as desirable in the conditions under which the war was being fought.[27]

Bob Harris's letters were replete with episodes of derring-do and stirring references to "the fighting K.R." and "the jolly K.R." And in mid-September, the old frontiersman came back to San Angelo, so full of enthusiasm for the imperial cause and the commercial potential of South Africa that he intended to return and re-enlist.[28] Whether he and Dave Atkins met is impossible to know; but, if they did not, Dave must have heard a great deal from second or third hand. It is certain that this true yarn, and others, were the source of an idea that he put on one side to germinate until the day came for him to adopt it as his own. That day would not be slow to arrive. He may already have calculated that when the State of Texas finally got around to hearing his case, it was likely to secure his conviction.

On December 3, a special venire of 108 jurors was called for the Atkins case, and the date of the trial set for the 14th. Came the day, but not the defendant or his witnesses—W.F. Holt, the precinct justice, and the cattlemen James and William Johnson. Atkins's attorney then stepped smartly up with a continuance plea from his client. Despite "due diligence," Dave had been unable to locate his witnesses; all he wanted was more time. Holt, the Johnsons, and Dave McGuirt could, between them, show that Hardin had been wearing a pistol when he was killed, that he had previously made it known that he would kill Atkins "if he ever crossed his path," and that State's witness George Bodry could have verified both lines of defense but had perjured himself. The court pronounced the case "continued by defendant's defaulting witnesses," solemnly levied a $100 fine upon each, and ordered them attached to appear at the May term, 1901. Atkins had been given the time he needed. Procedure ground on; at the end of the December, 1901, term the court ordered an alias capias to be issued for the errant defendant. By then he had been missing for more than a year.[29]

The Harrises and Bent had taken passage from New York to Southampton, England in the liner *St. Paul*, and from Southampton to Cape Town in the *Scott*.[30] Considerations of finance or personal security precluded Atkins from following their style and their seatracks. He would have to sail from New Orleans as a muleteer after signing on under an assumed name.[31]

The British authorities who were supervising the shipments were anxious to obtain the services of men experienced in the handling of livestock, especially those who said they would stay on after disembarkation to scout or fight; they did not bother with checks on identity or character. They also provided a ticket for the outward and return voyages, reasonable pay, and not very good food. Bob Johnson, of the Erie cattle spread, could hardly have been more obliging than they.

After decamping from Tom Green County towards the end of 1900, Atkins may have marked time for several weeks in the East and Midwest. But by early February he was in New Orleans and ready to deliver himself from an unpromising present to an uncertain future.

Dave saw the dangers that might confront him as a fighting soldier in South Africa as offering more attractive prospects than a trial for murder before a Texas jury of unpredictable sympathies. He boarded the requisitioned British and South American Steam Navigation Company cargo liner *Hostilius* at New Orleans, as one of a team of muleteers bound for Table Bay, beneath Cape Town.

The *Hostilius*, Captain J.L. Lewin, 2025 tons net and 3325 gross, and 350 feet from stem to stern, was almost new. But her first voyage, directly after her completion in Dumbarton in July, 1900, was almost her last. She had to be towed into Barbados after breaking a propeller shaft and subsequently, near the end of a six-month tramp, went aground off Bremen.[32] Still, she embarked from Liverpool in good order on January 22 at the start of her second trip; and, on February 12, docked at New Orleans to receive a consignment of Texas mules and their handlers. When she cast off on February 18, 1901, Dave Atkins was among those aboard.[33]

According to the reminiscences he dictated ten years afterwards, it was a wretched voyage, though its duration was much shorter than the twelve weeks his narrative allocated to it. She was not a happy ship and Atkins was not a happy would-be warrior. Officially, however, the voyage passed free of trouble.[34]

Hostilius docked at Cape Town on March 22, thirty-two days out of New Orleans. Here the mules were unloaded. Atkins remained aboard and, probably three days later, stepped ashore at East London.[35] A couple of days after his arrival he presented himself at the recruiting office of the Kaffrarian Rifles.

Unlike the practice in some of the other irregular regiments, the enlistment form adopted by the Kaffrarian Rifles posed very few questions. The applicant was required to furnish no more than a name, an age, a home address, and a civilian occupation. Atkins probably knew this before he left Texas. On March 27, 1901, he swore an oath of allegiance to King Edward VII, and, in return for a promise of pay "not less than five shillings [$1.20] per day," plus rations, clothing, and equipment, completed and signed an enlistment form. He was now 31293 Trooper Drake, J.W.[36]

⊰ 18 ⊱

AN ANNIVERSARY FOR
GEORGE SCARBOROUGH

Early in March, 1900, Assistant Superintendent Frank Murray, of the Denver office of Pinkerton's National Detective Agency, came to Alma to investigate reports that currency obtained in the Wilcox robbery was being passed in the locality. Some of the stolen bills had been placed on deposit at the bank in Silver City by the storekeeper at Alma.[1]

Murray began his search for information on the Wilcox robbers by looking for cowboy friends of theirs who had changed traceable bills on their behalf or would admit to having spent stolen money. Foremost among these undetected collaborators was Jim Lowe, bartender of the saloon annexe to the Coats and Rowe store. Lowe and Red Weaver were just back from Solomonville, which they had visited "about the time the races were being run." Murray became quite friendly with Lowe while he pursued his inquiries. Charles A. Siringo, the "cowboy detective" who followed Murray to Alma more than a year later, believed that the assistant superintendent never suspected Lowe of being Cassidy.[2]

William French contradicts Siringo, and, in this instance, is the more credible. He wrote that the Pinkerton man, whose name he misremembered as "Byrne" or "Burns," came to see him one morning, stated why he was there, and explained that some of the Wilcox suspects were now at the WS. He wanted to interview Johnny Ward.

French took this as a reference to Big Johnny Ward, whose criminality he already suspected. But, since he was not on the premises and Little Johnny Ward was, French sent for Little Johnny and was astonished to hear him admit to having spent such bills in the store and to see him pull more of them from his pocket. Ward had got them from Clay McGonagill, in payment for a couple of horses, just before McGonagill's departure with an alleged brother called Neale.[3]

Murray also showed a photograph of one man sitting and two or three others standing, all of them clad in "in the usual cowboy outfit." When French identified the seated figure as Jim Lowe, but denied knowing any other name for him, Murray informed him that the subject was known to the authorities as Butch Cassidy. French thought that one of the men shown as standing in the photograph might by

Capehart, but he was unsure: the picture "had been taken some years before, and Tom was many years younger than Jim [Lowe]."[4]

French's principal concern was that he "stood a good chance of losing the outfit [he] was so proud of." But, for the moment at least, he was to be spared this misfortune. Murray had seen and recognized Cassidy in Alma that morning, but had no intention of trying to arrest him; to attempt such an act in that neighborhood, he "would need a regiment of cavalry." The detective then took his leave, saying he would have to start looking for McGonagill.

When French saw Cassidy, later in the day, the outlaw "only grinned" as French described Murray's visit. Butch told French that he and Capehart "had already spotted" Murray; "they suspicioned who he was" when he returned to the village after his talk with French, and drank with him "to make sure." Cassidy let French know that he would have to leave the area "before very long," as he expected his friends to send for him; but "he liked the country very much" and would stay for the time being.[5]

Cassidy and Capehart warned their friends, at least five of whom brought their sabbatical rapidly to a close. Several of them vowed to kill Murray before they had to leave and he could do so. Doubtless they had just heard of the killing of Loney Logan, near Kansas City, Missouri, and arrest of Bob Lee at Cripple Creek, Colorado, both on February 28. The prominent role taken by Pinkerton operatives in the two cases had been well reported.[6]

Whether from humanity or in the interests of discretion, Cassidy helped Murray to get out overnight with a whole skin. The story of Butch's intervention comes from Siringo, and is not belied by his statement that Murray later insisted that Siringo was mistaken about Lowe being Cassidy, or by French's failure to mention the incident. If, as Siringo says, Murray acknowledged that he owed his life to Lowe, it is possible that his rejection of Siringo's identification of Lowe as Cassidy was his way of returning the favor. The absence of any reference to the affair in French's writings is not significant. French did not see or hear everything—and the WS hands, along with the local people generally, made sure that he did not. It was in everyone's interests, including his own, that he did not know too much.[7]

Five of Cassidy's pals headed north in a body. Their identities are obscured by a thicket of aliases, but the names that stand out amidst the underbrush are those of Tom Capehart, Will Carver, Thomas C. Hilliard ("Tod Carver"), Ben Kilpatrick, and Harvey Logan. A sixth, the Sundance Kid, had already left.

Siringo has Cassidy selling his saloon—more probably, a share in the concern—and riding away with Red Weaver on the morning after Murray's retreat. Actually, the interval must have been more like a week. French's foreman, Perry Tucker, wanted to quit before the WS had shipped all its cattle to Magdalena, and suggested Butch should succeed him. Knowing what he now did, French dared not fall in with the proposal, though he would have been happy for Cassidy to stay on in a lesser capacity until the rest of the cattle had been trailed to Magdalena for shipment. This did not suit Cassidy; though willing to accept Tucker's authority, he was not prepared to take orders from any newcomer. That, at any rate, was French's understanding; in reality, Cassidy was making excuses. The time had come for him to go anyhow.[8]

The weakest point in this part of French's narrative bears upon the enigmatical personage who can best be termed "William French's Tom Capehart." By French's account, Cassidy assured him that Capehart would stay on until Tucker's departure at the end of the next trail drive, and that, in the event, he remained on the WS until Cassidy had been gone for more than a month. He goes on to say that Capehart stayed mostly at the horse camp, making only rare appearances in Alma or at the ranch. This means that French would have seen very little of him. Even so, there is no getting past contemporary evidence that Capehart was among the five who left the WS ahead of Cassidy and Weaver and were next reported in Springerville, Arizona. What probably happened is that Capehart, perhaps with others of the gang, went with Tucker and the herd to Magdalena, and then headed for Springerville, a hundred miles almost due west. He may have holed up again at the WS horse camp for a few weeks later that spring.

Cassidy and Weaver left Alma some time between March 15 and 20. Before starting out they stole all the horses from the Bar 02 ranch, owned by N.M. Ashby, whose rustling activities (wrote French) had incurred their contempt and anger. By March 25 they were only a day behind the group of five that included Carver, Logan, Ben Kilpatrick, and Capehart.

On that day the advance party reached Springerville. They bought provisions and one of them left a letter, for collection from the post office by someone who would be in town shortly. Next day, Cassidy and Weaver rode in, leading their string of stolen horses. They called for the letter and rode on.[9]

For a clearer understanding of what ensued over the next two days, four simple but crucial facts should be noted.

First, the Springerville-St. Johns area was suffering from the attentions of a band of livestock thieves recently arrived from northwest New Mexico. Among the suspects was a man known locally as "Skeet" (or "Squit") Jones.

Second, no one in Springerville recognized any of their seven visitors or had any idea of who they were. But, since the seven were well armed ("with Mauser rifles," thought one correspondent), and had about the same number of extra horses, the suspicion arose that they were stock thieves, if not potential train robbers.[10]

Third, some of the local citizenry were headstrong, if not trigger happy. If they had known the character and caliber of the men they were pitting themselves against, they may well have proceeded with more deliberation.

Fourth, it was quickly learned that Cassidy and Weaver really had stolen the spare horses, albeit from another locality; thus material support was almost immediately forthcoming for the original suspicions.

Not long after they left Springerville, Cassidy and Weaver were arrested by Sheriff Edward Beeler and lodged in the Apache County jail at St. Johns. A passerby had reported seeing a freshly slaughtered cow and five men standing near it. Cassidy and Weaver were taken in because of their suspicious demeanor and apparent connection with the other five strangers. The five men were in St. Johns, purchasing further supplies, when Beeler's posse arrived with the two prisoners. Beeler did not molest them, not so much because their behavior was entirely innocent as because he needed more help. For the moment he concentrated on the two birds in hand.

Weaver gave his real name, while Cassidy identified himself as Jim Lowe. A telegram was sent to French for confirmation of their identities. Inquiries were also put out about the horses the men were leading.[11]

Next morning, March 27, Beeler set out with an enlarged posse, while another group of citizens was being assembled as a second force. Beeler soon overhauled the five, mainly because the latter exhibited a curious lack of haste for men who were supposed to be on the run; possibly they were loitering in the hope that Cassidy and Weaver would talk their way out of trouble and catch up with them. Shots were exchanged between the posse and the five, and two of the strangers' horses were killed. Though the posse had the best of it, they seem not to have pressed their advantage too hard and soon turned back to St. Johns.

The citizens' group did not see the Beeler's party, but assumed that the sheriff was still on the trail. They split into two sections. One section of four broke away, planning to outflank their quarry, get ahead of them, and lie in wait. But the suspects' northward line of retreat was a feint; they made a detour at right angles to their original course, then headed south. Their pursuers gave up the hunt.

The remaining four men, including Andrew Augustus ("Gus") Gibbons and Frank LeSueur, clung doggedly to the trail. They stayed together until afternoon, when two of them turned for home. LeSueur and Gibbons kept up the chase, still under the misapprehension that Beeler and his men were on the ground between the fugitives and themselves.

LeSueur and Gibbons were amateurs at this dangerous game. The five saw them from afar, doubled back on their tracks, and placed themselves in ambush among the cedars and boulders high on the mountainside. The two young men dismounted and led their horses. They walked right into the waiting rifles and died in a flurry of lead. Gibbons, who was in the lead, was wounded in the stomach and then shot in the back and finally three times through the head as he tried to stagger downhill. LeSueur died where he fell, from bullets through the neck and between the eyes. Their killers took their horses, weapons, money, and even their hats.

Local opinion was outraged when the news was brought to St. Johns on the 28th. Fury and shock were understandable; the hunted men had reacted with calculated and merciless ferocity.[12] "The sight was horrifying to the senses," wrote Gus's uncle Dick Gibbons, one of those who found the bodies, "To see the two boys that I had known since they were in the cradle . . . and for them to be shot down like dogs . . . made me sick. It was murder in its worst form . . . " and the assassins "had out-villained villainy."[13] All chillingly true; yet the present writer cannot disagree with the comment of Philip Rasch, author of a well-reasoned and well-researched study of these shootings and those that followed:

> While it may appear callous to say so, the young men were armed and presumably quite willing to take the lives of five men who could be charged only with suspicion of having killed a cow. The best of causes confers no immunity upon its adherents.[14]

Beeler had vowed from the beginning "to follow the outlaws and get them if it took all summer." After writing to Ben Clark to report the murders, the southward flight of the killers, and the detention of Lowe and Weaver, he raised another posse and returned to the chase on the 29th. But the killers were well ahead. That night the five tarried long enough in or near Frisco to steal seven horses.[15]

At about this stage one of the five turned northwards, towards Globe. Another took his place at the same time or a little later. By now the Beeler posse was catching up. At the Jim Crow Mine, near Carlisle, New Mexico, thirty miles north of Steins, the sheriff was only an hour behind. The story given to the press was that the posse, "learning of the splendid arms carried by the outlaws, decided not to push them to a fight and returned." In fact, Beeler followed the gang westward into Graham County, Arizona, but not too impetuously; the fate of LeSueur and Gibbons was proof of the folly of risking an ambush. The two young men had not appreciated the desperate character of the men they were pursuing. Beeler, doubly forewarned by their deaths and the knowledge that the criminals' firepower was superior to the posse's, showed sense in tempering courage with prudence. When the outlaws passed through Duncan, Arizona, on Sunday evening, April 1, they were again a long way in front of the pursuit. They seemed to be in no great hurry, for they halted awhile for Capehart to exchange words with people who knew him.[16]

From Duncan, the gang continued south. On Monday, April 2, a prospector named J.D. Mack was wounded from ambush in Pinery Canyon, which leads west from the Chiricahuas into Sulphur Spring Valley. Although the men who killed LeSueur and Gibbons were in roughly the same general area at roughly the time of the attack, a more precise correlation of time, place, and circumstance is lacking.[17] They are unlikely to have traveled quite that far into the mountains by the date in question. But they were unquestionably the authors of a far lesser crime whose consequences were far greater. Just as at Springerville a week earlier, they slaughtered a cow.

Late on Sunday, or early on Monday, the five made camp on the Triangle ranch, eighteen miles northwest of the town of San Simon and near the northern edge of Cochise County. They killed the animal, dined on some of it, and resumed their journey to the Chiricahuas. Later on the 2nd, Walter Birchfield, the ranch manager, found the carcass. Like the Apache County posses, he had no inkling of the identity of the perpetrators. He assumed they were petty criminals, most likely smugglers from Mexico. He rode to San Simon and sent a wire to a man who lived in Deming, was chief special officer for the New Mexico Cattle Raisers' Association, and held deputy sheriff's commissions in several Arizona and New Mexico counties, including Grant and Cochise. That night George Scarborough dropped off the S.P. train at San Simon and rode with Birchfield to the miscreants' campsite.[18]

Eight months after the Texas Canyon affair Scarborough, with Jeff Milton and Eugene Thacker, had run down "Bronco Bill," Will Johnson, and Daniel "Red" Pipkin, who were in sojourn in Arizona after a series of crimes in New Mexico. Scarborough killed Johnson and gave "Bronco Bill" the wound that terminated his short but lurid career in outlawry.[19]

A more recent "exploit" was the recapture of Pearl Hart, the much noted "female stage robber." Pearl, in company with a habitual drunkard whose name was variously given as Mike McGinnis and Ed Sherwood, had escaped from Tucson. It was their ambition to reach Casas Grandes, and their misjudgment to break the journey at Deming. In the morning Officer Scarborough, learning that the two celebrities had hit town, barged into their hotel room. Pearl informed him, amid much profanity, that she had nothing to wear to jail, as all her clothes had been taken to the Chinese laundry. Scarborough insensitively ordered her to don Mike's garments and stood his ground until she complied. As usual, he had got his man.[20]

Early on the morning of Tuesday, April 3, 1900, Scarborough and Birchfield reached the thieves' camp. Nearby was what was left of the Triangle cow, and they were soon heading south on the trail of the men who had killed it. As they approached the Chiricahuas they came upon a sure indication that the men they were after were not smugglers; they had dropped some .30-40 Winchester cartridges.[21]

This ammunition came originally with the Krag-Jorgensen bolt-action rifle adopted by the U.S. Army in 1892. Three years later the Winchester company chambered their model 95 lever action rifle and carbine for the .30-40 cartridge. Now, even five years on, these weapons were carried by only a few lawmen—and outlaws.

Scarborough had one; Birchfield, not being a professional peace officer, stuck by his 1894 model Winchester .30-30, which was more than good enough for ordinary day-to-day contingencies. A contest with desperate characters carrying .30-40 rifles was very much out of the ordinary; in this situation he was under-armed. The black powder cartridge from the .30-30 was twenty grains lighter than the .30-40 (160 grains, as opposed to 180); its muzzle velocity was below 2000 feet per second, compared with about 2300; and its accuracy dropped sharply once the range was stepped up from 150 yards.[22]

Even the heavier .45-70 was not good for precision shooting at any distance much beyond two hundred yards; whereas the .30-40 could be depended on at 250.[23] In diagrammatic terms, the supremacy of the .30-40 was palpable; but if reference must be had to a practical lesson, the defeat of the posse in Turkey Creek Canyon was well within recall.

Scarborough and Birchfield now knew they were in pursuit of big game—and big game that could retaliate with superiority in weaponry as well as in numbers. Birchfield, although a deputy sheriff, would rather not have been in the hunt; on his own admission, he would not have taken the trail of professional outlaws merely on account of a slaughtered beef. Nor would he have sent for Scarborough in such circumstances.

Scarborough, however, was the opposite case. Once on the ground, he was irrepressibly eager to come to grips with the desperate characters whom chance—or the fondness of range criminals for free beef—had thrown into his path. He would have heard of the murders of LeSueur and Gibbons by wire from Silver City to Deming, but probably did not see any connection between that episode and his present assignment. He knew, as everyone did, that Will Carver was likely to be in Cochise County, and may have suspected that confederates of the Las Cruces bank robbers were also there; but other men of questionable character may al\o have been about, including some whose names he had never heard. If there was a new gang in the making, he wanted to know about it, and preferably to unmake it before it got started.

Early in the afternoon they came to the remnants of a fire in Triangle Canyon, seventeen miles southwest of San Simon and well into the Chiricahuas. Here the five had stopped for dinner, leaving behind a pail with some coffee in it. The coffee was still warm enough to be enjoyed, and the two officers paid it the compliment of drinking it. Perhaps they asked themselves or each other whether the beverage had been left out of courtesy—or in haste. In either event, the five may have seen or sensed that they were being trailed.

Scarborough and Birchfield returned to the long haul up the canyon. As the trail wound higher and higher into the mountains, Scarborough became uneasy. This was the worst sort of country in which to be on the wrong end of an ambush. If there was any ambushing to be done, he wanted to be the one who was doing it. He told Birchfield, possibly to Birchfield's relief, that he believed he would turn back.

Everything that is known about Scarborough argues that he would not have turned tail. Any retreat on his part would have been temporary and tactical. In the event, no maneuvering was needed. Soon after Scarborough had spoken of his doubts, he and Birchfield ran onto the men they were trailing. It was now about two o'clock in the afternoon, and they were following the course of a waterless creek called Triangle Springs, eighteen to twenty miles southwest of San Simon.

Birchfield was the only one of those involved in the ensuing fight whose observations are preserved. He described the action at least twice in writing, and several times orally to people who subsequently quoted him. Understandably enough, his two written accounts are not a perfect fit for each other, while the details of his spoken descriptions depend on the ability of the eventual narrator to recall his words and repeat or paraphrase them accurately. He may also have disclosed facts or views to one person that he preferred to withhold from another. While his status as the sole eyewitness on record has to be both the strength and weakness of his testimony, the consistency of his various accounts in their main particulars entitles them to a large measure of trust. Variances over some of the lesser details are subject to ratiocination, but what seems to have happened is this:

About a mile into the canyon, the trail Scarborough and Birchfield were following diverged from the creekbed. It now ran downhill and to the south. The five men had gone into camp on a rockstrewn hill overlooking their recent trail, but on lower ground than the creekbed along which Scarborough and Birchfield were riding, though well out of their range. They seemed not to have noticed the two officers, but must have been expecting them to take the new, southerly trail beneath their position. Why else would they have made camp again so soon after their dinner stop?

Birchfield, who knew the country much better than his companion, proposed they follow the dry course of Triangle Spring to its head, cross a ridge, and descend into Dun Springs Canyon. Now that he had the game in his sights, Scarborough would not hear of retreat. Besides, the five men had not seen them; no sighting, no risk—yet. "No," he replied, "we're going back down and see who these fellows are."

Scarborough and Birchfield started down the trail and reined up sharply at the sight of two saddled but riderless horses about seventy-five yards ahead of them. They dismounted and went ahead on foot until their distance from the five was about two hundred yards. Still they had not been spotted, but they were now about level with the outlaws' position and with much poorer cover.

Scarborough told Birchfield that "there was no use to call on them to surrender." The obverse of this frank, realistic, and characteristic statement of policy is that it would have been even less use to let the outlaws begin the shooting. Since someone would have to shoot first, the implication could not be plainer: Scarborough and Birchfield would make the best of their advantage by letting their rifles announce their presence. Scarborough fired three or four times, and Birchfield once. None of their bullets took effect, and the five men scampered behind the boulders scattered across the hillside. All the advantage now lay with them.

For half an hour nothing much happened. When, just once, a head popped up from behind a rock, Scarborough fired at it; when it was smartly withdrawn, he fired twice more at the spot where he had seen it. Birchfield saw nothing to aim at and wasted no cartridges. As the minutes passed with no sign of activity from the hilltop, doubts settled on the two men; either their adversaries had slunk away, or they were lying doggo, waiting for the officers to lose patience.

Scarborough and Birchfield knew that, whether the risk to movement had passed or not, there was nothing to be said for their present situation. They decided to return to their horses, sheathe their rifles, and ride away in search of a better place to fight from. If they were fired upon before they could find one, they would stand their ground and fight.

The two officers got to their horses, drew their revolvers, and spurred toward a cluster of rocks, but before they could get there the men on the hill poured down a concentrated rifle fire from a range of 350 yards. A .30-40 slug knocked Scarborough out of the saddle at the first fire; a lucky hit on a moving target at that distance, even for the .30-40. As the officer tumbled to the ground, one of the men gave a great whoop. For Scarborough, it was the huntsman's halloo. Birchfield recognized the voice. "[I]t was old Capehart," he told his friend and former boss Henry Brock, of the Diamond A, "I'd a-knowed him anywhere."[24]

Birchfield's horse, though unhit, was so frightened by the whining lead and flying rock fragments that he threw his rider and tore away. Scarborough's horse had not run, so Walter seized his companion's .30-40 Winchester from the scabbard and jumped behind a sycamore. Several ricochets broke the skin of his arms and head and one bullet bored through his left shoulder.

The bullet had broken Scarborough's leg near the thigh. He was insensible and Birchfield thought him dead until he regained consciousness and called out to him. At first, Scarborough himself thought he was done for. He could hardly move, but was game enough to try. Birchfield then crawled over to help him. Although exposed to a sustained fusillade, Birchfield fetched rocks from a pile about thirty yards away and threw up a barrier to shield Scarborough and himself.

Two of the five, Capehart and Will Carver, knew Birchfield and liked him. They may have wanted very much to finish off Scarborough while he was still helpless; but when it became evident that they would have to kill Birchfield, too, the gang sheered off and thereafter held their distance. It is likely that, while Birchfield was building the wall of rocks, they had been shooting around him rather than at him. For his part, he probably did not want to shoot any of the men once he knew who some of them were, and never told his fellow-officers that he had recognized anyone. But he did his best to save Scarborough.

Although immobilized by his wound, Scarborough was characteristically undaunted. At about three o'clock he called out to the assailants: "We have one gun between us; I'm wounded, but if you will show yourselves, I'll fight the whole bunch." His opponents, of course, were not so foolish as to exchange their considerable strategic and numerical advantage for a display of death-or-glory Quixotry. As the day advanced, they continued to snipe at Scarborough from cover, bombarding him with rock splinters but doing him no further damage.

When the light faded, Birchfield mounted Scarborough's horse and spurred away. He rode through snow and sleet to get help from the San Simon ranch headquarters. Still the attacking party did not try to storm Scarborough's poorly protected position; they may indeed have gone before Birchfield left.

Birchfield found the ranch deserted; the staff had pulled out with the roundup wagon during the day. At three o'clock in the morning he had reached San Simon station, telegraphed the news and a request for a doctor, gathered some help, and started back. Scarborough, with his ugly wound in the right thigh, was unable to move when the relief party arrived several hours later. He was driven into San Simon at 2 p.m. and placed on the next train for Deming. Loss of blood and long hours of exposure to the cold had seriously weakened him. He died at home early on Thursday morning, April 5, after an operation to remove fragments from his shattered thighbone, four years to the day after his shooting of John Selman. He left a widow and seven children, six of them still at school.[25]

Scarborough's friends were far fewer than his enemies, but they spoke up feelingly for him, and a correspondent at Deming touched hyperbole in both tribute and invective: "The tragedy that marks his end raises a monument of ignominy against the cowards who ambushed him in a defile in the Chiricahua mountains . . . his end was no less heroic than Custer's. The difference was only in numbers . . . Five to two with the additional odds in favor of the first, in that they could lie in wait for their prey . . . The vulture is more magnanimous."[26]

Henry Brock, who heard the story of the shooting from Birchfield, said that his friend had deliberately led Scarborough into the trap: "He didn't tell me he got Scarborough up there in order to get him killed, because he didn't have to."[27]

But it is obvious that Birchfield's reactions were as spontaneous as Scarborough's. Brock himself related that Birchfield had improvised a shelter of rocks for Scarborough. The deputy would not have done this if he had been in league with the gang. Nor would he have undertaken a hard ride through foul weather and in darkness to bring help to the stricken man. His need for medical attention for his own wound only strengthened this argument. Birchfield knew that his own was a flesh wound, and not dangerous; but, since it did give him pain, he surely would not have wanted to aggravate it by taking on a long night ride in treacherous conditions. With nothing else to worry about, he could have waited for daybreak.

No doubt Walter disliked Scarborough, as Brock maintained, and would not have sent for him had he known whose trail they would have to follow; but this does not mean that he would have involved himself in such underhand (and dangerous) work as to conspire with outlaws to mislead and murder him. Yet it is fair comment on Scarborough's standing that Brock, a well regarded cowman, not only believed what he did of Birchfield, but approved of it.

A theory has been advanced that the slaughtered beef which was the direct cause of the affray was killed solely to lure Scarborough into an ambuscade. Robert DeArment, Scarborough's biographer, dismisses this as "ludicrous:"

> If Birchfield was not a party to the plan, what assurance did the gang have that he would send for Scarborough? If he was a conspirator, why did he go to such lengths in an attempt to save Scarborough's life?[28]

The Triangle cow was killed more than one hundred miles west of Scarborough's home in Deming, New Mexico. The outlaws could have no way of knowing that Birchfield would not associate them with the carcass, and, therefore—given his friendly feelings towards two or more of them—that he would report the felony to anyone. If he did make it into a case for criminal investigation, there could indeed be no certainty in the outlaws' minds that he would send all the way to Deming for help. Birchfield could have turned to any of a number of deputy sheriffs and stock detectives resident in Cochise County.

The notion that these desperadoes, already in hotfoot flight from two murders, would single out a beef for slaughter so that George Scarborough could be summoned to investigate, is preposterous. To go on from there to assert that they should then purposely attract pursuit by leaving a trail for him to trot along behind for forty miles, before riding obligingly into their guns, is asinine.

On the other hand, it does appear that the outlaws realized that they were being tracked by someone, and were preparing an ambush when Scarborough and Birchfield came upon them from an unexpected direction.[29] It is also clear that their failure to come down and see off the wounded Scarborough from close quarters does not show a lack of homicidal intent. As a Tucson press correspondent reported at the time, "Scarborough had been on the trail of the thieves for several weeks and pursued them into the roughest portion of Chiricahua [the Chiricahuas]. The thieves evidently planned to ambush the officers, and it seems that Scarborough fell into the trap easily." This dispatch was complemented by another from Benson: "The outlaws in some way discovered that they were being followed and laid a trap for the officers, who walked into it." It would be rash to dismiss that correspondent as a misinformed fool. The Deming report previously quoted is also uncompromising in labeling the killing an ambush, though the journalist's dogmatic acerbity hints of comment driven more by outrage than knowledge.[30]

The Benson reporter added, more controversially, "Scarborough evidently did not realize that he was on the trail of this murderous gang or he would not have been so easily trapped." The present writer has already stated his belief that Scarborough had a very good idea of just whom he was following, and that it was this knowledge, or suspicion, that whetted his appetite for a scrap and made him all the more determined to close with the malefactors.

Once the thieves recognized Scarborough, and saw he was down, they badly wanted to make sure of him; the intensity of the barrage they directed at him is proof enough. But they could not close in to dispatch him without doing so right under Birchfield's eyes, or without killing Birchfield first, both of which were out of the question.

"One April day in 1900," Lorenzo Walters wrote less than thirty years afterwards, "Max Stein, Tom Capehart, George Frank[s] alias Bill Carver and Frank Laughlin, holdup men and all around crooks, left Tombstone in a hurry . . . Their first stop of any note was over in the San Simon Country near the New Mexico-Arizona Line." He then gives an elaborate account of their decision to kill a beef and a perfunctory one of their fight with Scarborough and Birchfield.[31]

If Walters is correct, the men would have had to leave Tombstone no later than the first day of April, and could not have been up in Apache County when Frank LeSueur and Gus Gibbons were murdered near St. Johns on March 27. But, like many other Western authors who were close in time to the persons and events they wrote about, Walters took an easy-going view of such historical elements as names, dates, and facts. The four individuals whose identities are only partly circumscribed by the names he quotes could not have left Tombstone at the beginning of April, because they were among the five murderers of LeSueur and Gibbons.

The following is a listing compiled from five different sources of all the real and assumed names with which seven purportedly separate collective identities were invested by contemporary authority:

(1) John Hunter; Skeet (Squit) Jones; Dick Smith.
(2) William Morris; Coley.
(3) Tod Carver; Kid Carver.
(4) Tom Capehart; Wilson; Smith.
(5) Mack Steen; Bob Johnson.
(6) Jess Black; Franks.
(7) Unidentified.[32]

Six identities and a non-identity for five assassins, but the first three can be rolled into one, except that Hunter may be one alias too many for Thomas Hilliard, the individual behind them.

Once Tom Capehart and his aliases had been reconciled, it was obvious that he was well known throughout the southern section of the Arizona-New Mexico borderlands. Since he was also the possessor of some pronounced mannerisms, his description was more detailed than those initially available for any of the others. He was about 5'10" tall, weighed 170 pounds or a little over, was stoop shouldered "but quite well appearing," blue eyed, and amiable but not loquacious. He habitually smiled and ducked his head from side to side when he did talk.[33]

"Steen" and "Bob Johnson" were not Bob Johnson of the Erie outfit, but someone who may have known him or been employed by him. His height was given as six feet, and his weight as 180 pounds. His complexion was light, his eyes light blue, and when last seen was wearing a "very heavy sandy mustache." This description could easily have fitted either Ben or George Kilpatrick, but most probably belongs to the former. Ben was forever stealing the name of someone acquainted with him. Among those honored in this way at one time or another were Texas neighbors whose names he purloined: Cunningham, Rose, and (the writer believes) Beeson.[34]

As far as is known, Tod Carver was not kin to Will Carver. The name was false, anyway; he began life as Thomas C. Hilliard in San Saba County, Texas, not far from the home of the Ketchum brothers. At this time he was twenty-six years old. The circular described him as 5 feet 10 or 11 inches tall, about 160 pounds in weight, with black eyes, dark hair, and a slight speech impediment, and missing the forefinger of his right hand.[35]

A description compiled later for the Pinkerton Criminal History File is fuller, but inaccurate in several important respects: "age 25 to 30, height 5 feet 8 inches, weight 145, complexion dark, almost swarthy, hair dark, eyes brown, mustache dark brown and thin, beard if any dark or black . . . square shoulders and small feet, active movements, talks very fast . . . 1st finger off right hand, nr. 2nd joint." Eventually closer observation put his height at five foot ten, and his weight at 165 pounds; the curtailed forefinger confirmed his identity.[36]

The description of Jess Black, or Franks, cites a complexion as dark as the man's choice of alias, with eyes to match. His height was stated to be 5'8 or 9" and his weight about 175 pounds. Franks was the reddish-blond Will Carver, who often used black dye. But his actual height was more like 5'6" or 7" and his weight nearer 150 to 160 pounds.[37] Do the aliases denote two men, rather than one composite figure?

An enigma within the mystery arises from Siringo's account of his meeting in Alma with "Jesse Black, one of Jim Lowe's warmest friends, who had figured in the raid on Frank Murray." Since that meeting took place in the spring of 1901, a year after the murders and about the same time as Carver was killed in Texas, Siringo's Black could not have been the Black who was also identified as Franks. There are unlikely to have been two Jesse Blacks in that neighborhood within such a short space of time. Either the name Black got onto the suspects' list by mistake, or a whim of Siringo's led him to switch the alias to another Cassidy ally.[38]

All Siringo knew then was that this "Black" was a "hard case." Later, he says, Bert Charter ("an intimate of Cassidy") named him as Byron Sessions, from Utah. But Charter misled, or Siringo misheard; Sessions did not go to New Mexico. Who, then, was "Jesse Black" of Alma? Probably John Allred, some of whose kin had known the Sessions family in Utah.[39]

The final, unidentified suspect was said to have been short, dark, and thickset. Harvey Logan had accompanied Ben Kilpatrick from Wyoming. If he was still in that section of country—and no evidence exists to the contrary—he is likely to have stayed close to Cassidy, Kilpatrick, and the rest. That would make him the fifth member of the gang. Logan was dark, just over 5'6" and about 140 pounds in weight. He could have been either "Hunter" or the "Black" who had been merged with "Franks."[40]

Sheriff James K. Blair, of Grant County, New Mexico, named the killers as Capehart, Tod Carver, Black, "Franks," and an unknown "tall, well-proportioned man" who was "a hard fighter"—the member of the gang identified elsewhere as "Steen" and "Bob Johnson." Blair's "Black" and "Franks" correspond with Logan and Will Carver.[41]

The discrepancies in the actual and advertised heights and weights for Will Carver and Tod Carver illustrate the frequency with which such particulars are overstated by the untrained observer. Eye coloring, too, is notoriously difficult to recall, unless it happens to be a piercing blue or gray.

As for variances in complexion and hair color, Will Carver was not the only member of the gang to use dyes. Ben Kilpatrick used them, and some of the others probably did the same. So did many other criminals of the period. Even more widespread was the practice of regularly growing, shaving off, and regrowing facial hair, or changing its cut. The only trustworthy descriptions of wanted men were those compiled when they were in custody or in the morgue, and therefore no longer wanted.

The resolute and unyielding Sheriff Ed Beeler had ridden south through Graham County at the head of a fresh posse. They had arrived at San Simon on the morning of April 4, shortly before Scarborough, suffering intensely, was brought in by wagon. Beeler, together with Sheriff Jim Blair's Grant County posse and a party led by John Slaughter, followed the killers southward into Mexico, where all trace of the gang was lost. There Beeler heard that one of the Gibbons-LeSueur killers was working as a wood hauler near Globe, where he was known as Bill "Coley" Morris. Beeler arrested him at Cherry Creek on May 2. Witnesses identified him as one of the five who had ridden through St. Johns. He admitted knowing the other suspects but claimed an alibi, which Beeler believed. Accordingly, he was released. This was a mistake, for Morris was not a man but another alias for Hilliard, best known as Tod Carver. It is likely that he left the gang before they went to Cochese County. If so, he can be eliminated from the suspects' list for the Scarborough murder.[42]

Cassidy's residence in the Apache County jail was soon over.[43] In French's rendering of the story, Cassidy rather distrusted and despised Weaver, and was seeking some way of ridding himself of his unwanted company even before they were detained by the law. Their arrest gave him his opportunity; he was able to persuade the authorities in St. Johns that he, Jim Lowe, was a bona-fide traveler. This fellow Weaver, Cassidy went on, had tagged on to him just down the road. Cassidy was allowed to take the horses and go; he was soon back in Alma. Weaver remained in custody at St. Johns, "on the ground of his suspicious appearance and his not being able to give a more definite account of himself."[44]

French's version may have been accurate as far as it went, but it went nothing like the whole way. Weaver was released from the St. Johns jail later in April, but was then required to answer two charges of larceny of horses in Socorro County, New Mexico.[45]

On the 27th of the month he and Cassidy were no-billed on the first charge. Next day, a Saturday, they attended court in Socorro and offered a plea of Not Guilty to an indictment derived from the second charge. Their trial before District Judge Charles A. Leland was set for Friday, May 4, but when the day came only Weaver was in the dock. The likely explanation for the apparent cessation of proceedings against defendant "James Lowe" is that he took unspoken leave of Socorro and Grant Counties during the two dates. Coincidentally, or otherwise, William French was in town that week to supervise the loading of a trainload of cattle destined for the Springer ranch.[46]

Weaver's case was continued to the next term and he was granted bail in the sum of $1,000. There must have been an irregularity in his bond, for on June 14 he was in jail when the enumerator arrived to interview the inmates for the Twelfth Decennial Census. Red described himself as a native of Texas, born in 1874. Later his bond was secured and he was at liberty until the opening of the fall term of district court.[47]

Some time later French learned that a couple of mysterious strangers, equipped with unusually large kyacks (panniers), had visited the camp of a survey party on the old Maxwell Grant. These kyacks were the match of a pair which French had given to Cassidy just before Butch and Red left in mid-March. The rancher concluded that Cassidy and another man, probably Capehart, had reclaimed the buried Folsom loot. He could not have been wholly right, for Cassidy could not have been one of the pair. It is likely that the task of removing the treasure was delegated to Red Weaver.[48]

At about this time Reed Dean, his brother Dolph, and their friend Johnny Allred camped at the head of the Saliz, near Bull Springs, just on the Mexican side of the international border, and set about "gatherin' steers." Two of them charged towards "a big old steer standin' down under a juniper tree down yonder" on the high ridge, and almost overran a man on "a little dun horse." Instead of going up the nearby trail, the man on the dun horse made for the canyon. The crew saw that he had roped himself to the horse, and enjoyed a good laugh at the way he bobbed up and down and to and fro as he was borne down the mountainside and into the canyon. A few years later, they saw the serious side of the incident when they were given cause to believe that the man may have been burying the loot from the train robbery that had preceded Sam Ketchum's death.[49]

Red had to return to Socorro for the resumption of court proceedings against him, but again the case was continued and his bail was renewed. In late 1900 or early 1901, he again showed himself in Alma, well supplied with money and not caring who knew it.[50]

In the spring of 1900 more bad news from the north had reached Cassidy and the other outlaws in the southwest. On Tuesday April 17, George Currie was shot dead by officers in Utah, not far north of Robbers' Roost. His confederates, one of whom may have been Harry Longabaugh, escaped. It is possible that they were in Utah for a rendezvous with the seven who had been intercepted near St. Johns.[51]

Cassidy and the other six had been pursued in Arizona because they looked like thieves and some local people suspected them of having designs on a train on the Santa Fe-Pacific Railroad. Probably the gang had no interest at all in the Santa-Fe Pacific, but were intending to team up with Currie, Longabaugh, and others for robberies further north. If so, the plan was initially frustrated by the trouble that put two of them briefly behind bars in St. Johns, and forced the other five to turn back south. Their run-in with Scarborough a few days later may have caused several weeks' further postponement.

These reverses, and the passing of George Currie, necessitated delay, but not cancellation. Most of the band reached Utah during May. Cassidy's court appearance in Socorro would have compelled him to start north later than the others, but, early in the summer of 1900, he was reunited with them and with some who were already in the north, most notably Harry Longabaugh and William Cruzan.

⸰ 19 ⸰

BUTCH CASSIDY, THE SUNDANCE KID . . . AND WILL CARVER

Harry Longabaugh, alias Harry Alonzo, alias Frank Roberts, alias Frank Jones, with a future paved with fresh aliases a-plenty, but already nicknamed "the Sundance Kid," had been a fugitive for ten years. His story, like that of most of his companions, could be told in three words: cowboy, pilferer, outlaw. He came West from Pennsylvania as a fifteen year old in 1882, and worked on various ranches, beginning with his uncle's.[1] In 1887 he pleaded guilty to horse theft and was sentenced to eighteen months at hard labor in the new Crook County Jail at Sundance, in the northeast corner of Wyoming.[2] Early in the summer of 1892, he may have been one of a hard riding trio who plundered five stage coaches in the Mussel Shell country of central Montana within a period of fifteen days.[3] On November 29 of that year he took part in the train robbery at Malta, Montana, on the recently constructed Great Northern line, acquiring little loot and only a splash of short-lived notoriety.[4]

After staying out of trouble for almost five years he was arrested with Harvey Logan and Walter Punteney for the robbery of the bank at Belle Fourche, South Dakota, on Monday, June 28, 1897. Longabaugh was caught in bad company, had a bad record, and was planning to help the other two rob a bank elsewhere when they were all pulled in; but he may well not have been among the six Belle Fourche robbers, though Logan and Punteney were. Longabaugh and Logan, whose pose as the Jones brothers had not yet been unmasked, did not wait to be tried; on October 31, they broke jail at Deadwood and were not recaptured.[5]

On the other hand, there is a high degree of probability that Longabaugh took part in the train robberies at Humboldt, Nevada, on July 14, 1898, and Wilcox, Wyoming, on June 2, 1899, and in a saloon robbery at Elko, Nevada, on April 3, 1899, though he was not publicly accused of any of the three.[6]

Up to December, 1894, Harvey Logan, alias Tom Jones, alias Dickinson, alias Roberts, but worst known as "Kid Curry," gave no promise of the infamy that was to be his. But two days after Christmas that year he rounded off the celebrations in Landusky, Montana, by killing Powell "Pike" Landusky, founder of the town. For the next two years

271

he and his brother, Loney, made their living as rustlers and petty holdup men, under the guidance of "Flat nose" George Currie.[7] He and Loney rode with Currie, Punteney, Harve Ray, and Tom O'Day at Belle Fourche. He and Currie were most likely alongside Longabaugh at Humboldt and Elko. These three, with Loney, the Logans' cousin Bob Lee, alias "Bob Curry," and Ben Kilpatrick, were the Wilcox robbers. Currie and the Logans were the three who killed Sheriff Hazen and afterwards outran the posses that trailed them almost to the Montana and Idaho boundary lines.[8]

In the latter part of the year, as we have seen, Longabaugh, Ben Kilpatrick, and Harvey Logan made their way to Alma, New Mexico. Longabaugh soon left for Brown's Hole or Hole-in-the-Wall. Logan and Kilpatrick, along with Cassidy, Carver, Capehart, Hilliard, and Weaver, were following him north some weeks later when the arrest of Cassidy and Weaver, and the killing of Gibbons and LeSueur, compelled the diversion that led to their encounter with Scarborough and Birchfield.

A month after the killing of Scarborough, Logan, Kilpatrick, and others again moved north through Arizona or New Mexico. Capehart, Hilliard, and George Kilpatrick may have been in the party, which probably divided en route, three going some hours ahead of the others. Since they reached the Robbers' Roost area of Utah without causing any news, it is impossible to say exactly when they began their long ride or which route they took.

Cassidy, having been detained in Socorro, probably started out later, accompanied by Will Carver. Whether they trailed the main group to begin with, or headed directly for Brown's Hole, these two, and they alone, reached Powder Springs, in the extreme northwest of Colorado, sometime in June 1900.[9]

The party now led by Kid Curry may have intended to rendezvous with Cassidy and Carver, or they may have had plans of their own all along. If their program called for the first course, it was abandoned; if the second, another postponement was forced upon them. Late in May this band of roving murderers killed twice more.

Yet again, the machinations of blind chance fashioned a tripwire for tragedy. Sheriff Jesse Tyler, of Grand County, Utah, had been looking for Tom Dilley, a troublesome local hardcase and rustler, when he and other officers ran onto George Currie near Green River and killed him. Tyler was still searching for Dilley more than a month later. At noon on Saturday, May 26, Tyler and two deputies, Samuel Jenkins and Herbert Day, came upon three or more men camped with a score of horses in a willow grove on Hill Creek, forty miles north of Thompson Springs (now Thompson), Utah. Tyler believed from their crouching posture that the men were Indians, perhaps a party of Utes the posse had seen the previous day. He and Jenkins decided to talk to them anyway. They dismounted, and walked over to the camp, having left their rifles with the horses—proof that they expected no trouble. Day stood and watched from beside a rock fifty yards from the camp. Tyler's greeting drew a reply that Day did not catch, but it was obviously inimical, for the officers turned and began to run for their horses. They had no hope. The deadly .30-40 rifles spoke and the two men were shot in the back—Tyler twice, Jenkins five times. Day thought he heard Jenkins yell "Dilley," but Dilley was not there—he was on a thieving expedition elsewhere; the doomed deputy may actually have shouted "Da-a-a-y!"[10]

Day ran; the killers rifled the pockets of their victims, and rode away northeast. At Turner's cabin, twelve miles from the scene of the double murder, the men, or some of them, stopped to take the owner's best horses. "We are going up Hay Canyon and will cross White River," one of them informed Turner, "Just as soon as we get some money we'll pay you for the horses, providing we don't get killed. One thing is certain, we will never be taken alive."[11]

They seemed to be heading for Brown's Hole; but, since they did not link up with Cassidy and Carver, who arrived there soon afterwards, their true destination may have been Hole-in-the-Wall. Charles Kelly, without citing any authority, states that two of the original five then turned back south, while the other three made for Hole-in-the-Wall.[12] Kelly receives partial support from a contemporary report that one man, Hilliard, was tracked back to Arizona after the killings. It may be apposite that, after this, Tom Capehart was never seen by anyone he had known in New Mexico and Arizona, but Hilliard was. Whether Kelly is right or wrong, Kid Curry and Ben Kilpatrick did go into Wyoming and remained for four months.

The indomitable Ed Beeler showed up in Utah about a week after the killings. He scoffed at the identifications being bandied about by some of the press: the murderers of the two Utah officers were not the likes of Cassidy, Jim Rose, or Will Roberts, he insisted, but those who had killed three times in Arizona. The descriptions tallied; so, even more damningly, did the brands on their horses. He had followed the men for thirteen hundred miles through Arizona, New Mexico, old Mexico, Wyoming, and Utah, and he would "follow them to hell."[13]

Neither Beeler nor the Utah officers seem to have understood that a name coupled with the murders in Arizona, and a quite different name connected with those in Utah, could have been two separate aliases for a single man; thus the suspect named in Utah as Jim (or Joe) Rose could well have been the same as Apache County's "Bob Johnson." Rose was one of the many surnames in the alias wardrobe of that inveterate changer of names, Ben Kilpatrick. A man named Joe Rose, who was not Ben Kilpatrick, belonged to the so-called Bassett gang of outlaws in Brown's Hole, but he had no connection with the killings in Arizona and southern Utah.[14]

The confusion ran even deeper than that; Harvey Logan was identified in Utah as two of the suspects—once in his own name, and once as Will Roberts. Nor did Beeler realize that the "Jim Lowe" who had so lately and so briefly been his guest in the Apache County lockup was the notorious Butch Cassidy, now written of in Utah as one of the murderers of Tyler and Jenkins.

Cassidy can be exonerated of complicity. Eight days earlier the gang had passed through Moab, sixty miles south of the place where Tyler and Jenkins were killed. Obviously, at that time, the men were in no hurry. Traveling at even triple that rate, Cassidy could not have left Socorro in time to be anywhere near Moab by May 18. Moreover, if he had been there at an hour when the town was awake, he might well have been recognized. In fact, fear of recognition in such places as Moab would have deterred him from visiting them by day.

Yet, if a story told by Siringo is broadly true, Cassidy did follow the same route as that taken by the murderers. After getting out of the trouble that had caused his detention in Arizona, Cassidy trailed Logan's party north. He made no attempt to overtake them, because he mistook their sign for that of a posse on their trail. A note in one of the gang's "blind post offices" rid him of misunderstanding, but still he did not catch them up; perhaps he hung back on purpose, not wanting to run the risk of traveling with the killers across open ground.

Siringo names his informant as Bert Charter, so the story is likely to be true. He does not mention the Tyler-Jenkins shootings, but does allude to the LeSueur-Gibbons murders. He adds that Beeler led his posse all the way to Baggs, where Butch was in hiding at the time.[15] All this is consistent with the main facts drawn from other sources. It also explains, and is supported by, Cassidy's arrival at and departure from Powder Springs with Carver but without Logan or Kilpatrick. Logan did go to Brown's Hole, but not while Cassidy and Carver were there.

At this time, Logan was about thirty-three years old—the same as Longabaugh, a year younger than Cassidy, a year older than Carver. Even without the apocrypha, and allowing for the tendency of some writers to debit him with murders in which his companions had an equal if not the full share, it is clear that he was one of the most ferocious and violent criminals of his day, and one of the cleverest. If, as appears, he, Cassidy, and Carver had planned a joint criminal venture, it never matured. He schemed out one of his own.[16]

Bill Cruzan, who had served three years in the Colorado State Penitentiary for grand larceny but had yet to graduate from rustling to highway robbery,[17] joined him and Ben Kilpatrick in Hole-in-the-Wall or elsewhere in Wyoming. With them were two other men, unnamed at the time and never convincingly identified since; one or both of them (Tom Capehart being the foremost contender) could have been in the gang that had come from Arizona, or could have been recruited from the fraternity of Hole-in-the-Wall regulars.

At 8:30 p.m. on Wednesday, August, 29, 1900, the second section of Union Pacific train No. 3, westbound, was held up just beyond Tipton station, Wyoming, by these five. "Reliable sources" gave it out that the loot was $55,000; the Pacific Express Company said the robbers obtained only $50.14 and a package of watch parts.[18]

These "reliable sources" turned out to be an employee of Pacific Express—Messenger Ernest Woodcock, no less. The express messenger was not supposed to know the nature and contents of the sealed through safe, but no organization has ever succeeded in preventing its employees from talking to one another if they want to, and doubtless Woodcock "heard something" en route. But what he heard, and reported, need not have been correct; the loss to Pacific Express may have been nothing like $55,000.

Nor was it anything like $50.14. The official who broadcast this figure may have thought the precision imparted by the inclusion of the fourteen cents would carry an appearance of conviction. It carried less conviction than eyewitness reports that one sack of loot was so heavy that two men were needed to shift it, and that three gold $20 pieces were afterwards found in the debris of the car; no great acumen is required to discern a torn bag or broken box as the link between a weighty sackful of booty and three stray gold coins. Pacific's reference to the stealing of watch parts does not merit much notice; even if the gang could have placed them with a jeweler or "fence," they would scarcely have been worth bothering about.[19]

A story that three sacks of coins which they assumed to be gold turned out to be pennies, which Logan poured down the nearest prairie dog hole with the words, "They can't make us take that kind of money," has the circumstantial detail that solicits credence. But it does not deserve any; it comes from a source that names Logan's fellow robbers, besides Ben Kilpatrick, as Longabaugh, Carver, and O.C. Hanks.[20] At the time in question, Longabaugh and Carver, with Cassidy, were in Idaho, preparing to rob a bank in Nevada; Hanks, whom we shall meet shortly, was still an inmate of the Montana State Prison.

On September 2 Logan, Kilpatrick, and Cruzan reached Jim Ferguson's ranch at the foot of Black Mountain, where they had planned the robbery. They hid out on the mountain for three weeks, waiting for the posses to disperse. On the 23rd the three left Ferguson's and rode southwest. Cruzan turned back in eastern Utah and, in the longer haul, would have no cause to regret it. Siringo, who investigated the case for the Pinkertons, give no indication that anyone was involved in the robbery besides those three, presumably because he had no idea who the other two were or where they had gone.[21]

Towards the end of this period, on September 19, Cassidy, Carver, and the Sundance Kid had stirred up some excitement of their own by robbing the bank at Winnemucca, Nevada, of $32,340 in cash.[22]

In 1912 an English language newspaper in Buenos Aires, Argentine, published a first-person article describing the robbery, and, even more interestingly, the bandits' movements before and after it. The basis of the piece was an oral account given by the Sundance Kid to an unnamed person who later committed it to writing and sent it to the paper. It remained buried in a volume of back issues for more than eighty years, until it was found by the researcher Mike Bell and subsequently published, along with his analysis.[23]

The narrative is subject to several reservations: Longabaugh may have forgotten or misrepresented some details; the contributor may have forgotten or muddled others; and someone in the newspaper office may have added journalistic flourishes of his or her own.

There are, moreover, two conspicuous aberrations in the printed story. Longabaugh—or his confidant, or the journalist, or two or all three of them at different points—amalgamates the identities of George Currie and Will Carver into "George Carver." Then, further into the narrative, the account of the bandits' escape from Winnemucca is conflated with a description of the hunt that ended with the death of Currie.

These are easily set aside. The unassailable fact that Currie was cornered and killed after a hard chase in Utah five months before the Winnemucca raid obviates any difficulty over the first inconsistency, and makes sense of the second. The story that Longabaugh told his unknown friend in South America may have been longer and more complicated than the version which was eventually turned into a newspaper feature. His description of George Currie's last days may have been torn away from its context, but it has value as support for the belief that Longabaugh and Currie (but not Cassidy) were together in the spring of 1900, just before Currie's death. Some elements in the escape story may also have been derived from Longabaugh's recollections of the getaway after the Humboldt train robbery two years earlier. Humboldt and Winnemucca are just forty miles apart.

As for Will Carver, there is copious evidence from elsewhere that he was in the Winnemucca robbery. It may be significant that Longabaugh probably did not know him well, and may not even have met him until a couple of months before the Winnemucca robbery. In contrast, Longabaugh and Currie had been closely associated for years.

When the allowances and adjustments to the Buenos Aires story have been made, we are left with one of the most important pieces of historical rediscovery to be unearthed in the broad field of American outlawiana. In essence, it is Harry Longabaugh's own account of how he, Cassidy, and Carver planned and executed the robbery of the Winnemucca bank and effected their escape.

In the summer of 1900, where his tale begins (though he, or his narrator, sets it in 1902), Longabaugh was short of money. He "drifted over" to Powder Springs, hoping to encounter "some of the bunch," and was glad to find Cassidy and his new partner, Carver. This meeting of the three like minds probably occurred in late June. They waited a month for Harvey Logan ("our leader . . . the brainiest member of the bunch,"), then, when he did not appear, made up their minds to pluck the bank at Winnemucca.[24]

The first part of their plan called for two of them to buy extra horses at Twin Falls, Idaho, while Longabaugh inspected the bank. He reached Winnemucca on September 4 and, naming himself "Dave Jones," worked as a roadmender for three days while sizing up the bank and the town. He intended to take the train to Twin Falls, via Ogden, but a man he encountered near the depot seemed to recognize him, so he bought a "cayuse" and saddle, under his old alias of Frank Jones." During his three or four days in this small town he had also found occasion to air his other well-worn alias, "Alonzo." Evidently his range of pseudonyms was unimaginative, and his use of it more compulsive than intelligent.

Longabaugh, indifferently mounted as he was, needed six days to make the two hundred miles to Twin Falls. At Golconda, twenty-five miles east of Winnemucca, he appears to have stopped to collect a letter from one "Mrs. Mike," addressed to him as "C.E. Rowe" and mailed from Riverside, Wyoming, on September 1. He tore it up shortly afterwards, along with two slightly earlier ones from Douglas Preston, Cassidy's attorney. Later they were found and pieced together. All three may have referred to the sale of singed currency from Wilcox—or scorched gold from Tipton.[25]

Cassidy, Longabaugh, and Carver went straight from Twin Falls to Three Creek, where they held up James and Elizabeth Duncan's store for the groceries they would require on the trail.[26] The incident was reported as a robbery; but, in all the attendant circumstances, and bearing in mind Carver's longstanding acquaintance with the Duncan brothers, the "holdup" is likely to have been prearranged with Jim Duncan. Once he and his wife had reported a robbery, they could not easily be accused of having harbored or cooperated with felons. As it is, Longabaugh does not mention the Duncans by name; but he does say that when he and his companions were about to depart, the proprietor offered each of them a new hat. Another old friend, George Moore, supplied four good horses. Such gestures hardly reek of rancor.

The three outlaws made good time to Winnemucca, pausing to cache horses and supplies at various points along the 150 miles of their route. "Cowboy Bill" Carver, most uncharacteristically, was dressed like a hobo; right down to his hobnailed boots. On his way into town he killed a skunk, but did not come out of the engagement unmarked. For some time thereafter the outlaw could have been readily identified by the smell of his clothing.

Aside from Carver's encounter with the skunk, the entire operation was cleanly executed. The trio arrived in Winnemucca in the small hours of Wednesday, the 19th; entered the bank at noon; held up the cashier, three assistants, and a customer; and emerged a few minutes later with their booty, nearly all of it in gold coin. They were hotly pursued for a day or two, but shook the posses before they reached the Idaho line. Reference to contemporary newspaper sources shows that the pursuit, though not without moments of danger for the freebooters, was far less intense and sustained than the Buenos Aires story pretends. But, if it had been kept up into Idaho, it would have taken the same course as that described.[27]

Once arrived in Three Creek, the outlaws had to bury most of the money; the sack weighed more than 125 pounds, and they, their pack horses, and their saddle horses were exhausted. They paid Duncan twice the value of the goods they had taken from his store and left for the south.[28]

Here, near its conclusion, a fog of contradictions descends on Longabaugh's story, but proof exists for three important components: money was buried near Three Creek; Cassidy and Longabaugh recovered their shares before heading for Texas late in October; and Carver went his own way after the swag had been planted.

In the Buenos Aires version, the portion belonging to the hybrid "George Carver" stayed in its hiding place because George was killed before he had a chance to return for it. But as a matter of recorded history it did not stay buried. Its owner, Will Carver, came back from Texas nearly three months later and dug it up.[29] For reasons that will soon be apparent, Longabaugh may never have known about Carver's expedition.

In mid-October a man referred to as both "Alonzo" and "Swede" was said to have arrived in Rawlins, Wyoming, where he tried to exchange "burned" or "blackened" gold coins—and Longabaugh, alias Alonzo, was described (incorrectly) as a "Swedish-American" in a Pinkertons' circular.[30] There is no reason to suppose that any of the gold stolen in Winnemucca was defaced in this way, but the gold extracted from the wreckage of the Pacific Express safe at Tipton may have been. Rawlins is less than sixty miles from the site of the train robbery, and a similar distance from Encampment, the home of Longabaugh's correspondent "Mrs. Mike" and her husband, believed by Donna Ernst to have been Mike Dunbar.[31]

Longabaugh had taken no part in the Tipton stickup. Why, then, should he have been in Rawlins with some of the Tipton loot? Much of the answer may rest on the proximity of Rawlins to Jim Ferguson's Black Mountain ranch. At the height of the hunt for the Tipton robbers, Logan and Kilpatrick could have deposited much of the stolen coin with Ferguson, on the understanding that Longabaugh would collect it later from Ferguson or an intermediary. Harry had already negotiated the discount sale of much of the currency spoilt at Wilcox. Logan and Kilpatrick would have counted on his success in similarly trading off the plunder damaged at Tipton. Ferguson, and others, would have taken a cut. After discounts, bribes, and presents, the proportion of the Wilcox and Tipton booty that filtered through to the robbers would not have been enough to pay for more than a few months of retirement.

Winnemucca was different. Here the loot was in clean currency and coin. Even so, it was inconvenient that so much of it should have been in gold pieces—awkward to shift in bulk and too conspicuous for habitual use in everyday transactions.

The bank robbery, like the Humboldt train robbery two years earlier, was at first attributed to the "Shaw-Spencer gang," of Burns, Oregon.[32] Suspicion then fastened briefly on sundry local men who were thought capable of committing the crime. Only when these inquiries proved barren did official interest move to the individual who had come to Winnemucca as Dave Jones, made himself known in some quarters of the town as Alonzo, and taken temporary leave of it as Frank Jones. At last, but too late, they were on the right lines.[33]

According to Charley Siringo, whom the Pinkertons put onto the trail shortly after the Tipton robbery, Logan and Kilpatrick made their escape through western Colorado and southeastern Utah into New Mexico, claiming to be broke.[34] We see them next towards the end of October in San Antonio, Texas, with Will Carver.

Logan, as "Bob Nevilles," and Carver, as "Will Casey," disported themselves with two of Fannie Porter's young ladies, professionally known at that particular time as "Maude" and "Lillie;" when a surname was required, these daughters of delight slipped comfortably in and out of "Smith," "Walker," "Williams," and "Davis."[35] The two men drank heavily and took the girls on fast buggy drives through the city. Logan apparently had little money, but Carver did not mind letting it be seen that he was well in funds.[36]

Fannie, when asked later by a detective, denied having known Ben, but Lillie remembered him as "Dan;" he was, she said, athletic in appearance and an "expert bicycle rider," though "very quiet" and seemingly short of money. .

After a stay of three weeks, broken by an excursion to Fort Worth (partly for word of Cassidy and Longabaugh?) and another to Houston, the girls and their consorts said their goodbyes on or about November 18 and left town for a longer stay at Fort Worth. Maude, whose original name was Delia Moore but whose formal appellation was Mrs. L.D. Watson, wanted to visit her family in Kennedale, not many miles southeast of the city, but that was incidental to the men. They were in Fort Worth for a reunion.[37]

{ 20 }

"BEFORE HE COULD COCK HIS PISTOL"

When Cassidy and Longabaugh journeyed to Fort Worth, they probably did not travel in the comfort and style to which their recent access of wealth entitled them. If they had any opportunity to buy new clothing to replace the worn and dirty garments they had worn on their flight from Winnemucca, a heightened sense of caution could have warned them against doing so until they had put a couple of states between Nevada and themselves. Thus they might well have traveled by side-door Pullman, as stated in one early account of their careers, rather than as paying passengers.[1]

Whether they posed as tramps or as gentlemen, they would have taken the Colorado & Southern from Denver through Trinidad and Texline to Fort Worth. They would have arrived during the third week of November, no more than a couple of days before Carver, Logan, and Kilpatrick came in from San Antonio. Carver, whose trip from the north preceded theirs by several weeks, would have taken the same route. Most likely he, Logan, and Kilpatrick knew just when and where to meet Cassidy and Longabaugh.

Celebrations were due, and they were lavishly done. Soon after their reunion, the five commemorated the occasion for all time. On November 21, attired in the most fashionable city togs, and either inebriated or about to become so, they assembled at Swartz's photographic studio on Main Street for one of the most famous of all group portraits. Seated are Harry Alonzo Longabaugh, Benjamin Arnold Kilpatrick, and Robert Leroy Parker; standing, William Richard Carver and Harvey Alexander Logan. Only Parker, known in Fort Worth's saloons and brothels as Jim Ryan and to law-enforcement agencies throughout the West as Butch Cassidy, looks the camera directly in the eye. The Swartz View Company was just a few doors from Maddox Flats, the building in which they had taken furnished rooms. It was also close both to the hothouses of the red light district ("Hell's Half Acre") and the local office of that citadel of virtue, the Wells, Fargo Express Company.[2]

Carver and Logan still had the girls they had brought from San Antonio, and Will was going to marry his. But, amid all the gaiety and jollification, they were giving

279

thought to matters even more serious than the holy vows of matrimony between a train robber and his trollop.

Butch had already made up his mind to leave the country, and Sundance had agreed to go with him. They had cashed in on crime; unlike most of their kind, they wanted to turn the proceeds into investment capital to provide the basis for a profitable retirement. First, though, they needed a sanctuary. Cassidy had persuaded Longabaugh that they would find none anywhere in the United States, but would be comparatively safe in South America. The idea was discussed with the others, perhaps put to them as a proposal. They were uninterested. Carver's viewpoint was parochial; he would rather "die on dirt I know than live in some jungle."[3] Doubtless the full extent of his knowledge of the southern continent was something he may have heard about the Amazon and its forests.

Probably on November 23, Carver, Logan and their consorts left Fort Worth for a few days each in Houston and San Antonio. By the 29th they were back in Fort Worth, where, on December 1, Carver, under his current alias of "Will Casey," and "Lillie Davis," under her real name of Callie May Hunt, applied for a licence to marry. The ceremony was performed the same day by John P. Terrell, Justice of the Peace of Precinct Number One (Fort Worth), Tarrant County.[4]

That day or the next brought the dissolution of the Fort Worth Five. All had trains to catch.

Ben, Cassidy, and Longabaugh went to San Antonio, where for two weeks they mingled freely with Fannie Porter's household. Fannie was unable to remember this when interviewed by the *San Antonio Express* in 1902, but Lillie assured a Pinkerton detective that Fannie was well enough acquainted with Longabaugh to know he had had a gold false tooth replaced by a white one.[5]

Mr. and Mrs. Carver, alias Casey, were bound in the opposite direction. They were accompanied northward by Harvey Logan and Maude Smith, Walker, or Williams. At Denver the two couples stayed two nights at the Victor Hotel. Their next stopover was at Shoshone, just north of Twin Falls, Idaho, where much of the groundwork for the Winnemucca robbery had been laid out. Here Carver informed the bride that he was "going up the road" for a few days. Logan flattered Maude with a similar announcement.

The two men were gone for five days. When they came back they had the gold currency Carver had buried in the gulch near Three Creek after the Winnemucca stickup, though they did not risk telling the women about their good fortune.

After that, the return journey: stage from Shoshone to Twin Falls, Northern Pacific train to Ogden or Salt Lake City, and thence to Denver for about a week. While they were in Denver, Callie was shown, or saw, the produce of the Idaho soil extracted by her husband and Kid Curry. There were six or seven sackfuls of gold, Callie noticed, together with "a big bundle of paper money." Somewhere en route they had lost, or had stolen from them, a satchel containing "a big gun," over whose disappearance they gave vent to "considerable complaining and grieving."[6] Finally, it was back to Fort Worth. Maude went home to Kennedale; the others met Ben Kilpatrick in San Antonio, where the whole party booked into the Laclede Hotel on December 22.[7]

Butch and Sundance had just left San Antonio. With them was a young woman known as Ethel, whose name and background have yet to be proved. She and Longabaugh styled themselves "Mr. and Mrs. Harry Place." Cassidy hung onto his Fort Worth and San Antonio persona of James Ryan. Late in December they may have visited New Orleans. After a visit to Longabaugh's kin in Pennsylvania and a brief whirl in New York City, they sailed for Buenos Aires.[8]

On December 23, Carver gave Callie $167, mostly in gold, and packed her off to her parents in Palestine, east Texas; they never met again, though he may not have intended it that way. He, Logan, and Kilpatrick were about to leave San Antonio and make plans for another robbery.[9]

While they were still in town, Carver encountered his former employer Ed Jackson. After they had shaken hands, Carver asked Jackson not to tell anyone about their meeting. He closed their brief conversation with the remark that he would soon see Jackson "in his own country." By that he meant Jackson's own section of Texas; specifically, the town of Sonora, where Jackson and Lee Aldwell, another of Carver's one-time bosses, had set up the First National Bank earlier in the year.[10]

Carver must have known that Sonora, Texas, although not on any railroad, was now connected with the outside world by telephone. If he had had any sense, he would have guessed that about the first thing Jackson would do was put a call through to his partner. He did, and Aldwell told Sheriff Elijah S. Briant. The sheriff took the warning seriously and passed the word to a score or more citizens to be ready to intervene should Carver show himself in Sonora.[11]

Family sources say that Carver visited his mother and the rest of the Causeys at Christmas. A report by a Pinkerton operative dates the men's departure from San Antonio as December 30. As Bandera County, where the Causeys still lived, is within eighty miles of San Antonio, the likelihood is that Carver and his companions reached the Causey place on December 31. Will is said to have given his folks some money. If he did, they were wise enough not to advertise it.[12]

The three outlaws, still attired in their stylish city garb, were traveling in an elegant rubber-tired buggy. From Bandera they went north to Kerrville, birthplace of Ed, Jeff, and Dave Farr. After that they visited Fredericksburg, another twenty-five miles northeast. After that, it was Mason, forty miles to the northwest. Now they were on the road to San Angelo, but still in country where not even Carver was known.[13]

In each town, they stayed long enough to take more than a sidelong look at its bank, made themselves at home in its saloons, and told their story. It was not a bad one; they were in the market for good polo ponies. Polo was not much played in Texas, though Charles Metcalfe of the XQZ ranch and some of his friends had introduced it to Tom Green County five years earlier.[14] But at the end of the century there was a surge in the popularity of the game among the social elite in New York state, and a touring syndicate had bought many ponies from ranchers in Concho, Sutton, Irion, and Tom Green Counties for resale to Eastern polo clubs.[15]

In a saloon in Brady, forty miles north of Mason and seventy-five east of San Angelo, they were spotted by a visitor who thought he recognized Carver. This was H.E. "Boosie" Sharp, a bartender in Sonora whose home had formerly been in Brady.

Either he went for a word with John Wall, sheriff of McCulloch County, or Wall asked his opinion first. Sharp told Wall that he was not quite sure that Carver was among the three, but Wall did not like the look of them anyway and set off to the telegraph office to send out some inquiries. Whether suspicious, or by coincidence, the men left town at almost that moment.[16]

The men stayed in or near San Angelo for two or three weeks, without stirring a ripple of adverse interest. Towards the end of this period, Kilpatrick left for his parents' place in Concho County, partly in the hope of recruiting one or both of his younger brothers, George and Ed, into the incipient Carver gang. On February 3, Logan wrote to Maude, in her formal name of Mrs. L.D. Watson. Carver sent Callie $70 in paper money at about the same time.[17]

Callie was far from Carver's foremost preoccupation; he had plans for a big robbery. First, though, he wanted to wipe the slate with Rufus Thomas, the gambler and gunman who had helped to arrest Elzy Lay—and would have tried to arrest him, too. Thomas's good friend John Loomis wrote that Carver especially resented Rufe's intervention because he, Rufe, was not a regular officer.[18]

But Carver had brooded over the matter for so long, and was so determined to resolve it by killing Thomas, that Loomis's explanation may not go more than half way towards the truth. Carver and Thomas had known each other for a long while. It may be that something had passed between them that led Carver to see Thomas's action not merely as unwarranted, but as a betrayal, even a double cross. The much-traveled Thomas had moved back to San Angelo for the time being, and Carver knew it. He wrote to Thomas, identifying himself and threatening to kill him.[19]

Once arrived in San Angelo, Carver set about stalking Thomas out. He found him deeply engaged at the poker table, and waited for the game to end or for Thomas to leave it. But Thomas was a dedicated poker devotee as well as a gambler by profession. As a poker addict himself, Carver could not bear to break up the game. After two whole days of hanging around, he lost patience and left.[20]

That, in substance, is Carl Livingston's account, acquired in part from Thomas himself. John Loomis tells it a little differently. He adds the detail that Carver had made copious use of black dye to change the coloring of his hair and complexion. Loomis also contributes the information that Rome Shield and two Texas Rangers were sitting in at the table, all of them armed. Carver stepped into the room, took in the scene, and walked out. Thomas saw that he was being watched from the door but was too engrossed in the game to pay any attention to the onlooker.

Loomis, like Livingston, quotes Carver's explanation that he stayed his hand because he did not want to disturb such a big game, but does not accept it; he thought it likelier that Carver was deterred by the presence of Shield and the two Rangers.[21]

Shield, in fact, had just become an ex-sheriff; he had stood down in 1900, steadfastly refusing to say why, and his former chief deputy, Jake Allen, had been elected as his successor.[22] But the change in his status would not have affected his reaction to any attack on Thomas.

Carver's account with Thomas was still open; its closure would have to be deferred. He and Logan had to leave San Angelo and drive to Knickerbocker for a meeting with Ben Kilpatrick. The three men were in Knickerbocker by February 10 and remained until the 25th.[23]

Carver must have been wonderfully sure of being on friendly turf. And with good reason: here he was in the midst of folk who knew him, knew what he had been and what he had become; yet, for all the world heard about his presence on his home patch, he might as well have been in Mongolia, Montenegro, or Montevideo. He would not have deceived many of Knickerbocker's older residents by an application of black dye. Kilpatrick was hardly a stranger from afar, either. True, Logan was an unknown; but his presence with the other two made it improbable that he could have been taken for anything but a desperado.

The much respected pioneer Joe Tweedy, proprietor of the largest of Knickerbocker's three general stores, and one of the chief talkers and doers in that strongly Democratic community despite his secondary status as mainstay of the county's Republican party, would frankly admit to having sold them merchandise. He professed to have taken them for strangers, who were merely touring the neighborhood to buy horses.[24]

It was here that the first public utterance was given to the absurd fiction that the trio in the rubber-tired buggy claimed to be from Iowa. The notion that such obvious Texans as Carver and Kilpatrick would try to pass themselves off in such towns as Kerrville and Mason as from Iowa, does not merit a moment's consideration; even Logan, who may have been born in that state, would not have looked, acted, or sounded it, much less been so rash as to lay claim to it. Knickerbocker, where Carver was personally known to many, was about the last place on earth where they would have encumbered themselves with any such pretense. But they may well have portrayed themselves as representatives of a syndicate in Iowa.

"Woodyard Chipling," the urbane and ubiquitous Knickerbocker correspondent for the *San Angelo Standard*, evidently knew enough to appear to know nothing. If Phil Lee, constable for the Knickerbocker precinct, or W.F. Holt, still its J.P., said or did anything about their presence, it went unnoted and produced no result. No one sent for Sheriff Allen.

One author states that the men stayed with "friends on Dove Creek."[25] Most of this generally peaceful and well-behaved community must have been shielding the outlaws in one sense or another. Whether Carver, in particular, was the beneficiary of fear, sympathy, affection, or recollections of the camaraderie of bygone days, his status in that locality would be just as it was when he was riding with the Ketchums: as long as he and his partners got up to no mischief near home, hardly anyone would interfere with them.

This applied equally when they showed their faces in Sonora, shortly after February 25. Here they bought a dun or sorrel horse from George W. Morris, proprietor of the Maude S saloon, two doors down Main Street from the First National Bank. Morris owned race horses and his saloon was named after one. The men paid him $75 for the sorrel, saying they thought it might make a good polo pony. Carver walked into the bank to exchange several $20 pieces for gold certificates and chat with Cashier Lee Aldwell, his old employer.[26] The officers and citizens who had been put on the alert for a visit from Carver would surely have known that he was now in town. Their passivity is easily explained; since, so far, they had no grounds for suspicion that Carver posed a threat to the town, they were happy to let him come and go in peace. The fact that he had given Ed Jackson advance notice of his visit would have convinced many that he harbored no ill intent.

By March 1, Carver and Logan had moved on to Christoval, their headquarters for most of the next three weeks. For a time they were the guests of Pat Wilson.[27] Among Carver's other friends in Christoval was Bill Chaney, who later became a Pinkerton informant—probably the one who furnished the agency with a lively account of the Winnemucca robbery, as he had heard Carver relate it.[28]

Ben Kilpatrick had gone from Knickerbocker to the family farm in Concho County. His brothers Boone, George, and Ed were there, along with the rest of the family. The Kilpatricks were the focus of resentment and distrust at the best of times; at the moment, a row was simmering between them and their neighbor Oliver C. Thornton, who had been a state's witness in the assault charges brought against George Kilpatrick four years earlier. Thornton and the Kilpatricks were now at loggerheads over the family's refusal to prevent their hogs from straying across the land he farmed in a portion of the pasture owned by his employer. The employer was Ed Dozier, a past sheriff of Concho County, and, as such, no ally of the Kilpatrick tribe.[29]

Christoval was within forty miles of the Kilpatrick place, and Carver and Logan made several excursions to maintain contact with Ben. One tale of post-contemporary origin and dubious credibility has them planning to rob the bank at Eden; their arrival on horseback just ahead of closing time looked suspicious to the staff, and they locked the doors before the men could enter.[30] Rash as they could be, the Kilpatricks would not have been so foolish as to mount an attack on a bank almost on the doorstep of their parents' home.

Another story concerns Ed Dozier. Since it comes from Dozier's friend and neighbor John Loomis, it carries the timbre of truth.

Carver was a stranger to most in Concho County, but not to ex-sheriff Dozier. He knew that the outlaw was in the Eden neighborhood, and was not one to shrug the matter off. He declared that if he, and not his rival Jim Howze, were sheriff, he would run the gang out of the county. Carver heard about Dozier's pronouncement and sent word to him that he would settle matters with him personally. Dozier, as Loomis justly comments, "Had the reputation of a fighting man;" even so, the message made him "somewhat nervous, for Carver was a dangerous and desperate foe."[31] But the threat never materialized; an unforeseen but avoidable crisis was to drive Will out of Concho County for good before he could force the issue with Dozier.

Carver may already have chosen the First National Bank of Sonora as the scene of his next criminal exploit. Though their buggy tour of the district had given Logan, Kilpatrick, and himself an opportunity to select any one of half a dozen other banks, it is likely that the one at Sonora was always Carver's first choice of target. He may not have experienced much difficulty in talking Logan and Kilpatrick into agreement; his contribution to the glittering success at Winnemucca entitled him to extended professional credit. It had also gone to his head. He now made the mistake of talking about the gang's intentions to a cattleman who was supposedly a mutual friend of himself and Rufe Thomas.

This conversation occurred just before Carver made a second attempt to settle with Thomas. Carver could not find his man and, as before, had to leave San Angelo without accomplishing his mission. Thomas, it turned out, was sick in his hotel room at the time of Carver's visit. But he was up and about soon afterwards, when the supposedly mutual friend let him know about his second narrow escape from a run-in with "Cowboy Bill."[32]

John Loomis says that Thomas's cattleman informant, whose name he does not reveal, was not so much friendly with Carver as afraid of him. The man had once employed Carver and, claims Loomis, was "undoubtedly . . . paying [him] for protection." He told Thomas that Carver was set on robbing the Sonora bank and suggested that Rufe go there to warn the officers. Since the bearer of the warning could easily have conveyed it to Sonora himself, Thomas suspected a double cross and hesitated. As Thomas walked up the street pondering over how or whether he should act, he encountered Sheriff Briant, who chanced to be in San Angelo that day. Thomas resolved his dilemma on the spot. He told Briant what he had heard and the sheriff, with a specific warning to add to the general one that had not been acted upon a month earlier, again put his deputies and the constable on their guard and requested the vigilance of other citizens whose help he could rely on.[33]

Carver seems to have been well on the way to becoming fatally enveloped in a sense of his own invincibility. He had challenged and outfaced Rufe Thomas and given Ed Dozier something to worry about; sooner, rather than later, he would chance his arm once too often. Perhaps he was hunting fate.

When, towards the end of March, Ben Kilpatrick and the two strangers were seen near the Kilpatrick farm with the rubber-tired buggy and seven extra horses, they could not fail to excite suspicion. John F. Dodson, a neighbor, came upon the outfit by a spring in the pasture of the Molloy Cattle Company; only Ben Kilpatrick and one of the strangers were in camp with the horses, seven of which were tied and in corrals. Dodson later insisted that he had not been snooping; he had stumbled upon the camp by accident, while on a turkey hunt. Maybe so; but Dodson would not have forgotten that Ed Kilpatrick had been charged with stealing a Molloy horse three years earlier.

The stranger in camp was named as "Charles Walker;" the absent stranger was circulating as "Bob McDonald." Walker was the alias chosen by Carver, and McDonald was Logan's alter ego of the moment; but, at the time, this was either imperfectly understood by some of the few local people who saw them, or purposely misrepresented by several of the Kilpatricks. George Kilpatrick, however, later identified Walker as Carver with a firmness and in circumstances that make it most unlikely that he was lying or mistaken. Both Carver and Logan were at the Kilpatrick house on the morning of Wednesday, March 27, when Thornton renewed his complaint about the troublesome encroachments of the Kilpatrick pigs.

Thornton left his house shortly before noon to walk the mile to the Kilpatrick place. When, after an unexpectedly long interval, he failed to reappear, his wife set out with their dog to look for him. Her knock at the Kilpatricks' door drew no response; the place seemed deserted. She turned and was beginning to retrace her footsteps when the dog leaped away. She followed and soon found her husband.

Oliver Thornton was "lying over a log at the spring, with two bullet holes in his body, one through the forehead which came out at the back of the head, and another clear through the body going in at one side and out at the other." There was no blood near the spring, which, the reporter commented, "was singular if the man had been killed there instead of somewhere else and carried there."[34]

Although Eden was only six or seven miles from the farm, Ed Kilpatrick managed not to get there until six o'clock. By then Carver, Logan, and Ed's brothers Ben and George were long gone. Nothing was known of the whereabouts of the other Kilpatricks, except that they were not in when Mrs. Thornton called at the house.

Ed's version of events was that Ben, George, and "Walker" were playing croquet in the yard when Thornton "threw down on the crowd" with a Winchester and ordered them to keep the hogs out of the Dozier pasture. Ed replied that the hogs belonged to Boone, and that the croquet players wanted no trouble. Thornton's alleged rejoinder was that he "came there for trouble," whereupon Walker shot him, and then ran after him to shoot him a second time as he fled for his life. The dying man tumbled over a log by the spring, and Walker then stood over him and shot him once more.

But Ed was also reported to have said that Thornton "was shot for being a spy." If he did say that, the implications are that Thornton was making the long-running pig dispute a pretext for taking a good close look at the Kilpatricks' visitors, that he may well have been unarmed, and that he did not expect any real bother. This is consistent with the further statement that Thornton was "a quiet, peaceable inoffensive man, who was perfectly harmless." While such consistency in itself is proof of nothing, it is compatible with the balance of probabilities.[35]

Ed did not mention McDonald at all, but, by putting a heavy brown mustache on the supposed Walker and endowing him with a dark complexion and baldness, he as good as idenitified Logan as the killer. He may not even have realized that he was mixing up one alias with another; since he knew Carver by his real name, neither he nor his brothers would have dropped into the habit of thinking or speaking of him on any other terms. So far as Logan is concerned, Ed might not have known his right name, but he would have known that McDonald was a false one and would not have been assiduous in his use of it. Carver and Logan had adopted the names Walker and McDonald to screen their identities from potential enemies, not from their confederates.

George Kilpatrick would confirm that Carver was Walker, and that it was McDonald who killed Thornton.[36] As evidence of Carver's innocence of the murder of Thornton, though not of Logan's guilt, this looked ironclad. Both Will and George were suffering from serious gunshot wounds at the time, and Kilpatrick could not have been sure that he would survive or that Carver would not. It does not exclude the possibility that George himself or one of his brothers was the actual killer.

Seven months later, Boone Kilpatrick bluntly named Carver as the killer. He stated, further, that the killing was justifiable, because Thornton had a shotgun and was cocking it when Carver fired.[37] Neither assertion is to be trusted. By that time Carver was dead, but Logan was very much alive, and Boone, as will be seen, had several reasons for wanting the dead blamed for a misdeed of the living. His other assertion—that Thornton was the aggressor—runs against the grain of good sense.

John Loomis believed that "one of the younger members of the gang committed the crime to impress Carver with his toughness." This could only have been a reference to George or Ed Kilpatrick, who, like Ben, "were natural born criminals." After the killing of Carver, wrote Loomis, "it was easy to lay the blame for the killing of Thornton on him and thus protect the real criminal from a sentence that could have been hanging."[38]

His is a tenable explanation. Now that Ben was at his home again, and had brought with him two of the most notorious bandits in the West, the uninvited appearance of Thornton, even if unarmed, could no longer have been seen as an annoyance. He had become a menace.

Loomis thought that Carver was not capable of murdering a defenseless man in cold blood, but that the Kilpatricks were. He may have been right, but his comments on the crime suffer from a notable omission. He did not mention Logan at all, and may have known nothing about the man. If he had been familiar with Logan's career, and known that he was on the scene when Thornton was killed, he may well have looked in his direction before assigning the murder to the Kilpatricks.

After the murder, Carver arranged to meet Logan and the Kilpatricks with provisions four or five days later on Sol Mayer's T Half-Circle range, southwest of Eldorado. Logan and Ben quickly harnessed their team to the buggy and threw their saddles and range clothing inside. Then, with George, they drove away southward through the Molloy pasture.[39]

Carver struck off with the saddle horses. A day or so later he concealed them in the Bird and Mertz pasture on Rocky Creek, near Sherwood, sixty miles west of Eden—and eighty miles north of Sonora.[40] The gang was going through with its plan to rob the Sonora bank; these horses would form one of the escape relays.

The three in the buggy drove at speed, stopping south of Eden to cut the telephone wire to Eldorado, where the two Kilpatricks bought supplies the next morning. A little later the three paid "good prices" to Tom Palmer, rancher and former long-serving deputy sheriff, for the same number of horses.[41] They had an eighteen hour start, because the party from Eden that went to the Kilpatrick place on Wednesday evening, and took the trail from there, was soon overtaken by darkness. At six in the morning the posse broke camp and followed the trail towards Eldorado. During the day the wires were repaired and news of the murder was sent ahead to Sonora and elsewhere, with brief descriptions of the Kilpatricks and Logan.

The fugitives set up camp by a water hole on the T Half-Circle range, between Ozona and Sonora. Whenever they were approached by any of Mayer's cowboys, they pulled away, which the boys—who had not yet heard of the murder—may have interpreted as a sign of unsociability rather than criminality. On or about March 30, the gang stole oats and a quarter of beef from Mayer's ranch headquarters, sixteen miles west of Sonora; the disruption of their plans in Arizona and

Utah the previous year had not taught them the folly of petty pilfering from big cattle outfits.[42]

Upon leaving the T Half-Circle headquarters they drove into a thicket of live oak, abandoning the vehicle in a small clearing. Here those who were still in city clothes hastily donned range costume. They saddled three of the horses, threw a pack on the fourth, and hurried away.[43] Carver joined them in the T Half-Circle pasture on April 1. They doubled back north to pass the night at a ranch in Schleicher County, where they made their final plans for a descent on the Sonora bank. After the robbery, they would carry the loot to the Chaney place, divide it, and scatter.[44] They did not clip the wires between Eldorado and Sonora, nor those connecting Sonora with Ozona.[45] This may have been a calculated risk; their reasoning could have been that sabotage to the Eldorado-Sonora line would have betrayed their destination, if not their objective.

Events would show that failure to sever the telephone wires on April 2 was a foolish oversight or a serious error of judgment for, late that afternoon, a call from Al Haley, the T Half-Circle foreman, advised Briant of the theft. Haley gave the location of the suspects' camp, and said that their tracks were heading towards Sonora when last seen by the T Half-Circle hands who had been following them. The sheriff decided to give them a call in the morning if they did not appear in town before then. Although he did not know it, one of the men—either Logan or Ben—had been in town that very morning to view the bank from the inside while converting $100 into gold certificates.[46]

From the start, the expedition against the Sonora bank was an ill-conceived and perilous venture; the gang might more logically, and in greater safety, have crossed Schleicher and Sutton Counties to hold up the G.H. & S.A. in Val Verde County, especially after the murder of Thornton had upset their preparations and stirred up the whole section. But, bedazzled by the shower of gold that was the reward for five minutes' labor in the Winnemucca bank, they were bent on pressing ahead with their scheme. Sonora and Eldorado are only twenty-one miles apart, yet the plan required an interval of almost a week between their arrival in Eldorado and the consummation of the robbery in Sonora. Carver was too well known in Schleicher and Sutton Counties for those six or seven days to be anything but risky, even without the furore aroused by an unscheduled murder. After the Thornton killing, the outlaws were flirting with a death trap.

The Sutton County Courthouse stood, and stands today, at the head of Main Street and at right angles to it, dominating the Square that takes its name and fronted by Water Street. Parallel with Main Street were Plum Street (also known as Prospect Street), to the east, and Oak Street, to the west. An alleyway ran north-south between the backs of the buildings in Main and Oak Streets.[47]

From a viewpoint on the courthouse steps, the eye would sweep southwestwards across Courthouse Square and Water Street and range down Main Street. On the observer's left hand—the eastern side—the nearest building of consequence was the Hagerlund Brothers' store. Opposite Hagerlunds' was the Decker Hotel, with Becket's stable a short distance downstreet on the same side.

In those days in southwest Texas, the sheriff was nearly always a cattleman. Sutton County had cattleman-turned-druggist, Lije Briant, whose business premises were on the western side of Main Street between Becket's stable and the Barton saloon. Just below the saloon were the extensive Vander Stucken store buildings. A little further down, beyond the Main Street-Concho Avenue intersection, was "The Devil's Retreat," where Mike and Steve Murphy, brothers of editor-owner John "Pat" Murphy of the *San Angelo Standard*, published the *Devil's River News* every Saturday.

Crocket Street crossed Main Street a few yards downstreet from the newspaper office. This intersection marked the southern limit of the commercial district, other than the Victor Castillo store at the corner of Plum Street and Tom Green Avenue on the southern edge of town, and several drinking joints and dens of prostitution in "Mexico," the nearby Spanish-speaking quarter. A few steps south of the Castillo store, at the bottom end of Plum Street, and "Lillie's Place" opposite, was the west fork of Devil's Draw, almost parallel with Tom Green Avenue until it curved away to the north.

Facing the *News* building from the eastern side of Main Street was the McDonald Hotel. Directly upstreet from the hotel were a store, a restaurant, and the Favorite Saloon. A few doors further up from the Favorite were two more saloons, with only one other building to separate them. These were the Ranch saloon and George Morris's Maude (or Maud) S. The bank was a few yards north of the Maude S, immediately across the street from Becket's stable.

Ed Jackson and Lee Aldwell, in concert with other "prominent stockmen and business men," had moved to set up the First National Bank of Sonora in the spring of 1900. Bad weather delayed completion of the 24' x 50' stone building until well into the summer, but on Wednesday, August 15, its doors were finally opened. Besides Jackson, the president, and Aldwell, the cashier, the officers included E.R. Vander Stucken as vice-president and four directors. The institution was capitalized at $50,000, "every dollar paid in." The design incorporated a fireproof vault and "a modern fire and burglar proof safe."[48] Hence, when Carver and his pals moved into town to rob the bank, it had been functioning for just seven and a half months.

As dusk closed in on Tuesday, April 2, the four men rode in on the southern fringe of town from the northwest, following the Draw to the lower end of Plum Street.[49]

They intended to stick up the bank next day. They had all the ammunition and nearly all the supplies they needed. Their expensive horses, which had been feeding on grain for several weeks, would easily outrun and overstay the town plugs ridden by most of their first pursuers. They had at least one relay in place and could expect to be well clear before better-organized and better-mounted posses were put on their trail.

Their preparations were not quite complete. They needed, or at least thought they might as well get, a further sack of oats and a couple of other items. If the grain was all they were after, they would not have had to skirt the southern edge of town and ride up Plum Street. Oats, as Carver well knew, were readily obtainable at the combined bakery and store operated by W.J. (Jack) Owens in the Ogden building near the Oak Street end of Concho Avenue. If they had wanted nothing else, one or two of them could have slipped unnoticed up Oak Street, in and out of the bakery, and down Oak Street or the alleyway. Had they done that, the First National Bank of Sonora would have been held up the following day, very likely when the sheriff and his assistants were out of town, looking for them in the wrong place.

But the purchase of oats and one or two other commodities was only a secondary object. The nocturnal ride through the streets was chiefly for the benefit of George Kilpatrick, who later stated, perhaps truthfully, that he had never been in Sonora before. It is likely that Logan and Ben had looked over the town earlier in the day, when one of them had changed money at the bank. Now, to provide the younger Kilpatrick with a mental map of the entry and escape routes, and enable him to have a good look at the back door and frontage of the bank, Carver would take him through the town. To lend legitimacy to their purpose, they would inquire for grain at places where they did not expect to find any. They were armed only with pistols, having left their .30-40 rifles in camp.

Near the bottom of Plum Street the men halted outside the Castillo store to ask for baking powder, flour, and oats. The proprietor could sell them the powder and the flour, but not the oats. Logan and the older Kilpatrick then rode west along Tom Green Avenue and a short distance north to a small building by the Draw, south of the Oak Street-Concho Avenue intersection. Here, since housing was sparse, they were well away from prying eyes. It was now a little after eight o'clock. They dismounted and waited.

Will and George rode up Plum Street, between the "Mexican" houses and vacant lots, across Concho Avenue, behind the Ranch and Maude S saloons, the First National Bank, and the Hagerlund store. They entered Water Street, turned into Main Street, dismounted outside Becket's stable, and entered. Becket's stable—or, rather, its location—was what had drawn them into the center of town. It was directly across the street from the bank.

It was also not far from the Maude S. As the two men rode up to the stable, the saloon bartender, Boosie Sharp, was standing by the front door. Although it was now getting on for nine o'clock, he saw them well enough to think they could be two of the rubber-tire fugitives from Concho County. He did not recognize Carver as Carver, and might have been deceived by the outlaw's paint-and-dye disguise even in daylight. Boosie watched the men as they came out of Becket's, rode by, and swung into Concho Avenue. He followed, and saw two riderless horses hitched outside the Owens bakery. Then he hurried to the sheriff's office, in the courthouse. Briant quickly rounded up his deputies, former sheriff J.L. Davis,[50] who was on duty at the jail on the west side of Courthouse Square, and Henry P. Sharp, Boosie's brother. They met Constable W.D. Thomason in Main Street.

Carver and Kilpatrick must have considered their mission accomplished; before, during, and after the charade of asking the ostler to sell them oats (he had none, but could have sold them a barnful of hay, had they wanted it) they made the best of the opportunity to look across the street into the building opposite. Now they could put the play acting behind them, buy the oats, and rejoin Logan and Ben. They rode around the corner to the Owens store-bakery and went in. Their errand was a simple one, requiring no more than a few minutes. But that was all the time that was needed for Briant, Thomason, Davis, and the Sharp brothers to bear down on them.

It never occurred to Carver, a hunted man for four years and seldom so hunted as he was in these last few days, that one of them ought to have stayed outside to keep watch. George Kilpatrick seems unthinkingly to have followed Carver's unthinking lead. Perhaps Carver belatedly realized his oversight, for Boosie Sharp said that he glanced several times at the window or doorway while holding the sack open for Owens to pour in the grain. He could not have seen anything in the unlit street from the interior of the bakery, anyway.

Just over a year previously, on March 11, 1900, Briant had been shot and badly wounded by a wife-beating thief and rowdy named Hopson. Briant's mistake had been to attempt the arrest of an armed man without first drawing his own gun. Only the robust intervention of Deputy Davis had saved his life.[51] No needless risk would be taken this time. Briant drew his revolver and the other officers did the same.

The sheriff told Henry Sharp to watch the side door so that the men could not escape that way. He peered through the window into the dimly lit bakery. It was impossible to be sure about the men. But they could be sure about one of the horses; the flare of a Lucifer match showed Thomason the dun sorrel the men had bought from George Morris. That eliminated the last shred of doubt.

Briant decided not to wait for the men to step into the street. He led the way inside and ordered them to raise their hands.

Carver was still at the counter, but was about ready to leave; he was bending over the sack and tying the string. Kilpatrick was nearer the front door, but was not watching it.

Carver's right hand shot to the butt of his Colt's .45; he might have beaten the drop, but the gun got entangled in his suspender as he was drawing it. Briant did not wait at Carver's convenience. He fired, hitting Carver in the right forearm, forcing him to let go of the uncocked pistol. The outlaw was trying to pull his Smith & Wesson, left handed, when a bullet from Davis struck him in the chest and brought him down. He was groping for the Colt's when Henry Sharp rushed in and kicked it away.

Kilpatrick had responded to the command with the inarticulate, indeterminate movement of a man who did not know whether to fight or surrender. He was immediately shot down by Thomason.

Both Carver and Kilpatrick were now on the floor. All four officers kept firing until both of them lay still. Neither had fired a shot. Kilpatrick had not even begun to draw his .38 Army model revolver.

Their wounds were described in the report published on April 6 by the *Devil's River News* and repeated with only a few typographical variances in the same day's issue of the *San Angelo Standard*. For the *News*, the headline was WILL CARVER JOINS SAM. The *Standard* chose BEFORE HE COULD COCK HIS PISTOL.

> Carver was shot through the right lung, the ball passed through the body and lodged under the skin near the spine, [and was also hit] twice in the right arm and twice in

the right leg and once in the left arm. A ball also struck him near the left temple. Both his right leg and right arm were broken in two places . . .

The most dangerous wound Kilpatrick has is from a shot that entered his left breast and ranged out back of the shoulder; [he also has] two shots in the left arm and one in left knee, [and] a glancing ball also struck him in the left forehead . . .

Not everything meant for Carver had been aimed true. At least one bullet flew through the partition into the next room, where Owens's wife and son were baking bread, though without hitting either.

Out in the draw by the cabin in Oak Street, Logan and Ben Kilpatrick heard the shots and at once put the correct interpretation on them. They were seen, or heard, riding out of town "at full speed."[52] According to Roy Holt, they stayed for a few days with unnamed "friends on Dove Creek," then started out for Wyoming. That may be so; but Ben Kilpatrick, for one, tarried awhile in Fort Worth. So much for the later assertion that the Swartz photograph had made the town unsafe for them.

(They were, however, in Wyoming or Montana by June 6, when two men robbed the store and post office at Rincon, New Mexico. On the 12th, these robbers were in San Marcial, eighty miles further north but now headed southwards. At least one reporter took them for the pair who had fled Sonora after the killing of Carver.[53] It was a poor guess. Logan and Ben Kilpatrick had their eyes on a far bigger prize.)

Both the wounded men were believed to be dying. Stretchers had to be improvised from doors knocked off their hinges. Carver and Kilpatrick were placed on them, carried to the courthouse, and laid out for medical treatment on the desks of Briant and Davis. Doctors were sent for and one of them administered an opiate. Carver, apparently oblivious of his surroundings, gabbled incoherently, as if in the throes of a violent dream: "Keep shelling them, boys . . . Will you stay with me? . . . Will you swear it . . . Stay with the safe . . . Now we have them! . . . Die game!" and much more that was not recorded. As the effect of the drug weakened, the delirium receded and his words were rational, but few. When asked his name, he at first equivocated: he was "one of the Off boys." But the question was pressed, and he replied, "I'm one of the Carver boys, Will Carver."

Carver was now "sinking fast." Ben Binyon, who for years had worked alongside him on the Half Circle Six, came to see him. Did he remember Binyon? "Yes." Did he have a message for Binyon to take to his friends? "No."

Binyon stayed until Carver breathed his last, sometime between eleven o'clock and midnight. Lee Aldwell, his old friend and employer, whom he had intended to blackguard into emptying the bank vault the very next day, appeared shortly afterwards. He said nothing for publication other than that, up to a few years ago, Carver had been highly thought of, with "hosts of friends."

Kilpatrick looked at first as though he would take the same course as Carver, and may have thought so himself. He said that he had heard nothing about the gang's supposed plan of "making a run on the First National Bank;" but was more informative on the Thornton murder. He claimed not to have been "there" at the time of the murder, but stated that those who were had named McDonald as the killer.

McDonald, he said, "was a dark man about the size of Bill [Carver], maybe a little larger or a little smaller, but he thought smaller." Harvey Logan was roughly of Carver's size, but slighter of build and with a much darker natural complexion. As for his brother Ben, George lied. He alleged that Ben had left camp in the morning, and had not returned before he and Carver rode into town in the evening.[54]

Further examination suggested that George would pull through, so he was removed to the jail, which stood beside but some little way from the courthouse, facing the head of Oak Street. His mother was sent for and Mrs. J.L. Davis, the jailer-deputy's wife, whose living quarters were at the jail, told her young daughter to share her bed with the "she-devil." Another visitor from Concho County was Sheriff Howze, who confirmed the identifications but, unaware of the accumulation of evidence to the contrary, endeavored to dismiss the fourth man (McDonald) as a "myth."[55]

During the morning, several of Carver's old acquaintances came to look at him for the last time: George Hamilton, another former Sixes man, who had become Berry Ketchum's partner in the sheep business; Ed Jackson; Archie Kuykendall, of Sherwood, who had once roped a deer on the Sixes range; M.V. (Mike) Sharp, of Sonora; and the Misses Georgia and Eleanor Ervin, proprietors of the local millinery and candy store.[56]

An inventory was made of his personal estate. It was inconsiderable: "a very handsome Colt's .45, ivory handle and silver mounted, number 201916, one Smith & Wesson 38 hammerless;" a beltful of cartridges, some of them steel jacketed; a gold case Elgin watch; a silver case compass; a handsome diamond ring; two $20 gold certificates but no cash except for a $5 bill; a thin gold wedding band; and two small photographs—one of his late wife, Viana, the other of Laura Bullion. Otherwise, for the moment, there was only his horse and its accouterments. Afterwards, three of the other horses he and his companions had bought were found and credited to the estate.[57]

At half-past three in the afternoon D.B. Woodruff, the local J.P., and ex-officio coroner, conducted an inquest at the County Jail. He described the body as that of a "medium sized, well built man; weight, about 150 pounds, height about 5 feet, six inches; age, between 35 and 40. Light brown mustache, recently shaved; blue eyes; brown hair. Some traces of dye." Woodruff may have understated Carver's height by an inch or two, and he certainly overstated his age; Carver was 32 when he died. Woodruff's finding was a statement of fact that left only one verdict open: the fatal wounds were inflicted by "officers while in the proper and legal discharge of their duties as duly accredited officers of the State of Texas, after having duly demanded the surrender of the man, who was known to be a fugitive from justice and desperate man; and in our opinion they simply did their duty."[58]

On Thursday, April 4, Carver was buried at Sonora under the rites of the Methodist church. His friend George Hamilton paid the funeral expenses. Among those not in attendance were members of his wife's family; but, five days later, Elliott Byler and his son Jake did visit the graveside. They may have been given the wedding ring and the photo of Viana.[59]

Ed Jackson was appointed administrator of Will's estate and on June 29 the goods were put up for public sale, with Lee Aldwell as auctioneer. The proceeds amounted to $425. George Morris got his dun horse back for $40, thus turning a profit of $32. Boosie Sharp paid $32.50 for the Colt's six-shooter, while Jackson himself parted with $6 for the S & W five-shooter. Jackson also gave $125 for the diamond ring, Hamilton, with much reluctance, accepted reimbursement of the funeral expenses. The balance was sent to Carver's mother and sister.[60]

A month later the silver-mounted and elegantly chased Colt's revolver was placed on display at the Parlor saloon in San Angelo. The *Standard* remarked facetiously that the gun "kills with much less pain than the ordinary blued steel affair."[61]

Laura Bullion was then staying with James and Lucinda Lambert, who had moved to Cochise County, Arizona, just north of the city of Douglas. Perhaps she was expecting Will to meet her there. When she heard about his death, she made an entry in her memorandum book:

W.R. CARVER, killed Tuesday, April 2, 1901.

Beneath it she composed, or copied, a bitter—or affected?—rhyming couplet:

He has fled; I wish him dead, he that wrought my ruin,
O the flattery and the craft, which were my undoing.[62]

George Kilpatrick was soon on the mend; his five wounds had looked a lot worse that they were. The ugliest was to the head. The bullet had hit "George's hard head near the brow [and] furrowed under the skin to the back of the skull," and was easily removed. Sutton County had no hope of proving that he had conspired to rob the bank, or that he was guilty of the minor thefts from the Mayer ranch. He remained in the Sutton County Jail for three weeks, more of a patient than a prisoner.[63]

In mid-April, a grand jury in Concho County indicted both George and his brother Ed for the murder of Oliver Thornton. Both were denied bail and remanded to the Runnels County Jail at Ballinger, where Ed was taken on April 20. On the 26th, Sheriff Howze collected George from the Sonora jail for removal to Ballinger. At a habeas corpus hearing in Paint Rock, on Monday, April 29, both brothers were granted bail and released. A series of continuances delayed their trial until the following March.[64]

George's aspirations to outlawry were not blunted by his close call at Sonora. Three years later he renewed his association with Harvey Logan and began to make some progress in the career which had been retarded by the intervention of Elijah Briant and his men. Ed was to pursue similar inclinations, though in different company.

Will Carver had been dead for less than a week when luck turned sour on Red Weaver.

For six months, Red had disported himself as would befit a gentleman of wealth and leisure, reveling in his position as resident badman of Alma, New Mexico. The larceny charge against him had been deferred yet again, and looked likely to peter out. In the meantime, he had no difficulty in raising bond.

Then, one night, he attended a dance in Alma and turned his charm on Lydia Sipes, a relative of the three Holliman (or Hollimon) brothers, who did a little ranching and some rustling in that neighborhood. William, known as "Pad," the youngest of the three brothers, objected strongly to Red's behavior and the outlaw was put out into the road. (Or, in the more delicately tuned phrasing of the *Silver City Independent*, Holliman felt that "Weaver's reputation was such that he was not entitled to this courtesy.") On the following day, Monday, Weaver caught Holliman in the Coats & Rowe store, struck him in the face, drew his gun, and demanded satisfaction. Pad claimed to be unarmed but offered to settle up with Weaver in the morning.

Four accounts of the denouement are available. The fullest was assembled by Philip Rasch. It comes down to this:

Although Weaver was regarded as a four-flusher by French (and, according to French, by Cassidy), no one doubted that he was much too tough for the likes of Pad Holliman. As the hours dragged by, Holliman's friends urged him to get out of town while he still had a whole skin. He stubbornly refused to go. By daybreak, he had thought it over; and the more he thought about it, the more scared he became. At last he went outside and began to walk towards his horse, carrying his cocked .30-30 in one hand. Weaver was standing in the street, bent on canceling out his obligation to young Holliman. Pad, turning a corner, saw him at once and instinctively fired from the hip. He did not take aim; he was so frightened that he did not realize he had pulled the trigger. Yet there lay Red Weaver, stone dead, with an undischarged six-shooter beside him and a red splash of blood upon his forehead.[65] If, indeed, that was the course of events, it was, in law, a simple case of self-defense, and in fact, a sheer fluke.

The report in the *Independent* was only a week behind the event; but that alone is no warranty for greater authenticity. Alma and Silver City are seventy-two miles apart, were not connected by telegraph or telephone, and the anonymous bearer of the news was clearly partial to Holliman's side of the argument. Moreover, winners who remain near the field of battle have a tendency to be seen to have been in the right.

As the *Independent* told the story, Weaver and Holliman were walking towards each other. Holliman warned Weaver to stop or be shot; Red responded by drawing his gun; Holliman's rifle and Weaver's pistol spoke simultaneously when only a few paces separated the antagonists; Holliman's second shot smacked into the middle of Weaver's forehead; and Weaver was already falling, with much of the top of his head torn away when he got off a second shot, as futile as his first.

The newspaper's comment that Holliman bore "an excellent reputation where [he was] known" may have been shaped by misinformation or diplomacy. Weaver, being in no condition to argue, was given less shrift, but fair justice. It had been "common rumor for the past two or three years that he was in some way connected with the famous 'Black Jack' gang, but this was never proven. He had been arrested in both New Mexico and Arizona, but escaped conviction." The paper also commented that Red was "a familiar figure in Silver City about a year ago," but without explaining how or why. It could say nothing about his family or background except that he was about thirty and had come from Texas.[66]

The reported mode of Weaver's vanquishing was too prosaic for some pens. One imaginative correspondent of the day, not from New Mexico, pictured the two men "advancing towards each other, shooting at every step."[67]

This was miles from the truth, but William French traveled a fair step further a quarter of a century later, with a most vivid eye-witness account of something that he never saw; or which, if he saw it, did not happen the way he told it.

French said he had been to Graham for his mail and was riding through Alma when Elton Cunningham, who was working in the store, drew his attention to Holliman. Pad was prowling the streets with a Winchester, "looking for something or somebody, who did not happen to be in sight at the time." Cunningham told French that Pad was "in search of Red, who was in the saloon opposite . . . and there was liable to be trouble." Before French could take Cunningham's advice to take shelter in the store, Red "came out . . . with a pistol in his hand and the ball opened."

Bullets were flying everywhere, wrote French, and it was all he could do to dodge them and control his skittish mount. The two combatants were "enshrouded" in smoke, but at the end of it all Red was prostrate and lifeless, and Pad was standing over him. After Holliman shouldered his rifle and walked away, "apparently contented," Cunningham and French inspected the body. Evidently, said French, Holliman must have pressed the nozzle of his rifle against Red's snout before firing the fatal shot, for "the whole back was blown out of his [Weaver's] head." Weaver's pistol was empty, French added, while report had it that Pad "had exhausted all the cartridges in his magazine." French commented that it was "[n]ot very accurate shooting at a distance of two or three yards," and that Weaver "should have killed Holoman [*sic*] before he had time to get his gun off." As it was, nothing could be done with Red except carry him back into the saloon and spread him out on the billiard table.[68]

There was more wildness in French's narrative than in the shooting. The less melodramatic versions rest on stronger evidence than the unfailing readability but variable reliability of French's "Recollections." And Cunningham, named by French as a fellow witness, did not so much as mention the affair in any of the series of interviews he recorded with Lou Blachly.

Arthur Soule's comment that the affair "was more in the line of an ambush [than] a duel" hits the mark.[69] Support for it comes from our fourth witness, Marvin Powe, an O Bar O cowboy. Powe had talked to Weaver at the Cow Springs ranch, between Deming and Silver City, a few days before the fracas at the Coats & Rowe store. The ill-feeling between Weaver and the Hollimans was of long standing, and Red had already made up his mind to kill Pad. The word that came back to Powe was that Holliman stood behind a tree, waiting for Weaver to show himself. When he did, "he [Pad] stepped out and he shot him [Red] right between the eyes." Powe's belief was that the whole brood of Hollimans had been afraid of Weaver.[70] On the fatal day, the two were on the lookout for one another, with Pad on the defensive and the a *priori* odds favoring Weaver; but Holliman was the first to see his adversary, and castled his king with a well directed shot. A lucky shot? Only if Holliman fired from the hip, as he professed to have done. A dash of skepticism would not be amiss.

Thus passed Bruce Weaver, on Tuesday, April 9, 1901, to the loss or personal regret of no one.

Weaver could well have killed Holliman "before he had time to get his gun off" if Holliman had given him the time. Still, Pad's plea of self-defense was reasonable; it was he who was the threatened party. The local authorities unhesitatingly took that line. Holliman gave himself up at Mogollon and was bailed for $3,000 by the resident Justice of the Peace. When he appeared at the next term of county court his case was not referred to the grand jury.

Whatever the exact truth about the details of the encounter, the outcome proved that the result of a gunfight could not always be written down in advance.

Montague Stevens, owner of the SU outfit on the San Francisco, wasted few words in passing judgment on the loser: "Weaver was no good." We have seen that Holliman was not much better. That was the general view, and Stevens did not dissent from it: "They were both bad men as far as that's concerned." [71]

Tom Ketchum might have sneered at the profligate rashness of Will Carver's last months; he may never have thought very highly of Red Weaver. But from the standpoint forced upon him by his predicament, he must have envied them the style of their taking off. Tom could not change the cards he had been dealt; all he could do was try to play a bad hand well.

"I believe I'll keep my nerve," he had remarked to Saturnino Pinard and his deputy, Tom Gray, when they were returning him to Santa Fe after his trial and conviction.[72] During the long months of his imprisonment, he rarely showed any sign of giving way to fear. When the time came, he too would die game.

{ 21 }

OFF WITH HIS HEAD

Twenty months and a few days spanned Tom Ketchum's arrest and his dispatch into the hereafter. The interval allowed him ample time for reflection, but he never yielded to repentance. He regretted nothing, except for being caught and failing to kill Harrington or Kirchgrabber. He felt sour towards his fellow train robbers Bronco Bill and Elzy Lay because they were merely serving out prison terms—yet he would declare that he would rather be hanged than die of old age in a cell.[1]

Now and then, news would come through of his former associates; first, the arrest of Bud Upshaw, then the surrender and disappearance of Dave Atkins, and finally, near the end of the time left to him, the deaths of Will Carver and Red Weaver. In Tom Green County, about the first item on the criminal calendar for 1901 was a motion of the district attorney to dismiss a charge against Jose Ma Perez and Tom Ketchum.[2] No prior reference to this case has been found, nor any clue as to its nature, but its removal from the docket of a Texas court could have done nothing to lighten Ketchum's predicament in New Mexico.

As his future shortened, Tom affirmed his belief that "the gang" would rescue him, and many of the officers feared that he might have genuine cause for optimism.[3] Their worries, although understandable, were wholly irrational; as far as is known, the dwindling and scattered remnants of the outlaw freemasonry never gave a thought to helping Ketchum escape. He had quarreled with his few intimates—Carver, his brother Sam, and Atkins. Other criminals, who would not have conjoined their fortunes with his when he was at large with an impressive record of criminal campaigning in his warbag, were not going to spare a single moment's concern for him now that he was discredited, disabled, under heavy guard, and doomed for the gallows.

In appealing to the Supreme Court of the territory, Ketchum's attorneys again invoked the eighth amendment to the Constitution of the United States, contending that the death penalty was a "cruel and unusual" punishment for the offense charged. Bunker and Guyer submitted this argument on the morning of January 25, 1901, before Justices Crumpacker, McFie, McMillan, and Parker.[4] It had not swayed Chief Justice Mills, the trial judge, and it did not impress the Supreme Court. The plea was

298

summarily rejected, and official policy coldly restated, in the opinion delivered by
Justice Parker a month later. If Parker's reaction to the acquittal of the alleged Steins
Pass robbers has been correctly reported, it showed that he was hardly a fountain of
objectivity. His response to the plea of Ketchum's attorneys was reasoned but inex-
orable. He cited the judgment in the case of William Kemmler, the first man to die in
the electric chair, discussed three rulings of the Appeal Court of the Commonwealth
of Massachusetts, and went on to quote the comments of the judge who had handed
down the opinion in the cause of the State of Missouri vs. Williams:

> The interdict of the Constitution [is] against the infliction of cruel and unusual pun-
> ishments as amount to torture, or such as would shock the mind of every man pos-
> sessed of common feeling, such for instance as drawing or quartering the culprit,
> burning him at the stake, cutting off his nose, ears or limbs, starving him to death, or
> such as was inflicted by an act of Parliament as late as the 22 Henry VIII, authorizing
> one Rouse to be thrown into boiling water and boiled to death for the offense of poi-
> soning the family of the Bishop of Rochester.

Parker cited a number of other cases before stating his views on the act of February
23, 1887:

> It is hardly necessary to recall the incidents attending the ordinary train robbery,
> which are a matter of common history, to assure everyone that the punishment pre-
> scribed by this statute is a most salutary provision and eminently suited to the offense
> which it is designed to meet. Trains are robbed by armed bands of desperate men,
> determined upon the accomplishment of their purpose, and nothing will prevent the
> consummation of their design, not even the necessity to take human life . . . If the
> express messenger or train crew resist their attack upon the cars, they promptly kill
> them. In this and many other ways they display their utter disregard for human life
> and property . . . [5]

His colleagues concurred with his opinion that the statute was "not in violation
of the eighth amendment to the Constitution of the United States" and it was ordered
that the sentence be executed on March 22.[6] But a couple of days later the execution
was postponed until March 27, and on March 19 Governor Otero granted a stay of
thirty days to give Ketchum's attorneys an opportunity to produce new evidence.[7] It
is not apparent what sort of evidence they were looking for, as the case against
Ketchum was absolutely clearcut. About all they could hope for was that Tom might
part with enough information to induce the Governor to exercise clemency. In
default of this, Ketchum would hang on April 26.

During his eighteen months as a prisoner in the territorial penitentiary,
Ketchum received numerous visitors. Some of these were officers who tried to sound
him on the activities and associates of various outlaws still at large. One whose
motives were rather different was Ben Clark, sheriff of Graham County, Arizona. In
April 1897 Clark, then a deputy under William Birchfield, was a member of the posse

that killed Black Jack Christian. Nearly thirty years later Clark would write that he visited Ketchum "in order to remove all doubt" as to the identity of Black Jack.[8]These words make very little sense. Clark had seen the body of the man slain by the posse, and if there were doubts over whether it was that of Black Jack they were not going to be resolved by an inspection of Tom Ketchum.

But Clark's explanation cannot be taken at face value. It will be recalled that Clark had proclaimed the man killed at Cole Creek to be "Tom Ketchum, alias Black Jack" and had adapted the testimony of witnesses acquainted with Black Jack so as to make it appear that they were, too, believed the pseudonym to be Tom Ketchum's. Once the press had the story of Clark's intervention, it chose to interpret his statement as evidence that, since the man who died in Cole Creek Canyon was not Tom Ketchum, that man could not have been Black Jack. This false but facile conclusion blended smoothly with journalistic assumptions, or assertions, that the one and only Black Jack was Tom Ketchum; seemed to authenticate previously published articles in which the crimes and identities of Tom Ketchum and Black Jack were merged; and was taken as licence for the creation of more of the same.[9]

The comparative few who knew that the real Black Jack was Will Christian, the Oklahoma City jail breaker and Indian Territory outlaw, did not speak to, or were not spoken to by, the hacks who filled the columns of the larger newspapers. Not until the late 1920s, when some of the well-informed few began to speak for the record, did that fact begin to enter general circulation. It was common knowledge in Graham County long before Clark went into print in 1929. There was not much historical truth in his two-part magazine article, "William Christian, alias Black Jack," but the title of the piece amounted to a public admission of past evasion and error.[10]

Anyway, Clark visited Ketchum, in company with Sheriff Thomas S. Hubbell, of Bernalillo County New Mexico, and listened attentively while Tom gave them an untruthful account of his movements in Arizona.[11]

But Ketchum was still using the Black Jack monnicker to secure a little unearned income. More than fifty years later, the governor's son, Miguel A. Otero, Jr., by then a retired district court judge, told George Fitzpatrick of Santa Fe, that when he first went to see the outlaw, his view of the prisoner was blocked by a blanket covering the bars. Pinned to the blanket was Tom's "See Black Jack" note. The charge was still 25c.

Tom, apparently, always liked to see the six-year-old boy, and would reminisce to him. Young Miguel, for his part, contributed candy, peanuts, and an avid ear. The senior Otero wrote later that one day his son put in a plea for the condemned man: "Papa, Tom is an awfully good friend of mine, and I wish you would pardon him, as he promised me that he would be good and settle down."[12]

J.S. "Rox" Grumbles, a cattleman from Lincoln County, called on Ketchum a number of times. Grumbles was "much of a warbler," according to Jack Culley, and Tom would get him to sing a ballad "with a sad refrain at the end of each verse about 'a prisoner for life.'"[13] But if Tom was contemplating the gloomy prospect of a life behind grey walls after the commutation of his death sentence, he was troubling his mind without cause. Otero had not the least intention of canceling Ketchum's appointment with the executioner.

Berry Ketchum went along to the penitentiary on one further occasion, but still Tom refused to see him. More than this; he charged that Berry had introduced Sam and himself to train robbery. The three of them, Tom alleged, had obtained about a hundred thousand dollars, but Berry had held onto nearly all of it in order to set himself up as "a real Christian gentleman."[14]

This was fabrication, but it may have been engendered by a genuine sense of injury. Envy of the respected and prosperous elder brother could not have wholly accounted for his malevolence; there was real bitterness in Tom's criticism of Berry.

Whatever reasons underlay Tom's hostility towards him, Berry went to Governor Otero to express his disappointment at Tom's attitude. Before he left Santa Fe he gave the warden some money, to be spent on keeping Tom well provided with candy and cake and such trifles.[15] This gesture called for no great measure of his largesse, and his air of solicitude may have been feigned.

There was never any possibility that the sentence would be commuted by the Governor. Yet there were grounds, constitutionally unassailable, on which a reprieve could have been sought without recourse to Otero.

In law, any bill passed by the territorial legislature was invalid until it had been ratified by Congress. The statute that stipulated the death penalty for those convicted of train robbery had not been presented for ratification. Theoretically, therefore, it was null and void. In the event, Bunker and Guyer did not cite the point until Ketchum was beyond their help.[16] Perhaps it did not occur to them in time; perhaps, on the other hand, they felt constrained from using the argument by the enormity of its implications.[17]

As the day appointed for the execution drew close, the authorities, preserving as much secrecy as was possible, laid out plans for the delivery of Tom Ketchum from the territorial penitentiary to the Union County jail. At midday on Tuesday, April 23, Ketchum was told he would be leaving for Clayton that afternoon—two days earlier than had been advertised. Shortly after three o'clock, he was placed, heavily manacled, in a steel-lined mail car. Among the guards were ex-Sheriff Harry C. Kinsell, of Santa Fe; Salome Garcia, who, as Sheriff of Union County, was to act as executioner; Tom A. Gray, Garcia's deputy; H.J. Chambers, a detective from Chicago, who had been invited to assist García in the arrangements for the hanging; W.H. Reno, as official representative of the Colorado and Southern Railway; Joe Napier; Harry Lewis; and Sheriff Putnam, of Elbert County, Colorado. The prisoner, it was reported, "chaffed good-naturedly" with his escort and "nonchalantly said good-bye" to the officials of the penitentiary.[18]

He was taken to Clayton via Lamy Junction, Las Vegas, Raton, and Trinidad. The strained nerves of the guards were badly jarred when the train came to a sudden and unscheduled halt on the stiffest grade on the Raton Pass. For a few moments they imagined that friends of Ketchum, bent on a rescue act, had held up the train.

"I don't want ever to be so scared again," said Joe Napier, in relating the incident to Jack Culley. "A rescue by Tom Ketchum's gang wasn't goin' to be a garden party exactly. I don't reckon it was more than a few minutes till we knowed what had happened, but it seemed to me a week."

The cause of the delay was soon found to be a minor and rather commonplace accident: the couplings had broken apart on the grade, cutting off the car occupied by Ketchum and his guards. It was a simple matter to reconnect the train, and the journey was completed without further alarm. "But," said Napier, "I believe the last thing to fade out of my memory'll be the moment when I looked outa that train door and seen the Black Jack coach was cut off."[19]

At half-past five on Wednesday morning Ketchum rode into Clayton for the last time. He noted the stockade which had been erected outside the courtyard to prevent all but the privileged holders of tickets from witnessing his final moments, and suggested that it should be torn down so that everyone could watch. He was given permission to examine the scaffold and eyed it critically.

"It looks good," he opined, "but I think they ought to hang Harrington on it first, and if it works all right, they might try me."[20]

Eight o'clock on the Friday morning was the time set for the execution. Throughout, Ketchum retained both his composure and his waggish if sometimes malicious sense of humor. He slept soundly and ate heartily of the food carried to the jail from the Eklund Hotel. Altogether he was more assured and at ease than those who were charged with the task of ending his life.[21]

Never before had there been a legal execution in Union County. There were officers everywhere in town. Two men were posted on either side of the gate to the prison yard. It was their duty to turn away anyone who could not show a pass, and to admit no one without having first made a search for weapons. Otero, still afraid that the plans might fall awry in spite of all the precautions, sent Lewis "Cap" Fort to Clayton with instructions to supervise Sheriff Garcia's preparations for the execution. Fort, García, and Chambers, it turned out, held very diverse opinions on the rudiments of an art in which none of them was expert.

A fifteen foot rope, "of first class Manila hemp," had been supplied at a cost of $20.80 by the Chief of Police at Kansas City, along with a suggestion that there should be a drop of seven feet. Chambers disagreed emphatically; as he saw it, "four feet six inches would be plenty for a man of Ketchum's weight—193 pounds." Fort then lengthened it to five feet six inches, only for García to extend it by a further six inches. Fort and Chambers, as if anxious to have the final say, then got together and altered it to five feet nine inches. There the grisly comedy was concluded—unless it is true, as was alleged, that Garcia surreptitiously readjusted the drop to the seven feet originally proposed.[22]

Sheriff Garcia, already nervous, was thrown into consternation by a message, bearing what appeared to be the signature of Governor Otero and the Great Seal of New Mexico, which ordered him to postpone the execution for another thirty days, at the request of President McKinley. The telegram was handed to Garcia at about eight o'clock on Wednesday night. Ketchum heard about it, "was almost overcome," and broke into a dance. Then, recovering himself, he exclaimed, "By God, I'll write a letter to Papa McKinley tomorrow." Garcia wired Otero for confirmation, and received a disclaimer. When the news was given to the prisoner, "his face was a study for a few moments." After that, he relapsed into silence.[23]

The author of the "bogus respite" was never unmasked. Whoever he was, he caused a good deal of excitement and succeeded in allowing Ketchum to remain breathing for five hours longer than the authorities had decreed.

No Baptist minister squandered his time by visiting the outlaw; if the tenets of that faith had ever drawn any credence from Tom Ketchum, he had long since disencumbered himself of these and all other religious pretensions.

As was usual in such circumstances, a Catholic priest undertook to interest himself in Tom's future welfare. Father Dean would travel from Trinidad with a message of solace. Tom did not want to hear him or see him:

"Don't want no preacher. They don't do no good."

Later, his attitude appeared to soften. He told the jail officials that they could send for the priest.

Ketchum whiled away much of Wednesday and Thursday playing cards. He did not expect a reprieve, and was not short of a card-playing metaphor as a means for self-expression: "The cards are shuffled for me to hang, and I'll have to go."[24]

During Thursday, he was seen by a number of callers. Besides John Guyer and his brother George, there came separately or together Albert Thompson; E.A. Bingham, special correspondent of the Denver *Evening Post*; and their no less able but unidentifiable counterpart from the Denver *Rocky Mountain News*. One or both of the Guyers represented the *Denver Times*; Thompson was reporting for the *Denver Republican* as well as for the local press.[25]

When Ketchum "objected to being called Black Jack," Thompson humored him by addressing him only as Tom. "All day," wrote Bingham, "he spoke with much profanity of his indifference to his fate."

He also spoke, with or without profanity, of the fate he wished he could settle upon his enemies. Reno was one who came in for special mention: "I'd like to have a gun on him for a second—even with only this left arm."[26]

At 10 p.m he told his visitors that he wanted to turn in, as there would be no bed for him the following night. Before they left, he asked attorney Guyer to prepare a letter about the Steins Pass case, to be signed by him and addressed to the President:

"I think it my duty to do this, don't you?"

"Yes, of course I do."

"I'll tell you a lot of things in the morning."

"Have you any feeling against anyone concerned in the prosecution?"

"You bet I have. The railroad company put up lots of money to convict [me]. I'll tell you in the morning about it."

"Have you any fear of death, Tom?"

"Not a bit,"

"Going to die like a man, are you?"

"You bet your life," the *Times* had him reply; or, as the *Post* heard him, "Bet your God-damned life I am."

Finally, when the visitors were turning to go, "Tell Harrington I'll meet him in hell for breakfast."

Ketchum then changed his mind about going straight to bed. Instead, he "entertained his guards with humorous stories of his experiences, for some of which he undoubtedly drew upon [i.e. improved upon] his memory, others [being] authentic." His claim to have been present when George Musgrave killed George Parker at the Diamond A roundup in 1896 did not enhance his reputation for veracity. He alleged that each man had slain the other; but Parker was unarmed and defenseless, and Musgrave was still at large in 1901.[27]

Before he retired for his last night above ground, Tom was again asked whether he wanted to see the priest. He replied that he would rather have some music.

Was there anything else Union County could do to lighten Ketchum's last night? Ketchum thought so; it could supply him with a woman. Sheriff Garcia was a liberal-minded man, but the limitations of his authority and the constraints of his susceptibilities precluded compliance.[28] Tom had already shown an interest in hearing some music; he would have to be satisfied with that.

Ketchum responded with a further plea. It was one that went the rounds. The *Denver Times* called it "a strange request." Other descriptions were more decorative. In William French's paraphrase, the condemned man "sent back word" to the powers-that-be that "they might kiss—let us say a certain unorthodox portion of his person, to use a more printable expression," and should, therefore, "bury him with his face downwards, thus avoiding the necessity of turning him over." In another version of the tale, Ketchum designated Harrington as the putative beneficiary of his request.[29]

Probably Ketchum fell asleep and did not hear the rumble of the southbound train that paused at midnight to unload the coffin he would occupy a few hours later. The train also brought Father Dean from Trinidad. At 12:30 a.m. the priest entered the death cell.

Father Dean's efforts met with an immediate and decisive rebuff.

He began by inviting the condemned man to make his confession. Tom said he would rather sleep. When Dean persisted, Ketchum signified his willingness to confess, provided only that the priest would confess to him too. If the priest would get a fiddler, added Ketchum, they could dance together. The priest withdrew.[30]

After that, Ketchum again fell into slumber. He passed an easier night than Reno, who was up until the small hours, or Garcia, who did not go to bed at all. He awoke at 4:40 a.m., arose at seven, and donned the shabby old clothes in which he had arrived—work pants and a "rough flannel shirt." Soon he was breakfasting on potatoes, steak and eggs, biscuits, and coffee. Then he took a bath.

At 9 a.m. the barber was ready for him. Tom's hair and mustache were trimmed and his chin shaved. Nearby was the new clothing, suitable for the occasion, which the county had purchased for him. Freshly bathed and barbered, attired in a black suit and white shirt, with a white tie and black Oxford shoes, he would make a neatly turned out corpse.

The execution was to have taken place at 11 o'clock, but Garcia had decided to put it off for a couple of hours. Ketchum would be allowed, or expected, to tell his life's story to the press, and would then be given a good dinner.

At about 9:30 a.m. the Guyers arrived to dispose of the first item of the day, the letter asking President McKinley to intercede in the case of Alverson, Hovey (alias Hoffman), and Warderman. It was drafted by John Guyer and signed by Ketchum.

> . . . There are now three men in the Santa Fe penitentiary, serving sentences for the robbery of the United States mail at Steins Pass, Ariz., [sic], in 1897, viz: Leonard Albertson [Alverson], Walter Hoffman and Bill Warderman. They are as innocent of the crime as unborn babes.
>
> The names of the men who committed the crime are Dave Atkins, Ed Bullin, Will Carver, Sam Ketchum, Bronco Bill and myself. I have given to my attorney in Clayton means by which articles taken in said robbery may be found where we hid them, and also the names of witnesses who live in that vicinity, who will testify that myself and gang were in that neighborhood both immediately before and after the robbery.
>
> . . . I wish to do this much in the interest of these innocent men, who, as far as I know, never committed a crime in their lives . . . [31]

Probably it was nothing more than spite that led Tom to implicate "Bronco Bill" in the Steins affair. While Bill's whereabouts at the time of the holdup are unknown, it seems plain that there were only five of the robbers and that he was not among them. The most that can be said is that Ketchum and Walters probably met in southwest New Mexico or southeast Arizona in 1897. It is improbable that Walters would have joined Tom's gang even if invited to do so. The two men were next door neighbors in the penitentiary, but their contacts were not friendly.

The reference to an "Ed Bullin" was repeated in too many reports to have been a misprint, though some newspapers emended the spelling to "Cullen" or "Cullin," the name given by Tom in his oral references to the Steins holdup and the one actually borne by the cowboy and camp cook whose first criminal venture was ended by Guard Jennings's shotgun. The "Bullin" in the letter intended for President McKinley may rather have been a slip of Tom Ketchum's pen or tongue, which suggests that a member of the Bullion family—a mere acquaintance—may have been unaccountably at the forefront of his mind at that moment. If so, it was the sort of unforced disclosure that, in any ordinary situation, Ketchum would never have made. But, with the shadow of the noose edging ever closer on this, his last morning on earth, some weakening of his habitual watchfulness would have been understandable.

Whatever the explanation, this signed statement is the sole and unsupported authority for the claim, not advanced at the time of Ketchum's death but repeated many times in later years, that Laura Bullion's supposed brother Ed was the man killed at Steins. As we have noted, Laura Bullion's only brother was Daniel, who was alive and in Texas long after the Steins Pass contretemps.

After signing his confession, Tom cast off his old clothes and boots and changed into the outfit in which he was to appear before the public. One of the Guyers fixed the one-armed prisoner's tie for him. Then, just before ten o'clock, Thompson was admitted. With him was Deputy Marshal Frank Hall, who had arrived in town the previous night and whom Ketchum seems by now to have regarded almost as a friend.

When Thompson wanted to know whether he had any statement to make, he replied that he had not "much of anything to say" just then but would make one later.

"Not nervous this morning, are you Tom?" Thompson inquired.

"Feel my pulse," the condemned man replied, holding out his arm.

Thompson did so, and, as he later told his friend Albert Law, it "showed not the slightest tremor."

Ketchum addressed himself mainly to Hall rather than to Thompson. The outlaw's main concern appeared to be the whereabouts of a silver-handled revolver, which had been taken from him when he was arrested, and since passed to Hall. He told Hall that he had stolen the gun and asked him to "return it to its rightful owner."

By about 10:30 a.m., Bingham of the *Post*, the *News* reporter, and several other journalists or acquaintances were gathered in the jail corridor. A stenographer was summoned and Ketchum began to talk.[32]

He again spoke scathingly of Berry:

"The assistance he has rendered me in my present trouble was to send me $150. I don't call that much."[33]

His sentence, he thought, was "a little unjust" for the crime:

"The lawmakers of this territory did not make the laws to protect the people, but to protect the moneyed corporations."

"The crimes that I have committed," he continued, "I do not deny at all—none of them;" but before he finished speaking he had denied some of them.

After giving a detailed account of the Steins Pass episode he reiterated that he had not meant to wound the mail clerk, Fred Bartlett, in his last holdup. Next he discussed Black Jack, refused to divulge his real name, but maintained that he was not the man killed near Clifton in 1897 and that he was still alive.

"There are a dozen men in southern Arizona who will swear that I and Black Jack are two different persons," he said. This was an understatement (though he referred only to Bill Lutley, Burt Cogswell, John Banke, "and most of the Erie cowboys")—but none of them had thought enough of Ketchum to come forward with this information after his arrest. Black Jack, he said, "was the cause of my becoming an outlaw. Les Dow, the officer, saw Black Jack at the Deer Creek tank affair, and in 1898 he told me that if I was ever tried for Black Jack's crimes I would never get free, for I looked too much like him. I thought if I was going to be hanged for another man's crimes I might as well have some of my own." But Ketchum had made himself a fugitive killer eight months before Black Jack's gang began operations. Moreover, it seems unlikely that he and Dow could have had any such conversation, as the officer had returned to Eddy almost directly after the fight and was murdered there less than three months later. Tom erred in citing 1898 as the year of the supposed meeting, for Dow had been killed in February of 1897.

There followed assorted lies:

"I never killed anyone in my life, and never shot but three men in my life. I know exactly who killed Herzstein at Liberty in 1895 [1896]; but I don't wish to tell you. They are men I don't wish to get into trouble. I was crippled in Texas at the time.

Then the men who committed that murder are alive and free. Yes, sir; alive and got their liberty, while I have merely tried to hold up a railroad train and have got to die for it." He again declared that he was in Alamosa, in southern Colorado, at the time of the first of the three holdups near Folsom, but, as before, generously gave himself credit for having planned the robbery. Next, he proceeded to accusations of the sort that have always been difficult to substantiate:

"I feel that my attorneys did all they possibly could, but the prosecuting attorney and all were bought by the railroad company, and it was cut and dried from start to finish to hang me. I believe they used money during [doing?] the execution and conviction both. I have been told that, but I do not wish to tell exactly who told me. I have been told that they put up money to Mills and to others to prosecute me; also that they put up money to see that the execution went off."

Before he moved on from the general to the particular he referred to the personal oversight over which he had brooded ever since his arrest:

"If I had known that it was a capital offense for robbing a train in your territory I would certainly have killed someone." Very glib; as he said, he could easily have shot down Kirchgrabber, or Drew, or Scanlon, after Harrington had wounded him; but the chances are that, at the time he was too badly hurt to think of anything but flight.

"I feel sore against Harrington," he vouchsafed. "And hope that I will meet him in hell inside of six months. I also hold ill will against old Fort and against Reno, and hope that I will be able to meet them there inside of a year . . . I think I will have a supper ordered for them." Fort and Reno, no doubt, were gratified by the degree of magnanimity afforded them, as compared with Harrington. Still, his plight was not without its compensations: "One good thing about going to hell is that I'll have two good arms when I get there."

"I can't tell exactly, but I believe if there is a hell there will be a lot of people out of this territory that will go there . . . My belief is to treat everybody right. I can take the Bible and prove or disprove anything. From reading the Bible, if I profess any religion, it will be the Holiness religion."

When one of the journalists asked him whether "he had any definite ideas about the hereafter," he replied with an answer and a question: "No; have you?"

Having delivered himself of these thoughts on hell, life, and divinity, he spoke briefly of the Powers murder. At no point did he mention the killings at Camp Verde or the train robberies in Texas.

Both Pinard and Garcia, he admitted, had treated him well. In fact, he left everything he owned to Saturnino Pinard. A photographer took two pictures of him. He asked for copies to be sent to a kinswoman, Eva Prodman, who was living in Lodi, California, and to his nephew Lee Smith, the eldest son of John Wesley Smith and Tom's sister Elizabeth.

At some point after being sentenced he had recalled a jest made by Will Carver one day when the gang were hiding out in Hole-in-the-Wall, probably in the winter of 1898–99: "Tom, if the law ever captures and hangs you, come back and tell me how it feels. I might want to try it myself some day!" Now he attributed almost the same gallows jest to Bill Walters:

"Bronco Bill told me before leaving Santa Fe prison that if it did not hurt to let him know as he wanted to be hung, too," he confided, with another flash of spite towards the man whose great offense, in Ketchum's eyes, was not that he had killed, but that he had dodged the scaffold.

In one brief passage he spoke his own epitaph:

> My advice to the boys of the country is not to steal horses or sheep, but either rob a train or bank when you have got to be an outlaw, and every man who comes in your way, kill him; spare him no mercy, for he will show you none. This is the way I feel about it, and I think I feel right about it.

This, very likely, was the attitude that had carried him into outlawry and accompanied him ever since, rather than one that had emerged from the bitter fruit of reflection during the long months of captivity. By "boys of the country" he probably meant the young men of rural America, rather than the youth of the United States as a whole; but he would not have minded who heeded his counsels.

The press conference ended sometime between 11:30 and noon. Ketchum had a few parting words for Albert Thompson: "Well, good-bye old man. I shall be shaking hands with Sam in hell tonight."

John Guyer, a good amateur musician, had already sent for his violin. A harmonium and guitar accompaniment was provided by George Guyer and a man named Epimenio. Together, at Tom's request, they played "Just as the Sun Went Down." The outlaw listened in silence as they played the Amelia Waltzes and the "Mocking Bird" with variations. He was served fried chicken for dinner and attacked it with relish, avowing that he didn't "want to go to hell hungry because it's a long time till supper." John Guyer waited for him to finish before saying goodbye:

"Well, Tom, I've done all I could for you and unless you especially request it, I do not want to see the end. I feel that I cannot witness your execution."

They shook hands and Tom answered, "Yes, Guyer, you have done for me all any man could have done. I will not ask you to see me die." Then a parting glint of the old malignance: "Tell Harrington I'll meet him in hell soon."

Guyer must have been alone in his sensibility that day. As the hour approached, just about everyone else became affected by a craving to partake vicariously in the forthcoming event.

All the stores were closed. The saloons were open and trading briskly. Idle talk flowed with the liquor. Public sentiment, as far as it could be gauged from what was heard on the streets and in the saloon-bars, was not so much for Ketchum as against the authorities, the railroads, and other entrenched interests. It was generally held that the man should not die for the crime of which he had been convicted, but probably few of the prospective spectators felt too strongly about the issue. The atmosphere, as reconstructed by the newspaper reporters—none of them strangers to hyperbole—was that of a macabre and somewhat muted carnival.

At about twelve o'clock the first of the invited guests sauntered into the stockade. Several photographers were perched upon a platform above the wall of the jail.

One man set up his camera by a gap in the fence but the hole was covered and he had to seek a vantage point elsewhere. The one photographer allowed into the jail yard mounted his camera directly in front of the gallows. By one o'clock the yard was overrun with expectant onlookers, more than a hundred of them, including some latecomers without tickets. Almost the last to arrive was Dug Clark, a cowpuncher from one of the ranches over the Colorado line. He was known to a number of people in Clayton; but none of the assembled officers had ever seen him before and they watched him keenly as he walked over "to a spot where he could command a good view of the jail door and of the scaffold."

The scaffold stood close to the north wall of the jail. From the windows on the second floor of the courthouse, almost directly above the gallows, Cap Fort, Albert Thompson, and several others watched for the appearance of the principal actor and his entourage. Sheriff O.T. Clark, of Las Animas County, Colorado, was waiting on the platform. The crowd was tense and quiet. Those who were unable to get into the yard gathered in morbid little groups outside the stockade and on the sidewalks, or stayed in the saloons.[34]

The morning had been clear and bright. At one o'clock the sun lay shrouded and the wind skimmed the dusty prairie in sharp gusts from the south, scattering sand and grit amongst the crowd. The wind was buffeting the stockade at thirteen minutes past one when the door of the jail opened and Tom Ketchum emerged, flanked by Sheriff Garcia and Detective Chambers and followed by several deputies and jailors, together with the priest, whose patience evidently exceeded his powers of persuasion. In Garcia's pocket was a hood of black muslin.

Although Tom's left arm was chained to his side, he walked firmly to the corner of the jail. There, it seemed to those who were nearby, "a distinct and unmistakable look of recognition" passed between Ketchum and the cowpuncher. Without pausing, Ketchum turned the corner and, looking downwards, quickly ascended the thirteen steps. Only the limp from his old leg wound made his movements look a little unnatural.

Besides Ketchum himself, the party on the scaffold comprised Sheriffs Garcia and Clark, Detective Chambers, Trinidad C. de Baca, Deputy Sheriff Perfiris Casadus, and Father Dean. Reymundo Arguello, the jailor, was standing against the wall below, with John McCandless and Doctor J.C. Slack. McCandless was to lift the body and Arguello would cut the rope when Slack pronounced Ketchum dead.

Ketchum had declined to address the crowd. He stepped directly onto the trap and looked down.

"It's all right," he said, perhaps relieved because he could safely stand there. He told García that he wanted no pictures taken, but the photographers were already snapping away and nothing could or would be done to stop them. He had another request to make:

"Please dig my grave very deep."

Then, or so it was thought, "his eyes straightway sought the stalwart cowpuncher and rested upon him with a peculiar expression for fully ten seconds," the other man returning the look.

"Hurry up, boys," he said impatiently, as they were binding his legs, "Get this over with. Give me my black cap."

The noose was pulled down and adjusted, Tom helpfully moving his head from side to side as Garcia or an assistant tried to get the hood in place. The wind flapped at the hood and, to the annoyance of the prisoner, it had to be removed for a few moments. Then it was put back and pinned to Ketchum's coat; his view of the prairie beyond the stockade was shut out forever. The noose was drawn over his head and tightened, with the knot under the left ear.

Then, in a voice that carried clearly across the yard, he said: "Let 'er go."

"Not quite ready," returned the sheriff. One or two of the men on the platform touched Ketchum's hand: "Good-bye, Tom."

Garcia, grasping the hatchet, was standing by the control rope. Because the thought of the part he must play had made him nervous, he had fortified himself from the bottle and was now "a little tipsy."

"Are you ready?" he inquired, when he was.

"Ready. Let 'er go," Ketchum muttered through the hood.

Tom needed all his nerve. Garcia took a huge swing at the control rope and missed it, burying the blade deep into the boards.

Beneath the scaffold the crowd was laughing and smiling while Garcia struggled frantically to wrench the hatchet loose. A witness reported that it took the sheriff several minutes to tear it clear, and it must have seemed so; but actually the time was just seventeen or eighteen minutes past one when Garcia was ready to try again. His second blow smote cleanly through the twine, the trap flew back, and Ketchum plunged downward "with the speed of a meteor"—all the way to the ground.

The spectators in the yard saw the body jerk, then tumble towards the earth, to alight on its feet for an instant before it pitched forward, blood spurting forth from the black cap.

Unbeknown to his father the sheriff, young Fructuoso Garcia was watching through a large knothole in the fence; he later admitted to feeling faint. Someone behind the courthouse windows, seeing the rope leap up, went hysterical with rage. Thinking that the rope had broken and that Ketchum had survived the drop, the man yelled: "Hang him again! Hang him again!"

As Fructuoso Garcia remembered it, another voice, or perhaps the same one, bawled: "Get another rope for that son of a bitch. Let's hang him right this time."

The words of Reymundo Arguello tell most vividly just how Ketchum died, and appear to give the nay to at least one hardy tradition.

> . . . Then Sheriff Garcia cut the rope. We were under there waiting. It was awful down there. I was scared. Then the body came hurtling through the trap door. The body didn't stop and hang as I thought it would. I was supposed to cut the rope after McCandless lifted the body up. I reached down and turned the body over. Blood spurted out. It went all over my clothes. I looked away, toward the photographers. In the pictures my eyes stuck out of my head. The head [Ketchum's] didn't fall over one side and the body the other, as people say. The black hood was pinned to Black Jack's

shirt with *muy grande* pins, horse blanket pins, I guess. If those pins hadn't held the hood in place the head would have rolled away. It had been jerked off right where the hair comes around.

Yet photographs taken close up from two different angles show clearly the hood lying beside the headless trunk, in corroboration of accounts such as those in at least four Denver dailies and those that Guyer telegraphed to the *San Angelo Standard* and *Santa Fe Daily New Mexican*: "The fall severed his head from his body," he told the *Standard*, " . . . The head remaining in the black cap, rolled to one side, then the rope released it and it [the rope] flew high in the air."

John Guyer may not have seen the execution—he had told Ketchum that he would not watch—but his brother George may have been among the journalists who did. Those who reported the execution as eyewitnesses included E.A. Bingham, Albert Thompson, one of the Guyers, the anonymous correspondent for the *Rocky Mountain News*, and at least one other. All state that the head was torn clear of the body when the trap was sprung.

The fact could not have been otherwise. Everyone saw the rope whip back, and it was intact. The noose could not have jerked free without first pulling off both the head and the hood that enveloped it, despite the pins. Reymundo Arguello and his companions were the witnesses nearest to the event, and Arguello told what he believed he had seen; but the suddenness and proximity of the horror put him in the worst position to report accurately, not the best. He and the other men below the platform would have been tense, anyhow; but at least they believed they knew what to expect, and would have been mentally prepared for it. They were ready to face the spectacle of a man dangling at the end of a rope, and for the task of removing the noose when life was extinct. Their senses may not have been able to assimilate the ghastliness of the sight that met their eyes as the body plunged to the ground before them, splattering blood about. They must have been unhinged for a few seconds, or longer. Extreme shock impinging upon extreme tension can induce effects kindred to hallucination.

The camera did not lie, nor were head and hood detached after the fall of the body but before the photography. The head was later sewn back onto the trunk by Dr. Slack or E.J. Sipe, deputy coroner of Las Animas County, Colorado, and the hood replaced. Lastly, the "*muy grande* pins" were reattached. They would hold firm now.

Officers looked about them for the cowpuncher, whom they had taken to be one of Ketchum's gang, but he was gone. Days later they learned his name. There is no explanation for the apparent understanding between Ketchum and Dug Clark. They may have known each other; or the entire scene could have been a delusion projected in overstressed minds.

The crowd had dispersed quickly. Not all of them returned to the saloons. One, a lawyer, arrived home with his shoes all bloody. His wife made him wash them in a trough before she permitted him to enter the house by the back door. His nine year old daughter, who in adult life became Clara Toombs Harvey, also brought back first-hand knowledge of the hanging. She had been out riding, and happened to be passing the stockade when the trap dropped.[35]

Ketchum would not be getting a family funeral. All that was reported was that Berry had "declined" to take charge of the remains. Elzy Lay's friend Elton Cunningham seems to have been more closely informed than the press. According to him, Berry was asked by telegram what he wanted done with his brother's body. His answer took the form of a question: "Can't you eat it?"[36]

Cunningham's story is credible. After his arrest, when he was thought likely to die from the effects of Harrington's buckshot, Tom had insisted that Berry should not be allowed to take charge of his body. Then, and at every opportunity thereafter, he had spoken of his oldest brother with a rancor barely distinguishable from hatred. Whatever the rights and wrongs that had lain between them, and wherever their origin, the antipathy was mutual. Tom had charged Berry with having fattened himself on the stealings of his younger brothers. Now Berry proposed that a meal should be made of Tom's remains. Union County, New Mexico, could not have asked for a clearer invitation to bury the deceased outlaw at public expense. Berry may also have heard about, and called to mind, Tom's quip that the prison authorities were fattening him up so that they could eat him.

At half-past two the plain white coffin was lifted onto a spring wagon and trundled out of the courthouse yard. Fort and Thompson followed this informal hearse to a hill some way north of town, arriving just as the gravedigger was about to lay the coffin to earth. The casket was opened at Fort's behest and the men stared down at the remains, admiring the dexterous handiwork that had restored the head to the body. Then the lid was replaced, the coffin lowered, and the soil shoveled into the hollow. There was no mourner, no minister, and no monument for Tom Ketchum. There was, however, a spectator: "a woman of the lower stratum" drawn merely by curiosity, sniffed the *News*.[37]

Billy Reno was interviewed directly after the execution, and several times again in the next two or three days. He let it be known at length and in detail that he disbelieved almost everything Ketchum had said. Such was his faith in Ketchum's penchant for mendacity that he scoffed even at those of Tom's statements that happened to be truthful.[38]

Many theories were tendered to explain Ketchum's death by decapitation. It was intended that way to ensure a mercifully instantaneous death; it was intended that way to ensure that Ketchum should not create a precedent by surviving the drop— these were the premises of two of the numerous conjectures.

A more tenable hypothesis was argued thus: on the Thursday night the officials decided to test the rope, or the mechanism, by attaching a two hundred pound sandbag to the noose and dropping it through the trap. The rehearsal went off beautifully, but the participants neglected to remove the sack. In the morning the rope was as rigid as wire.[39]

Some maintained that Tom had hurled himself forward when the trap dropped, so as to be sure of avoiding death by suffocation. This would have been a rare feat, more especially because his legs were bound.[40]

The explanation most commonly accepted was the obvious one: between them Fort, Garcia, and Chambers had hopelessly botched the job. Several newspapermen reported that the drop was one of seven feet. If this were true, it would seem that, after Fort and Chambers had set the drop at five feet and six (or nine) inches, someone must have meddled with the apparatus yet again. So, either the Chief of Police at Kansas City, who had recommended a seven-foot drop, did not know what he was talking about, or something must have been amiss with the rope. An unidentified newspaperman who telegraphed the story to the *San Francisco Chronicle* implied as much: he reported that "the noose was made so it slipped easily . . . the weight of the body, with the easy running noose, caused the rope to cut the head clean off." Clearly, he meant that the rope had been treated. In his *Early History of Clayton*, though not in his later book *They Were Open Range Days*, Albert Thompson was more specific. According to him, the substance used was soap, and the man who applied it was Sheriff Garcia. Thompson said that Garcia, "mortally afraid" that some of Ketchum's erstwhile running-mates would attempt a rescue, "decided to soap the rope to make sure that it slipped properly." Sam Howe, Reno's former Chief in the Denver Police Department, who had seen many an execution, told the *Post* that, for a man of Ketchum's size, the "regulation drop" was no more than three feet; "that distance nearly always breaks the neck."

"But," he concluded, with dry pragmatism, "The execution was successful, wasn't it?"[41]

Yet another theory was floated in the *Post* by two of the best known detectives in the West, David J. Cook and James McPartland, and amplified by Howe in the *Denver Times* several days later. All three declared that the rope was too slender to withstand the force of the drop. William Reno had given Howe what he believed to be a piece of the execution rope. The rope was only three-eighths of an inch thick, too thin to support a man of Ketchum's weight for a gallows drop of three feet, much less five. In Howe's opinion, which amounted to the same as that of Cook and McPartland, "the five-eighths-inch rope [was] the best, though some were "considerably wider."

Howe's assertion was referred to Sheriff Garcia, who refuted it in the columns of the same paper. Since he, Garcia, still had the entire rope, Reno could not have given part of it to Howe. The explanation may be that what Reno obtained was a section of the smaller control rope, which Garcia had cut to release the trap. Either Reno mistook this for the hanging rope, or Howe misunderstood Reno.[42]

In the end, the chief blame rested with Fort, since he was the governor's emissary, sent out to make sure that there were no mistakes. Garcia, however, was the main target of the critics. One newspaperman went so far as to say that the sheriff planned to present the rope to his daughter as a keepsake. Garcia's response to the sneers and accusations was ineffable:

> Tom Ketchum's head being severed from his body was caused by his being a very heavy man. Nothing out of the ordinary happened. No bungling whatever. Everything worked nicely and in perfect order. Salome Garcia, Sheriff.[43]

"Not a strong argument," is the just comment of Arthur Soule, "since weight is the primary factor to consider when hanging a man."[44]

Ketchum's hometown newspaper had reported most of his crimes but had refrained from connecting his name or those of his partners with any of them, until Sam's arrest rendered further discretion pointless. After that, he made regular appearances on its front page, the last of them on the day following his execution, which it called "The Most Horrible . . . Known in Modern Times." Thereafter it published not a word about him.[45]

Neither editor Murphy nor ex-Sheriff Shield rose to the invitation of "Woodyard Chipling" to tell all they knew about the criminal operations of Tom and his partners. Doubtless there were people in Tom Green County who would not have cared for public reminders of their dealings with the Ketchum gang. That did not mean there was not a great deal of talk, some of it serious, some facetious. John Loomis repeats deadpan a story that was "spread in the San Angelo country," which held that Berry "bribed the officers to hang a waxen image instead of Tom," who escaped and was still living. Berry's reaction to that one would be worth knowing about.[46] As it was, Berry had nothing whatever to say; or if he had, it stayed off the record.

Long afterwards Gerome Shield did furnish Albert Thompson with an account of some of what he knew. Thompson intended to make full use of Shield's material, but published only a little of it.[47]

Although the means may have been questionable—"cruel and unusual," indeed, though not intentionally so—the result of Salome Garcia's ministrations was beyond all quibble: the worst desperado and killer in the Southwest was no more.

Yet, albeit in a grotesque way, those who had prophesied against the event were proved right. Gerome Shield had offered to bet boxes of cigars against it, many other officers had predicted against it, and Tom Ketchum himself had repeatedly made his promise against it.

They never hanged him.

22

EMPTY SADDLES AND
LONELY GRAVES

It was far more a sign of social and economic transition than an argument for the deterrent effect of capital punishment that there was no really serious outbreak of outlawry in New Mexico after the execution of Tom Ketchum. An unforeseen result of the Territory's anti-train robbery legislation was that its enforcement acted as a deterrent against its future use. Public unease at the harshness of the statute was magnified into disgust by the Clayton carnival of blood and bungle. "Such acts perpetrated in the name of justice are sad commentaries upon Twentieth Century Civilization," lamented the *Raton Range*. "The more we observe the ways of men and dogs, the more respect we have for dogs."

Whatever else he had done at other times, Ketchum was sent to the gibbet merely—to quote some of his own words—for "stopping an engine." He had behaved recklessly and viciously in doing it, but decapitation was a grossly disproportionate penalty. The case, and the attendant publicity, was of no service to New Mexico's campaign for Statehood.

Since, however, the territorial government did not budge, the United States Congress took the decision away from it. An act of July 1, 1902, removed from the Territorial courts the jurisdiction in all cases of assault upon a railroad locomotive, car, passenger, or railroad or federal employee, in any United States Territory. The act placed these cases within the exclusive jurisdiction of the United States. Maximum punishment upon conviction was twenty years' imprisonment, or a fine of $5,000, or both, at the court's discretion.

Two who thought that New Mexico was still the land of opportunity for the would-be outlaw were Henry Hawkins, sometimes known as Bill Hawkins or Bill Daniels, and a fellow who called himself Ed McCorkle.

In the last days of 1901 Hawkins emerged as the leader of the "Mesa Hawks," a bunch of third rate bad actors whose operations attracted much publicity for a few weeks in the winter of '01–02. Their brief corporate career ended in March 1902 with the capture of four of them.[1] Frank Potter and Frank Isbell vanished altogether. Hawkins made a fleeting reappearance on Wednesday afternoon, December 10, 1902,

316 THE DEADLIEST OUTLAWS

when he and McCorkle stuck up the Sierra County Bank at Hillsboro. They rode out of town with several thousand dollars, vanished somewhere beyond the Black Range, and were never caught.[2]

In his reminiscences, brought to the printed page by his son, Ben W., the rancher Ben E. Kemp named one of the bandits as Big Ed Kilpatrick. Kemp's identification was assured, but matter-of-fact, showing no wish to make a particular point out of it. He could only have been referring to the larger of the two bandits, the one who had been using the name McCorkle; he did not know the other robber, but the detailed descriptions issued after the holdup depict Hawkins as much the smaller of the two.[3] In March of that year, Ed and George Kilpatrick had been tried and cleared at Ballinger, Texas, of the Thornton murder. In mid-February, 1903, Ed was on a visit to Sanderson, Texas, from Sheffield, where he appears to have been living at the time. He could easily have been in New Mexico for much of the interval between the two dates.[4] After February of 1903 nothing more was heard of him from anywhere.

The Congressional act of July 1, 1902, like the Territorial act of 1887 which it had superseded, produced unexpected consequences at the first challenge. On July 30, 1904, a Rock Island train was held up and looted at Logan, northeast of Tucumcari. Four likely-looking suspects were soon in the jug. One, whose connection with the others was nebulous, if not nil, was killed by a jail guard. The other three, to the surprise of most, were convicted; but only in November 1906, at their third trial. They were tried before William J. Mills, who had officiated at Elzy Lay's trial. Since the Logan case belonged to the federal jurisdiction, Mills (like Frank W. Parker in the Steins Pass trial) was able to exploit an old and discreditable law whereby no stenographic record of the testimony heard in a federal case would be kept unless the judge ruled otherwise.

Mills did not rule otherwise. Nonetheless, it is certain that the three defendants did not receive a fair trial, certain that they were convicted against the evidence, and next to certain that they were innocent. Grounds exist for suspicion that the escapade was carried through by a trio headed by the elusive Hawkins. But the main point of interest is that, had the defendants been tried under the provisions of the territorial law, with its mandatory death penalty, the jury, confronted with such insecure evidence, would probably not have had the nerve to convict at any stage and would most likely have thrown the case out at its first hearing. A jury weak enough, or a courts system dishonest enough, to send defendants to prison against the evidence, is unlikely to send them all the way to the gallows against the evidence. Obviously, there might well have been no Logan case at all if train robbery had been a capital offense in 1904; but that is another, and irrelevant, consideration.[5]

Elsewhere in the West trains would still be held up, or occasionally a bank would be raided, in the style which had been reproduced so often in the last decade or so of the old century. A few gangs of outlaws arose at different times in the first years of the twentieth century, but almost always their first major crime was also their last. As for the men who had taken to outlawry when the Ketchums were still riding, they carried on until they were caught or killed, unless they read the omens in time to leave the United States for another continent.

If Ed Kilpatrick was one of the Hillsboro robbers, he could not have been discouraged by George's mishap in Sonora in 1901, or by Ben's undoing in the fall of the same year. Nor, in the longer run, were George and Ben; both would shake off defeat and invite more of the same by returning to crime.

The plans discussed in Texas between Carver, Logan, and the Kilpatricks had included dispersal as well as robbery. Carver's unwillingness to follow Cassidy and Longabaugh to South America may have been related less to the ties of parochial sentiment than to his mainly unrealized investment in the Folsom robbery of 1899. He would surely have known where to find the buried loot, for word of its whereabouts penetrated prison walls to reach Elzy Lay. Whether or not Carver intended to resume his erratic "courtship" of Laura Bullion, he would not have skipped the country without first collecting his share of the cached money. But he was killed before he could develop whatever schemes he had been carrying in his head. His demise caused Harvey Logan and Ben Kilpatrick to revise their own plans. It was also a turn in the road for Laura Bullion.

Soon after Carver's death Bill Chaney visited her in Arizona. Chaney, in words reported as hers, "sort of felt sorry" for Laura.[6] She was not happy in Cochise County with her Uncle Jim Lambert and Aunt Lucinda. Her sister Fannie ("a charming young lady," was the verdict of the *San Angelo Standard*), had married R.M. Hanks, assistant postmaster of San Angelo, at Sherwood on Tuesday, October 23, 1900, after a long courtship, and now lived with him at San Angelo. Since then there had been little contact between the two girls.[7] Her grandparents Elliott and Serena Byler, who had done all they could for her, were ageing; all their daughters had made their own homes elsewhere, and she could hardly impose on them.

Chaney's role was that of pander for Ben Kilpatrick, but she did not mind. She accompanied him to Fort Worth, where, as she primly expressed it, he "introduced" her to Ben.[8] In reality, she would have known him already, perhaps for ten years or longer.

Kilpatrick went to Montana; Logan, most likely, had already gone when Laura and Ben met in Fort Worth. By unknown means, and in an unknown place, the two men met Orlando Camillo Hanks, a thirty-seven year old Texan just released from the Montana State Penitentiary at Deer Lodge. Logan and Kilpatrick needed a third pair of hands, and would not have depended on chance to provide it.

"Charley" Hanks had left his home in DeWitt County, Texas, to evade a charge of criminal assault. He was not close kin to the Hanks who had married Laura's sister. After leaving Texas, he worked in New Mexico and the northern cattle ranges for a few years, tried his hand at rustling, then reached for bigger things. On the night of August 25, 1893, he and three others stopped an eastbound train on the Northern Pacific near Greycliff, Montana, and robbed the express car and all the passengers. One month later the gang were trapped on the Blackfoot Reservation and three of them were killed, along with a posseman named Schubert. Camillo Hanks, last of the Greycliff robbers, was tried for the murder of Schubert and convicted on January 10, 1894, under the name of Charles Jones. His term of imprisonment at Deer Lodge expired on April 30, 1901.[9] Almost at once he got in touch or was put in touch with

Logan and Kilpatrick. It is likely that he had a past acquaintance with Logan, or friends of Logan, and that the meeting was prearranged.

Laura may have traveled with Ben for part of the way; if she spoke the truth a few months later when she told of working as a dance hall girl in Wyoming, she could not have been referring to any other period in her life.[10] By September she was with the Bylers again. But not for long; they were about to sell up and move to Arizona,[11] and she expected to rejoin Ben when he came back from Montana. His return may already have been overdue by then.

Barely two months after Hanks's release, he, Logan, and Kilpatrick held up west-bound train No. 3 on the Great Northern Railway at Exeter Switch, near Wagner, Montana, a mile or two west of the scene of a robbery by the Sundance Kid more than eight years earlier.

The holdup, one of the most celebrated of the era, began at twenty minutes past two on Wednesday afternoon, July 3. When it was over, the three bandits were in possession of currency worth $40,500 less than its face value. A nominal forty thousand dollars of the booty comprised banknotes enroute from the Treasury to the Montana National Bank at Helena, tens and twenties, which lacked the signatures of the president or vice president and cashier of the bank, A.L. Smith and Thomas C. Kirts. A further $500 was in incomplete notes for another bank. For the rest, there were nine complete Helena banknotes that had been sent to Washington as specimens; eight gold watches; three hundred and sixty money order blanks of the Great Northern express company; and some sealed packages whose contents were never described but could have included legitimate currency. The shortness of the interval before the robbers set about adding false signatures to the imperfect bills suggests that the unflawed ones could not have amounted to much. Similarly, the fact that the signatures were in the wrong names—J.W. Smith and Allan Hill—indicates that the bandits would not have hung onto the nine sample notes, or even bothered to memorize the signatures on them.

The posses were out for nearly a week without sighting the robbers. Only one of the three, Harvey Logan, was correctly identified. Another, Kilpatrick, was mistaken for Harry Longabaugh, the Sundance Kid. Later the Pinkertons were to name Cassidy as one of the gang. Before the case was solved Hanks was misidentified at different times as Logan and Cassidy, while Logan, as well as Kilpatrick, was confused with Longabaugh. Cassidy and Longabaugh had left North America nearly five months previously.[12]

Three weeks after the robbery James Winters, who in 1896 had killed Johnny Logan, a brother of Harvey, was ambushed on his ranch near Landusky.[13] Although the absence of direct evidence left ample room for doubt, the common belief was that Harvey Logan had ridden back on his tracks to dispose of his old grudge against Winters.

On or just before 7 September, Logan, Kilpatrick, and Hanks turned up in Fort Worth, scene of much of the gang's foolishness the previous autumn. At about the same time, Delia Moore, as "Annie Rogers," left Fannie Porter's house in San Antonio and traveled to Fort Worth, coincidentally—or perhaps just ostensibly—to see a sick relative. After a week or so she went to Dallas and thence to the small town of Mena, in southwest Arkansas. On or about September 11 or 12, Logan called on Fannie. She was not surprised to see him; he arrived just ahead of a telegram addressed to her but intended for him. It was from Annie. He left for Mena that night. They took a southward train through Texarkana and alighted at Shreveport, Louisiana, for a stay of several days.

On September 18, they moved on to Memphis, where they remained for the rest of the month, living and being entertained in bawdy houses, exchanging several hundred dollars' worth of stolen currency, and spending several hundred dollars more. Charley Hanks was with them, though it is not clear whether he had been traveling with Annie all along, or followed afterwards, with Logan or alone.[14]

Early October found the three of them in Nashville. There, on the 14th, Rogers was arrested as she tried to exchange more than $500 in Wagner ten dollar bills. Logan got out of town; Hanks continued to board at the cheap lodging house he had booked into four weeks previously. On the 26th of the same month two policemen attempted to capture Charley, but he lunged free, fled down the street, and, after a madcap chase across the town, got away on a stolen horse.[15]

Early in September, Elliott Byler had gone to Tolpa, Coleman County, to say goodbye to one of his married daughters. About a week later he sold his property to John Wesley Smith, brother in law of Berry, Sam, and Tom Ketchum. He and Serena were about to join the Lamberts near Douglas, Arizona. "One by one the old land marks are passing away," lamented "Pickwick," the current purveyor of "Knickerbocker Knicknacks." The Smiths arrived from San Saba County to take possession, and on September 16 the Bylers, "accompanied by Miss Laura Bullion," took the train from San Angelo to Big Springs and thence to Arizona. Another Knickerbocker correspondent, "Old Nick and Bridget," remarked that the old couple would be sadly missed, but had nothing to say about their granddaughter.[16]

Laura could have done little more than see them through to their destination before turning back for Fort Worth, where Kilpatrick was waiting. They lived for about three weeks in Hite's (or Hyde's) Flats as Mr. and Mrs. Cunningham, thereby pilfering the good name of several families well known to them in Tom Green and adjoining counties. In October they spent a week or two at the health and tourist resort of Hot Springs, Arkansas, where they posed for a souvenir snapshot while seated in a buggy. During the last week of the month they went to Memphis, which Harvey Logan and his consort had visited a month earlier. Finally, on the morning of November 1, they registered at the Leclede Hotel in St. Louis, Missouri, as Mr. and Mrs. J.W. Rose, this time filching the name of a well-established Concho County ranchman.[17]

Here they passed the hours and the days filling in the signature blanks on the stolen bills. They also did a little shopping. Unluckily for them, a cashier noticed the Montana bills just after a merchant had paid them into the bank. At once the hunt was on for the merchant's customer. On Tuesday evening, November 5, perhaps because Bullion was unwell, Kilpatrick went out alone. That night he was tricked and trapped as he caroused in a brothel.

Worried at his failure to reappear, Laura was on the streets early next day. The bad news was in the morning papers. She swiftly made ready to go, but the police were at the hotel desk ahead of her. A valise containing more than $7,000 in Montana notes was among the items that changed hands in the next few moments.[18]

At police headquarters Kilpatrick was saying nothing. Bullion, while seeming to break down under the grilling of Chief of Detectives Bill Desmond, lied merrily all the way down the garden path. The officers thought they had Harry Longabaugh, and Laura encouraged them in their false belief. The "stubborn silence," which Ben maintained "like a burro," nourished an official ignorance that was further complicated by a rival theory that the prisoner was Harvey Logan. There were no physical similarities whatever in the appearance of the two outlaws, other than the one that Kilpatrick had created by treating his hair and mustache with black dye.

But Kilpatrick, with mustache, did look a little more like the Longabaugh of the Fort Worth photo than the clean-shaven Kilpatrick shown sitting beside him. The prisoners kept the police on the wrong track. Even during her second interrogation, when she gave Desmond a mainly true account of her own background, the woman did not undeceive the police about the identity of her companion. On November 8 two of the city's principal dailies, the *Globe-Democrat* and the *Post-Dispatch*, printed a set of observations and opinions that revealed the limitations of Desmond's knowledge and perspicacity. He suspected Bullion of participation in the actual holdup: "I wouldn't think helping to hold up a train was too much for her. She is cool, shows absolutely no fear . . . I have known boys to be accomplices in such undertakings and she would look like a boy when dressed in male attire. She has a masculine face."[19]

A reporter from the third of St. Louis's great newspapers, the *Republic*, scoffed at the notion. The reporter had this to say of "the frail wisp of diminutive femininity" who perched on a vast highbacked chair opposite the burly and grizzled Chief of Detectives: "By no stretch of imagination could anyone looking at Laura Bullion conceive of her participating in any wild night ride after a daring raid, or engaging a posse to cover the retreat . . . after the accepted manner of bandit queens in well regulated novels. On the contrary, Laura would be much more at home on the steering gear of an Arkansas plow, or piloting a potato digger, or frying flapjacks for the men folks."

That writer may have veered too far in the opposite direction. Bullion was far less of an untutored yokel than the man (or woman) from the *Republic* portrayed her as or made her sound like. If Laura you-alled or reckoned or bad-grammared more than she customarily did back home in Knickerbocker, nervousness or journalistic licence might equally have done it for her; alternatively, and more probably, she was acting a part.

Still, she was neither a gun-toter nor a train robber. She may have been telling the truth when she said she could hardly shoot or ride. This last was settled by Chief of Police Matthew Kiely, who interviewed Laura after Desmond had finished with her. After listening to her account of where she had been and what she had been doing in the spring and summer of 1901, Kiely said he was satisfied that she had taken no active role in the train robbery.[20]

On November 14, Sheriff Howze of Concho County telephoned Jake Allen, his counterpart in Tom Green County, that he and more than a score of his fellow-citizens recognized Ben Kilpatrick from a newspaper photograph of the "Longabaugh" being held at St. Louis.[21] The following day the prisoner finally admitted as much to Desmond. By then he had been confidently greeted as "Longabaugh" by a man falsely claiming to be the district attorney who had prosecuted the real Longabaugh at Sundance, Wyoming, "in 1889." Even after that, he was authoritatively pronounced to have been one of the Winnemucca robbers by George Nixon, whose bank Longabaugh, Cassidy, and Carver had so memorably emptied of funds scarcely more than a year before Kilpatrick's arrest. The make-believe D.A. and the banker had spoken eloquently, though unwittingly, for the uncertainties of eyewitness testimony.[22]

Kilpatrick and Bullion faced a seventeen-count federal indictment alleging currency offenses. Their attorney—Charles P. Johnson, who in 1883 had successfully defended Frank James for murder committed during a train robbery—could have mounted an interesting defense. He would have argued that, since the names appended to the incomplete bills were fictitious, the defendants could not have been guilty of forgery. Another point to emerge was that the notes were a liability upon the U.S. government from the moment they left the treasury; it made no difference how they were signed, or whether or not they were signed at all. But Ben could not afford the luxury of the law's delays that must precede a trial. He knew that the governor of Montana was about to have him extradited for train robbery, a capital offense in that state. When the case was called in federal court on December 12, he at once changed his plea to one of guilty and was sentenced to fifteen years' imprisonment. Laura did the same next day and received a five-year term.[23]

Harvey Logan had returned to Tennessee, his family's home State. In Knoxville he began to unload more of the Wagner banknotes. A pool room brawl led to a gunfight in which the outlaw was wounded by a policeman. Less than two days later, on December 15, the fugitive, bleeding, bedraggled, and exhausted, was found shivering in the snow near Jefferson City, thirty miles east of Knoxville.[24]

Charley Hanks kept almost constantly on the move. Reputedly he first went to Calaveras County, California, after his narrow escape from the officers in Nashville. He may also have stayed awhile with kinsfolk in New Mexico before showing his face in Texas. He then visited his mother, Mrs. Laura Cox, in Abilene, and sold some of the stolen currency to a brother, Wyatt Hanks, in Callahan County. He again left Texas, but returned in the spring of 1902, from the east. On April 15, he set out for San Antonio to enjoy a little barroom fun. Night became morning; Charley became demonstrative and troublesome. At about 3 a.m. he was shot dead by one of three officers who had been summoned to suppress his rowdy behavior. His mother confirmed his identity; brother Wyatt was one of three men subsequently arrested for receiving stolen money.[25]

The great Wagner express robbery case was closed, but others were in the making. Remnants of the old gangs, reinforced by some newcomers to the profession, were still operating from the traditional hideouts in Wyoming and Utah. Four of them chose the unconventional hour of ten o'clock in the morning of July 14, 1902, to waylay a Denver and Rio Grande train crammed with tourists admiring the scenic grandeur of the wild Saguache country. They halted the train at the foot of a steep mountain pass two miles east of Chester, near Sargents, Colorado, dynamited the two express safes, and rounded off the entertainment by inviting the sightseers to form a line beside the coaches and to hand over their money and valuables. Siringo identifies Bill Cruzan as one of the gang, though over-dependence on an unchecked memory makes him move the robbery to a site near Grand Junction.[26]

Recollections of the days when Harry Longabaugh and Harvey Logan were prowling about Carbon County, Montana, with ambitions on the bank at Red Lodge, were stirred on Monday, December 1, 1902, by the robbery of the bank at Bridger, twenty miles northeast of Red Lodge. Jesse Linsley, a convicted horse thief, and a character known as "Lonesome Joe," forced Cashier J.F. Trumbo to hand over $3,748 and rode hard for their holdout, Pat Murphy's ranch on Fishtail Creek, near the Wyoming line. In an effort to throw off the sheriff's posse, they almost completed a circular course one hundred miles in diameter. The trick failed. On Thursday, December 4, the posse rode up to Murphy's cabin and arrested him, the two robbers, and a fourth man.[27] Cashier Trumbo's reunion with Jess and Joe was held in the county jail at Red Lodge, but now it was they who were in the cage.[28]

Montana's law providing for capital punishment in train robbery cases was no more successful in preventing holdups than similar laws in New Mexico, Arizona, and several southern states. The turn of the Burlington & Quincy's train no. 6, which used the Northern Pacific tracks, came at Homestake, east of Butte, in the first minutes of February 12, 1903. A red lantern halted the train on a curve, the locomotive crew was overcome and the passengers intimidated, the money cars pulled ahead, and the express company's through safe blasted open in what had become the familiar fashion.[29]

None of this could compare with the coolness, cleverness, and audacity of Harvey Logan's escape from the jail at Knoxville, on June 27, 1903. Logan rode out of town on the sheriff's horse, lost his pursuers in the mountains of North Carolina, and then vanished for months on end. There was no shortage of rumors as to his whereabouts, but the officers had to wait until the following spring for a real lead. Logan was then reported to be with the unreformed George Kilpatrick and others in the neighborhood of Ozona, Texas. This sighting went the way of the others: the men left while the officers were still discussing what they should do.[30]

George Kilpatrick, the presumed Logan, and a third man—Dan Sheffield, most likely—made their next recorded appearance in Colorado. Late on Tuesday night, June 7, 1904, the Denver and Rio Grande Western's train no. 5, westbound, was held up and robbed at Parachute, between Grand Junction and Glenwood Springs. The robbers employed the standard technique. So, in announcing its loss as only $10, did the Globe Express Company. The company's statement was contradicted by various witnesses. Some said that each robber carried a sackful of loot away from the wrecked express car; others who saw the fleeing trio next day claimed that all three horses were heavily burdened. Possibly the loot, though bulky, included only a small sum of cash (though not as little as $10).[31]

It was said at the time, and has been repeated many times since, that if the bandits had waited for the oncoming Colorado Midland express to pass over the same tracks, they would have cashed in for $150,000. Perhaps so; but upon what—or whose—authority was this assertion voiced? Only a few officials of the express company would have known how much money was aboard the train that was not robbed, and none of them is credited as the source of the rumor.[32]

A report that a consignment of $12,000 was overlooked[33] in the robbery that did take place is less implausible; if a package marked for that sum was lying among the debris, someone else would have seen it if the bandits did not. Whether the report was true or not, its existence tends to support the suspicion that the express car was not "running light" on the night of June 7. Denver was not just a terminal city for three lines of railroad; it was an important trans-shipment point. Nothing lodged in the through safe at Denver could be removed (except by safe-crackers) until the train reached Salt Lake City. Packages would have been placed in as well as taken out of the way safe at intermediate points. Logan and his chums may not have blundered as badly as has been supposed in choosing the Rio Grande express.

The bandits' failing was in the inadequacy of their escape plan. They had not taken sufficient pains to acquaint themselves with terrain to which two of them may have been utter strangers and which not even Logan knew well. Worse; although they seem to have had an accomplice with spare horses, they failed to make contact with him. The horses they stole would not have been as good as those they missed.

Hard pressed by the posses, they were forced to abandon their original mounts and, allegedly, to cache the plunder. They stole more horses but made poor progress. On Thursday evening they were trapped in a rocky draw near Glenwood Springs. Two of them managed to scramble to safety; the third, too badly wounded to go with them, killed himself.[34]

In the pocket of the dead outlaw was found a letter from Ola Kilpatrick, addressed to Tap Duncan. When it was learned that Tap was alive and in Texas, the suggestion was briefly heard that the body was that of Jim York, another former resident of San Saba County. Four or five photographs were taken of the body, as was the standard practice, but the corpse remained on ice until the end of the month, waiting for a name. Finally, Lowell Spence, the Pinkerton operative who had trailed Harvey Logan for the whole of 1901, positively identified Logan from the posthumous photographs. Others disagreed. Exhumation of the body settled nothing.[35]

On November 1, two men held up the bank at Cody, Wyoming, and murdered the cashier, Frank Middaugh. For several days afterwards the papers were full of stories that Logan was one of the robbers. Two local thugs whose ambitions far exceeded their capabilities were the next suspects, but were soon shown to be innocent of this particular crime. Others were arrested, or accused, but none charged, and the crime remained unsolved.[36]

Nothing happened that would still the rumors about Kid Curry. He had got out of the mountains disguised as a prospector, it was said, and away to South America.

But, like much else that is romantic, the tale was wrong from stem to root. Harvey Logan was dead. Comparison of the photos of the deceased Parachute robber with those taken of Harvey Logan in his lifetime allow no room for doubt that Logan was indeed the wounded train robber who committed suicide rather than submit to recapture.

William Ellsworth Lay, alias William H. McGinnis, was a model prisoner and a "trusty" at Santa Fe; although a long-term prisoner, he did not incur a single demerit. Possibly his fellow inmates thought of him less warmly. Sometimes he would accompany Superintendent Bursum on buggy-rides around the city.

Twice he helped the authorities to subdue mutinous convicts. On the second occasion, according to the reminiscences of Miguel Otero, he was actually asked to ride out of the prison gates to summon the territorial militia. Bursum seems to confirm this in a letter to Butch Cassidy's first biographer, Charles Kelly.[37] But their recollections are at odds with those of Walter Hovey, who was still serving time for the Steins affair. Hovey wrote that it was he who made the ride into town to spread the alarm, and he was telling the truth. His version is upheld by the *Santa Fe Daily New Mexican*, which describes the incident on the evening of its occurrence, February 22, 1904, with a warm tribute to Hovey's "bravery and loyalty."[38]

Otero and his friend Bursum were either deceived by faulty memory, or guided by a need for Lay to be shown in the best possible light to justify the magnanimity accorded him. This does not mean that Lay may not have played a part of some other sort in the quelling of the riot. Otero, who had been sympathetic towards Lay ever since the outlaw's trial, was still governor. When Bursum, another sympathizer, spoke up for Lay, the governor was ready to listen. If the whole story is in the correspondence, Bursum was actuated solely by concern for the state of the prisoner's health; Lay was suffering from inflammatory rheumatism. Otero at once commuted the sentence of life imprisonment to one of ten years; with remission for good conduct, the outlaw would be free on January 10, 1906, after six years and three months in the penitentiary.

Lay's letter of thanks expressed his gratitude in profuse terms. Otero's response was to do more; he offered Lay a place in the convict gang that had been set to work on the construction of a "scenic road." The consideration would be a further twenty-six days remission of his revised sentence ("extra leave allowed"). Road-building, apparently, was the very thing for the relief of inflammatory rheumatism. Lay rose to the scenic challenge and was duly released on December 15, 1905.

William French's statement that the former bandit went to Alma after being let out of prison is confirmed by Jack Stockbridge, who had sheltered Sam Ketchum, Carver, Lay, and Weaver directly after the train robbery and was now living near Alma, and H.A. Hoover, a resident of Alma in 1905. Hoover noted in his diary that he had seen "McGinnis" in town on Christmas Day, and later talked with Lewis (sometimes referred to as Louis) Jones, with whom Lay boarded for about eighteen months.[39]

The Joneses, originally from Texas, had lived in western New Mexico since 1885. Early in 1897, two of the Black Jack Christian gang had held up their store in Upper

San Francisco Plaza (familiarly known as Frisco, but now Reserve, New Mexico) and robbed it of $180 and a big sack of peanuts.[40] They had moved to Alma and opened a large general store there a year or so before Lay was discharged from the penitentiary. Apparently he had never met either of them until he approached them for accommodation shortly after his arrival in 1905 but, as Lewis observed, he seemed to trust them. Perhaps he really did know them; he could have met them in 1899, during his time on the WS. If so, he, and they, judged it wise to pretend otherwise. If not, he undoubtedly knew of them, and they of him.

Probably, too, all of them would have heard about the errand that had brought Berry Ketchum from southwest Texas to the vicinity of Bull Springs, on the Sonora side of the Border below Bisbee and Douglas, Arizona. As much of the story as is known comes from Reed Dean, a local cowman and a friend of the Jones brothers.

"Berry come out . . . [and] camped there at the old Cottonwood camp where Jones Canyon and Cottonwood came together and he went up the ridge, up the old Hell Roarin' Trail that went out on top to Bull Springs and right around the rim of the mountain and come down the Jones Canyon ridge and he stayed there about two weeks makin' that round and finally all at once he was gone . . . That's all we know now . . . only that he acted as though he knew it was hid there and I believe it is yet." Dean concluded that Berry had known roughly where the money was hidden, but not its exact location. He did not know whether Ketchum had been acting on directions from Lay.[41] The likelihood is that he was not. If Lay had wanted Berry to dig up the money, he would have made sure he knew enough to find it.

When Dean heard about Berry's expedition, he remembered the encounter a year or two earlier between his roundup crew and the rider beside the juniper tree in the mountains near Bull Springs. He had no idea of this man's identity, except that if, as he now presumed, the stranger had been burying the stolen money, he could not have been Berry Ketchum.

Dean believed that Berry's mission had been a failure. He was more right than he ever knew. What the Jones brothers never told him was that Elzy Lay had assumed executive control of his own financial affairs.

Lewis Jones told Hoover that Lay wrote a number of letters in the hope of tracing his sometime partners. When the last of his letters was returned to him, marked "unclaimed," like all the others, he announced that he was going off to dig up a box of money which was "buried under the root of a juniper tree on the Mexican border;" all being well, he would be back within two weeks. Thirteen days after his departure he rode up to the store with fifty-eight thousand dollars "wrapped in a slicker."[42]

Corroboration comes from Stockbridge, who saw a great deal of Lay during that period: "When he come down to Alma that time I saw him a good many different times there. He stayed there for three or four months around waitin' to try to get contact with some of his fellers after he went and got that money and brought it back."[43]

William French is also in agreement. He surmised that Lay had headed for Alma after his discharge simply to collect his share of the Folsom loot.[44]

Hoover opined that the $58,000 "was not from the Folsom train holdup" but "more than likely . . . from some other train robbery." He maintained that the messenger at

Folsom saved all the money in his care; argued that the gang could not have traveled the four hundred miles from Folsom to the Mexican border before Lay was caught; and asserted that Lay himself was supposed to have remarked that the express company had been tipped off, "for they got nothing" out of the holdup.[45]

French, Dean, and Stockbridge were right, and Hoover wrong. The fatuous tale that has an express messenger hiding money to which he had no access obtained far more credence than it deserved. French himself tells of how and why he formed the conclusion that the booty had been cached in Colfax County and that Butch Cassidy had set out to recover it. Obviously the rancher never knew for sure that the money had been brought south, and he did not venture to guess who might have brought it. But then he did not look for the explanation behind the sudden affluence of Bruce Weaver. As for Hoover's third point, it is hardly surprising that Lay would not want it thought that he proposed to collect and live off the proceeds of the Folsom or any other robbery. In any case, when express company officials expected an attempt at robbery they did not hold back their scheduled shipments. They hired guards.

There is, finally, the question of how Lay was able to learn where the money was to be found.

Charlie Siringo, the "cowboy detective," who for years moved unsuspected among the friends and confederates of the outlaws, claims that he was asked to "smuggle" into the Santa Fe penitentiary the key to a code through which Lay would be able to keep in touch with his comrades outside. He visited Lay, whom he described as "a pleasant fellow but a hard-looking 'mug,'" in the summer of 1902. The cipher, if Siringo is to be believed, was childishly simple: a confidential message would be conveyed by every fourth word of an ordinary note.[46] Siringo does not say whether or not he informed the penitentiary officials of this but probably he did not. Had he done so, Lay might not have retained the exemplary prison record that enabled him to earn maximum remission after the commutation of his sentence, while Siringo himself would have been unmasked as soon as Lay's contacts realized that their code was no secret to the authorities. By using this or a similar device, any of those few who knew where the Folsom loot had been secreted could have passed the word to Lay. The message could have been sent by an intimate of the deceased Carver or Weaver, or of the departed Cassidy.

Thus, Elzy Lay's impeccable conduct while he was in prison should not be wholly ascribed to his mild temperament and persuasive manner; he had plenty to look forward to.

Lay stayed on with the Jones brothers for several months after his trip to the border. During all this time the money, covered by gunny sacks, reposed in a corner of the small stockroom next to the main store building. Finally Lay, and the money, went to Wyoming on horseback. He did not go alone; riding with him was the greatly wanted George Musgrave, of the old High Five or Black Jack gang, and a man known as Jack Dempsey. Musgrave's current alias was "Bob Cameron." His first meeting with Lay may have been in Cochise County in the fall of 1898, or near Alma early in 1899.[47]

The three men ended up in Baggs, Wyoming. On the way there Elzy learned that his wife, the former Maude Davis, had divorced him. Eighteen months after his arrival at Baggs he eloped with Mary Calvert and married her at Thermopolis on March 27, 1909. Musgrave, now calling himself George Murray, had married Mary's best friend Jeanette Magor on November 2 of the previous year. George's pal Dempsey was redirected to the Wyoming State Penitentiary in October, 1908; he had been stealing horses almost from the day he got into Baggs.[48]

Lay remained a wanderer almost to the end of his life, but was esteemed and trusted wherever he went. His reformation owed much to his strength of character; but that fifty-eight thousand dollars must have helped, too. He wrote to tell the Jones brothers that he had invested $40,000 in a cattle ranch. In the years that followed he knew many vicissitudes. For a time he was an oil-field scout. He opened saloons at various places, and was once employed as a payroll guard. At the time of his death, on November 10, 1934, he was superintendent of a waterworks in Los Angeles.[49]

Berry Ketchum, unlike his brothers (and discounting Sam's brief marital interlude), was a family man. His marriage to Barshie Shields produced three daughters: Nora Blake, Alice Doty, and Barsha Green.[50] His wife's persistent ill-health and the ignominy of his brothers' downfall did not dampen his random and roguish sense of fun. In March, 1900, this diehard Democrat announced that he had acquired the new Republican campaign badge and would "present it to Joe Tweedy," Knickerbocker's principal G.O.P. workhorse. The device, said the Democratic paper, was "very [*sic*] unique and cannot fail to attract attention wherever it is displayed. Doc [S.L.S] Smith says it is the best thing ever invented."[51] Unfortunately the paper provided no illustration or precise description.

While his brothers rose and fell in the profession of robbery at arms, Berry steadily advanced in his career as a stockman. He took out ten-year leases on 3840 acres in Schleicher County (three sections on April 25, 1896, three on December 10, 1897) and 2240 in Tom Green County (a half section on September 14, 1899, and three sections on April 25, 1900). His success was not unchecked; in 1899, for example, a man named Carl Weiss sued him and won. The cause of the action is unknown.[52]

Though his home ranch was only three miles from Knickerbocker, he seems always to have found Sherwood more congenial, and made himself noticed there during the Fourth of July celebrations of 1901. Otherwise his time and attention were still divided between his Dove Creek and Independence Creek properties. In the high summer of 1901 he again moved his family to the Pecos County ranch, in the hope that a change of air would be of benefit to his wife's health. She got no better, and had to be sent to a specialist in Coleman shortly after returning to Tom Green County.[53]

At the end of September the two older girls started school at Knickerbocker, but Berry was not set on a permanent move to Independence Creek. By mid-October Barshie was well enough to accompany him there on another visit. In January, 1902, Berry and his crew drove a herd of cattle to their new range by the Pecos. Dave Atkins's brother Walter, who often worked for Berry, went to live on the Pecos in February. By late March, Roxie Baze, a relative of Tom Hardin's widow, and a former schoolmate of the Bullion sisters, was staying on Berry's ranch, probably to keep house during Barshie's illness and until the Ketchums were ready to occupy it full-time. In April, Berry leased out the Dove Creek pasture to Gus Thomas and John

Wesley Smith. Late in August "Senorita," the latest in a succession of Knickerbocker correspondents for the *San Angelo Standard*, noted that, while Berry was about to return to the ranch, taking "[s]everal of our boys" with him, "Mrs. Ketchum and children will remain here."[54]

H.A. Holmes, in the 1960s a Justice of the Peace in Pecos County, remembered him well:

> He was a tall heavy set man with a full beard. He was rough spoken. I have seen him many times. That was before the days of the automobile and he drove a pair of mules to a small buck board.[55]

Louis Montgomery, a native of San Saba County who spent his last years in nearby Brady, had a story which nicely illustrates Berry's reputation for toughness:

> When I was rodeoing they had a mean bucking horse that came off the Ketchum ranch and they called him Berry Ketchum because he was so tough.[56]

But if Berry Ketchum was known as a hard man, he was always a straight one in his dealings with his neighbors. Jim Harkey, a nephew of Dee Harkey, was in his employ for twenty years and told Mr. Holmes that "he never worked for a better man than Old Man Berry Ketchum."[57]

Berry died on March 31, 1914, at San Angelo, a rich man and a respected one. His daughter Nora married Gus Thomas Duncan, one of the sons of Bige Duncan and Berry's sister Nancy. Not for nothing had Gus Thomas and Bige Duncan been called "the inseparables;" Bige had even taken his friend's name for his third son.[58]

The Kilpatricks moved southwest soon after Berry Ketchum, making their new home in Crockett County, not far from Ozona. In September 1902, Boone Kilpatrick married Truda Sheffield, daughter of the man after whom the town was named. Truda's brother, Dan Sheffield, was about to turn outlaw; Boone's brother Felix, whom Mr Holmes characterized as "fully as mean as Ben, if not meaner," seemed to be similarly inclined. Ed Kilpatrick was rarely and then only briefly present. He was never brought to book for the Hillsboro bank robbery but was killed accidentally a few years later. George Kilpatrick left home in the spring of 1904 to take part in the Parachute train robbery. He never returned, though in March, 1905, he wrote at least once to a sister from Marlin, near Waco, Texas. Dan, who was believed to have gone north with him, did return to his home turf.[59]

In 1910 Felix Kilpatrick married Myrtle McDonald, a cousin of Dan and Truda. Felix owned a small ranch at Hondo, New Mexico, and was killed there in June 1913 by Sheffield, with Myrtle in evident complicity. Since the three of them had been living in New Mexico under assumed names, they must have been hiding from someone or running from something. Whatever the background of the case and the circumstances of the killing, Sheffield was acquitted and no charges were brought against cousin Myrtle.[60]

Laura Bullion's time was served in the Missouri State Penitentiary at Jefferson City.[61] After the expiry of her sentence on September 19, 1905, she followed Ben, who had been transferred to the new U.S. Penitentiary at Atlanta, Georgia. She took a room in an Atlanta boarding house under the name of Mrs. Freda Arnold, but was not permitted to visit Ben.[62]

Felix Kilpatrick had outlived his brother Ben by a year. Ben served nine and a half years as a federal prisoner—three years and three months in the Ohio State Penitentiary, Columbus, and the balance at Atlanta. He kept in touch with his family and with former associates, especially Laura after her release.

Ben Kilpatrick served hard time; he was an unruly and rebellious prisoner, and the regime was strict, with harsh punishments for petty infractions. Every letter he wrote was read and copied by the prison authorities before mailing, and so was every letter addressed to him before he was allowed to see it. Even letters between members of Ben's family were halted in transit and read by detectives: an illegal practice, but one sanctioned by the history of government everywhere. Some of his letters were not sent out at all, and some of those addressed to him were withheld.

Sometimes a letter would be smuggled into him, or out of the prison on his behalf. Detection incurred punishment, or the suspension of "privileges." He worried about the whereabouts of George, who was not heard from again after the spring of 1905, but apparently made no reference to Ed. He seemed well posted on recent train robberies and was anxious to learn whether George had been involved in any of them. Much of this correspondence survived and has been seen and quoted by James Horan (not always faithfully), by Dale Schoenberger, and particularly by Arthur Soule.[63]

Kilpatrick's attitude began to change about two years after his transfer to Atlanta. He had fought the system to a stalemate, but even if he kept up the fight the system would come out on top in the end by making him serve the full fifteen years. If he toed the line he could get out in nine and a half. He affected humility and contrition and worked conscientiously. The officials, thinking they had crushed him, treated him more humanely. The deputy warden noted that he was the best workman on the stonecutting gang.[64]

Ben's apparent reformation coincided with, and may have been influenced by, the induction into the stonecutting team of H.O. Beck, whose many aliases included Ole Hobek and J.B. Flood. Beck's background, visible personality, and criminal record were utterly different from Kilpatrick's. He was from Minnesota, of Norwegian or German parentage, and ten years older than Ben. Although he, like Ben, had been sentenced for currency offenses, he had manufactured counterfeit money, as distinct from adding detail to legal tender stolen at pistol point.[65]

But he was widely traveled and mentally dedicated to crime. Unknown to the authorities, he nourished ambitions to make his way as a train robber. He may already have enjoyed some success in that field; at any rate, the direction of his later career shows that he must have been familiar with an incident near Memphis, Tennessee, on April 22, 1901. Just before midnight on that date, the westbound express of the Choctaw, Oklahoma and Gulf Railroad had been boarded by six robbers at a point known as Bridge Junction, or Iron Mountain Crossing, on the Arkansas side of the Mississippi River. The detached express car was hauled half a mile up the line, the safe blown, and at least $3,000 extracted before the bandits scampered down the embankment and vanished in the cane brakes near Hulbert, Arkansas. Whether or not Ole Beck had any direct knowledge of this crime, he would be present each time when it was twice re-enacted.[66]

Whatever the prison rules dictated, Ben and Beck must have talked long and earnestly. The transformation in Ben's attitude and conduct was recognized in August, 1909, by the restoration of his "privileges;" he had regained hope of qualifying for early release. His friend Beck, who had made a point of being a model prisoner, was freed on the 27th of the same month. The two stayed in contact while Ben kept up his campaign to secure remission or a pardon. In the spring of 1911, Beck visited San Angelo, calling himself Howard Benson. He traveled to Christoval by car and to Sheffield by buggy, then slipped away without paying the livery stable's bill. He had gone to talk to Kilpatrick's friends and certain of his kin.[67]

Kilpatrick's program succeeded. The remission he had lost for misconduct was restored, and on June 11 he was discharged from the penitentiary. He was now thirty-seven; Laura, who was now living in Birmingham, Alabama, was thirty-five. He intended to go straight to Birmingham for a reunion with her, but the authorities if Concho County, Texas, had their own ideas. He was immediately rearrested and taken to Paint Rock to face trial for the murder of Oliver Thornton ten years earlier. Laura Bullion is said to have followed him to Texas and to have stayed there at least until March, 1912, living mostly with Ma Kilpatrick or Boone.

Ben was allowed bail at a habeas corpus hearing three weeks later and stayed in Boone's sheep ranch until the case was ready for trial. Apparently, however, the evidence was too weak to justify further prosecution, for on September 4 the proceedings were abandoned. Bige Duncan, Berry Ketchum, Tom Palmer, and William C. Jones would have testified for the defendant; so, more surprisingly, would Lee Aldwell, J.L. Davis, and Elijah Briant of Sonora.[68]

Once clear of the Thornton affair, he went back to Boone's ranch, though not for long. While there, he found or created the means to replace his cheap prison-release clothing with "a fifty-dollar Stetson, tailor-made suits, and a pair of handmade boots." On several occasions he called on Marvin Hunter, editor of the weekly paper at Ozona. Hunter was fooled:

> He was a genteel, likeable fellow, who looked you square in the eye, and had nothing about him that would ever lead one to believe that he had trodden the outlaw's trail. One day in my office Kilpatrick told me he had "gone dead wrong," to use his own language, and that he realized the folly of it all. He said he had fully reformed in prison, and it was his intention to lease some land near Sheffield, get a flock of sheep, and convince the world that he could be a good citizen instead of an outlaw. And I sincerely believe that was his intention; but, alas, for good intentions![69]

Ben's friend Ole Beck, meanwhile, was working as a ticket agent for a firm in Memphis. Early on Wednesday, November 1, 1911, the westbound train was again held up and robbed between Bridge Junction and Hulbert, Arkansas. On this occasion the bandits' main source of revenue was the U.S. mail car. About the only other difference between this and the robbery at the same place ten years before was in the lettering on the cars and locomotive: the Choctaw, Oklahoma and Gulf had been taken over by the Rock Island system in 1902.[70]

Three months later, on Tuesday, February 6, 1912, the same train was robbed in the same way at almost the same spot. As in November, the registered mail may have yielded better returns than the express safe. The February robbers, like the November gang, took the obvious line of retreat: by boat across the river to Memphis, with subsequent dispersal. Soule, the first writer to turn the spotlight on these incidents and to link them to the last phase of Ben Kilpatrick's career, has found that Beck resigned from the Memphis ticket agency on the day before the robbery and that Kilpatrick was in Texarkana three days after it.[71] Texarkana was an easy mainline rail journey from Memphis, via Little Rock.

Soule cites a string of robberies in Oklahoma and Texas during the first two months of 1912 which he thinks could have been committed by Kilpatrick and Beck. One was the "robbery in a sandstorm" on February 15, when two men robbed the bank at Seminole, Texas, near the southeastern corner of New Mexico, and rode away into immediate and utter oblivion.[72] If Kilpatrick and Beck were in the recent Hulbert robbery, they could hardly have had the time to return to southwest Texas and carry out the Seminole robbery. Ben did not even leave Texarkana until the 12th, and then his immediate destination was Fort Worth for a meeting with Beck. The pair might have been guilty of one or two of the other robberies; so, alternatively, might friends or kinsfolk of Ben who had confederated themselves with the two ex-convicts. But no connection has been established; the plain fact is that these were unsolved crimes. On the other hand, Kilpatrick's ambition to bring train robbery back to southwest Texas is documented in blood.

Ben was seen again in Sheffield before the end of February; he even had another talk with Marvin Hunter. Two weeks after that last interview with Hunter, Ben Kilpatrick rode up to the Berry Ketchum ranch with another man, claimed by Jim Harkey to have been his (Harkey's) first cousin, Nick Grider. Jim shod two of Berry's horses and gave them to Ben and his companion, Nick. This was the preface to one of the last train holdups ever attempted in the tradition of that fading figure, the hardriding badman of the Old West.[73]

Grider? He may have been the man who was with Ben at the Ketchum ranch, and he may have been part of the conspiracy to rob the train. But he was not Kilpatrick's partner in the actual stickup. That role belonged to Beck, whose experience in such work may have been the equal of Ben's.

Kilpatrick and Beck rode down through Terrell County to the Galveston, Harrisburg and San Antonio tracks, less than forty miles south of the Berry Ketchum ranch. By Tuesday, March 12, 1912, their preparations were complete. They headed for Dryden, halfway between Sanderson, the county seat, and Lozier, scene of Tom

Ketchum's first train robbery.[74] That evening the two young sons of the pumpman at Dryden saw the men beneath the water tower. The two lads took them for hobos, but thought them "pretty nice folks" all the same.[75]

In the first minutes of the 13th, Kilpatrick and Beck stepped into the locomotive cab of the westbound express, now known as No. 9, shortly after it pulled out of Dryden. All went according to the old-established pattern as the train was stopped and the mail and express cars were run up the track a mile from the detached passenger coaches. Beck kept the crew under guard while Kilpatrick went through the two cars. Everything proceeded to plan in the mail car, where Kilpatrick made the clerk gather up the registered pouches and toss them outside for later collection. But in the express car the messenger, David Andrew Trousdale, cleverly distracted Ben's attention, then broke his neck and smashed his brains out with three blows of an ice mallet. Trousdale now took the dead man's semi-automatic seven-shot .401 carbine and waited for the second bandit. Growing impatient after what was said to have been an hour's wait, the messenger fired a couple of shots. As Beck started to climb into the car Trousdale shot him through the head.

The bodies were taken on to Sanderson and photographed. Kilpatrick was identified almost at once. A week passed before Beck could be named as the second man. Those who recognized him as Howard Benson may never have realized that Benson was merely an alias for Beck. Others named Ben's partner as Ed Welch, an old acquaintance with family connections in San Angelo who was a fugitive from a murder charge.

Forty years later, on his eightieth birthday, Jim Harkey told H.A. Holmes what he knew of the holdup and named Nick Grider as Ben's companion, saying that "it had been so long since it happened that he knew there would never be anything done about it." Holmes unhesitatingly believed his friend, and, in 1970, the author unhesitatingly believed Holmes.[76] But it is now certain that the man buried alongside Ben Kilpatrick near the scene of their downfall was Beck, not Grider. Possibly, however, it was Grider who had charge of the two pack horses and two saddle horses found near the spot where the train had been stopped. Tracks found nearby showed that a fifth horse had been ridden away. If Grider was the third horseman, he may have extended precipitate flight into permanent departure. Harkey might have believed that his cousin was killed at Dryden, or affected to do so to explain Nick's disappearance.

Soule uncovered evidence that Felix Kilpatrick, his wife Myrtle, and Dan Sheffield were co-conspirators in the holdup plans. His suspicion that Laura Bullion was also mixed up in the scheme is supported by the belief of Laura's cousin, Bernice Byler Haag, but there is no real evidence against her.[77] The most that can be said is that if, as would appear, she was living with the Kilpatricks at the time, Ben is likely to have told her what he was going to do.

None of this is necessarily inconsistent with the findings of another researcher, C.F. Eckhardt, whose informants believed that the confederate who escaped was Alfred "Big Boy" Shelton, husband of Ben's sister Ola. Eckhardt also learned that all four of the abandoned horses bore Berry Ketchum's brand.[78]

Laura Bullion was now homeless and destitute. Her estrangement from her own family was complete; her sister, Fannie Bullion Hanks, would have nothing to do with her and, during her time at Jefferson City, Laura had vowed not to see her or her husband ever again: "[T]hey need not be uneasy for I never intend they shall ever hear a thing about me after I leave here. I would not go back there, not for anything in the world." But she had kept in touch with her cousin Bernice, and was able to approach her father, Laura's Uncle Jake Byler. He gave her enough money to leave Texas and start life anew. She lived in various Southern cities as Freda Lincoln, describing herself as a widow and working as a seamstress. She died in Memphis, Tennessee, on December 2, 1961, aged eighty-five.[79]

Even as late as 1916 outlawry of the old horseback kind was not extinct in the United States, but it was kept alive principally by bank robbers in Oklahoma and the adjacent fringes of its neighbor states.[80] Staidness and outward respectablility were steadily overtaking the last of the wilder communities further West. Late in the first decade of the twentieth century there were still desolate and almost trackless stretches of open space and the isolated, mountainous localities where an outlaw could find allies as well as cover; but the rapid development of the telephone network greatly lessened the chances of escape to such places after a robbery. As the *San Angelo Standard* observed after the death of Will Carver, "The magic of the telephone and telegraph is rapidly making this country unsafe for such gentry, and their ultimate extinction is only a question of a few short years."[81] By "this country" the San Angelo editor meant southwest Texas, but his words could be applied with almost equal force to many of the areas of the American West that were more thinly settled—much of Wyoming and Montana, for example, as well as the bulk of Arizona and New Mexico.

Progress, as it is called, was beginning to manifest itself in other ways, too. The "horseless carriage" of the early nineties was ridiculed by all but a handful of novelty- seekers. In 1899 the "locomobile" commanded small bands of enthusiasts in the bigger cities but remained something of a freak to the ordinary public, who regarded its advocates as dangerous eccentrics. In 1902 the automobile was in vogue with the wealthy, and in 1904 its manufacturers were peddling the notion that every household was entitled to own one.[82] Several more years elapsed before the new mode of transport even started to make any real impression on the rural West, and by then most of the bad old ways were dying out side by side with most of the good old ways.

But the 180-degree revolution is rare in any sphere of history, and this era of rapid change in the American West was not among the exceptions. The bad new ways that came on the heels of the old were but the same *mores* in fresh guise. Banditry was not extinguished; like most human institutions, it survived by adaptation. Practitioners who could not reform or adapt had a straight choice: emigrate or die.

Many of the "wanted men" of the American West followed the example of Butch Cassidy and the Sundance Kid by going to one or other of the South American republics. Here there could be peaceful oblivion for those who sought it. For those who did not care to settle down, there was immense scope for banditry.

Cassidy and Longabaugh, with the woman known as Ethel (or "Etta"), lived quietly on a ranch at Cholila in southwest Argentina for nearly five years before going back to the old ways of robbing and dodging. It can fairly be said that they were forced into a criminal future by their criminal past. The turning point was the robbery by two Americans of the Banco de Londres y Tarapaca in Rio Gallegos, at the southern end of Patagonia, on February 14, 1905, when the equivalent of nearly $24,000 was taken. The robbers had introduced themselves locally as Brady and Linden; further north, their names were Bob Hood and Grice (or Gray, or Day). They were also known to Cassidy and Longabaugh. Cholila and Rio Gallegos are seven hundred miles apart; but the intervening spaces were sparsely populated, and Cassidy and Longabaugh were suddenly conspicuous—and vulnerable. Even if they were not suspected of robbing the bank, they were sure to become the focus of official interest. Butch, Sundance, and Ethel dared not stay. After making arrangements to sell up, they crossed the mountains into Chile.[83]

At the end of June, Longabaugh took Ethel to San Francisco. He came back without her (though she may have returned later) and, on Tuesday, December 19, 1905, he, Cassidy, and two other Americans robbed the Banco de la Nacion, in Mercedes (originally Villa Mercedes de San Luis), 400 miles west of Buenos Aires and 250 east of the frontier with Chile. The stickup and getaway were as well managed as they had been for the Winnemucca raid five years earlier. Cassidy, Longabaugh, and their companions escaped into Chile with 14,000 pesos—worth almost as many U.S. dollars.[84]

Cassidy and Longabaugh lived in Chile for a short time, then worked as stock handlers in Bolivia for two years. The final phase of their outlawry began and ended in that country in 1908. On May 25 and again on August 19 two American bandits robbed the paymaster of a railroad construction company at Eucaliptus station. Cassidy and Longabaugh may have been responsible for at least one of these holdups. Beyond all reasonable doubt they were the pair who robbed another paymaster at Huaca Huañusca on November 4 and were shot dead in San Vicente two days later.[85]

Ethel's later history remains a mystery. The Rio Gallegos robbers have yet to be unmasked. Apparently both were natives or former residents of Texas, but no clues have been unearthed as to their real names. That is doubly unfortunate, because there are suggestions that "Brady" may have been related to Ethel.[86] He may also have been "Bob Evans," an outlaw who was killed on December 9, 1911.[87]

William French says Tom Capehart accompanied Cassidy to South America, and that he died alongside Cassidy; but here, French confuses Capehart with Longabaugh, perhaps knowingly. Henry Brock heard that Capehart was in Peru, with Cassidy and others. Whatever the truth in that, Brock, or his informant, may in their minds have arrived at Peru by way of Patagonia. Leonard Alverson knew that Capehart had turned outlaw but never learned what finally became of him.[88]

We have already shown that Capehart and Longabaugh were two different men. The idea that Longabaugh was using the name Tom Capehart along the Arizona-New Mexico border can be dismissed out of hand. It would be ludicrous to suppose that Longabaugh (or anyone else) would have borrowed Capehart's name in country where the real Capehart was well known to one and all, lawmen not least. Perhaps

Capehart really did go to South America; he might even have been one of the uniden-tified individuals who rode into outlawry down there. But the only certainty about Tom Capehart's later life is that nothing is certain.

As far as is known, Dave Atkins was alone among Western outlaws in looking for safety in the midst of the war in South Africa, though a number of men from the San Angelo area had visited the region in 1900, and Charley Perry, the sheriff-embezzler from New Mexico, was already there. Hostilities between the British Empire and the "Boer republics" of Transvaal and Orange Free State had opened in October, 1899 and produced a salutary series of defeats for the imperial forces. But by the following October the struggle seemed to be all but over: in May the Orange Free State had been annexed to the Crown and reconstituted (with dubious legality) as Orange River Colony, and the annexation of the South African Republic, or Transvaal, fol-lowed in October.[89]

Events soon showed that the end had not even begun; the war now entered its final, but protracted stage. It became a Guerrilla War. This was something that the professional stupidity of many senior British officers and the institutional stupidity of the War Office prevented the imperial forces from being any good at. Whitehall and the top brass had only recently absorbed the lesson that uniforms of khaki were better suited than jackets of scarlet for an army campaigning on the veldt or in the uplands. Slowly and reluctantly, it was surrendering its diehard prejudice against mounting large forces of infantry, and setting aside its doubts about the value of irregular forces raised in the colony of Cape of Good Hope.

Such attitudes changed because circumstances invalidated them. In this instance, the choice had been to adapt, or lose. Hitherto, the British military estab-lishment had tolerated only token units of mounted infantry; the Boers, in contrast, had little else, apart from some good artillery. Now the imperial forces had to grap-ple with terms set by the enemy.

Adaptation was not easily achieved. Most of the English infantrymen were townees who had to be taught to ride. The British Isles could not produce enough horses. Worst of all, the military command had no idea of how to make use of the horses at its disposal, and in fact disposed of most of them by sheer wastage.

The War Office met the first problem by making wider use of the forces best able to counter guerrilla warfare. These were the regiments, often containing only a few hundred men, which had been raised in South Africa. Many who enlisted in these outfits, including some of their officers, were born in South Africa or had set-tled there; some had left England, Scotland, or Ireland specifically to join a unit of this kind; some were "Cape Dutch" adherents of the imperial cause; and some, finally, were from Canada, Australasia, or the United States. They were inherently likely to be of much more use in anti-guerrilla sorties than on the parade ground. Only a few of their most effective officers, notably the unconventionally brilliant Mike Rimington and Henry Scobell, were Englishmen whose careers were, or had been, in the Regular Army.

The imperial government overcame its second difficulty by placing larger over-seas orders for saddle horses and transport mules. Almost from the beginning of the war, these animals had been bought in Texas by British Army agents and shipped out from New Orleans. Usually, their handlers came home on the next available ship. Some accepted invitations to enlist and fight against the Boer. Now, with animals being exported in greater numbers, more vessels crossing the ocean to deliver them, and the keenness of the British to recruit good horsemen who would fight, a fugitive possessing the right qualifications could ensure a free ticket from jeopardy to obscurity without much risk of detection.

The Kaffrarian Rifles were officially "embodied" on October 18, 1899, as Cape Colony Volunteers. The "K.R.," were conceived as mounted infantry but soon reorganized on the same lines as cavalry, with Squadrons replacing Companies. In October, 1900, when the war appeared to be over, the force was stood down. Early in November it was disbanded. When the alarm was sounded again in January, many of the old sweats returned, but plenty of vacancies remained open.[90] Dave Atkins was among those who responded. There can be little doubt that the idea came to him, directly or indirectly, from Bob Harris, whose adventures with the Kaffrarian Rifles had been highly publicized in San Angelo long before his homecoming in September.[91]

The oath to which Atkins and all other recruits were required to subscribe included the phrase "South African Mounted Irregular Rifles," but the free-and-easy regimen implied in that description was no prohibition against the longueurs of foot drill and the petty tyranny of deliberately mindless fatigues. Atkins, as Trooper Drake, had to endure this tedious nonsense, like the rest of the men, and did not forget it.[92] The four hundred or so in the ranks of the Kaffrarian Rifles were of the right material for guerrilla warfare, but some of the officers seconded to them from regular units of the British army may not have been. Still, despite the worst that War Office maladministration could do, the K.R. and many other of the Irregular outfits did excellent work throughout the war.

Dave Atkins, as Trooper Drake, was allocated to F Squadron, under Captain H.V.F. Shine. The K.R. men were part of a column commanded by Colonel C.P. Crewe, of the Border Horse, which in March of 1901 had just returned from a successful campaign in the Orange Free State.[93]

Cape Colony was not only at war; it was in the war. In December 1900, Commandant P.H. Kritzinger's guerrillas had invaded the Cape Midlands from the Orange Free State to seek recruits from the Cape Dutch settlers, attack the railway and telegraph systems, and generally make mischief. They were still in the colony in April, 1901, when the K.R. were sent up the Eastern Railway to Stormberg Junction, in the mountains 150 miles northwest of East London. But Drake and his fellow recruits did not even receive their horses until they were sent to Rosmead Junction, a hundred miles west of Stormberg, after two more weeks of field training and drill. Towards the end of April, he at last found action. His patrol was fired upon from the hills but succeeded in getting by far the best of the ensuing engagement.[94]

Shortly afterwards, the K.R. rushed to Murraysburg, a small town in the wool-growing and horse-breeding country a hundred miles southwest of Rosmead Junction, but off the railway. They were too late; the Boers had already sacked the place. Next, they were ordered to the Orange Free State to deal with guerrillas who had wrecked and plundered a train near Heuningneskloof, south of Bloemfontein. After a two-day battle the Boers fled, abandoning 140 horses; more than they had taken from the train.[95]

Towards the end of that month Trooper Drake and his comrades spent three days in the lightly garrisoned village of Jamestown, a short distance northeast of Stormberg Junction. On June 2, soon after their departure, Kritzinger's commando overwhelmed the defenders. One fully-informed commentator observed, with pitiless terseness, that the defense by the Town Guard "was the reverse of heroic."[96]

The campaign against sporadic guerrilla and insurgent activities dragged wearily on, with only occasional flashes of excitement. At the apex of the imperial military pyramid, General Sir Herbert (later Earl) Kitchener put his faith in large-scale strategy founded upon attritional principles. For the Cape irregulars, the ebb and flow of counter-guerrilla operations would go on until the larger issue was resolved.[97]

In July 8 an official inventory recorded the strength of the Kaffrarian Rifles as 301 men, 374 horses, and two machine guns. They were still part of Crewe's column.[98]

In August the K.R. were in Graaf Reinet, an important rail center near the Valley of Desolation, in the Great Karoo. Drake was there, or in nearby Murraysburg, when the news came through on September 5 that Scobell's column of Lancers, Yeomen, and Cape Mounted Rifles surprised Hans Lötter's insurgent commando between Graaf Reinet and Cradock. Lötter, as a Cape insurgent, was deemed to be a rebel and a traitor. A month later he was put before a firing squad. Murderer and train robber Atkins, alias Trooper Drake, thought the punishment unjust. Others in the field took the same view. So did many in England.[99]

Towards the end of September, the regiment was posted to Burghersdorp, which occupied a site in the mountains thirty miles southwest of Aliwal North, an important rail center on the Orange River. Burghersdorp itself was a sizable town and the oldest in the eastern Cape. "That was," Dave Atkins told his niece, perhaps humorously, "about the strongest guarded town in South Africa."[100]

On December 14, they headed for Jamestown, fifty miles to the east. Next day, during a surprise attack on a laager near Jamestown, the regimental adjutant, Captain J.M. Fairweather suffered his third wound of the campaign. The ferocity of the exchanges is described in graphic detail in Atkins's reminiscences.[101] Drake himself experienced a close call on December 28. He was pitched from his horse while in the midst of the guerrillas his detachment had ambushed near a farmhouse. He secured a remount by shooting a guerrilla out of his saddle, only for the horse to fall beneath him as he raced towards what should have been safety. Sadly for the horse, but fortunately for the rider, the British trooper who had fired at Drake had underaimed. Drake had already been presumed killed, and thus was mistaken for a charging Boer.

After the engagement, the dead horse was inspected by Major (later Colonel) R.H. Price. He recognized it as one he had recently left at the farmhouse because it was sick.[102]

Price took over the command of the Kaffrarian Rifles early in January and led them back to Burgersdorp. They would be quartered there for the rest of the war.

Quartered there, but not confined there; they spent much of the next three to four months elsewhere.

Shortly after its return to Burgersdorp, the regiment was sent forward to help mop up Boer guerrillas in the Free State, or intercept those filtering south across the Orange River. Atkins, alias Drake, saw plenty of action. As he said of one lively encounter, "[The Boers] must have knew that I was with the English that morning the way the bullets was singing about my head . . . If people treated me the way the Boers treated the English I would never go around them any more. But the English would hang around [the Boers] like a 17 year old boy after a feisty 19 year old girl."[103]

The success of Kitchener's bludgeoning but systematic policy of building block-houses and wire fences, burning crops and farms, and concentrating Boers and pro-Boer blacks in prison camps, had convinced all but a minority of Boer "bitter enders" that the fight could not go on.

These "Bitter Enders," wanted to prolong the war by moving it to the sparsely-peopled western Cape. Their desperate campaign would fail, but one of its inciden-tal effects was to make life interesting for Dave Atkins during the rest of the South African summer. He and his comrades were dispatched from Aliwal North to catch one band of irreconcilables; it was a long, hard chase, during which Atkins/Drake may have learned how it felt to be a posseman.

From Aliwal North, the regiment was sent southwest to Aberdeen ("very pretty location for a town," said Atkins). From then onwards, aside from a lot of travel and a couple of sharp little battles with the last of the bitter-enders, regimental maneu-vers took the form of bureaucratic in-fighting with rival sections of the British impe-rial effort.[104] The war was at last coming to a close. Corporal Drake, as he had become, had to prepare some sort of a future for Dave Atkins, criminal.

In February or March, 1902, he had addressed a note to the *San Angelo Standard*. A month or more must have elapsed before his advertisement was received, but on April 19 it appeared in print:

Notice

Any one wishing to know the whereabouts of J.W. Droke will reach him by address-ing as follows:

J.W. Droke, 31293 Kaffrarian Rifles, F. Squadron, Burghersdorf, South Africa, Cape Colony or Elsewhere.[105]

"Burghersdorf" is a former variant spelling for Burghersdorp which Atkins later repeated in his reminiscences. Whether "Droke" was the result of a misreading by the San Angelo editor, or whether Atkins himself substituted it for the far commoner Drake as a simple device to attract less comment, is impossible to say. The latter seems the likelier. San Angelo did have at least one family of Drokes, but Drakes were plentiful in Tom Green and nearby counties. Anyone in the Knickerbocker area expecting to hear from Atkins, in the name of Drake, would not have been misled by the alteration. Nor would a letter addressed to 31293 J.W. Droke have failed to reach

31293 J.W. Drake. The sense of the message is obvious. Atkins judged that the time had come for him to take soundings from someone who knew about his assumed identity and flight to South Africa.

On May 31, 1902, the Treaty of Vereeniging brought the war to its conclusion. As always, military demobilization could not be accomplished overnight. The Kaffrarian Rifles were not officially pronounced non-effective until June 30, and their discharge order was not issued until July 29.[106] Only then did Dave Atkins step out of his role as Tommy Atkins.

His last three weeks in South Africa were spent in Cape Town, where he was made drunk by former K.R comrades, who then assaulted and tried to rob him. He fought them off but was arrested for indecent exposure before he could rearrange his disheveled clothing. He jumped bail and took ship for England, disembarking at Southampton. He booked into a hotel, seduced an entirely willing chambermaid (we have his word for it), and left for London early next morning. He made a three-week visit to the Kentish seaport and holiday resort of Folkestone, with a side trip to Dover (without taking a cross-channel ferry, apparently), then returned to London and booked passage for the United States from Liverpool by way of Queenstown (now Cobh). At Ellis Island, he was required to endure the standard immigration procedures.

A visit with a friend in Vermont was spoiled by the friend's widowed sister, who, after several weeks' ostensibly intense courtship, vanished from his life at precisely the moment he lost his suitcase and its contents, which included money. We do not know where he got the money, but soldierly looting was a commonplace of the Boer War, and a man of Dave's experience and proclivities would not have missed the opportunities that service in an irregular unit sometimes afforded.[107]

In December, 1902, after two years' absence, Atkins returned furtively to Knickerbocker. Doubtless he had heard of the return of Grandpa and Grandma Byler early the preceding April, after only six months in Arizona.[108] If no prior word had reached him of the fate of Carver, Tom Ketchum, Ben Kilpatrick, and Laura Bullion, he would have been brought up to date by now.

For a while, he was much in the company of his old friend, Bill Chaney, soon to become his mortal enemy, whom he describes in his memoirs as "a little dark skinned object built in the shape of a man." Bill, the memoirs tell us, admitted that Will Carver had given him "Montana money," by which he can only have meant the Winnemucca loot, buried in Idaho by Cassidy, Longabaugh, and Carver and recovered at different times by these three and Harvey Logan. Now Chaney wanted to hire Atkins for $10 to kill Ed Jackson and take from his body the diamond ring that had once belonged to Carver. When Atkins indignantly refused—the ring alone was worth $360—Bill tried to draw him into a scheme to hold up the San Angelo-Sonora mail hack.

Atkins again declined. He may not have known that Chaney was now an informant for the Pinkertons, under the code-name "Dog," but he did learn that Chaney wanted to arrest him and had sneaked off to Sheriff Jake Allen for the requisite authority and papers. "He got both," recalled Dave, "thinking I was a damn fool and never knew anything, only what he told me. Thought he could come to me as he usually did, sit and chat with me until he got the right kind of a chance, and then shoot me."

A day or two later, on or about November 18, 1903, Atkins lay in wait for him in a pasture near Christoval, and opened fire, wounding Chaney's horse. Chaney got off three shots in return before the horse collapsed. The turncoat, unhorsed, screamed threats and obscenities at the departing Atkins, and, in the days that followed, raised a shooting party to kill or capture him and his allies. Official reaction took the form of a piece of paper dated January 1, 1904, and entitled # 1485: *State of Texas versus Dave Atkins; Assault with Intent to Murder W.H. Chaney.*

Obviously Dave was no longer suited to the local climate. After warning his friends about Chaney he again left Texas. He was soon boarding another steamship at New Orleans, this time for Belize, in the colony of British Honduras, where he knifed a man to death. A year or so there, and in the neighboring Honduras republic under the name of George Young, with not much more than an attack of yellow fever and an alleged meeting with Butch Cassidy to show for it, was enough. After touching down briefly in Guatemala and Mexico he traveled by train via Laredo to San Antonio, Texas.

He kept the name George Young and made his next fresh start at Quail, Collingsworth County, in the Texas Panhandle, in May 1905, and remarried at Wellington, on May 8, 1906, when he was still only thirty-two. The subject of his temporary affections was the widowed Mrs. Amelia Oldham. Three years later, he was away again, to Mexico, Guatemala, and Costa Rica. Upon his return he decided to test the air in his home county. During 1910 and early 1911 he dictated his reminiscences. Later that year, he sailed for South America.[109]

His adventures during the new decade are worth almost a chapter in themselves. Probably the high point for him arrived during August, 1916, in Chama, New Mexico. He and Bill Chaney participated on opposite sides of a land war, which ended for Chaney when he became one of the many fatalities in a prolonged "revolver battle." He hit the low point on Monday, August 30, 1919, with his arrest in Jones County, Texas, followed by a free automobile ride to San Angelo. Tom Green County had not forgotten about the murder of Tom Hardin.

The original bill of indictment had been lost, but a substitute was filed on September 4, 1919, with Sam Moore again listed as co-defendant. At his trial, in January 1920, Gerome Shield took the stand on his behalf with testimony about Hardin's quarrelsome behavior in San Angelo. For the benefit of form and the record, District Judge Charles E. Dubois rendered a model exposition of the self-defense and no-retreat doctrines of Texas homicide law to jurors who may have known them already. The jury found no excuse for Atkins, but they did specify the lightest punishment available after a murder conviction: a five-year prison term. His motion for a new trial was denied. Charges against Moore were dropped.[110]

When he came out of prison, Atkins no longer needed, and showed no further inclination, to roam the earth. But the restlessness and instability at the marrow of his character broke out into violence again in 1932. He was adjudged insane and placed in the State Hospital, Wichita Falls, where he remained until his death in 1964 at the age of ninety. His was the longest life of all, and the loneliest death.[111]

Len Alverson, Bill Warderman, and Walter Hovey, alias Hoffman, received a full pardon from President Theodore Roosevelt on March 29, 1904—a month after Hovey had helped defeat the prison mutiny, but nearly three years after Tom Ketchum had publicly stated that none of the three was implicated in the Steins Pass holdup, and one year after Antonio Borrego, Assistant Cell-house keeper at the New Mexico Territorial Penitentiary, had sworn before a Notary Public that Sam Ketchum, three or four days before his death, had likewise disassociated them from complicity in the affair.[112]

In his recommendation, the outgoing U.S. Attorney General, Philander Chase Knox, reported that the conduct of the three prisoners had been "unusually good" and that all of them "rendered great services to the authorities by disclosing and aiding in suppressing mutinies, capturing escaped convicts, and saving property during fire and explosion." Roosevelt told the three by letter that he knew they were victims of a "great injustice" and, characteristically, suggested that each should return to Arizona and "face the world like a man." Only Alverson took the first half of the advice. Jess Benton, who had so wanted the ranch in Texas Canyon, took possession shortly after the men were convicted. Alverson maintained that Benton and his partner, Jim Wolf, simply filed homestead rights and moved in. Benton's version is that John Cush had to mortgage the property in order to pay the lawyer who defended him; the lawyer then sold the ranch and cattle to Benton.[113]

Most of Alverson's own cattle had been sold to meet lawyers' bills. After his release he went back to claim those that were left. All he found was "one big red steer." He stayed in Cochise County and on October 8, 1938, dictated his reminiscences to Mrs George F. Kitt.[114]

Luckier than most was Bill Cruzan, who had taken part in at least two train robberies. When Charlie Siringo called at his hideout somewhere in the Colorado mountains, Bill was not at home. He was never captured.[115]

Sam Ketchum now lies under the main road between Santa Fe and Albuquerque. His burial place was near the corner of the Odd Fellows cemetery. Much later, when plans were made to widen the road by thirteen feet, the authorities had the choice of arranging for the body to be moved to a new grave and leaving it undisturbed. They decided upon the latter course.[116]

Some twenty-five years passed. Then Sam's great-grandson, Berry Spradley, located the cemetery and placed a marker near the grave of the man who, in Tom Chaney's phrase, "was a mighty good man to die an outlaw."[117]

The grave of Tom Ketchum was not left undisturbed. In 1933 it was announced that the body would be disinterred and taken to the new cemetery, a half mile east of the old graveyard. Ketchum was to be raised at 2 o'clock, on the afternoon of Sunday, September 10. The committee in charge of the proceedings included Carl Eklund, Tom Gray, and Albert Thompson, all of whom had witnessed the execution, thirty-two years earlier. Another of the members was Jack Potter, who had known Ketchum as a trail hand.

The people came to see, and the ceremony went off as planned. There was an audience of more than a thousand for Henry H. Errett, Superintendent of Schools for

Union County, when he climbed onto a truck beside the open grave to begin his discourse on Ketchum's life and death. He began by explaining that they had not met to honor or pay homage to Ketchum, "but rather to drive home to everyone that crime eventually exacts the toll of suffering, misery, death and disgrace." He finished by stating that the inner casket would be opened so that the crowd could inspect what was left of the outlaw.

Those who crowded up to the coffin were struck by Ketchum's durability, for the body was "in a fine state of preservation."

> His jet black hair and long thick mustache had turned a maroon red. His skull was in fine condition. The black suit he wore had turned to a reddish gray color and was decomposing. The lower jaw had dropped, his eyeballs were gone but their deep sockets were intact. Very little flesh covered his face. The coat sleeve was neatly folded over the stump of his right arm.

At four o'clock the body was put into a new coffin and driven away to the cemetery. There was some talk of a commemorative monument being erected, and highway signs being put up outside Clayton "advising tourists of the tomb of one of New Mexico's reputed most infamous and bloody killers;" but, more than fifty years later, there was still no marker over the grave.

There matters stood until the late 1980s, when Berry Spradley planted the engraved stone that now surmounts the burial spot. The epitaph is spoken by Shakespeare:

> And how his audit stands
> Who knows save heaven.[118]

None would gainsay that.

It is always tempting to seek to fit a character into perspective by comparing him with his equivalent in modern times. Such comparisons, at best, are meretricious and superficial. Tom Ketchum was one of the most daring and dangerous criminals of his own generation and type; yet he hardly stands in close affinity with such as Floyd, Dillinger, or the Barkers. Undeniably, he was a bad man, often black-humored, always at odds with the world, tainted with meanness, and shot through with a streak of sheer viciousness. For all that, and more, he was infinitely superior to the slimy and loathsome creatures of the city underworlds of his day and ours. Further than that one can barely go, but Jack Culley has this to say of Ketchum and his like:

> And if you are an admirer of the simple qualities of courage and endurance and self-reliance in men—well, these men had them . . .
> If we ever thought about the moral aspect of the matter, we were likely to argue that our western bandits were better people than the robber barons, . . . who preyed upon the public in the industrial field. They did not rob widows and orphans. Be that as it might, we recognized the bandits as cowpunchers like ourselves . . .

Such exploits as theirs, indeed, have the stuff of the great sagas and ballads in them, the hero-tales that have thrilled mankind in all ages.[119]

Idealized and over-simplified this may be. Yet a mountain of factual assertion cannot stand in the way of a rivulet of romantic imagery. Perhaps, then, the undeniable appeal of legend and folklore is the touchstone to a higher and more elemental truth than the sort of truth which is a thing of record.

But perhaps, again, the whole question is resolved more conclusively, more in the spirit of the range, and more impartially, by another of Tom Ketchum's contemporaries.

The flowers which Jack Potter placed in the open casket, that September afternoon in 1933, were accompanied by a card bearing these six words:

"To a cowboy who went wrong."[120]

⫷ 23 ⫸

MYTH, MISTAKE, AND MUDDLE

(I) One Dead Mexican

Among the drolleries beloved of "western" hacks whose tiresome penchant was to array historical personalities in the garb of fiction, is the story of how Tom Ketchum, keen to try out his new rifle, and bent on settling a wager with another of the gang as to which way a man would fall from his horse after being shot, wantonly picked off a Mexican who was riding some distance away.

This jolly little tale, with painstakingly "recreated" conversation, was first committed to cold print in Albert Thompson's book *They Were Open Range Days*.[1] Thompson says that the shooting took place in "the Big Hatchet Mountains, southwestern New Mexico," and that Ketchum admitted it to Jerry Leahy.[2]

Is it not strange that Ketchum should choose as his confidant a man who felt fully at ease with the role of putting a rope around his neck? And must we accept the authority Thompson confers upon himself on the strength of statements he attributes to others? Thompson says that he first interviewed Ketchum through the good offices of his friend, Sheriff Salome Garcia, just before Tom went to trial. But Garcia did not become sheriff until January, 1901, three months after Ketchum's conviction.[iii] At the time of the trial, Saturnino Pinard was still sheriff. This does not prove that the interview could not have taken place. But it does show, at the very least, that Thompson got his sheriffs and his chronology mixed up and did not check his memory.

Some of the inconsistencies between Thompson's recollections of Ketchum's trial and the relevant passages in the official transcript are too pronounced to be explained by the discretion of the court clerk or the faulty memory of the newspaperman. But they are not so great as to deprive his observations of all interest or value. If a defective memory subtracted something from his courtroom impressions, he may have drawn on his imagination to supplement the remainder. But he did attend the trial and his account of the proceedings deviates more from the detail than from the essence.

Less indulgence is due his assertion that he asked Tom whether "Laura Bullen [*sic*] ever engaged with you in a robbery or train holdup." This, purportedly, was one of a series of questions Thompson put to Ketchum just before his execution.

Ketchum, he adds, made no reply to it. In reality, the question could not have been asked. Bullion did not become a public figure until after her arrest in St. Louis in November, 1901, when Chief of Detectives Desmond of that city foolishly encouraged two daily papers to circulate his mistaken belief that she could have taken part in the Wagner robbery.[4] By then, Ketchum had been dead for more than six months. It was common knowledge in Tom Green County at that time that she had been Will Carver's mistress, but the local newspapers had refrained from saying so. Hence we may be sure that Thompson would not even have heard of Laura Bullion in April 1901.

Desmond's speculative balloon was almost immediately deflated by his superior, the St Louis Chief of Police; but not everyone who had seen the original assertion took notice of the refutation.[5] The likelihood is that Thompson learned of Bullion's supposed notoriety years afterwards from a piece of catchpenny prose in some weekend supplement. He may have liked the story and seen the basis for a question he would have asked Ketchum, had Ketchum been spared enough time on earth to be asked. He might then have convinced himself that his retrospective musings would justify a pretense that he had actually posed the question.

The palpable fact that Albert Thompson sometimes made things up is no excuse for disbelieving everything he wrote; historiography cannot afford such short cuts. Fortunately, we do not need to guess whether Ketchum really did confide in Leahy. Whatever Ketchum told Leahy, or did not tell him, for whatever reason, we have to confront two newspaper stories—quite dissimilar in detail, but with one important feature in common—which appeared shortly after Ketchum had been captured. The first is taken from the *Trinidad Chronicle-News*, as quoted by Titsworth:

> . . . One day a Mexican rode into San Angelo, Texas, wearing a magnificent sombrero, all a-glitter with silver braid. Black Jack coveted it, and he knew but one way to get it. The Mexican was not quick to give up the hat, but soon had no use for it, for dead men's heads are just as well uncovered. Ketchum looked very well in that hat.[6]

About a month later, the *El Paso Herald* carried a piece which was reprinted in the *Santa Fe New Mexican* on October 7, 1899.

> . . . The nature of the man is shown by a well authenticated story to the effect that, during his boyhood days on the ranch, one of his chief sources of pleasure was gained from a somewhat peculiar habit he had of hiding behind the chaparral on some lonely hill and from this vantage point shooting at—and seldom missing—the Mexican herders on the plains below. . . .

These tales, themselves untrue, may have launched this enduring fabrication upon its merry way. John Loomis combined the two in a story he ascribes to Rome

Shield, who claimed to have received it from Ketchum during their meeting in the Santa Fe penitentiary in September 1899.

It seems that Ketchum "succumbed to the blandishments" of a senorita while he and another of the gang were hiding out in a small town in Mexico. The girl's lover caught her in Ketchum's company, but was shot dead by the second outlaw before he could interfere.

Confident of being pursued, the two desperadoes lay in wait on a rocky hillside fifteen miles beyond town. Sure enough, a posse of fifteen or more rode clippety-clop into the ambush. His eyes alighting on the "unusually fine sombrero" worn by the leading Mexican, Tom requested his pal to leave that man to him, "for he wanted the hat." The sidekick, to Ketchum's chagrin, promptly put a bullet through the sombrero and its owner's head, ruining the hat. Still, the story had a happy ending for Tom; he and his chum killed about six more Mexicans before returning to the United States ("without further incidents").[7]

The "sombrero story" is a lavishly free adaptation of a scene from real life in which the main part belonged to William Christian, the real Black Jack. In late October or early November, 1896, Christian and one or more companions, while traveling from the scene of one robbery in Cochise County, Arizona, to the site of the next, encountered a man "sporting the dream of a cowboy hat, with all the spangles and trimmings that made its owner prouder than a president and envied by every knight of the lariat who saw it." Christian tried on the hat, and, since the size was right, insisted on a swap. He then dug into his pocket and gave the previous owner the $12 it had cost him.[8]

There was no wager, no shooting, and Tom Ketchum was in no way involved in the transaction. But he was a killer, and he had been saddled (not altogether unwillingly) with Black Jack's identity and notoriety; therefore, the tale could be transplanted to Texas and its incidental details stretched and glossed to fit a new set of reference points. The El Paso reporter dispensed with the bespangled sombrero, but retained the West Texas background and turned a single murder into a succession of killings by sniper fire. Thompson then shifted the locale back to the Arizona-New Mexico border, and concocted a fresh set of details. Others elaborated the embroidery. This is Elton "Cunny" Cunningham, talking to Lou Blachly on December 10, 1955:

> . . . Jim Lowe (Butch Cassidy) didn't think much of Black Jack Ketchum. He said Sam was a perfect gentleman but Black Jack was a S.B. He told me one thing, that he was with him and they'd done something [and] they were riding away, Jim Lowe, Tom Ketchum and Sam Ketchum and one of the others, I don't know [which]. There was four I think and they met a Mexican on the road ridin' a little old pony. And he said, "Buenos dias," and they spoke to him and rode on and Tom Ketchum stopped and he says, "That damn Mexican will go back to town and tell he saw us." He wheeled his horse and went back. Jim Lowe told me he could see him from the road . . . [Ketchum] stopped the Mexican, pulled him over on his horse, pushed his foot in the stirrup, kicked the horse in the belly, and the horse went on down the road and drug this

Mexican to death. Jim said from that time on he had nothing to do with Tom Ketchum. He said a brute like that he didn't know. But this Sam Ketchum, his brother, was fine, he was just fine.[9]

This was a yarn that Cunningham told Blachly twice, with little variance, although in the alternative version he seemed at one point to credit Lay as his source.[10] Cunningham's closeness to both Cassidy and Lay is no proof that the story he told Blachly came from either. Nor does his momentary disagreement with himself over which of the two he heard it from mean that he heard it from neither. He was speaking to Blachly at a remove of over a half century from the subject—enough of an interval to qualify a modicum of inconsistency for the benefit of the doubt. But Cunningham's inconsistencies were few; the least that can be said for him is that he had a clear recollection of the story as he liked to tell it. He may have misplaced some details, and invented others as fancy or expediency directed; but he did not make the whole thing up, though someone did. Elements of it were in circulation long before Blachly's interviews with Cunningham and other old-timers.

Loomis tells almost the same story as Cunningham, though more cursorily. He attributes it to an unnamed man who knew Ketchum "intimately." As he tells it, Tom—seized by one of his more playful moods—tied the foot of an unsuspecting Mexican in the stirrup, frightened the horse into bolting, then "sat and laughed" while the horse dragged and kicked the man to death.[11]

Was this grim little anecdote born in Texas or New Mexico? Almost surely, Loomis and Cunningham never met; most likely, neither ever heard of the other. But did they have a common informant? Or was it one of those stories of uncertain pedigree that were told and retold in saloons and around campfires from Bisbee to Roswell to San Angelo?

Besides the cowboy's forced sale of his ornamented sombrero to Black Jack Christian, there are two incidents in the life of Tom Ketchum which may have been twisted by word of mouth into a rough and ready formula for such creations as these. One was the murder of Jap Powers, who was not of Mexican ancestry, but who was ambushed near San Angelo. The other was the murder of Merejildo Gallegos—who, if not a Mexican, was at least of Spanish descent. A more significant constituent may have been Ketchum's well-founded reputation for brutality. The stories were untrue from beginning to end, yet people in the Southwest were ready to believe them, or to repeat them as if they did.

One possibility remains. Ketchum, in conversation with Leahy, might have made some vague allusion to the Powers or Gallegos murder. If he also told Leahy that he had killed a man merely to put a rifle to the test, then surely the district attorney was being ribbed. That, given Ketchum's impish and quirky sense of humor, and his propensity for malicious practical jokes, may be the true explanation of the story's origin.

(II) "They Got John Legg"

Of all the officers who were involved in the hunt for the Ketchum gang, William H. Reno was the most widely quoted. His part in the war of words that followed the Turkey Canyon fight has already been described. Although the frequency of his appearances in the columns of the Denver newspapers might encourage the suspicion that he was garrulous and publicity conscious, he was neither. Denver had five daily newspapers which competed fiercely for news and circulation. Crime news was a staple circulation booster, and reporters for the rival sheets were constantly in the hunt for interviews with police officers, railroad and express company detectives, and postal inspectors.[12]

Thus Reno could not easily have avoided the attentions of journalists, and it would not have looked good to his employers or to the wider public if he had tried too strenuously to do so. It was also usual for reporters or editorial staff to ginger up an interviewee's oral prose, the effect sometimes being to convey a false impression of the subject's character. Reno was one whose public persona may have been over-colored by journalistic licence.

This does not mean that there were not times when Reno said too much or got adrift of the facts. After the execution of Tom Ketchum, he declared that the outlaw was "lying all the time" in his last statement.[13] Actually, Ketchum was not lying all the time; only part of the time. Besides, Reno could tell a pretty wild story himself. One reporter, an avid listener as Reno was holding forth during the train journey back north, recorded the following specimen:

> Sitting at the window of a Pullman car yesterday morning, Billy Reno looked out over the brown, uncompromising plains and smiled, inscrutably. "They got the man who started me on this chase," he said, with charming insouciance. "Who was he?" someone asked. "John Legg. He wrote me in 1897 that Black Jack [Ketchum] and his gang were coming north. A little later they did the job at Folsom, N.M. Next year they killed Legg at Fort Sumner, N.M." Again that smile, and the train put behind a few more of those sad New Mexico miles.[14]

Legg worked for several years as a deputy sheriff in Lincoln County and sometimes served as a deputy United States marshal. In August, 1894, he killed one William McLehaney, known as "Portales Bill."[15] His part in the pursuit of Tom and Sam Ketchum after the murder of Herzstein and Gallegos has been told.[16] In October of the same year, 1896, he rode with one of the posses that made a feeble pretense of giving chase to Black Jack Christian's gang,[17] who held up four stage coaches during that month. He was shot and killed at Fort Sumner, but not by the Ketchums or any other outlaw band. The fracas that resulted in his death arose from a quarrel over a Poker hand. Legg was killed by James Blanton—like Legg, a gambler and a hardcase, according to the *Roswell Record*—on March 22, 1899. A shot fired by Legg, apparently intended for Blanton, wounded a man named Gillespie.[18]

It is quite possible Reno truly believed that Legg met his death at the hands of the Ketchum outlaws. If he did, this is yet another case of an officer laboring under the double burden of an untrustworthy informant and his own gullibility. Even so, the lapse did not typify Reno's professional conduct. He had a long and successful career in law-enforcement and was one of the most persistent and conscientious of all the officers who investigated the various train robberies committed by the Ketchums.[19]

The failings of many individual lawmen, and the need for greater cooperation between the different agencies of law and order, were sorely exposed during the campaign against such groups as the Ketchum band. In theory, this ought to have had the healthy and constructive effect of awakening the public into electing or securing the appointment of better men. More than one writer on western outlawry has contrived a tidy conclusion by propounding this as though it were fact. One might assert with an equal regard for consistency that the current prevalence of violent crime is proof of the very reverse. In truth, today's officers, like those of yesteryear and times more distant, are no more and no less than a fairly typical sample of humanity in general.

(III) The Identity of G. W. Franks

The most gratuitous malformation in the tangled chronicles of the Ketchum and Hole-in-the-Wall gangs was conceived forty years after the events to which it relates. In it Harvey Logan, alias Kid Curry, is substituted for Will Carver as "G.W. Franks," the man whose shooting so unnerved the posse in Turkey Creek Canyon. Its origins are easily traced.

The story was introduced by Charles Kelly in *The Outlaw Trail*.[20] Its purported source was William French's book, *Some Recollections of a Western Ranchman*. Kelly also cited French's book as his authority for the absurd statement that Tom Capehart was another alias for Harvey Logan. Thus it was Kelly's assumption that G.W. Franks, Tom Capehart, and Harvey Logan were all of them the man who held back the posse in the Turkey Canyon fight. James D. Horan, in the first edition of *Desperate Men*, followed Kelly and imparted a few touches of purplish prose; in the second edition of the book, and various other writings, he added quite a few more.[21] Brown Waller, whose book on Harvey Logan, *Last of the Great Western Train Robbers*, is largely an ill-organized pastiche of contemporary newspaper accounts, struck a curious compromise between the evidence of his own extensive research and his unwillingness to dissent from Kelly and Horan.[22] He concluded that there must have been two Tom Capeharts and that both Logan and Carver used the alias "G.W. Franks."

Time, now, to look at what French actually wrote. Far from stating that Capehart was Franks, he does not mention Harvey Logan at all, from the first page of his *Recollections* to the last. What he does say is that he believed Capehart to be Franks.[23]

French relates how Cassidy told him that Tom Capehart had just returned to the WS range with news of Lay's capture, then describes his own subsequent conversation with Capehart:

I then asked Tom, whom [*sic*] it was evident must be the man Franks, how Mac [Lay, alias McGinnis] had been taken.

... That he did not intend to commit himself was evident from the start, for he made no direct allusion to the cause of Mac's trouble, saying merely that he had been wounded, shot twice through the body ... [24]

Capehart's account of the arrest of Lay, as he heard it at Lusk's ranch or camp, and retold it to French, has been examined in Chapter 17. We have seen, also, that Tom told French that he was apprehensive of being taken for the fugitive "Franks," since from the description being circulated he might have been Franks, or again he might not; and that French therefore deduced, or assumed, that Capehart really was Franks.[25] This poses a separate question, but before it is considered something should be said about the whereabouts of Harvey Logan at the time Charles Kelly says he was at Alma, Folsom, Turkey Canyon, and Chimney Wells.

It is certain that Logan was one of the six who robbed the Union Pacific at Wilcox, Wyoming, on June 2, 1899. This occurred while Sam Ketchum, Lay, and Franks were in or near Cimarron, New Mexico—three hundred miles south of Wilcox. The investigation disclosed that Logan, with two companions, was roaming through Wyoming for several weeks prior to the robbery.[26] Cassidy and Lay were still working for William French during the earlier part of this period. Lay, as has been related, quit the WS late in April or early in May. Cassidy stayed on in Alma.

Directly after the Wilcox holdup the six robbers split into two groups of three. George Currie and the Logan brothers drew the keener pursuit and killed Sheriff Hazen a few days later. Since they are known to have retreated north, it is clear that Harvey Logan could not have been in New Mexico at the time of the Folsom robbery. Nor could he have joined Lay after the Turkey Canyon fight.[27]

This last point is enough to defeat F. Bruce Lamb's attempt to bundle fact with fantasy by excluding Harvey Logan from the Folsom robbery but arranging for him to arrive at Turkey Creek Canyon just ahead of the Elliott-Farr-Reno posse. Lamb claims, quite credibly, that Logan spent much of the winter of 1903–4 at a ranch in Fremont County, Colorado, owned by Bruce's father Frank and Frank's brothers, Tom and John.

Lamb further states that Harvey Logan, with Cassidy and Longabaugh, stopped at the ranch directly after the Wilcox robbery. He goes on to describe, in words ascribed to Logan, how Cassidy and Longabaugh "elected" Harvey to go to Turkey Creek to "check up on [their] wandering sidekick," Elzy Lay. Logan arrived just as Lay and Sam Ketchum were about to depart; Will Carver and Ben Kilpatrick had left during the morning. Surprised to hear that the gang had already committed the robbery, he berated Lay and Ketchum for their dilatoriness. Ketchum retorted that they were safe in their hideout and would sleep there that night. But Logan had scarcely unsaddled his horse when Lay was shot down and the battle opened. Logan's alleged narrative continues into an account of the fight and Lay's eventual capture, with himself in the role usually allotted to Carver/Franks. As a diversion, he has Lay let him into a secret; he and Tom Ketchum had taken $50,000 from a train at Grants, and hidden the lot in "Cave 44" in Wild Cat Canyon, among the southern Chiricahuas. Elzy even gave Logan a map, showing the exact location of the cache. That knowledge made Logan a figure of great potential wealth, for he has already salted away Lay's and Ketchum's receipts from the Folsom enterprise.

Logan's story then moves on to Capehart's ride to Alma, with himself as Capehart. After that, the putative Logan speaks of the efforts of French and Cunningham to raise bail money for Lay. Finally, with Lay convicted and behind grey walls, Longabaugh and Logan recovered both hoards of buried loot and used some of it to pay for his early release.[28]

Altogether, a ripping good yarn.

Now for a few facts. First, Longabaugh was among the three Wilcox robbers who traveled northwest after the holdup, and could not have been in southern Colorado by early July; second, Logan headed due north from Wilcox with his brother and Currie, and was still in the north a month later; third, Kilpatrick was not in the robbery at Folsom, and could not have been, because he was in Wyoming with Longabaugh; fourth, Cassidy did not take part in the Wilcox robbery and was in southwest New Mexico throughout the period under review; and fifth, neither Ketchum nor Lay participated in the big train robbery at Grants.[29]

Since Logan could not have been at the Lamb ranch by the end of June, or in Turkey Canyon by July 16, we are left with a further question: did the story begin with Logan himself? Bruce Lamb presented it in the first person, as though it had come straight from Logan. The narrative is continuous, and in colloquial language, such as Logan himself might have used, especially if he had been born about forty years later. How did the Lambs manage to retain an absolute grasp of such a coherent and detailed statement for seventy-five years without making and keeping any formal record of it?

We may reasonably accept that the fugitive, on the run after escaping from the Knoxville jail, spent several months of 1903–4 on the Lamb ranch. We may also believe that he had first met the Lambs a few years earlier, and that he and sundry friends had dropped in at the ranch more than once before the fateful Wagner robbery of 1901. We can even live with the idea that, while at the Lamb ranch during 1903–4, Logan may have talked to the family about shared acquaintanceships and, perhaps, about episodes in his past career.

But can we credit the notion that he spoke of his escapades in minute detail, illuminating his narrative with conversation recalled verbatim? That Bruce Lamb's uncle remembered everything he had heard and retold it to the nephew, word perfect? That the uncle never put Logan's fireside reminiscences into writing? That, consequently, the outlaw's tale lay intact in Bruce's memory until the day came for him to write it down and tell the world? And, above all, that even had he possessed the requisite narrative and inventive powers, Logan would have wanted to fabricate such a motley of consummate twaddle? Only one answer is possible.

So, as well as having no part in his own story, Logan could have had no part in its composition. How, then, was the story constructed? The answer is obvious from the standard printed sources. It was done mainly by inserting Logan into the relevant section of French's *Recollections*, and adding a few cues taken from Siringo, Hoover, Walter Noble Burns, and, possibly, Alverson's reminiscences or someone who had quoted them in print.

Long before Lamb's literary debut, Miguel A. Otero had put Harvey Logan among the Folsom bandits, and for the oddest reason. He thought that G.W. Franks and Will Carver were both aliases for Harvey Logan. No comment is needed.[30]

Sam Ketchum, soon after being captured, referred to one of his companions as "the Kid." Kelly seizes upon this as a reference to "Kid Curry" (Harvey Logan), thereby demonstrating a failure of both research and intelligence.[31] When making his statement, Sam refused to name his companions; he could have been talking about either of the two, since both were much younger than he. Since, however, both were well into their thirties, and neither had ever been known as "Kid," he is likely to have used the nickname to make it easier for him not to disclose the identity of either.[32]

Kelly, incidentally, says that Lay was one of the Wilcox robbers.[33] This is as untenable as the assertion that Logan was at Folsom, thanks to castiron evidence that Lay was in northeast New Mexico throughout the month of June, 1899.

Jack Culley accepted French's conclusion that Tom Capehart was Franks, in preference to evidence from George Crocker that Franks was Carver.[34] Let us allow that French reported truthfully what he had seen or heard on the subject. But Capehart, as French admitted, "did not intend to commit himself;" he told French no more than what he thought French was entitled to know. Capehart only learned of the arrest of Lay several hours after it had taken place, and so could not have been the man who had accompanied Lay to Lusk's camp the previous evening and who was watching the hill during Lay's struggle to escape from the posse. If Capehart did not mention the presence of Will Carver or any other third party, it would have been because he thought it best that French should not be told.

French's story may be taken to show that Capehart was in Lay's company after the Turkey Canyon affair; but there is unquestionable evidence that "G.W. Franks" was Will Carver. There are the findings of Carl Livingston, whose occasional howlers should not obscure the fact that much of his information came from people who were in a position to know,[35] including, in this instance, Cicero Stewart, Rufe Thomas, and, indirectly, William Reno. There are references in the case papers for the McGinnis murder trial that make it obvious that Carver was the chief object of suspicion.[36] There are the reminiscences of John Loomis, who was a friend of Rufe Thomas and had been friendly with Carver.[37] There are the statements of Albert Thompson and George Crocker, both of whom might from time to time be careless or even inventive on the finer details, but who nevertheless could draw upon first hand knowledge, were close to others with the same advantage, and were generally trustworthy on matters of importance.[38] Mack Axford's account of the events is derived chiefly from what he was told by Carver.[39] When the *San Angelo Standard*, in reporting Carver's death, said that Carver was Franks, it was merely repeating something that was regarded as an established fact.[40] Among those who had established the fact was Gerome Shield, the sheriff at San Angelo, who was as well posted on the Ketchum gang in Texas as anyone outside their own small circle, and was in touch with express and railroad officials in New Mexico.[41] Another was Shield's friend Wilson Elliott, formerly of San Angelo; whatever his executive failings, Elliott cannot be accused of ignorance of the movements, crimes, and personal appearance of the Ketchums and Carver.[42] He and Reno were among the witnesses whose testimony caused a Colfax County grand jury to indict "Franks, alias Carver" with the murder of Edward Farr.[43] All we lack is a sworn admission from Carver himself.

Just before his execution, Tom Ketchum did his best to throw the question wide open.[44]

"The name of the man in the Turkey Creek canyon fight, supposed to have been Franks," he said, "I won't tell because he is alive and at liberty. I know the man well enough—have known him for fifteen years, but I won't tell who he is."

Since Ketchum knew of Carver's death in Sonora, three weeks earlier, it is impossible to hazard a guess as to whom he might have had in mind. Franks was Carver, and the chances are that Ketchum must have been well aware of this. One explanation could be that here, as so often elsewhere, he was lying—perhaps deluding himself into the hope that by withholding information or by appearing to withhold it, he might gain a last-minute reprieve.

Stories were set afloat that G.W. Franks was a "mystery man" with no other known identity who returned to Colfax County many years later to dig up the loot. A more refined variant of this yarn turned this or some similar personage into a kind of parrotless Long John Silver of the Southwest. This creation was given a temporary sobriquet (Pegleg Sullivan); the least semblance of a home background (his sole relative was a niece in Kansas City, whose letters to him were addressed to Bill Karnes—thereby removing whatever point there might have been to his adoption of Sullivan as his Cimarron incognito); and a history (he was none other than the long-lost Tom Capehart, latterly returned from South America, minus one leg).

The Sullivan-Karnes-Capehart thesis reads like a vision descried in the bottom of a beer glass by someone with too much drinking time on his hands. It was told to Agnes Morley Cleaveland, and given an audience by her book *Satan's Paradise*.[45] Prospective readers who know this author only through the magical prose of her deservedly much-praised *No Life for a Lady* are hereby warned.

Cleaveland's acquaintances in Cimarron may have heard that someone—somewhere—came looking for the buried money, and that a man who many swore could only have been Franks was seen in the locality long after the robbery. Both rumors sprang from actual incident, but there was no connection between them. The money, as has been stated, was taken out of the ground about a year after the robbery: the man alleged to have been Franks was an obscure drifter and recluse named Irvin "Black Bob" McManus.[46]

During 1904, Black Bob worked as a cattle detective for the Mesa de Mayo Land & Cattle Company, of Trinidad, Colorado, where he was well known and attracted no adverse notice. But, in February 1905, he and others were alleged by L.A. "Lon" Meredith to have been plotting to rob a rancher of the proceeds of a cattle sale. McManus and his friends retaliated by bringing a cattle-killing charge against Meredith in adjacent Union County, New Mexico.[47]

At this point Meredith's brother-in-law, Deputy Sheriff William T. Thatcher, muscled into the case. He and Deputy Sheriff George W. Titsworth convinced themselves that they could convince others that Black Bob was "G.W. Franks." On that premise, Thatcher obtained a warrant from Colfax County, where Ed Farr had been killed in 1899. On April 5, 1905, they crept up on McManus while he was building a corral by his cabin, "in a wild, rocky cañon far from any other habitation." He was taken to Trinidad, and thence to Raton, New Mexico. Then, said the *New Mexican*, someone with a good memory for faces identified him as Frank Potter, one of the three members of the old Mesa Hawks gang still at large (the others being Henry Hawkins and Frank Isbell).[48]

Jeff and Dave Farr could do better than that. They were confident that the prisoner was the G.W. Franks who, they insisted, was the marksman who had slain their brother. Jerry Leahy, who was still district attorney of Colfax and Union Counties, would have none of it. He declared that the prisoner bore "not even the slightest resemblance" to the real Franks.[49]

Leahy suspected the Colorado men of trying to put one across him, and his anger showed. He investigated claims that McManus was wanted for crimes committed elsewhere, and found them baseless. Later he found that a third Colorado deputy, Henry Haley, who had assisted Thatcher and Titsworth in manufacturing a case against McManus, was about to face trial in Union County on four charges of horse theft. And a similar charge was outstanding against Thatcher's convict brother-in-law, Lon Meredith. All three deputies, he further noted, held their commissions by virtue of their positions as guards for the Colorado Fuel and Iron Company.[50] At that time, and for the next decade, the C.F. and I. controlled and practically owned Las Animas and Huerfano Counties.[51]

Leahy notwithstanding, Governor George Curry of New Mexico pardoned Meredith on the ground that McManus, whose testimony had contributed most to the conviction, was a fugitive from justice at the time of the trial. So he was; but he had been found to be innocent of the charge of post office robbery from which he was fleeing. The outcome of the Lon Meredith case made no difference to him; he had shown that he was no more Potter than he was Franks, and was long gone from the area when Meredith was released in March, 1909.[52]

Since Jeff and Dave Farr had never seen the real Franks, it would be interesting to know what led them to identify McManus as their brother's killer.

Did they knowingly misidentify him? If so, why? But if not, why would they not accept the indubitable evidence that "G.W. Franks" was William Carver, and that he had been dead since April, 1901?

Some people are very obstinate.

❧ NOTES ❧

BIBLIOGRAPHICAL ESSAY

Although the bulk of the material for this book has been drawn from archival, newspaper, and other unpublished or hitherto largely untapped sources, some assessment should be offered of the principal published works in which the Ketchum brothers and their comrades in crime feature with any prominence.

Prior to 1970, there were two books on Tom Ketchum: Ed Bartholomew's *Black Jack Ketchum: Last of the Hold-up Kings* (1955) and F. Stanley's *No Tears for Black Jack Ketchum* (1957). Both books are short; both are chaotic. Evidence of research is not non-existent, but it is patchy, superficial, and unsystematic. Their subject matter is derived for by far the most part from secondary sources and restricted mainly to the three holdups at Folsom, New Mexico., the fight in Turkey Creek Canyon and its consequences, Tom Ketchum's trial, and his execution. Both authors attribute to the Ketchum gang many of the crimes committed by Black Jack Christian's band in the summer and fall of 1896, while almost wholly ignoring the Ketchums' banditry in Texas. Stanley makes extensive, though uncritical, use of the *Santa Fe Daily New Mexican*. Neither he nor Bartholomew attempted to locate trial transcripts or any other court records.

A unique exhibit in Stanley's book is a long quotation from the unpublished recollections of Mason Chase, a ranchman who lived near Cimarron and was a friend of James H. "Billy" Morgan, an important figure in the Turkey Canyon affair. Chase's recollections are gossipy in places and show malice toward some.

Ed Bartholomew traveled through and took close note of much of the country traversed by the Ketchums in southwest Texas and, especially, northeast New Mexico. On the Philmont Scout Ranch, in the mountains west of Cimarron, he photographed a huge carving of a face, uncommonly like Tom Ketchum's, chipped out of the side of a boulder. Otherwise, the best feature of his book is the chapter on the death of Will Carver, much of which also appears in Bartholomew's *Kill or Be Killed*.

Bartholomew and Stanley stray wildly off-trail in depending on Lorenzo D. Walters's *Tombstone's Yesterday* (1928) for the history of the Ketchum gang. Walters, who was briefly a policeman in Tucson, Arizona, was in a position to write authoritatively of the early years in Tombstone and its environs, but lacked the ability or inclination to do so. One or two of his chapters have no facts for the narrative to stand upon. Others are no better than semi-fiction. Much of what he wrote about the Ketchums (in a chapter consisting mostly of thinly but not always accurately paraphrased newspaper reports) belongs by rights to his chapter on Black Jack Christian. For example, he charged the Ketchums with holdups committed by the Christian gang at Nogales, Rio Puerco, San Simon, Huachuca Siding, and other places in Arizona and New Mexico. While he points out that Ketchum was muddled with Christian, his mishandling of the subject is merely a demonstration of the confusion he recognizes but makes no attempt to unravel. His book does include one or two anecdotes about Tom Ketchum that may well be true.

Bartholomew and Stanley were not the first to choose Ketchum as the subject for a full length biography. In 1926, a sketchy little piece entitled "'Black Jack', The Texas Outlaw," was published in Marvin Hunter's *Frontier Times* magazine under the byline of A.W. Thompson. Albert W. Thompson may already have been planning a fuller treatment of Ketchum's life. He was a former owner of the Clayton, New Mexico, *Enterprise*, and a minor politician, and had been allowed to meet and talk to Ketchum several times while the outlaw was being held in Clayton for trial and execution. In that era, almost all news journalism was anonymous, but there are strong internal indications that it was Thompson who reported Ketchum's last days and execution for the *Denver Republican*. If so, his contemporary reporting is more trustworthy than some of his recollections of it.

During 1930, Thompson collected material from "a score or more of men and women," supplemented it with re-creations of his conversations with the imprisoned outlaw, pepped it up with assertions made on dubious authority or none, mixed in lashings of raw fiction, and served up the potpourri as a typescript of fifty thousand words called *The Story of Black Jack Ketchem*. The misspelling is his, and recurs throughout the text.

If Thompson entertained thoughts of securing a publisher then and there, he was persuaded or obliged to postpone their implementation. His pen was not idle during the ensuing interval. He wrote assiduously for the local press, and early in 1933 contributed a series of articles on Ketchum to the Clayton *Union County Leader*. These were incorporated in a short book, *Early History of Clayton, New Mexico*, which appeared later that year. Here Thompson concentrated mainly on the closing scenes of Ketchum's outlawry, drawing upon his monograph of 1930, which he said he hoped to publish one day. By now, he was sometimes spelling the Ketchum family name correctly.

Then, in 1945, when most of those who could question his narrative had passed on, and the memories or sensitivities of others had dulled, he returned to the 1930 manuscript and retouched it here and there. All to no avail: a further small book, *They Were Open Range Days*, came off the press in 1946, but its treatment of the Ketchum story was merely an abridgment of the 1933 version, and the longer work of 1930 remained unpublished at Thompson's death in 1951, at the age of eighty-six. His daughter-in-law, Goldianne, seems not to have known of its existence. In her own book on the history of Clayton, published in 1962, she stated that Albert was never able to write his projected biography of Tom Ketchum.

All too readily, the present author assumed that the "longer writing" Thompson mentioned in 1933, if ever completed, had been consigned to the fireback or wastebasket. This changed only in 2005, with the arrival of a letter from Berry Spradley, Tom Ketchum's great grandnephew, who had located and read the document in Albuquerque. It will be referred to herein as the *Albuquerque ms*.

The character and limitations of Thompson's project are most aptly illustrated by words plucked from his foreword. He justly observes that many of the tales attached to the Ketchums were "as ridiculous as they are grossly misleading, exaggerated, or false," and maintained that his object was "partly" to correct these canards, only to add: "Some fiction is, naturally, woven into the story." He then insists that, nonetheless, his narrative "in the main . . . depicts the life of the bandit and his followers faithfully." The net result is, of course, an increase in the stock of tales that are "grossly misleading, exaggerated, or false." This would not matter much, if we could be sure that all his fiction is recognizable as such; but not all of it is. Despite copious research and reflection, a few instances remain where this writer cannot be sure whether Thompson is quoting Ketchum truthfully or putting posthumous words into the doomed prisoner's mouth.

Thompson shows no command of chronology until his narrative reaches the late summer of 1897; but, despite the scarcity of dates (and the few that are given are wrong), his success in unlocking the memories of several people who had known Tom well in southwest Texas before he turned outlaw give value to the early pages of the manuscript. Some of the later pages owe at least as much to the assistance of a railroad detective, William Reno, as to Thompson's contact with Ketchum. On the whole, however, the uncertainties and variables with which Thompson's chronicle is riven make it a piece of work better encountered near the conclusion than at the beginning of a research project.

In citation, Thompson's informal *Early History of Clayton, New Mexico*, will be identified as *Clayton ms.*, because the author worked from a copy of Thompson's typescript, rather than from the resultant book.

One writer who did make a real (though not wholly successful) effort to disentangle the Ketchums from the Christians was J. Evetts Haley, in *Jeff Milton: A Good Man with a Gun* (1948), a book which the present author has long cherished as a wonderful piece of writing and, altogether, one of the two or three finest works of Southwestern historical literature known to him. Haley was occasionally misled by such storytellers as Frank King, but the book's chief and besetting defect is in its implicit proposition that Jeff Milton was perfection personified.

Erna Fergusson's *Murder and Mystery in New Mexico*, which was also published in 1948, includes a chapter called "How Black Jack Lost His Head." Since that author's father, Harvey Butler Fergusson, was a well-known New Mexico lawyer, who had appeared for the defense in the Fountain murder case (which also gets a chapter), it is not surprising that she located, and made some use of, the transcript of Ketchum's trial. Her other material comes from the writings of Jack Culley and Miguel Otero, and from the variable memories of named and unnamed old-timers. Thus her sources are a mixture of the good, the not so good, and the dubious or worse; and, since she makes no apparent attempt to distinguish between them, the same is true of her presentation. She seems, in places, to have written for effect as much as for history.

Only in recent years has much been brought to light on the Ketchum brothers' principal allies in crime, Will Carver and Dave Atkins, as individuals with lives and characters of their own. *From Cowboy to Outlaw: The Story of Will Carver* (1995), by Donna B. Ernst, and *Den of Outlaws* (2000), by Barbara Barton, are by no means free of errors; but these, for the most part, are too obvious to count for much. The sum of what is right in each book amounts to far more than what stands to its debit. Ernst includes a wealth of genealogical data on the Carvers, as well as particulars on Will's brief marriage and a good account of his last days and hours. Barton's unique contribution is to bring Atkins out of the shadows; without it, the present writer might not have known where to begin to document the long interval between Atkins's retirement from banditry and his death in a home for the insane. Barton, writing from the Ketchum brothers' home town of Knickerbocker, is also good on several aspects of their lives in that section of Texas, and on Laura Bullion's family. More recently still, our knowledge of Bullion and her kin has been further advanced in Ernst's *Women of the Wild Bunch* (2004).

In 1926, Charles A. Siringo, whose fifteen years as a Texas cowhand had been followed by twenty-two years as an operative for Pinkerton's National Detective Agency (usually referred to hereinafter as P.N.D.A.) and by a third career in authorship, included a few pages on the Ketchum gang in the manuscript of a book which was to have been entitled *Bad Men of the West*. His volume of reminiscences, *Riata and Spurs*, was published early in 1927, only to be withdrawn almost immediately because his former employer, the Pinkerton agency, objected to some of the content, even though it had been published in almost identical form fifteen years previously as *A Cowboy Detective*, Siringo's first book. When *Riata and Spurs* reappeared, later that year, it was in an expurgated ("revised") edition, with eleven chapters of the *Bad Men of the West* project brought in to replace the material to which the agency had taken exception. The chapters from *Bad Men of the West* seem to have been written more to entertain more than to inform—a formula designed, doubtless, for a public that expected no more and no less. We may say of them that they are the work of a writer who, in this instance, did not strain himself to achieve more than the approximate truth. That, at any rate, is an impression which his pages on the Ketchums do nothing to dispel. They are preceded by a statement that "the original 'Black Jack' . . . went by the name of William Christenson." Aptly enough, he gets William Christian's name about half right.

Siringo's personal reminiscences (*A Cowboy Detective* and the original edition of *Riata and Spurs*) have faults, but they are not the same ones. These recollections suffer from a paucity of dates, and from their author's looseness of construction and disregard for chronology, but they are as truthful as his memory will allow. A further proviso is that Siringo was inhibited or prohibited from using the real names of many of the people who figure in these volumes. Nevertheless, they are valuable raw material for any researcher prepared to invest time and patience in them.

Edward Wilson's *An Unwritten History*, published in 1915, seems to have been the first book to state that Tom Ketchum was never called "Black Jack" by those who knew him personally and who knew, or knew of, the real Black Jack or High Five gang. Carl B. Livingston, of Roswell, New Mexico, was the first to put that fact into something like general circulation, and (a handful of little-noticed 1890s newspaper items aside) the first to publicly link the Christian surname with the Black Jack alias. His articles were published in the *Roswell Record* and soon afterwards, in 1930, in *Wide World* (which reprinted them in 1955). Most of his material came from eyewitnesses, and much of it was accurate. One or two of his informants seem, however, to have exercised their imaginative or inventive faculties more than their memories. A more grievous fault lies in Livingston's melodramatic presentation of a ludicrous thesis that the Christian, Ketchum, and Hole-in-the-Wall gangs were just components of a single far-flung outlaw combine operating under the collective corporate banner of the "Black Jack Gang." The various gangs were linked, but only on an informal or ad hoc basis; geographical and personal considerations ensured that they could never have solidified into a unified entity.

"William Christian, alias Black Jack," by Ben R. Clark, followed on the heels of the initial publication of the Livingston account. It appeared as a two-part article in *Progressive Arizona and the Great Southwest* (1929–30).

B.D. Titsworth's "Hole-in-the-Wall-Gang," in common with much of Albert Thompson's output, was first seen in the *Union County Leader*. Soon afterwards, in 1957–8, it was reprinted in *True West*. It consists chiefly of newspaper clippings collected by Titsworth's father, a Texan who served for many years as a peace officer in southern Colorado. One of the Titsworths inserted the year into the dateline of each of the newspaper item—an unfortunate interpolation, since the year indicated is not always the right one. Titsworth, the son, adopted a watered-down version of the Livingston super-gang fantasy: he merged the Ketchum and Cassidy-Logan gangs, recruited one "Red Bob" McManus to their already teeming ranks, but excluded the Christian gang (either through good judgment or because he had never heard of it).

Around Western Campfires, by Joseph "Mack" Axford, is a highly interesting record of what its author did, saw, and heard—and he did, saw, and heard a great deal—in the West of the later 1890s and early 1900s. Reassuringly unpretentious in tone, and always entertaining, it is one of the best books of frontier reminiscence.

Cattle, Horses and Men of the Western Range is a first rate book. Its author, Jack Culley, was one of those typically untypical Englishmen of a breed now almost extinct. He was also a top notch cowman. Like most of its type, his book proffers erroneous statements on matters he is reporting from second or third hand, but the mistakes are easily spotted and do not detract markedly from its quality.

William French's substantial fragment of autobiography, *Some Recollections of a Western Ranchman*, was first published in 1927; in 1965, the remainder of the author's original text was restored with the publication of a companion volume, *Further Recollections of a Western Ranchman*. Even more than with most Western memoirs, an effort has to be made to impose a verifiable chronological framework on a narrative containing few dates, and most of those few incorrect. Comparison of French's version of events with contemporary or more detailed accounts is usually unflattering to French. Nevertheless, the two volumes have much to offer to the researcher with the patience or tenacity to dig below their urbane surface. The man French, incidentally, has been described as an Englishman and an Irishman. He was neither; or, rather, both: he was a junior member of the Anglo-Irish Protestant landholding "ascendancy"—a class which contrived to become more Irish than the Irish whilst yet remaining more English than the English, though in his instance the Celtic genetic strain was stronger than he sometimes chose to pretend.

From time to time, reference has been made in the pages that follow to other writings usefully germane to the Ketchum gang, especially those of Miguel A. Otero, Albert Thompson's daughter in law Goldianne (Mrs. Harry Thompson), Jack Potter, Howard Bryan, Mary Laurine Doherty and Emma Adams, and Arthur Soule. Potter was a resident of Clayton; as with Thompson and Titsworth, much of what he wrote was first seen in the *Union County Leader*. It is obvious that he and Thompson freely swapped their recollections. Such other comment on these sources as seems due has been entered in the main text or appended to citations in the Notes.

Since 1970, a number of persons whose lives and names were connected with those of the Ketchums have become the subjects of published monographs. *Bureaucracy, Blood Money, and Black Jack's Gang* (1984) was the last and most ambitious attempt of this writer to describe and explain the career of Black Jack Christian, but it was not until 2002 that the story of the gang's most colorful and resilient member, George Musgrave, was definitively and vividly told in what is probably the most fully-researched study of western outlawry ever published, *Last of the Old-Time Outlaws* (2002), by Karen Holliday Tanner and John D. Tanner, Jr. A few years earlier, Robert K. DeArment's *George Scarborough: The Life and Death of a Lawman on the Closing Frontier*, answered the long-unheard call for a biography of Jeff Milton's friend and saddle partner. This is a fine book, in which the author does not render unto Scarborough that which is not Scarborough's, though the present writer thinks it possible to justify a more austere view of some of Scarborough's attitudes and actions towards the end of his life.

The literature on some of those nearer the periphery of the Ketchum story is more voluminous than that on the Ketchums themselves. The following can be recommended without much reservation: Donna Ernst, *Sundance, My Uncle* (1992) and *Harvey Logan: Wildest of the Wild Bunch* (2003); Sylvia Lynch, *Harvey Logan in Knoxville* (1998); Anne Meadows, *Digging Up Butch and Sundance* (1994; rev. ed. of 2003 cited hereunder unless stated otherwise); and Richard Patterson, *Butch Cassidy: A Biography* (1998). All are seminal.

Larry Pointer's *In Search of Butch Cassidy* (1977) embodies a wealth of original research, but, viewed on its central ground, has to stand as a failure because it is founded on the false premise that, far from being killed in South America, Cassidy returned quietly to the United States and lived on as William Phillips, author of a third-person narrative manuscript, which Pointer believed to have come from Cassidy's hand. In reality, and beyond sustainable doubt,

Cassidy died in Bolivia in 1908 and had nothing whatever to do with Phillips, whose manuscript was a semi-fictitious and semi-informed attempt to reconstitute incidents in Butch's life in outlawry.

Brown Waller's *Last of the Great Western Train Robbers* is a kind of scrapbook journey through the career of Harvey Logan. Waller's sincerity of purpose is not in doubt, even if the purpose is not always accomplished. The book consists mainly of barely rephrased articles from a great many newspapers, indiscriminately assembled, precariously connected, and occasionally remote from Waller's avowed subject. It cannot, therefore, be rated as a prime source; but, with careful use, it becomes a worthwhile adjunct to the closely researched, clear-minded, and well-organized writings of Ernst, Lynch, and Patterson. Pearl Baker was raised in the Robbers' Roost country, and her matchless knowledge of her native topography, its inhabitants, and their ways, illuminates the pages of *The Wild Bunch at Robbers Roost*. But her narrative material is mostly anecdotal, and her presentation of it shows little or no grasp of the imperatives of historical writing. Inconsistencies pass by unremarked, and attempts to check reminiscence against record are conspicuously few. It is not unkind to liken the result to the curate's egg.

No researcher in recent years has cleared out more historical thickets in the domain of Southwestern lawlessness and law-enforcement than Bob Alexander. His books are as entertaining as they are revelatory. Volume II of his *Lawmen, Outlaws, and S.O.Bs* (2004) has five well documented and well illustrated chapters appertaining to Tom Ketchum's story or offshoots of it.

When the first edition of the present book went to press late in 2006, the writer had not heard of the monumental two-volume *Tom Green County: Chronicles of our Heritage* (2003). Had he known the work, he would have been spared errors and omissions which, it is hoped, have been repaired in this second edition. Even more important, he would have benefited from a greater breadth of understanding. Massive as they are, these volumes will not, and cannot, tell every reader everything about everyone and everything with a place in the formal and informal history of Tom Green County; but where there are not facts, there are likely to be clues. They have helped inestimably in the preparation of several chapters of this second edition of *The Deadliest Outlaws*.

There are two histories of Irion County, Texas, of which the author has seen only the earlier, by Leta Crawford (1966). It is short, but good. Crawford's father, Fayette Tankersley, belonged to a pioneering ranching family and was part-owner of the famous 7D outfit; so, one feels, the book might have had more to say about the Ketchums than it does.

As a general work of reference, Sammy Tise's *Texas County Sheriffs* can, here and there, be almost as dangerous as it is indispensable. Fortunately, Tise himself was only too aware of the dangers, and very commendably lessened them by drawing attention to them. His primary source was the State Election Registers filed in Austin. He had seen the records held in some county seats, but not all; consequently, the book will not record anything like every instance in which a sheriff had to be replaced before the end of his elective term.

Special mention must be given to the writings of Larry D. Ball, beginning with his thesis from the late 1960s, *Southwestern Conditions and Outlawry at the Turn of the Century*. Two masterworks of scholarship and good writing have followed: *The United States Marshals of New Mexico and Arizona, 1846–1912* (1978) and *Desert Lawmen: The High Sheriffs of New Mexico and Arizona, 1846–1912* (1992). Both should be in the saddlebags or road safety kit of any prospector who ventures into the treacherous terrain of the history of law enforcement in the further reaches of the American Southwest.

NOTES TO CHAPTER 1

Much of this introductory chapter is an overview of the documented chronicle that follows. Citations from it will, therefore, be confined mainly to direct or indirect quotation.

1. Albert W. Thompson, *Albuquerque ms.*, 1930, 6–7, 90 *Clayton ms.*, 1933, 42; John H. (Jack) Culley, *Cattle, Horses and Men of the Western Range*, 47–8, 55; Howard Bryan, *Robbers, Rogues and Ruffians*, quoting Robert W. "Stuttering Bob" Lewis, 252 (repeated in Bryan, *True Tales of the American Southwest*, 39): John A. Loomis, *Texas Ranchman*, 63–4; Joseph "Mack" Axford, *Around Western Campfires*, 62; Leonard Alverson, *Reminiscences*, as told to Mrs. George (Edith Stratton) Kitt, 9; Walter Hovey, ed. Doris Sturges, "Black Jack Ketchum Tried to Give Me A Break!" *True West*, Vol. 19, No. 1, Whole No. 110 (April 1972), 6–11, 48–52 (50); Ben W. Kemp and Jeff C. Dykes, *Cow Dust and Saddle Leather*, 165–6 (the book is a biography of Kemp's father; Ben E.); Denver, Colorado, *Rocky Mountain News*, 14 March 1900 ("tiger in human form"); ibid., 27 April 1901 ("foreign to his nature"); *Denver Evening Post*, 26 April 1901 ("unloved leader"); *Denver Times*, 25 April 1901 ("ignorant and brutish"); Trinidad, Colorado, *Chronicle-News*, 21 August 1899; San Angelo, Texas, *Standard*, 5 August 1899 ("most overbearing man"), 26 August 1899 (quoting Taft), 9 September 1899 (quoting Knickerbocker letter from "Woodyard Chipling," dated September 6); Miguel A. Otero, *My Nine Years as Governor of the Territory of New Mexico*, 121–4; Jack Potter, *Lead Steer and Other Tales*, "Riding with Black Jack," 107–117 (113) (Reprinted in *Sheriff and Police Journal*, May 1941, 9, 17, 19, 25, 29, a copy of which is preserved in the Pinkerton File, *Ketchum Gang*, Library of Congress, Washington, D.C. Manuscript Division: Box 90, Folder 6. All citations hereunder relate to the *Lead Steer* printing); Elton A. Cunningham, Mogollon, New Mexico, to Lou Blachly, 2 January 1955, transcript of tape recording 129—Transcript No. 3, pp. 5, 7–8, quoting Elzy Lay (The Center for Southwest Research, University of New Mexico, Albuquerque; hereinafter, UNM).
2. *Denver Post*, 29 April 1901 ("called 'Dad'"); Culley, 57; Bryan, Axford, and Alverson, all loc. cit., Thomas Green Chaney, to Ruby Mosley, 20 January 1938, Federal Writers' Project (FWP hereinafter); A. Thompson, *Albuquerque ms*, iv, 11; Santa Fe, New Mexico, *Daily New Mexican*, 21, 25 July 1899.
3. W.H. Reno, Letter, 12 September 1899, in *The Chicago Detective*, October 1899 (in Pinkerton File); State of Texas, County of Sutton: Death Certificate, 3 April 1901; Alverson, loc. cit., Loomis, 66; Roy D. Holt, "The End of Will Carver," *True West*, Vol. 15, No. 4, Whole No. 99 (May-June 1970), 36–8, 86–7, 90 (38 and 86); Axford, loc. cit., A. Thompson, *Albuquerque ms.*, 11, 69; ibid., *Clayton ms.*, 41; Bryan, *Ruffians*, 263–4, quoting Frank Shelton; *San Angelo Standard*, 6 April 1901; Sonora, Texas, *Devil's River News*, 6, 13 April 1901; Donna B. Ernst, *From Cowboy to Outlaw: The True Story of Will Carver*, 3–4; J.H. Yardley, to Elizabeth Doyle, 17 November 1937, (FWP); Thomas Green Chaney, to Ruby Mosley, 20 January 1938, ibid.
4. James D. Horan and Paul Sann, *Pictorial History of the Wild West*, 195; Axford, 62–3; *New Mexican*, 7 September 1899; *San Angelo Standard*, citing Shield, 26 August, 9 September 1899; Dave Atkins, with notes by A.C. Atkins, "From Mother's Son to the Owl Hoot Trail;" "Dave Atkins in South Africa;" "The Highway is My Home;" ms., (hereinafter *Atkins ms., I, II, and III*), West Texas Collection, Angelo State University (WTC, ASU hereinafter).
5. Arthur Soule, *The Tall Texan: The Story of Ben Kilpatrick*, is good on Ben's background and family history and on the last ten years of his life, though weak on the outlawry of the 1890s and inclined to magnify Kilpatrick's part in it.
6. See Chapter 13, n.52 and Chapter 23 (iii): "The Identity of G.W. Franks."
7. Jeff Burton, *Dynamite and Six-shooter*, 5.

8. William M. Griffith, Tucson, Arizona, to Attorney General (Joseph McKenna), Washington, D.C., 9 December 1897, repeating text of letter dated 19 November 1897 which the Department of Justice had denied having seen. (Letters Received: Department of Justice Year File 13065–[18]96 [cited hereinafter as LR: Justice Year File])

9. Creighton M. Foraker, Santa Fe, New Mexico, to Attorney General, 9 October 1897, in ibid.

10. Leta Crawford, *A History of Irion County, Texas*. 37; Kemp and Dykes, 165–6; Axford, 63; W.H. Hutchinson, *The Life and Personal Writings of Eugene Manlove Rhodes: A Bar Cross Man*, 50; Denver, Colorado, *Rocky Mountain News*, and *Republican*, both 28 April 1901.

11. Kemp and Dykes, 166.

12. Much of this paragraph is taken from information supplied by Major Aud Lusk, of Carlsbad, New Mexico, the rancher's younger son, to Philip St. George Cooke, of Santa Fe, on 3 September 1969, and repeated by Cooke to the author later that day. Also, Axford, 259–261, whose informants included Will Carver. Contemporary news accounts of Lay's arrest contain no hint of any kind of previous arrangement, or understanding, between Lusk and the Ketchum gang.

13. Culley, 53.

14. Dispatch from San Antonio, Texas, 19 June, in St. Louis, Missouri, *Globe-Democrat*, 20 June 1897.

15. Potter, 111.

16. San Antonio dispatch of 30 September, in St. Louis *Globe-Democrat*, 1 October 1897.

17. Jack Huchinson, to Lou Blachly, interviewed during 1957 (exact date not stated), transcript of tape recording #169, 27–8 (UNM).

18. Clark Secrest, "Black Jack Died Game: The Bandit Career of Thomas E. Ketchum," *Colorado Heritage*, Autumn 2000, 53–60 (53).

19. Leta Crawford, ibid., 36.

NOTES TO CHAPTER 2

1. The ubiquity of the family name is a matter of observation. References in the *Dictionary of American Biography*, newspapers, and census returns attest to its presence in the States named, and others in New England, Middle West, and Upper South in the 1850s or earlier. Ketchum is the prevalent form, but the original Ketcham is widely found also. Occasional variants are Kitcham, Ketchem, and so on. Berry Spradley, a great-grandson of Sam Ketchum—his mother, Wallene (Mrs. E.C. Spradley, 1919–2001), was the daughter of Sam's son, William Berry Ketchum (1876–1951)—has provided the author with detailed summaries of his thirty-five years of ancestral research (Spradley to author, I—20 November 1973 and c. 1 March 1974; II—11 September 2003; and III—c. 10 October 2003, identified hereafter as Spradley, Family History, I, II, and III).

2. Spradley, Family History, I. and II. Temperance Ketchum's first two children were James W. and Joseph, born in 1842 and 1845 respectively, but both died before or during the move to Texas. Another boy, Abner, was born in San Saba County on February 2, 1856, but died soon afterwards. Elizabeth was born on March 20, 1848.

3. Spradley, Family History, I. *Eighth Census of the United States, 1860: State of Texas—County of San Saba*, Sheet 11, entries 76, 78; *Ninth Census of the United States, 1870*, ibid., S. 9, lines 12–16.

4. "Advance sheets" for *Resources, Soil and Climate of Texas*, by A.W. Speight, State Commissioner of Statistics, in San Saba, Texas, *News*, 13 January 1883.

5. "Description of San Saba County," in *San Saba News*, 25 December 1880. The article was, in part, a promotional prospectus, designed to foster local self-confidence and attract capital and immigration. Hence the risk of drought was glossed over. The *News* columns knew better; thus, a "Richland local" in the issue of 29 August 1882: "No rain yet, but a number of long faces." Such plaints were common.

6. "Description of Richland Valley," ibid., 23 December 1882.

7. *1870 U.S. Census, Texas*, loc. cit., and entry 77; Spradley, Family History, I.

8. Spradley, Family History, I. On the morning before his execution on 26 April 1901, Tom said he was "forty years old the last day of last October," thereby overstating his age by three years. Maybe his memory faltered under the gravity of the occasion. The Denver *Rocky Mountain News* and *Republican*, in almost identical reports published on 28 April 1901, carried the fullest account of his death-cell statement.

9. Spradley, Family History, I; J. Marvin Hunter, "Jim Ketchum's Last Stand," *Frontier Times*, Vol. 24, No. 12 (September 1947), 544, incorporated in Spradley, Family History, III; F. Stanley, *No Tears for Black Jack Ketchum*, 23, quoting J. Evetts Haley, *Fort Concho and the Texas Frontier*, 155; Barbara Barton, *Den of Outlaws* (2000), 8–10; Mrs. Helen Ketchum, widow of Jim Ketchum's son Van, to Nellie B. Cox, February 1938, FWP. Tom Ketchum stated that the family members killed on that occasion were both uncles (*Rocky Mountain News*, 27 April 1901).

10. Spradley, Family History, I; *San Saba News*, 25 December 1880.

11. Spradley, ibid.

12. *1870 Census*, loc. cit.

13. Spradley, ibid. The cemetery is at Harkeyville, three miles west of San Saba town. .

14. Ibid.

15. An early example of the misleading reports of Tom's educational attainments ("A College Man," declared the headline) appeared in the *Rocky Mountain News*, 8 November 1897. The culminatory nonsense, garnishing him with a degree from Harvard, and accompanied by a crude line drawing shamelessly presented as a depiction of Black Jack, was decanted upon readers of the *San Francisco Chronicle*, 21 March 1898. Its publication coincided with, or was germinated by, a rollicking extravaganza wired from El Paso the previous day. The product of this haphazard brew of fact and fable was a composite figure created out of Tom Ketchum, Black Jack Christian, and a minor wrongdoer named John (or Howard) McDonald. The same story, with sundry additions, subtractions, elaborations, and variations, is found in many other organs, the versions in the *San Angelo Standard*, 12 August 1899 ("Black Jake"), *The National Police Gazette*, 6 January 1900 ("His Only Romance a Bar-Room Wedding"), and *Denver Post* 26 April 1901 ("Black Jack's Evil Deeds") being especially outlandish. An earlier emanation from the *Denver Post* (18 July 1899, but probably cooked up in 1897 and doled out a time or two thereafter), ingeniously consolidates all the main ingredients of the stew into a personage named Jacob Emmons: a native of Vineland, New Jersey, well connected and well educated, who worked as a cowboy for eleven years before enlisting as a U.S. Army scout at Fort Whipple, Arizona; inherited $1,500 in 1893; left the army; dissipated his inheritance within a month; drifted into Sonora; and reappeared on American soil as the murderous cut-throat Black Jack. The story of Mr. Emmons, fact or fiction, contains little that would have been recognizable to Messrs. Christian, Ketchum, and McDonald.

16. *San Saba News*, 14 February 1880, 24 June 1882; A. Thompson, *Albuquerque ms.*, iv, 16.

17. *San Saba News*, 23 December 1882, 3 February 1883. The latter item reported that the public school at Richland Springs was of recent construction. Any school in previous use there must have been run on ad hoc lines. Shield was born on 22 March 1862 (*San Angelo Standard*,

30 March 1895). He spoke of his boyhood acquaintance with Tom Ketchum while waiting for a train at Trinidad, Colorado (unidentified and undated newspaper item, presumably *Trinidad Chronicle-News*, 2 September 1899, reproduced in B.D. Titsworth, "Hole-in-the-Wall Gang," Part II, *True West*, Vol. 4, No. 3, Whole No. 18 (January-February 1957), 20–23, 30–32 (20).

18. Spradley, Family History, I; *Rocky Mountain News*, 27 and 28 April 1901.

19. *1870 U.S. Census: Texas—San Saba County*, (Exclusive of Town of San Saba), numerous entries on S. 6, 7, 8, and 10; ibid., Town of San Saba), S.1, L.5 and 7. Outside the town there were also four households of Montgomerys and two large collections of Kuykendalls. Chris Weatherby, "From No Account to Plain Mean," *Old West*, Vol. 10, No. 4, Whole No. 40 (Summer 1974), 26–7, 64–5 (26) gives the location of the Duncan place as "near the north mouth of Richland Creek." See also Dee Harkey, *Mean as Hell*, (1st ed.) 1–6, 11, 20.

20. Weatherby, 26.

21. *Index to Probate Cases of Texas, from January 30, 1866 to June 28, 1939*: Case no. 29, Thomas E. Ketchum—a minor, filed 17 March 1880; Weatherby, 26; El Paso, Texas, *Herald*, in *New Mexican*, 7 October 1899.

22. Shelton, "Recollections," 1932, quoted from Albuquerque, New Mexico, *Tribune* by Bryan, *Ruffians*, 253–4 (but Shelton seems to err in charging Ketchum with the robbery of a store in Knickerbocker—see Chapter 4, n. 52 and relevant text).

23. Weatherby, 26.

24. *Denver Republican*, 27 April 1901.

25. Harkey, 21.

26. Spradley, Family History, I.

27. *1870 Census*, ibid., (Exclusive of Town of San Saba), S. 9, L. 17–26. The household was enumerated as A.E. Duncan, 47; his wife, Mary M., 38; Harriet, 16; Alex. A.. (a misreading or mishearing of Abijah), 13; Jane, 9; James P., 8; Richard, 6; Julia A, 4; Ann B., 3; and George T., 1.

28. Many of the county's cattle and horse brands were shown in successive issues of the *San Saba News*; for example, on 10 September 1881 and 14 February 1882. But some ranchers declined to advertise, maintaining that their brands were already familiar to all, or that it would be a mistake to make them familiar (*San Saba News*, 15 December 1883).

29. *San Saba News*, 23 December 1882.

30. Ibid., 24 December 1886; 14 January, 1 April 1887; Spradley, Family History, I, II, III; *Tenth Census of the United States, 1880: State of Texas—County of San Saba*, Precinct 1, page 6. Although the Nicholas Ketchums, were not closely related to the family of Green Berry Ketchum, Nicholas's profession was the germ of an oft-repeated tale that Tom and his brothers were the sons of a physician. As far as this writer has learned, this began with Albert Thompson in 1930 (*Albuquerque ms.*, 8) and first occurred in print three year later in Thompson's *Early History of Clayton* (*Clayton ms.*, 40); it was omitted from Thompson's *Open Range Days*. The story was repeated in 1939 by Thompson's friend Jack Potter ("Riding with Black Jack," 110) and re-emerged in Ed Bartholomew, *Black Jack Ketchum: Last of the Holdup Kings*, 9, as part of an incorrect statement that the father was still living when Tom's family moved to Tom Green County. Further appearances followed in close succession: Part I of B.D. Titsworth's "The Hole-in-the-Wall Gang," *True West*, Vol. 4, No. 2, Whole No. 17 (November-December 1956), 4–10, 30–2(4), but previously published in the Clayton *Union County Leader*, dates unknown; Stanley, 6–7; Goldianne Thompson, William H. Halley, and Simon Herzstein, *Clayton, the Friendly Town in Union County, New Mexico*, 144. (Goldianne Thompson was the widow of Albert's son Harry.) Neither Albert Thompson nor Potter says how he got the story. Tom Ketchum, whom Potter knew and whom Thompson interviewed, is not its source: just before his execution he said simply, "My father was a cowman" (*Rocky Mountain News* and *Denver Republican*, 28 April 1901). Probably Potter took the story from

Thompson, who may have been misled by a flaw in the memory of Gerome Shield or some other Texas informant.

31. Spradley, Family History, I.

32. Ibid., and *Tenth U.S. Census, 1880: Texas—San Saba County*, Precinct 9, p. 2.

33. Otero, 122, where the former governor recalls a conversation with Berry Ketchum after Tom's refusal to see Berry.

34. A. Thompson, *Albuquerque ms.*, 19; Loomis, 64.

35. Austin, Texas, dispatch, in *San Francisco Chronicle*, 29 July 1899.

36. *Rocky Mountain News* and *Denver Republican*, both 28 April 1901.

37. A. Thompson. *Albuquerque ms.*, 11.

38. Ibid., 12.

39. Ibid.

40. *San Saba News*, 7 January 1882.

41. Ibid., 28 January 1882.

42. The killing of a granger, W.A. Brown, by T.G.T. Kendall, and the State governor's insertion of a force of Rangers to protect Kendall against Brown's friends, was an early illustration of the mounting tensions between large and small ranchers, and an unheeded warning for the far worse troubles that lay ahead. (*San Saba News*, 1 June 1878; C.L. Sonnichsen, *I'll Die Before I'll Run*, 208–210).

43. Harkey, 20–21.

44. Ross McSwain to author, in conversation, 31 May 2008. McSwain has spent many years studying the San Saba Mob. See n. 54.

45. *San Saba News*, 3 November 1883.

46. In ibid., 24 February 1883, Sam Ketchum's name occurs twice in the list of those taking bed and breakfast at Mrs. M.I. Bostick's hotel in San Saba town. That is the last seen of him in the author's microfilm copy of a very incomplete file of that newspaper.

47. *Tom Green County: Chronicles of Our Heritage—Volume I: General History* (hereinafter cited as Tom Green County, I), 146, "Knickerbocker Community" by Katharine T. Waring, which states that the Ketchum family and Abijah Duncan were residents before the flood which destroyed Ben Ficklin, the original county seat, in 1882. The author does not believe any of them were more than temporary or transient residents before about 1885. See n. 48.

48. Knickerbocker was founded in 1877 by four sheepmen from New York State: Joseph Tweedy, J.B. Reynolds, and W.T. and Lawrence Grinnell. Their choice of name for the infant settlement was a whimsicality, sprouting from the Grinnell brothers' familiarity with the humorous *History of New York* written by Washington Irving under the pseudonym "Diedrick Knickerbocker" (Barton, 2–4).

Barton's statement (12) that Berry Ketchum moved to the Knickerbocker area in 1880 is incorrect; the exact date has yet to be determined, but is believed to have been near the turn of 1884–85. The Ketchum brothers knew the westward trails and may have lingered in the San Angelo locality for weeks at a time before that date, but that is not the same as settling there. Spradley, Family History, I, states that Sam was a Half Circle Six employee for the second half of 1885.

49. *San Saba News*, 19 December 1885. Similarly charged and similarly dealt with at the same session of court, were Willis Johnson, who may have been merely the namesake of the current sheriff of Tom Green County (1884–92), and J.T. Rutledge, a future sheriff of Irion County.

50. *Tenth U.S. Census, 1880: Texas—Tom Green County*, Precinct No. 2, p. 4. Spradley, Family History III, says that George W. Ketchum, the oldest son of the James Ketchum who had been slain in 1867, had settled on Dove Creek in the 1870s. The 1880 Census has no entry for this George; and, while this is absolute proof of nothing, the probability is that one George was

taken for the other. It seems inconceivable that the two were actually one; for a start, the George whose presence was recorded by the enumerator was living not in or near Knickerbocker, but in a section of Fort Concho whose inhabitants were mostly natives of Mexico, as he claimed to be.

51. Spradley, Family History, I; *Ninth U.S. Census, 1870; Texas—San Saba County*, S.1, L. 1–3; *Tenth ibid., 1880—San Saba County*, Precinct 9, p. 3; *Rocky Mountain News*, 27 April 1901. See also Chapter 3.

52. For early references to Rutledge and various Kuykendalls, see *San Saba News*, 19 December 1885; to Tap Duncan, ibid., 2 December 1887, 23 November 1888; York, ibid., 27 April 1887; and to Cheney, ibid., 27 April and 23 November 1888. The Cheney family is listed (with that spelling) in the 1880 *U.S. Census, San Saba County*, precinct 5, p. 1, not far from the household of Mary Ellen Ketchum, widow of the murdered James. William H., was then 18—the eldest of the five children of William C. Cheney, a widower. The family name was, and is, often spelled Chaney, which is how Cheney is pronounced. (Thomas Green Chaney, to Ruby Mosley, 30 January 1938—FWP); also, extract from ibid., in Spradley, Family History, III. Thomas Chaney, enumerated like the others as Cheney, was three years younger than his brother Will.) The Shield family seems to have made no mark in San Saba and had moved on by 1880, but Rome Shield's name figures in well over one hundred items in the *San Angelo Standard* from mid–1892 to the end of 1902, alone.

▪   Harkey, 22, says his brother, Sheriff Joseph M. Harkey, arrested Bige and Dick Duncan for stealing harness and other accouterments, and that a "Mr. Trobridge" subsequently had them charged with horse theft. The gaps in the microfilmed files of the *San Saba News*, and the unavailability of the court records, preclude verification (or refutation), though it is certain that Barlow Trobridge lived near the Ketchums and Duncans, and that George W. Trowbridge was a resident of Locker, a few miles north of Richland Springs.

In February 1889, Dick Duncan and Walter Landers battered to death the widow Naomi Williamson, her widowed daughter Lavinia Holmes, her mentally retarded son Ben, and her younger daughter Beauleah (affianced to Dick). The murderers tied the bodies to a wagon, dragged them through the dirt, lashed them to rocks, and pitched them into the Rio Grande near Eagle Pass. Dick was arrested several months later and convicted. The principal witnesses for the defense were Abijah Duncan, Sr. and Dick's younger brother, Tap. After a lengthy debate over the competency of the Texas court, Dick was hanged at Eagle Pass on September 18, 1891. The tombstone erected by kinsfolk includes the phrase "Murdered at Eagle Pass," an opinion that cannot easily be supported by fact or reason. Landers was never apprehended. (Weatherly, as cited; dispatches from San Antonio, Austin, and Eagle Pass in St. Louis, Missouri, *Globe-Democrat*, 1 and 6 March, 5 and 9 December 1889; 16 May 1890; 8 July, 4 August, 18 and 19 September 1891.)

53. *San Saba News*, 7 January, 10 June, 16 December 1887. Dee Harkey's book mentions none of this.

54. These events are brilliantly described and at least partly explained in Sonnichsen, *I'll Die*, 206–231. There was much that Sonnichsen was unable to learn or felt unable to say, for some of which see Ross McSwain, *See No Evil, Speak No Evil* (published November 2008).

NOTES TO CHAPTER 3

1. Sources as in Chapter 2, n. 15. The alleged background and purported history of the Jacob Emmons personage was mismatched first with the identity of Black Jack of the High Five gang and then with that of Tom Ketchum, as their two distinct lives and personalities became inter-

twined and began to merge into a hybrid half-factual figure with some of Tom Ketchum's attributes and background. The name of Emmons soon became absent from most of the retellings, variants, and ornamentations of the Black Jack yarn; the name of Ketchum often replaced it.

2. Charles Kelly, *Outlaw Trail*, rev. ed., 23–5, named Sam and Tom Ketchum as the owners of the ranch, but only because he read too much into the manuscript recollections of the bank robber Tom McCarty. McCarty's partner in crime, Willard Erastus Christiansen, alias Matt Warner, referred to the Ketchum ranch without drawing any connection between it and the outlaw brothers from Texas (Warner, as told to Murray E. King, *The Last of the Bandit Riders*, 95–7; but Christiansen/Warner was far from the last of the bandit riders). McCarty wrote only that a Sam Ketchum owned the ranch near Milford, which was quite true; but he was not the Sam Ketchum from San Saba and Tom Green counties, Texas (Jon M. and Donna McDaniel Skovlin, *In Pursuit of the McCartys*, 31–6, 41, 70–1).

3. Thomas Edgar Crawford, ed. Jeff C. Dykes, *The West of the Texas Kid*, 43–5. Like many other bearers of a nickname with "Tex" or "Texas" in it, Crawford was not a Texan. He came from Ohio.

Although Tom Ketchum was not called "Black Jack" by anyone who met him before his arrest in 1899, and never spoken or written of as such before 1897, that in itself does not disprove T.E. Crawford's story; irrespective of the honesty or dishonesty of his narrative, he could have referred to Ketchum as "Black Jack" just to make the character more readily recognizable to the reader.

4. John Rolfe Burroughs, *Where the Old West Stayed Young*, 50.

5. *Tom Green County, I*: Suzanne Campbell, "Brief Overview . . . ." 1–2; "Creation and Organization . . . ," 21–2.

6. *San Angelo Standard*, 24 June 1893 ("Report of the Commissioner of Agriculture, 1891–2"); 29 December 1894 ("After Seventeen Years: San Angelo Then and Now"); 16 November 1895 ("Great San Angelo").

7. *Tom Green County*, I, 5; endpage maps: front: modern Tom Green County, back: Tom Green County, 1874 (also in endpages of Volume II, *Family Histories*, hereinafter cited as *Tom Green County, II*); Marker, Tom Green County Historical Commission, Concho Park, San Angelo; maps, as cited in n. 5. Use has also been made of DeLorme's *Texas Atlas and Gazetteer* (Yarmouth, Maine, 2001), 54–5; and, for statewide reference, Maps.com *Atlas of Texas: Historical and Thematic Maps*.

8. The deadliest flood was the one that carried away the county seat, Ben Ficklin, in 1882. The town was never rebuilt, and the county seat was moved to San Angelo. In the spring of 1900 the waters of the North Concho were reported to be "nearly as high as in the Great Flood of 1882." (*Tom Green Times*, 26 August 1882, rep., *San Angelo Standard*, 3 September 1898; *Standard*, 7 and 14 April 1900.) Storms of less intensity, but whose effects were ravaging nonetheless, happened in several intervening years. The flooding of Menardville (now Menard), in June, 1896, was the subject of an effective photograph by Noah Rose, in Oran Warder Nolen, "Noah H. Rose—Frontier Camera," *Old West*, Vol. 4. No. 3, Whole No. 15 (Spring 1968), 30–35, 50 (34).

9. Barton, 43–5, for the early years of the Half Circle Six as a cattle outfit.

10. *San Angelo Standard*, 15 April 1899.

11. Loomis, 53.

12. Mrs. Elender Ervin had arrived in San Angelo in 1886 (Ervin to Nellie B. Cox, 5 January 1938, FWP).

S.L.S. Smith's medical services and position on the board of the Concho National Bank were regularly advertised in the *San Angelo Standard*, for instance in the issues of 20 July and 24 August 1895.

13. Barton, 12.
14. Seaton Keith to Nellie B. Cox, 8 February 1938, FWP.
15. Keith was a member of the San Angelo's champion team-of-four in the "whist carnival" at Dallas in October 1899. W.A. Guthrie, for some years an editor and co-proprietor of the *San Angelo Standard* and a fellow member of the whist four, declared that Keith was probably the best player of all. References in the *Standard* include those in the issues of 18 October 1899 and 29 September 1900. See also, Keith to Cox, ibid., *Tom Green County.* II, 187, 235, 321, 448; Loomis, 71, 85–6.
16. A. Thompson, *Albuquerque ms.*, 11.
17. Keith, interviewed Cox, as cited.
18. Sayles's principal work was *The Annotated Statutes of Texas* (1895). He died on 22 May 1897 (*San Angelo Standard*, 29 May 1897).
19. Trinidad, Colorado, *Chronicle-News*, 2 September 1899, in Titsworth, II, 20.

If the *San Angelo Standard* had reported the dog-chasing and congregation-chousing incident, there would be no chronological problem. But it did not; during that period, it often chose not to report the lesser misdemeanors of local offenders. On 10 June 1893, it reported that Shield had shot a mad dog on the streets of San Angelo; but this could not have been connected with the Ketchum incident: Shield had been in office nearly seven months, and, moreover, Tom was in New Mexico. Support for the redating comes out of Shield's own mouth. After visiting Ketchum's hospital cell in August 1899, he commented that had not seen Tom since 1892 or 1893. (He might have added, but did not, that he had tried hard enough to catch sight of him in the meantime—on at least two occasions while Tom was watching him. See Chapter 10.)

In 1930, Shield furnished Albert W. Thompson, of Clayton, with a written account of Tom's life in Texas, which Thompson used in the preparation of the *Albuquerque ms.*, and to a far lesser extent, for his *Early History of Clayton, New Mexico*, of 1933. In Thompson's later book, *They Were Open Range Days*, Shield was again quoted (182) as having written that he arrested Tom in 1892.

20. J. Willis Johnson was elected in 1888 to his third successive term. Nor did Shield serve in 1890–92. Records of election returns at the Texas State Archives, as cited in Sammy Tise's book *Texas County Sheriffs*, show that Shield was first elected sheriff on November 4, 1890. This is incorrect: Shield was not even a candidate for the sheriff's office, although he did run for the post of stock inspector, and was elected. Johnson was easily re-elected sheriff that year, and went on to serve a full fourth term. At the time of the 1890 electoral campaign, Shield was defendant in a murder case. He was acquitted about three weeks after the election. Two years later, the local Democratic Party nominated him as its candidate to succeed Johnson. Shield came out top of the poll on November 8, 1892, and, in accordance with the laws of Texas (until 1922), assumed office upon approval of his bond. One of his first official acts was to appoint Johnson as a deputy, along with a couple of Johnson's own former deputies (*San Angelo Standard*, 22 March, 8, 15, 22 November 1890; 19, 26 November, 3 December 1892; *Dallas News*, 29 November 1890; Tise, 403).
21. Spradley, Family History, III.
22. *Tenth U.S. Census, 1880: San Saba County*, Precinct 5, p. 6. Eula, a boarder with the Joseph Neeper household, was enumerated as "Ula."
23. Spradley, Family History, III.
24. Ibid., I; Barton, 39.
25. For some of his transactions in livestock and land see *San Antonio Standard*, 26 November 1892; 25 July, 21 November, 19, 26 December 1896, 25 September 1897; 30 July 1898; 2 April 1899. His involvement in, or attendance at, the races at Sherwood and Ozona is noted in ibid., 3 March 1894 and 20 July and 31 August 1895.

26. Ibid., 14 May 1892.

27. Ibid., 3 April 1897.

28. Ibid., 9 October 1897.

29. Ibid., 9 and 16 March 1901.

30. Ibid., 18 March 1899.

31. Bartholomew, 8, and Barton, 61, say that the brothers worked for R.F. Tankersley, though Barton's assertion that they did so "after the murders in New Mexico" is plainly wrong. The murders were those of Levi Herzstein and Merejildo Gallegos (see Chapter 5), which occurred in 1896, and the Ketchums did no cattle work in Texas after that. Bartholomew, 6, also has Tom working alongside Jack Miles, the roping champion-to-be, on the ranch of the well-known San Angelo pioneer, Jonathan Miles. Bartholomew offers no source, but the statement is readily credible. (Jonathan Miles's eventual fall was not much less spectacular than Tom's, but it is not a story that belongs here.) Elsewhere (ibid. 8), Bartholomew writes, again with plausibility but without proof, that Tom was employed by the vast Prairie Cattle Company, whose brands included the Cross L, formerly of San Saba County, and LIT (purchased in 1881 from George Littlefield). In 1889 the Cross L ran cattle on the range north of the new town of Clayton, New Mexico; the LIT pasture was just to the southeast of Clayton, in Hartley County, Texas. Dave McCrohan said that Sam and Tom worked on his father's ranch for two years "and made good dependable hands at the time" (McCrohan to Ruth Mosley, 20 January 1938, FWP).

32. Harvey E. Chesley, *Adventuring with the Old Timers: Trails Traveled, Tales Told*, 118 and 128 (Note).

33. V.H. Whitlock (Ol' Waddy), *Cowboy Life on the Llano Estacado*, 7, 8, 137; Chaney, to Mosley, as cited, FWP.

34. Whitlock, 18–19, 133–7.

35. Chesley, 118. W.M. "Bob" Beverly served as sheriff of Midland County from 1908 to 1912 (Tise, 373).

36. Donna B. Ernst, "Unraveling Two Outlaws Named Carver," WOLA *Journal*, 30–32 (30). Ernst thinks that Tom's companion would have been Tod, rather than Will.

37. Edward Wilson, *An Unwritten History: A Record from the Exciting Days of Early Arizona*, 60.

38. The Burrow and Cornett-Whitley gangs attracted a huge amount of attention during 1887–8 from such Texas dailies as the *Houston Post, Austin Statesman*, and *San Antonio Express*, and from several out-of-State papers, notably the *St. Louis Globe-Democrat*. G.W. Agee, *Rube Burrow, King of Outlaws, and his Band of Train Robbers*, published in 1890, concentrated mainly on the second, post-Texas phase of Burrow's lawlessness. It was reprinted in *Old West*, Vol. 4, No. 3, Whole No. 15 (Spring 1968), 67–96.

The Cornett-Whitley gang received coverage in Jeff Burton, "The Most Surprised Man in Texas," *Frontier Times*, Vol. 47, No. 2, New Series No. 82 (March 1973), 18–21, 50–53, 69; Burton, "'The Great Manhunt' : Correspondence from 'W.B.S.' : Some Scenes of Violence and Gunplay in Texas," English Westerners' *Brand Book*, Vol. 18 (1975–6), 11–34; Robert W. Stephens, *Bullets and Buckshot in Texas*, 60–86, 204–215; Gary Fitterer, ms., "'He Will Rob No More,'" (chapter 12 from unfinished biography of Alfred Allee) (copy to author, courtesy Chuck Parsons); Parsons, "The Fate of Several Texas Outlaws in the Indian Territory," *Okolha*, Vol. 1, No. 4 (Winter 2004), 9–13.

The best collective contemporary source for the robberies specifically mentioned in this paragraph of text is the *Globe-Democrat*, which printed more telegraphic material than any other newspaper in America (its nearest competitor in this respect was the rival *St.Louis Republican*—renamed *Republic* during 1887). See the issues of 18, 20, 21, 22, 26, 30 June 1888 (Big Horn); 15, 16 July 1888 (La Junta); 16 April 1889 (Grover); 26, 30 June 1889 (Telluride); 5 August 1889 (Cheyenne, near Tascosa, Texas); 8, 9 August 1889 (Thompson Springs); 9, 10,

12 June 1890 (New Salem); and 31 July, 1 August 1890 (Trinidad). The quotation is from W.S. Parkhurst, a Denver & Rio Grande conductor, at a railroaders' convention in St. Louis (*Globe-Democrat*, 13 May 1891).

39. *Territory of New Mexico, Statutes of 1887*, Chap. 19, S. 1; *Compiled Laws of 1897*, Sec. 1151.

40. Albert Thompson, *Clayton ms.*, 41; Goldianne Thompson, Halley, and Herzstein, 140–1. Stanley, 120–8, contains much historical material on Clayton, mostly drawn from the files of its first newspaper, the *Enterprise*.

41. A. Thompson, *Clayton ms.*, 48; *New Mexican*, 5 September 1899, derived from Ketchum's statement to Miguel Desmarias (whose name has often been misspelled Desmarais), the prison surgeon who cut off the outlaw's wounded and festering right arm. Desmarias said that Ketchum "refused alcoholic stimulants" even at the conclusion of the operation. Speaking directly to the press, just before his execution, Tom said that he "was never drunk in his life," which may have done only partial credit to his abstemiousness (*Rocky Mountain News, Denver Republican*, both 28 April 1901).

42. Quoted in A. Thompson, ibid., 41. Hinkle later served as governor of New Mexico.

43. Potter, 110, and Thompson, loc. cit.

44. George Fitzpatrick, Santa Fe, New Mexico, tape recording, February 1964, re-recorded for the author in Santa Fe by Colin Rickards and Phil Cooke, with Fitzpatrick's permission, October 1967. Fitzpatrick edited *New Mexico* magazine and had compiled material on the Ketchum gang from first-hand sources over a period of many years.

45. A. Thompson, *Albuquerque ms.*, 66.

46. William Cooley Urton, to Georgia B. Redfield, Roswell, New Mexico, 3 September 1936 (transcribed 14 September 1936) and 20 January 1939 (FWP). William Cooley Urton (1878–?) was the eldest son of William G. Urton (1843–1929), a stockholder in the Missouri-based Cass Land and Cattle Company and prime mover in the establishment of the 7HL outfit in eastern New Mexico. The Cass Company's brand became the Bar V after its acquisition of the neighboring JJ outfit in 1889.

47. *Trinidad Chronicle-News*, 2 September 1899. Shield had just met Tom for what he said was the first time since "about 1892 or 1893."

48. *San Angelo Standard*, 3 December 1892.

49. Ibid., 4 March 1893.

50. Tom's sojourn at the Rhodes ranch is in Hutchinson, 50. Although no date is given, the visit could hardly have taken place earlier than Ketchum's last season with the Bar V's (1893) or after his engagement by the VV's in the spring or summer of 1894.

51. *San Angelo Standard*, 30 September 1893. Less than a year earlier the Coleman, Texas, *Voice* had described Miles as "the champion roper of the world." (In ibid., 26 November 1892.)

52. Potter, The Trail Drives of Texas, (1920), contributor; Cattle Trails in the Old West, 1935. Lead Steer and Other Tales (1936). Jack Myers Potter was born in Caldwell, Texas, in December 1864. Jack, like his father, was loose-footed as a young and youngish man, and seldom at home. In 1882 he was hired by the New England Livestock Co. and remained with the company until it sold out in 1893. He purchased the Escondido ranch, near Clayton, in 1894. In his writings—most of which postdate his retirement from ranch management in 1928—he does not always attempt to distinguish between history and romance. In the judgment of his friend J. Frank Dobie: "Jack Potter's imagination is a joy; his fancy, when he turns it loose, is as refreshing as rain on a drouth-browned mesa . . . Here is the stuff of history, it being understood that history is something more than naked literalness." (Dobie may have been the supreme arbiter of such questions; he might almost have been writing about himself.)

53. Potter, 107–110. In the "Sheriff and Police" reprint, 17, the name Bose is given as Rose. This has a more convincing ring to it, but, whichever form is correct, the man behind the name can-

not be identified. Perhaps his real name was neither Bose nor Rose; the name Slim may also be an invention. But the story itself rings true.

54. The author has lost the reference to this quotation, but no special insight is required to conclude that its application may have been rather general.

55. Loomis, 32, 63–4.

56. *San Angelo Standard*, 6 October 1894.

57. Ibid., 3 October 1896.

58. Ibid., 13, 20, 27 October and 3 November 1894.

59. R.F. Tankersley was quite frequently mentioned by the Knickerbocker correspondents of the *San Angelo Standard*. Thus a "Knickerbocker Local" of 2 September 1893 reported that he had been rounding up his cattle "preparatory to shipping some fat cows to market," while on 28 October of that year "Knickerbocker Gleanings" noted that he had driven cattle down to the Pecos for the winter, and commended his example to others. The names of the Collynses were even oftener in the paper. On 30 January 1894, G.W. Shield, M.B. Pulliam, Bailyn Collyns, Drumm & [William] Collyns, and William Hiler, sheriff of Sterling County, were among the dozen cowmen who published a proclamation advertising their intention to prevent by all lawful means "the unwarranted tresspass [sic] of drifting sheepmen" (*San Angelo Standard*, 24 February 1894).

The wedding of Charles Collyns and Pearl Collins was recorded in ibid., 1 May 1897.

60. Ibid., 7 July 1900, where for the first time those convicted in County Court on gaming charges were identified by name. The change of policy may have reflected the editor's awareness of a shift in public attitudes; it may no longer have been the prevailing view that such misdemeanors were too trifling for exposure of the names of offenders in the columns of the local press.

61. The Legal Tender ("Restaurant, Bowling Alley and Billiard Hall"), was one of many San Angelo saloons to place a weekly advertisement in the *Standard*; the issue of 23 July 1898 has a typical example. Crenshaw worked and played in partnership with Rome Shield. Together they pursued and captured a notorious murderer and highwayman, Will Simmons; arrested another killer, H.H. Rushing, and took charge of an unsuccessful panther hunt "on Pecan Mountain at the head of east Grape Creek" (ibid., 14 July 1894, 21 and 30 November 1895).

62. The *San Angelo Standard* and *Devil's River News*, in their joint report of Will Carver's death published on 6 April 1901, mentioned the Ketchum-Carver gaming partnership, but without saying more than that the arrangement had lasted "only a short time a few years ago." The statement was repeated unadorned in numerous books and articles, the earliest being Part II of Carl B. Livingston's three-part series "Hunting Down the Black Jack Gang," (London, *Wide World*, September 1930, reprinted April 1955), 12–23 (20) of reprint. Much more recently, Soule, 16, has cited unspecified County Tax Returns as disclosing that Sam Ketchum "operated a saloon or gaming table in San Angelo in 1895." Such records presumably would not classify the premises as a gambling hall, for the more than sufficient reason that gaming in a public place was unlawful in Texas. Still, the year could well be the right one.

63. *San Angelo Standard*, 18 August 1895.

64. Atkins's background, origins, and early life are well described by A. C. Atkins, Introduction to *Atkins ms.*, I, 1 and Barton, 12–15. See also correspondence and notes in Joel Tom Meador files and "John J. Atkins," undated press cutting in B.D. Arthur, *Scrapbook No. 3*, (WTC, ASU).

65. *Tenth Census. 1880: State of Texas-McCulloch County*, where George W., (later known as Bud), then seven years old, is shown as the eldest child of George R. Upshaw (age 30, b. Missouri) and his wife Delphine (age 23, b. Texas). At that time, there were three younger boys (Charlie, Edwin, and Alex); later, at least two more children were added (a son, Dee, and a daughter, L'Ada). The family was living in Tom Green County in the early 1890s, if not earlier.

They moved to Val Verde County circa 1896, where, in January, 1898, George, Sr., unarmed, was fatally shot in the back by Roy Bean's son, Sam, from the Jersey Lilly saloon in Langtry. A trial jury decided that these circumstances did not add up to murder; Sam himself was knifed to death in Del Rio in 1907. Also during the early 1900s, L'Ada Upshaw was married on the Pecos High Bridge. (Joel Tom Meador File, West Texas Collection, Angelo State University; C L. Sonnichsen, *The Story of Roy Bean: Law West of the Pecos*, 154–7, 188, [pb ed.,]; Douglas Lee Braudaway, *Val Verde County*, 58–9; Braudaway, *Railroads of Western Texas: San Antonio to El Paso*, 45.)

It has not been established whether the George Upshaws were closely related to a family listed in the 10th Census as resident in Precinct 13, San Saba County. Thomas A. Upshaw and his wife Mary Jane were from Alabama; their first children, John and Juliette were born in Louisiana; the rest—Mary, Jane, Sarah, and Jeremiah—in Texas. Jeremiah was listed as a female; but so, as we have seen, was Tom Ketchum. This can be attributed to the enumerator's haste or carelessness. In the instance of the Thomas Upshaw household, the mistake may have been facilitated by the fact that the entries preceding Jeremiah's were for females.

NOTES TO CHAPTER 4

1. *San Angelo Standard*, 1 December 1894 (Miller's purchase); ibid., 21 January, 18 June 1892 (rental of Loomis's pasture) and 29 July 1895, (his leasing of the "pecan privilege"); ibid., 23 October 1897 (Metcalfe's sale of the XQZ). Metcalfe's life and career are summarized on a Tom Green County Historical Commission marker in grounds of the courthouse at San Angelo.
2. *Tom Green County*. I, 19, 20, 63, 140, 227–9. The *San Angelo Standard*, 12 August 1893 reported the death of James Spears.
3. The *San Angelo Standard* teems with references to these and other local cattle outfits. A few are: 14 January, 8 April 1893 (Fayette Tankersley and the 7D); 18 February 1893 (Charles Metcalfe and the XQZ); 8 July 1893, 24 February 1894 (Bailyn Collyns); 5 August 1893 (Will Collyns's purchase of interest in the DOK); 14 May 1892; 14 September 1895 (Drumm and Will Collyns sell nearly 3000 steers); 21 December 1895 (brands of Joe, Ike, Tom, and Will Funk); 21 April, 12 and 19 May, 30 June 1894, 23 March 1895 (Comer Bros., and life on the 4 Cross L); 19 August 1893, 7 February and 10 November 1894, 20 April 1895 (Blake Taylor). Among the local ranchers who attended the Texas Cattlemen's Convention in Fort Worth in 1894 were M.B. "Nub" Pulliam, Seaton Keith, E.T. Comer, Joseph Funk, Will Collyns, and John Ryburn of the Half Circle Six (ibid., 17 March 1894). Others prominent in the cattle industry of the San Angelo area during the later 1880s and 1890s were Leasel B. Harris and his sons, Frank and Ralph; Jonathan Miles; John R. "Sarge" Nasworthy; Maximilian Z. Smissen; the Turner family; and the Blocker, Sugg, and Yates brothers. See also *Tom Green County* I, 2 (arrival of R.F. and Annie Tankersley), 86 (Funk brothers), 106 (R.F. Tankersley), 156, 157 (John Loomis), 184–5 (Water Valley), 219–228 (Ranching), 228–234 (Farms and Ranches), 219–239 (early ranches in the Water Valley area); 86 and II, 229, 240 (Funk brothers); ibid., II, *passim*, various family histories. On July 1, 1880, Annie Tankersley registered her own brand: OICU; Metcalfe's XQZ brand was registered on March 3, 1884. See also Loomis, 21–4, 27–31, 83–8; Barton, 13, 17, 158–64, 212. For specific references to the Half Circle Six, or (6), see n. 6.
4. *San Angelo Standard*, 8 April, 13 May, 1 July 1893; 26 May 1894; Roy D. Holt, "The End of Will Carver," *True West*, Vol. 15, No. 4, Whole No. 99 (June 1970), 36–8, 86–7, 90 (38). The program necessarily varied from ranch to ranch and from year to year; in 1895 the Comer outfit's spring roundup was completed before the middle of May (*Irion County Record*, in ibid., 18 May 1895).

5. *San Angelo Standard*, 1 July 1893; 11 July 1896; 2 July 1898; 29 June, 13 July 1901.

6. For fall and winter roundups on the Half Circle 6, Frank Tankersley's, and other ranches, see ibid., 10 December 1894; *Ozona Courier*, in ibid., 22 October 1892. In January 1895 the *Devil's River News* reported that 5000 head of Mexican cattle were being driven north through Sutton County to D.P. Gay's ranch near Ballinger. (Item repeated in *San Angelo Standard*, 19 January 1895.)

7. The owners of Garrett and Levy were James T. Garrett, of Knickerbocker and Arden, and R.J. Garrett and M. Levy, both of whom lived in Falls County.

8. Spradley, Family History, I; *San Angelo Standard*, 24 December 1892; 13 May, 24 June, 30 September, 25 November 1893, 20 January 1894; 9 November 1895; Holt, loc. cit.

9. *San Angelo Standard*, 15 December 1894, 12 January 1895, 17 and 31 December 1898, 7 January, 4 February, 14 October 1899, and 28 May 1900.

10. Ibid., 11 June (reward notice) and 9 July 1892 (role of Bob Lowe); 8 July, 14 and 21 October, 9 December 1893. Tom Ketchum's removal and misuse of a Door Key horse is disclosed in ibid., 2 September 1899. Irion County was organized in 1889.

11. Barton, 28–34, 39, 45, 116, 212. The *San Angelo Standard* recorded the death of O.L. Tweedy on 17 November 1894 and Joe Tweedy's extension of the store on 28 September 1895. Early in March, 1900, he suffered both the burglary of his store and Berry Ketchum's (apparently good-natured) mockery of his efforts on behalf of the G.O.P. (Ibid., 10 March 1900.) See also Chapter 3.

12. Ibid., 4 June, 29 October 1892; 20, 27 May, 10 June 1893; 12 October 1894; 27 March, 1 May 1897.

13. Ibid., 6 June, 29 August 1896; 27 March 1897.

14. *Atkins ms.*, I, Introductory note by A.C. Atkins and n. 2, 26–7 (WTC, ASU); *Tenth U.S. Census, Texas: Tom Green County*, Precinct No. 1, p. 7: the other Atkins children were Sarah, 16; John, 14; May, 12; and Lillie, 3. (Dave, whose initials were D.E., was enumerated only as Edward.) See, also, Joel Tom Meador Files-Atkins family, inc. letter to Meador from A.C. Atkins, Fort Stockton, Tex., 1980; "John J. Atkins," B.D. Arthur Scrapbook 3 (both WTC, ASU). For the Baze family, see *Tom Green County* 1, 146 and II, 34–9 (Michael Polk Baze, 38); also *Tenth Census, 1880: Texas—Tom Green County*, where M.P. Baze, though familiarly known as Polk, is listed simply as Michael Baze.

15. Barton, 12–14.

16. *San Angelo Standard*, 21 January 1893; *Atkins ms.*, I, 3, and A.C. Atkins n. 1, 25.

17. Barton, 61–2; Butte, Montana, dispatch to Dallas, Texas, *News*, in *San Angelo Standard*, 17 March 1900. The latter seems to have been based on Shield's own words. For more on the history and outcome of Atkins's trouble with Hardin, see Chapters 6, 17, and 22, with references.

18. *Tenth U.S. Census, 1880: Texas—Tom Green County*, Precinct No. 3, p. 2 (Bylers); Precinct No. 2, pp. 12 and 28, and Precinct No. 3, p. 3 (various Tankersleys). Fereby, the youngest of their four married daughters, was yet to follow Elliott and Serena Byler from Arkansas; their only son, Jake, was then in New Mexico. Richard F. Tankersley, a native of Mississippi, was then 48; his wife, Chonita, was a seventeen-year-old native of Mexico. His divorced first wife Anna (Annie), mother of their nine children, was a hotel keeper in San Angelo; she died in 1902. Among the children were Fayette, G.W. (Wash) and H.M. (Mart), all three of them among the leading stock raisers and ranchers of Irion and Crockett Counties. *San Angelo Standard*, 15 February 1902, See also Joel Tom Meador Files—Laura Bullion (WTC, ASU); *Tom Green County*, II, 78; Author's visit to Sherwood, Tex., Cemetery, 31 May 2008; Carolyn Bullion McBryde, "The Thorny Rose," True West, April 1992, 21–7 (212); Barton, 16.

Fereby Byler Bullion's three older sisters were Susan (or Susanna), Charity, and Lurena. Jacob A. Byler died at Mertzon, Texas, on 12 March 1944.

19. Barton, 16–17; for Reuben Madison Hanks and Mary Frances Bullion Hanks, see *Tom Green County*, I, 89, where Fannie's birthplace is given as Parker County, Texas.

20. Barton, 16–17, 22, 41–3.

21. Ibid., 41–5; McBryde, 22; *San Angelo Standard*, 14 and 21 January, 25 February, 25 March 1893; *Tom Green County Marriage Book*: A.A. Allen-Manty Byler, c. 009, and Charles P. Allen-Mary Byler, c. 022 (WTC, ASU).

22. Barton, 49–50; McBryde, loc. cit.

23. *San Angelo Standard*, 1 July 1893, 13 October 1894, 6 June 1896, 26 November 1897, 9 June 1900. The words spoken by or attributed to Laura are from the *St. Louis Globe-Democrat*, 7 November 1901. The article was reprinted in the *Standard* of 14 November.

24. Holt, 38; Loomis, 66; Shelton, in Bryan, *Ruffians*, 263–4; *San Angelo Standard*, 5 August, 9 September 1899, 6 April 1901; *Devil's River News*, 6 April 1901.

25. *Tenth U.S. Census, 1880: Texas—Uvalde County*, Vol. 31, E.D. 134, S.22, L.38 (household of Richard T. Carver); ibid, Bandera County, Precincts 1 & 2, p. 17 (Causy-Carver household; note the enumerator's spelling of the family name of the stepfather of the two Carver children); State of Texas, County of Bexar, License of Marriage, 2 April 1872; Walter S. Causey: Family Compilation Sheets, 15 September 1995, derived from contemporary official records, George Alfred Carver and Walter Scott Causey (Sutton County Historical Society, Sonora, Texas); William Richard Carver, Pedigree Chart, compiled 18 September 1995 (Sutton County H.S.); Letter, "Uncle Dick" (Richard Carver) to Mrs. Fannie Hill, 4 August 1915; Ernst, *From Cowboy to Outlaw*, 1–2 and Supplement, "Carver Genealogy," 21–6. (The latter work was published without annotations, but Mrs. Ernst kindly provided the author with a copy of the draft Notes.)
In 1939, J. Marvin Hunter described Carver as a "pretty good old country boy" from Bandera County in "'Black Jack' Ketchum and His Gang," *Frontier Times*, Vol. 16, No. 7 (April 1939), 315–320 (315). In the *Album of Gunfighters* (Warren Hunter, 1951, reprinted 1955, 1959), 82, Marvin Hunter and Noah H. Rose associated Carver's family with the Pipe Creek neighborhood, and disclosed that Carver had been living with a stepfather, but without any mention of the name Causey. Holt, loc. cit., specifically and erroneously identifies Bandera County as Carver's birthplace. Obviously Holt, who in most respects was well informed, was unaware of the facts about Carver's origins and upbringing.

26. Holt, 38; *State of New Mexico: Bureau of Public Health*: Certificate of Death—Francis [*sic*] Emeline Hill, 26 July 1934; "Mrs. F.E. Hill," from unnamed Arizona newspaper, c. 29 July 1934; Ernst, *From Cowboy to Outlaw*, 23–4; *Tenth U.S. Census, 1880: Texas—Uvalde County*, loc. cit.

27. *San Angelo Standard*, 6 April 1901; *Devil's River News*, 6 April, 6 July 1901; Holt, loc. cit.

28. Ernst, *From Cowboy to Outlaw*, 3, supported by draft Note citing the research of John Eaton, of Sonora, Texas (Ernst to author, undated, early August 2001). She is incorrect in saying that the Sixes (Half Circle Six) was "later called the T Half Circle." These were two separate ranching enterprises. The T Half Circle belonged to the brothers Max and Sol Mayer, of Sonora, Texas; the owners of the Half Circle Six at this time (later, the operation was divided) were Stilson, Case, Ryburn and Thorpe.

29. Holt, 38.

30. "Carver Family Compilation Sheets," as cited (Richard T. Carver); Ernst, *From Cowboy to Outlaw*, "Carver Genealogy," 22–3.

31. Holt, loc. cit., *San Angelo Standard* and *Devil's River News*, both 6 April 1901.

32. *State of Texas; Tom Green County*: License of Marriage, William Carver and Miss V.E. Byler, 9 February (certified 10 February) 1892; "Family Compilation Sheets," and "William Carver Pedigree Chart," (where Carver's death was misdated "2 April 1902"); Holt, 37; Loomis, loc. cit.

33. *San Angelo Standard*, 14 May, 16 July 1892; 25 March, 9 September, 14 October 1893; 20 September 1894.

34. William Richard Carver/Viana E. Byler, "Family Compilation Sheets"; Ernst, unpublished addendum to *From Cowboy to Outlaw*, citing research notes by Joe[l] Tom Meador, of Eldorado, Texas, with further addition by Jo-Ann Palmer: " . . . [Elliott] Byler wouldn't put [the] stone with Carver's name [on it];" also, Ross McSwain to author, at Sherwood cemetery, 31 May 2008: "No one knows where Viana is [buried]."

35. Holt, 86; Loomis, loc. cit., Shelton, in Bryan, *Ruffians*, loc. cit.

36. Alverson, 9.

37. *San Angelo Standard*, 12 November, 10 December 1892; 4 March, 8 April 1893.

38. Ibid., 9 September, 7 October 1893.

39. McBryde, 23: " . . . Knickerbocker rumor maintains Laura . . . intermittently worked for Fanny Porter between 1891 and 1895. Bernice Haag [née Byler, a cousin of Laura's] said that Laura attended dances in the Knickerbocker area in 1896, indicating she returned from her escapades in San Antonio around that time." We can tighten the timeframe. Laura is known to have been variously in Knickerbocker, the Devil's River country, and Water Valley from March 1893, to September 1894, and to have been in Knickerbocker before the end of 1896. If, in addition, Haag's memory is accurate in placing Bullion at Knickerbocker for at least part of 1895, Laura's "escapades" in San Antonio could only have taken place during part of 1891/2 and part of 1895/6.

40. Ibid., 22.

41. St. Louis *Republic*, 8 November 1901.

42. St. Louis *Globe-Democrat*, 7 November 1901.

43. St. Louis *Republic*, 8 November 1901.

44. *San Angelo Standard*, 16 November 1901.

45. Quotations from several of Laura's letters are in McBryde, 25; Soule, 87–93; and in Dale T. Schoenberger "The Tall Texan," *True West*, April 1992, 20, 28–32 (29–30). See also n. 79.

46. Holt, 37, 86 (citing Bob Evans).

47. *San Angelo Standard*, 9 September, 7 and 14 October, 4 November 1893.

48. Ibid., 28 October, 4 November 1893.

49. Ibid., 3 November 1894. In that issue, one "Hyena," writing from Arden, identified "Zoe" as "a certain 'lean and hungry Cassius'"—a clear reference to Cassius M. Cash. In "Knickerbocker Knews," a week later, "Zoe" tried to laugh off the charge, and hinted that "Hyena" was a clergyman, but nothing was heard from "Zoe" thereafter. Cash and his wife left Knickerbocker shortly afterwards, but soon returned. "Zoe" did not.

50. Ibid., 19 May 1894.

51. Ibid., 14 September 1895.

52. Ibid., 1 December 1894, 28 September 1895. Leta Crawford, *A History of Irion County, Texas*, 36. The reference to Burleson is incomprehensible, unless a person of that name later acquired the former Hardin store. As far as the author can determine, there were no Burlesons in Tom Green County before 1900, although there were plenty of them in San Saba County.

53. Houston, Texas, *Post* and *Dallas News*, from St. Louis dispatches of 6 and 7 November, in *San Angelo Standard*, 9 November 1901; *St. Louis Globe-Democrat*, 7 November 1901. The dispatches to the Houston and Dallas papers named Sherman, Texas, as the place from which one of these letters was mailed, but Sherwood, Texas, is much likelier to be correct.

54. *San Angelo Standard*, 11 January 1896.

55. *St. Louis Globe-Democrat*, 7 November 1901.

56. *San Angelo Standard*, 1 February 1896.

57. Ibid.

58. Alverson, loc. cit. The fiction that Carver fled Texas because he had killed "an overbearing bully" in self-defense, and could not afford to fight his case in court, was first publicized by

J. Marvin Hunter in "'Black Jack' Ketchum and his Gang"—*Frontier Times*, Vol. 16, No. 7 (misnumbered 6) (April 1939), 315–320 (315). Hunter does not say where he read or heard the tale, and, to be just to him, does not vouch for its truth.

Bob Johnson succeeded Tom White as Erie foreman at about this time (Lynn R. Bailey, "*We'll All Wear Silk Hats*," 156).

59. Carlsbad, New Mexico, *Argus*, 25 August 1899.

60. Ernst, *Cowboy to Outlaw*, "Carver Genealogy," 22–5; "Frances Emeline Hill—Obituary," from unidentified Arizona newspapers (Sutton County Historical Society).

61. Alverson, loc. cit.

62. Easily the fullest and best-researched account of the High Five or Black Jack gang is Karen Holliday Tanner and John D. Tanner, Jr., *Last of the Old-Time Outlaws*, 22–155. For the first homicides charged against the Ketchum brothers, see Chapter 5, *infra*.

63. Ernst, 5.

64. *San Angelo Standard*, 26 December 1896.

William S. Veck (1826–1900) fought in the Mexican War of 1848, joined the California gold rush, and settled in Fort Concho about 1868. He married Katie Wuertemburg in 1872; Lottie was the first of their six daughters. Veck became San Angelo's leading merchant and banker. (Ibid., 26 October, 9 November 1895; 1 February, 7 March, 5 September, 10 October, 26 December 1896; 20 February, 6 March 1897; 24 March 1900; *Irion County Record*, in ibid., 21 March 1896.)

The story of Sam and Joe Moore was very different. They began as trusted ranch hands. Then Sam joined Dave Atkins in hurrahing the town of Knickerbocker. These festivities ended with the murder of Tom Hardin. Sam and Joe then ventured more widely into crime, with singular ill-success. They were caught almost red-handed by Rome Shield after a comically inept attempt to rob a general store at Christoval, and were later the chief perpetrators of a ludicrously clumsy scheme to pass counterfeit currency. Shield commented after the Christoval fiasco that "Black Jack or any member of his gang would feel like taking the bunglers . . . and giving them 300 with a wet rope." Yet they eluded serious punishment on these and other charges. Between misdeeds, Sam married Alice Ervin at the M.E. church in Knickerbocker, "to the inspiring strains of Lohengrin's wedding march." Joe married Minta Drennan in San Angelo next day, apparently without any encouragement from Wagner. It may or may not have significance that Sam became an office holder in the Knickerbocker branch of the Ancient Order of Woodmen. His fellow functionaries were some of the town's most influential citizens, such as Joe Tweedy and James F. Hester. Small wonder that Sam's "perennial cheerfulness" was a matter of public note. (*San Angelo Standard*, 11 January, 6 June, 11 and 25 July, 25 December 1896; 27 March, 15 May, 18 September 1897; 15 July, 19 August, 7 October, 25 November, 30 December 1899; 17, 24, and 31 March 1900; 19 January, 24 August, 2 November 1901.) See also Chapter 6.

65. *St. Louis Republic*, 8 November 1901.

66. *San Saba News*, 27 April, 23 November 1888; *St. Louis Post-Dispatch* and *St. Louis Republican*, both 8 November 1901.

67. Soule, 14; Barton, 7, 43–4. Soule writes that "Ben, Sam Ketchum, Will Carver, and Dave Atkins are said to have worked on the T Half Circle Six off and on between 1881 [?] and 1891." His reference to a "T Half Circle Six" outfit is an obvious error; see n. 28. Soule must mean the Half Circle Six, which did employ Sam and Tom Ketchum, Carver, and Atkins, and may have hired Ben also.

68. *Tenth U.S. Census, 1880: Texas—Coleman County*, Justice Precinct 10, S.6, L.1.

69. Soule, 1–6, 8–10.

70. Loomis, 67.

71. A single clause in one sentence in a letter to Ben from his sister Ola, dated 26 March 1905, sums up the state of the relations between the Kilpatricks and their neighbors in both their new home and the previous one: "[T]hese devils here [Ozona] are worse than them at P[aint] R[ock]." (Quoted in Soule, 87.) Extracts from other letters to Ben from his mother and Ola are in James D. Horan, *The Wild Bunch*, 187–3. Horan repeats this material in *Desperate Men*, revised and enlarged ed., 361–2. Here, as often elsewhere, Horan is careless or worse. A letter which Horan says was written to Ben by his father, George Kilpatrick, Sr., was actually addressed to the outlaw's sisters. Nor is it certain that the writer was not Ben's brother George, Jr. Soule (loc. cit.,) ascribes it to the father; but McBryde (24–5), who evidently saw this letter and others similar to it, names the writer as George, Jr., Soule says that the prison file on Ben Kilpatrick has no record of any letter sent to Ben by his father or his brother George, much as he had wanted to hear from the latter. He did receive at least one letter from his brother Felix (Soule, 88–9).
72. Soule, 7.
73. Chapter 7, *infra*; Hunter, "Black Jack Ketchum and his Gang," 315, and "The Way of the Transgressor," *Frontier Times*, Vol. 19, No. 3 (December 1941), 125–8 (125).
74. As Schoenberger points out (28), Ben, at a fraction of an inch under six foot, "was tall, if measured by nineteenth century standards, but today he would not be a very 'Tall Texan.'"
75. *San Angelo Standard*, 30 July 1892; Loomis, 57.
76. Soule, 14.
77. Ibid., 9–10, citing court records.
78. Ibid, 9, 13–14 ; Hunter, "Ketchum and his Gang," 315; "Transgressor," 125.
79. Excerpts from the lengthy jail correspondence, drawn mostly from Ben's side of it, are given in Soule, 87, 90–95, 98–9, 101–2, and Schoenberger, 28–32. McBryde, 25, quotes from several of Laura's letters. See n. 45.
80. Bryan, *Ruffians*, 254.

NOTES TO CHAPTER 5

1. *Rocky Mountain News*, 28 April 1901. In the very similar rendering of the stenographic record of Ketchum's statement published in the *Denver Republican* of the same date, the ungrammatical "done" is substituted for "did." A shorter version printed in the *Denver Times* the previous evening, apparently based on the reporter's own notes, has Ketchum saying that Wright took the horse not from Tom, but from Tom's nephew. (Ketchum had several grown or adolescent nephews.)
2. Loomis, 64
3. Ibid., 63–4.
4. Ibid., 27–8. The novels of Anthony Trollope (1815–82) would not have been widely read or known in late 19th century Texas. Nowadays they are not widely read or known even in England (even though several have been successfully adapted for television).
5. *San Angelo Standard*, 2 and 30 December 1893.
6. Ibid., 14 July 1894.
7. Note by Jo-Ann Palmer, Sutton County Historical Society, copy supplied to author; Ernst, *From Cowboy to Outlaw*, 4.
8. *San Angelo Standard*, 14 December 1895, 30 May 1896; San Angelo dispatches of 13 December and 25 May in *St. Louis Globe-Democrat*, 14 December 1895 and 26 May 1896; Loomis, 63–5. In the first of the two *Globe-Democrat* items, the victim was miscalled "Jack," an obvious misrendering of "Jap." This error may have been replicated in other dispatches to engender one more, wherein "Jack" was supplanted by "John."

9. *San Angelo Standard*, 14, 21 December 1895; 30 May 1896.

10. Ibid., 1 February 1896.

11. Ibid., 8 February 1896.

12. A. Thompson, *Albuquerque ms.*, 14.

13. Barton, 74–5.

14. Ibid., *State of Texas vs. Tom Ketchum, No. 1198—Murder; vs. J.E. Wright, no. 1199—Murder; vs. S.E. Powers, No. 1200—Murder; vs. Bud Upshaw, No. 1201—Murder*: Bills of Indictment filed 16 May 1896.

15. Writs of Capias, Nos. 1199 and 1200, 16 and 23 May; Precept to Serve Indictment, No. 957, 27 May 1896 (Powers); Bail bond, 21 July 1896 (Wright); *San Angelo Standard*, 30 May; San Angelo dispatch in Little Rock, Ark., *Arkansas Gazette*, 26 May 1896.

16. *San Angelo Standard*, 11 January 1896; A. Thompson, *Albuquerque ms.*, 14, *Clayton ms.*, 41, citing written information received in 1930 from G.W. Shield. In the former, Thompson describes Powers as "a respectable citizen of Tom Green County" who had "in some manner . . . incurred the displeasure of a certain element there, for what reason is not disclosed." If he took this from Shield, the ex-sheriff was being more discreet than candid.

In *Open Range Days*, 182, Thompson mentions the Powers affair only in passing. Horsehead Crossing was near the site of Girvin (pop. approx. 50), close to the meeting point of Pecos, Crane, and Crockett Counties and thirty-three miles northeast of Fort Stockton. It was also the site of a station on the old Butterfield stage line. For its history, characteristics, and exact location, see Clayton W. Williams, "That Topographical Ghost—Horsehead Crossing," *Old West*, Vol. 11, No. 2, Whole No. 42 (Winter 1974), 22–5, 50–2; Patrick Dearen, "Horsehead to Castle Gate: Trailing the Past," *True West*, Vol, 39, No. 8, Whole No. 292 (August 1992), 22–7.

17. *San Angelo Standard*, 1 February 1896.

18. A. Thompson, loc. cit.

19. *State vs. Wright, No. 1199*: Subpoenas, undated and 17 September; *Motion to Attach*, 26 September; *Witness Attachments* (two), 2 October 1896; *State vs. Powers*, No. 1200: Subpoenas dated 25 May, 28 October, 18 November 1896; Witness Attachments (two), dated 18 November 1896; Application for Attachment and Subpoena, by B. W. Rucker (?), undated (prob. late November 1896); *San Angelo Standard*, 19 December 1896, 1 May 1897. The spelling of the names given here is in every instance the same as that used in the respective document.

For the Upshaws' move to Val Verde County, see Chapter 3, n. 65. A. Thompson, *Albuquerque ms.*, 19, mistakenly says that, after the murder of Powers, Tom went to work for the Bar Vs and the LFDs. The error arose from Shield's failure to supply dates and Thompson's own failure to look for them, which led him to place the murder in the late 1880s. We have seen that both Sam and Tom did work for these and other cattle outfits during the early 1890s—before the murder.

20. *State vs. Wright, No. 1199—*December term 1897; *State vs. S.E. Powers, No. 1200—*May term 1899: Motions of District Attorney D. D. Wallace for dismissal.

21. San Angelo dispatch, May 25, in Little Rock *Arkansas Gazette*, 26 May 1896.

22. The fullest contemporary accounts of the events that began with the arrival of the Ketchum brothers on the Bell ranch in the spring of 1896 appeared in the Las Vegas, New Mexico, *Daily Optic* and *Santa Fe Daily New Mexican*, some of those in the latter being reproduced or condensed from the former.

The *Optic's* informant was A.O. Milice, of the Bell ranch, and the paper published the descriptions of the killers on 18 June 1896. The text quoted herein is given in Bryan, *Ruffians*, 261–2. The present writer was, regrettably, able to see very little of the *Optic* in the original; but the *New Mexican*, also of 18 June (unlike the *Optic*, it was an afternoon or evening newspaper), carried a slightly shortened version of the description, omitting the references to the temperament of the first man and the caliber of his rifle. See also *New Mexican*, 23, 25, 26 June, 2 July 1896; *Las Vegas Optic*, in ibid., 20 June, 20 July 1896; Roswell, New Mexico, *Record*, 19 June 1896; Santa Fe dispatch, 1 July, in *Globe-Democrat*, 2 July 1896. Las Vegas is about 110 miles west of the Bell headquarters and roughly ninety miles northwest of the scene of the murders.

Among the accounts of those who were alive at the time, that of Jack Culley (34–6), is easily the best. As a senior employee of the Bell at the time, Culley knew most of those involved in the case. Potter, 110–111, was also close to good sources, though he set the incidents in August, 1894. Thompson, *Albuquerque ms.*, 50 ff, *Clayton ms.*, 41–2, assigned the action to 1891, the last of a procession of errors that began with his misdating of the Powers killing; see n. 18. In *Open Range Days*, 183, he mentions the Herzstein and Gallegos murders only in passing and without any date.

B.D. Titsworth, presumably steering by Thompson's *Early History of Clayton*, followed him in placing the Liberty affair in 1891 (I, 5).

Fabiola Cabeza de Baca Gilbert, *We Fed Them Cactus*, 61–2, is at fault in saying that the store was robbed at gunpoint. She, too, misdates the crime, attributing it to 1898, but includes several touches of original information gleaned at first hand.

Charles A. Siringo, *Riata and Spurs* (rev. ed.,) 193–4, says that "Elza Lay, *alias* Bob McGinnis" joined the Ketchums on the Bell and assisted in the burglaries. There is no possibility that more than two men were present and, moreover, Lay was in Wyoming at the time in question. Siringo also errs in stating that three of the pursuers were killed. He quotes a cowboy named Banty Caldwell—later a Hollywood stunt rider—who helped to bury the dead, as saying that Herzstein's body had eleven bullets in it. This is evidently true. Bryan's (ibid., 260–263) is a good straightforward account, which, as mentioned above, includes the full descriptions of the malefactors as first circulated by the *Las Vegas Optic*.

23. San Antonio dispatch in *St. Louis Globe-Democrat*, 16 September; Marfa, Texas, *New Era*, in *San Angelo Standard*, 21 September 1895 and 27 March 1897; *Ozona Courier*, in *Standard*, 12 December 1896; Sonora, Texas, *Devil's River News*, in *Standard*, 27 November 1897; *Standard*, 2 December 1899; Secrest, 57 (note); Bob Alexander, *Lawmen, Outlaws, and S.O.Bs*, 179; ibid., II., 43–55 (E.E. Townsend and the Valentine robbery); Alexander to author, 17 May 2006, with enclosures, comprising copies of Bills of Indictment (Presidio County, Texas); press reports from the *El Paso Times*; and an article by Everett (E.E.) Townsend, published in the December 1933 issue of *Voice of the New Mexican Border*. Townsend, 181, recalled that the taller of the two bandits, whom he took to be Tom Ketchum, was blue-eyed. Tom Ketchum's eyes were not blue.

24. Culley, 34.

25. A. Thompson, *Clayton ms.*, 49.

26. See Chapter 14, text at n. 49; Chapter 15, text at n. 6.

27. Culley, 35. The cowboys said the man was Tom Ketchum. Culley maintained that it was Sam, not Tom. Culley's own statement that the man wore a black beard argues that the cowboys were right.

28. Bryan, *Ruffians*, 263: Gilbert, ibid.

29. Culley, 36. The amount stolen from the post office is in *Annual Reports of the Post Office Department for the Fiscal Year Ended June 30, 1897*: Report of the Assistant Attorney-General for the Post Office Department, Exhibit A, 42–66 (56), where it is shown that Morris Herzstein's claim for $44.69 was allowed.

30. *Roswell Record*, 30 July 1896.

31. *New Mexican* and *Globe-Democrat*, both 2 July 1896; *Optic*, in *New Mexican*, 20 July 1896

32. *Roswell Record*, 30 July, 14 August 1896. James D. Shinkle, *Reminiscences of Roswell Pioneers*, 227–230. The fullest account of Perry's overall career is in Robert K. DeArment, Deadly Dozen,

115–33. On June 1968, during a visit to England, a Perry family descendant, Mrs. Emmett White, of Roswell, told the author and journalist Colin Rickards that Perry was killed in South Africa several years after his arrival there. Perry died "in a fight near Johannesburg . . . He was found behind his dead horse, his ammunition all spent, surrounded by empty cartridges and 'about thirty or so' dead Africans." Mrs. White believed that Perry had been named after Christopher Columbus (Memo., Rickards to author, 9 June 1968, and in conversation).

Harkey, 98–9 (69–70 of paperback reprint), wrote interestingly of his participation in the futile chase, but named South America as Perry's destination and included Carver in the Herzstein burglary and murders. The first error may be dismissed as a permissible lapse of memory; there is less excuse for the second.

33. *Optic*, 17 June; *New Mexican*, 18, 26 June, 20 July; *Globe-Democrat*, 20 July 1896.

34. *New Mexican*, 4 September and 11 November 1899; Otero to Murphy, 16 November 1899 (*Records of the Territorial Governors*—State Archives of New Mexico). The *New Mexican* scribe of November 11 misplaced Liberty in Union County, which strengthens the impression that the reporting was guided by neither insight nor information.

35. *Rocky Mountain News* and *Denver Republican*, 28 April 1901.

36. *New Mexican*, 23 June 1896.

37. The criminal career of the Christian brothers in Indian Territory was more extensive and lasted longer than Glenn Shirley acknowledged in his excellent, but far from exhaustive survey *West of Hell's Fringe*, 283–300. The fullest and most accurate account is in Tanner and Tanner, 25–39. Jeff Burton, *Bureaucracy, Blood Money, and Black Jack's Gang*, (London, The English Westerners' Society, 1984), *The Brand Book*, Vol. 22, Nos. 1 & 2 (Winter 1983 and Summer 1984), 1–66 (1–2) summarizes the many crimes in Indian Territory ascribable to the Christian gang, but includes a minor robbery (at Glenn) that was proved to have been the work of impostors, and excludes their last, a botched attempt to rob a store at Kiowa in mid-January of 1896. It was this failure that precipitated the brothers' flight to New Mexico and thence to Arizona.

38. Kemp and Dykes, 165.

39. A. Thompson, *Albuquerque ms.*, misallocates this intermission to the summer of 1897, a mistake he would not have made had he known that the Lozier robbery had occurred that spring and that Tom and his partners had consequently been obliged to spend the next few weeks dodging the posses.

40. Alverson, 9. See also Chapter 4.

41. Jesse James Benton, "Cow by the Tail," Part III, *Frontier Times*, Vol. 39, No. 2, New Series No. 34 (March 1965), 6–11, 38, 40, 42, 44, 46–51, 59–60, 71 (46).

42. Alverson, 4–6; Hovey, 7–8, 10–11, 48, 50.

43. Axford, 22–6; William French, *Some Recollections of a Western Ranchman*, 259.

44. Two dispatches from Santa Fe dated 6 February and 29 April 1897, each published in the following morning's edition of the *Globe-Democrat*, illustrate the rapidity with which the details of the Herzstein-Gallegos case were forgotten, and the identities of the High Five and Ketchum gangs muddled and subsumed into one chaotic patchwork. In the February account, Black Jack and "Red" Anderson were said to have crossed the Texas Panhandle from Indian Territory, worked briefly on Waddingham's Bell ranch, robbed the Liberty post office and killed Levi Herzstein and a companion misnamed Merejildo Trujillo. The killers were said to have belonged to the Dalton brothers' gang. Since the Christians were allied to members of that gang, it would not have been surprising if the author of the dispatch had pinned the names of Will and Bob on the murderous pair. Instead, the correspondent stupidly aligned the report with the groundless assertion that Black Jack was Howard (or John) McDonald, a minor criminal who had just been arrested in El Paso, Texas. In reality, the Christians had left Indian Territory in late January, and moved on to Arizona two months later, Will acquiring the

nickname Black Jack and Bob calling himself Tom Anderson. Both were at work in Cochise County, Arizona, at the time of the burglary and murders in eastern New Mexico. The dispatch of 29 April incorporated some of the same misinformation in its report of the killing of Black Jack, while tacitly repudiating the McDonald nonsense. Similar dispatches appeared in other large newspapers, such as the *Rocky Mountain News*, at the same time.

45. Ben R. Clark, "William Christian, alias Black Jack," *Progressive Arizona and the Great Southwest*, December 1929, 24–5, and January 1930, 20–22.

46. Siringo, *Riata and Spurs* (rev. ed.,), 193, was first to go into print with the Bucket of Blood version, a year before the Brewery Gulch variation made its public debut in Lorenzo D. Walters, *Tombstone's Yesterday*, 131. Almost in the same breath Walters says that Sam and Tom were born at San Diego, Texas, and taken to Kingston, New Mexico, when quite young—two statements of no ascertainable ancestry, both representative of their author's inventive tendencies. Despite that, and the errors in Siringo's few scrappy pages (192–9) on the Ketchum gang, the author feels that the Bucket of Blood/Brewery Gulch anecdote is, at worst, close to the spirit of the truth; this, or something like it, may accurately convey the circumstances in which Ketchum claimed, or accepted, the accolade of Black Jack's notoriety.

Both variants of the saloon story have been repeated, reworded, or repackaged many times since. For example, Bartholomew, 19, has a recolored rendering of the Walters version, credited to Joe Chisholm's book *Brewery Gulch*.

47. Tanner & Tanner, *Last of the Old-Time Outlaws*, 119, citing *Albuquerque Daily Citizen*, 30 April 1897.

48. Albuquerque dispatch, 28 April in last edition of *Globe-Democrat*, 29 April and morning edition, 30 April 1897.

49. Fred Higgins, Deputy U.S. Marshal, to Edward L. Hall, U.S. Marshal of New Mexico, 30 April 1897; Clark to William K. Meade, U.S. Marshal of Arizona, 2 May 1897; Wilson, 59.

50. The controversy is described and analysed in detail in Burton, *Bureaucracy*, 33–9, and Tanner & Tanner, ibid., 120–130.

51. Barton, for example, unquestioningly refers to Tom Ketchum as Black Jack throughout.

52. Hutchinson, loc. cit.

NOTES TO CHAPTER 6

1. Alverson, 9–10.

2. Ernst, *From Cowboy to Outlaw*, 5.

3. San Antonio dispatches in *Globe-Democrat*, 3, 4, 7 September; Austin dispatch in ibid., 9 September; Del Rio, Texas, dispatch in *San Francisco Chronicle*, 4 September; San Antonio dispatch in ibid., 7 September 1891. The San Antonio dispatch in the issue of September 4, which states that the through express safe was blown open, seems to have been put out by Andrew Christeson, Wells, Fargo's divisional superintendent, or on his authority. The messenger was J. Ernest Smith, who almost four years earlier had killed two train robbers just east of El Paso. The Samuels robbers, like the pair who had died near El Paso, had to blow open the door of the express car before Smith would step outside; unlike their predecessors, however, they denied him the opportunity for greater heroics.

4. Del Rio dispatch in *Globe-Democrat*, 23 October; San Antonio dispatch in ibid., 28 October 1891; Carolyn Lake, ed., *Under Cover with Wells Fargo: The Unvarnished Recollections of Fred Dodge*, 143–4.

By far the fullest and best account of the Samuels episode and its outcome is in Alexander, *Outlaws, Lawmen, and S.O.Bs*, 10–28. Alexander shows that the surname of the man who clung to the robbers' trail until they were overtaken was Sitter, not (as has usually been written) Sitters; the final "s" was added to the name by a later generation of the family. Frederick Wilkins, *The Law Comes to Texas*, summarizes some of the facts (299–300).

5. Jeffrey Burton, "The Duellists of Devil's River," in *Vignettes in Violence*, ed. Barry C. Johnson—English Westerners' Society Special Publication No. 11A, 2005, 61–94 (61–2).

6. Ibid., 62. The quotation is from the *El Paso Times*, 31 December 1896. Also, John R. Hughes, Ysleta, Texas, to Adj. Gen. W.H. Mabry, Austin, 1 January 1897.

7. Rolly Shackelford and Alex Purviance received five-year terms, but Purviance fell mortally ill before sentence, and was released almost at once. Newman and Frank Gobbles, the first of the four to be arrested, escaped punishment.

8. San Antonio dispatch in *Globe-Democrat*, 15 May 1897.

9. San Antonio, Texas, *Daily Light*, 14 May and *Daily Express*, 15 May; San Antonio dispatch in *San Francisco Chronicle*, 15 May; *San Angelo Standard*, 22 May 1897.

10. Brook Campbell, to Elizabeth Doyle, 17 November 1937, FWP. Campbell mentioned no date; but if, as the writer believes, his story is true, and given the circumstances stated, it is hard to see how the incident could have happened at any other time.

11. *San Angelo Standard*, 6 March 1897.

12. Ibid., 6 June 1896; 18 September 1897; 15 July 1899; 19 January 1901.

13. Ibid., 27 March 1897; *Atkins ms*, I, 3, A.C. Atkins, n. 2, 26; *Inquest over the dead body of T.R. Hardin, by George Becker, J.P., Prec. No. 4, Tom Green County, March 21, 1897*: testimony of Boyd Cornick, M.D; S.D. Kay; Sam Moore; Sam Moore, recalled; George Bodry; Carl Philip Schwalb. W.K. Brown was not asked to testify at the Inquest, yet did so at Atkins's trial in 1920.

14. Ibid., 24 April 1897.

15. *Atkins ms.*, I, 3–4, A.C. Atkins, nn.3 and 4, 28; Barton, 80–81. In *Atkins ms.*, ibid., n.3, A.C. Atkins states that a Baze descendant told him that the provider of the horse was one of the Baze family.

16. *Atkins ms.*, I , 4–5; Barton, ibid.

17. *San Antonio Light*, 14 and 15 May 1897.

18. The proceedings at and near Lozier station after the arrival of Ketchum, Carver, and Atkins drew generous attention from the press, including *San Antonio Light*, 14 and 16 May; *San Antonio Express*, 15 and 16 May; San Antonio dispatches in *Globe-Democrat*, 15 and 19 May, *El Paso Times* and *San Francisco Chronicle*, both 15 May; and Del Rio dispatch in *San Angelo Standard*, 22 May 1897. Express Messenger Joyce dictated his recollections in 1922. They were published in "Main Lines," Superintendent's Newsletter, San Antonio Division, Southern Pacific Lines, Vol. 2, Nos. 5–6, May-June 1967, 5ff (typed copy to author from Xanthus "Kit" Carson, Albuquerque, New Mexico, January 1968). Joyce adds many interesting (and, one must hope, accurate) details to the contemporary accounts, but seriously understates the extent of the company's loss to the bandits. He misdates the robbery to May 10—an excusable, though slightly surprising, slip of the memory.

Atkins ms. I, 5, contains the only reference to the abandoned plans to rob the train on the 13th. Atkins says nothing about the robbery except that the engine was boarded and the train run ahead about a mile to the point at which the safe was exploded.

19. Del Rio dispatch, May 14, in *San Angelo Standard*, 22 May; *San Antonio Light*, 16 May 1897. The duration of the holdup, and the damage to the mail car and its contents, are in *Annual Report of the Post Office Department, 1897*, "Report of the General Superintendent of the Railway Mail Service," 538, where the time of the stoppage is put at 1:50 a.m.

W.H. Jones served as sheriff of Val Verde County from May 2, 1885 to December 1890 and again from November 8, 1892 to November 8, 1898 (Tise, 505). Lozier is now in Terrell County, which was detached from Pecos County on 8 April 1905.

20. *Light,* ibid.
21. 15 May 1897.
22. Barton, 81.
23. San Antonio dispatches in *Globe-Democrat,* 19, 21, 27 May, 20 June 1897; Austin dispatch of August 3 in *San Angelo Standard,* 19 August 1899; *Atkins ms.,* I, 5. The fact that the San Angelo paper held the Austin dispatch for two weeks is an instance of its editor's apparent reluctance to print any report naming Tom Ketchum or his partners in connection with any piece of criminal news, while they were still at large. But on August 19 the editor knew that a man had just been captured during an attempt to rob a train in New Mexico; he may have made a reasoned guess that the bandit taken into custody was Tom Ketchum, and used it as an opportunity to print this item of interesting but slightly stale news.
24. Hughes to Mabry, 18 May 1897 (Texas State Archives, Austin).
25. Same to same, 27 May 1897.
26. Same to same, 2 June 1897; *Atkins ms.,* I, 5.
27. *San Antonio Express,* 15 May; *Globe-Democrat,* 15, 21 May, 1897. None of these reports openly connected Ketchum, Carver, Atkins, or Upshaw with the Lozier robbery or Powers murder, but a report in the *New Mexican* of 21 August 1897, though imperfectly informed, did confirm that a group of four men, on the run from crimes committed in Texas, had taken refuge in southwest New Mexico. See text at n. 36.
28. See Chapters 20 and 22.
29. *San Francisco Chronicle,* 15 May 1897.
30. *Globe-Democrat,* 20 June, 8 July 1897.
31. The report in ibid., put the haul from the two safes at $10,000, including seven or eight thousand dollars from the through safe. In the first report of the *San Antonio Express* 15 May 1897, "a reliable source" was quoted as stating that the sum stolen "was not less than $10,000, and may be much more." The railroad officials who predicted a loss of no more than $300 were given space in the *San Antonio Light,* 15 May 1897. Next day, however, the *Light* reckoned that the through safe must have contained at least $15,000. Even this estimate, or guess, fell far short of the true figure.
32. *San Antonio Light,* 16 May 1897.
33. The tale that the heavier shipments had been diverted onto another route appeared in the *San Antonio Light,* 14 May and, more elaborately, in the *San Antonio Express,* 15 May and *San Angelo Standard,* 22 May 1897. The Globe-Democrat, 20 June 1897, quoted the Wells, Fargo company's admission that the robbers had decamped with $42,000. The company's last public word on the matter, adjusting the loss to $48,980, reached the *San Angelo Standard* on 19 August 1899.
34. "Main Lines," loc. cit.
35. *San Angelo Standard.* 19 August 1899.
36. *New Mexican,* 21 August 1897.
37. The evidence is most fully collated and considered in Tanner & Tanner, *Last of the Old-Time Outlaws.* 119, 126–7.
38. Austin dispatch of August 3 in *San Angelo Standard,* 19 August 1899.
39. Hutchinson, loc. cit.
40. Turkey Creek Canyon and its surrounding terrain are closely described here and in Chapter 13 on the basis of information quoted in the text, or cited hereunder and in the Notes to that chapter. The author has not visited the canyon, but Ed Bartholomew did, in the early 1950s. His observations are recorded in *Black Jack Ketchum,* 84–8.
41. *District of New Mexico—Fourth Judicial District: No. 626—United States of America vs. Charles B. Collings et al.,* Bill of Particulars; A. Thompson, *Albuquerque ms.,* 61, 68, *Clayton ms.,* 42; Otero, 111; Livingston, I, 347; Santa Fe *New Mexican Review,* 24 November 1898.

Livingston, whose information came from someone connected with the investigation of the Folsom robbery, says that Collings was a Texan, the *Review* that he was superintendent of the Aztec. Larry Reno did not believe that Livingston's source could have been his grandfather, William H. Reno, as there was little recorded contact between the two men (though they might have spoken over the telephone). (Lawrence R. Reno to author, 2 August 2003.) Another possibility is that William Reno's finding reached Livingston secondhand, by way of Albert Thompson. Livingston's series on the Ketchum and Christian gangs was published in Roswell just as Thompson was assembling his Ketchum monograph, and Thompson does quote a letter from "one of his [Tom Ketchum's] recent biographers" whom he does not name but who may well have been Livingston. It will become apparent, anyway, that William Reno took a leading role in the investigation and the preparation of the case against Collings. The author's conclusion that Weaver and Collings were two names for the same man will be explained in Chapter 13.

42. Titsworth, I, 5–6. This portion of Moore's anecdote may be true, but some of the other detail commands disbelief. Prominence is thrust upon "Black Bob McManus . . . the most mysterious member of the gang," who was alleged to have stood guard while the others were playing Poker. In 1905–6 George Titsworth made himself look silly by striving to prove, in the face of good evidence and good sense, that McManus, a personal enemy of several years' standing, was "G.W. Franks" of the Ketchum gang. Evidently, after the passage of nearly half a century, when McManus's name was only a dim echo from the past even to the older people of the locality, and the details of his embroilment with George Titsworth had vanished from public memory, Titsworth the son took it upon himself to revive his father's empty accusations as if they had been established as fact. Jack Potter was another who sought to anoint McManus with undeserved notoriety. Potter, presumably with intent to amuse, relates how Chris Otto, a sheepman who stopped a train in order to board it as a passenger, was mistaken for "Black Bob McManus, the desperado." See *Cattle Trails of the Old West*, rep. *Old West*, Vol. 12, No. 3, Whole No. 47 (Spring 1976), 58–9. In reality, McManus had little or nothing to do with the gang; "G.W. Franks" was Will Carver. See Chapter 23.

43. *U.S.A. vs. Collings*, as cited: Bill of Indictment, April term, 1898; Bill of Particulars.
44. Ibid.
45. *Atkins ms*, I, 6.
46. Donald F. Myrick, *New Mexico's Railroads*, 135–6.
47. Mary Laurine (Owen) Doherty and Emma (Hardesty) Adams, *The Folsom, New Mexico, Story and a Pictorial Review*, includes a contribution from Thomas E. Owen, who refers (20) to "the nice level flat" as "an ideal place to rob a train." It is questionable whether any stretch of open country could have been anything but a poor site for an assault upon an express car, especially when the lights of a stationary train—even if partly hidden in a cut—might have been visible from the nearest settlement, as at Folsom. But the spot selected by the Ketchum gang was ideal for a getaway. Larry Reno has made the point that "a veritable network of roads . . . and trails" met near the holdup site. A pursuing posse would have to determine whether the malefactors had traveled east toward Clayton, south or southwest toward Fort Union and Las Vegas, southwest toward Springer, northwest toward Raton, north towards Folsom and the Colorado line—or west towards Cimarron (Reno to author, 2 August 2003).
48. The description of Twin Mountain and its setting is from A. Thompson, *Open Range Days*, 184. The clearest account of the robbery, based largely on an interview with the express messenger, is in a Fort Worth dispatch of September 4 in the *Globe-Democrat*, 5 September 1897. The Denver papers (except the Times) relied wholly on dispatches from Trinidad: see the *Rocky Mountain News* and *Republican*, both 4, 5 September; *Post* and *Times*, both 4 September only. The *Rocky Mountain News* of 5 September has the fullest report, but includes the suspect state-

ment that both the engineer and fireman were "bludgeoned" before the car door was opened: all other sources agree that only the messenger was assaulted. Shorter reports are in the *New Mexican* and *San Francisco Chronicle*, both 4 September 1897, from Denver dispatches. The account in A. Thompson, *Albuquerque ms.*, 72–8, has several virtues: the author knew the terrain intimately, was well acquainted with Harrington, received information at first or second hand from other members of the crew, corresponded or talked with William Reno, and was altogether too close to the personalities and events to indulge in any wild flights of fiction in describing this robbery. He did, however, take liberties with some of the finer detail. Thus his account of the transaction in the express car, whether or not his informant was Messenger Drew, differs rather from the one that Drew gave the *Globe-Democrat* reporter on the day after the holdup. Thompson maintains that only one bandit stuck up the engine crew, but all the news accounts agree that two robbers entered the cab and ordered the train stopped. In these and similar instances the writer has preferred the press version. The *Globe-Democrat* report is askew in stating that Harrington ordered the train to be "backed four miles" after the robbery. Such a maneuver would have been both senseless and desperately dangerous if it had not been mechanically impossible. "Four miles" must have been a telegrapher's or transcriber's mistake for "for a mile." What happened is that the robbers, before leaving, ordered the train ahead, but it halted after a mile and was reversed to the scene of the attack. Thompson goes badly off course in naming "William H. McGinnis" (Elzy Lay) as a participant and "Bronco Bill" (William Walters) as an accomplice.

Thompson's *Clayton ms.*, 42–3, retells the story, but with less detail. Otero, 112–3, duplicates material in *Clayton*, including the incorrect references to Lay and Walters, but adds several items of original data; likewise Erna Fergusson, *Murder & Mystery in New Mexico*, 95–6, 98, 102. Owen, in Doherty and Adams, 20, adds a couple of nice stories of local provenance, but is wrong in saying that the robbers disconnected the mail and express cars before blowing the safe. He also places a greatly inflated figure on the loss sustained by the Pacific Express Company.

The names of the engineer and fireman are given correctly and in full in the Witness List in *U.S. vs. Collings* et al., as cited.

49. Doherty and Adams, loc. cit.

50. *Globe-Democrat*, 5 September 1897; A. Thompson, *Albuquerque ms.*, 77–8.

51. From particulars received by J.E. Harley, Superintendent of the Atchison, Topeka and Santa Fe Railway in New Mexico, wired to H.S. Lutz, the company's agent in Santa Fe, and passed by him for publication in the *New Mexican*, 4 September 1897.

52. Titsworth, I, 6–7 (quoting his father, George Titsworth, who mismatches time and event— obviously he kept no diary or other contemporary written record, and trusted a weak memory to rustle up the dates); various dispatches in *Rocky Mountain News*, 5, 6, 7 September; Denver *Post*, 6 September, and Trinidad dispatch in Denver *Republican*, 8 September (where the Peenland trio are miscalled "Beden"); Clayton dispatch of September 6 in *New Mexican*, same date; Trinidad, Colorado, dispatch in *San Francisco Chronicle*, 6 September; Clayton dispatch in *Globe-Democrat*, 9 September 1897; A. Thompson, *Albuquerque ms.*, 80–81.

George Titsworth says the pursuit began on July 17 (the right date is September 4): recounts that seven were arrested (the suspects may have numbered seven, but only five were detained); exaggerates the importance of the episode (which occurred only because the posse was on the wrong trail); omits the names of the arrestees; and neglects to add that only two were held to face charges (both of whom soon broke jail). B.D. Titsworth precedes his father's recollections with a newspaper clipping which purportedly relates to the robbery of September 3, but actually describes the one that occurred at the same place on July 11, 1899.

A. Clayton dispatch in the *Chronicle*, 22 September 1897, reported the escape of the Cowans from the Union County Jail, Clayton, on the 20th.

53. *Atkins ms.*, I, 6–7, Trinidad dispatch, Sept.7, in *Denver Republican*, 8 September 1897.

54. The plundered train pulled into Fort Worth at 7 p.m. on the 4th, two hours late. The local correspondent for the *Globe-Democrat* alleged "a general belief that the bandits got between $12,000 and $15,000." Pacific Express put the range from $5,000 to $15,000. For once, an express company was overestimating its probable loss; but since the officials would have pitched their estimate on the low side, we may conclude that the gang was badly out of luck that night. The Denver papers, as cited in n. 47, were soon placing the amount at $3,000 or less. Later information fixed the loss at $3,500. Livingston, I, loc. cit., A. Thompson, *Albuquerque ms.* 80, *Clayton ms.*, 43; Otero, loc. cit., and Titsworth, I, 6, all echoed this figure. Their unanimity suggests a single source, but it is likely to have been authoritative. If Tom Ketchum's statement that his share of the booty was $500 was truthful, then the total haul could have been as little as $2,000. But Tom also claimed not to have been present when the train was robbed; all he had done (said he) was plan the holdup. His story does not bear scrutiny. See n. 61 and accompanying text.

55. George S. McGovern and Leonard F. Guttridge, *The Great Coalfield War*, 64, 80–81, 118, proffer a few glimpses into Reno's earlier and later career, but the book is biased towards the union interests and, consequently, inimical to Reno, his colleagues, and his employers. More detail of Reno's professional life, and a fairer perspective, are provided by an article in the Denver *Republican*, 18 July 1899, and obituaries in the *Denver Post* and *Trinidad Chronicle-News*, both 28 October 1935.

56. Posses were still on the ground after the release of the Peenlands on September 7. Alverson, loc. cit., says that the gang appeared in the vicinity of Tex Canyon in September 1897 (it may actually have been about October 5–9), and states that Carver was the only one of the four who had been there before. Tom Ketchum's words are from his last statement, printed in *Rocky Mountain News* and Denver *Republican*, 28 April 1901.

57. Alverson, 4; *Atkins ms.*, I, 7.

58. *Murder & Mystery in New Mexico*, 102

59. *U.S. vs. Collings et al.*, as cited, Bill of Particulars; Livingston, I, loc. cit., *Rocky Mountain News*, 1 April: *New Mexican*, 11 April 1898. Collings was arrested near Bisbee, Cochise County, late in March, 1898.

60. *Rocky Mountain News*, 24 August, reprinted in *San Angelo Standard*, 2 September 1899.

61. Titsworth, I, 6, No corroboration exists, leaving the obvious possibility that Ketchum lied to Titsworth, or that Titsworth made the whole story up. The author is inclined to accept it; at worst, it carries far more conviction than the Alamosa statement. If Tom really had been in the Alamosa district for several weeks, as he pretended, he would have been able to cite witnesses who had seen him there. As it was, his account was wholly unsupported. This, its inherent improbability, the availability of a credible alternative, the findings of William Reno, and the admissions of Atkins (who, without naming anyone apart from himself in connection with the first Folsom case, mentions Tom Ketchum just once in the contect of the Lozier robbery, and shows clearly that the three Lozier robbers participated in the Folsom stickup) combine to disprove Tom's Alamosa tale.

NOTES TO CHAPTER 7

1. Alverson, 10.

2. Tombstone dispatch in *Globe-Democrat*, 16 August; condensed report in ibid., 19 August; Bisbee, Arizona, *Lyre*, 16 August, in Safford, Ariz., *Graham Guardian*, 20 August 1897.

3. Foraker to U.S. Attorney General, 9 October 1897, in LR: Justice Year File 1896–13065; *Bisbee Lyre*, loc. cit.

4. Santa Fe dispatch in *Globe-Democrat*, 17 October, where the marshal went on to say that it was "generally conceded that the original Black Jack was still at large;" Foraker to Attorney General, 9 October 1897, ibid. Many other reports confirmed and complicated the pattern of contradiction. Thus, a Phoenix dispatch in the *Globe-Democrat* of 24 May alleged that Black Jack was still at large, and that Tom Ketchum was the man killed at Cole Creek the previous month; but a dispatch from Santa Fe published in the same paper on 3 July 1897 tagged the dead man "Black Jack Ketchum." There was a multitude of such items, though not all of them depended on the confusion of identities between Tom Ketchum and Will Christian. For example, a story in the Deming, New Mexico, *Headlight*, reprinted in the *New Mexican*, 17 August 1897, having observed that Black Jack seemingly possessed "the nine lives of a cat," cited "[r]eliable information that 'Black Jack,' Jeff Davis [George Musgrave] and Anderson [Bob Christian]" had been seen lately near "the Animas country" in the extreme southwest of New Mexico. At that time, almost no one realized that the gang had a new recruit, George Musgrave's older brother Van, who was as dark as Christian and Ketchum and bigger than either. He is likely to have been the supposed Black Jack of the Deming report. See also n. 5 below.

5. A letter from Robert C. Ross of the Texas Rangers, undated but evidently written and sent on 20 or 21 October 1897, apprised Foraker of "reliable information for stating that Tom Ketchum was with Black Jack and others in Chihuahua." Foraker forwarded this document to the Attorney General in Washington on 25 October 1897, along with a letter of his own and other materials.

6. *New Mexican*, 21 August 1897. These incidents are treated in detail in Tanner & Tanner, *Last of the Old-Time Outlaws*, 132–5 and 305, nn. 6–11, and, especially, Alexander, *S.O.Bs II*, 239–46 and 248–9, nn. 35–59.

7. *Deming Headlight*, loc. cit., *New Mexican*, 25 August 1897; Tanner & Tanner and Alexander, both loc. cit.

8. Solomonville, Arizona, *Graham County Bulletin*, 19 November 1897.

9. Concho (County), Texas, *Herald*, in *San Angelo Standard*, 16 January 1897.

10. Ibid.

11. Ibid.

12. Soule, 14.

13. Donna B. Ernst, "Before the Wild Bunch Struck a Bank in Winnemucca, Nov., They Hit a Store in Three Creek, Idaho," *Wild West*, December 2001, 10 and 64 (10).

14. *Atkins ms.*, I, 17. For an appraisal of the literature on Cassidy, Currie, Logan, and Longabaugh, see bibliographical introduction to the Notes to Chapter 1.

15. San Antonio dispatch in *St. Louis Globe-Democrat*, 1 October 1897.

16. San Antonio dispatch in ibid., 22 October 1897.

17. *Atkins ms.* I, 7. According to the typescript, Atkins said that the gang stayed in "the [Turkey Creek] canyon" for six weeks after the Folsom robbery. Whether he did say this, whether his amanuensis was hurried into a mistake, or whether the error is in the transcription, that statement cannot be correct. The gang would not have risked tarrying in the Cimarron area for anything like that long after their commission of a sensational robbery in the next county; more important, and as has been shown, there is actual evidence that they did not remain there for much more than a week after their return from Folsom. They would have arrived in Turkey Canyon about the beginning of August and are known to have left for Arizona in mid-September.

   Another undoubted error in the typescript names "the Solane" as a stopping point. A.C. Atkins, as editor and transcriber, argues convincingly that Solano, N.M., the nearest point etymologically, is too far off the outlaws' route to fit the reference and, further, that the use of the definite article shows that Atkins was talking about a geographical feature, or a corporate entity—*not* a settlement. But A.C. Atkins's conjecture that the gang might have headed for the Bell ranch is unsustainable: first, as he soon learned, the Bell has never been called "the Solane"; second, the Ketchums' murder of Herzstein and Gallegos (and their theft of ranch property) guaranteed that the outlaws would not put in an appearance there; and third, Dave Atkins's narrative states clearly that the gang's object was to avoid human contact in that part of New Mexico.

The present writer has no doubt that "the Solane" was a mishearing or misreading of "the Salado." Salado Creek is both logically and topographically in the right place: it was a watering spot that lay plumb in the path of their approach from the northeast and their planned route to the southwest.

18. *Atkins ms.*, I, 7–10.

19. *Atkins ms.*, I., 10. A.C, Atkins was puzzled by the manuscript reading of "Cherokee ranch," but here "Cherokee" can only be a misspelling of Chiricahua (Anglo pron, Cherry-cow)—an obvious lapse on the part of a note-taker who several times wrote down "Chiricahua Mountains" correctly. The outlaws were on the range of the Chiricahua Cattle Company.

20. George Scarborough was a distinguished exception. See Chapter 18.

21. *Atkins ms.*, I, 10. The history of the Chiruicahua and Erie cattle companies is well told by Lynn R. Bailey in *We'll All Wear Silk Hats*.

22. One "Marton Ketcham" was on the payroll of the San Simon Cattle and Canal Company during 1897. In all probability this was the individual whose name appears successively as James M. Ketchum, M. Jacob Ketchum, and Marlson Ketchum in the San Saba County Census Returns for 1860, 1870, and 1880, and as Marion Ketchum in *San Saba County History*, 169 (where it is also stated that he married Elizabeth Cheney [Chaney?]). He was born in 1859, the second child and eldest son of James Ketchum, who was killed by Indians in 1867. His younger brother Peter had moved to Tom Green County, and certainly had contact with Berry and Sam during the 1890s.

23. Alverson, 10–12; Axford, 63.

24. Walter Noble Burns, *Tombstone: An Iliad of the Southwest*, 370–1, in a passage merging the identities of Tom Ketchum and Will Christian into one. (Both men used the hideout, first Christian, then Ketchum.) Also, Soule, 33–4, citing F. Stanley, *The Alma Story*, who says that it was from there that Elzy Lay, after leaving prison, recovered a hoard of booty from a train robbery. (See Chapter 22.) Livingston, I, 352–3, describes how Tom Ketchum directed officers to a similar hideout in the Chiricahuas, near Turkey Track horse camp "forty miles north of Bisbee," in the hope that they would be ambushed when they reached it. See Chapter 16.

25. Alverson, 9.

26. Axford, 62, 256; Kemp, 166; A. Thompson, *Albuquerque ms.*, 63; *Clayton ms.*, 42. In the Albuquerque version, Thompson has Ketchum add: "They called us 'The High Five' at first." The Ketchum gang was never called the High Fives (except to uninformed commentators, like Thompson himself, who did not know that the High Five gang was the Christian gang); and it is most improbable that Ketchum ever said that it was. Obviously, Thompson had given way to his recurring tendency to indulge in fictional flourishes. The absence of this sentence from *Clayton* leads the author to suppose that the rest of the *Albuquerque* passage may have been Thompson quoting Ketchum, as distinct from Thompson quoting his own imagination.

27. Axford, 62–3; Alverson, 9 (insertion); Hovey/Sturges, 50.

28. *Rocky Mountain News* and *Denver Republican* 27 and 28 April 1901; only the *News* of the 27th has Ketchum referring specifically to "Moritos" (La Morita). We have only Tom Ketchum's word for this, and Tom was anything but a steadfast devotee of the truth. But the

author is strongly disposed to believe him here. Two circumstances tend to support his story: first, Atkins was the first to quit the gang—and it is not likely that he would have stayed in it for long after a row with Tom Ketchum; second, his murder of Tom Hardin while drunk made his over-fondness for alcohol a matter of record (a record to which his own reminiscences offer several further illustrations). It is certain that the authorities did learn early in December that a holdup attempt on the S.P. was imminent.

29. Los Angeles dispatch in *San Francisco Chronicle*, 11 December 1897; Foraker to Attorney General, 12 December 1897, stating that he had been advised on December 4 that a Southern Pacific train would be held up within the next ten days and that he was cooperating with the railroad and express companies, as well as with U.S. Marshal Griffith of Arizona. For the George Scarborough assertion (partly dependent on the erroneous statement that Scarborough had been deputized by Foraker, but still a credible hypothesis), see DeArment, *Scarborough*, 174–6 and Alexander, *S.O.Bs. II*, 70. But see, also, Chapter 9, n. 5.

30. *Rocky Mountain News* and *Denver Republican*, both 28 April 1901.

31. Ross, El Paso, Texas, to Foraker, 15 October 1897, copy in LR: Justice Year File 13065–1896.

32. Ross to Foraker, circa 20 October 1897, copy enclosed with copy letter from Louis M. Buford, U.S. Consul, Paso del Norte (Juarez), Mexico, 21 October 1897, ibid.

33. Cornelius C. Smith, Jr., *Emilio Kosterlitzky: Eagle of Sonora and the Southwest Border*, is the standard biography. Also, Larry D. Ball, *The United States Marshals of New Mexico and Arizona Territories, 1846–1912*, 208, 229, 230; Ball, *Desert Lawmen: The High Sheriffs of New Mexico and Arizona, 1846–1912*, 220–222; Dane Coolidge, *Fighting Men of the West*, 195–214; Allan A. Erwin, *The Southwest of John H. Slaughter, 1841–1922*, 241, 319; J. Evetts Haley, *Milton*, 202–3, 258–260, 281, 286–8, 359–362.

34. Denver dispatch in *San Francisco Chronicle*, 16 October; Santa Fe dispatch in *Globe-Democrat*, 17 October 1897.

35. Titsworth, I, 5. His principal source was the *Trinidad Chronicle-News*.

36. *Trinidad Daily Advertiser*, 4 November 1897.

37. Ibid., 5 November 1897; Titsworth, loc. cit.

38. Titsworth, loc. cit.

39. This chain of incident is comprehensively described in Tanner & Tanner, *Last of the Old-Time Outlaws*, 135–149. The Tanners' research revealed, among much else, that the outlaw hitherto known only by his alias of Theodore James was Calvin Van Musgrave. See also Burton, *Bureaucracy*, 42–51.

40. Axford, 254–5. The words actually spoken were, "Tell Them Old Bill Dalton has come to life again." (Tanner & Tanner, ibid., 142, citing Albuquerque, New Mexico, *Daily Citizen*, 8 November 1897.) The speaker could only have been Bob Christian, who, alone of the gang, had known Dalton, been accessory to some of his crimes, and could have felt impelled to mention him by name. By then, Dalton had been dead for well over three years, and his name might not have been to the forefront of the public mind in New Mexico even in 1893–94, when he attained so much notoriety in Indian Territory. It is not to be wondered that, in later accounts, "Old Bill Dalton" was displaced by the familiar and more eye-catchingly evocative "Black Jack."

41. Axford, 256; Foraker, Santa Fe, to Buford, El Paso de Norte, 25 October 1897, LR: Justice Year File 1896–13065.

42. Santa Fe dispatch in *San Francisco Chronicle*, 8 November 1897.

43. Telegrams and letters in LR: Justice Year File 1896–13065, viz., Foraker, Deming, N.M., to Attorney General, 6 and 7 December; Griffith, Tucson, Ariz., to Attorney General, 9 December (telegram); Foraker, Santa Fe, to Attorney General, 12 December; Griffith to Attorney General, 9 December (letter), enclosing copy of his earlier letter of 19 November; same to same, 22 December 1897.

NOTES TO CHAPTER 8

1. In his ante-mortem statement, reproduced in its fullest form in the *Rocky Mountain News* and *Denver Republican*, both 28 April 1901, Ketchum specifically named Cullen. In the letter Tom addressed to President McKinley, which was published in many newspapers in the days following the execution, the name appears variously as Cullen (e.g. unidentified report and Associated Press dispatch, both reprinted in Hovey, 53); Cullin (e.g. special dispatch from Clayton in *Denver Post*, 26 April and *New Mexican*, 27 April; *Silver City Independent*, 30 April); and Bullin (e.g. *Denver Times*, 26 April, *Rocky Mountain News* and *New York Times*, both 27 April 1901). Only later was it corrupted into Bullion. Ketchum's mind had good excuse for wandering occasionally as he wrote, or dictated, that letter: his neck was only three hours from the noose. He had known both Cullens and Bullions: mental stress could have caused him to muddle one with the other. If so, at least one press correspondent spotted and corrected the error, and at least one did not. Alternatively, Ketchum made no mistake, but a correspondent or compositor did, the coincidental outcome being a name similar to one that became notorious with Laura Bullion's arrest later that year. Ed's surname is misspelled "Cullin" throughout Ketchum's oral statement, as transcribed and printed in the *News* and *Republican* of 28 April 1901. Haley, 281 ff., makes the same mistake. A form of Ketchum's letter reprinted in the *Trinidad Chronicle-News*, 22 June 1930, appears to mark Cullen's literary debut as "Ed Bullion." He recurs as such in Stanley, 48, unsourced, and Bartholomew, 10–11, 42–3, adopted from Stanley.

Barton, 52, was the first to cite the *Twelfth U.S. Census, 1900*, to show that Dan Bullion was living in Texas two years after the Steins affair. More specifically, the census taken in Brewster County in June states that he was aged 19, Texas born, and living alone at or near Marathon. No great significance hangs on his statement that both his parents were born in Missouri (his mother was born in Arkansas); a year later, his older sister, Laura, could not say whether she had been born in Missouri or Arkansas. In 1917 he appeared before the Local Board for Lincoln County, N.M., as a volunteer for military service. The entry on Registration card No. 336 describes him as 37 years old, a mechanic, nearest relative Mary M. Bullion, living at Carrizozo, medium height and build, with gray eyes and black hair. (Information provided by WTC, ASU.)

2. *Ninth U.S. Census, 1870; Texas—San Saba County (Exclusive of Town of San Saba)*, S, 8, L.13–14, 4 July 1870; *Tenth* ibid., 1880—*Bandera County*, Precincts 1 and 2, p. 17 (also recorded on Sheet 9, line 1), 23 June 1880. The family spelling is given as "Cullin" in 1870 and "Cullen" in 1880. Ed's niece, Becky Gaines, confirms that Cullen is the correct form and has provided his date and place of birth (John Tanner to author, 13 August 2004).

3. Foraker to Attorney-General, 12 December 1897 (LR: Year File 13065–1896); *New Mexican*, 13 December; El Paso dispatch in *Globe-Democrat*, 15 December 1897.

4. Haley, *Milton*, 281.

5. Axford, 37. Very similar stories, with variations and adaptations, have been told elsewhere and about other cowcamp characters. Lynn R. Bailey, "*We'll All Wear Silk Hats*," 93–4, 173 especially, demonstrates the unlikelihood of either of the Shattucks figuring in any such encounter. Even so, the present writer does not share Bailey's general disdain of Axford's book, and is at a loss to understand how Axford's use of the anecdote might be construed as a sign of hostility toward the Shattucks, the more so as Axford does not name the Shattucks anywhere.

6. Haley, loc. cit., *Atkins ms.*, I, 10.

7. Benton, *Frontier Times* serialization, III, 46.

8. Telegram, Foraker, Deming, to Attorney-General, 7 December 1897, as cited; Letter, Santa Fe, same to same, 12 December (LR: Justice Year File 13065–1896); Griffith to Attorney General, 22 December (in ibid.); Los Angeles dispatch in *San Francisco Chronicle*, 11

December; *Silver City Enterprise,* 10 and 17 December; *New Mexican,* 13 December 1897. In his letter of December 12, Foraker said that the posse comprised four deputies from Arizona, four from New Mexico, and six men hired by Wells, Fargo—fourteen in all. Other contemporary sources, including Foraker himself when interviewed for next day's *New Mexican,* put the number at sixteen. See Chapter 9, n. 1 and text.

9. Ibid.

10. Personal observation, June 1972, August 1986, and (especially) 3 August 2001 and 5 August 2005; Robert Julyan, *The Place Names of New Mexico,* 341; Marjorie White, "Death Pass in the Peloncillos," *Frontier Times,* Vol. 10, No. 4, New Series No. 42 (July 1966), 42–3, 68–9. The place name is often printed as "Stein's," the form used by both Haley and White, but Julyan omits the apostrophe, and has been taken here to be the stronger authority. Contemporary press usage seems, however, to have been mostly on the side of the apostrophe. The manner of articulation is also at dispute. Julyan advises that "Steens" is the pronunciation in local use; but, in conversation with the author in 2005, the proprietors of the former Charles store (Larry and Linda Link) insisted that "Stines" is correct.

11. White, 42.

12. Jeffrey Burton, *Constable Dodge and the Pantano Train Robbers,* 24–28.

13. Tucson dispatches in *Globe-Democrat* and *San Francisco Chronicle,* both 26 February 1895; William M. Breakenridge, *Helldorado: Bringing the Law to the Mesquite,* 400–401; Nelle Merwin, "The Great Willcox Train Robbery," *Golden West,* Vol. 2, No. 2, January 1966, 23, 54–6; Maurice Kildare (pseudo., Gladwell Richardson), "The Willcox Double Robbery," *Real West,* June 1968, 31–3, 50–51, 63; Colin Rickards, "There Were All Kinds of Gunfighters," [Bill Traynor], *Old West,* Vol. 6, No. 1, Whole No. 21 (Fall 1969), 22–3, 60–62.

Breakenridge, a railroad detective in 1895, said in his autobiography that the Steins robbers of that year were Grant Wheeler and Joe George, who had plundered a train at Willcox on January 30. But the *Chronicle* report includes a statement from Breakenridge dismissing any notion that the men who succeeded at Willcox could have been those who flopped at Steins Pass less than a month later: the latter attempt, he announced at the time, "was the work of very green hands." This earlier pronouncement is the one to believe. Kildare's article is based on interviews with Breakenridge. As such, it is an expanded version of the *Helldorado* account, and of little merit. Kildare's "Sheriff Jim Fry of Cochise County" was Camillus S. Fly, who held office from the beginning of 1895 to the end of 1896. Contemporary press reports nominate Wheeler and George as the Steins Pass bunglers, but leave no doubt that they were accompanied by two or three other men for the Willcox sortie—a point that Breakenridge evades. Joe George's real name was said to have been David Sizer.

A reference to Joe George in White, 43, confuses the lucrative robbery at Willcox with the failure at Steins.

14. Tanner & Tanner, *Last of the Old-Time Outlaws,* 90–91.

15. District of New Mexico, Third Judicial District: *The United States of America versus William Warderman et als., No. 1217—attempt to rob the mail,* a True Bill (with Witness List and Subpoenas); *No. 1218—violating postal laws:* (Subpoenas); *Atkins ms.,* I. 11.

16. Charles H. Jennings was the second son of Sidney D. and Harriet Gertrude Jennings, residents of Kings County, N.Y., *10th Census*—Film on T9–0855, p. 347A. (Details from John D. Tanner, Jr.) Tom Ketchum's subsequent attempt to implicate Bronco Bill Walters was engendered by malevolence and a violent sense of resentment, as explained in Chapters 16 and 21, and is easily refuted. This apart, we are indebted to Tom for identifying the tasks performed by each individual member of the gang, and see no reason to quarrel with the broad outline of his account (*Rocky Mountain News* and Denver *Republican,* 28 April 1901). It is likely, moreover, that some of his references to "Bronco Bill" may relate to Will Carver, who was sometimes

nicknamed "Cowboy Bill" in Texas and was also noted there as an exceptionally fine rider. In one of these references to "Bronco Bill" the name "Bill Carver" follows in parentheses. It cannot be determined whether the parenthetical additions embody Ketchum's or the reporter's attempt at clarification. But Ketchum's letter to McKinley does name Carver and Bronco Bill separately.

We have the benefit of Dave Atkins's disclosures as well as Ketchum's. Atkins pointedly did not name any of his confederates (though, later in his narrative, he makes it plain that those arrested for the crime were not among them). His version of events has been incorporated in the main text; nothing in it is incompatible with the picture that can be built up from the other sources, and many of its details correspond with those given in material he would not have seen or known about. Unusually for informal reminiscences, Atkins's contain many dates; and all of them are right, or nearly right. His dating of the Steins Pass episode is in the latter category: he cites December 7, instead of December 9.

The author has also tried to reconcile discrepancies at several points in the following contemporary press accounts. *Deming Headlight*, 10 December: *Rocky Mountain News*, 10 and 11 December; Los Angeles, California, *Times*, 10 December, reprinted in *Chronicle*, 11 December; Phoenix *Arizona Republican*, 12 December; *New Mexican*, 10 and 13 December; *Globe-Democrat*, 11 December; Tucson *Arizona Daily Star*, 10 and 11 December; Enterprise, 17 December 1897. These are the principal areas of inconsistency:

(i) The preliminaries. The *Headlight* has four bandits descending on the station "[s]hortly before" the train came in. An El Paso dispatch in the *Globe-Democrat*, says the first pair of robbers entered the station agent's office at eight o'clock and "were chatting indifferently when, half an hour later, the headlight was seen coming around a curve;" whereupon they held up the agent and three more robbers appeared, after which the agent was forced to set a red light. The hasty dispatch to the *New Mexican* of the 10th, also from El Paso, had nothing to say about the robbers' arrival and early actions—the five merely "stepped out from their hiding places" when the train was halted by the danger signal. A Lordsburg dispatch in the *L.A. Times* stated that the railroad station was held up at "6 p.m." and that the train did not pull in until nine; and Express Messenger Adair, interviewed for the same newspaper at Shorb, near Los Angeles, put the time of the attack on the train at 8:30 p.m. (The particulars in the *Rocky Mountain News*, 10 December, were much the same as those in the following morning's *Globe-Democrat*.)

A. Thompson, *Albuquerque ms.*, 88–91, overloads his narrative with passages of "reconstructed" conversation, but cannot be disregarded, because some of his information seems to have come from the St. Johns. From them he learned that the five robbers arrived at 6:15 p.m., which comes close to the *Times*'s "6 p.m." and confirms that the gang hung about the station for more than two hours before showing their hand. The St. Johns' story provides a credible explanation of how at least two of the bandits occupied themselves during their two-hour wait for the train. According to the account given to Thompson, the wife was intimidated into cooking a meal for the men (in reality, perhaps only for two of them—Atkins and Cullen). This social detail eluded all the press reports; but this may have been because, at the time, the St Johns thought it best to keep quiet. The author suspects that Charles and Daisey St. John did not need to be dragooned into sharing their supper; at the least, they would have recognized the pointlessness of defiance. Thompson was given to understand that the robbers were already masked when they rode in, and that they remained masked while they were taking supper. The author does not believe it; the visitors could not have consumed meat and vegetables through cloth masks. After the holdup, and at the trial of three men accused of it, St. John professed himself unable to identify the bandits, because they had worn masks. But the probable truth is that the masks would have been donned only when the arrival of the train was imminent: the St. Johns may have known full well who was visiting the station, and may not have wanted to identify them. Nor would they have wanted the express and railway companies and the local peace officers to realize this. Both ends would be served by the pretense that the bandits were masked throughout.

Finally, the best argument for the Thompson narrative is that, in all crucial particulars, it squares with the one that Atkins dictated almost twenty years before Thompson began work on his. Atkins, too, relates that the gang turned up at the station at about six p.m. ("two and a half hours before train time") and that they ate a leisurely supper with the St. Johns. About the only difference is that Thompson has the bandits eating a cooked meal, whereas Atkins says that they excused Mrs. St. John from cooking and were content with fruit, bread, and milk. A statement by Atkins that only four of the gang went into the station house will be correct: the fifth man would have stayed outside to keep watch.

Atkins's account was a family memoir, of whose existence Thompson could not have been aware. Besides, a reading of Thompson's works is proof that Thompson knew next to nothing about Atkins, and made no visible effort to learn more.

A short paragraph in *Annual Report of the Post-Office Department for the Fiscal Year Ended June 30, 1898*, "Report of the Superintendent of the Railway Mail Service," 627–730 (682), presumably derived from Postal Clerk Albright's official memorandum, times the stoppage at "about 8 p.m."

The author's conclusion is that the reports in the *Globe-Democrat*, *L.A. Times*, and *Star*, between them, get closest to the truth.

(ii) The amounts stolen. All accounts agree in the one essential: the bandits' takings were derisory. Tom Ketchum admitted stealing the telegraph operator's rifle, but disassociated himself from the rest of the program of petty thievery: "Ed Cullin [*sic*] went into the depot and secured a few dollars in money—I don't know exactly how much—somewhere between $7 and $11. I received none of the money myself, as I did not want it." It is known that the Post Office, located in the Charles store, coughed up $9: St. John, who had been in charge of the office that night, submitted a claim for that sum on behalf of the nominal incumbent, Emma Rodgers, who was fully reimbursed by the Department before the end of the fiscal year (*Annual Report of the Post Office Dept., 1898*, 95). ("It took about twelve dollars worth of swearing to get the papers in shape," the sardonic editor of the Lordsburg *Western Liberal* commented on 21 January 1898, referring to St. John's visit to the U.S. Commissioner on the 18th.)

The Lordsburg correspondent of the *L.A. Times*, ibid., provided a round figure of $11.20 for the moneys blackguarded out of the railroad company, express company, and post office. Then, in its issue of 13 December 1897, the *New Mexican* published Marshal Foraker's summary of the night's depredations: the robbers had filched $2 from the post office, 25c. from the express office, and about $10 from the station agent. Foraker may have been referring to St. John's personal cash loss, as distinct from what was obliged to surrender from the post office till. If not, most of St. John's $10 was the $9 belonging to the post office. Hence the two-dollar contribution may have come from the till of the Charles store, just a few feet away from the post office counter. All that was said about McMullen's loss was that "but little money was secured" from him and St. John (Deming dispatch in *Rocky Mountain News*, 11 December 1897). On the basis of the available data, therefore, the proceeds are unlikely to have exceeded $30, and may not have amounted to half of that.

Something else: if money was found on Cullen's body, not a word was said about it in print. More than an hour separated the disappearance of the robbers and the appearance of the Foraker posse. It is not inconceivable that one or more of the citizenry of Steins turned a profit on the night's transactions. Another question turns on Engineer Tom North's value as a witness. When interviewed for the *Arizona Daily Star* issue of 11 December 1897, he professed an inability to identify his assailants by face or voice; he "could form no idea of their features" because they "wore full masks," and they had spoken very little, "communicating with each other almost entirely by signs." Yet, if the press reporting of the subsequent trial is any guide, he could confidently identify two of the bandits from the witness stand more than two months after the attack on the train.

The report that the engineer had detached only one of the two coupling chains came not from North but from "A Local Story" in the *Phoenix Republican*, taken from "[t]wo or three" incoming passengers whose homes were in Phoenix. Many of the disagreements over factual detail may have been resolved at the trials of the accused, but no official record was made of the testimony, and press accounts of the court proceedings are few and sketchy. See Chapter 9. North had been in the employ of the Southern Pacific for sixteen years. He was the fireman on November 24, 1883, when eastbound train no. 19 was derailed and robbed at Gage, New Mexico, and the engineer killed.

17. *New Mexican*, 7 September 1899; *Rocky Mountain News* and *Denver Republican*, both 28 April 1901.

18. *San Angelo Standard*, 26 August 1899.

19. The fullest description of the battle is Adair's. He and Albright were interviewed at Shorb, near Los Angeles, by a correspondent for the *L.A. Times* of 10 December. A dispatch from Deming in the same issue depicted the fight as Jennings had seen it. Both items were reprinted in the *San Francisco Chronicle*, 11 December 1897. A dispatch from Phoenix, Arizona, in the *Rocky Mountain News*, same date, was taken almost wholly from a passenger.

20. Deming dispatch in *Rocky Mountain News* and *Globe-Democrat*, both 11 December 1897. The St. Louis paper supplemented the telegraphic news with a profile of Stoeger compiled by a city reporter. Stoeger was thirty years old, Austrian by birth, and a traveler for the American Brewing Company. Adair told his *L.A. Times* interviewer that the conductor and brakeman had already warned the approaching Limited. This confirms the obvious, since these two members of the crew had been left at the depot with Agent St. John.

21. The passenger whose account was telegraphed from Phoenix to the *Rocky Mountain News* thought that the occupants of the express car kept the doors closed until almost the end of the siege and that Cullen was killed because he "very imprudently" stuck his head inside in the false belief that the defenders were surrendering. But the men in the express car were reported as saying that the doors were open throughout the fight.

Cullen's parting exclamation was variously rendered as "Boys, I am gone," and "Boys, I am dead." Adair told the reporter who interviewed him at Shorb that Cullen had uttered the latter cry twice before dying, but it seems likely that each phrase was heard once. Both the *Deming Headlight*, 10 December, and the Deming dispatch in the *St. Louis Globe-Democrat*, 11 December 1897, state that Cullen's corpse was carried to Tucson—an understandable, but incorrect, assumption; the body was taken from the train at or near San Simon, where the officers were waiting. Marshal Foraker's men then boarded an eastbound train and unloaded the dead man at Lordsburg (Foraker to Attorney-General, 12 December 1897).

22. Ibid., Griffith to Attorney-General, 22 December, LR, as cited; *New Mexican*, 13 December; Lordsburg dispatch to *Los Angeles Times*, 10 December, reprinted in *San Francisco Chronicle*, 11 December 1897; Haley, 283–4.

23. Foraker to Attorney-General, 12 December; *New Mexican*, 13 December; El Paso dispatches in *Globe-Democrat*, 11 and 15 December 1897; *Rocky Mountain News*, 3 June 1900.

24. *Deming Headlight*, 10 December; Deming dispatch in *Rocky Mountain News*, 11 December; San Simon and Silver City dispatches in *New Mexican*, 14 December 1897.

NOTES TO CHAPTER 9

1. *U.S. vs. Warderman et al.*, Praecipe and Subpoenas, Nos. 1217 and 1218; *Silver City Enterprise*, 10 and 17 December; San Simon and Silver City dispatches in *New Mexican*, 14 December; Tucson dispatch in *San Francisco Chronicle*, El Paso dispatch in *Globe-Democrat*, both 15 December; *Deming Headlight*, and Las Cruces, New Mexico, *Rio Grande Republican*, both 17 December 1897; *Arizona Daily Star*, 15 and 16 December 1897, 16 January 1898; *Annual Report of the Attorney General of the United States for the Year 1898*, 236, 274, 276; John Tanner to author, with enclosures, 24 June and 13 August 2004; Haley, 281, 283–4; DeArment, 176, 182.

Although Milton took the oath on December 6, 1897, Duffy did not sign the commission until December 13 or file it until the 18th. Webb was commissioned on December 16, and Graham on December 18. Hood received a commission on April 18, 1898, long after the completion of his work on the case. The Scarboroughs were among those first summoned by Foraker, but neither was given a commission in connection with the case; as mentioned below, George Scarborough was first commissioned as a field deputy three months later. The organizers of the posse—Foraker, Griffith, and Thacker—did not take to the saddle after the holdup at Steins Pass. White, a deputy marshal since July 7, 1897, and Graham apparently did not come into the case until after the initial pursuit.

2. For an appraisal of Haley's biography, see Bibliographical Essay (preceding endnotes to Chapter 1). Examples of Milton's old-age excesses of self-appreciation are cited in Evans Coleman to *Arizona Republican*, 23 December 1937, and Burton, *Bureaucracy*, 57 (n. 28).

3. For an appraisal of DeArment's biography, see Bibliographical Essay.

4. DeArment, 95–112, 142–156; Haley, 228, 233–251; Leon Claire Metz, *John Selman, Gunfighter*, 2nd edition, 198–203; Metz, *Dark Angel of Texas*, 247–252; J. Marvin Hunter, "George Scarborough, Peace Officer," *Frontier Times*, Vol. 24, No. 9 (June 1947), 436–7. Hunter's sister was the wife of Scarborough's brother-in-law, Frank M. McMahan.

5. See Holmes Maddox, "George Scarborough—U.S. Deputy Marshal and Pioneer," *The Cattleman*, June 1947, rep. *Frontier Times*, Vol. 24, no. 9 (June 1947), 437–9 (438). Maddox states that the U.S. marshal for Arizona had sent Scarborough into the field "to catch Black Jack and his gang." If this were so, the arrangement must have been informal and unofficial, for Scarborough was never commissioned in Arizona. The dates of his commission in New Mexico, and a summary of expenses claimed and allowed, are in *ARAG 1897*, 276–7.

Maddox, loc. cit., dated Scarborough's arrival in Arizona to the summer of 1898 and the Steins Pass holdup to "about Christmas that year 1898." The correct year in each instance is 1897.

6. DeArment, 92.

7. Los Angeles dispatch in *Chronicle*, 11 December; *Star*, 15 December; *New Mexican*, 13 December; *Enterprise* and *Headlight*, both 17 December 1897; Tanner to author, 13 August 2004; Foraker, Santa Fe, to Attorney General, Washington, 12 December, and Griffith, Tucson, to Attorney General, 22 December 1897 (LR: Justice Year File 13065–1896); Haley, 281. The *Headlight* story says that Milton's party left Nogales on the previous Friday, December 10—an obvious mistake. The author doubts that White was with Milton's party at this time; see n. 21.

8. Haley, 204.

9. *New Mexican*, 12 and 13 December; Tucson dispatch in *Chronicle*. 15 December; *Star*, 15 and 16 December 1897; Maddox, 438, DeArment, 177; A. Thompson, *Albuquerque ms.*, 95–6. Thompson claims certainty of knowledge that Sam Ketchum and Carver were at Galeyville at the time of the Steins affair, and that the rider who was stated (but only by Maddox) to have headed west from the Cienega ranch—and who, says Thompson, may or may not have been Tom Ketchum—joined them there, but produces not a vestige of evidence for either assertion. Both statements were engendered by the false assumption that the Ketchum gang were respon-

sible for the recent train robbery at Grants, New Mexico, on which Thompson (ibid., 82–8) contributes a chapter that is fiction from beginning to end, and inept fiction at that. At the root of it all, yet again, was the unquestioning belief that the original Black Jack gang, which carried out the Grants robbery, was the Ketchum gang. In fact, there was hardly any contact between the two groups.

Haley, loc. cit., relying on a ms. by Mildred Taitt Milton, has Jeff Milton leading the party which took the longer route. The contrary but contemporary version in the *Star* and *Chronicle* is likely to be correct.

10. DeArment, 178: "Scarborough produced a pair of overalls he had found along the trail." It is not stated how, or at what point along the trail, the overalls were found.

11. Silver City, New Mexico, *Independent and Grant County Democrat*, 14 December; San Simon and Silver City dispatches in *New Mexican*, 14 December; Tucson dispatch in *Chronicle*, El Paso dispatch in *Globe-Democrat*, both 15 December; Star, 15 and 16 December; Silver City dispatch of December 14 in *Rio Grande Republican*, 17 December; *Enterprise* and *Headlight*, both 17 December 1897; Hovey/Sturges, 11, 14–15, 48; Alverson, 12–15; Benton, III, 47. Alverson says that Vinnedge was also arrested in the house, which is plainly wrong; if "Cushey" was nearby when the posse showed up, he managed to evade it.

Differences in the news reports over whether the arrests occurred on the Sunday or the Monday could imply journalistic misunderstanding or, more probably, the reluctance of some possemen to admit to having lingered in or near Tex Canyon for a day and a half, as they certainly did. Obviously the officers had no advance agreement as to precisely what story to tell.

Hovey/Sturges, 48, say the posse rode in on November (meaning December) 11; but the 11th was Saturday, and on that day the two sections of the posse were still approaching the lower Chiricahuas. The press reports, taken together, fully bear out Hovey's statement, which Alverson supports by implication, that the arrests happened on the day after the arrival of the posse. It is certain that the men were taken from Tex Canyon on the Monday, reached San Simon on the Tuesday, and were delivered to Griffith in Tucson on the Wednesday.

12. Alverson, 19.
13. Hovey/Sturges, 48, and ibid.
14. Alverson, 10; *Globe-Democrat*, 15 December; *Headlight*, 17 December 1897.
15. Alverson, 13.
16. Hovey/Sturges. 48, and ibid.
17. Tucson dispatch in *Chronicle*, 15 December; *Headlight*, 17 December 1897; Haley, 284–6.
18. San Simon dispatch in *New Mexican*, 14 December; *Headlight*, 17 December 1897; Hovey/Sturges, loc. cit.
19. Griffith to Attorney General, 22 December; *Star*, 16 December 1897; *Headlight*, ibid., Alverson, 15; Hovey/Sturges, loc. cit.
20. *Star*, 16 December 1897; Hovey/Sturges, loc. cit.
21. Alverson, 13–14. His and Hovey's failure to mention Scott White as good as proves that White was not in the posse (n. 5). Alverson had been a deputy sheriff under White, and the two men were friends. Later, White was a witness for the defense at the trial of Alverson and his companions. Had he been present during the arrests, Alverson would not have had cause to single out Milton as the only one of the posse of whom he could speak well.
22. Hovey/Sturges, loc. cit.
23. Ibid.
24. *Headlight*, 17 December 1897; *New Mexican*, 28 February 1898; Alverson, 12; Benton, loc. cit. and ibid.
25. Silver City dispatch in *New Mexican*, 14 December 1897.

26. Foraker to Attorney General, telegram, 14 December; Denver dispatch in *Chronicle*, 16 December 1897.
27. *Headlight*, 24 December 1897; Haley, 286. *U.S. vs. Warderman. et al.*, No. 1217: Arrest Warrant (Vinnedge), 16 February, Removal Warrants, 19 and 21 February 1898.
28. *Headlight*, 24 December 1897.
29. Alverson, 15.
30. El Paso, Texas, *Times* in *Arizona Daily Citizen*, 8 January; Star, 16 January; *Citizen*, 17 January 1898.
31. *Star*, ibid.
32. Griffith to Attorney General (John W. Griggs), 13 September 1898 (LR: Justice Year File 13065–1896).
33. Ibid.
34. Foraker to Attorney General, 9 and 20 April 1898.
35. John Tanner to author, 19 September 2003.
36. This sequence has occasioned extensive correspondence between John Tanner and the author.

No press report has been found of Vinnedge's arrest and arrival in Tucson; but the trial papers show that he was collected from there on February 19 for removal to Silver City, and court protocol would require his return to the U.S. District of New Mexico within three or four days of being lodged in the Tucson jail. "I can't see that Milton would have reached Steins [after arresting Vinnedge] earlier than the evening of February 16" (Tanner to author, 24 June 2004). The author believes that Milton was at Steins Pass on the night of February 16–17, awaiting the morning's eastbound express for Deming and thence Silver City, having arrived with Vinnedge about twenty-four hours earlier and put him on a westbound train after the necessary exchange of telegrams.

Even more opaque are the circumstances in which the arrest was made. Milton told Haley that Scarborough (no first name) had accompanied him on the search for Vinnedge; but on 13 February 1898—precisely when Vinnedge's arrest was imminent—Childers informed Thacker by letter that Scarborough (no first name) was in Silver City and that he, Childers, would "keep him here." The use of the unqualified surname in each instance strongly implies that both references would be understood as applying to George, the senior and by far the more notable of the two Scarboroughs in the case. Since Silver City and Tex Canyon are 110 miles apart by straight line, the two statements are in direct opposition: one or the other must be eliminated or rationalized. The author's belief is that George Scarborough was in Silver City when Milton arrested Vinnedge. Ed Scarborough, who later turned bad and wore prison stripes, may well have been with Milton; but Milton, for some hidden reason, wanted it to be thought that George was along.

That is not all. Griffith's letter of 13 September 1898 was designed to support Milton's claim for expenses incurred from February 6 in the alleged pursuit of Bronco Bill Walters. More than forty years later, Milton stuck to the same tune in his interviews with Haley. It was all arrant and patent nonsense, for at that time Walters was not an accredited outlaw and did not begin his preparations to rob a train until the middle of March. The author's conclusion is that Milton's expedition was aimed partly at intimidating sympathizers or potential imitators of the High Five and Snaky Four. It was also speculative; the posse would hope to run onto some of the actual malefactors, or at least uncover clues to their whereabouts. But the only tangible product of Milton's long sortie was the arrest of John Vinnedge. Something more would be needed to justify the expense claims of Milton and his confrères. Griffith obligingly supplied it in his letter to Attorney General Griggs. Milton, it seems, sustained the deception to the end of his days.

(John Tanner to author, ibid., 24 June, and 13 August 2004, author to Tanner, 3 November 2003, 31 May 2004, and 26 July 2004; *U.S. Court for the First District of Arizona*—Removal Order and Execution, John Vinnedge, 19 February 1898, (with trial papers, *U.S. vs. Warderman et al.*, No. 1217); Griffith to Attorney General and other correspondence relating to Walters in LR: Justice File Year 13065–1896; Childers, Silver City, N.M., to J.N. Thacker, Tucson, A.T., 13 February 1898 (U.S. Marshals' Service—General Correspondence of the U.S. Marshals, Arizona, MS 820, Arizona Historical Society, Tucson).

Although, unaccountably, he places the holdup and his own arrest in November instead of December, Hovey is correct in saying that Vinnedge was arrested "some nine weeks later" than the other five (Hovey/Sturges, 48).

37. *U.S. vs. Warderman et al.*, Nos. 1217 and 1218—True Bill of Indictment; *U.S. vs. Thomas Capehart et al.*, True Bill of Indictment. The Indictment for No. 1218 is not extant, but its substance was stated in detail in the judge's instructions to the jury and adapted for use in No. 1220, which was intended to provide scope for the prosecution of the defendants as accessories after the fact to the post office robbery. Evidently the Indictment for No. 1220 was filed on 25 February 1898; but, although the jacket seems to be the original, the document filed within it cannot be.

The Indictment, as it exists, charges Capehart and Vinnedge as accessories to post office robbery and Warderman, Hoffman, Marshall, and Alverson as principals: yet all six were tried together in March for attempted mail robbery, and in September for post office robbery. It looks as if the extant version of the indictment may have been an improvisation, of dubious legality or none, designed to allow the United States another shot at convicting two of the three who had twice been acquitted as principals.

38. *U.S. vs. Warderman et al.*, as cited, Nos. 1217 and 1218: Warrants dated 16 and 21 February 1898, stipulating $5,000 bail for each defendant in each case; Silver City dispatch in *New Mexican*, 28 February 1898.

39. *U.S. Warderman et al.*, No. 1217: Motion, 24 February 1898. James Sherman Fielder practiced law at Silver City and Deming in partnership with a brother, Idus Lafayette Fielder. Both were natives of Georgia, Idus being twelve years the elder. Lawyer Jim seems not to have believed in the courts as the rightful arbiters of all disputes. On 8 October 1895 this "brilliant young attorney," having taken at least one drink too many, fell out with Charles L. Cantley, City Marshal of Silver City, and killed him in a gunfight.

As if the defense of the Texas Canyon crowd were not enough to occupy his thoughts and energies, Jim Fielder soon had to contend with the news of his sister's suicide. Mrs. J.W. Fayman, later known as Mrs Josie Black, had once been the best music teacher in Los Angeles. Her life changed when a "prominent Nevada capitalist" came between her and her marriage. Latterly she had traded herself as "Pauline," singer and piano player in a Phoenix saloon. On February 27, 1898, she imbibed a fatal mixture of alcohol and morphine. Her envoi was scribbled across the back of a photograph. It concluded: "[D]on't telegraph my brother in Silver City." (Silver City dispatch via Santa Fe, *Globe-Democrat*, 10 October 1895; John Tanner to author, 28 December 2003, enclosing articles from Phoenix *Arizona Republican*, 28 February, 3 and 4 March 1898.)

40. Bill Doty, Archivist, National Archives and Records Service, Pacific Region, Laguna Niguel, California, to author, 11 July, and in conversation, 6 August 2001; Santa Fe dispatch in *New Mexican*, 5 March 1898; Hovey/Sturges, 48–9.

41. *Territory of New Mexico, U.S. Third Judicial District*, Docket: 162, 164, 167, 170, 171, 173 (2, 3, 4, 7, and 8 March 1898).

42. Tanner and Tanner, 23–4, 162, 168.

43. Childers, Albuquerque, to Attorney General (John W. Griggs), 28 March 1898. (LR: Justice Year File 13065–1896.)

44. *U.S. District Court*, ibid., Docket, 152 (25 February 1898). The author has taken a juror named José Smith to be a Spanish-American.

45. *Enterprise*, 4 March: Silver City dispatches in *New Mexican*, 28 February, 7 March 1898.

46. Hovey/Sturges, 49. Graham apparently did not enter the case until after the raid on the Tex ranch.

47. *Enterprise*, 4 March; Silver City dispatch in *New Mexican*, 7 March 1898.

48. Hovey/Sturges, 11, 48.

49. Alverson, 14–5.

50. Childers to Attorney General, as cited; Silver City dispatch in *New Mexican*, 7 March 1898.

51. *U.S. vs. Warderman, et al.*, No. 1217: Instructions to the Jury.

52. Ibid., Verdict; *U.S. District Court*, ibid., Docket, 172 (8 March 1898); Silver City dispatches, in *Globe-Democrat*, 10 March; *Enterprise* and *New Mexican*, both 11 March 1898; Haley, 290. Haley credits Milton with swearing out the warrants under which the acquitted men were detained for a second trial.

53. Childers to Attorney General, as cited.

54. *Compiled Laws of New Mexico, In Accordance With an Act of the Legislature, Approved March 16th, 1897*, (Santa Fe, *New Mexican* Printing Company, 1897).

55. *U.S. District Court*, ibid., Docket, 173, 176 (8 and 9 March 1898).

56. *Enterprise*, 3 June 1898.

57. Hovey/Sturges, 49.

58. Ibid.

59. *U.S. vs. Warderman et al.*, Writ of Removal—Silver City to Las Cruces; Hovey/Sturges, 49–50, though Hovey does not mention Marshall's period of liberty between the two trials.

60. The names in the Praecipe and the individual Subpoenas issued in connection with No. 1218 are almost the same as those for No. 1217. See also *U.S. District Court*, ibid., Docket, 197, 200, 202, 203 (12, 14, 15, 16 September 1898).

61. *U.S. vs. Warderman et al.*, No. 1218, Affidavit for Poor Person, 1 September 1898.

62. *Independent*, 20 September 1898.

63. Ibid.

64. Ibid. The issue of 27 September 1898, which may have provided more detail on their defense, is lost.

65. Hovey/Sturges, 49–50.

66. Alverson, 16.

67. Hovey/Sturges, 50.

68. *U.S. vs. Warderman et al.*, No. 1218: Instructions to the Jury.

69. *U.S. District Court*, ibid., Docket, 209 (21 September 1898).

70. Ibid., 213; *U.S. vs. Warderman et al.*, No. 1218: Commitment to the Penitentiary, 27 September 1898; *Independent*, 4 October 1898.

71. Alverson, 16.

72. *U.S. vs. Thomas Capehart*, No. 1220: True Bill of Indictment; *U.S. vs. Warderman et al.*, No. 1221, True Bill of Indictment; *U.S. District Court*, ibid., Docket, as cited, 215 (Nolle Prosequi, No. 1220—23 September 1898), and 230 (Nolle Prosequi, No. 1221—7 February 1899). See n. 76.

73. *U.S. vs. Warderman et al.*, No. 1218: Commitment to the Penitentiary, executed by Foraker, 28 September 1898.

74. Hovey/Sturges, loc. cit. Hovey's statement that he, Alverson, and Warderman were each fined $10,000 is a needless exaggeration. The sense of his words would not have lost much force if he had kept to the right figure of $500 per head punitively and $7,000 between them to meet the costs of their prosecution.

75. *Affidavit*, Antonio Borrego, 17 April 1903, relating to statement by Sam Ketchum "three or four days" before his death on 24 July 1899 (that is, on or about 21 July, though misdated 7 August 1899 in the affidavit); *Rocky Mountain News*, 27 April 1901; Hovey/Sturges, 51; A. Thompson, *Open Range Days*, 182, quoting letter from Gerome Shield, in which Shield says Tom Ketchum admitted to him that he and his gang were the Steins Pass robbers. Hovey/Sturges state, loc. cit., that both Tom Ketchum, whose letter is reproduced therein, and Bronco Bill admitted participation in the Steins Pass affair, but he was mistaken over the latter. Perhaps Hovey confused Walters's arrest with that of Sam Ketchum, whose confession he does not mention.

76. *U.S. vs. Capehart*, No. 1218 (an apparent renumbering of No. 1220, presumably in error; see n. 72).

77. *New Mexican*, 8 December 1898.

78. Livingston, I, 347; A. Thompson, *Albuquerque ms.*, 81.

79. *Rocky Mountain News*, 1, 9 April; *United States District of New Mexico—Fourth Judicial District: United States of America vs. Charles B. Collings et al.*, No. 626; Writ of Arrest, 11 April 1898.

80. *New Mexican*, 13 April 1898; *U.S. vs. Collings et al.*, True Bill of Indictment.

81. Ibid., Demurrer to Indictment, 15 April 1898.

82. Ibid., Motion to Quash, 15 April 1898.

83. Ibid., Affidavit for Service; Order upon U.S. Marshal to pay, both 23 November 1898.

84. Ibid., Praecipe for Subpoenas; Witness List. Wilson Elliott's prior acquaintanceship with the members of the gang—besides being an inferential certainty, since his background was the same as theirs—is established by his conversation with Gerome Shield, reported in the *San Angelo Standard*, 5 August 1898.

85. Santa Fe *New Mexican Review*, 24 November 1898.

86. *U.S. vs. Collings, et al.*, List of Jurors, 21 November 1898.

87. *Rocky Mountain News*, 8 January 1899.

88. Reno's letter to Romero is in the case papers, *U.S. vs. Collings*, as cited, along with an unsigned receipt, same to same, dated January 22, 1899.

89. Hovey/Sturges, 8.

90. Chapter 21, text at n. 31 and ff.

91. A. Thompson, *Albuquerque ms.*, 95–6.

92. *Jeff Milton*, 265.

93. G. Thompson and others, 147.

94. *Atkins ms.* I, 12; A.C. Atkins. nn. 18 and 19.

NOTES TO CHAPTER 10

1. Erwin, 262–3, citing Fred Moore, a mutual friend of Slaughter and the outlaws. At the time in question, he was with the outlaws, who made sure he did not get away to warn the rancher.

2. *San Angelo Standard*, 25 September 1897.

3. *New Mexican*, 7 September 1900.

4. Axford, 62. It is not known whether they had met Elzy Lay by early 1898, but they all knew the Kilpatrick brothers and may already have considered an approach to one or more of them.

5. Barton, 77; photograph on 78.

6. *San Antonio Daily Express*, 30 April 1898.

7. Del Rio dispatch in ibid., Del Rio and El Paso dispatches in ibid., April 29; also, *San Angelo Standard*, 7 May 1898.

8. The second and more successful of the Comstock train robberies received extensive press attention. Dispatches from Del Rio, Alpine, Comstock, and Houston were amply supplemented by information gathered at first hand in San Antonio for the *San Antonio Express*, 30 April 1898. The *San Angelo Standard*, 7 May, kept its readers informed with dispatches dated April 29 from El Paso, San Antonio, and an article reprinted from the Houston, Texas, *Daily Post*, 4 May 1898, which was drawn from the informal report of Wells, Fargo's divisional superintendent, Gerrit A. Taft. An El Paso dispatch to the *San Francisco Chronicle*, 30 April, incorporates an interview with Dick Hayes, the express messenger, whose home was in El Paso. The telegrapher, or someone on the staff of the *Chronicle*, went astray in nominating the eastbound train as the object of the attack, while a reference to Hayes having a rifle may have sprung from a misunderstanding: Hayes may have spoken of his Winchester, and his interviewer may then have assumed that "Winchester" always meant rifle. In fact, Hayes was armed with a Winchester shotgun. The account in the *El Paso Times* of 30 April was drafted after the train's arrival in that city and appears not to have come from the same hand as the dispatch to the *Chronicle*. The first report to go into print was the one in the *San Antonio Light*, 29 April 1898. Details were sparse, and the lengthier account which might have been expected in the next issue was pre-empted by a rush of news on the Spanish-American War, the consuming press sensation of that spring and summer.

The time of the stoppage was differently recorded from one dispatch to another, because the news crossed timezones east and west and because of delays or misunderstandings in the transmission of the news. Annual Reports of the Post Office Department . . . 1898: "Report of the Superintendent of Railway Mail Service," 627–730 (695), records that the train was held up at 11:50 p.m., but that would only have been the time at which the robbers halted the engine to detach the passenger cars. The locomotive was commandeered at the depot at about 11:30 p.m.
9. One of the participants in the Wilcox, Wyo., train robbery of 2 June 1899 used what was obviously a false voice and spoke in what may have been a consciously assumed dime-novel vernacular (Pointer, 151). A dozen years later, on the morning of 13 March 1912, while holding up a train at Baxter Curve, seventy miles west of Comstock, Ben Kilpatrick also disguised his voice by pitching his tone artificially high. He gained nothing from the ruse, for the messenger killed him and his companion then and there (Soule, 171). See Chapter 22.
10. *San Francisco Chronicle* and Alpine dispatch in *San Antonio Express*, both 30 April; *Houston Post*, 4 May 1898.
11. *San Antonio Express* ("Information Gathered Here"), *San Francisco Chronicle*, and *El Paso Times*, all 30 April 1898.
12. Ibid., *San Antonio Light*, 2 May; *San Angelo Standard*, 7 May 1898.
13. Pieced together from all the sources cited in n. 8. Minor inconsistencies have been reconciled as smoothly as possible.
14. *Light*, 29 April 1898.
15. *Chronicle* and *San Antonio Express*, 30 April 1898.
16. Ibid., and *Houston Post*, 4 May 1898. Several accounts, such as the earliest one in the *Light*, 29 April 1898, alleged that registered mail was stolen, but *ARPOL, 1898*, loc. cit., says" [t]he mail car was not entered by the robbers, and the mail car was not molested, though the clerk was ordered to the ground and the blast of the explosives used on the express car caused some damage to both the mail car and its contents."
17. Houston dispatch in *San Antonio Express*, 30 April 1898.
18. *Houston Post*, 4 May 1898.
19. Dodge, ed. Lake, xii.
20. Del Rio dispatch in *San Antonio Express*, 30 April 1898.
21. Comstock and Alpine dispatches, in ibid.

22. Comstock dispatch, loc. cit.
23. Burton, "The Duellists of Devil's River," 63–66. Newman's companions were all from the vicinity of Sonora, Sutton County.
24. Reprinted in the *San Angelo Standard*, 7 May 1898.
25. Ibid., and Del Rio dispatch, loc. cit.
26. *ARPOD, 1898*, loc. cit.
27. See Chapter 14.
28. Loomis, 65–6.
29. St. Louis, Missouri, *Republic*, 8 November, reprinted in *San Angelo Standard*, 16 November 1901.
30. *San Angelo Standard*, 11 June 1898; Burton, "Duellists," 66–93. Newman later betrayed his partners and Bill Taylor killed him on 6 August 1900. (Burton, ibid., 81–3.) Information on three of the four Coleman bunglers that was unavailable when "Duellists" was published early in 2005 was passed to the author later that year.

Pierce F. Keton served twelve years in the Texas State Penitentiary, not seventeen, as previously written. He was pardoned on 13 March 1911, followed his brothers John and Matthew to Bisbee, Arizona, and died there of pneumonia on 8 January 1914, aged 48 years (the Registrar wrote "49"—the product of poor arithmetic) and eleven days. Jeff Taylor did not die in prison, as stated in "Duellists," but escaped on 25 October 1910. He was then about 43 years of age. Apparently he was never recaptured. The Taylor brother who died in the Huntsville penitentiary was John, on 8 July 1894, aged about 35. He had escaped in 1878, pending an appeal against conviction for the theft of a mare in Coryell County, but was recaptured fifteen years later and sent back to complete a ten-year term. Yet another brother, Jim, was pardoned on 19 November 1897, about halfway through a five-year term for horse theft in Menard County. He was about 28 at the date of his release. Bill Taylor's later history remains an open book. At the time of his third and definitive escape in December, 1901, he was 38 years old.

The author is indebted to John Tanner for copies of the Ketons' mortality and burial records, and to Chuck Parsons, of Luling, Texas, who, with the generous assistance of Donaly Brice, Sam Fowler, and Matt Okaty, of Texas State Archives, Austin, kindly furnished copies of pages from the Convict Ledgers and official correspondence relative to these men..
31. Report of General Manager L.S. Thorn, Texas & Pacific Railway, in special dispatch, from Dallas, Texas, to St. Louis, Missouri, *Post-Dispatch*, 2 July, reprinted in *San Francisco Chronicle*, 3 July 1898.
32. Chesley, 118.
33. The adventurist excitement aroused by the Spanish-American War dominated the news pages at the expense of nearly everything else that ordinarily would have been prime news during the spring and early summer of 1898. Few newspapers were willing to sacrifice much space for a train robbery in West Texas, even a notably successful one. Thus the *San Antonio Express*, normally generous in the allocation of print to criminal cases, allotted only a single cursory paragraph, followed by a couple of other short pieces in the next few days. Thorn's telegram to the *St. Louis Post-Dispatch* gave only a little further detail. Fortunately, the press in Fort Worth, one of the principal stations on the line, showed greater interest, and the *San Angelo Standard*, 9 July 1898, assembled something like a full picture, copied principally from the Fort Worth press but with additional dispatches from El Paso, Midland, and Fort Worth. An item in the Abilene, Texas, *Reporter*, 9 July 1898, though brief, included a few further particulars. More than thirty years later, further incidents in the robbery were revealed in the recollections of Frank Shelton, who as sheriff of Martin County, was at the head of the pursuit, were published in newspapers in Texas and New Mexico (Bryan, *Ruffians*, 271, citing Albuquerque, New

Mexico, *Tribune*; Barton, 87, citing Midland, Texas, *Reporter-Telegram*, 27 December 1998, an item based in part on an earlier printing of Shelton's reminiscences).

34. Bryan, quoting Shelton, loc. cit.

35. *San Angelo Standard*, 9 July 1898.

36. A Dallas dispatch in the *San Antonio Express*, 3 July, suggested lower and upper limits of $1,000 and $30,000 respectively. The range predicated in the *St. Louis Post-Dispatch* story of 2 July was from $10,000 to $50,000; the "thoroughly reliable" source for the loss of one particular consignment of $5,000 cash was quoted in a Fort Worth dispatch of July 2 published in the *San Angelo Standard*, 9 July 1898. Shelton's statement is in Bryan, loc. cit. The $30,000–$50,000 estimate occurs in an Austin dispatch of July 11 in the *Standard*, 23 July 1898. Barton, loc. cit., says $500, which must be an understatement, probably caused by someone's omission of one or two noughts from a figure shown in an older source.

Tise, 373, states that H.R. Wells became sheriff for a single two-year term after the election of November 1898; but in fact his period of office began in February, 1898, when he was appointed sheriff following the resignation of William Davis "Dave" Allison (Bob Alexander, *Fearless Dave Allison*, 64, n. 126, where Wells's initials are given as H.W).

37. *San Angelo Standard*, 9 July 1898.

38. *St. Louis Post-Dispatch*, 3 July; *Abilene Reporter*, 9 July; Big Springs, Texas, dispatch of July 2, in *San Angelo Standard*, 9 July 1898.

39. The erroneous report (badly mangled in places by an incompetent dispatcher or typesetter), was part of a Fort Worth dispatch in the *San Antonio Express*, 5 July, and recurs as an addition to a Big Spring dispatch in the *San Angelo Standard*, 9 July 1898. Another dispatch from Fort Worth, in ibid., reported correctly that the bandits, all mounted, were headed for San Angelo.

40. Sherwood, Texas, *Irion County Record*, in *San Angelo Standard*, 16 July 1898; Bryan, quoting Shelton, loc. cit.

41. Anonymous informant (probably Hardy Jones), to Nellie B. Cox, January 1938, FWP. As the anonymous passage is preserved alongside material contributed by Jones under his own name, and as both Jones and the unnamed informant arrived in that part of Texas in 1879, the great likelihood is that Jones was the anonymous interviewee. Jones is the subject of an obituary notice from an unnamed and undated newspaper (probably 1940s) in B.D. Arthur *Scrapbook* 3, (WTC, ASU).

42. *Irion County Record*, loc. cit.

43. Letter from "P & H," Midland, July 9, in *San Angelo Standard*, 16 July 1898.

44. Tanner & Tanner, *Last of the Old-Time Outlaws*. 155–6.

45. Harkey, 159–160.

46. He was indicted and eventually arrested for the murder of Jap Powers, but disappeared from the case after his release on bail. *San Angelo Standard*, 16 and 23 December 1899, 3 February 1900 and Chapter 17, n. 17.

47. Leta Crawford, 36–7. She gives no date, but all the known facts and circumstances point to late July or early August, 1898.

48. *San Angelo Standard*. 13 August 1898 ("Knickerbocker Knick Knacks").

49. Ogden, Utah, dispatch in *San Francisco Chronicle*, 15 July 1898; Ernst, *Sundance*, 100–103; Ernst, "George S. Nixon," WOLA *Journal*, Summer 2001.

50. Winnemucca dispatch in *San Francisco Chronicle*, 13 March 1900; Ernst, "Nixon," loc. cit., and *Sundance*, 102–3. One of the acquitted men was James Madison Shaw, who, as "J.J. Smith," had taken part in the Canyon Diable, Arizona, train robbery of 1889, and, after his release from prison, had betrayed the hiding place of the Black Jack Christian gang in April, 1897. Also accused, and briefly held in Nevada, was Daniel "Red" Pipkin. He was soon returned to New Mexico and thence to Arizona, where eventually he was convicted of horse theft. Burton,

Dynamite and Six-Shooter, 177; Karen Holliday Tanner and John D. Tanner, Jr., ms., untitled, on Bronco Bill Walters (2003), 89–95.

51. Ernst, "Nixon," loc. cit., and "Winnemucca," 10, 64; Mike Bell, "Did the Sundance Kid Tell His Own Version of What Happened at the Winnemucca Bank Robbery?" WOLA *Journal* Vol. 10, no. 1 (Spring 2001), 5–17; Bell to author, 12 May 2002.

52. *San Angelo Standard*, 5 August 1899; Santa Fe dispatch in ibid., 2 September 1899; *New Mexican*, 25 August 1899.

53. *San Angelo Standard*, 30 July 1898.

54. Ibid., 5 August 1899.

55. Alverson, 19–20.

56. The text of the Reward Poster is in A. Thompson, *Albuquerque ms.*, 65–6. Doubtless the loan of a copy of this document was part of the help Thompson received from William Reno.

57. Axford, 62–3; *Atkins ms.*, I, 12. As to Andy Darnell and Frank Johnson, see Bailey, 151–7; also, Alverson, *Reminiscences*. 24–5: "The Killing of Billy King." Andy Darnell seems not to have been kin to the no less troublesome Tom Darnell, though they were of kindred temperament and, for that reason, both died from violence created by themselves (John Tanner to author, 5 October 2008).

58. *Atkins ms.*, I, 12–13.

59. William French, *Some Recollections of a Western Ranchman*, 256–7; French, *Further Recollections of a Western Ranchman*, 505–7. The pagination of the two volumes is continuous, as though they were two parts of a single book.

French gives no dates, but says he spent a week or ten days in Ireland, traveled to Brindisi and thence to Cairo for a meeting with Henry Wilson, the principal stockholder in the WS. From Cairo, the two men went to Jerusalem, arriving there "shortly after the visit of the All Highest [Kaiser Wilhelm II of Germany]." As he "did not want to be away from the ranch too long and wanted a few days in Ireland" he did not stay long in Jerusalem, so he returned to America by way of Jaffa, Alexandria, and Europe. The fulcrum of any attempt to reconstruct the timing of his itinerary must be any dates that are absolutely known. Kaiser Wilhelm II entered Jerusalem on Saturday, 29 October 1898, and departed early the following week. French's arrival at the Holy City would not have been more than two or three days before or after November 8. His outward passage from Alma to Ireland would have taken from twelve to fourteen days; say, fourteen. Add to that ten days for his stay in Ireland, five days for his travel from Ireland to Brindisi, and eight days from Brindisi to Jerusalem via Cairo (where he appears not to have stayed long—perhaps a couple of days), and we have a total of thirty-seven days of traveling and visiting. This figure is not absolutely provable, but it is close enough, for French could hardly have carried out that program in fewer than thirty-five days or required more than forty for its completion. Thus we can say with something near certainty that he must have left Alma in the last days of September at the earliest, and no later than October 7. As French "did not want to be away from the ranch too long and wanted a few days in Ireland," not many days passed before he began the return leg of the journey, from Jaffa and thence Alexandria. We may take November 15 as the notional date of his homeward departure. He may have needed seven days to reach Ireland by the Messageries Maritimes route to Marseilles, and thereafter overland and by ferry to Ireland. His "few days in Ireland" probably amounted to no more than one week. The sea voyage and the overland trip to Alma could have occupied as many as fourteen days if he was traveling at leisure, or badly delayed, but could have been done in ten if he was in a hurry, as he seems to have been, or if nothing untoward happened (and he says that nothing did). On that basis, he would have reached home in mid-December, 1898; no earlier than the 10th, but not later than the 20th, depending on whether he left Jerusalem shortly before or shortly after November 15, and other variables. It will be seen that French was in Alma early in 1899; see n. 63.

60. Most comprehensively and dependably in Patterson, *Cassidy.*

61. John Tanner, Jr., Fallbrook, California, "[L]ay Family History," copy to author, 28 July 2001; Harvey Murdock, "Elzy Lay," speech given at Buffalo, Wyoming, 22 July 1999, transcription by John Tanner, copy to author; Jim Dullenty, "Elzy Lay's Outlaw Career Ended in Prison," *Newsletter* of the National Association of and Center for Outlaw and Lawman History, Vol. II, No. 4 (Spring 1977), 12–15. At his trial, and then at his induction into the New Mexico Territorial Penitentiary, Lay gave his birthplace as Illinois. Murdock, Lay's grandson, accepts this as correct, but the stronger evidence is that Lay was born in Ohio and during his infancy taken first to Illinois and then to Iowa.

62. Bailey, 162–7; Axford, 34–7. The title of the Erie Cattle Company passed to Matthew and Jeptha Ryan on February 27, 1900 and its corporate identity was ended on September 5 that year.

63. French, *Some Recollections*, 255, 257–9, 278; *Further Recollections*, Introduction (by Jeff C. Dykes), x–xi, 505–7; Axford, 41–51. As is common with works of reminiscence written in old age and unsupported by diaries or other memory aids, both authors are sparing with dates, and often wrong about the ones they do mention even when they are only meant to be approximate. French says (*Some Recollections*, 260) that he thought Lay quit the WS at about the end of September or early October, 1899, but it can easily be proved that he left at about the end of April or early in May of that year. Axford, 41, writes that he and others were engaged for the fall roundup by Perry Tucker, French's newly reappointed foreman under the authority of a letter received from French. The letter is also mentioned by French himself, who says (257–8) that it was sent "[a] week or two after" his return to the ranch, on the advice of his retiring foreman, Clarence Tipton, and that four or five weeks elapsed before Tucker showed up with Cassidy ("Jim Lowe") and Lay ("William McGinnis"). Axford and others accompanied Cassidy and Lay, or followed shortly afterwards. All would have given notice to Bob Johnson, the Erie foreman; hence the interval between Tucker's receipt of the letter and his arrival with the newly recruited crew. It is obvious, therefore, that Cassidy, Lay, and their companions must have begun work on the WS in February, 1899, notwithstanding Axford's reference to "the fall roundup." Lay's period of employment there could not have extended much further than ten weeks.

64. French, *Some Recollections*, loc. cit., and 260; Axford, loc. cit. In the early 1890s, McGonagill's father, G.I. McGonagill, was sheriff of recently formed Ector County, in southwest Texas. At the beginning of the 20th century, still in his very early twenties, Clay McGonagill became a riding-and-roping champion, making a good living on what came to be called the "rodeo circuit" (Whitlock, 112–5, 169, 171). See Chapter 18, n. 3.

65. Murdock, as cited. In stating that Cassidy advised Lay against having anything to do with the Ketchums, he may have been expressing a conclusion, rather than repeating a documented fact; but, if so, it is one that is consistent with the recollections of Cunningham, who spoke admiringly of Sam but scathingly of Tom, and William French, who excoriated both brothers. Neither man ever met either Sam or Tom; the opinions of both were formed from hearsay, and French's were driven by understandable anger.

66. Bryan, *Ruffians*, 253; *True Tales*, 40, and retelling by Chuck Hornung, "They Called Him 'Stuttering Bob': Robert W. Lewis, New Mexico Lawman," NOLA *Quarterly*, XXII, 4 (October 1998), 3–19 (3). Hornung calls the ranch the Bar N: French, *Further Recollections*, 373, 398, calls it the N Bar.

NOTES TO CHAPTER 11

1. *Roswell Record*, 12 May and 18 August; Carlsbad (formerly Eddy) *Argus*, 18 August 1899; Livingston, II, 12–14. *The Record* of May 12 alludes to a report on the thieves in its previous issue (5 May 1899), but it is not there, though plenty of space is found to report the capture of another gang of horses thieves; doubtless the story published on the 12th, but not its forerunner, was copied without credit from another newspaper. The *Record* of August 18 blamed the offense on the "Acoo thieves"—an apparent reference to the trio who had robbed Alamogordo Lumber Company's pay office in April. Both it and the *Argus* of the same date misstate the Cass Company's brand as the Bar F; the earlier *Record* item correctly gives it as the Bar V. See nn. 11 and 12.

2. Axford, 63. His is the only explanation to be supported by the citation of specific evidence. Siringo (*Riata and Spurs*, rev. ed., 194) says simply that Tom "had a disagreement with his brother Sam" shortly before the projected train robbery, backed out of the plan, and rode angrily away, "telling the gang that he was going back to Texas." Up to this point, the story could be true; for the rest of it, see Chapter 14, n. 37.

Thompson, *Clayton ms.*, 44, says that, in the fall of 1899, the gang were "quartered in the hills of eastern Arizona" when, "for some undisclosed reason," Tom fell out with Carver, Lay, and Bronco Bill, and that Sam, for the first time, sided with the others, leaving Tom to keep his own company. But by the fall of 1899, Sam was dead, Lay and Tom were prisoners, and Bronco Bill, who had never been with the gang anyway, had been in custody for well over a year. It looks certain, moreover, that the breach did not occur until the gang reached eastern New Mexico. In other words, Thompson knew as little of the circumstances of the row as he admitted knowing of its cause, but felt obliged to write something.

Titsworth, I, 8, also places the fateful quarrel in Arizona, and attributes it to a dispute over the division of the loot from a holdup at Jerome. There was no Ketchum gang holdup at Jerome. The only serious crime any of the gang ever perpetrated in Arizona was Tom's lone descent on a store at Camp Verde, where he took two lives but.apparently, no booty (see this chapter). That was just nine days before the second Folsom robbery, or two months after the probable date of the rupture. Thus Titsworth, or his newspaper source, was as uninformed as Thompson.

Otero, 113, correctly dates the altercation to the spring of 1899, but otherwise follows Thompson.

3. *Territory of New Mexico vs. William H. McGinnis, Cause No. 2419—Murder*: testimony of James Hunt.

4. French, *Some Recollections*, 260.

5. *Territory vs. McGinnis*: testimony of Hunt, Agapito Duran, and James H. Morgan. Bryan, *True Tales*, 70.

6. *Territory vs. McGinnis*: testimony of Duran.

7. Ibid., testimony of James Correy and Duran.

8. Ibid., testimony of Hunt and Morgan. In court, both men avoided mention of the suspicions they had formed while the strangers were in Cimarron, and counsel for the Territory did not encourage them to do otherwise; suspicion not arising from any specific action is evidence of prejudice, not of the criminality of the individual under suspicion. But their testimony does show that they had been keeping a keen eye on the visitors. Culley, 37, citing George Crocker; Stanley, 57–8, quoting Mason Chase ms; Ernest V. Ludlum, *Southwest of the Border of Illinois*, 183–5; Marinell Ash, Edinburgh, Scotland, to author, 18 September 1983 and 13 January 1984. Both Chase and Ash state that Morgan recognized members of the Ketchum gang in Cimarron. Morgan had helped Dr. Ash's grandfather, Alvin Ash, a runaway from home, to

ecome a cowboy in Texas in the 1880s. In 1899 Alvin was a cowman and deputy sheriff in Colfax County, New Mexico. Marinell Ash adds that it was well known in Gila, N.M., where Morgan lived out his last few years, that "he had been a Pinkerton employee when he was working at Cimarron . . . using the freighting business as a cover." It will be seen that he was also an informant for Marshal Foraker. In the early 1890s, Morgan was "a well known figure along the Pecos River." For a while he hauled freight between Eddy and Roswell, driving a six-teen-mule team (Whitlock, 112, 137, 184). See also Chapter 16, n. 44.

. Bryan, *Ruffians*, 265, 282. Agnes Morley Cleaveland, *Satan's Paradise*, 98–101, would have us believe that the gang all boarded at Henry Lambert's St. James Hotel, imbibed Lambert's "care-fully hoarded rare liquors," gambled there for high stakes, and paid for everything in gold pieces. Thirteen-year old Fred Lambert, the third of Henry's four sons, kept bar, says Cleaveland; but, when not keeping bar, he was competing with the Ketchum brothers, Bob [*sic*] McGinnis, "Booger Red" [Weaver], and Bill Franks at target shooting against the back wall of the stone jail—an exercise in which Fred held his own against all of them, except McGinnis. Once, we are informed, young Lambert engaged Tom Ketchum in soul-to-soul conversation. Cleaveland gives the year as 1900; but, if these things happened at all, they could only have happened in 1899, when Fred Lambert would have been twelve, not thirteen.

But could they have happened/? This much could be true: young Lambert may have helped out at the bar, and may have seen Sam Ketchum, "McGinnis," "Franks," and "Red" there and elsewhere in town just prior to the second Folsom robbery. He could not have seen or talked to Tom, because Tom was not within four hundred miles of Cimarron at the time; he was in the general vicinity of Prescott, Arizona. Thus these souvenirs from the Lambert-Cleaveland album of memories of old Cimarron have no claim upon anyone's serious attention, although Stanley, 40, gives them his.

0. Ludlum, 184–5.

1. El Paso special to *Los Angeles Times*, 10 April, reprinted in *San Francisco Chronicle*, 11 April; Redding dispatch in ibid., 27 July; ibid., 31 July 1899. This last article is devoted to Sheriff Charles F. "Doc" Blackington, of Socorro County, New Mexico, who had collected Gentry from the Redding jail and was enjoying an extended break for refreshments in San Francisco, where he went out of his way to attract notice. The notice was not unduly complimentary. As the *Chronicle* scribe observed, "Whether it is the cool nerve of the man that prompts him to jug-le loaded revolvers under the noses of unoffending bartenders, or whether such actions are prompted by an uncontrollable desire to be considered a real bad man from a bad country, is, in the case of the Sheriff from New Mexico, an open question. Blackington is rapidly acquir-ing a reputation at the Palace Hotel and at certain resorts in the tenderloin that would provoke the envy of the toughest bandit of the country . . . [H]e is enjoying the full limit of sport and pleasure that the town affords . . . ." In speaking of a friend of Gentry's, who was planning to rescue the bandit, Blackington told the *Chronicle*: "Say! I've simply got that fellow lashed to the mast, and if he gets too sociable I'll make him look like a dirty deuce in a new deck."

A Globe, Arizona, dispatch in the *St. Louis Globe-Democrat*, 2 February 1898, glances at Gentry's earlier career in crime, which began the previous November with a raid on "the peaceful Mormon hamlet of Heber [Arizona]."

2. *El Paso Times*, 2 May, in *Roswell Record*, 5 May, with an afterpiece from Eddy, New Mexico; El Paso dispatch in *San Francisco Chronicle*, 3 May; Alamogordo dispatch of May 3 in *Santa Fe Daily New Mexican*, same day; *El Paso Times*, 3 May, reprinted in *New Mexican*, 4 May with additions from the *New Mexican* office; *El Paso Herald*, in ibid., 5 May 1899; Tanner and Tanner, *Last of the Old-Time Outlaws*, 153–8 and Notes, 310–1; Tanner and Tanner, "Shoot-out at Parker's Well," *True West*, Vol. 46, No. 9, Whole No. 377 (September 1999), 20–25. Harkey, 91–201, was generous in the praise he bestowed upon himself and correspondingly disparaging

of his companions, especially Stewart, who, as sheriff, was in charge. Stewart angrily rebutted Harkey's aspersions, asserting that, far from having more than three hundred shots aimed at his person (as he claimed in his autobiography), Harkey kept out of the fight and did not join Stewart and Tom Tucker until the outlaws were under arrest (Stewart, interviewed by Lou Blachly, December 1957; quoted Tanner & Tanner, *Last*, 157). In 1970, the present author commented that, in this instance, "Harkey . . . for once . . . seems to have been entitled to whatever honors were going" (*Dynamite and Six-shooter*, 200). That view was the product of deficient research and insufficient appreciation of Harkey's flair for invention. Tom Ketchum's name was put forward in a bid to pin an identity to a member of the gang who first tried to cloak himself in the egregious pseudonym of "Thomas Thomas." He turned out to be Jim Knight (or Nite). Another notable name mistakenly introduced into the dispute over the identities of the four was that of Van Musgrave's younger but more badly wanted brother George. A third man falsely alleged to have been among the arrestees was the youngest Musgrave brother, Volney, who was then awaiting trial for cattle theft.

13. Ketchum's statement that he was in the Sacramento Mountains in southern New Mexico was made shortly before his execution, and in part corroborates (or is corroborated by) a report that he passed some of the summer of 1899 on Gene Rhodes's ranch near Engle (Walters, 147–8). But, although Ketchum may have been there, Rhodes himself was not: he had just left for New York to marry Mrs. May Davidson Purple, and did not return until mid August (Sonnichsen, *Tularosa*, 216). As previously stated, the fullest version of Ketchum's remarks before he went to the scaffold is in the *Rocky Mountain News* and *Denver Republican*, both 28 April 1901.

14. The first account to reach the outside world was a dispatch from Prescott, published in the *Phoenix Herald* and *San Francisco Chronicle*, 4 July 1899 and in various weekly papers over the next few days: two Graham County papers, the *Safford Arizonian* and *Graham Guardian*, both published the story on the 6th, the *Guardian* calling the affair a "Tripple [*sic*] Tragedy," which implied that Boyd's wound was much worse than it was.

The Prescott correspondent maintained, erroneously, that the store had been visited by "two masked men," one of whom remained outside while the other entered the premises and committed the murders. This may well have been the belief, or the impression, of the excited messenger who carried the news to Prescott, a forty mile ride from Camp Verde, but it was false. Otherwise, little variation is to be found in the reporting of the incident.

Sheriff Munds gave a short but clear resumé of the facts of the crime to the *Santa Fe Daily New Mexican*, 4 September 1899.

Maurice Kildare (one of the many pseudonyms of the prolific Arizona author Gladwell Richardson) uses contemporary issues of the Flagstaff *Coconino Sun* and Prescott *Courier* together with his exhaustive local knowledge, for a thorough and absorbing reconstruction of the background, the crime, and the pursuit ("Who Killed Rogers and Wingfield?" *Real West* 61, July 1968; 13–14, 55–7, 72). His dismissal of the case against Ketchum is unpersuasive. The great defect in Kildare's approach is implicit in his choice of title. He almost presupposes Ketchum's innocence, yet makes no attempt to retrace his movements, consider the evidence against him, or marshal any factual support for the conclusion that Ketchum's notoriety and timely capture made him a suitable nominee for scapegoat status. Kildare's recital of a string of plausible but unbuttressed alternatives, framed in his own mind or suggested to him by local old-timers, makes interesting reading but does not amount to anything like a case. A possibility not to be ignored is that Kildare, like many magazine writers of his era (he was born in 1903), may have believed that mystery sold better than exposition.

Richard W. Sturgis, "I Trailed Black Jack Ketchum," *True West*, Vol. 10, No. 6, Whole No. 58 (August 1963); 40–1, 52–4, depends wholly on the memory of Frank Wingfield, who was

ghty-five when he told his story; but such were the horror of the crime, and his prominence
the hunt for the killer, that he must have spent much of the intervening sixty-three years
inking about the affair. He might have suppressed or altered some of the detail, but he would
ot have forgotten much. Kildare is extremely critical of Frank Wingfield's behavior during the
ase, and perhaps with some cause; but Frank's own narrative reflects some of what he had
arned of the case in the succeeding years. Wingfield's certainty that Ketchum was the culprit
sts on a far stronger basis than Kildare's actual or professed skepticism.

It is of small moment whether the gunman, just before killing Rogers, said "Don't do it,
ack," (as in the local press accounts cited by Kildare) or "That won't do, Mack," (the words
Frank Wingfield recalled them). More important is the dispute over motive. The county
eriff said flatly that the latecomer's object was robbery, and Frank Wingfield always believed
e same. Kildare was sure that the intruder approached the store with the set intention of
lling both Rogers and Wingfield. None considered a third and quite tenable possibility that,
hatever their prior relations, the stranger wanted nothing more of the storekeepers than the
pportunity to purchase some provisions. Isaac Elmer Jones, like Frank Wingfield a Verde
lley octogenarian in the 1960s, included a crisply worded description of the double murder
his reminiscences (Harold Farmer, "The 'Old Timer' of Verde Valley," *Pioneer West*, Vol. 1,
o. 4—November 1967, 38–41, 63–4). Jones believed that the motive was robbery and
clared that his identity was never known. But Jones was only nineteen at the time, appar-
tly took no part in the pursuit, and would have had no strong reason for remembering
pects of the case that did not impinge on his immediate experience.

. Sturgis, 40.

. Kildare, 56.

. Sturgis, 54; Kildare, 57; Phoenix dispatch in *San Francisco Chronicle*, 31 January 1900, when
utberth was still under bond. Later Cutberth was accused of being Dave Atkins (*Phoenix
rizona Republic*, circa 2 February, in *San Angelo Standard*, 10 February; *El Paso Times*, 4, 6,
d 8 February 1900). (See Chapter 17, at nn. 19, 20, and 21.)

. Prescott dispatch, July 22 in *Los Angeles Times*, 23 July 1898.

. Farmer/Jones, 63.

. Kildare, 56–7.

. A. Thompson, *Albuquerque ms.*, 7 and *Clayton ms.*, 44. For events from July, 1899, onwards,
e former manuscript has little of substance that is not repeated more economically in the lat-
r, which, as has been stated, was Thompson's final draft for the *Early History of Clayton*. In
ost instances hereafter, therefore, citation will be restricted to the later and shorter work.

. Sturgis, Kildare, both loc. cit., *Rocky Mountain News*, 29 August; *New Mexican*, 4 September
99.

. Jerome, Arizona, dispatch in *Rocky Mountain News*, 26 August; Jerome dispatch in uniden-
ied Colorado newspaper in Titsworth, I, 33.

. Mack Rogers's half brothers, James and Oliver, had been in the Verde Valley for some years
hen Mack arrived early in 1898 (Kildare, 13). It is not known where he had lived in Texas.

. 27 April 1901.

. Kildare, loc. cit., "In spite of sparse news reports of the day, and even fewer legal records
d statements of pioneers of that time, there is one definite conclusion: somebody got away
ith murder!" Farmer, 63, "We never did find out who the killer was."

. Edward L. Bartlett, Solicitor General, Territory of New Mexico, to M.A. Otero, Governor,
November, re application of the Governor of Arizona for the extradition of Thomas
etchum, alias George Stephens, alias Charlie Bishop; Otero to N.O. Murphy, Governor of
rizona, 14 November 1899, denying the requisition.

. Kildare, 56; Sturgis, 53.

29. Sturgis, 40, 53; Kildare, 13, 56–7.
30. Kildare, 57. Bishop died in 1937.

NOTES TO CHAPTER 12

1. *Territory vs. McGinnis*, testimony of Hunt, Duran, and Morgan. Owen's recollection of McJunkin's account of his encounter with the gang is in Doherty and Adams, 20–1, and is outlined in at least one earlier book, G. Thompson and others, *Clayton, The Friendly Town of Union County, New Mexico*, 149. If, as Owen says, McJunkin was the man who guided the officers to the Daugherty Spring campsite after the robbery, it is strange that he was not called upon to testify at Lay's trial. That aside, Owen's memory is askew when he names this as the place where one of the gang tore up the letter (actually, the envelope or wrapping of a package) which Titsworth later glued together. The fragments were recovered from the spot where the gang camped the following morning, a mere half-mile from the scene of the holdup.
    In 1908, in an arroyo on the XYZ ranch, McJunkin and one or two companions came across the bones of what they took to have been wild horses but which turned out to be the remains of a species of bison that flourished in the Pleistocene era. Archaeological excavations carried out in 1926, four years after McJunkin's death, found that the beasts had been slain by arrows which showed that human habitation had existed in the area far earlier than had previously been thought, or assumed. See Mildred F. Mayhall, "George McJunkin's Pile of Bones," *Old West*, Vol. 10, No. 2, Whole No. 38 (Winter 1973), 19, 54–5.
2. Ibid., testimony of Morgan. Witness testified that Foraker had telegraphed him on July 1 to take a posse to look out for Ketchum, "Franks," and "McGinnis," and admitted that he had been in touch with the marshal about the three suspects even before then. When prosecuting counsel asked him to state the exact date of the earlier communication from Foraker, the defense objected and was sustained by the court. He did admit that he had been "employed in looking after and watching" the suspects.
3. Such as Conductor W.S. Parkhurst, *Globe-Democrat*, 13 May 1891, and an unnamed former engineer of the Utah and Northern, *New York Sun*, in ibid., 7 November 1894.
4. Secrest, 55.
5. *Territory vs. McGinnis*, testimony of Frank Harrington, J.A. Tubbs, and H.P. Scott; Amarillo and Trinidad dispatches in *Rocky Mountain News*, 13 July; Trinidad dispatches in *Denver Republican*, 12, 13 July, and *Denver Post*, 13 July; *Denver Times*, 12 July; *New Mexican* 12 and 14 July, the latter being a condensation of the material in the *News*; Trinidad *Advertiser Standard*, 12 July 1899; *Trinidad Chronicle-News*, 13 July 1899. rep. Titsworth, I, 6; Livingston I, 344–6; A. Thompson, *Clayton ms.*, 44–5, and *Open Range Days*, 184; Otero, 113–5; Waller 121–3; Secrest, 56. The *News* has the best coverage of the Denver papers. The report in the edition of the *Post* seen by the author is brief; it includes a few lines of the story printed almost simulataneously by the *Chronicle-News*. That in the *Times* was compiled from uncredited dispatches, by implication from Clayton ("46 miles from the scene"); when the facts ran out, the correspondent or the *Times* office invented a few more.
    Although Thompson and Livingston interviewed members of the train crew, both their accounts of the holdup erred in stating that only one bandit stepped into the locomotive cab. Livingston's version is also marked by the oddest of the various divergences from the narrative consensus. He relates how an unnamed member of the gang, posing as a cripple, bought a ticket from Trinidad to Folsom and was helped aboard by Harrington and Brakeman Bob Hawkins. When the engine paused at the water tank just outside Folsom, the supposed invalid dived through the window, leaving his crutches and cane on the seat. He had, allegedly,

scrawled a note to inform his confederates at Folsom that the train crew were unarmed. The confederates not only omitted to destroy the note but, while riding away after the robbery, obligingly dropped it where the pursuing officers could find it. Carl Livingston said it was W.H. Reno who spotted the note, but the story may have come to Livingston secondhand from one of several trainmen and not direct from Reno; see Chapter 6, n. 41. That aside, Livingston's reproduction of passages of conversation from the engine and cars before and during the holdup is mostly incredible. Far more reliance can be placed on Engineer Tubbs's remarks to the Colorado paper cited above and on the stand at the "McGinnis" trial.

6. *Territorial vs. McGinnis*: testimony of Harrington and Tubbs; Livingston, I, 346.

7. Otero, loc. cit., G. Thompson and others, 150. Only two months after the robbery, Foraker told the Albuquerque correspondent of the *Chicago Chronicle*, in an article reprinted in the *San Francisco Chronicle*, 14 September 1899 (not in all editions), that the bandits had obtained $30,000. The moneyed corporations may have viewed such a disclosure as a public indiscretion, for the marshal was close to railroad and express officials who were close to the facts. Otero, however, may not only have been closer still, but, long before he wrote his memoirs, could have acquired information not available to Foraker (or to himself) a mere two months after the event.

8. *Rocky Mountain News*, 17 July 1899.

9. A dispatch from Trinidad, July 12, first published outside Colorado in that evening's *New Mexican*, included a succinct statement of the two sides of what had become through the years a wearyingly familiar issue of news and propaganda: "[T]he express messenger says there was nothing of value in [the safe]. Others say it contained a large amount of money." The *Trinidad Advertiser-Sentinel*, 13 July 1899, presented only the first half of the equation: "[T]here was nothing in the express safe. Supt., Webb, of the C & S, and Wells Fargo Express Agent Snover state positively that no money was secured by the robbers." Express Messenger Scott never wavered from this stance. On the stand, he insisted that the gang had taken nothing, except for a saddle tree and some fruit. In a review of the case nearly six years later, the *Rocky Mountain News* (8 April 1905), having forgotten the belief it had voiced in 1899, barely deviated from this line; it declared that "the bandits secured less than $100." Twenty-five years after that, Livingston was still being told that the stickup had been profitless—and he believed it (I., 346-7). Charles Kelly, Butch Cassidy's first and none-too-punctilious biographer, who was without much knowledge of, or interest in, the Ketchum gang, lazily accepted the same view (*Outlaw Trail*, enlarged edition, 251). James Horan (*Desperate Men*, first ed., 228-9), merely took Kelly's account and elaborated it for the sake of effect rather than in the cause of truth. Nonetheless, the "others"—those who reckoned the safe "contained a large amount of money"—were right, and were bound to be. The Colorado and Southern linked the rising cities of Denver and Fort Worth. Since both were important trans-shipment points, connected with other railroads, express matter would be unloaded as well as taken aboard en route, but it is likely that the train would usually be carrying at least as much money at the end of its trip as at the beginning. Reno's unwillingness to put a figure on the loss (or to assert that there had been none) went on the record in the *Denver Republican*, 27 April 1901, and *Denver Post*, 28 October 1935.

10. *Territory vs. McGinnis*: testimony of Martinez and Apodaca. The newspaper articles cited in n. 5 embody the differing opinions on the number of men and horses at the holdup. A statement from Trinidad in the *Rocky Mountain News*, 13 July 1899, that "there were four men in the robbery, but only three men rode away, two men riding one horse" makes little literal sense. The intended message may have been "there were four men in the robbery, but only three horses were ridden away, two men riding one horse." Nevertheless, a fourth horse was there or nearby.

11. Jack Stockbridge, to Lou Blachly, 16 March 1955, tape 394, transcript pp. 10–11; ibid., 18 March 1957, tape 380, transcript pp. 2–3. If Stockbridge's words were transcribed accurately, he put the distance between Folsom and the XL horse pasture at "probably one hundred and fifty miles." Despite the intermission of sixty years, he would surely have remembered that the two points were nothing like that far apart. The author has not heard the original recording, but has heard other interviews taped by Blachly in which the quality of the sound is not good, and thinks it likely that Stockbridge was misheard. What he may have said was that the horse camp "was probably under fifty miles" from the holdup site—an estimate tolerably close to the actual distance of thirty-five miles.

Another of Stockbridge's statements confounds credulity: he told Blachly that he had been able to inspect the four rifles without their owners' knowledge. This would have been an intolerable breach of etiquette in any instance; and, in this particular instance, a reckless rejection of good sense. The men would not have left their rifles with the horses, anyway; they would have kept them within reach. One of the four may, however, have let Jack look at his long-barreled .30–40. He may also have noticed that the other weapons were of carbine length and, in the uncertain light, mistaken them for .30–30s.

A final, and obvious error, is his assertion that Tom Ketchum was among the four. Here, however, he was merely repeating what he had heard, or assumed, at the time. There is no reason to doubt that all four were strangers to him. The author believes that Stockbridge's narrative is factual at its core, and not to be dismissed merely because the narrator could not resist the opportunity to make a good story sound even better.

12. *Territory vs. McGinnis*; testimony of William H. McGinnis.

13. Ibid., testimony of Morgan.

14. Foraker, Albuquerque, to Attorney General, Washington, D.C., 12:37 p.m. 13 July 1899; *Territory vs. McGinnis*, testimony of C.M. Foraker.

15. Ibid., testimony of Foraker and Wilson Elliott.

16. Ibid., testimony of Titsworth and W.H. Reno; Trinidad dispatches in *Denver Republican*. 12 July, *Rocky Mountain News* and *Denver Post*, 13 July 1899; Waller, 123.

17. Trinidad dispatch in *News*, ibid., and Waller, loc. cit.

NOTES TO CHAPTER 13

1. *Territory vs. McGinnis*; testimony of Juan C. Martinez, George Titsworth, and W.H. Reno; Trinidad dispatch in *Rocky Mountain News*, 13 July; Associated Press dispatch of 17 July 1899, quoted in Titsworth, I, 8: Doherty and Adams, 21; A. Thompson, *Clayton ms.*, 46; Stockbridge to Blachly, tape 380, transcript p. 3, tape 394, transcript pp. 11–12, UNM.

Stockbridge insisted that the engagement in Turkey Creek Canyon happened on the same day as the visit of the Colorado officers to the XL because both the officers and the bandits they were tailing went straight from the horse camp to the scene of the encounter. He was wrong; the outlaws were traveling quite slowly, passed Raton on the morning of the 13th, and did not turn into the canyon until the early hours of the 15th; while Farr, for his part, went by train from Springer to Trinidad later on the 15th.

A minor discrepancy occurs between Titsworth's testimony and that of Reno because Titsworth's memory skipped a day, making him say that he returned to Folsom on July 12. That could not have been so, and it is not only obvious, but certain, that the correct date was the one given by Reno, July 13.

2. *Territory vs. McGinnis*: testimony of Titsworth, Martinez, C.M. Foraker, and Wilson Elliott.

3. Colorado City, Texas, *Clipper*, 11 April 1885, in *Frontier Times*, Vol. 18, No. 7 (April 1941), 306; *Territory vs. McGinnis*; testimony of Elliott; *San Angelo Standard*, 5 August 1899. For the Wells, Fargo Reward Poster, see Chapter 10, text at n. 56.
4. *Territory vs. McGinnis*: testimony of Foraker, Elliott, and Morgan. Ludlum, 185.
5. *Territory vs. McGinnis*: testimony of Foraker, Elliott, Morgan, and James Hunt.
6. Ibid., testimony of Elliott; *San Angelo Standard*, 5 August 1899. A. Thompson, *Clayton ms.*, 46, offers some support.
7. *Territory vs. McGinnis* and *San Angelo Standard*, both ibid; *Denver Times*, 26 April 1901. Ludlum, 187, says simply that Morgan tracked the fugitives to Turkey Canyon.
8. See nn. 62, 63, 64 and text ff.
9. *Territory vs. McGinnis*: testimony of Foraker (recalled).
10. Ibid., testimony of Reno. In an interview for the *Rocky Mountain News*, 20 July 1899, Reno stated that "Mr. Elliott was . . . in charge of the posse of five men sent out by United States Marshal Foraker, but not of sheriff Farr or myself." Foraker had indeed requested, and received, permission to hire no more than five men (telegram to Attorney General, 13 July 1899: LR: Justice Year File 13065–1896, and note on document jacket, same date). But in a report to the Attorney General, 28 August 1899, in ibid., Foraker referred to Farr as one of his possemen. And in his testimony in the McGinnis trial, Reno stated that he and Farr were members of the posse led by Elliott. This contradiction will be examined in the text.
11. *Territory vs. McGinnis*: testimony of Foraker.
12. Ibid., testimony of Elliott, Morgan, and Perfecto Cordova.
13. The description of the fight up to this juncture has been constructed mainly from conclusions drawn from the testimony of Elliott, Cordova, Morgan, David Farr, and the defendant, in *Territory vs. McGinnis*. The analysis at the base of those conclusions is summarized in Chapter 15 of the present work and set out in greater detail in Burton, "'Suddenly in a Secluded and Rugged Place . . .' : The Territory of New Mexico versus William H. McGinnis: Cause No. 2419—Murder," *The Brand Book*, 1971–72 (London, The English Westerners' Society, 1972), 46–81. Farr's testimony is straightforward and dependable throughout, and Morgan's mainly so. Elliott, Cordova, and the defendant all had reason for fabrication or evasion—and their testimony shows as much. Defendant testified that he had been unconscious throughout the fight. His post-trial admission that he was Farr's killer is from Axford, 257–9.
14. Axford, loc. cit. Axford's information came from Carver, several weeks after the fight, and from statements attributed to Sam Ketchum. Axford's recollections extend more than seventy years into the past, and when his memory of what he did, saw, and heard can be checked against other sources, or, in their absence, subjected to a credibility test, it nearly always repels disbelief. In common with most "old timer" authors, Axford wrote without the assistance of diary entries or any other prompting device, except occasionally the memories of friends; consequently, his book has few dates, and some of those few a year or two out. Where mistakes occur, such as confusion between the details of two similar incidents, they are generally the product of a failure of recall.

In the instance of his account of the shooting of Farr, difficulty arises from his reference to Sam Ketchum as an indirect source. Lay would have spoken to Sam about the fight during the first hours afterwards; but Sam was captured only two days later, and from that time until his death a further six days after that, had no opportunity to speak to anyone except officers and officials of the law, the express company, the railroad, and the penitentiary. His response to their questions was a steadfast refusal to incriminate anyone but himself; save once by implication, when he asserted the innocence of the three men who had been imprisoned for the Steins Pass holdup. Two possibilities are open. One is that Axford's hearsay began with the

McBrides, or someone else on the Lambert ranch; if, as it would seem, the bandits had regarded these people as their friends, Sam might well have talked to them frankly in the interval between his reception and his arrest. The other explanation is that Axford's sole source was Carver. Since Carver called on him only a few weeks or months after the fight, and described the Turkey Canyon fight as he saw it, as well as the visit to the McBrides, the flight to Chimney Wells, and Lay's subsequent capture, there is no reason to suppose he would not have mentioned what Ketchum and Lay had told him about their part in the fight. Even if the second suggestion is correct, the slip of memory is unimportant. The reliability of Axford's anecdote is established by his observation that the bullet scars on the trees showed that "the man down the hill [Lay] was the one who won the battle." The killing of Sheriff Farr may, or may not, have been the factor that determined the outcome; but it is certain that the jurors heard, and accepted, testimony that the man in the higher position (Carver) was the killer. (They also heard, but did not understand, or did not heed, the testimony of Dave Farr, who concluded from a careful examination of the site that the fatal bullet came from the lower position.)

The *New Mexican*, 18 July 1899, quoting another dispatch from Springer, reported the diameter of the tree and the bullet's probable point of impact.

15. Reno described his part in the action in a dispatch to the *Las Vegas Optic*, 19 July, reprinted in the *New Mexican* of the same date; in the *New Mexican*, 21 July; in the *Denver Post*, 18 July; in the *Rocky Mountain News*, 20 and 25 July; in the *Denver Republican*, 18 and 20 July; and, finally, and more briefly, in a letter dated September 12 published in *The Chicago Detective*, October 1899 (clipping in Pinkerton file, as cited). For reasons to be explained in Chapter 15, and to the palpable discomfort of defense counsel in *Territory vs. McGinnis*, Reno was not called upon by the Territory to testify on the fight.

16. *Territory vs. McGinnis*; testimony of Elliott; *Rocky Mountain News* and *Trinidad Advertiser-Sentinel*, 19 July; *Santa Fe Daily New Mexican*, 21 July; *San Angelo Standard*, ibid. In the *New Mexican* item, Foraker for some unknown reason denied that two of the bandits' horses had been killed.

17. Only Wilson Elliott, quoted in the *San Angelo Standard* of 5 August 1899, included the torn valise in the inventory. It was also he who attested to the number and location of the spent cartridges ejected from Carver's rifle.

18. *Territory vs. McGinnis*; testimony of Elliott, Morgan, and McGinnis; dispatches from Springer and Las Vegas or East Las Vegas (N. Mex.,) in *New Mexican*, 17, 18, 19 July; *New Mexican* (from first-hand), 21 July; *Albuquerque Journal-Democrat*, 17 and 18 July; *Denver Evening Post, Republican, Rocky Mountain News,* and *Times,* all 19–25 July, inclusive; Trinidad Advertiser-Sentinel, 19, 20, 22 July 1899; Titsworth, I, 8–9, quoting Associated Press dispatches from Springer; Axford, loc. cit. In the *Advertiser-Sentinel* story of 19 July 1899, Love is misidentified as Smith.

Siringo, writing in 1926 (*Riata and Spurs*, rev. ed., 195–7), claims the authority of (unnamed) eyewitnesses, but the facts and his account of them are far apart; he states, for example, that Love was kneeling next to Farr when both were shot. He rightly places some emphasis on the tree-piercing properties of bullets fired from steel-jacketed cartridges, but says incorrectly that "both sides" were using them. Had this been so, the battle might have turned out differently: as it was, Morgan was the only member of the posse whose rifle is known to have been capable of discharging smokeless cartridges with steelnosed bullets. Siringo's version of the escape of Ketchum, Carver, and Lay is balderdash.

Culley, 38–9, is brief, but finds room for sweeping errors; he opens the battle at 4 p.m. (over an hour prematurely), has ten in the posse (three too many), and ends with a flourish of fictitious melodrama ("William McGinnis—tall, elegant, soft-spoken bronco rider—as he rode off wounded in four places, stopped and waved his hat to the survivors of the posse. 'Adios, boys!'

he shouted; then turned and disappeared over the crest of the hill.") The hat flourishing episode occurred a month later, but the hat-waver was the unwounded Will Carver and he was about to put distance between himself and the posse that had just caught Lay/McGinnis. See Chapter 14.

   Chase ms., in Stanley, 59, went one better than Culley; he put the strength of the posse at eleven. Chase's account, when all is said and done, is mostly gossip, and truthless gossip at that. He claims (Stanley, 61) that Reno kicked Ketchum and had to be restrained at gunpoint by the purportedly kindhearted old ranchman. This statement can be neither proved nor disproved, but Chase's manifest unreliability elsewhere makes a strong case for disbelief. He says, for instance, that Sam's wound was in the right shoulder; if he had been half as close to events as he pretended, he would have known that it was in the left shoulder. The Dean Canyon rancher must have talked and listened to Morgan, but misquotes or is misled by him more than once; for example, he has Morgan telling Jim Hunt that the three visitors he had encountered at the door of Hunt's store were "McGinnis, Sam Ketchum and Franks, three of the toughest men in southern New Mexico and Arizona." No such conversation could have taken place, because Morgan did not know Lay, alias McGinnis, at all. Chase said that the three men arrived in Cimarron as a group and went about as a group for "more than three months." The record of the testimony of Hunt and Morgan at the McGinnis trial shows that Lay/McGinnis was in Cimarron and its vicinity town for not quite two months, that he and Weaver arrived ahead of Sam and "Franks," and that he was not seen in their company until a week or ten days before all four left town. Chase goes on to state that Morgan told him that he, Morgan, had crawled to a rock overlooking the position of the suspect who had done most of the shooting (Carver) and brought the fight more or less to its close by putting him out of it. That may be what Morgan told Chase, but it was untrue in every particular. Lastly (Stanley, 62), he declares that "[t}he boy [Jim McBride] who came to Cimarron to notify Mr. Detective [Reno] is still [1924] waiting for his reward." Actually, the railroad paid up almost at once. Moreover, Elliott's depiction of McBride as a friend of the gang, if not a collaborator, is more credible than Chase's portrayal of the renter as an ordinary good citizen who had taken pity on a stricken stranger. See comments below on the Elliott and Axford versions.

   Livingston's description of the Turkey Canyon engagement (I, 348–9) is fanciful in the extreme. It would have been more accurate had William Reno acceded to Livingston's requests for information on the fight, but he did not. (Lawrence R. Reno to author, as cited.)

   Only Axford states (though Elliott strongly implies) that Carver and Lay accompanied Ketchum to the Lambert or McBride ranch, but his account is not only well sourced (see n. 14); it also makes better sense than Sam's story that he had struggled to the cabin alone and on foot. Sam might have told the others to abandon him, but it is not to be credited that they would have done so, with what they supposed to be a friendly hearth only three miles away.

   Elliott's disclosure that the three men had gone to Ute Creek after the battle comes close to supplying corroboration for Axford (Springer dispatch in *San Francisco Chronicle*, 21 July; *Trinidad Advertiser-Sentinel*, 22 July 1899). Even if Carver and Lay had gone on ahead of Sam Ketchum, Lay's condition would have obliged them to halt at the cabin in Ute Park where Sam was later arrested. Hence all three would have been there together, whether they arrived at the same time or not. The likelihood is that the three left the canyon together, and kept together until they stopped at McBride's cabin, where Sam told the others that he could go no further. Elliott did not identify the source of his information, but it could hardly not have been one or more of the people at McBride's. We shall see that, as a witness, Elliott was often untrustworthy. But, on the character of the McBride people, and the nature of their relationship with the train robbers, his statements seem to the author to have the smack of credibility.

Waller, 123–8, has the fullest account of any of the secondary sources, but only because of his belief, or supposition, that "Franks" was his biographee, Harvey Logan. Waller makes conscientious, but not always perspicacious, use of the *Rocky Mountain News* and *New Mexican*.

19. Butch Cassidy arranged for Carver to place the watch in safekeeping with Elton Cunningham, who eventually sent it to Bige Duncan. (Blachly/Cunningham interviews, February 1952, #126, 30; 2 January 1955, #129, 10; 10 December 1955, #128, 15–16.) Blachly seems to have believed, or wanted to believe, that Cunningham was given the watch by Harvey Logan. He prodded Cunningham into saying that the man's name sounded something like Harvey. Carver also sounds something like Harvey. Since both Logan and Carver were otherwise unknown to Cunningham, Blachly asked him to identify the man from a copy of the group photograph taken in Fort Worth a year later. He told Cunningham that Carver had been killed in San Angelo, Texas. Cunningham said that he had given the watch to "the one killed in San Angelo." Since there is no longer any excuse for doubting that Carver was "Franks," it is obvious that Sam could not have handed the watch to anyone but Carver.

20. Springer dispatch in *Las Vegas Optic*, 19 July, reprinted in Titsworth, I, 9–10; *Trinidad Advertiser-Sentinel*, 25 July 1899; *Chase, ms.*, quoted Stanley, 60–61; Bryan, *Ruffians*, 278–80; Culley, 39. Bryan cites a hunting mishap as Sam's explanation for his indisposition, and Culley, an accident at a sawmill. Probably, however, Sam did not try to conceal the truth from the McBrides—but the McBrides judged it wise to conceal Sam's candor.

21. *San Angelo Standard*, 5 August 1899.

22. *Territory vs. McGinnis*: testimony of Elliott, Morgan (recalled), and Foraker (recalled); *New Mexican*, 17, 19, 21 July; *Trinidad Advertiser-Sentenel*, 19, 22, 25 July; *Rocky Mountain News*, 20 and 25 1899; Ludlum, 187; *Chicago Detective*, loc. cit.

23. Foraker was quoted by Marion Littrell, in Las Vegas dispatch to *New Mexican*, 17 July; but in the *New Mexican* of 21 July he explained that he was merely passing on the news that Reno had just brought to Cimarron. The truth here seems to be that Foraker misunderstood Reno: what Reno is likely to have meant is that he and the two men with him had all received wounds and that he had heard nothing from Elliott's group. Elliott's erroneous statement that he was the only member of the posse not to have been wounded is in the *San Angelo Standard*, 5 August 1899.

24. *Territory vs. McGinnis*: testimony of Elliott. The misconception that Love's wound was caused by an "explosive bullet" began with W.H. Reno (Springer dispatch in the *Las Vegas Optic* of 19 July, reprinted that evening in the *Daily New Mexican*), but Reno may only have been repeating what he had been told. A widely diffused Associated Press release inflated this report into an assertion that all the bandits had used explosive bullets. The canard was exposed almost as soon as Love's wound was examined by a doctor (*Trinidad Advertiser-Sentinel*, 19 July 1899, which, however, exemplified the continuing confusion by calling Love "Smith").

25. *Territory vs. McGinnis*: testimony of Foraker (recalled); Ludlum, loc. cit.

26. *Territory vs. McGinnis*: testimony of Foraker (recalled) and Elliott. A Springer dispatch to the *Rocky Mountain News* and *Denver Republican*, both 19 July 1899, mentions Foraker's arrival in Springer on the 18th, "having about seventy-five pounds of dynamite," although all other sources, including his own testimony at the McGinnis trial, indicate that he had about half that much. From Springer, the marshal traveled by rail to Albuquerque, via East Las Vegas and Las Vegas.

27. Springer dispatch of 17 July in *New Mexican*, same date; ibid., 18 July, correcting the error; *Rocky Mountain News*, 21 July 1899.

Identical or similar dispatches from Springer were carried by many other papers; see n. 18.

28. *Rocky Mountain News*, ibid., Ludlum, loc. cit.

29. French, *Some Recollections*, 263–4.

30. A Springer dispatch in the *New Mexican*, 17 July, confirms that Reno was the first to report the news over the telephone. In an article in the *Rocky Mountain News*, 21 July 1899, railroad officials referred to a telegram from him, also received on the 17th.

31. Springer dispatch in *Rocky Mountain News*, 19 July 1899, stating that the inquest had been held late on the night of the 17th.

32. *Trinidad Advertiser-Sentinel*, 19 and 20 July; Springer and Trinidad dispatches in *Rocky Mountain News*, 19 July 1899.
Farr's funeral was held in his home town, Walsenburg, at 3:30 on the afternoon of July 19. Trinidad and Walsenburg dispatches in *Denver Times*, 18 and 20 July; Walsenburg dispatches in *Denver Post*, 19 July and *Rocky Mountain News*, 20 July; *Trinidad Advertiser-Sentinel*, 20 July 1899; undated [July 19] Trinidad dispatch in Titsworth, I, 10.

33. Springer dispatch, 18 July, in *Albuquerque Journal-Democrat*, 19 July. *Las Vegas Optic* and *New Mexican*, 18 July. A shortened version of the story is in an East Las Vegas dispatch in the *Rocky Mountain News*, 19 July 1899.

34. Ibid.

35. *Territory vs. McGinnis*: testimony of Elliott; Springer dispatches in *New Mexican*, 18 July and *Rocky Mountain News*, 19 July; *Trinidad Advertiser-Sentinel*, 19 and 20 July 1899; clipping from unidentified Colfax County newspaper [*Raton Range, Gazette*, or *Reporter?*], enclosure in letter from Marinell Ash, Edinburgh, Scotland, 13 January 1984. Dr. Ash's grandfather was the Alvin Ash mentioned in the report.

36. Springer dispatches in *Denver Post*, 19 and 20 July; *Denver Republican, Denver Times*, and *Rocky Mountain News*, all 20 and 21 July; Springer dispatches to Las Vegas or East Las Vegas, in *Daily New Mexican* and *Las Vegas Optic*, 19 July, *Albuquerque Journal Democrat*, 20 July, and unidentified paper in Titsworth, I, 10; *New Mexican*, 21 July; *Trinidad Advertiser-Sentinel*, 20 and 22 July; *Raton Range*. 27 July 1899. The *Range's* informant was Louis Kreeger, who had not been a member of the arresting party but who would have heard the details from Reno and his helpers. Kreeger misnamed Clause as Claude, and misrepresented him as a son of the McBrides—a good example of the ease with which the most elementary facts can be mangled, even in transmission from a participant to a colleague.

37. *Chase, ms.*, in Stanley, 61–2.

38. Springer dispatch in *Rocky Mountain News*, 21 July; *Trinidad Advertiser Sentinel*, 22 July 1899; A.P. dispatch from Las Vegas in unid., newspaper in Titsworth, I, 10–11.

39. *San Angelo Standard*, 5 August 1899.

40. Culley, 39–40; Bryan, *Ruffians*, 280–282; Ludlum, 185.

41. Springer dispatches in *Las Vegas Optic*, 19 July reprinted in *Albuquerque Journal-Democrat*, 20 July; *Denver Republican*, 20 July; *Rocky Mountain News*, 20 and 21 July; Santa Fe dispatch in ibid., 22 July; *Denver Times* and *New Mexican*, both 21 July; *Trinidad Advertiser-Sentinel*, 22 July 1899. All the charges were preferred by Reno.

42. A.P. dispatch from Springer dated 21 July 1899, in Titsworth, I, 9–10, reprinted from *Las Vegas Optic*.

43. Springer dispatch in *San Francisco Chronicle*, 21 July; *Trinidad Advertiser-Sentinel*, 22 July 1899; Axford 257–8.

44. *Territory vs. McGinnis*: testimony of McGinnis.

45. Springer dispatches as cited in n. 36. (The Springer reports were widely disseminated. Part of one was incorporated in a review of the case published by the Boston, Mass., *Illustrated News* of 12 August 1899.)

46. Springer dispatches of July 17 and 20, in *New Mexican*, 17 July, and *Denver Republican* and *Rocky Mountain News*, both 21 July; telegram from Reno to Colorado & Southern officials, in *News* and *New Mexican*, 22 July 1899.

47. A Springer dispatch in the *Denver Times* and *Rocky Mountain News*, 20 July, said that Love was "worse" at the Chase ranch. Another from the same place, published next day in the same papers and the *Denver Republican*, and echoed by the *Denver Post* on the day after that, said he had died there. Yet Chase's manuscript account of the Turkey Canyon affair, in Stanley, 57–62, not only makes no reference to any such event but do not mention Love at all except as one of several unnamed possemen who were wounded. A Springer dispatch of 20 July, via Las Vegas, and published in that afternoon's *New Mexican*, confirms the date, and puts the place of death as Springer and the time at 3:30 a.m. The *Trinidad Advertiser-Sentinel*, 21 July, also mentioned that Love had died in Springer the previous morning. Ludlum, 187, is direct and smacks of authenticity.

48. Ludlum is supported by the *Denver Times*, 22 July 1899, which quotes a Springer dispatch of the same date, saying that Love had been buried in Cimarron on the 21st. The erroneous reports that Love died or was buried at Springer may have sprung from editorial carelessness in the rewriting or compression of dispatches originating from that town. (Titsworth, I, 9, from an unidentified clipping, quotes a Springer dispatch of the 21st as stating that Love had died there that morning, thereby getting the time wrong as well as the place.)

49. Sources as for n. 41.

50. Springer dispatch in *Denver Republican* and *Rocky Mountain News*, 20 July; *New Mexican*, 21 July 1899. Many other papers repeated Sam's statement, literally or in paraphrase. In later years it was widely circulated by Kelly, 253–4, and Horan, *Desperate Men*, 1st ed., 229–230. See n. 52.

51. Press sources, ibid.

52. Both Kelly and Horan, ibid., seemed determined to believe, without evidence, that "the kid" of Sam's statement was Harvey Logan, notorious in Montana and Wyoming as "Kid Curry." Bruce Lamb introduced an ingenious variation, whereby Carver is acknowledged to be "Franks," but the perpetrator of the damage wrought on the posse is held to be Logan, who, fortuitously and providentially enough, had arrived in the outlaw camp in Turkey Canyon only a few minutes before the shooting started (Lamb, "Shootout at Turkey Creek," *New Mexican*, 5 May 1978, Supplement 4–5). Soule, 32, 36, accepts this without demur, citing Lamb, *Kid Curry*, 192–4). Culley, 39, plumps for Capehart—an opinion wholly dependent upon his over-reliance on French. Dullenty, "Elzy Lay's Outlaw Career," 14, advances the name of George West Musgrave, but produces no evidence (which is just as well, because none exists, or could exist). Lay and Musgrave were much in each other's company in later years, but that is not evidence of an earlier association, criminal or otherwise. Fern Lyon, of Los Alamos, New Mexico, puts the view that "the kid" in question was Harry Longabaugh, "the Sundance Kid" ("Butch Cassidy and the Sundance Kid,") *New Mexico*, Vol. 50, Nos. 11–12, November/December 1972, 36–44). Her theory seems to have rested on the belief that Tom Capehart, as portrayed by French, was neither more nor less than Harry Longabaugh under a *nom de guerre*, and an unawareness that Capehart existed as anything other than as an alias. Kelly and Horan trafficked in the uninformed view that Tom Capehart was the alias worn locally by Harvey Logan. This is another balloon that cannot fly; not only did Capehart exist in his own right, but he was a familiar and generally popular figure throughout the rangelands of Grant and Cochise Counties. Would Longabaugh, or Logan, pose as Capehart in sections of the Southwest where the real Capehart was so widely known? While there is something in French's Capehart that does not belong to the real Capehart, the likely explanation for the inconsistencies may lie with French's inability to subdue his imagination. His belief that Capehart was "Franks" may have been genuine, but he appears to have drawn upon snatches of reading about Butch Cassidy's later life in South America to dress the Capehart he knew in some of the Sundance Kid's clothing. See "The Identity of G.W. Franks," Chapter 23 (iii).

53. Donna B. Ernst, "Unraveling Two Outlaws Named Carver," WOLA *Journal*, Fall 1997, 30–2; Ernst, "A Deadly Year for St. Johns Lawmen," NOLA *Quarterly* (January-March 2001), 18–21; Philip J. Rasch, "Death Comes to St. Johns," ibid., Autumn 1982, reprinted 1999 in Rasch, *Desperadoes of New Mexico*, 53–72.
54. *New Mexican*, 25 July; *San Angelo Standard*, 5 August 1899.
55. Springer dispatch in *Rocky Mountain News*, 20 July 1899.
56. Raton, N.M., *Reporter*, 26 July 1899.
57. Tom J. Trujillo, Records Supervisor, Penitentiary of New Mexico, Santa Fe, to Philip St. George Cooke, 18 March 1968, letter passed to the author by Phil Cooke.
58. *New Mexican*, 21 July 1899.
59. Springer dispatch in *Denver Republican* and (abridged) *Rocky Mountain News*, both 20 July 1899.
60. *Republican* and *News*, ibid. A report of the findings of an investigation by Dave Farr and others, in the *Rocky Mountain News* and *Trinidad Advertiser-Sentinel*, 25 July 1899 (and reprinted in *Raton Range*, 27 July 1899) ended the public quarrel. See Chapter 14.
61. Springer dispatches in *Denver Republican* and *San Francisco Chronicle*, both 21 July, and *Denver Times*, 22 July; *Trinidad Advertiser-Sentinel*, 22 July 1899.
62. Springer dispatch in *Rocky Mountain News*, 22 July 1899. The story did not reach the columns of the *New Mexican* until July 25, when it was appended to the report of Sam Ketchum's death.
Rincon was the junction of two stems of the Atchison, Topeka and Santa Fe Railroad. Deming was the interchange point for westbound traffic on the Southern Pacific and the Silver City branch line of the Santa Fe.
63. Ibid.
64. *Rocky Mountain News*, 21 July 1899, citing Reno's telegram from Springer to Colorado Southern officials in Denver.

NOTES TO CHAPTER 14

1. *New Mexican*, 21 July 1899.
2. "Bronco Bill" Walters, with Bill Johnson and Daniel "Red" Pipkin, robbed a Santa Fe train at Belen on 24 May 1898. The next day, Walters and Johnson killed three members of a pursuing posse. The only comprehensive account of Walters's life and crimes is Karen Holliday Tanner and John D. Tanner, Jr., untitled ms., July 2002, copy supplied to author; ms., more recently rev. and awaiting publication.
3. *New Mexican*, 21 July 1899, where the name of the Wells, Fargo route agent is misspelled "Powers." The spelling is confirmed in John Tanner to author, 19 September 2003, citing information from Robert J. Chandler, archivist and historian at the Wells, Fargo Bank, San Francisco, California. Powars was sometimes referred to as a Superintendent—a solecism, but not one that offended company protocol.
4. *New Mexican*, ibid.
5. Ibid., *Rocky Mountain News*, 21 July, citing telegram from Springer to the C & S office in Denver; Springer dispatch, in ibid., 22 July; *Trinidad Advertiser-Sentinel*, 25 July 1899.
6. *New Mexican*, 21 July 1899. The statement that two of the bandits' horses had been shot was carried in dispatches published in numerous papers during the previous two days: *San Francisco Chronicle* and *Trinidad Advertiser-Sentinel*, both 19 July; *New Mexican*, 20 July, for example. It was repeated many times thereafter, most conspicuously by Elliott in the *San Angelo Standard*, 5 August 1899, and during the testimony in *Territory vs. McGinnis*. Foraker's

grounds, or motives, for disputing it cannot be gauged; ordinary misinformation, or misunderstanding, may have been speaking for him.

7. *New Mexican*, 21 July 1899.

8. Ibid.

9. As was implicit in his statement, quoted in the *Rocky Mountain News* and *Denver Republican*, both 20 July 1899, that he could "stand a little thing" like the unanesthetized probing of his wound by the physician who attended him at Springer.

10. *New Mexican*, 25 July 1899; Bryan, *Ruffians*, 283. Desmarias's fee for his attendance on Sam was included in the bill for $415.90 which Foraker passed on to the Department of Justice in the fall of 1899 (Foraker to Attorney General, misdated October 30 (for September 30?), received 7 October 1899 (LR: Justice Year File 13065–1896).

11. Antonio Borrego, affidavit before N.B. Hamblin, Notary Public, 17 April 1903; Alverson, 17; *Rocky Mountain News*, 27 April 1901; *San Angelo Standard*, 5 August 1899; Trujillo to Cooke, as cited; Bryan, *Ruffians*, loc. cit.

12. *New Mexican*, 25 July 1899; Trujillo to Cooke; Bryan, *Ruffians*, loc. cit.

13. *New Mexican*, 25 and 27 July; *San Angelo Standard*, 5 August 1899.

14. *San Angelo Standard*, ibid.,

15. *New Mexican*, 27 July 1899.

16. *Rocky Mountain News*, 25 July 1899.

17. Reno, letter to *Chicago Detective*, as cited.

18. *Trinidad Advertiser-Sentinel*, 25 July 1899.

19. Ludlum, 187.

20. Bryan, *Ruffians*, 282.

21. The history of this controversy receives detailed and dispassionate treatment in Barry C. Johnson *Case of Marcus A. Reno* (English Westerners' Society. 1969).

22. Fort Worth dispatch in *Houston Post*, 28 July, reprinted in *San Angelo Standard*, 5 August; Austin dispatches in *San Francisco Chronicle*, 21 and 29 July and *Santa Fe Daily New Mexican*, 31 July 1899; Bartholomew, 16.

23. *San Angelo Standard*, 5 August 1899.

24. Ibid.

25. Otero, 117.

26. *Rocky Mountain News*, 6 and 8 August 1899.

27. See Chapter 18.

28. French, *Some Recollections*, 266–7; Titsworth, I, 30–31 (apparently an interpolation by the compiler's father, George Titsworth: "They could have ridden that four hundred miles on good horses in eight days very easily after McGinnis got well enough to ride that distance").

Culley, 40, is a condensation of French, loc. cit. The essence of the French/Culley account is that Lay, tended by Capehart, rested in Lincoln County for a month before going on to Chimney Wells. Otero's version is much the more credible.

Chimney Wells was sometimes called Clayton Wells.

29. *Carlsbad Argus*, 25 August 1899. Eddy was renamed Carlsbad after a popular vote on 23 May 1899.

30. There is little scope for argument about how the law caught up with Lay, alias McGinnis; in general, the sources complement each other, with few contradictions or errors, though in the first telegraphic reports, Lusk's name is given as "Lord." The proximate sources are the *Carlsbad Argus*, 18 August; *Carlsbad Current*, 19 August (issue not seen by author, but used by Bob Alexander, *S.O.Bs. II*, as noted below); Carlsbad dispatches (probably from the office of the *Carlsbad Current*) in *New Mexican*, 16 and 22 August (the latter reprinted in the Phoenix, Ariz., *Arizona Bulletin*, 8 September); *Roswell Record*, 18 August (from Stewart's telegram to

Sheriff Fred Higgins); Carlsbad dispatch in *San Angelo Standard*, 19 August; *Denver Post*, (dispatches uncredited), 17 August 1899: *Territory vs. McGinnis*, testimony of M.C. Stewart. Among the later accounts, only those of French and Culley (both loc. cit.,) are seriously defective; Livingston's was, until recently, the best (II, 13–18), though—not surprisingly, seeing that V.H. Lusk was one of his informants (Stewart and Thomas evidently were others)—he makes no suggestion of a prior acquaintanceship or understanding between the rancher and the outlaws. Almost forty years after the publication of the Livingston series, Lusk's grandson repaired the omission, on the authority of what he had been told by both Virgil and John (Aud Lusk, interview by Phil Cooke, as cited). Axford, although writing in the mid–1960s, seems to have been able to stick close to what he says he heard from Will Carver. His memory may have been refreshed by conversations with others down the years, but the present writer has no difficulty in accepting the authenticity of his account (Axford, 259–261). Loomis, 64–5, based his version on his recollections of what he was told by Rufe Thomas, whom he knew well. The erroneous statement that the incident took place on "Clabe Merchant's ranch on the Black river" would have arisen from a failure of Loomis's memory, not Thomas's. Titsworth, I, 32, aside from the passage quoted above, seems to be a paraphrase of the dispatches from Carlsbad to the *New Mexican* and other papers, into which one of the Titsworths—compiler B.D. or his father, George—introduced the name of "Black Bob McManus" where the original had shown "G.W. Franks." Waller, 131–2, uses a variety of news dispatches, slightly paraphrased. His chief editorial contribution, evidently directed by too uncritical a reading of Charles Kelly, is to substitute the identity of Kid Curry for that of "Franks." See "The Identity of 'G.W. Franks,'" Chapter 23 (iii). Finally, the best-informed, as well as the most recent, is the account in Alexander, *S.O.Bs. II*, 105–110 and 123–5, in a much-needed chapter on the life of Cicero Stewart.
31. Livingston, II, 12–14.
32. *Carlsbad Argus*, 25 August 1899; Livingston, II, 18; Alexander, loc. cit., (the sole source for the exact location of the Dagger Draw mentioned in the text—Eddy County has more than one Dagger Draw).
33. This paragraph is rationalized from a passage in French, *Some Recollections*, 268. The author accepts—not without some hesitation—that French's story is essentially true and that the man who gave him a deliberately incomplete description of the affair was the real Tom Capehart, but has tried to take account of the obvious shortcomings of French's memory and comprehension. For instance, Capehart could not have got the story from the senior Lusk, because Virgil was receiving medical treatment in Carlsbad. Capehart must, therefore, have spoken to John Lusk.
34. "Tom Johnson" in the dispatch from Carlsbad to the *New Mexican* of 16 August, which was published just a few hours after the arrest; "John Thompson" afterwards, until it was established that he was French's former employee, "Bill McGinnis."
    The quotation is from the *New Mexican*, 22 August 1899. In the *Arizona Bulletin* reprint of 8 September, the Andy Jones brand was given as BD Connected and the inscription "in plain gothic letters" is rendered as JO YOUMAN "with the 'm' inverted and indistinct."
35. *Carlsbad Argus*, 18 August 1899.
36. *San Angelo Standard*, 26 August 1899, where Shield unhesitatingly identified "Franks" as Carver.
37. Ketchum's admission that his first intention was to hold up the Santa Fe at Wagon Mound occurs in *Territory vs. Thomas Ketchum: No. 136—Assault on Railroad Train with Intent to Commit a Felony* (District Court—Fourth Judicial District): Testimony of George W. Titsworth. Ketchum never confirmed it; but nor did he ever dispute it.
    Siringo, *Riata and Spurs*, rev.ed., 194–5, says that, after leaving the rest of the gang, Tom initially headed for Texas, but "cooled down," wheeled his horse westwards toward Folsom, and

decided, as a joke on his former gang, to hold up the train single-handed, not realizing that they had advanced their plans and held it up "only a few days previous." As usual, Siringo is remote from any sense of chronology. Aside from the intrinsic unlikelihood of this part of his story, one would think from his manner of telling it that the interval between the quarrel and Tom's lone attack on the train was more like a week and a half than three and a half months.

38. Doherty and Adams, 21. This demolishes a story from Culley, 43, that, on the afternoon of August 16, Ketchum "rode his big brown up the front street" of Folsom, where he was known to one and all; dismounted outside Jim Kent's saloon; and lost "a thousand dollars in gold and silver." He could not have been in both places at the same time, and Culley's yarn is inherently ridiculous.

39. To enumerate the accounts of Tom's last holdup and ensuing downfall would be to recite much of the Bibliography; to haul each one up for minute inspection would require nearly another book. These are the prime contemporary sources: *Territory vs. Ketchum*, as cited—testimony of F.E. Harrington, Joseph H. Kirchgrabber, Charles P. Drew, John W. Mercer, C.C. Waller, Joseph E. Robbins, F.F. Clarke, H.D. Lewis, George W. Titsworth, Fred Bartlett, F.W. Hall, Saturnino Pinard, and F.J. Dodge; dispatches from Clayton and Trinidad in *New Mexican*, *Albuquerque Journal-Democrat*, and *Rocky Mountain News*, 17 August; *Denver Post*, 17 and 18 August; Wichita Falls, Texas, dispatch of 17 August in *San Angelo Standard*, 19 August 1899, and *New Mexican*, 5 September 1900. The *Journal-Democrat* jeered at the captured and so far unidentified bandit as "An Amateur;" the *New Mexican*, more levelly, chose the headline "A Robber Foiled." The most significant of the later writings are Arie W. Poldervaart, *Black Robed Justice*, 179–181; Titsworth, I, 10 and 30; Livingston, I, 349–351; A. Thompson, *Clayton ms.*, 46–7 and *Open Range Days*, 185–6; Fergusson, 103–106 (taken mainly from the trial transcript, although she does not say so); Culley, 43–6; Doherty and Adams, 21–2; Secrest, 56. Stanley, 105–6, appears to have used the *New Mexican* and Titsworth. The material collected from interviews by Fitzpatrick and later recorded on tape is also valuable. Bartholomew's account, 76–8, is unsourced, but accurate as far as it goes.

Fred Bartlett, the mail clerk, described Ketchum's gun as a pistol; but the robber was too far away, and Fred's head was poked into the line of fire for too short a time, for him to have discerned what kind of gun it was. The only weapon that Kirchgrabber saw in Ketchum's hands was a Winchester, but of course he would have been facing ahead when Tom stole up on him from behind. He could not have confronted Ketchum until he had stopped the locomotive, and by then the bandit had switched to the rifle which, as reaffirmed by an article in the *New Mexican* of 5 September 1900, was "slung across his back" when he crawled over the tender. Poldevaart, who had read the trial transcript, also concluded that Ketchum held up Kirchgrabber with his revolver. It is clear from the testimony of all (save Bartlett) who saw Ketchum after he had left the engine, that the bandit was covering them with a Winchester, occasionally gripping it one-handed.

John Mercer, who took Tom's six-shooter, described it as a Colt's .44. Everyone else who saw the piece, or claimed to have seen it, said it was a .45. Mercer also stated that the revolver was loaded in all six chambers, and that four or five rounds remained in the Winchester. Ketchum himself offered no testimony at his trial.

40. *San Angelo Standard*, 9 September 1899.

41. *Rocky Mountain News*, in ibid., 2 September 1899.

42. Ibid., 2 and 9 September 1899; A. Thompson, *Clayton ms.*, 47; Thompson, *Open Range Days*, 185; Trinidad dispatch of 21 August 1899 in Titsworth, I, 30.

43. Thomas Owen, in Doherty and Adams, 22, implies that Ketchum fired before Harrington. All other sources, including repeated statements by the two principals, agree that Harrington beat Ketchum to the trigger.

44. *Territory vs. Ketchum*: testimony of Mercer and Waller; Fitzpatrick. The train had left Texline, 75 miles southeast of Folsom, at 2 a.m. Thomas Owen (Doherty and Adams, 22) contributes a variant. When Ketchum raised his revolver, the conductor berated him: "We just came to help you but if this is the way you feel, we will go and leave you." This produced instant capitulation: "No boys, I'm all done, take me in." Some or all of these words may have been spoken, though they were not reported at the time. The general effect of the two versions is the same.

45. *Territory vs. Ketchum*; testimony of Waller, Robbins, Clarke, Lewis, and Pinard. Also, Titsworth and A. Thompson, both loc. cit; Pinard, San Diego, Calif., to Jack Potter, Clayton, N.M., January 1, 1928, in Potter, *Riding with Black Jack*, 114–5; Pinard, quoted Culley. 46; Fructuoso Garcia (son of Sheriff Salome Garcia), Clayton, New Mexico, interviewed by Phil Cooke, 22 June 1968 (notes supplied to author).

Pinard had been awoken in the small hours of the 17th and had boarded the northbound freight when it halted at Clayton, at about 4 a.m. In his letter to Potter, cited above, he stated: "I never received any reward." Since it was he, officially, who put Ketchum under arrest, he may reasonably have expected one. Harrington, however, had done all the hard work, and he did receive a reward.

46. *Territory vs. Ketchum*; testimony of Robbins and Lewis.

47. Ibid., testimony of Lewis and Pinard, G. Thompson and others, *Clayton*, 150, identify the doctor as Ringen; but in the copy seen by the author, his name is crossed out and that of Harry Lautemann entered in the margin, in what appears to be Goldianne Thompson's hand. Doherty and Adams 20, also misidentify the doctor as Ringen. Lautemann is the doctor named in Pinard's testimony.

48. *Territory vs. Ketchum*, testimony of Lewis.

49. Ibid., testimony of Pinard; *New Mexican*, 17 August; *Denver Post* and Denver dispatch in *San Francisco Chronicle*, 18 August 1899; Livingston, I, 361; Titsworth, loc. cit., and Owen, in Doherty and Adams, 22.

NOTES TO CHAPTER 15

1. *Territory vs. Ketchum*, testimony of Pinard; Pinard to Potter, in *Riding with Black Jack*, loc. cit; *Denver Post*, 17 and 18 August 1899. The interposition of the federal authorities, and District Attorney Leahy's support for it, rankled with the sheriff. At the trial he was called by the defense and cross-examined by Leahy.

According to Harry Lewis's testimony, the special train which carried Reno, George Titsworth, himself, and others from Trinidad arrived at Folsom between 8:30 and 9 a.m.

2. *Territory vs. Ketchum*; testimony of Robbins; *Denver Post* and Denver dispatch in *San Francisco Chronicle*, 18 August 1899.

3. Foraker, Albuquerque, to Attorney General, 28 August 1899 (LR: Justice Year File 13065–1896).

4. The four previous occasions on which a lone bandit overcame the entire crew of a train before pillaging the express or mail occurred at Flomaton, Alabama, 1 September 1890; Kent, Texas, 16 May 1893; Pacific, Missouri, 24 May 1893; and Uintah, Utah, 14 October 1896. Rube Burrow, the Flomaton robber, is believed to have taken part in as many as seven previous train holdups, but the Kent, Pacific, and Uintah bandits were all debutants.

5. *Denver Times*, 26 April 1901; Trinidad dispatch of August 21, 1899, in Titsworth, I, 30.

6. Pinard, quoted in Culley, 46, says incorrectly that forty-two pellets were extracted. A. Thompson, *Clayton ms.*, hatched the canard that Espey performed the surgery in Trinidad, but

corrected himself (after a fashion) in *Open Range Days*, 186. Even so, Titsworth, loc. cit., and Owens, in Doherty and Adams, 22, repeat the error. In his *Albuquerque ms.*, of 1930, Thompson first wrote that the arm had been taken off in Trinidad, but inserted a correction later. See n. 36.

7. *Territory vs. Ketchum*; testimony of Titsworth and Lewis.

8. Ibid., testimony of Titsworth (G); Titsworth (B.D.), I, 30; Livingston, I, 351.

9. McCronan to Mosley, FWP. McCronan describes her only as "the Ketchum girl," which seemingly must eliminate Tom's sisters, the younger of whom was already past forty—scarcely a "girl."

10. Solomonville *Arizona Bulletin*, 11 August 1899.

11. Titsworth (B.D.) and Livingston, both loc. cit., *San Angelo Standard*, 26 August 1899.

12. *New Mexican*, 25 August; *Carlsbad Argus*, 1 September 1899; Livingston and Titsworth, ibid.

13. *San Angelo Standard*, 26 August 1899.

14. Ibid.

15. Telegram dated 25 August 1899, in ibid.

16. *Carlsbad Argus*, 25 August 1899.

17. *New Mexican*, 23 and 25 August; Trinidad dispatch in *Denver Post*, 24 August; *Carlsbad Argus*, 25 August 1899; Alexander, *S.O.Bs.* II, 110–111; Livingston, loc. cit.

18. Issue of 23 August 1899, reprinted in Titsworth, I, 31; Alexander, ibid., 111 and 125, n. 40, reveals that Lay was photographed at the Las Animas County jail (and the book carries the result on p. 112).

19. Carlsbad dispatch of August 23 in *Albuquerque Journal-Democrat*. 24 August; *Argus*, 25 August 1899.

20. Ibid., and Livingston, loc. cit.

21. *Argus*, 1 September 1899. For the most searching investigation of the manner of Christian's death, see Tanner and Tanner, 122–5. The Tanners cite J. Evetts Haley's interview with Dee Harkey, in which Harkey refers to information received from a member of the posse and is, for once, a convincing witness.

22. *Trinidad Chronicle-News*, 24 August; Raton, New Mexico, *Gazette*, 31 August 1899.

23. *Chronicle-News* and *Gazette*, ibid., *New Mexican*, 25 August; Trinidad dispatch in *San Francisco Chronicle*, 27 August; *Rocky Mountain News*, in *San Angelo Standard*, 2 September 1899; Livingston, I, 51–2.

24. Raton *Gazette*, 31 August 1899.

25. *New Mexican*, 28 and 31 August 1899 (2nd ed.). The two pieces were combined and published as one in the *Albuquerque Journal-Democrat*, 30 August 1899, where the whole is credited to the *New Mexican* even though that paper had apparently not yet printed the later paragraphs! (Presumably the Santa Fe editor had sent or wired them, pre-publication, to his counterpart in Albuquerque.) The writer believes that the later paragraphs originated in Denver, but has not yet connected them with any specific newspaper there. Those paragraphs were also reprinted in Bryan, *Ruffians*, 294–5.

26. *Rocky Mountain News*, in *San Angelo Standard*, 2 September 1899.

27. Ibid.

28. *New Mexican*, 28 August; dispatch from Santa Fe in *San Angelo Standard*, 26 August 1899; Livingston, I, 352; Trujillo to Cooke, as cited; Lay entered the penitentiary records as William K. (not H.) McGinnis.

29. *New Mexican*, 25 August 1899.

30. Jerome dispatches of 25 and 26 August in *Rocky Mountain News*, 26 August and unidentified Colorado newspaper in Titsworth, I, 33; *Rocky Mountain News*, 29 August; *New Mexican*,

4 September 1899. Titsworth, loc. cit., appends the fullest description of the items found with Ketchum's horses (including a new Winchester .30–40), adding mistakenly, and unaccountably, that the animals were not recovered until they had drifted to "a small town near Texline." Other considerations aside, the nearest small town to Texline, Texas, was (and is) Texline, Texas.

31. *New Mexican*, 28 August; *Albuquerque Journal-Democrat*, 30 August; Trinidad *Chronicle-News*, 2 September; *San Angelo Standard*, 9 September 1899; Loomis, 65–6.

32. *New Mexican* and Journal-Democrat, ibid., *Standard*, 2 September 1899.

33. Taylor was prominent in the local government of San Angelo and his advertisements were a fixture in the weekly *Standard*. The other local saddler was Dunn.

34. *Trinidad Chronicle-News*, 2 September 1899.

35. *Phoenix Herald* in Solomonville *Arizona Bulletin*, 8 September 1899.

36. *New Mexican*, 2 September; *San Angelo Standard*, 9 September 1899; Fitzpatrick; Culley, 46, citing material gathered by Fitzpatrick; Thompson, *Open Range Days*, 186; Foraker to Attorney General, undated letter received 7 October 1899, Justice Year File 13065–96. Thompson says that the amputation took place "several months" after Ketchum's arrival at the penitentiary. Ketchum had been in Santa Fe for just nine days when the arm was removed.

37. Lordsburg *Western Liberal*, 8 September 1899.

38. "From Knickerbocker," in the *San Angelo Standard*, 9 September 1899.

39. Loomis, 67.

40. *New Mexican*, 4 September; *San Angelo Standard*, 9 September (reprint of foregoing); *Rocky Mountain News*, 6 September 1899; Jerome dispatches, as cited.

41. The governor's attitude was given forceful and unambiguous expression in Otero to N.O. Murphy, 14 November, as cited, and *New Mexican*, 10 and 11 November 1899. Kedzie was referring to the acquittal of Oliver Lee for the murder of Henry Fountain.

NOTES TO CHAPTER 16

1. An A.P. dispatch in Titsworth, I, 31, quotes a Santa Fe special telegram to the *Denver Republican*, 26 August 1899, as calling the prisoner Ezra L. McGinnis. Titsworth, II, 30–31, also reprints an interview for an unidentified Colorado newspaper given by William Reno in Clayton, New Mexico, on 27 April 1901, in which reference is made to "Ezra Lay McGinnis." But the author has found no evidence that the outlaw was formally unmasked as William Ellsworth Lay until after his release in 1905, although Otero may have known the truth long before that date. William J. Mills, a fifty-year old native of Connecticut, had been appointed Chief Justice of New Mexico on 19 January 1898. His career up to then is summarized in the *Silver City Enterprise*, 21 January 1898.

2. Stats. L., XVII, 283–330; *New Mexican*, 15 September 1899.

3. *New Mexican*, ibid. The Indictment of "William H. McGinnis," No. 2419, is in the case papers, *Territory of New Mexico vs. McGinnis*, Transcript of Record. The Indictment of "G.W. Franks, alias William Carver," No. 2428, is preserved in the Colfax County District Court Records, Criminal Cases #2402 - #2908, 1899–1907: Box 6—Serial #13275 (New Mexico State Records Center and Archives, Santa Fe) (Copy to the author from Karen Holliday Tanner.) George J. Paice was foreman of the grand jury. The witnesses were W.H. Reno, J.H. Morgan, Perfecto Cordova, Agapito Duran, and Wilson Elliott. Evidently the grand jury did not issue indictments for the murder of Love.

4. *New Mexican*, 2 and 5 October 1899.

5. Lou Blachly interviews, as cited: tape recording #127—February 1955, transcript 29–30.

6. Ibid., tape recording #129, 2 January 1955, undated clipping from *Raton Range*, transcript, 1. Jack Stockbridge, who attended Lay's trial told Blachly that Cunningham, when drunk, confided to him that money had been raised to enable Lay's attorney, Andrieus Jones, to bribe the messenger into denying that he could identify the defendant as one of the robbers; the object, according to Stockbridge, was to forestall a prosecution on the mandatory capital charge of train robbery. Cunningham may have told such a story to Stockbridge, but it could not have been true. First, when Lay stood trial for murder, the messenger was allowed to testify on the subject of the robbery and specifically identified Lay as one of the bandits. Secondly, an indictment for murder always took priority over any other, even though the death penalty applied only where the defendant was convicted in the first degree. Stockbridge stated in error that Lay avoided the death penalty by pleading guilty to murder, but this is a simple instance of a very old man being let down by his memory on a technicality which did not impinge upon him personally (Stockbridge to Blachly, Tape No. 394, 18–19).

7. *Territory vs. McGinnis*; case papers.

8. Ibid. Geronimo is in central Graham County, Arizona, six miles northwest of Fort Thomas and forty miles west of Morenci.

9. The jurors were J.M. Charretta, Jacinto Flores, W.H. Butler, J.A. Rush, Cristobal Rivera, Robert Love (foreman), Marcelino Martinez, Richard Fitzgerald, Patrick Boyle, Francisco Gurna, Frank Anderson, and Charles Rathbun. The proceedings that led to their selection were summarized in the *Raton Range*, Blachly tape recording #129, transcript, 2.

10. The governor put his position in the most explicit terms in Otero, 129–131, though he was mistaken in stating that Lay rode into town to report a mutiny in the penitentiary. The convict who performed that service was Walter Hovey. See Chapter 22.

11. *Territory vs. McGinnis*; testimony of James Hunt. The early stages of the trial were reported in the *New Mexican*, 5 and 6 October 1899.

12. Extensive use is made of the testimony of these witnesses in Chapters 11 and 12.

13. Ibid. The *New Mexican*, 7 October 1899, summarized the proceedings of the 5th, which lasted until 11 p.m. The reporter commented that "[t]he court room was inadequate for the people who tried to obtain admittance. And many were turned away."

14. This view is propounded at greater length in Burton, "'Suddenly in a Remote and Secluded Place'," 53–4 and 75 particularly.

15. Act of February 26, 1891, *Compiled Laws of New Mexico*, sections 1063–1069 inclusive.

16. *Pace* Otero, loc. cit., not every ruling was adverse to the defense. But only a few were not.

17. *Territory vs. McGinnis*: testimony of Chapman.

18. Ibid., testimony of Reno.

19. Ibid., Elliott, cross-examination.

20. Ibid., and re-examination.

21. Ibid., testimony of Cordova.

22. Ibid., and cross-examination.

23. Ibid., re-examination.

24. Otero, 129.

25. *Territory vs. McGinnis*: testimony of Morgan.

26. Ibid., testimony of Farr.

27. Ibid., testimony of Stewart.

28. Ibid., Interlocution at close of case for the Territory.

29. 31; Lawrence R. Reno, quoting his grandfather's papers, in address to 10th Annual WOLA Convention, El Paso, Texas, 22 July 2000, and letters to author, 4 September 2001 and 18 June 2002; Foraker, interview with Albuquerque correspondent of a Chicago newspaper in *San Francisco Chronicle*, 14 September 1899 (not in all editions). On 20 July 1899 the *Trinidad*

Advertiser-Sentinel said of Sam: "[T]here is no doubt but what he is the man who killed Sheriff Farr . . . " While the statement is unsourced and could have been conjecture dressed up as reporting, it could also have been derived non-attributively from information furnished by Reno, whom the correspondent appears to have met in Springer.

Yet, after Elzy Lay's conviction, Billy Reno put on a public change of mind: he now believed, or implied that he believed, that Sam Ketchum's admission of guilt was a sham to protect his uncaught comrades (W.H. Reno, interview in *Denver Post*, 28 April 1901, reprinted but not identified in Titsworth, II, 31,)

30. Acquittal, or a verdict of excusable homicide, would have precipitated a prosecution for train robbery that was most unlikely to fail.

31. *Territory vs. McGinnis*: testimony of Miguel Lopez.

32. Ibid., cross-examination.

33. Ibid., testimony of McGinnis. The closing phase of the trial was capably epitomized in a Raton dispatch to the *New Mexican*, 9 October 1899.

34. *Territory vs. McGinnis*: testimony of McGinnis.

35. Ibid., cross-examination.

36. Ibid.

37. Ibid.

38. Ibid., testimony of Elliott, recalled: examination and cross-examination. The importance of this passage cannot be overstated, for counsel has come close to wringing from the witness an admission that, contrary to his earlier statement, his first bullet was aimed at the defendant.

39. No full record of the closing speeches has been found. The passage given here was singled out by the defense and quoted in para. 12 of Motion for a New Trial, *Territory vs. McGinnis*.

40. Ibid., Instructions to the Jury, 7 October 1899.

41. Ibid., Motion for a New Trial, 10 October 1899—para 11.

42. Ibid., Proceedings of 7 October 1899; Exception filed nunc pro tunc as of October 7th and overruled.

43. *New Mexican*, 9 October 1899: *Territory vs. McGinnis*; verdict; sentence.

44. Records of the Penitentiary, Trujillo to Cooke, as cited; also, Tanner & Tanner, *New Mexico Territorial Penitentiary (1884–1912) Directory of Inmates*, 107–8. He was described as temperate, a tobacco user, and literate (but not educated above the 8th grade); his parents were Methodists, but he could not (or would not) say whether they were alive. He was now listed under his "correct" alias of William H. (not K.) McGinnis.

A word on some of the principal witnesses at his trial:

William H. Reno left the service of the Colorado Southern System several years later and joined the Colorado Fuel and Iron Company, becoming head of their "secret service." He died on October 27, 1935, aged seventy-three, after a long, varied, and successful career in law enforcement. His grandson, Lawrence R. Reno, was preparing a biography, of which the present writer has a copy of the *Outline*, but died early in 2007 before he could complete it.

Marshal Foraker's faith in Wilson Elliott remained unshaken. On January 6, 1900, Foraker employed Elliott as an office deputy, at $75 plus fees and expenses. But on February 28, less than eight weeks later, Elliott's appointment was terminated (*ARAG, 1900*: 360—Exhibit S).

George Titsworth, too, continued in law enforcement, working at times for C.F. and I. In the 1930s he was living in Valdez, Colorado. See also Chapter 23 (iii), "The Identity of G.W. Franks."

In the late 1930s Alvin Ash found "Billy" Morgan "nearly blind and living rough, down south of Hachita, [New Mexico]" and took him to El Paso for treatment. He stayed at Ash's house, "but didn't like being indoors and would pace round and round the back yard." Later he was "looked after by local families" near Gila, N.M., until his death in the mid 1940s (Marinell Ash to author, 13 January 1984).

45. *Territory of New Mexico vs. McGinnis, Appellant,* No. 873.
46. Charles A. Siringo, *A Cowboy Detective* (first published 1912), 364–6. Material in pages 339–380 of this book is repeated in the original version of Siringo's *Reata and Spurs* (published in 1927, but withdrawn for revision after objections from the Pinkerton agency), 229–251.
47. *New Mexican,* 2 and 3 October 1899; Livingston, I, 352. The *New Mexican* misnames Ketchum's partner as *Frank* Attlebury; Livingston does not mention Attlebury at all and makes no reference to a co-conspiriator. The *New Mexican* report of 2 October recurs, slightly edited, in the *Tombstone Prospector,* 10 October 1899. Details from Attlebury's prison record are in John Tanner to author, 9 October 2002; also, Tanner & Tanner, *Directory,* 97.
48. *New Mexican,* 2 October 1899; Livingston, I, 352–3.
49. *New Mexican,* 2 and 3 October 1899; Livingston, loc. cit. For Martin, see Tanner & Tanner, *Directory,* 13.
50. Livingston, loc. cit. James Emmit McCauley, *A Stove-Up Cowboy's Story,* 37, has a sketch of Steve Roup, who was well known in Cochise County as a cowman and a very handy fellow with a gun. For Roup's death, see ibid., loc. cit., and 45; also (a rather different version, where Roup is called Rook) in Axford, 40. The comments of Alexander, *S.O.Bs II,* 114, and 126, n. 53, are apposite and have been taken into account.
51. See Chapters 18 and 19.
52. Alexander, *S.O.Bs II,* 126, n. 52, citing a statement in *Carlsbad Current-Argus,* 26 May 1955, that "the Eddy County sheriff detected the trap in time to avoid it."
53. *San Angelo Standard,* 24 September 1898, 27 January 1899. Otero, 122–3, says Sloan *did* hunt for the illusory hoard. Anecdotal material on the Sugg brothers may be found in Leta Crawford, 40–41, and Loomis, 29–31. Scattered glancing references to the brothers' ranching and other interests in the San Angelo locality occur in *Tom Green County,* I and II.
54. *New Mexican,* 10 November 1899.
55. Bartlett to Otero, 11 November 1899 (the emphasis is Bartlett's); *New Mexican,* same date.
56. Otero to Murphy, Phoenix, Arizona, 14 November 1899.
57. Otero to Morrison, Prescott, Arizona, 15 November 1899.
58. *Rocky Mountain News,* 16 November; *San Angelo Standard,* 18 November 1899; Stats. L., XVII, 320 (R.S. 5473).
59. Alverson, 20–1.
60. *New Mexican,* 5 September 1900.
61. Ibid., Childers, Albuquerque, to Attorney General, 29 May 1901 (LR: Justice Year File 13065–1896).
62. Fitzpatrick, tape recording; Bryan, *Ruffians,* 297.
63. Fitspatrick, ibid.
64. *New Mexican,* 5 September; Clayton dispatch of September 4 in ibid., 6 September 1900.
65. A. Thompson, *Clayton ms.,* 48.
66. *New Mexican,* 6 September 1900.
67. Ibid., *Territory of New Mexico vs. Thomas Ketchum,* No. 136, as cited: Indictments, Order of Court, and Plea of Defendant; A. Thompson, *Clayton ms.,* loc. cit.
68. A. Thompson, ibid., 40; *Open Range Days,* 181–2. Albert Law, a native of Clayton, and a close friend of Thompson's despite being thirty years his junior, provided the information that Thompson was nicknamed "Pinhead." Law became editor of the Dalhart, Tex., *Texan* (Law to Phil Cooke, 16 November; Cooke to author, 20 November 1967).
69. *New Mexican,* 7 September 1900.
70. Clayton dispatch of September 6 in ibid., 8 September 1900.
71. Ibid.
72. A. Thompson, *Clayton ms.,* 49, retold in *Open Range Days,* 186.

73. *Territory vs. Ketchum*; testimony of Charles P. Drew.
74. Ibid.
75. Ibid., cross-examination.
76. The most significant testimony of these witnesses has been incorporated in Chapter 14.
77. Secrest.
78. *Territory vs. Ketchum*; testimony of Hall and Pinard.
79. Ibid., testimony of Dodge.
80. A. Thomas, *Clayton ms.*, 50; *Open Range Days*, 167; *New Mexican*, 10 September 1900: Clayton and Fort Worth dispatches of September 8 to *Dallas News*, in *San Angelo Standard*, 15 September 1900.
81. Fort Worth dispatch of September 10 to *Dallas News*, in *San Angelo Standard*, 15 September 1900.
82. *Territory vs. Ketchum*, Motion for New Trial; Motion in Arrest. *New Mexican*, ibid.
83. *Territory vs. Ketchum*; Sentence of Court.
84. Culley, 47.
85. *New Mexican*, 13 September 1900.
86. *Rocky Mountain News*, 13 September 1900.

NOTES TO CHAPTER 17

1. French, *Some Recollections*, 266–8. See Chapter 14, n. 33, and text relating thereto.
2. *Carlsbad Argus*, 18 and 25 August; Carlsbad dispatches of August 18 and 22 in *San Francisco Chronicle*, 19 August, and *San Angelo Standard*, 26 August; Alexander, *S.O.B.s II*, 110, 125 n. 35, quoting *Carlsbad Current*, 19 August 1899.
3. See Chapter 20.
4. Dispatches from Omaha, Laramie, Ogden, Salt Lake City, Denver, and Cheyenne, in *San Francisco Chronicle*, 3, 5, 6, 7, 9, 13, and 14 June 1899; ARPOD, . . . *1899* . . . "Report of the General Superintendent of the Railway Mail Service," 623–810 (695), where the number of robbers is put at five, presumably because the sixth was not seen from the train; Siringo, *Cowboy Detective*, 305–14, 320–6 (intermittently); Kelly, 239–248; Horan, *Desperate Men* (rev. ed.,), 243–252 Horan and Sann, 212–3 (especially reproduction of express and railroad reward poster dated 12 January 1900, identifying the Logan brothers and Bob Lee, with a full description of Lee); Waller, 94–116; Pointer, 149–154; Horan, *Outlaws*, 252–3 (especially reproduction of express and railroad poster dated 10 June 1899, describing George Currie and the Logan, alias Roberts, brothers); Patterson, 143–150; Soule, 29–31; Ernst, *Logan*, 31–5.

Kelly and Pointer are drawn off course by desire to recruit Cassidy to the robber force. Horan, in *Desperate Men*, characteristically ignoring his own research materials, allocates the robbery to three men only, names Elzy Lay as one of the three, and invents some snappily vivid dialogue for them. (We have cited proof that Lay was in New Mexico on the date of the Wilcox holdup.) Waller trailed the two bandit trios through the newspapers more assiduously and for longer than anyone else, but several times misidentifies members of the gang (he, too, puts Elzy Lay among the robbers), besides confusing one fugitive trio with the other. The two reward notices were compiled from two separate sets of details and do not refer to exactly the same men. The earlier one was derived from a sheepherder's recognition of Currie and the "Roberts" (Logan) brothers shortly after the Wilcox robbery. The basis of the second poster was the flight of Loney Logan and Bob Lee from Harlem, Montana, in January, 1900; Harvey Logan's name was included because of his relationship with Loney, but as he was not known in Harlem no description of him was appended. A casual reading of the particulars on the two notices might lead to confusion between George Currie and Bob Lee: first, because Lee, like his cousins the Logans, sometimes called himself Curry; and second, from the coincidence that for both George and Bob the most conspicuous facial feature was a nose that flattened near its base. But George Currie undoubtedly was the Logans' companion in the flight from Wilcox and in the Teapot Creek fight. Bob Lee was one of the trio who headed northwest from Wilcox. Circumstantial evidence suggests strongly that Longabaugh and Ben Kilpatrick were the other two. Longabaugh was closely linked to George Currie and Harvey Logan during the year preceding the Wilcox stickup, and in touch with Logan after it. Kilpatrick rendezvoused with Logan when the pursuit had faded, and rode with him to New Mexico, where Ben drew attention to himself and his confederates by spending bills identifiable as being from the Wilcox loot. The Pinkertons specifically identified Longabaugh as one of the Wilcox robbers (Robert A. Pinkerton to H.G. Burt, President of the Union Pacific Railroad, 14 February 1903, reproduced in Horan and Sann, 231). Ernst believes that Lee was guilty only of receiving stolen currency (for which he was sentenced to ten years in the Wyoming State Penitentiary, and served six and a half), and that the sixth man was Will Carver. But Carver's proven presence in the vicinity of Cimarron, New Mexico, at the time of the Wilcox robbery, gives him a perfect alibi for the latter crime. See Chapters 11, 12 and 13.

5. French. *Some Recollections*, 271–2; Siringo, *Cowboy Detective*, 353–6. See also Chapters 18 and 19.

6. Cunningham, interviewed by Blachly, tape recording #128, 9–10; F.E. Gilpin, interviewed by Bill McGaw, in The *Southwesterner*, January 1962, 7. Cunningham also said that Longabaugh was not in the locality for long. He was not tubercular, as Cunningham's use of the term "lunger" would imply, but he suffered for years from a persistent ailment, variously said to be sinus[itis] and catarrh (Meadows, 37, 272). Other references are as in n. 5.

7. French and Savage, loc. cit. The stolen Portland banknotes are listed in the reward notice of 12 January 1900, in Horan and Sann, loc. cit.

8. El Paso dispatch in *San Francisco Chronicle*, and *New Mexican*, both 13 February 1900; Ball, *Desert Lawmen*, 189; Harold Edwards, "Pat Garrett and the Las Cruces Bank Robbery," *True West*, Vol. 45, No. 2, Whole No. 358 (February 1998), 8–13 (8–9). The nearest to a precedent was the robbery by a lone bandit of a large general store at San Marcial that also operated as a bank, though not formally recognized as one. This crime occurred on 1 December 1892. The robbery of the bank at White Oaks, also in 1892, was not the result of an armed assault by day; the premises were entered by burglars who blew the safe and escaped with its contents.

9. *San Francisco Chronicle*, ibid., *New Mexican* 14, 16, and 17 February 1900; Ball, loc. cit., Edwards, 9–13.

10. *New Mexican*, 16 and 17 February 1900.

11. Edwards, 9–13; *U.S. District Court, Third Judicial District of New Mexico*, as cited: Docket, 202, 213. See also Chapter 9.

12. Edwards, 10–11.

13. Ibid., 11–13; DeArment, 227, 232; Philip J. Rasch, "Death Comes to St. Johns," NOLA *Quarterly* (Autumn 1982), reprinted 1999 in *Desperadoes of Arizona Territory*, 53–72 (66).

14. Edwards and DeArment, loc. cit., John Tanner to author, 6 November 2000, enclosing entries for Brooks in records of New Mexico Territorial Penitentiary. He was received from Grant County on 2 October 1900, to serve five years for larceny of a horse, and released on 26 June 1904. He was a native of Albany, Texas, 28 years old when he began his sentence. Lizzie Weaver was fifteen when she married him. Also, Tanner & Tanner, *Inmates*, 109.

15. Edwards, loc. cit., Tanner to author, 27 June 1900, enclosing records for Wilson and Wilbur from *U.S. Census, 1900*, and the Territorial Penitentiary. Both entered the penitentiary on 30 April 1900. Wilson, #1342, informed prison officials that he was born at Ogdensburg, N.Y., but

specified California as his and his parents' birthplace when questioned by the census enumerator. He gave April, 1868, as his date of birth. His term was commuted from ten years to eight, of which he served six, being released on 3 June 1906. Oscar J. Wilbur, #1343, appears in penitentiary records as a native of Old Colorado Post, Coleman County, Texas; in the census return, he is Irish born, naturalized in Pennsylvania, in 1888. He was pardoned by Governor Otero on 9 October 1900, three months before his formal date of discharge. He was 37 years old. Also, Tanner & Tanner, ibid., 107.

16. *San Angelo Standard*, 24 March 1900.

17. Ibid., 16 and 23 December 1899; 3 February 1900.

18. Phoenix dispatch in *San Francisco Chronicle*, 31 January; Phoenix *Arizona Bulletin*, circa 3 February, in *San Angelo Standard*, 10 February; *El Paso Times*, 4 February 1900.

19. *El Paso Times*, 4, 6, and 8 February 1900.

20. *San Angelo Standard* and *El Paso Times*, ibid.

21. *San Angelo Standard*, 10 March 1900.

22. Ibid., 17 March 1900 (two items: Butte, Montana, dispatch of March 12 to *Dallas News*, and a note on Shield's telegram to Deputy Sheriff S.B. "Dick" Runyon that he had taken charge of Atkins).

23. Bob Harris, Smith, and Miles wrote extensively of their experiences at sea and abroad. Their letters, and those of others from Tom Green County who took passage for South Africa, whether addressed to kinsfolk, friends, or the editor in person, were published in the *San Angelo Standard*: those from Miles on 31 March, 5 May, 7 July (two) and 14 July 1900; those from Smith on 5 May, 4 August, 15 September 1900, 1 June and 7 December 1901. Miles, Smith, and Doc Moss sailed together, but Miles and Moss gave up good jobs within a month of their arrival in Mozambique and returned to Texas from Cape Town soon afterwards. Smith, a bachelor, stayed in Southern Africa for eighteen months, fell seriously ill in England, and eventually resumed his old duties at the Landon Hotel. All three had avoided the war. William S. Veck, nephew and near-namesake of San Angelo's principal merchant and banker, traveled to South Africa by way of Southampton and London, but soon decided that his future lay in South America. George Bent followed a similar course. A young artist, Jack Kelly, went out with a consignment of horses. Not long after his return to Texas he was drowned while trying to cross a river in flood.

For Bob and Felix Harris, see nn. 26, 28, 30.

24. *Rocky Mountain News*, 14 and 16 March; *San Angelo Standard*, 24 March 1900.

25. Ibid., 5 May, 8 and 22 December 1900.

26. Ibid., 13 and 20 January (the latter including an article reprinted from the New Orleans, La., *Picayune*), 24 and 31 March 1900.

27. John Stirling, *The Colonials in South Africa, 1899–1902*, a history of "the Services of the Various Irregular Corps Raised in South Africa and the contingents from Australia, Canada, and New Zealand, India and Ceylon," has a good sketch of the organization and operations of the Kaffrarian Rifles on 112–6.

Initially, the corps comprised two sub-divisions, styled "companies," as befitted infantry. Later, these smaller units were redesignated "squadrons," in accordance with the practice in cavalry regiments. There were eight of these, Squadrons A to H inclusive.

28. Published in the *San Angelo Standard*, 19 May, 23 June 1900. His impending return was announced in ibid., 25 August and 15 September 1900; an "unconfirmed" report of his capture was published in the issue of 5 May 1900 but had no truth in it. Before the end of the year he was back with the imperial forces in South Africa. Six months later he resigned, sick of a war which, he was convinced, would end only when the country was in ruins. His impressions are in ibid., 15 June 1901.

29. Ibid., 8 and 22 December 1900; 11, 18 May, 7 September, 7 and 28 December 1901; *State of Texas vs. Atkins, No, 1239—Murder*: Defendant's Motion for Continuance, 14 December 1900.
30. The Harrises arrived in Cape Town on 14 February 1900.
31. *Atkins, ms. II*, is Dave's story of the voyage and his military service in South Africa, as dictated to a niece, towards the end of 1910. Extensive, though uncritical, use is made of it in Barton, 136–55. This material, slightly rearranged but uncorrected, reappears in Barton's article, previously cited, of which pages 27–9 are concerned with Atkins's South African episode. New Orleans was already the established shipment point for Southwestern livestock. Hence it was the natural port of exit for Texas and Southern mules and horses purchased by the United Kingdom government for use in South Africa (*San Angelo Standard*, 25 November, 16 December 1899; 20 January, 17 and 31 March, 21 April 1900).
32. *Lloyds Register of British and Foreign Shipping from 1st July 1899 to 30th June 1900*, Vol. 1, Steamers: No. 713—*Hostilius*; *Lloyds Weekly Shipping Index*, Vol. XLII—6 July 1900–18 January 1901; Casualties and Miscellaneous Reports, in ibid., 3, 4.
33. *Lloyds Weekly*, as cited, Vol. XLIII—25 January–24 May 1901.
34. *Atkins ms.*, II, 2–3; Barton, 138; *Lloyds Weekly*, XLIII. The transcript names the port of departure as "Newhampton," which is followed in the A.C. Atkins typescript by a set of editorial parentheses enclosing the word "England." The vessel sailed from New Orleans. (There is no English seaport with the name "Newhampton" anyway.) The niece who wrote down Dave's dictated recollections may have been overhasty, or unable to keep pace with his speech; or A. C. Atkins may have been misled by her script or by a tear in the original manuscript.
35. *Lloyds Weekly*, XLIII. *Hostilius* anchored in Table Bay on 22 March 1901 and began her homeward trip from East London on March 31. Her date of arrival at East London is not given, but can safely be assigned to the 25th or 26th, because the port was about two days' sailing time from Cape Town and Atkins is known to have enlisted in East London on the 27th. *Atkins ms.*, II, 4 says that the ship had to wait at Cape Town "for orders."
36. The extant Enlistment Forms for the Kaffrarian Rifles are in File WO 126/74 at the Public Records Office, Kew, Surrey, but they comprise only those for members of Squadrons A and B whose service ended in March 1901 or earlier. The Kimberly Regiment and the East Griqualand Mounted Rifles, whose Enlistment Forms are in the same file as those for the Kaffrarian Rifles, demanded far more personal information from applicants for recruitment. The oath of allegiance for these and similar corps included the phrase "South African Mounted Irregular Forces." The Nominal Roll for the Kaffrarian Rifles, a converted accounts ledger, is in PRO File 127/11. Atkins's name was first entered on page 21 (originally numbered 281) as J.H. Drake; later, the second initial was crossed out and replaced by a W. In the typescript of *Atkins, II*, followed by Barton, loc. cit., his alias is given as "L.H. Drake" but, as will be shown, the initials he used were J.W. The error in the typescript may have arisen from the partial fading or transcriber's misreading of the original longhand. He may have intended to adopt the surname Droke, rather than Drake. See Chapter 22.

NOTES TO CHAPTER 18

1. Siringo, *A Cowboy Detective*, 339–40; French, *Some Recollections*, 270; Cunningham, interviewed Blachly, tape 128, 17. Cunningham does not mention Murray by name, and says he was not in Alma when the detective visited the place, but reports what he heard.
2. Siringo, 353–6, portrays Cassidy as the owner of a saloon; Gilpin, interviewed McGaw, loc. cit., identifies Cassidy's place of work as the barroom in the Coats and Rowe store; Cunningham, loc. cit., said flatly that Cassidy did not own a saloon. It is not unlikely that

Cassidy worked for a share in the profits of the liquor side of the store's trade, making him less than a proprietor but more than an employee.

3. French, *Some Recollections*, 270–272; for the background and early life of McGonagill (whose name French misspells McGonigal), see Whitlock, 112–115, and for his earlier range career, see Axford, 27–9, 41. Soon afterwards, McGonagill joined the professional rodeo circuit. Late in 1902 he and Joe Gardner won a prize of $10,000 by defeating John Hewitt and Fred Baker, both of San Angelo, in a team roping contest (*San Angelo Standard*, 3 January 1903). The *San Francisco Chronicle*, 5 April 1906, welcoming him home as one of nine cowboys from Texas and New Mexico who had just returned from a four-month tour of Uruguay and Argentina, reported that he had "thrown a steer in the record time of 21 1–2 seconds." The early part of the visit is well described by Daniel Buck in *South American Explorer*, No. 37, June 1994, 3–9. Among McGonagill's companions was Bill Connell, already the joint owner of a ranch in Argentina. Connell's story that Butch Cassidy attended one of the troupe's shows in Buenos Aires is questionable, but not wholly incredible.

4. French, *Some Recollections*, 272–4.

5. Ibid., 274.

6. Siringo, *A Cowboy Detective*, 354–5. French, ibid., speaks of his temporary retention of Cassidy and Capehart without mentioning the sudden departure of several of their friends.

7. Siringo, ibid., 355–6.

8. French, *Some Recollections*, 275.

9. Ibid., 275–6; Siringo, 356; Rasch, "Death Comes to St. Johns," 53–4; Donna B. Ernst, "A Deadly Year for St. Johns Lawmen," NOLA *Quarterly*, Vol. 25, No. 1 (January 2001), 18–21 (18); Ernst, "Unraveling Two Outlaws Named Carver," WOLA *Journal*, Fall 1997, 30–2.

10. Rasch, loc. cit., Ernst. "A Deadly Year," loc. cit., Special dispatch, Navajo Springs, Arizona, to *Los Angeles Times*, in *San Francisco Chronicle*, 30 March and Solomonville *Arizona Bulletin*, 6 April 1900.

11. Ernst, "A Deadly Year," 19; Rasch, "Death Comes," 54; French, *Some Recollections*, 276–7.

12. The fullest stories of the ambush are a dispatch from J. M. Brown, a St. Johns schoolteacher, published in the Salt Lake City, Utah, *Deseret Evening News*, 1 April 1900, and a series of diary entries by Richard Gibbons, an uncle of Gus. A copy of most of the diary for March 27 and 28 is in a manuscript held by the St. Johns Historical Society. Lengthy extracts from the original appear in C. LeRoy and Mabel R. Wilhelm, *A History of the St. Johns Arizona Stake* (Orem, Utah, Historical Publications, 1982), 238–242, comprising much of the material in the StJHS manuscript and a few further lines not included in it. The *Deseret Evening News* item seems to be the principal source used by Waller, 141–3. An undated article by Roscoe G. Wilson (sic), "Two St. Johns Lads Killed by Outlaws," in the StJHS ms., collection, is derived mainly from the Gibbons diary entries, but incorporates statements by Dr, James Gibbons, who blamed the Bronco Bill gang for the killings—an impossibility, since that gang had been broken up twenty months beforehand. ("Wilson" was a misspelling. Roscoe G. Willson, 1879–1976, was born in South Dakota but spent most of his long life in Arizona. His books *No Place for Angels: Stories of Old Arizona* and *Pioneer Cattlemen of Arizona* were compiled from his column for the *Tucson Daily Star*—John Tanner to author, 19 April 2005.) Additional details of the ambush are in the Navajo Springs dispatch to the *Los Angeles Times*, in *San Francisco Chronicle*, 30 March and Solomonville *Arizona Bulletin*, 6 April 1900, the latter with a note on the detention of Weaver and Ed [sic] Lowe; Rasch, "Death Comes," 54–6, which includes references to the *St. Johns Herald* and *Holbrook Argus*; and Ernst, "A Deadly Year," 18–19, which draws upon the files of the StJHS. James H. McClintock, *Arizona—The Youngest State*, 486, allots only four sentences to the double murder.

13. Gibbons diary, loc. cit.

14. Rasch, "Death Comes," 56.
15. *Tombstone Epitaph*, 9 April; Rasch, loc. cit., from Holbrook, Ariz., *Argus*, 14 April 1900.
16. *Arizona Bulletin*, 13 April 1900.
17. Rasch, ibid., citing *St. Johns Herald*, 28 April 1900.
18. DeArment, *George Scarborough*, 222–3.
19. Ibid., 200–7; Albuquerque dispatch to *San Francisco Chronicle*, 7 August 1898; Henry Brock, Lou Blachly interviews, as cited, tape 13, 10 October 1953 (author's notes from original recording, Zimmerman Library, UNM, Albuquerque, September 1969); Haley, 294–301, where the killing of Johnson and wounding of Walters is wrongly transferred from Scarborough to Milton; Karen Tanner and John D. Tanner, Jr., untitled manuscript on William Walters, copy in possession of author, 76–80 and note (38) on 82, where Evans Coleman reproves Milton for claiming credit that was not his due.
20. El Paso dispatch in *San Francisco Chronicle*, 21 October 1899; DeArment, *George Scarborough*, 220–1.
21. Tucson dispatch in *San Francisco Chronicle*, 5 April; Deming dispatch of April 5 (misdated April 4), in Solomonville *Arizona Bulletin*, 13 April; Benson dispatch to *Phoenix Arizona Republican*, in *Safford Arizonian*, 14 April; *Tombstone Epitaph*, 9 April 1900; Brock, to Blachly, 12–15 June 1952, "The Ambush of Black Jack," subsection "Death of George Scarborough," Zimmerman Library manuscript, 5–9; Maddox, 438–9; Waller, 143–4.
22. John Tanner to author, 20 May 2005, on the specifications and characteristics of the various firearms and cartridges.
23. Ibid.
24. The quotation is from Brock, ibid., 7. Also, John Tanner to author, ibid.
25. Hunter, "Scarborough," 437; DeArment, *George Scarborough*, 228–30.
26. *Arizona Bulletin*, ibid.
27. Brock to Blachly, ibid., 6. The same view appears, reworded, in ibid., 9.
28. In *George Scarborough*, 228–230. The present writer was an adherent of the decoy theory (though not of the conspiracy scenario) in *Dynamite and Six-shooter* (135–6). That was in 1970; further research, and further thought, have since changed his mind about the former.
29. *San Francisco Chronicle*, ibid. It was the correspondent's erroneous understanding that at this point Scarborough and Birchfield had a third officer with them.
30. *Chronicle, Arizona Republican*, and *Arizona Bulletin*, all ibid.
31. Walters, 170.
32. Three different reward notices were issued. Those first accused were "John Hunter, alias Skeet Jones, Bob Johnson, one Wilson alias Smith, and one Coley." The second set of names comprised "Tom Capehart alias Wilson, William Morris alias Coley, Tod Carver, Jess Black alias Franks, and Mack Steen or Johnson." When it emerged that the name Morris was merely an alias for Tod Carver, a further revision was necessary. The final list consisted of Tom Capehart, alias Wilson; Tod Carver; Mack Steen, alias Bob Johnson; Jess Black, alias Franks; and an unknown. This last notice was published in the *St. Johns Herald*, 26 May 1900, by which date the aggregate reward for the killers of LeSueur and Gibbons had risen from $2000 to about $5000. (See Rasch, 59–60; Ernst, "A Deadly Year," 30.)

Other variants of the suspects' register occur in the earliest reports. The Jerome, Ariz., *Mining News*, 9 April, mentioned only John Hunter, alias Dick Smith; Bob Wilson; and Tom Carver (quoted in John Boessenecker, Union City, Calif., to author, 27 February 1984). The *Tombstone Epitaph*, same date, offers the names of John Hunter alias Dick Smith, Bob Johnson, Wilson, alias Smith, Kid Carver, and an unknown. The list in the *Safford Arizonian*, 14 April 1900, is the same, except that Carver is named as Tod, rather than Kid—the latter was probably a copyist's or printer's error. McClintock, loc. cit., evidently depended on one of the earlier sources. He gives only four names: John Hunter, Ben Johnson, John Wilson, and John Coley. "Ben" could have arisen from another copying slip. If so, it is merely coincidental that it is the first name of the man whose true identity lay behind the alias Bob Johnson, viz., Ben Kilpatrick.

The question of identity is discussed intelligently and at length in DeArment, *George Scarborough*, 224–246, though several of his shots are wide. His suggestion (241) that the killer Bob Johnson may have been the ranch foreman of that name is untenable; as a senior employee of the Erie company, the real Bob Johnson could have cleared himself without difficulty. No evidence has turned up to show that he was even momentarily under suspicion. DeArment also states that "in 1970, Jeff Burton confidently named Capehart, clearly meaning Logan, as a gang member" (*Dynamite and Six-shooter*, 135–6). A closer study of the latter work will show that its author, while displaying every confidence in identifying Capehart as one of the killers (a view with which DeArment concurs), is at pains to demonstrate that Capehart could not have been Logan, going so far as (180) to describe the Kelly-Horan position that Capehart was "just another alias for Harvey Logan" as an absurdity. DeArment's rejection of attempts to put Cassidy among the attackers is convincingly argued, although evidently he was then unaware of the most convincing argument of all: the fact that Cassidy was under arrest at the time of the fight. See nn. 11 and 43 and relevant text.

33. Rasch, ibid., 59–60; DeArment, ibid., 239.

34. Kilpatrick's use of the names Rose and Cunningham, among others, was dwelt upon by the press at the time of his arrest in St.Louis, Mo., in November, 1901, and is noted in Chapters 4 and 22 of this work. At San Saba in the spring of 1888 a Ben F. Beeson was cleared of charges of aggravated assault and false imprisonment on motion of the district attorney (*San Saba News*, 4 May 1888). The name and its owner could hardly not have been known in Kilpatrick's home quarter, Concho County, Texas. There is no direct evidence that Kilpatrick misappropriated it, but it may be significant that Baker, 11 and 102, places an otherwise unknown Ben Beeson among the Wilcox and Tipton train robbers. She also, correctly, puts Ben Kilpatrick on the scene of both crimes. The present writer believes that, if any of the outlaw gang ever passed himself off as Ben Beeson, it would have been Ben Kilpatrick. Probably Baker knew Robbers' Roost as thoroughly as anyone has ever known it, and was as well informed on its inhabitants and habitués as anyone of her generation ever could be. But she was not knowledgeable about the origins and byways of those, like the Kilpatricks, who rarely or never visited the Roost, or only occasionally went north from Texas. Thus she might well have taken the man, Ben Kilpatrick, and his alias-of-the-moment, Ben Beeson, as two distinct entities.

35. Ernst, "Two Outlaws," 30–1.

36. Two descriptions of Hilliard, both derived from PNDA sources, appear in Ernst, "Two Outlaws," 30 and 31.

37. See Chapters 1 and 20.

38. Siringo, *A Cowboy Detective*, 355, 369.

39. Ibid., 369: Burton, research file, Byron Sessions.

40. The Pinkertons' descriptions of Logan, slightly modified from time to time to account for changes in his facial appearance, were widely distributed. Examples are reproduced in Horan & Sann, 211 and 225, the latter from Knoxville, Tenn., *Sentinel*, 27 June 1903, after Logan's escape from the local jail, and in Lynch, 23 and 144, the second of these being in Spanish for circulation in South America.

41. DeArment,*George Scarborough*, 238–9, quoting Blair, interview in *Silver City Independent*. 17 April 1900. James Knox Blair's life and official career are described in his obituary, *Silver City Enterprise*, 7 February 1941, in the *Silver City Daily Press*, 27 July 1968 ("Sheriffs' Issue"), and in Bob Alexander, *Lawmen, Outlaws*, and *S.O.Bs*, 55–6, 57–60, 204–6, 208–210, and 214–5.

42. Maddox, 439; DeArment, ibid., 252–4; Rasch, "Death Comes," 58–9.

43. Rasch, "Death Comes," 54; Ernst, "A Deadly Year," 19. Cassidy's residence in the St. Johns jail in late March and early April vanquishes allegations that he was a party to the killing of Scarborough. Livingston, II, 23, in relating that Cassidy both planned and, with others (whom he did not name), executed the assassination of Scarborough, cites as authority an anonymous "New Mexico man" who had met Butch in "a certain South American republic." The fact that the story cannot have been true does not rule out the possibility that Livingston knew a man who had met Cassidy in South America, or claimed to have done so, or who knew someone who claimed to have done so. The Lohman family, originally from the San Angelo area of Texas but long established in Livingston's home town of Roswell, New Mexico, had South American connections through George Lohman, a good friend of George Musgrave. Cassidy was killed in South America before Lohman got there, but Lohman would have been well placed to pick up old and doubtless garbled stories about Cassidy in South America. John Tanner suggests that Lohman's source is at least as likely to have been Musgrave's wife Jano (the former Jeanette Major) as Musgrave himself. She was sister-in-law to Bert Charter, an accomplice and close friend of Butch Cassidy in Wyoming and Colorado. (Tanner to author, 19 April 2005.) Others from the Arizona and New Mexico ranges, such as Clay McGonagill (n. 3), visited Argentine during Cassidy's lifetime. DeArment, *George Scarborough*, 242–3, considers Michael Williams's article "Iron Men of Arizona" (*Pearson's Magazine*, September 1928), wherein the killing of Scarborough is attributed to Will Carver, Cassidy, Capehart, "and a man whose name never got known." Williams credits as his source "a great friend of the gang" whose name could not be revealed "for obvious reasons." Both Livingston and Williams were proponents of the decoy-and-entrapment theory which DeArment roundly, and justly, derides. See n. 32.

44. French, *Some Recollections*, 276–7.

45. Ernst, "A Deadly Year," 19–20.

46. Ibid., 20.

47. Ibid.

48. French, *Some Recollections*, 277–8. For the reasoning behind the author's contention that Weaver shifted the treasure from Colfax County to the Alma neighborhood, see Chapter 22.

49. Reed Dean, to Lou Blachly, 24 September 1952—Tape Recording #130, 22, UNM. See Chapter 22, nn. 41 and 42.

50. Ibid., and Ernst, "A Deadly Year," loc. cit.

51. Thompsons [formerly Thompson, and originally Thompson Springs], Utah, dispatch in *San Francisco Chronicle*, 20 April 1900; Kelly, 261–2; Waller, 45–7; Baker, 103–5. The most detailed of the secondary accounts is Waller's, its main source being the *Deseret Evening News*.

NOTES TO CHAPTER 19

1. Donna B. Ernst, *Sundance, My Uncle*, 1992), is the fully documented biography of Harry Longabaugh, the Sundance Kid, though the continuing research of Ernst, her husband Paul, and others, proves that it is far from the last word on its subject. Longabaugh's nativity is not recorded, but census and family bible establish his approximate date of birth (Donna Ernst to author, 21 April 2003).
See also Pointer, 98–9; Meadows, 26–31 (all printings), and Patterson, 111–8.

2. Ernst, ibid., 39–47.

3. Billings dispatch in *Globe-Democrat*, 4 June; Helena dispatch in ibid., 22 June 1892.

4. Great Falls dispatch in ibid., 30 November 1892; Pointer, 99; Ernst, *Sundance*, 79–83; Patterson, 120, 294–5; Meadows, 31–2. Pointer gives the date of the robbery as 12 December

1892—a mistake copied from one of the P.N.D.A. reward posters referring to Longabaugh, first illustrated in Horan and Sann, 219.

5. Deadwood, S.D., dispatches in *Globe-Democrat*, 29 and 30 June, 1 July, 2 and 3 November; Helena dispatch in ibid., 27 September 1897; Horan and Sann, loc. cit., 85–7; Baker, 97–8; Waller, 75–85; Pointer, 99; Horan, *The Outlaws*, 252 (reward poster, Butte County Bank, 28 July 1897); Ernst, *Sundance*, 85–7, Logan, 18–27; Patterson, 125–7; Meadows, 32, 318; R.I. Martin, "A Lively Day in Belle Fourche," *True West*, Vol. 9, No. 4, Whole No. 50 (April 1962), 43, 47–8. Those first accused were George Currie, Harvey Ray, Tom O'Day, and two men referred to as "the Roberts brothers" (Harvey and Loney Logan, though at times Longabaugh also used the name Roberts during this period). The names of Longabaugh and Punteney were added later. Harvey Ray was a personage in his own right, not a mere alias for Harvey Logan. Neither Ray nor Loney was indicted. Those billed were Currie, O'Day, Punteney, Longabaugh, and Harvey Logan, the last two as "Frank and Tom Jones"—five indictees, though the robbers appear to have numbered six. (Many sources, however, take the view that there were only five in the gang.)

No one was ever convicted of the robbery. An alibi was found for Punteney, and the jury liked it well enough to acquit him, in the face of a wealth of eyewitness and circumstantial evidence that declared him guilty. More ludicrous still was the subsequent acquittal of Tom O'Day, who had been caught redhanded. In contrast, the conventional belief that Longabaugh was among the guilty, restated in Ernst's *Sundance*, has been unsettled by her later researches, which have uncovered apparently secure evidence that he was nowhere near Belle Fourche on the day of the robbery. (Patterson, 296–7; Ernst, *Logan*, 21.) Baker says that Currie, like Longabaugh, took no hand in the robbery, and that "Willie Roberts (called Indian Billy, although he was a Mexican from New Mexico)" planned it; but Will Roberts was only an alias for Harvey Logan, who was neither an Indian nor a Mexican.

6. Chapter 10, nn. 49–51; Baker, 100–101; Ernst, *Sundance*, 104–6.

7. Chapter 17, n. 4.

8. Waller has little on Logan's early life, but provides (69–71) a good account from contemporary newspaper sources of his killing of Powell Landusky on 27 December 1894. The most interesting account from any source is Jim Thornhill's, given to his friend Ross Santee and reproduced in Santee's *Lost Pony Tracks*, 172–3. Santee's portrayal of Thornhill's social attitudes is unflinching ("[N]o race as a whole was worth the powder to blow it to hell. To Jim the human race as a whole was a failure. Only the individual counted, no matter his color or creed—and a friend could do no wrong.") and repeats statements from him characterizing Harvey Logan as an extreme misanthrope (171); see also Kelly, 117–8. Soule, 27, supplies the essence of the biographical background that Kelly, Horan, Waller, and others left unexplored. Ernst, *Logan*, 7–9, takes this forward in what is by a long way the fullest and best treatment of Kid Curry's life and crimes; the murder of Landusky and the proceedings arising therefrom are covered on 11–13 and 83–6, with excerpts from the testimony at Loney Logan's trial for the killing. (Loney was acquitted; Harvey the actual killer, was never tried.)

9. As will be seen, they stayed in Brown's Hole for about a month, waiting in vain for Harvey Logan, before moving on into Idaho, where they remained for several weeks while laying plans to rob the Winnemucca bank. Cassidy could hardly have reached Brown's Hole much earlier than the middle of June; on the other hand, the timespan imposed by the course of subsequent events predicates a date no later than early August for the beginning of their journey from the Hole to Idaho.

10. Thompson's and Salt Lake [City], Utah, dispatches in *San Francisco Chronicle*, 28 May 1900; Thompson's Springs dispatch in ibid., 29 May 1900; Kelly, 263–4; Waller, 147–152; Baker, 87–8; DeArment, 234–6; Patterson, 252; Rasch, "Death Comes," 62; Ernst, *Logan*, 37–8.

11. Waller, 150.
12. Kelly, 265.
13. DeArment, *George Scarborough*, 235–6.
14. John Rolfe Burroughs, *Where the Old West Stayed Young*, 201, quoting the ms. reminiscences of Jesse S. Hoy, a pioneer cattleman of Brown's Park.
15. Siringo, *A Cowboy Detective*, 367–8. Beeler's heroic efforts obviously did not satisfy the electors of Apache County, Arizona, for in November 1900 they turned him out of the sheriff's office. On 12 January 1901, in defense of his own life, he killed an enemy of long standing, Monterey "Monte" Slaughter. His unprotected back was powerless against bullets fired into him from behind by two of Slaughter's kinsmen just three months later. He died that night, 11 April 1901, not quite twenty-five years old. See Karen Holliday Tanner and John D. Tanner, Jr., "Revenge: the Murder of Ed Beeler," WOLA *Journal*, Vol.XIII, No. 1 (Summer 2004), 2–7; Ball, *Desert Lawmen*, 66, 210–211; Siringo, *Cowboy Detective*, 353, 268; Phoenix dispatches to *San Francisco Chronicle*, 16 April 1901.
16. Any joint timetable for the reunion of the two sections of the gang would have been wrecked by the bloody meeting with Tyler and Jenkins and the ensuing hue and cry.
17. Horan and Sann, 192–3. William Cruzan, 27 years old, was received at the Colorado State Penitentiary on 22 March 1895 from Mesa County, to begin a four year term for grand larceny as Colorado State Prisoner #3722. He was released on 12 May 1898. (R.W. Adkisson, Supervisor, Bureau of Classification and Records, Colorado State Penitentiary, Canon City, to Colin Rickards, 12 August 1969, copy from Rickards to author).
18. Cheyenne, Denver, and Pocatello dispatches in *San Francisco Chronicle*, 31 August 1900; Cheyenne dispatch of August 30 (the year 1898 mistakenly inserted by the compiler) to unidentified Colorado newspaper, reprinted in Titsworth, I, 7; Siringo, *A Cowboy Detective*, 339–53, 367–8; Kelly, 273–6; Horan, *Desperate Men*, 1st ed., 238–9; rev. ed., 267–9 (where he alleges that Longabaugh and Harvey Logan robbed the passengers, and purports to substantiate his misstatement with a list he says was compiled by the Pinkerton agency); Horan and Sann, 208, 215–6; Waller, 153–7; Pointer, 165–9, (based mainly on the spurious Phillips ms. but with material added from contemporary sources); Horan, *The Outlaws*, 254 and 301 (n.11): Patterson, 161–3 and 306–8 (nn. 15–32, inc.,); Soule, 41–3; Ernst, *Logan*, 39–42.

Kelly and Horan, in particular, are driven by a desire to have Cassidy on the scene—a position for which Patterson furnishes a labored, and fallacious, attempt at justification. Patterson's suggestion is that Cassidy, Longabaugh, and Carver could have traveled west by rail, and thus have time in hand to pluck the Winnemucca bank. This theory cannot withstand the first whiff of common sense, much less analysis, and is consigned to the wastebasket by the *Buenos Aires Standard* presentation of Longabaugh's narrative (Bell, cited n. 23 *infra*).

Ernst, *Logan*, 39 and 42, cites the Pinkertons' belief that the fourth and fifth men in the Tipton gang were Jim Ferguson and Jack Ryan and their suggestion that the two be arrested as accessories before and after the fact. The present writer suspects that this recommendation conveys the full extent of their guilt, and that one or two of the men who came north with Logan and Ben Kilpatrick are likelier to have been among the actual executants.

In "Think You Used Enough Dynamite, Butch?" (English Westerners' *Tally Sheet*, Vol. 47. No. 1—Winter 2000, 1–13), Dennis Cross conscientiously reviews many of the secondary sources. He is good on the robbery and the pursuit (3–6), but his discussion on the question of identity is far less satisfactory, partly because he handicaps himself by ignoring the earliest and most valuable published source: the writings of Siringo, who investigated the case for the P.N.D.A. and spent several months on the trail of three of the gang. Another serious limitation is explicit in Cross's title, which is lifted from the script of George Roy Hill's filmic extravaganza, "Butch Cassidy and the Sundance Kid." Cross at once admits the unlikelihood of the words having been uttered at the scene of an actual train robbery. But the choice of title accurately conveys Cross's readiness to swallow the premise that both Cassidy and Longabaugh were in the Tipton robbery. He follows others in accepting Kelly's yarn of Cassidy's rendezvous with the lawyer, Douglas Preston, at Lost Soldier Pass—a non-existent arrangement, and a non-existent place. He even considered the proposition that Laura Bullion would have assisted at the robbery if Ben Kilpatrick had taken part in it. He eliminates her from suspicion on the authority of his own feeble argument that Kilpatrick must be excluded from suspicion because the trainmen—surprised if not frightened, and in pitch darkness—could not assert that one of the robbers was six foot tall, as Ben was. Neither Cassidy nor Longabaugh—nor, for that matter, Will Carver—was or could have been present, and the "evidence" cited in support of Cassidy's supposed involvement varies from the honestly mistaken to the flagrantly fictitious.

Kilpatrick certainly was present. Neither then, nor after her arrest for currency offenses, was it suggested that Bullion could have participated in the robbery. Had she been accused of the crime, her innocence could have been established at once; she was in Texas when it happened. Moreover, she was still Carver's consort, not Kilpatrick's. The three whom the Denver office first connected with the robbery were Harvey Logan, Bill Cruzan, and "a man who might be Longabaugh." Siringo's investigation confirmed the first two names, and inserted that of the hitherto unknown Kilpatrick for the notional Longabaugh.

19. Pocatello dispatch in *San Francisco Chronicle*, 31 August; Patterson, 163, citing *Denver Republican*, 2 September 1900; Horan and Sann, 216, illustrating Pacific Express Company reward poster.
20. Anon., ed. Alan Swallow, *The Wild Bunch*, 80–2). This is a book wholly unlike any other in the canon. Its opening section resembles a 1950–ish essay by a high school pupil of no special ability. The rest is a mixture of the conjectural, the erroneous, the fictional, and the semi-factual, with several injections of what may well be genuine and unique inside information. The anonymous author may have been Frank Lamb, whose son Bruce wrote extensively and, for the most part, inauthentically, about Harvey Logan during the later 1970s and afterwards. Lamb, senior, seems to have known Logan well and to have sheltered him after his escape in June, 1903.
21. Lowell Spence, "Logan's Log," first part in Horan, *Desperate Men*, 1st ed., between 272 and 273 (228 and 231 of UK ed.,), the document in full in Ernst, *Logan*, 46–8; Spence, a senior P.N.D.A. operative, was put on Logan's trail after the Wagner robbery of 3 July 1901, and made use of data gathered by Siringo and others.
22. Some contemporary sources say $32,640. It is possible that neither figure is correct. A few years later the Pinkertons put the loss at $40,000.
23. "Did the Sundance Kid Tell His Own Version of What Happened at the Winnemucca Bank Robbery?" (WOLA *Journal*, 2001, loc. cit.) Bell's answer to his own question is a ringing and closely reasoned affirmative, with which the present writer is fully in accord on grounds to be explained below. The original article, contributed to the *Buenos Aires Standard* of 17 April 1912 by an informant of Longabaugh but told in the first person as if every word had come direct from the outlaw's own lips (a palpable impossibility), was first reprinted as "An Interview with the Sundance Kid" in ibid., Vol. 5, No. 4 (Summer 1995), 13–16. Bell incorporated the results of the most recent research in the second reprint.
24. Ibid., (rev.) 6. On page 11, Bell takes the phrase "our leader . . . the brainiest member of the bunch" as a reference to Cassidy. Yet the narrative seems to refute this in its own terms: since Cassidy was one of those who were waiting for the absent "leader," and since the article goes on to state that the trio of Cassidy, Longabaugh, and Carver waited fruitlessly for a month before setting out on the Winnemucca expedition, the narrator must have been referring to someone else. As the "leader," or "Napoleon" (as he is also called) cannot have been Cassidy,

the reference could only have been to the sole plausible alternative: Harvey Logan. Longabaugh, or his amanuensis, does not explain Logan's failure to turn up, but the probable answer is that the murderous encounter with Tyler and Jenkins (also unmentioned in the article) forced the Logan party into a change of plan.
25. Ibid., 6, 11–12; Patterson, 169–171 and 309 (nn. 55–60 inc.).
26. Bell (rev.), 11–12; Ernst, "Winnemucca," 10, 64.
27. Winnemucca dispatches in *San Francisco Chronicle*, 20, 21, 22, 23, 25 September 1900; *Globe-Democrat*, 12 December 1901 (Nixon's account, in which he positively identified Ben Kilpatrick as one of the three marauders, although Ben was at Jim Ferguson's ranch near Dixon, Wyoming, on the day of the bank robbery—story copied in *San Antonio Standard*, 21 December 1901): Horan, *Desperate Men*, 1st ed., 239–42, and *The Outlaws*, 255–6; Kelly, 277–81; Waller, 157–60; Baker, 191–3; Pointer, 169–71; Patterson, 166–72; Ernst, "George S. Nixon," 3–4; Bell, (rev) 7–10. In the original edition of *Desperate Men* (240–41) is a report contributed in 1909 by an anonymous informant (Bill Chaney?) whose information obviously had come direct from Carver. This document, except in the form of occasional passages of paraphrase, does not appear in the revised edition (Winnemucca robbery described 272–5, Bison printing). For Moore, see Chap. 6, 83.
28. Bell (rev.), 10.
29. Proof of Carver's return to southern Idaho in December, 1900, is contained in a statement volunteered to a Pinkerton man a full year later by the second Mrs. Carver, née Callie May (or Mae) Hunt, alias Lillie Davis. Her revelations are most faithfully summarized in Ernst, *Sundance*, 148–9, and *From Cowboy to Outlaw*, 10–12, and printed in full in the same author's *Women of the Wild Bunch*, 38–43. Horan was the first to unearth this document and utilize it for publication (*Desperate Men*, 1st ed., 244–5), but, as so often with this author, the factual substance is carelessly (or wilfully) misused. In this instance, he at one point substitutes Logan's name for Carver's. In *The Wild Bunch*, 107–9, and the revised edition of *Desperate Men*, traces of the material reappear, beribboned with the fictional furbelows so characteristic of Horan's type of "historical" writing. See also Patterson, 176 and 310 (n. 16); but, *pace* Patterson, Carver (as William Casey) did marry Callie on 1 December 1900 and the certificate of marriage is still on file.
30. Lynch, 15, (early 1901—poster in English); Horan, *The Outlaws*, 267 (1903—poster in Spanish).
31. Patterson, 170–1 and 309 (nn. 57–64 inc.), citing articles by Lee Berk and Donna Ernst.
32. Winnemucca dispatch in *San Francisco Chronicle*, 18 February and 21 September 1900; Ernst, "George S. Nixon," 2–3.
33. Ernst, ibid., 3; Bell, 11–13; Patterson, 169 and 309 (nn. 53–4).
34. Siringo, *A Cowboy Detective*, 342.
35. Knoxville dispatch of December 17 in *San Angelo Standard*, 21 December; *San Antonio Express*, 18 December 1901, reprinted in ibid; Lynch, 16, 17, 69, 107, 109; Spence, "Logan's Log;" Waller, 161; Ernst, *From Cowboy to Outlaw*, 10–11, and *Women*, 32–42, 44–6.
36. "Lillie Davis," statement to Lowell Spence, 4 December 1901, extracts transcribed from Pinkerton archives by Donna Ernst, copy furnished to author by Sutton County Historical Society, Sonora, Texas; full text in Ernst, *Women*, loc. cit. In *Desperate Men*, 1st ed., 245, Horan switches the identity of "Dan," the expert bicyclist, from Ben Kilpatrick to Butch Cassidy.
37. Sources as for n. 35.

NOTES TO CHAPTER 20

1. Livingston, II, 19.

2. Ernst, *From Cowboy to Outlaw*, 10–11, *Logan*, 43–5, and *Women*, 32–4; Patterson, 175–7 and 310–311, nn. 11–25 inclusive. Patterson does not believe that the gang's rapid dispersal was caused by Fred Dodge's chance viewing of the group photograph. He argues that neither the photo nor any visit by Dodge to Fort Worth in 1900 is mentioned in the detective's published reminiscences (Dodge, ed. Carolyn Lake, *Undercover for Wells Fargo*). The objection is fallacious; Dodge's recollections, as edited by Lake, end in mid-sentence during his account of a train robbery investigation in mid-November 1893—seven years before the photo was taken. Lake states in an editorial note that the Dodge family moved to San Antonio in September 1900, which suggests that he could not have been far from the hunt for the men in the photo (196, 223).

    Livingston, loc. cit., writing in 1930, still believed that Longabaugh was just another name for Ben Kilpatrick and identified the fifth man in the picture as "a notorious criminal named Ole Hobek, who had lately taken to train robbing." But Hobek, real name H.O. Beck, also alias Magner, Flood, and Benson, a former and future convict, had no connection with any of the Cassidy or Ketchum gangs until he met Ben Kilpatrick in the U.S. Penitentiary, Atlanta, late in 1907, and is not known to have robbed a train anywhere until after his release in 1909 (Soule, 113–129).

3. Holt, 91.

4. *State of Texas, County of Tarrant: Rites of Matrimony, Certificate No. 9965, 1 December 1900—Mr. William Casey and Miss Callie M. Hunt.*

5. *San Antonio Express*, 18 December, and *San Angelo Standard*, 21 December 1901; "Lillie Davis," statement, 4 December 1901.

6. "Lillie Davis," ibid.

7. "Logan's Log" and ibid.

8. Patterson, 183–6 and 314–5 (n. 69–92 inc., citing the research of Donna and Paul Ernst, Ed Kirby, Dan Buck, and Anne Meadows); Meadows, 36–7.

9. "Lillie Davis," statement.

10. Holt, 87. See also n.48.

11. Sonora, Texas, *Devil's River News* and *San Angelo Standard*, both 6 April 1901; Loomis, 67.

12. Ernst, From *Cowboy to Outlaw*, 12; Hunter and Rose, 82.

13. Livingston, II, 18–9; Holt, 87; *Devil's River News* and *San Angelo Standard*, 6 April 1901.

14. *San Angelo Standard*, 28 December 1895.

15. Ibid., 29 April, 13 May, 7 and 21 October (this last including an item from the *Concho Herald*) 1899, 15 September 1900.

16. Holt, 87.

17. "Logan's Log;" "Lillie Davis" statement.

18. Loomis, 67.

19. Ibid.

20. Livingston, II, 19–20.

21. Loomis, loc. cit.

22. *San Angelo Standard*, 12 and 19 May, 17 November 1900.

23. "Logan's Log."

24. *San Angelo Standard*, 6 April 1901.

25. Holt, 90.

26. *San Angelo Standard* and *Devil's River News*, 6 April 1901; Jo-Ann Palmer, Secretary, Sutton Council Historical Society, Sonora, Texas, to author, undated [March 2002].

27. "Logan's Log."

28. See Chapter 19, n. 27. Horan, *The Wild Bunch*, 184, (repeated in Horan, *Desperate Men*, rev. ed., 363) cites correspondence between Chaney and the Denver office of the P.N.D.A. On 27 February 1906, Chaney wrote that Ben Kilpatrick's older brother Boone was "a straight man as far as I know."

29. *San Angelo Standard*, 30 March 1901. Dozier was elected sheriff of Concho County in November, 1892

30. Holt, 87, refers to this story as a "report" without saying whether he believed it.

31. Loomis, 66.

32. Ibid., 67.

33. Livingston, II, 19; and ibid.

34. *San Angelo Standard*, 30 March, reprinted in *Devil's River News*, 6 April 1901.

35. Ibid., Ernst, *From Cowboy to Outlaw*, 13–14 and *Logan*, 50, where it is stated that Ed Kilpatrick had "sent his sisters away to join their parents at a nearby sheep camp." Tom Chaney also understood that "Old Will [Carver] and [Ben?] Kilpatrick took some old guy [Thornton] for a spy." (Chaney to Mosley, FWP).

36. *Devil's River News* and *San Angelo Standard*, 6 April 1901.

37. *Globe-Democrat*, 12 December, reprinted in *San Angelo Standard*, 21 December 1901.

38. Loomis, 66–7.

39. *San Angelo Standard*, 6 April, reprinted in *Devil's River News*, 13 April 1901; Livingston, II, 19–20 (in which Thornton is incorrectly referred to as a sheriff). MacBryde, 23, says that the gang camped on the Byler ranch immediately after the murder, which cannot have been so; they might, however, have sheltered there a week or so later.

40. *San Angelo Standard*, 13 April 1901. The surmise then was that the horses had been abandoned on April 4 by the men who had fled from Sonora on the night of the 2nd, but the combined facts that three of the men at the Kilpatrick place when Thornton was killed fled the scene by buggy—and without their saddle horses—and that the fourth man later met them on the T Half Circle range, favor the conclusion that this fourth man had planted the saddle horses as a relay to assist their flight. This accounts for the temporary separation of the fourth man from the others. This man was surely Carver, the only one with the detailed knowledge to prepare the retreat and the local connections to place the horses with someone in the Sherwood vicinity who could be trusted to keep an eye on them. The Kilpatricks and Logan appear, moreover, to have visited Sonora earlier that day. The gang are also known to have bought fresh saddle stock on March 31 or April 1.

41. *Devil's River News* and *San Angelo Standard*, 6 April 1901.

42. Besides the T Half Circle, Sol and Max B. Mayer owned one of the two principal general stores in Sonora; the other belonged to the brothers John and James Hagerlund. Max married the daughter of another local cattleman, F.M. Drake.

   On 22 October 1899, two Syrian peddlers were murdered near the T Half Circle ranch headquarters by Manuel Esquivel and Mauricio and Alvino Garca, two of whom were later killed by officers.

43. *San Angelo Standard* and *Devil's River News*, 6 April 1901; Livingston, 20; Holt, 87.

44. Palmer to author, 12 February 2002, citing a statement from the rancher but not naming him; Chaney to Mosley, FWP; Ernst, *Logan*, 50–51. Carver had many friends on both sides of the Tom Green-Schleicher County line, such as John Rae and Tom Palmer, but seems to have been closest to the Chaneys. Tom Chaney stated that the gang intended to go to the W.H. Chaney place *after* the robbery.

45. The wires in and out of Sonora had been completed only a year or two earlier.

46. Ernst., From *Cowboy to Outlaw*, 15; also, Logan, 51.

47. Jo-Ann Palmer, sketch map, prepared for author, March 2002; street plan in John Eaton, *Will Carver, Outlaw*, 100.
48. *San Angelo Standard*, 21 July and 25 August 1900.
49. See n. 43, 46, 47; Mrs. Palmer, in a comment accompanying sketch map, as cited, points out that Carver knew all along that he could obtain oats from the Owens bakery, and if he had had no other reason for visiting town at night, he could have gone straight to the bakery, bought the oats, and returned to camp without being noticed.
50. Davis had been elected sheriff for the usual two-year term in 1892 (*San Angelo Standard*, 12 November 1892).
51. Ibid., 17 March 1900.
52. Holt, 90.
53. El Paso and Albuquerque dispatches in *San Francisco Chronicle*, 7 and 8 June; El Paso dispatch of June 12 in *San Angelo Standard*, 15 June 1901.
54. *San Angelo Standard* and *Devil's River News*, 6 April 1901.
55. Ibid., and *Devil's River News*, 13 April 1901; Palmer to author, 12 February 2002 and 12 June 2007.
56. Ibid., and Ernst, *From Cowboy to Outlaw*, n. 17. *Irion County Record*, in *San Angelo Standard*, 2 February 1896, reported that Archie Kuykendall had roped a deer.
57. Ibid. The *Standard* version of the report of 6 April 1901 misprinted the number of the .45 as 20,916.
58. *Certified Copy of Inquest: Will Carver, 3 April 1901*.
59. *Devil's River News*, 13 April 1901; Holt, 91. Details of the funeral are in Ernst, *From Cowboy to Outlaw*, 19, from research credited to Jo-Ann Palmer.
60. *Devil's River News*, 6 July 1901, as quoted in Ernst, loc. cit. Some of the particulars in Holt are at variance with the foregoing. Palmer, notes for author, March 2002, in margins of a copy of Holt's article, provides corrections.
61. *San Angelo Standard*, 27 July 1901. Holt, loc. cit., adds that Boosie Sharp received $65 for the gun.
62. *Globe-Democrat*, 7 November, in *San Angelo Standard*, 16 November 1901; Ernst, *Women*, 22.
63. Livingston, II, 20–1; Sutton County Historical Society, ms. addenda to Ernst, *From Cowboy to Outlaw*, copy to author, quoting R.E. Taylor, of Midland, Texas, whose father, Dr. A.L. Taylor, treated both the wounded men.
64. *San Angelo Standard*, 27 April, *Devil's River News*, 27 April and 4 May 1901; Soule, 47–8, citing Concho County court records.
65. Phillip J. Rasch, "Finis for Red Weaver," (London, English Westerners' Society *Brand Book*, Vol. 2, No. 3 (January 1956), 17–18, is brief but well sourced. Rasch quotes Holliman as having told Deputy Sheriff Percy Bonebrake that he was was "so scared he didn't even know he fired." As for the spelling of the name of Weaver's killer, French (*Some Recollections*, 222 and thereafter), who knew the family over a period of several years and may have been more literate than other contemporary commentators—certainly more so than the brothers themselves—uses the form Holomon. Nonetheless, French was ignorant of the youngest brother's first name; he surmised, incorrectly, that "Pad" was short for Patrick. Rasch accepted the form Holliman, used also by the *Silver City Independent* and by Siringo, *A Cowboy Detective*, 356, who refers to Pad as Jim. H.A. Hoover, *Tales from the Bloated Goat: Early Days in Mogollon*, 48, who also knew the family, has their name as Hollimon. The author has undogmatically plumped for Holliman.
66. *Silver City Independent*, 16 April 1901.
67. Afton, Wyoming, *Star Valley Press*, 25 April 1902, quoted in Soule, 37.

68. French, *Further Recollections*, 508–9. Cunningham makes no reference to the killing anywhere in his four recorded conversations with Lou Blachly.
69. Soule, loc. cit.
70. Powe to Blachly, tape 236, undated, transcript p. 1.
71. Stevens to Blachly, tape 334, 28 January 1953, transcript p. 11. See Bryan, *True Tales*, 13–32, for an excellent short account of Stevens's life. Bryan, like Lou Blachly, interviewed Stevens many times.
72. Culley, 48.

NOTES TO CHAPTER 21

1. His reflections, rationalizations, and recriminations were most fully reported in the *Denver Rocky Mountain News* and *Denver Republican*, 28 April 1901. See n. 29.
2. *San Angelo Standard*, 5 January 1901.
3. *New Mexican*, 5 September 1900.
4. No. 896—*Territory of New Mexico vs. Thomas Ketchum, Appellant*, in *Reports of Cases Determined in the Supreme Court of the Territory of New Mexico, from February 1, 1897 to August 30, 1901*—Charles G. Gildersleeve, Reporter, Volume X, 718–25; *New Mexican*, 25 January 1901.
5. *Reports*, ibid., 723–4.
6. Ibid., 725; El Paso dispatch February 25, in *San Angelo Standard*, 2 March 1901. The hearing is summarized in Poldervaart, 182.
7. *Rocky Mountain News*, 20 March; telegram, Santa Fe, March 22, 2:50 p.m., in *San Angelo Standard*, 23 March 1901; Stanley, 130.
8. Clark, II, 21.
9. Burton, *Bureaucracy*, 35–9; Tanner & Tanner, *Last of the Old-Time Outlaws*, 126–8 and 304 (n. 26).
10. Wilson, 59, was the first to state between book covers that the original Black Jack was not Tom Ketchum, though he either did not know the Christian surname or chose to suppress it. That was in 1915, a dozen years before the publication of Charles Siringo's assertion that he had learned in the fall of 1925 that the man was William Christenson, "one of my dear cowboy chums" in the early 1880s (*Riata and Spurs*, rev. ed., 192). (But since Christian was only nine years old in 1880, he could scarcely have been a cowboy contemporary of Siringo, whose range-riding days ended in 1884; besides, Siringo would surely not have misnamed Christian as "Christianson," had he known him personally at any time or in any station in life.) At about this time (1927), however, Carl Livingston was beginning to collect material for a series of articles on what he loosely called the Black Jack gang. Livingston learned from Charles Ballard, Fred Higgins, and others in eastern New Mexico that Black Jack was one of the Christian brothers, and approached Clark on the same subject. This, and the publication of Livingston's series in the *Roswell Record* a year or two later, may have forced Clark's hand. His two-part article, "William Christian, alias Black Jack," appeared in *Progressive Arizona and the Great Southwest* at the beginning of 1930, a few months before Livingston reached a sizable international readership with publication in the popular monthly magazine, *Wide World*. Among the many persons living in the Southwest in the 1920s who knew that one or other of the Christian brothers was Black Jack were Len Alverson, Mack Axford, Fred Bennett, Hiram Dow (son of Les Dow, who killed Bob Hayes, of the Black Jack gang, but was murdered three months later), Dee Harkey, Sam Hayhurst, Jim Herron, A.L. Peck (once editor of the Nogales, Ariz., *Border*

Vidette), Tuck Potter, and Scott White, most of whom put their reminiscences onto paper in later years and might have done so before that, had they been asked.

11. See n. 8.

12. Fitzpatrick; Otero, 121–3. See also Chapter 16.

13. Fitzpatrick, Cooke, tape recording, Otero, loc. cit., Culley, 55–6. Culley states (53) that Grumbles was an uncle of Idelle Culley, Jack's daughter-in-law.

14. Otero, loc. cit.

15. Ibid.

16. *Rocky Mountain News*, 27 April 1901.

17. Its validity could not have been conceded without undoing the whole work of territorial government and undermining the very basis of its existence. The case that it was invalid any-way was well put by the Attorney General of Colorado, in *Rocky Mountain News*, ibid. Ketchum's attorneys may have taken the same view.

18. *New Mexican*, 25 April 1901; entry in register of Territorial Penitentiary, with note of order of removal issued by W.J. Mills, Trujillo to Cooke, as cited. A. Thompson quotes the prison entry in *Clayton ms.*, 50, and *Open Range Days*, 187, though in the latter he erroneously cites Ketchum's prison number as 132, instead of 130. Ketchum's early removal was anticipated, and its reasons set out, in the *Raton Range*, 18 April 1901, quoted Stanley, 130–1.

19. Culley, 48–9.

20. Clayton dispatches of April 24 in *San Francisco Chronicle*, and April 25 in unidentified newspaper quoted Titsworth, II, 23; *Raton Range*, 25 April 1901, quoted Stanley, 132.

21. Fitzpatrick and ibid.

22. *Rocky Mountain News* and *Denver Post*, both 27 April, reported a drop of five feet six and five feet nine, respectively; a Clayton dispatch of April 26 in the *San Francisco Chronicle* and (abridged) in *Santa Fe New Mexican*, 27 April 1901, stated that Ketchum had been given a seven-foot drop.

23. *Denver Post* and *Denver Times*, both 25 April; Denver dispatch in *San Francisco Chronicle*, 25 April; *New Mexican*, 27 April 1901; Titsworth, II, 21 (rep. part of *Times* report, unattrib-uted). The slender Pinkerton file on the Ketchums shows that at least three New York papers reported the "false reprieve"—the *Times* and *Sun* on April 25, the *Journal* next day.

24. *Denver Times*, 25 April 1901.

25. Bingham's dispatches carried his by-line—a rarity for domestic news reports in those days. The identification in Thompson and the Guyers as the *Republican* and *Times* correspondents can be supported by both internal and external evidence: for example, the *Times* correspon-dent's reference to having fixed Ketchum's tie (which he described as "white," although it looks darker than that in the pre-execution photographs of Ketchum), at a time when only the Guyers were with him, and the reappearance in Thompson's published works of at least one exchange reported in the *Republican*. Both Thompson and George Guyer were career journal-ists (among other things).

26. *Denver Post*, 26 April 1901.

27. *Denver Republican*, 27 April 1901. George Musgrave shot and killed George Parker on October 19, 1896. (Tanner & Tanner, *Last of the Old-Time Outlaws*, 69–72.) In 1910 Musgrave stood trial at Roswell, New Mexico, and was acquitted. He died in Paraguay on August 15, 1947.

28. French, *Further Recollections*, 511–2. None of the newspapers seen by the author refer directly to this natural but impracticable desire; but the *Denver Post*, 26 April 1901, seems to have done so by implication: "He has been given everything that his fancy dictated, but one other request he urged frequently was denied him."

29. French, ibid., 512. The *Denver Times*, 26 April, reprinted with additions in next day's *New Mexican*, recorded that "Ketchum made the strange request that he be buried face downward," without any hint of the scurrilous overtones supplied by French. *The Rocky Mountain News*, 27 April 1901, was no less plain-colored. We may believe that French wrote what he heard; and the remarks French, or his informants, attributed to Ketchum may have been true to the desperado's character. The failure of family newspapers to report them says nothing for or against the veracity of French's story. The variation co-starring Harrington is in Bryan, *Ruffians*, 305.

30. *Denver Post*, 26 April; *Denver Republican* and *Rocky Mountain News*, 27 April 1901.

31. The letter was printed in many newspapers, including the *Denver Post*, 26 April, reprinted *New Mexican*, 27 April, *Rocky Mountain News* and *New York Times*, both 27 April, and *Silver City Independent*, 30 April 1901. The *News* referred to Ed Bullin, the *Times* to Ed Bullen, and the *Post* and the *Independent* to Ed Cullin, but the other names were also misspelled: Alverson as Albertson, Warderman as Waterman, and Hoffman, sometimes, as Huffman. The text is also given in Hovey/Sturges, 51, with Ed's name given correctly as Cullen, and A. Thompson, *Albuquerque ms.*, 93–4, where Ed makes another appearance as Bullin.

32. *Denver Times*, 26 April; *Denver Republican* and *New Mexican*, both 27 April 1901; Fitzpatrick; Cooke, tape recording; A. Thompson, *Clayton ms.*, 51, *Open Range Days*, 188; Law to Cooke, as cited.

33. As to the extent of Berry's assistance to Tom, the *Denver Evening Post*, 26 April, put the figure at $250, but the *Denver Republican*, 28 April and the *Rocky Mountain News*, 27 and 28 April, all say $150. The *Denver Times*, 25 April, stated that Berry had paid for Tom's appeal. The quotation in the text is from the *News*, 27 April.

In its issue of 28 April, the *News* declared that it was printing Ketchum's ante mortem statement "as taken down by a stenographer word for word." Its direct competitor, the *Denver Republican*, also announced on the same day that it was reproducing the statement in its entirety. Neither paper was quite as good as its word. Comparison of the two discloses one or two passages in the *News* that are missing from the *Republican*, and several paragraphs or sentences in the *Republican* that the *News* skipped; as between the two, the *Republican* is very slightly the longer. In a few places, the *News* made Tom's speech more grammatical—or, just possibly, the *Republican* made it less grammatical—than it really was. The *Denver Post* published a condensed version, with variations of its own, and its evening rival, the *Denver Times*, did not add much to the excerpts it published on the 26th. The extracts in the *San Francisco Chronicle* are similar to, but not the same as, those in the *Post*. Most of the textual inconsistencies are in the phraseology or in the spelling of proper names, rather than in the substance. A notable exception is that, in the summary of Ketchum's remarks sent by Guyer to such papers as the *New Mexican* and the *San Angelo Standard*, Leahy joined Fort and Reno as one of those whom Ketchum hoped to greet in hell within the twelvemonth. On this point the Guyer version is likely to be correct; the stenographer used by the *News* and *Republican* may have failed to catch Leahy's name. The obvious explanation is that both Guyer and a *Post* reporter made their own notes and transcriptions from Ketchum's statement, or parts of it. Some differences in the wording of the various press accounts could have been reportorial, others editorial.

Tom's anecdote about his conversation with Carver in Hole-in-the-Wall is in Titsworth, II, 21. It bears a stronger semblance of authenticity than his later attempt to ascribe similar words and sentiments to Bronco Bill Walters.

34. There are innumerable accounts of the outlaw's last hours, minutes, and moments. The *Clayton Enterprise* provided exhaustive coverage for its own readers and shorter telegraphic accounts for papers as far afield as San Francisco and New York. Its main reports were the same as those in the *Denver Post*. Press interest elsewhere was most intense in Denver, with five

dailies (*Republican, Times, News, Post,* and *Colorado Sun*) and Trinidad, with two (*Chronicle-News* and *Advertiser-Sentinel*). The *Santa Fe Daily New Mexican* of 27 April published six dispatches from Clayton and Denver, including two items from the previous evening's *Denver Post* and two from the *Denver Times*; one of the latter was slightly enlarged by the correspondent who dispatched it. Stanley, 133–9, uses the *Clayton Enterprise*, copiously supplemented by his own imagination; more interestingly, he reprints (142–5) the recollections of an eyewitness, George Hayden, first published in the Amarillo, Texas, *Sunday Globe News,* 24 July 1955. Salome Garcia had invited Jack Ellison, a deputy sheriff from nearby Hartley County, Texas, to attend the execution, and Hayden accompanied him. Bartholomew, 93–5, is brief, but accurate in most respects; no particular source is identified or identifiable. Larry D. Ball, in his early study "Black Jack Ketchum: The Birth of a Folk Hero," Jonesboro, Ark., Arkansas State University, *Mid-South Folklore,* Vol. 1, No. 1 (Spring 1973), 19–25, relies mainly on the Denver *Rocky Mountain News.* Secrest, 57–9, bases his account principally on the reports of the *Denver Times.* The newspaper accounts on which the present writer has chosen to depend are, chiefly, the *Rocky Mountain News,* 26, 27, and 28 April; *Denver Republican,* 26, 27, 28 April; *Denver Post,* 25, 26, 27, 28, 29 April; *Denver Times,* 25, 26, 27 April; and *San Francisco Chronicle,* 27 April 1901, whose dispatch from Clayton contained passages absent from the Denver papers seen by the author. (The fifth Denver paper, the *Sun,* was not looked at.) The Clayton dispatch of April 26, in Titsworth, II, 22–3, and uncredited, like most of Titsworth's clippings, was copied almost verbatim from the *Clayton Enterprise* or *Denver Post* (most of whose reporting came from the same writer or writers). The *New Mexican* was an afternoon or evening paper, but, since the whole of its extensive coverage came from reporters employed by the Clayton and Denver press, most of it had to wait for the issue of the 27th before getting into print. The *San Angelo Standard,* 27 April 1901, published John Guyer's telegram unaltered and over his name. As the Ketchums' local paper, its treatment of the execution is significant; it allotted all due prominence to the drama and horror of the event, but put nothing below the headlines except the Guyer telegram. Many of its readers had known Tom before he acquired notoriety; some had been more closely in touch with him thereafter than they might have cared to make public. Editor Murphy's grounds for printing not a word about Tom's background, and saying nothing about the evidence or suspicions connecting him with various crimes in Texas, may have been that all that needed to be known about these things was known already, and that what was not known would do as well to remain that way.

Among sources other than contemporary newspaper articles, those most valued by the author have been the Fitzpatrick and Cooke tape recordings, information from Guyer included in Goldianne Thompson and others, 151–2, and Otero, 125–7.

Albert Thompson described the closing scenes of Ketchum's life in the *Albuquerque ms.,* 181–94 and *Clayton ms.,* 50–51. His 1930s recollections occasionally tally with what he wrote for the *Denver Republican* in 1901; often they do not.

Onlookers from behind the stockade may have taken photographs, or attempted to do so, but the only photographer who was allowed into the yard and whose name is known is W.A. White, from the studio of G.J. Wheatley. Five scenes from the execution have been published, all of which were his. Various witnesses noted the time as Ketchum walked up to the foot of the gallows, but their reports are not always in accord. Albert Thompson wrote that Ketchum was brought outside at twelve minutes past one; other press correspondents differed over whether the condemned man was taken into the yard at 1:14 or 1:15; Guyer stated that Ketchum ascended the scaffold at 1:17 and took the long drop at 1:21; and the *Rocky Mountain News* reporter, whose watch must have been ahead of the others, reported that the trap was sprung at 1:23. It is likely that Ketchum started his last walk a minute or two before a quarter past one and was jerked to eternity four or five minutes afterwards. The true explanation for the reporters' disagreements over the exact time may be that some correspondents were too preoccupied with the drama onstage to think of looking at their watches until afterwards.

35. In *Not So Wild, the Old West*, Clara Toombs Harvey mentions that her father, the lawyer O.T. Toombs, was present at the execution, but not that (through chance or otherwise) she was riding past the stockade when the trap was sprung. This was among the stories garnered by Phil Cooke in Clayton in 1968.

Less than a year later, Guyer himself looked briefly as if he might become a subject for a hanging. On 27 March 1902 he shot and killed William E. Searls, who had been appointed to succeed him as postmaster (*San Francisco Chronicle*, 28 March 1902). According to the press correspondent, there was some talk of a lynching before Guyer was arrested and jailed by Sheriff Garcia. But Harvey states that the killing was justifiable and that the decision not to prosecute Guyer met with general approval.

36. *Rocky Mountain News* and *Denver Post*, 27 April 1901 (part of the latter rep.Titsworth, II, 30, unattributed); Cunningham, to Blachly, tape recording 129, as cited, 9.

37. A. Thompson, *Clayton ms.*, 51, and *Open Range Days*, 190–1.

38. *Denver Post*, 28 April 1901 (rep. Titsworth, II, 31, unattributed.).

39. Goldianne Thompson and others, 152–3.

40. The *Rocky Mountain News*, 27 April 1901, included the assertion in its headline ("Tom Ketchum Hurls Himself Downward"). Refutation was immediate; for example, that after-noon's *Denver Post*. That did not stop others from believing it; see Culley, 50, citing the opin-ion of a friend, Albert Shaw.

41. Clayton dispatch in *San Francisco Chronicle* and *Denver Post*, both 27 April 1901; A. Thompson, *Clayton ms.*, 40.

42. *Denver Post*, ibid., *Denver Times*, 2 and 9 May 1901, cited in Secrest, 59–60. Howe was mis-taken in saying that the drop was one of just five feet. For an authoritative insight into the mechanics and protocols of the executioner's art, see John Ellis, *Diary of a Hangman*, 25, 63, 93, 197, 207, 224, and many other places. The essence of Ellis's formula was the lighter the pris-oner, the longer the drop, though he would also take account of age and sex. Thus a man weighing 118 pounds but almost six foot tall received eight feet; another who was scarcely over five foot tall, but weighed 138 pounds, was allocated seven feet; and a woman five foot eight in height and weighing 130 pounds was given six feet ten inches—ten inches greater than the drop required for a man of the same height and weight. Since Ellis (who eventually commit-ted suicide, though not by hanging) officiated as principal or assistant at 203 executions in the United Kingdom, he spoke from a position of authority. He did say, however, that some of his predecessors had preferred a shorter drop.

43. *Denver Post*, 26 April 1901, reprinted next day in various papers, including *New Mexican*.

44. Soule, 51.

45. *San Angelo Standard*, 27 April 1901. Fred Dodge, who was below the scaffold when the body parted company with the rope, described the execution as the "most revolting and gruesome" he had ever seen (Hunter, *Album of Gunfighters*, 146). The headline of the *Silver City Independent*, 30 April 1901, included one of the same adjectives, though with a different spelling: "Black Jack's End was Grewsome." It must have been one of the half-dozen most bar-barously mismanaged legal executions enacted in the United States during the past quarter-century. The government of the Territory of New Mexico was not so much aghast at the squalor of the proceedings as appalled by the number of people who had seen them and the festive atmosphere surrounding them. The territorial legislative assembly, convening on January 19, 1903, amended the statute regulating the management of executions by providing that, thereafter, all executions were to be "conducted privately" before no more than twenty witnesses "including members of the medical profession, officers of the law, clergymen and

representatives of the press, "as nominated by the county sheriff and approved by the district judge." The new law also required the sheriff to cause an enclosure to be erected around the gallows, at a cost to the public purse of no more than $200 (*Acts of the Legislative Assembly of the Territory of New Mexico, Thirty-seventh Session*: Chapter 76—Approved March 17, 1903).
46. Loomis, 66. The unheeded invitation from "Woodyard Chipling" had appeared in ibid., 9 September 1899.
    At the time of the execution, two young brothers named Francis and Harrison Hamer were working as wranglers for Berry Ketchum. Both were to earn fame in the field of law enforcement. Harrison Hamer is best remembered for his part in the hunt for the Newton brothers' gang in the 1920s, Frank for his central role in the destruction of Clyde Barrow and Bonnie Parker. Harrison Hamer's great-grandson married the great-granddaughter of Elizabeth Smith, née Ketchum—a sister of Berry, Sam, and Tom (Berry Spradley to author, 18 and 19 July 2005).
47. A. Thompson, *Clayton ms.*, 41, 47–8, further compressed in *Open Range Days*, 182. The imprint of Shield's contribution is far more apparent in the early chapters of Thompson's unpublished *Albuquerque ms.* It is easily inferred that Shield and one or two other of Thompson's informants in Southwest Texas, offered statements with which they did not wish their names to be publicly connected.

NOTES TO CHAPTER 22

1. The Mesa Hawks spent several months stealing cattle in eastern New Mexico, then held up the post office at Revuelto, a saloon and general store at newly founded Tucumcari, and the post office and store at Fort Sumner, where Frank Potter killed a boy named Felipe Bobien (or Beaubien). After that, the gang scattered. Four of its members were soon captured; as far as is known, the other three—Hawkins, Potter, and Frank Isbell—were never caught. Some of the press reports about them were unfounded or over-sensational, partly because the activities and identities of other criminals were confused with theirs. An extended article in the *Rocky Mountain News*, printed in March or April of 1902 (unfortunately the author failed both to keep a copy of the piece and to take a note of its date) put their operations on a more consistently factual basis. Other sources include: *Indictment*, Guadalupe County, N.M., 31 March, certified copy 17 November 1902, in 57 Congress, II Session, *Senate Document 36*, Exhibit A, 239; dispatches in *San Francisco Chronicle*, 25 January, 10 February, 1 March; *New Mexican*, 21 October, 11, 13, 15, 17 November; *El Paso Times*, 13 February, 6 and 9 March; *Chicago Tribune*, 23 January; Clifton, Arizona, *Copper Era*, 3 April 1902; John Tanner to author, 27 June 2000, with New Mexico Territorial Penitentiary records for George Cook, Witt Neil (or Neil Witt), alias Shorty Daniels, John W. Smith, and George R. Massagee; ibid., 19 April 2005, citing Frederick W. Nolan, "Here He Lies," WOLA *Journal*, Vol. XII No. 1 (Spring 2003); ibid., 4 and 17 October and 10 November 2006, with copies of numerous primary and secondary research materials; Joseph Miller, ed., *The Arizona Rangers*, 43–7 and 254–5—Appendix F, "Report of Captain Burton Mossman of Arrests from October 2, 1901 to July 30, 1902, where the capture of two of the gang is antedated by more than a month; Bill O'Neal, *The Arizona Rangers*, 21–2, where George Massagee is confused with George Musgrave and a non-existent "Canley Musgrave" introduced, among other errors in a brief account of the Mesa Hawks (though in most other respects the book is good).
    Douglas H. Connell, "Battle on Mesa Redonda," *True West*, Vol. 15, No. 6, Whole No. 88 (August 1968), 37, merely hints at a murderous drama in which the Hawks were marginally involved; for something like the full story, see John (Dub) Bedingfield, "The Spikes-Gholson

Feud," *Real West*, Vol. 26, No. 206 (December 1985), 18, 32–35, copy to the author from John Tanner.

2. Reward notice and descriptions of Hawkins and McCorkle in *New Mexico Mounted Police; Wanted Posters Book 1*, State Archives of New Mexico, Santa Fe; Santa Fe and El Paso dispatches in *San Francisco Chronicle*, 14 and 16 December; *New Mexican*, 12 and 13 December 1902.

3. Kemp and Dykes, 168–170, according to which the bank robbers, one of whom Kemp named as Big Ed Kilpatrick, changed horses at his camp in the Black Range. Kemp, Sr., had known Kilpatrick for several years, and he certainly knew something about the Hillsboro bank robbery, for he was at first accused of having had a hand in it. On page 154 of the book, he says, or is made to say, that Big Ed Kilpatrick's "legal" name was Ben Kilpatrick and that he was killed during an attempt to rob a Southern Pacific train. This piece of misinformation may have been inserted by Dykes; or, if it was not, he should have known enough to be able to correct it. The Kemps and Dykes patently did not know that Ben Kilpatrick had a brother named Ed, did not know the date of the Hillsboro robbery, and did not know that Ben was in prison at the time of its occurrence.

In March 1905, two tramp bandits were killed at Separ, New Mexico, and one of them was named as McCorkle. It was soon learned, however, that the pair were George and Edwin Gates, two of the most-traveled desperadoes in the United States. (*New Mexican*, 18, 20, 29 March, *San Francisco Chronicle*, 11 and 16 April 1905). John Boessenecker, *Badge and Buckshot*, 200–237, has a good account of the Gates boys' crime rampage. One of the principal characters in Eugene Manlove Rhodes's *The Trusty Knaves* is a fugitive outlaw known as Bill Hawkins, whom another of the characters persistently misnames Henry Hawkins, and who turns out to be the Oklahoma bandit, Bill Doolin, lying low after breaking jail. Rhodes's preface carried the statement that the incidents depicted in the novel were of actual occurrence; when Doolin left the ranch, wrote Rhodes, "he rode straight to his death." The author does not believe it. Only seven weeks separated Doolin's escape on July 5, 1896 and his death on the following August 25. All the indications are that he remained in Oklahoma and Indian Territory throughout that period. Rhodes does not explain why he chose the name Hawkins for his outlaw; but then, in 1931, when the novel was published, few people even in New Mexico remembered the local outlaw, Henry Hawkins, alias Bill Hawkins, whereas Doolin's name and notoriety had been kept alive by the writings of Graves, E.D. Nix, and a lengthening succession of others. Rhodes must have known of the real Hawkins, may well have known him personally, and may have sheltered him. At the very least, therefore, he took Hawkins's name but substituted the persona of the more glamorous Doolin. The real Hawkins may, or may not, have figured in one or more of the incidents or conversations in the story. If so, the year would have been more like 1902 or 1903 than 1896.

4. Soule, 47–8.

5. Stats. L., XXXII, 728—Chap. 1376, Sec. 3; Karen Holliday Tanner and John D. Tanner, Jr., "Good Rewards but Bad Justice," working draft (copy with author)—final version. "Rewards and Justice Did Not Mix: the Logan, New Mexico, Train Robbery," *Journal* of the Wild West Historical Association, Vol. I, No. 1 (February 2008), 13–28 and 50. The indictment charged the defendants with the theft of money and other property to the value of $1,000—exactly $1,000 more than the loss publicly acknowledged by the express company.

The four alleged suspects were caught in the Chickasaw Nation by Deputy U.S. Marshal Tillman "Tom" Lilly and others, "after a six weeks search." A Las Vegas, N.M., dispatch of 19 November 1904 in that evening's *New Mexican*, reporting the arrival of John and James Black and John Murphy at the county jail, mentioned that the fourth man, Tom Boswell, was killed in an attempted jail break "a week ago last Saturday." The Blacks (real names, Bob and Joe Bishop) and Murphy (real name, Zerah "Zay"McPherson) were convicted in federal court at their third trial in November 1906 and sent to Leavenworth. (Tucumcari dispatches in *New*

Mexican, 1 and 2 August; reward offer in ibid., 6 August; Las Vegas dispatch in ibid., 19 November 1904; ibid., 15 and 19 May 1905; El Paso dispatches in *San Francisco Chronicle*, 31 July, 1, 2, 4 August 1904. Richard Graves, *Oklahoma Outlaws*, 12–13, describes the capture of the gang in Indian Territory, as related by Madsen. See, also, Ball, *U.S. Marshals*, 201–3, 212.) The case has been discussed by John Tanner and the author in a series of twenty letters written between February and October, 2007.

5. *St. Louis Post-Dispatch*, 7 November, and *St. Louis Republic*, 8 November 1901; Horan, *The Outlaws*, 260.

7. *San Angelo Standard*, 6 January and 27 October 1900; McBryde, 26–7.

8. *St. Louis Republic*, 8 November 1901.

9. Helena dispatches in *Globe-Democrat*, 20 and 30 August, 5 October 1893, 11 January 1894; Boston, Mass., *Herald*, in ibid., 30 October; letter, Blackfoot Agency, Mont., October 14, to *New York Sun*, in ibid., 6 November 1893; *San Francisco Chronicle*, 20 April 1902; Horan and Sann. 219 (details on P.N.D.A. reward poster; the same data is shown on a later poster, in Lynch, 15); Waller, 40–1.

10. McBryde, 22.

11. *San Angelo Standard*, 11 September 1901.

12. Dispatches from Great Falls, Havre, Anaconda, and Malta, Mont., and St. Paul, Minn., in *San Francisco Chronicle*, 4, 5, 6, 7, 8, and 9 July 1901; *Dallas News*, 28 October, in *San Angelo Standard*, 2 November; St. Louis dispatch of November 13 in ibid., 16 November 1901; Kelly, 282–6; Waller, 167–178; Anon., (Lamb?) ed., Swallow, 88–95; Pointer, 181–3; Patterson, 187–191; Soule, 54–6; and (the best) Lynch, 8–16 and Ernst, *Logan*, 51–5. Kelly includes Cassidy and Longabaugh among the robbers; the putative Lamb does the same, adding that Jim Thornhill "had charge of the relay horses;" Pointer includes Thornhill in an assault force of four, but excludes Cassidy and Longabaugh; Waller thinks Longabaugh could have been the one otherwise identified as Hanks; and Patterson, while non-committal about Cassidy's participation, believes there were four or more robbers on the scene. All are wrong in at least one respect. The three robbers were Logan, Kilpatrick, and Hanks, and they are unmistakably described in the reward notice in Horan, *Outlaws*, 253. This, however, did not stop Horan from appending a note that the trio were Cassidy, Logan, and Longabaugh; but then, Horan was miraculously able to ignore the findings of his own research.

13. Waller, 178–183; Ernst *Logan*, 55; "Logan's Log."

14. Knoxville, Tenn., dispatch, *San Antonio Express*, 18 December, reprinted in *San Angelo Standard*, 21 December 1901; Lynch. 102–5; Waller, 185; Ernst, *Logan*, 57.

15. Nashville, Tenn., dispatch in *Chicago Tribune*, 28 October 1901; Waller, 184–7, though Rogers's arrest is misdated October 10; Lynch, 18, 26–34 (verbatim, from Nashville, Tenn., *American*) Ernst, *Logan*, 59. Hanks was initially mistaken for Cassidy; but the error was soon apparent, except to Livingston, who, nearly thirty years later, in II, 21, and III, 94–5, invokes the anonymous authority of "a reliable man now in New Mexico" to misidentify Hanks as Cassidy and Rogers as Laura Bullion.

16. *San Angelo Standard*, 14, 21, 28 September 1901.

17. The real J.W. (Jim) Rose lived near Eden, close to the Kilpatrick place. From time to time his buying or selling or shipping of cattle would be mentioned in the *Conch Herald* and *San Angelo Standard*. On 16 December 1901 the *Standard* called Ben Kilpatrick's theft of Rose's name "a grave injustice to a good man and good citizen."

18. St. Louis dispatches of November 6 and 7 in *San Angelo Standard*, 9 November; *Globe-Democrat*, 7 November, reprinted in ibid., 16 November 1901.

19. The passage in quotation marks is an amalgam of the *Post-Dispatch* and *Globe-Democrat* variants of whatever form of words Desmond used.

20. *St. Louis Republic*, 8 November 1901. All the St. Louis papers covered Kilpatrick's interrogation in detail.
21. *San Angelo Standard*, 16 November 1901.
22. *Globe-Democrat*, 9 November 1901.
The visitor's account of Longabaugh's arrest in 1889 was grossly inaccurate. This, and his misidentification of Kilpatrick as Longabaugh, at first convinced the author that he was a hoaxer and an impostor. He could not have been either B.F. Fowler, district attorney of Crook County, Wyoming, when Longabaugh was convicted of theft, or H.A. Alden, who succeeded Fowler in 1889. The author's suspicion was that he may have been mentally unsound, or the worse for drink, or both, and that the reporter may have spotted this: there could have been a smirk behind the *Globe-Democrat's* description of the visitor as "a citizen of St. Louis . . . connected with one of the breweries." At that time the writer had not seen Wayne Kindred's article "The Hunt for the Great Northern Train Robbers," NOLA *Quarterly*, Vol. XXV, No. 1 (January-March 2000), 1, 3–9. Kindred finds that the man revisited the *Globe-Democrat* offices a couple of days later, identified himself as Charles Fesenfelt, repeated that he had prosecuted Longabaugh in Wyoming in 1889, and admitted that was no longer sure that the St. Louis prisoner was him: ibid., 7 and 9 (n. 9), citing *Globe-Democrat*, 11 November 1901.
Nixon's encounter with Kilpatrick, and his account of the Winnemucca robbery of 1900 were reported in the *Globe-Democrat* of 12 December 1901.
23. St. Louis dispatches of November 27, December 12 and 13, in *San Angelo Standard*, 30 November and 21 December 1901.
24. Lynch, 40–79, has the definitive account, with Waller, 201–15, as a serviceable alternative and Ernst, *Logan*, 60–61, as a concise one. Also, Knoxville dispatches of December 14, 15, 17 in *San Angelo Standard*, 21 December 1901.
25. Hanks's killing was reported, and his career, including his visit to Calaveras County California, summarized in the *San Francisco Chronicle*, 20 April 1902. Bartholomew, 99–100 uses the *San Antonio Light*, and both Waller, 197–9, and Soule, 72–3, follow the *San Antonio Express*, 16 April 1902 and successive dates. Most surprisingly, the *San Angelo Standard* found no room for the shooting, though on 21 June 1902 it copied an item from the *Coleman Democrat*, reporting the arrest of Charley's brother, Wyatt Hanks, for handling currency stolen at Wagner.
26. Dispatches from Salida, Denver, Telluride, and Gunnison, Colo., in *San Francisco Chronicle* 15, 16, 20 July; Salida dispatch in *San Angelo Standard*, 19 July 1902; George G. Everett, *The Cavalcade of Railroads in Central Colorado*, 54–8, reprinting dispatches in *Rocky Mountain News*, 15 and 16 July 1902. Siringo, *A Cowboy Detective*, 366, implicates Cruzan but does not identify the site of the robbery, beyond stating vaguely that it was "east of Grand Junction." But it can be established that he was writing about events in the summer of 1902 (see n. 45) and there was no other D & R.G. train robbery in Colorado during that year.
27. Butte, Mont., dispatch in *San Francisco Chronicle*, 5 December 1902.
28. Red Lodge, Mont., dispatch in ibid., 7 December 1902. Linsley's photograph and description are in Horan and Sann, 192.
29. Butte, Mont., dispatches in Coffeyville, Kansas, *Daily Journal*, 12 February, and *San Francisco Chronicle*, 13, 15 February 1903.
30. Waller, 206–41; Soule, 73–4; Lynch, 136–53; Ernst, *Logan*, 64–70.
31. Denver dispatch in *San Francisco Chronicle*, 9 June 1904; Anon., ed. Swallow, 114–6; Waller 246–9; Soule, 74–7; Lynch, 154–6; Ernst, *Logan*, 71–4. Gary Williams, "New Facts About Kid Curry, last of the Wild Bunch," *The West*, Vol. 1, No. 1 (March 1964), 6–9, 68–70 (70), though several of Williams's "new facts" were already old errors. This and the following section of the Swallow book, whose anonymous author may have been Frank Lamb, are almost the only

parts of it that appear to have been derived from an "inside" source—which is not to say that every one of the book's statements about the Parachute episode is accurate or truthful. Swallow's author names the third robber only as "Bill," a Wyoming man with a wife and two children. The purposeful vagueness could have been the creature of invention posing as discretion. Soule seems inclined to believe, on debatable authority, that this third man was a Wyoming cowboy, originally from Texas, calling himself Charlie Stevens, possibly an extension of the even more pseudonymous "Bill." Dan Sheffield's credentials look to be the strongest.

32. Anon., ed. Swallow, 115; Waller, 248; Soule, 76; Lynch 156; Ernst, *Logan*, 74; all citing or alluding to contemporary newspapers.

33. Lynch, 161, n.7, citing report in the Glenwood Springs, *Avalanche Echo*, n.d.

34. New Castle [*sic*], Colo., dispatch in *San Francisco Chronicle*, 10 June 1904; Anon., ed. Swallow, 116–20; Waller, 249–52; Soule, 76–8; Lynch, 157–8, Ernst, *Logan*, 75–6.

35. Anon., ed. Swallow, 120–1; Waller, 255–6; Soule, 79–80; Williams, 70; Ernst, *Logan*, 76–81; Daniel Buck, "New Revelations About Harvey Logan Following the Parachute Train Robbery," WOLA *Journal*, Spring 1997, 6–13. Soule's belief, or assumption, that George Kilpatrick was mortally wounded by the posse cannot be sustained; George was living in Texas in March 1905, though in poor health (McBryde, 24–5). Soule shows from letters written by Ben (101–2) that the older brother was concerned by the absence of any news from or about George, but George's silence could have sprung from the justifiable fear that any letter from him to any of his relatives might be intercepted. Anon., ed. Swallow, 121 and 125, says that George was killed "when he became entangled in his rope after roping a steer belonging to Berry Ketchum . . . about 1917." This cannot be literally true, for Berry died in 1914, but may be somewhere near the truth. It may, however, relate not to George, but to his brother Ed, whose death is also said to have been accidental.

36. Cody, Wyo., special to Kansas City, Mo., *Times*, in *San Francisco Chronicle*, 2 November; Cody, Thermopolis, Casper, Cheyenne, and Basin, Wyo., and Denver, Colo., dispatches in ibid., 3, 4, 5, 6, 10, 16, 17 and 23 November 1904. For a detailed review of the crime and investigation, see Roy O'Dell, "Bank Robbery at Cody, Wyoming: A Who Done It?," English Westerners' *Tally Sheet*, Vol. 42, No. 2 (Summer 1996), 59–64.

37. Otero, 130–1; Kelly, 258–9.

38. See n. 112.

39. French, *Some Recollections*, 282–3; H.A. Hoover, "*The Gentle Train Robber*," New Mexico, January 1956, 44–5, and *Tales From the Bloated Goat: Early Days in Mogollon*, 49; John Tanner, letters to author, 20 May 1997, 27 June 2000, 23 May 2001, and in conversation, Fallbrook, California, 5 August 2001.

Kelly, 259, supports French; yet, on the preceding page, he quotes a statement from Otero that Lay's wife had told him that contrary to French's published recollection, Elzy did not visit the ranchman after leaving the penitentiary. But in 1905–6, Lay had no wife; Mary Calvert, of Baggs, Wyoming, did not become the second Mrs. Lay until 1909. Hence she was in no position to know whom Lay did or did not visit in Alma during the eighteen months of his stay. On the other hand, French could not often have been found on the Alma ranch in 1905–6, because the main WS operation was now in Colfax County and, from 1900 onwards, French was generally there. But if he visited Alma at all during that period, he and Lay could hardly not have met.

40. Dean, to Blachly, 23–4, UNM; Tanner and Tanner, *Last of the Old-Time Outlaws*, 108, 198 (n. 11, citing statement by Lewis Jones). Jones said that Black Jack, meaning Christian, carried out the robbery unassisted; Dean, who claimed to have seen Black Jack (but seems to have believed it was Ketchum, not Christian) earlier that day, told Blachly that McGinnis, who was nearby, joined Black Jack shortly afterwards and helped him rob the store. Dean's information

came from Walter Jones, who, unlike Lewis, was, in the store at the time of the holdup. Unfortunately, no reference to the robbery, or to the futile pursuit (described by Dean) that ensued, can be found in any newspaper; it is possible that the Jones brothers may have kept the story from the local press correspondents, rather than risk being treated as informers by the outlaws. The Tanners allocate the robbery to late January or early February, 1897; but the present writer is inclined to place it in mid-March of that year, when the reconstituted High Five or Black Jack gang is definitively known to have visited Frisco and to have stolen a number of horses from the neighborhood, as Dean relates. The latter date would be enough to rule out Ketchum, who had just returned to Texas. Either date would eliminate Lay/McGinnis, who was in Utah during the first four months of 1897. (Moreover, the friendly relations that existed between Lay and the Joneses after his release are hardly likely to have sprung from any participation by him in a felonious attack on premises owned and maintained by them.) Dean's "McGinnis," in this context, may have been a muddled reference to George or Van Musgrave. In any event, the robbery can safely be attributed to one or more of the Christian gang.

41. Dean, ibid., 25.

42. Lay's reappearance in Alma, his recovery of the loot, and his time with the Joneses, are in H.A. Hoover's useful but mistitled article "The Gentle Train Robber," ibid., and the chapter "William H. McGinnis, Train Robber," in Hoover's *Tales of the Bloated Goat*, as cited, 49–50, 52–3. His departure with George Musgrave for Baggs, Wyoming, and subsequent marriage to Mary Calvert, are in Tanner and Tanner, 174–6.

43. Stockbridge, to Blachly, no. 380, 2, UNM.

44. French, *Some Recollections*, 282.

45. Hoover, "Gentle Train Robber," 45, *Bloated Goat*, 52–3. In the former, Hoover declares that it was "a matter of record" that the express messenger had removed and hidden the valuables from the safe "and spun the knob" on its door. In fact, the messenger did no such thing; he could not have extracted the contents of the safe and then "spun the knob" because he could not have opened it. A through safe could only be unlocked at its destination and, usually, at one or two important intermediate stations, where the agent (but not the messenger) knew the combination. Only the local safe, or way safe could be opened by the messenger.

46. Siringo has almost no use for dates, but a chronological frame can easily be constructed for the narrative sequence of *A Cowboy Detective*, 338–366. His trip to the Alma district can only have happened in the late spring and early summer of 1902, though Siringo inadvertently lays a red herring by conveying the impression that the bank at Winnemucca had been robbed shortly before he called on Elzy Lay in the New Mexico Territorial Penitentiary. In fact, the two events were separated by twenty months, but his memory had telescoped the interval by the time he wrote about them. The Pinkertons sent Siringo out on the trail just after the Tipton train robbery of 29 August 1900. He spent the next few months in Utah and western Colorado, under instructions from Assistant Superintendent Frank Murray to make his way to Alma (340–8) from southern Utah. He reached the vicinity of St. Johns "a few days" after the murder of ex-Sheriff Beeler (14 April 1901) and arrived in Alma when the killing of Red Weaver (9 April 1901) was still of recent memory. He then returned to the Grand Junction neighborhood by way of Silver City, White Oaks, and Denver (356–9). In August he and Harvey Logan's friend Jim Ferguson traveled to Ferguson's former home near Dixon, Wyoming (360–1). When Ferguson turned back for Grand Junction, Siringo pushed on to Rawlins, Wyoming, where he remained throughout the winter of 1901–2 (361–3). While there, he made friends with Robert "Bert" Charter, an intimate of the outlaw gang. The following spring (1902) he and Charter joined Ferguson in Grand Junction. That summer they were to travel to Rawlins on horseback, but before they started out Siringo, at

Ferguson's request, visited Lay in the penitentiary, having first passed Ferguson's "secrets" to the prison authorities. From Santa Fe he went to Palisade, Colo., where he presented Ferguson with proofs of his meeting with Lay. Finally he started out for Rawlins with Bert Charter and Bert's younger brother. Near the Wyoming line they heard of the D. & R.G. train robbery of 14 July 1902 (366). Charter then told Siringo the inside story of Cassidy's and Weaver's flight from Alma in March 1900 (367–8). He then tells of spending the fall "in and around Rawlins." At this point he breaks away from his narrative line to introduce the story of the Wagner train robbery of 1901 and the capture of Ben Kilpatrick and Logan. His idea may have been to suggest that he had a hand in the investigation of this crime, but it is obvious from his timetable for September 1900–late 1902 that he could not have had any direct connection with it.

47. Hoover, "Gentle Train Robber," 45, *Bloated Goat,* 52; Tanner &Tanner, *Last of the Old-Time Outlaws,* 151, 175.

48. Tanner & Tanner, ibid., 175–9 and 315 (n. 11).

49. Hoover, "Gentle Train Robber," 45, *Bloated Goat,* 53; James Landon Lay and Descendants, "Family History Report," comp. John D. Tanner, Jr., copy to author August 2001.

50. H.A. Holmes, Sheffield, Texas, to author, 26 October 1968; Spradley to author, July 1974, and "Family History," 3; idem., October 2003, "Modified Register for John Shields." H.A. Holmes belonged to a Texas ranching family. For many years his father lived in New Mexico, during which time, as the son told the author, he was "unfortunate enough" to have Roswell for his birthplace. The family moved to Sheffield in 1906, and H.A. Holmes "worked cattle for a good many years up and down the Pecos River and followed the trail herd, stood guard around the herd, ate beans out of a tin plate, drank coffee out of a tin can, and slept on a wet saddle blanket; that is, when the cook wouldn't let me sleep in the chuck wagon."

51. *San Angelo Standard,* 10 March 1900.

52. Ibid., 16 December 1899, 14 June 1902.

53. Ibid., 11 November 1899; 13 July, 24 August, 14 September 1901.

54. Ibid., 5 and 19 October 1901; 1 and 15 February, 22 March, 12, 19, 26 April, 30 August 1902.

55. Holmes to author, 26 October 1968.

56. Louis E. Montgomery, Brady, Texas, to author, 30 April 1969. Montgomery's grandfather, Luther Montgomery, was the first while settler of San Saba County. As a youth in the late 1890s, Louis worked for "Bee" Newman, father of the bandit Bud Newman, of Carta Valley, Texas.

57. Holmes to author, 26 October 1968.

58. Ibid., *San Angelo Standard,* 26 May 1900; Spradley to author, July 1974, and "Family History."

59. Soule, 9, 87; Holmes to author, 3 December 1966 and ibid. (Holmes knew both Boone and Felix and was a pallbearer at Boone's funeral.) McBryde, 20–1, says George "spent much of the rest of his life traveling from one mineral bath to another seeking relief" from the pain of his bullet wounds. Horan, *Desperate Men,* rev. ed., 361, like Soule, misidentifies the sender of the Marlin letter as George, Sr., but, unlike Soule, covers the error by omitting the reference to "sis." It is an error that needed to be covered, for, on page 286 of the same work, Horan has George, Jr., being killed alongside Carver in 1901 and Ma Kilpatrick collecting the bodies and addressing Sheriff Briant thus: "You killed my son. We Kilpatricks will never forget that."

60. Soule, 193–5.

61. Soule, 66–92; McBryde, 24–6.

62. Soule, 92; McBryde, 26.

63. Soule, 65–9, 83–144; Dale T. Schoenberger, "The Tall Texan," *True West,* April 1992, 20, 28–32; Horan, *Wild Bunch,* 180–5, repeated in *Desperate Men,* rev. ed., 281, 361–3. On 281

Horan misidentifies the Kilpatrick place as "the Bullion ranch in Concho County." Laura's family never had a ranch anywhere; she had been raised on the Byler farm in Tom Green County.

64. Soule, 125, quoting Deputy Warden to Warden, 10 August 1909.

65. Ibid., 114–21.

66. Various dispatches in Little Rock, Ark., *Arkansas Gazette*, 23, 24, 25 April; Memphis, Tenn., and Little Rock, dispatches in *San Francisco Chronicle*, 23 and 24 April, 18 May 1901. The last of these quoted a telegram from Shawnee, I.T., alleging that five suspects had been arrested there, the sixth escaping.

67. Soule, 187–8.

68. Ibid., 143–152; 155.

69. [J. Marvin Hunter] "Black Jack Ketchum and his Gang." 315–20, (319), *Frontier Times*, Vol. 16, No. 7 (misprinted as No. 6) (April 1939); idem, "The Way of the Transgressor," ibid., Vol. 19, No. 3, December 1941, 125–8 (128). The two passages differ only in punctuation, the earlier being quoted in the present work.

70. *New York Times*, 2 November 1911; Soule, 158–9. The reference to the Rock Island's purchase of the Choctaw is from Clifford B. Hull, *Shortline Railroads of Arkansas*, 42–3.

71. *New York Times*, 8 February 1912; Soule, 159–61; 164–5 (newspaper sketch of scene).

72. Jerry M. Sullivan, "Heist in a West Texas Sandstorm," *True West*, Vol. 21, No. 22, Whole No. 120 (December 1973), 125–8 (128); Soule, 161.

73. Soule, 162–3; Holmes to author, 3 December 1965. Jim Harkey, a member of the San Saba County pioneer family, waited until his eightieth birthday before telling Holmes that, as an employee of Berry Ketchum, he had shod two of Berry's horses for Ben Kilpatrick and Jim's first cousin, Nick Grider. He was sure that Grider was Kilpatrick's companion in the holdup that followed. Holmes's information was included in *Dynamite and Six-shooter*, 166–7. Since then, Arthur Soule has proved that it was Ole Beck, alias Hobek, alias Magner, alias Flood, alias Benson, who boarded the train with Kilpatrick. The author is certain that Holmes's story was truthful, and no less sure that Holmes placed absolute faith in what Harkey told him. It may be that Grider was the man with Kilpatrick when the horses were shod. The pair could then have joined Beck and others, possibly with a car and at least one other horse, at a rendezvous nearer Dryden.

74. The most comprehensive treatment of the holdup at Baxter's Curve is in Soule, 163–82, compiled from the *San Antonio Express, San Angelo Standard-Times*, and *Dallas News*, supported by official documents. It is well supplemented by an account compiled in 2001 by C.F. Eckhardt in 2001 and drawn to the author's attention by Berry Spradley ("The Last Gasp of the Wild Bunch: Ben Kilpatrick at Baxter's Curve;" Spradley to author, April 2004). The *Express* interviews with Trousdale and the Postal Clerk, M.E. Banks, were reprinted in *Frontier Times*, Vol. 4, No. 11 (August 1927), 52–5, and, though, uncredited, form most of the basis for the account in Bartholomew, 103–8.

Waller, curiously, remarks (12) that "for some reason the San Antonio papers failed to cover the drama," but makes good use (194–7) of the *El Paso Morning Times*, 14 March 1912. Stanley, 191–4, likewise cites no source, but provides a fuller picture of the proceedings, evidently from an unnamed and unidentifiable newspaper. Stanley's source stated that Kilpatrick took $60,000 consigned to the bank at Alpine, but asked particularly for the El Paso shipment ($30,000), which Trousdale had hidden. Soule, 179, interestingly but undogmatically, considers the possibility that not only might Trousdale have met Ben while employed on a Texas ranch, circa 1900, conspired with him in 1912 to rob Wells, Fargo, and then spectacularly scuppered the deal, but that he could have put up to it by certain law enforcement officials who wanted Texas to be rid of Ben Kilpatrick. The present writer would not be a bit surprised should further research prove some of this to be correct.

75. Eckhardt, 3.

76. Holmes to author, as cited.

77. Soule, 164, 174–5; McBryde, 26.

78. Eckhardt, 4, 6.

79. McBryde, 27.

80. David Murray, *From Doane to Dillinger*. Murray's chronicle is invaluable as a synopsis of armed robbery in North America from 1775 to 1939. From the beginning of 1914 to the end of 1916, for example, Murray enumerates some eighty cases of armed bank robbery in the United States, the great majority of them in Oklahoma. In at least one-third of that number, the perpetrators rode in and out of town on horseback (and there were still other instances that Murray has missed). Even a decade and more afterwards, there were bank robbers who relied upon the saddle horse. A new and greatly enlarged edition of *From Doane to Dillinger* was completed in December 2008.

81. *San Angelo Standard*, 6 April 1901.

82. As will be evident from perusal of a run of any of the larger newspapers and popular periodicals of the period, such as the *Chicago Tribune, San Francisco Chronicle*, and *The Strand* and *Harmsworth's* of London. Sometimes the articles were copied in the local press. As early as December, 1895, a reporter for the *New York World* was assured by Thomas Alva Edison that the horse was doomed: in ten years' time, Edison prophesied, the "horseless vehicle" would cost less than a carriage and pair, and would be cheaper to maintain. He did not think the new contraption would be powered by electricity. The interview was reprinted in the *San Angelo Standard*, 28 December 1895.

83. Meadows 63–70, (all three ed.,) 362–3 (Afterword in 3rd ed.). The pagination of Meadows's book to 361 is the same in all editions, with some rewording at 69–70 to allow for the insertion in the 2nd ed., of evidence shedding doubt on the participation of Cassidy and Longabaugh. Still later, the doubt solidified into certitude, hence the Afterword. See, also, Daniel Buck and Anne Meadows, "Leaving Cholila: Butch and Sundance Documents Surface in Argentina," *True West*, Vol. 43, No. 1, Whole No. 315 (January 1996), 21–7. An earlier look at the Rio Gallegos episode is Buck and Meadows, "Wild Bunch Bank Hold-up in Argentina," NOLA *Journal*, Vol. XV, No. 3 (Winter 1988), 4, 5, 18.

84. Meadows, *Butch and Sundance*, 79, 85, 87, 120–1. Meadows believes Place returned to South America and took part in the Mercedes, Argentina, bank robbery of 19 December 1905, before accompanying Longabaugh to Denver, Colo., where they separated for good. Also: Buck, "The Wild Bunch in South America: Part I—escape from Mercedes," WOLA *Journal*, Vol. 1, No. 1 (Spring-Summer 1991), 3–6, 21; ibid., Part IV, "A Maze of Entanglements," Vol. 11, No. 1 (Fall 1992), 18–21, concluded 13, esp. 20—quotation from *La Prensa*, Buenos Aires, 27 January 1906.

85. Meadows, *Butch and Sundance*, 99–100, 143, 193, 228–38, 240–3, 261–74, 278–80, 343–53; Murray, under dates cited; Meadows and Buck "Showdown at San Vicente," *True West*, Vol. 40, No. 2, Whole No. 298 (February 1993), 14–21.

86. Meadows, *Butch and Sundance*, (2nd ed.,) 69–70; Buck and Meadows, "Hold-up in Argentine," 5; idem, "Leaving Cholila," 26. The view expressed herein that the Rio Gallegos robbers were from Texas is the author's. It rests on the following proposition: Brady is a small town in south-central Texas; the bandit who took it for his name claimed to have stayed on a ranch near Vance, a village in southwest Texas so obscure beyond its own locality that he must have been familiar with the area to have heard of it; the ranch in question belonged to the

father-in-law of a Rio Gallegos druggist named Allsop; bandit Brady apparently said he was the brother of an American woman then living in southern Argentina, whose description resembled that of "Etta Place"; and, finally, Linden is also the name of a Texas town, and a surname sufficiently common in Texas and the South to recommend itself as an alias. It may, of course, be no more than a double coincidence of juxtaposition that McColloch County, of which the city of Brady is seat, is immediately east of Concho County, home of the Kilpatrick brothers, the eldest of whom, William, married a Miss Sarah Allsop in 1896, and lived for some time thereafter in Brady (Soule, 8). A last point: the pair who robbed the Rio Gallegos bank were known to have visited the Cholila ranch of Cassidy and Longabaugh. This circumstance suggests that one or both of them may have known one or both of Cassidy and Longabaugh in North America. It certainly led to the sale of the ranch and the departure of its owners for Chile.
87. Pointer, 203; Bruce Chatwin, *In Patagonia*, 58–9; Buck and Meadows, "Leaving Cholila," 25.
88. French, *Some Recollections*, 238; Brock/Blachly, interview, 8; Alverson, 19. Since none of these sources seems to depend on either of the others, and since all three are unlikely to have been mistaken, the probability must be that all three were right. French, however, was wrong to believe, or assume, that Capehart was Cassidy's partner in South America, while Brock's memory may have been at fault in assigning Capehart to Peru: after the passage of fifty years, Peru, Paraguay, and Patagonia might have been as one to the old cowman. The author's conclusion is that Capehart did go to South America; but, if he kept in touch with Cassidy and Longabaugh, it was definitely not as a fulltime associate of theirs.
89. For an understanding of the causes, course, and social context of the South African War of 1899–1902, the author has depended chiefly on the following studies: Rayne Kruger, *Goodbye Dolly Gray*; Eversley Belfield, *The Boer War*; Thomas Pakenham, *The Boer War*; Emanoel Lee, *To the Bitter End*; Peter Trew, *The Boer War Generals*; David Smurthwaite, *The Boer War, 1899–1902*; Martin Marix Evans, *Encyclopedia of the Boer War*.
   The views that follow are a distillation of this reading, though they were not contradicted by the recollection of impressions gathered by the author during his enforced term of service with the armed forces of the Crown a half-century after the Boer War.
90. Stirling, 114.
91. See Chapter 18.
92. *Atkins ms.*, II, 4–5; Barton, 140–1.
93. The officers named in Atkins's dictated memoirs were Price, Shine (as Shire), Crewe (as Crew), Austin, Anderson, and Lukin. All can be identified from the *Army Lists* published quarterly by the War Office in London, April 1901–July 1902 inclusive. The initials and status of Shine and Crewe are in the text. R.H. Price joined the K.R. as a lieutenant on 5 April 1901, was made second-in-command with the local rank of major, and had become C.O. and colonel by October 1901. R. Anderson, as a Sergeant-major, received a Mention of Despatches from Lord Roberts on 2 April 1901, and was subsequently commissioned. The Nominal Roll of the K.R. shows that G.C. Austin enlisted in the K.R. as a sergeant in January 1901; his commission as a lieutenant followed a few months later. H.T. Lukin became C.O. of the Cape Mounted Rifles, the regular army of Cape Colony, which often campaigned alongside the K.R.
94. *Atkins, ms.*, II. 6; Barton, 141.
95. *Atkins*, ibid., 7–8; Barton, 142. In the typed transcript of Atkins's recollections, Heuningneskloof is rendered as "Hemming"—an obvious misreading of Heuning as handwritten. (Barton has taken it as "Herning.") Either Dave Atkins could not remember the name in full, or he did, but could not or did not spell it out for the benefit of the kinswoman who was transcribing his words.
96. *Atkins*, ibid., 8; Barton, 144; Stirling, 108; Cape Town dispatch of June 5, in *San Angelo Standard*, 8 June 1901.

97. Kitchener's strategy, like the man himself, has always divided opinion. The most thoughtful and concentrated scrutiny of man and strategy is Trew, 88–136, with 100–25 for the South African phase of his career.

98. Stirling, 115.

99. Ibid., 108–9; Kruger, 439–40; Pakenham, 527–8, 561; Marix Evans, 157; *Atkins*, 9; Barton, 147.

100. Atkins spelled the name Burgersdorf, in accordance with common practice at that time. The spelling of many South African placenames seems to have been a contentious issue, presumably through tensions between old Dutch, modern Dutch, and Afrikaans.

101. Stirling, 115. Atkins mentions the adjutant several times (usually with disparagement) but does not identify him by name. His account of the scrap in which Fairweather was wounded includes a date, and it is correct—December 15 (*Atkins ms.*, II, 13–14 and 16). If Atkins did not keep a diary, he must have had an extraordinarily good memory for dates; his reminiscences include many, and those that are not spot-on are never more than a couple of days out. When, however, he placed incidents within the context of a period of weeks or months, he often undershot or overshot the factual mark, whether purposely or not.

102. *Atkins ms.*, II, 14–16; Barton, 152.

103. *Atkins ms.*, II., 16–20 (quotation on 18).

104. *Atkins ms.*, II; 17–27. A place which the transcript calls "Abbershire" can only be Aliwal North, even though it is thirty miles from Burgersdorp—not sixty, as the transcript says. As likely as not, Dave called it Aliwal North; the niece to whom he was dictating wrote down something like "Allerwellnth;" and A.C. Atkins, working from a torn or faded original, read it as "Abbershire." "St. Lulena," as the name of an island for internment, which mystified A.C. Atkins, definitely should have been rendered as St. Helena.

105. *San Angelo Standard*, 19 April 1902. The name as entered in the Nominal Roll, WO 127/11, certainly looks like Drake.

106. Note on inside front cover of Nominal Roll.

107. *Atkins ms.*, II, 28; Barton, 155–6.

108. *Atkins ms.*, II, 28–9; III, 2–3; *San Angelo Standard*, 12 April 1902.

109. Atkins, ms., III, 2–16; Barton, 210, where it is stated erroneously that Atkins began a prison term in 1911; *State of Texas* vs., Dave Atkins (wording as in text); *San Angelo Standard*, 2 September 1919; *Los Angeles Times*, 16 February 1920.

110. *State of Texas vs. Atkins*, No. 1239—January term, 1930: Indictment, Capias, Subpoena applications, Judge's instructions, Verdict, Motion for New Trial (amended), and Jurors' expense claims (WTC, ASU); *San Angelo Standard*, 27 January, and San Angelo dispatch of March 9 in *Dallas Morning News*, 10 March 1920. The author was first advised of Atkins's eventual trial and conviction by Charles E. Avery, San Antonio, Tex. (letter to author, 25 January 1987).

Thomas Green Chaney, to Ruby Mosley, FWP, 4, said that Bill Chaney fought a duel in New Mexico with his brother-in-law Frank Stidham, which ended with both men dead. Evidently Atkins had heard something about this, for at the time of his arrest he alluded to it as a "trumped up" affair (*Standard*, ibid.).

111. Notes and letters in Joel Tom Meador File (WTC, ASU); Barton, 211.

112. *Annual Report of the Attorney General of the United States, 1904*, 134; Alverson, 5, 17–8; Hovey, 51–2, where he predates both the riot and his release by one year.

113. Alverson, 17–8; Benton, III, 47.

114. Alverson, 1, 18.

115. Siringo, *A Cowboy Detective*, 369. In a confidential letter of 14 February 1903, to H.G. Burt, President of the Union Pacific Railroad, to solicit financial support for a project to

send two detectives to South America to search out Cassidy and Longabaugh, Robert Pinkerton described these two as "the last of the 'Wild Bunch,' except William Cruzan." (Horan and Sann, 231.)

116. *The New Mexico Territorian*, Vol. I, No. 11 (June 1962), 6 (article and photograph); Spradley to author, 4 October 2003, with photograph; Thomas Green Chaney, to Mosley, FWP.

117. The monument was put in place by the Historical Commission of Clayton, and Berry Spradley chose the epitaph (Spradley to author, 11 October 2003). Sam Ketchum's son William Berry Ketchum (1876–1951) and his wife, the former Mattie Louise Hines (1886–1961) had four children. The youngest of their three daughters, Wallene Ketchum (1914–2001) married Earnest Clifton "Tom" Spradley (1914–2002) in 1939. Berry Spradley is their son, John Berry Ketchum (1915–73), the only son of William and Mattie Ketchum, married an Englishwoman in 1945. Their three children live in England.

118. Potter, *Lead Steer*, 114, "Sheriff and Police," 25; Titsworth, II, 31–2; A. Thompson, *Clayton ms.*, 52–3, *Open Range Days*, 193–4 (the former being by far the more detailed); Spradley to author, 15 October 2003, with photograph. The quotation is from *Hamlet, Prince of Denmark*, III, 3, 82.

119. Culley, 57.

120. Potter, loc. cit.

NOTES TO CHAPTER 23

One Dead Mexican

1. At 191–3.

2. Ibid. Compare with the text in A. Thompson, *Clayton ms.*, pp. 39–54 of draft of *Early History of Clayton, New Mexico* (for Chapters 13–16), where there is no reference to the alleged incident.

3. Garcia was chosen to succeed Saturnino Pinard in the regular elections held in the fall of 1900. Details of the terms served by all who served as sheriff during New Mexico's (and Arizona's) territorial period are in Larry D. Ball, *Desert Lawmen*, 354–71.

4. St. Louis, Mo., *Post-Dispatch* and *Globe-Democrat*, both 9 November 1901.

5. *St. Louis Republic*, 8 November 1901. Desmond's notion that Laura Bullion, whose background and upbringing were those of the ordinary farmgirl, and who consequently had done little riding and less shooting, was a hard-bitten and hard-riding desperado, was rejected by James D. Horan in the original edition of *Desperate Men* (1949); he did not believe in it, and neither did the Pinkertons. Nevertheless, he did caricature her memorably, but misleadingly, as "a gum-chewing nineteenth century gun moll." (We do not know even that she habitually chewed gum, only that she did so while the St. Louis police were interrogating her.) In *Pictorial History of the Wild West* (1954), by Horan and Paul Sann, the young woman is, on no stated evidence, advanced in the criminal hierarchy to the status of horse-holder, supposedly complaining in a letter to her mother in Fort Worth of the bleakness and loneliness of Hole-in-the-Wall (180). She might have spent some time in Hole-in-the-Wall in the summer of 1901, but she could not have written about it to her mother in Fort Worth, because her mother, who had never lived in Fort Worth, died in 1891. When Horan came to write a supplementary work, *The Wild Bunch* (1958), he incorporated a good deal of new material on the outlaws, but by no means all of it was factual. Laura Bullion now emerged as a participant in the Wagner train robbery; as she was a member of the gang, wrote Horan, it was not thought "strange" that she should take part in a "raise" alongside them. The *Wild Bunch* additions were carried into the

revised edition of *Desperate Men* (1962), sometimes at the expense of more authentic or more carefully written passages in the first edition. Barbara Barton (*Den of Outlaws*, 2000) adopted this more glamorous reading of Laura's role, and takes it a bit further. She counts her in as a participant at Tipton (99) as well as at Wagner (130) and has her "decked out in cowboy clothes and six-guns."

6. Titsworth, II, 20.
7. Loomis, 63.
8. *Tombstone Prospector*, 9 November 1896.
9. Tape recording #128, 15–16 (misnumbered 14–15 in original typed transcript).
10. Tape recording #129, 8–9.
11. Loomis, 66.

"They Got John Legg."

12. "William H. Reno," Obituary Notices in *Denver Post* and *Trinidad Chronicle News*, both 28 October 1935 (clippings courtesy Lawrence R. Reno); Larry Reno to author, 4 September and 26 October 2001, 18 June 2002, 27 June and 2 August 2003.
For the daily newspapers published in Denver during the later 1890s, see Chapter 21, n. 34.
13. Interviews (two) in *Denver Post*, 28 April 1901 (quoted without attribution in Titsworth, II, 31).
14. Ibid., 27 April 1901 (Titsworth, unattributed, ibid.), 23.
15. *Roswell Record*, 17 August 1894.
16. See Chapter 5. Legg is named in the *New Mexican*, 25 June, 2 and 20 July 1896, the last being copied from the *Las Vegas Optic*.
17. *Roswell Record*, 23 and 30 October 1896; E.L. Hall, U.S. Marshal of New Mexico, to Attorney General (Judson Harmon), 20 January 1897 (LR: Justice Year File 13065–1896).
18. *Roswell Record*, 24 and 31 March 1899.
19. "William H. Reno—Veteran Colorado Manhunter," *Trinidad Chronicle-News*, 22 June 1930 (Courtesy Lawrence R. Reno); Larry Reno, correspondence as cited at n. 12.

The Identity of G.W. Franks

20. 250, 252–3, 256–7.
21. 1st ed., 228–9; rev. ed., 253–7.
22. 121
23. The name Capehart first enters French's narrative in *Some Recollections*, 259. At that point French does not connect the name or identity of Capehart with any other.
24. Ibid., 266.
25. Ibid., 267.
26. Waller, 94. Waller names them as Harvey Logan, George Currie, and Elza (Elzy) Lay, but Lay was in New Mexico at the time in question. Since Bob Lee, Loney Logan, and Harry Longabaugh comprised the second of the two groups that were converging on Wilcox, the third man in the first group could only have been Ben Kilpatrick. See Chapter 17, at n. 4.
27. After killing Sheriff Hazen, of Converse County, the Logans and Currie had pressed on in a northwesterly direction for a rendezvous with the other three robbers. The meeting took place early in July. Harvey Logan and Ben Kilpatrick spent the rest of that summer on a jaunt through Wyoming, Nebraska, Kansas, Arkansas, and Texas, finally to go to ground near Alma, New Mexico. See Chapter 17, at nn. 4 and 5.

28. Lamb, "Shootout," 4–5.

29. See Chapter 17, at nn. 4 and 5.

30. Otero, 111.

31. 253.

32. See Chapter 13, at n. 52 and 53.

33. 241–3.

34. 38–9.

35. Livingston, II, 18. On 17–18, Livingston describes Reno's actions after Lay's arrest with the familiarity that seems to bespeak first-hand information. Reno's grandson, Lawrence R. Reno, is certain that there was no written communication between the two men, except for a request by Livingston for a photograph, which Reno ignored. It is possible that Livingston took notes from earlier telephone conversations. The only other possibility, as elsewhere in Livingston's chronicle, is that Livingston secured information at second hand from people who knew Reno well. (Larry Reno to author, 4 September 2001, 2 August 2003.) Albert Thompson did meet William Reno, and got a lot of help from him; he *might* subsequently have passed some of Reno's information to Livingston.

36. *Territory vs. McGinnis*: Wilson Elliott, cross examination by A.A. Jones; William H. McGinnis, questioned by E.V. Long as to whether he had ever called himself Carver. At neither point was it suggested that the authorities believed that "G.W. Franks" was Carver's current *nom de guerre*—odd because the grand jury's recent indictment of "G.W. Franks alias William Carver" proves that the connection had already been established. Long may have been hoping to trap the defendant into an admission in open court that Franks was Carver—or he may merely have forgotten about the indictment. It is apparent that Elliott knew from the outset that Carver was likely to have been in the robbery.

37. 67.

38. Thompson, *Clayton ms.*, 44–6; Culley, 39–40, citing Crocker.

39. 256–61.

40. *San Angelo Standard*, 6 April 1901.

41. Ibid., 5 August 1899.

42. Ibid., and *Territory vs. G.W. Franks alias William Carver, Cause no. 2428—Murder*: True Bill of Indictment—September term, 1899. A third witness, the freighter and part-time detective, James "Billy" Morgan, may also have known that Franks and Carver were different names for the same man.

43. *Rocky Mountain News*, 27 April 1901.

44. *Satan's Paradise: From Lucien Maxwell to Fred Lambert*, 104–6; Cleaveland and Lambert were joint owners of the copyright (which bears out the impression that Lambert supplied much of the story published under Cleaveland's name). Bryan, *Robbers*, 312, provides more detail but a more sober tone in retelling the story, on the basis of an interview with Lambert in 1958, about forty years after the death of the alleged Franks/Capehart.

45. District Attorney Leahy's investigation into McManus's background disclosed that he had come from Indian Territory and had never been charged with any offense there. McManus's obscurity is probably the strongest argument in his favor; if he had ever been guilty of serious wrongdoing in the past, it is likely that Leahy's inquiries would have led to its disclosure. The sole basis for the prosecution of McManus seems to have been his role in the conviction of a man who, like Titsworth and Thatcher, was an ally and ofttimes servant of the Colorado Fuel and Iron Company. McManus's reclusive way of life made him an easy mark. Despite the ignominious collapse of the prosecution, the Titsworths, father and son, seem to have been determined to portray McManus as a member of the gang. Their rationale may have been that, since next to nothing was known about McManus, he could be passed off as a man of mystery and,

as such, justly an object of suspicion. B.D. Titsworth, perhaps on the strength of misinformation from his father, went so far as to insert McManus's name in a newspaper report of the arrest of Elzy Lay near Carlsbad, representing McManus to have been the man who watched from the hill as Lay was arrested (Titsworth, I, 4–6 and 30). We have already seen at length that the watcher on the hill was Will Carver—the one and only real G.W. Franks.

46. Trinidad dispatch in *Rocky Mountain News*, 8 April 1905.

47. *New Mexican*, 7 and 8 April (Trinidad and Raton dispatches, same dates) and 8 May; Trinidad dispatch of April 7 in *Rocky Mountain News*, 8 April 1905.

48. *New Mexican*, 10 April 1905 (Trinidad dispatch, same date); John Tanner, "Black Bob McManus," Research Notes from Governor George Curry, penal papers—Territorial Archives of New Mexico (New Mexico State Record Center, Santa Fe), copy to author.

49. Tanner, "Black Bob McManus."

50. George S. McGovern and Leonard F. Guttridge, *The Great Coalfield War*, 28–32, 108–114.

51. Tanner, "Black Bob McManus."

52. Ibid.

BIBLIOGRAPHY

PUBLIC DOCUMENTS AND RECORDS. OFFICIAL PUBLICATIONS, ETC.

Affidavit: Antonio Borrego to Notary Public, April 17, 1903.

Territory of Arizona:

General Correspondence of the U.S. Marshals: W.K. Meade (1893–97) and W.M. Griffith (1896–1901), Letters Sent and Received, 1896–1901. Arizona Historical Society, Tucson.

An act defining certain offenses against the public peace (February 28, 1889). Arizona State Library, Archives and Public Records, Phoenix.

Documents held by Sutton County (Texas) Historical Society:

Marriage Certificates: Walter Causey/Martha Carver; William Carver/V.E. Byler; William Casey/Callie M. Hunt (copies).

Marriage Records: Comanche County (copy); Index to Marriages in Tom Green County.

Death Certificates: Martha Jane Causey; Frances Emeline Hill (née Carver) (copies); note from Death Certificate of Viana Byler.

Inquest Proceedings: Will Carver.

Records of the Bureau of the Census (RG 29):

Eighth Census of the United States 1860: State of Texas: Counties of Atascosa and San Saba.

Ninth Census of the United States, 1870: State of Texas: Counties of Atascosa and San Saba.

Tenth Census of the United States, 1880: State of Texas: Counties of Atascosa, Bandera, Baylor, Coleman, San Saba, Shackelford, Throckmorton, Tom Green, and Uvalde.

Twelfth Census of the United States, 1900: State of Texas: Counties of Brewster, Sutton, Tom Green, and Val Verde; *Territory of New Mexico—City of Santa Fe* (Territorial Penitentiary).

Thirteenth Census of the United States, 1910: County of Tom Green

State Archives of New Mexico:

Acts of the Legislative Assembly, Thirty-fifth Session: 19 January–19 March 1903. Santa Fe: The New Mexican Printing Company, 1903.

Acts of the Legislative Assembly of the Territory of New Mexico, Thirty-seventh Session (1907). Santa Fe: New Mexican Printing Company, 1907.

New Mexico Statutes – Annotated. Compiled by Stephen B. Davis, Jr., and Merritt C. Mechem. Denver, Colo.: W.H. Courtright Publishing Company, 1915.

Records of the Adjutant General: Report of the Adjutant General from March 1, 1882 to January 1, 1884.

Records of the Territorial Governors, 1846–1912:

Miguel A. Otero (1897–1906): Correspondence re: request for extradition of Thomas Ketchum to Arizona, November 1899.

George Curry (1907–1910): Exhibits Regarding the Application for Pardon on behalf of Lon Meredith (Roll 179, frames 286-473: abstract by John D. Tanner, Jr.).

Records of the Mounted Police, 1905–1911: Scrapbook: Wanted Posters, Book One. Although the force was not formed until 1905, its records include "flyers" for criminals who had been connected in one way or another with members of the Ketchum gang.

Records of the Territorial Penitentiary: Admission Records from November 2, 1886.

State of New Mexico: Records of the Territorial Supreme Court

Reports of Cases Determined in the Supreme Court of the Territory of New Mexico. Columbia, Mo.: E.W. Stephens Publisher, 1902.

Territory of New Mexico vs. Thomas Ketchum—No. 136, Assault of Train with Intent to Commit a Felony. Indictments, Sentence, Testimony and other case and trial papers.

Territory of New Mexico vs. Thomas Ketchum, Appellant—No. 869.

Territory of New Mexico vs. William H. McGinnis—No. 2419, Murder. Indictment, Sentence, Affidavits, Testimony and other case and trial papers.

Territory of New Mexico vs. William McGinnis, Appellant—No. 873.

State of New Mexico: Territorial District Court Records

Territory of New Mexico vs. G.W. Franks, alias William Carver—No. 2428, Murder: A True Bill.

Territory of New Mexico vs. G.W. Franks: Warrant and Endorsement. Colfax County—Criminal cases: Nos. 2402-2908 (1899–1907).

State of Texas:

Texas State Library and Archives Commission

Convict Record Ledgers: VOLS, 1998/088—153 and 154, B Series:
    (1891–1895): Nos. 7341–12177
    (1898–1902): Nos. 17159–22080

Governor's Correspondence: Pardon-Jim Taylor (1896–97)
                                    Pardon-P.F. Keton (1897)

Application for Reward and Proclamation of the Governor (re: Bill Taylor), March 1918.

Correspondence of Adjutant-General of the State of Texas: Letters from John R. Hughes, January, May, and June 1897.

Angelo State University, San Angelo (Porter Henderson Library, West Texas Collection)

State of Texas vs. Tom Ketchum (No. 1198), J.E. Wright (No. 1199), S.E. Powers (No. 1200), and Bud Upshaw (No. 1201): Murder. Indictments, Subpoenas, Applications for Attachment of Witnesses, Requisition Application and Bail Bond (Upshaw), Motions for Dismissal, and sundry other papers relative to Powers murder case.

Inquest Proceedings: T.R. Hardin.

State of Texas vs. Dave Atkins—No. 1272, Murder. Indictment, Applications, Motions; and sundry other papers relative to proceedings in Hardin murder case, 1897–1901.

State of Texas vs. Dave Atkins—No. 1485, Assault to Kill. Indictment (Chaney case).

State of Texas vs. Dave Atkins—No. 1239 and No. 2172, Murder. Applications, Motions, Judge's Instructions and Charge, Verdict, and other papers relative to trial of Atkins on substitute indictment.

Tom Green County Marriage Books, 1875 through 1938.

(*See also* under Manuscripts and Miscellaneous headings)

State of Texas, County of Presidio:

State of Texas vs. Tom Ketchum and Tom Holland—No. 674, Murder; No. 675, Robbery.

State of Texas vs. Tom Holland, Tom Ketchum and S.L. Holland—No. 676, Conspiracy to Murder; Conspiracy to Rob.

(Indictment, Capias, and Sheriff's Return for each case)

State of Texas, County of San Saba:

Index to the Probate Cases of Texas—San Saba County, from January 30, 1866 to June 28, 1939.

United Kingdom of Great Britain and Northern Ireland:

Public Records Office, Kew, Surrey—National Archives of England and Wales:

War Office Papers: WO 126/74 Enlistment forms (Kaffrarian Rifles, etc.); WO 127/11 Nominal roll (Kaffrarian Rifles).

United States Government:

Statutes at Large of the United States of America: Vol. 17; Vol. 18, Pt. 1. Washington, D.C., Government Printing Office, annually. Vol. 18, Pt. 1 consists of the Revised Statutes of 1873–4.

Compiled Statutes of the United States; Supplement 1903. John A. Mallory, Compiler. St. Paul, Minn., West Publishing Co., 1903.

United States Department of Justice:

Annual Report of the Attorney-General of the United States 1896; 1897; 1898; 1899; 1900; 1904. Among the annual Exhibits are statistical summaries of criminal and civil cases commenced, terminated, and pending in each district court; tables showing the numbers and places of confinement of federal convicts; itemized details of the salaries, periods of service, and expenses claimed by and allowed to the individual marshals, deputies, and attorneys of each district; and the Report of the Pardons Attorney.

Letters Received: Department of Justice Year File 13065-1896. This file was opened in 1896 and closed in 1901, after the death of Tom Ketchum. It contains all the correspondence received by the Attorney-General of the United States concerning the operations of the Black Jack gang, the Ketchums, Bronco Bill, and others in Arizona, New Mexico and Mexico, ranging from the reports of the United States Marshals to the complaints of private citizens.

United States Post Office:

Annual Reports of the Post Office Department of the United States: 1896; 1897; 1898; 1899. The annual Exhibits include details of claims for losses arising from the robbery and burglary of individual post offices; summaries of most train robberies with particulars of losses, damage, and injuries sustained and delays incurred; and, occasionally, accounts of "Special Cases."

United States Senate:

Territory of New Mexico—Statehood Bill, November 12, 1902: 57th Congress, 2nd Session, Senate Document 36. Includes evidence submitted to Senate Committee by judicial and legislative officials and law-enforcement officers at various towns in New Mexico.

United States District Courts, Criminal Cases:

United States of America vs. Bob Christian; United States of America vs. William Christian, etc. Various documents of the U.S. Courts for the Western District of Arkansas and the Eastern District of Texas appertaining to the Christians, members of their family, and certain of their associates in the Indian Nations, 1886–1896. (National Archives and Records Administration, Southwest Region, Fort Worth, Texas.)

United States of America vs. Charles B. Collings et al.—No. 626, Conspiracy. Indictment, Affidavits, Bill of Particulars, Verdict, and other case and trial papers. (Records of the U.S. Fourth Judicial District of New Mexico, Criminal Case Files 1887–1910, N.A.R.A., Rocky Mountain Region, Denver, Colorado).

United States of America vs. William Warderman, et al. —Nos. 1217, 1218, etc., Attempt to Rob, etc. District Court Docket, February-September 1898; Indictments, Subpoenas, Instructions, Exceptions, Verdict, and other case and trial papers. (Records of the U.S. Third Judicial District of New Mexico, N.A.R.A. Denver).

MANUSCRIPTS

(A) Louis B. Blachly: Interviews with Pioneers—Tape Recordings and Transcripts

During the late 1940s and until the later 1950s Lou Blachly recorded interviews with many veterans of the New Mexico cattle industry. This material, comprising several hundred spools of tape, was placed in the safekeeping of the Zimmerman Library in Albuquerque. Few transcriptions had been made when the author listened to several of the tapes in September, 1969. By the early 1980s, Blachly's recordings had been constituted into the Pioneers' Foundation Oral History Collection, under the auspices and control of the University of New Mexico, and many, if not most, had been transcribed. The repository of the material is now designated The Center for Southwest Research and it is the author's understanding that the process of transcription is now complete.

The following transcripts have been consulted:

Henry Brock, "The Ambush of Black Jack" and "The Killing of George Scarborough" (part transcript of tape recording, ref. no. unknown, 12-15 June 1952); 10 October 1953, #13.

Elton (E.A.) Cunningham, 10 December 1955, #128; 2 January 1955 [1956?], #129.

Reed Dean, 10 August 1952, #132.

Jack Huchinson, 1957 (exact date not stated), #169.

Mrs. Morons McKeefry and Mrs. Emma Trotter, February 1952, #206.

Marvin Powe, n.d., #236.

Montague Stevens, 28 January 1953, #334.

Montague Stevens and Louis McCrea, n.d. [1953], #341.

Jack Stockbridge, 16 March 1957, #394; 18 March 1957, #380.

(B) "American Life Histories": Manuscripts from the Federal Writers' Project 1936–40

J.A. Byler, San Angelo, to Elizabeth Doyle (1937).

Brook Campbell to Elizabeth Doyle (1937).

Thomas Green Chaney, San Angelo, to Ruby Mosley (1938).

Mrs. Eleanor [Elender] Ervin, San Angelo to Nellie B. Cox (1938).

Hardy Jones, San Angelo, to Nellie B. Cox (1938).

Seaton Keith, San Angelo, to Nellie B. Cox (1938).

Mrs. Helen Ketchum, San Angelo, to Nellie B. Cox (1938).

Dave McCrohan to Ruby Mosley (1938).

Ernest Marshall, Maverick, Texas, to Anne McAuley (1936).

J.H. Yardley, San Angelo, to Elizabeth Doyle (1937).

(C) MISCELLANEOUS

"Reminiscences of Leonard Alverson," as told to Mrs Geo. F. Kitt. Arizona Pioneers' Historical Society [now Arizona Historical Society], Tucson.

The Reminiscences of Dave Atkins: "From 'Mother's Son to the Owl Hoot Trail"; "Dave Atkins in South Africa—Alias L.H. (sic) Drake"; "The Highway is My Home." Transcribed and Annotated by Arthur C. Atkins. Angelo State University, San Angelo, West Texas Collection.

"A Little Outlaw Gang," by Evans Coleman. Arizona Historical Society.

"'He Will Rob No More,'" by Gary Fitterer. Chapter from unfinished biography of Alfred Allee, courtesy Chuck Parsons.

"Red Pipkin, Outlaw," by John D. Tanner, Jr., and Karen Holliday Tanner. Working draft, July 2002, copy to author.

"Red Bob McManus." Research notes by John D. Tanner, Jr.

"The Story of Black Jack Ketchem (sic)," by Albert W. Thompson (1930). Zimmerman Library, University of New Mexico, Albuquerque. (Unpublished monograph, parts of which formed basis of Thompson's later writings on the Ketchum Gang.)

Untitled, marked "W.A. Thompson" 1933. State Archives of New Mexico, Santa Fe. Draft typescript for Albert W. Thompson's book *Early History of Clayton, New Mexico*, published later in 1933.

Untitled, by Karen Holliday Tanner and John D. Tanner, Jr. Working draft on life and outlaw career of William Walters; with endnotes and revisions, 2002–2004.

INTERVIEWS

In June of 1968, Phil Cooke, of Santa Fe, interviewed Fructuoso Garcia and other senior residents of Clayton, New Mexico, obtaining a good deal of unpublished personal reminiscence. Later, in September, 1969, Mr. Cooke interviewed Major Aud Lusk—younger son of Virgil H. Lusk—of Carlsbad, New Mexico. This material was dictated to the author.

George Fitzpatrick, also of Santa Fe, and editor of *New Mexico* magazine, generously made available the results of his own research on Tom Ketchum. Most of Mr. Fitzpatrick's information came from first hand. It was recorded in 1964 and re-recorded for the author by Phil Cooke and Colin Rickards. Among those interviewed were Reymundo Arguello and Miguel A. Otero, Jr.

THESIS

Larry D. Ball. *Southwestern Conditions and Outlawry at the Turn of the Century.* (1968).

NEWSPAPERS

Abilene, Texas, *Reporter*, 1894–1900.
Albuquerque, New Mexico, *Journal-Democrat*, July 18, 19, and 20; August 17, 24, and 30, 1899.
Albuquerque, New Mexico, *Tribune*, May 24, 1949.
Atoka, Choctaw Nation (Indian Territory) *Indian Citizen*, 1895–1896.
Carlsbad, New Mexico, *Argus*, August 18 and 25, September 1 and 29, 1899.
Clifton, Arizona, *Copper Era*, April 3, 1902.
Dallas, Texas, *Morning News*, September 3, 1919; March 10, 1920.
Deming, New Mexico, *Headlight*, December 10, 17, 24, 1897.
Denver, Colorado, *Evening Post*, September 1897, July 1899, April 1901, October 28, 1935.
Denver, Colorado, *Republican*, September 1897, June–July 1899, April 1901
Denver, Colorado, *Rocky Mountain News*, 1896–1901; July–August 1904; April 8 and November 1905.
Denver, Colorado, *Times*, September 1897, July 1899, April 1901
Durango, Colorado, *Weekly Democrat*, December 6, 1906.
El Paso, Texas, *Times* (exact title varies). August 17, 18, and 20, September 4, 1895; June 8, July 7, 1896; May 15-20, November 19 and 20, 1897; January 18, 19, 20, and 22, April 30, 1898; February 4, 6, and 8, 1900; February 13, March 6 and 9, July 29 and 30, August 1, 1902.
Jerome, Arizona, *Mining News*, April 9, 1900.
Kansas City, Missouri, *Daily Drovers' Telegram*, July 2-5, 1898.
Las Cruces, New Mexico, *Rio Grande Republican*, December 17, 1897.

Las Cruces, New Mexico, *Sun News*, July 21, 2002.

Lordsburg, New Mexico, *Western Liberal*, January 21, 1898, September 8, 1899.

Los Angeles, California, *Times*, April 30, 1898; July 14, 18, 23, 1899.

Oklahoma City, Oklahoma, *Daily Oklahoman* and *Weekly Oklahoman*, 1895; *Times-Journal* 1895–1896.

Phoenix, Arizona, *Arizona Republican*, numerous selected issues, 1894–1900.

Raton, New Mexico, *Gazette*, August 31, 1899.

Raton, New Mexico, *Range*, July 27, 1899; April 25, May 2, 1901.

Raton, New Mexico, *Reporter*, July 26, 1899.

Safford, Arizona, *Arizonian*, July 6, 1899; April 14, 1900.

Safford, Arizona, *Graham Guardian*, August 20, 1897, July 16, 1899.

Saint Louis, Missouri, *Globe-Democrat*, 1888–1898.

Salt Lake City, Utah, *Deseret Evening News*, April 1, 1900.

San Angelo, Texas, *Standard*, 1885–1891 (various issues); May 1892–January 1903 (all issues); September 2, 1919, January 27, 1920.

San Antonio, Texas, *Express*, December 29, 1896; May 16, 17, 1897; April 30, May 1, July 2, 3, 4 (late edition), 5 (early edition) 1898.

San Antonio, Texas, *Light*, 1897–1898.

San Francisco, California, *Chronicle*, 1889–1904.

San Saba, Texas, *News*, 1882–1888.

Santa Fe, New Mexico, *Daily New Mexican*, 1896–1905.

Silver City, New Mexico, *Daily Press*, July 27, 1968.

Silver City, New Mexico, *Enterprise*, February–May and November 30, 1883; September 1897–June 1898; February 7, 1941.

Silver City, New Mexico, *Independent and Grant County Democrat* December 14, 1897; September 20, October 4, 1898; April 16, 23, 30, May 7, 1901.

Solomonville, Arizona, *Graham County Bulletin*, 1896–1897; *Arizona Bulletin*, August 11, September 8, 1899; April 6, 13, 1900.

Sonora, Texas, *Devil's River News*, April 6, 13, and 27; May 4, 1901.

St. Johns, Arizona, *Herald-Observer*, August 29, 1942.

Tecumseh, Oklahoma, *Herald*, 1894–1896.

Tecumseh, Oklahoma, *Leader*, 1894–1896.

Tombstone, Arizona, *Epitaph*, April 9, 1900.

Tombstone, Arizona, *Prospector*, 1896–1897, October 16, 1899.

Trinidad, Colorado, *Daily Advertiser*, November 4 and 5, 1897; *Daily Advertiser-Sentinel*, July 12, 19, 20, 21, 22, and 25, 1899.

Trinidad, Colorado, *Chronicle-News*, June 22, 1930.

Tucson, Arizona, *Arizona Daily Citizen*, January 8 and 17, 1898.

Tucson, Arizona, *Arizona Daily Star*, December 10, 11, 15, 16, 17 and 18, 1897; January 16, 1898.

Washington, D.C. *Sunday Star*, April 16, 1905.

BOOKS

Adams, Clarence S. and Joan N. *Riders of the Pecos and the Seven Rivers Outlaws*. Roswell, N.M. Old-Time Publications, 1990.

Alexander, Bob. *Fearless Dave Allison: Border Lawman*. Silver City, N.M.: High-Lonesome Books, 2003.

———. *Lawmen, Outlaws, and S.O.Bs*. Silver City, N.M.: High-Lonesome Books, 2004.

———. *Desert Desperadoes: The Banditti of Southwestern New Mexico*. Silver City, N.M.: Gila Books, 2006.

———. *Lawmen, Outlaws, and S.O.Bs: Volume II*. Silver City, N.M.: High-Lonesome Books 2007.

Axford, Joseph "Mack." *Around Western Campfires*. New York: Pageant Press, 1964; slightly rev. Tucson: University of Arizona Press, 1969.

Bailey, Lynn R. *"We'll All Wear Silk Hats."* Tucson: Westernlore Press, 1994.

Ball, Eve. *Ma'am Jones of the Pecos*. Tucson: University of Arizona Press, 1969.

Ball, Larry D. *The United States Marshals of New Mexico and Arizona Territories, 1846–1912* Albuquerque: University of New Mexico Press, 1978.

———. *Desert Lawmen: The High Sheriffs of New Mexico and Arizona, 1846–1912* Albuquerque: University of New Mexico Press, 1992, 1996.

Baker, Pearl. *The Wild Bunch at Robbers Roost*. Rev. ed. New York: Abelard-Schuman, 1971.

Bartholomew, Ed. *Kill or be Killed*. Houston: Frontier Press of Texas, 1953.

———. *Black Jack Ketchum; Last of the Hold-Up Kings*. Houston: Frontier Press of Texas, 1955.

Barton, Barbara. *Den of Outlaws*. Knickerbocker, Tex.: Barton Books, 2000.

Belfield, Eversley. *The Boer War*. London: Leo Cooper, 1975; rep. 1993.

Broadaway, Douglas Lee. Railroads of Western Texas: San Antonio to El Paso. Chicago: Arcadia Publishing, 2000.

———. *Del Rio, Queen City of the Rio Grande*. Charleston, S.C.: Arcadia Publishing, 2002.

Breakenridge, William M. *Helldorado: Bringing the Law to the Mesquite*. First pub. Boston Houghton Mifflin, 1928; reprint Lincoln: University of Nebraska Press, 1992.

Bryan, Howard. *Robbers, Rogues and Ruffians: True Tales of the Wild West in New Mexico*. Santa Fe: Clear Light Publishers, 1991.

———. *True Tales of the American Southwest, Pioneer Recollections of Frontier Adventures* Santa Fe: Clear Light Publishers, 1996.

Burroughs, John Rolfe. *Where the Old West Stayed Young*. New York: Bonanza Books, 1970; first pub. 1962.

Chatwin, Bruce. *In Patagonia*. London: Picador, 1979; first pub. 1977.

Chesley, Harvey E. *Adventuring with the Old-Timers: Trails Travelled, Tales Told*. Midland, Tex. Nita Stewart Haley Memorial Library, 1979.

Cleaveland, Agnes Morley. *Satan's Paradise: From Lucien Maxwell to Fred Lambert*. Boston Houghton Mifflin, 1952.

Coolidge, Dane. *Fighting Men of the West*. New York: Bantam Books, 1953; first pub. 1932.

Crawford, Leta. *A History of Irion County, Texas*. Waco, Tex.: Texlan Press, 1966.

Crawford, Thomas Edgar. *The West of the Texas Kid, 1881–1910*. Norman: University of Oklahoma Press, 1962.

Culley, John H. (Jack). *Cattle, Horses and Men of the Western Range*. Los Angeles: Way and Ritchie, 1941.

DeArment, Robert K. *George Scarborough: The Life and Death of a Lawman on the Closing Frontier*. Norman: University of Oklahoma Press, 1992.

———. *Deadly Dozen: Twelve Forgotten Gunfighters of the Old West*. Norman: University of Oklahoma Press, 2003.

———. *Deadly Dozen: Forgotten Gunfighters of the Old West: Volume 2*. Norman: University of Oklahoma Press, 2007.

Doherty, Mary Laurine (Owen) and Emma Adams, (Hardesty). *The Folsom, New Mexico Story and a Pictorial Review*. Folsom: The Folsom Museum, 1976.

Dunn, Jerry Camarillo, Jr. *The Rocky Mountain States: The Smithsonian Guide to Historic America*. New York: Stewart, Tabor and Chang, 1989.

Eaton, John. *Will Carver, Outlaw*. San Angelo, Tex.: Anchor Publishing, 1972.

Ellis, John. *Diary of a Hangman*. London: Forum Press, 1997, 2000.

Ernst, Donna B. *Sundance, My Uncle*. College Station, Tex.: Creative Publishing, 1992.

———. *From Cowboy to Outlaw: The True Story of Will Carver*. Sonora, Tex.: Sutton County Historical Society, 1995.

———. *Harvey Logan, Wildest of the Wild Bunch*. Souderton, Pa.: Wild Bunch Press, 2003.

———. *Women of the Wild Bunch*. Souderton, Pa.: Wild Bunch Press, 2004.

Ernst, Robert (assisted by George R. Stumpf). *Deadly Affrays: The Violent Deaths of the U.S. Marshals*. ScarletMask Enterprises, 2006.

Erwin, Allen A. *The Southwest of John Horton Slaughter*. Glendale, Calif.: Arthur H. Clark Co., 1965.

Evans, Martin Marix. *Encyclopedia of the Boer War*. Santa Barbara, Calif.: ABC-Clio, 2000.

Fergusson, Erna. *Murder and Mystery in New Mexico*. Albuquerque: Merle Armitage Editions, 1948.

French, William. *Some Recollections of a Western Ranchman, New Mexico, 1883–1899*. London: Methuen, 1927; reprint New York: Argosy-Antiquarian, 1965.

———. *Further Recollections of a Western Ranchman*. New York: Argosy-Antiquarian, 1965.

Gilbert, Fabiola Cabeza de Baca. *We Fed Them Cactus*. Albuquerque: University of New Mexico Press, 1954.

Graves, Richard. *Oklahoma Outlaws*. Fort Davis, Tex.: Frontier Book Co., 1968; first pub. 1915.

Haley, J[ames]. Evetts. *Jeff Milton: A Good Man with a Gun*. Norman: University of Oklahoma Press, 1948.

Harkey, Dee. *Mean as Hell*. Albuquerque: University of New Mexico Press, 1948.

Harvey, Clara Toombs. *Not so Wild, the Old West*. Denver: Golden Bell Press, 1961.

Hilliard, George. *A Hundred Years of Horse Tracks: The Story of the Gray Ranch*. Silver City, N.M.: High-Lonesome Books, 1996, 1998.

Hoover, H.A. *Tales of the Bloated Goat*. El Paso: Texas Western Press, 1958.

Horan, James D[avid]. *Desperate Men*. First edition New York: G.P. Putnam's Sons, 1949; With Postscript, London: Hammond, 1952; Rev. and enlarged, Lincoln: University of Nebraska Press, 1962, 1997.

―――. *The Wild Bunch*. London: Landsborough Publications, a Four Square Book, 1960; first pub. New American Library, 1958.

―――. *The Outlaws*. Avenel, N.J.: Gramercy Books, 1995; first pub. 1977.

Horan, James D. and Paul Sann. *Pictorial History of the Wild West*. New York: Crown Publishers, 1954.

Hull, Clifford B. *Shortline Railroads of Arkansas*. Norman: University of Oklahoma Press, 1969.

Hunter, J. Marvin and Noah H. Rose. *The Album of Gunfighters*. N.p., Tex.: Warren Hunter, 1959.

Hutchinson, William H. *The Life and Personal Writings of Eugene Manlove Rhodes: A Bar Cross Man* (Norman: University of Oklahoma Press, 1956.

Kelly, Charles. *The Outlaw Trail*. New York: Devin-Adair, 1959.

Kemp, Ben W., with J[eff] C. Dykes. *Cow Dust and Saddle Leather*. Norman: University of Oklahoma Press, 1968.

Kruger, Rayne. *Goodbye Dolly Gray*. London: Pimlico, 1996; first pub. 1959.

Lake, Carolyn (editor). *Under Cover for Wells Fargo: The Unvarnished Recollections of Fred Dodge*. Boston: Houghton Mifflin, 1969.

[Lamb, Frank]. Ed. Alan Swallow. *The Wild Bunch*. Denver: Sage Books, 1966.

Lee, Emanoel. *To the Bitter End*. London: Penguin, 1986; first pub. 1985.

Miller, Joseph (ed.). *The Arizona Rangers*. New York: Hastings House, 1972.

Murray, David. *From Doane to Dillinger: Armed Robbery in America from the War of Independence to the End of the Great Depression*. Inverness, Scotland: privately printed, 2001; draft 2nd ed. (revised and enlarged) 2008.

McCauley, James Emmit. *A Stove-Up Cowboy's Story*. Dallas: Southern Methodist University Press, 1965.

McClintock, James H. *Arizona, the Youngest State*. Chicago: S.J. Clarke Publishing Co., 1916.

McGovern, George S. and Leonard F. Guttridge. *The Great Coalfield War*. Boston: Houghton Mifflin, 1972.

O'Neal, Bill. *The Arizona Rangers*. Austin, Tex.: Eakin Press, 1987.

Otero, Miguel Antonio. *My Nine Years as Governor of New Mexico, 1897–1906*. Albuquerque: University of New Mexico Press, 1940.

Poldervaart, Arie W. *Black-Robed Justice*. Historical Society of New Mexico, 1948.

Potter, Jack M. *Cattle Trails of the Old West*. Clayton, N.M.: Laura R. Krebhiel, 1936; reprint in *Old West*, Vol. 12, No. 3, WN 47 (Spring 1976).

―――. *Lead Steer and Other Tales*. Clayton, N.M.: Leader Press, 1939.

Ringgold, Jennie Parks. *Frontier Days in the Southwest*. San Antonio: The Naylor Co., 1952.

San Saba County History, 1856–1983. San Saba County Commission, 1983.

Santee, Ross. *Lost Pony Tracks*. New York: Charles Scribner's Sons, 1953.

Shinkle, James D. *Reminiscences of Roswell Pioneers*. Roswell, N.M.: Hall-Poorbaugh Press, 1966.

Siringo, Charles A. *A Cowboy Detective*. Chicago: W.B. Conkey, 1912; reprint Lincoln: University of Nebraska Press, 1988.

———. *Riata and Spurs.* Original and revised editions. Boston: Houghton Mifflin, 1927.

Sonnichsen, Charles Leland. *The Story of Roy Bean, Law West of the Pecos.* New York: Devin-Adair, 1943; reprint, Greenwich, Conn.: Fawcett Publications, 1972.

———. *Tularosa: Last of the Frontier West.* New York: Devin-Adair, 1960.

Stanley, F. *No Tears for Black Jack Ketchum.* Denver: World Press, 1958.

Tanner, Karen Holliday and John D., Jr. *Last of the Old Time Outlaws: The George West Musgrave Story.* Norman: University of Oklahoma Press, 2002.

———. *New Mexico Territorial Penitentiary (1884–1912): Directory of Inmates.* Fallbrook, Calif.: Runnin' Iron, 2006.

Thompson, Albert W. *They Were Open Range Days.* Denver: World Press, 1946.

Tise, Sammy. *Texas County Sheriffs.* Albuquerque: Oakwood Printing, 1989.

Tom Green County Historical Preservation League. *Tom Green County: Chronicles of our Heritage: Volume 1, General History; Volume 2, Family Histories.* Abilene, Tex.: H.V. Chapman & Son, 2003.

Waller, Brown. *Last of the Great Western Train Robbers.* Cranbury, N.J.: A.S. Barnes & Co., 1968.

Walters, Lorenzo D. *Tombstone's Yesterday.* Tucson: Acme Printing Co., 1928; reprint Glorieta, N.M.: Rio Grande Press, 1969.

Warner, Matt [Willard Erastus Christiansen], as told to Murray E. King. *The Last of the Bandit Riders.* Caldwell, Idaho: Caxton Printers, 1940, reprint New York: Bonanza Books, 1970s.

Wilkins, Frederick. *The Law Comes to Texas: The Texas Rangers, 1870–1901.* Austin, Tex.: State House Press, 1999.

Wilson, Edward. *An Unwritten History: A Record from the Exciting Days of Early Arizona.* Phoenix: H.H. McNeil, 1915; reprint Santa Fe: Stagecoach Press, 1966.

Wilson, John P., ed. *Pat Garrett and Billy the Kid as I Knew Them: Reminiscences of John P. Meadows.* Albuquerque: University of New Mexico Press, 2004.

ARTICLES

Anon. Report from *El Paso Herald Post*, May 25, 1949. *Frontier Times*, Vol. 28, No. 10 (July 1951).

Anon. "Nervy Express Messenger Kills Two Train Robbers." Orig. in *San Antonio Express* 15 March 1912. Reprinted in *Frontier Times*, Vol. 4, No. 11 (August 1927).

Anon. "Reburial of 'Black Jack' Recalls Last Train Holdup." Orig. in *Fort Worth Star-Telegram.* Reprinted in *Frontier Times*, Vol. 11, No. 1 (October 1933).

Ashton, John. "Billy Anson and the Quarter House." *The Cattleman*, September 1948.

Ball, Larry D. "Black Jack Ketchum: The Birth of a Folk Hero." *Mid-South Folklore*, Vol. 1, No. 1 (Spring 1973).

Bedingfield, John (Dub). "The Spikes-Gholson Feud." *Real West*, Vol. 28, No. 206 (December 1985).

Bell, Bob Boze ("Based on the Research of Bob Alexander and Jeffrey Burton"). "The Blast at Steins Pass: Black Jack Ketchum's Gang vs. Three Express Guards." *True West*, Vol. 55, No. 4, Whole No. 463 (April 2008).

Bell, Mike. "Interviews with the Sundance Kid." *Journal*, Western Outlaw Lawman Association (WOLA), Vol. IV, No. 2 (Summer 1995).

―――. "Did the Sundance Kid Tell His Own Version of What Happened at the Winnemucca Bank Robbery?" *Journal*, WOLA, Vol. IX, No. 1 (Spring 2000).

Benton, Jesse James. "Cow by the Tail." *Frontier Times*, Vol. 38, No. 6, Vol. 39, Nos. 1 & 2, New Series 32, 33, 34 (November 1964; January and March 1965), book serialization.

Buck, Daniel. "The Wild Bunch in South America." *Journal*, WOLA: Part I, "Escape from Mercedes," Vol. 1, No. 1 (Spring–Summer 1991); Part IV, "A Maze of Entanglements," Vol. II, No. 1 (Fall 1992).

Buck, Daniel (see also Anne Meadows). "New Revelations about Harvey Logan." *Journal*, WOLA Vol. VI, No. 1 (Spring 1997).

―――. "Cowboys Meet Gauchos." *South American Explorer* No. 37 (June 1994).

―――. "Leaving Cholila: Butch and Sundance Documents Surface in Argentina." *True West* Vol. 43, No. 1, Whole No. 315 (January 1996).

―――. "Wild Bunch Book Holdup in Argentina." *Quarterly*, National Association of Outlaw and Lawman History (NOLA), Vol. XV, No. 3 (Winter 1988).

Burton, Jeff [rey]. "'Suddenly in a Secluded and Rugged Place . . . : The Territory of New Mexico Versus William H. McGinnis: Cause No. 2419—Murder." English Westerners' Society, *The Brand Book*, Vol. 14 No. 3 (April 1972); Vol. 14, No. 4 (July 1972).

―――. "Bureaucracy, Blood Money, and Black Jack." English Westerners' Society, *The Brand Book*, Vol. 22, Nos. 1 & 2 (Winter 1983 and Summer 1984 double issue).

―――. "Tom Ketchum and His Gang." *Wild West* (December 2001).

―――. "The Duellists of Devil's River." English Westerners' Society, Golden Jubilee Publication *Vignettes in Violence* (October 2004).

Carson, Xanthus "Kit." "That $100,000 Loot in the Malpais Country." *True West*, Vol. 11, No. 6, Whole No. 64 (August 1964).

Clark, Ben R. "William Christian alias Black Jack." *Progressive Arizona and the Great Southwest* (December 1929, January 1930).

Connell, Douglas H. "Battle on Mesa Redonda." *True West*, Vol. 15, No. 6, Whole No. 88 (August 1968).

Cooke, Phil, ed. *The New Mexico Territorian* (most issues, 1961-2).

Dearen, Patrick. "Horsehead to Castle Gap: Trailing the Past." *True West*, Vol. 39, No. 8, Whole No. 292 (August 1992).

Denhardt, Bob. "The Personal Notes of William Anson." *Western Horseman* (November–December 1941).

Dobie, J. Frank. "Belling the Lead Steer." *Old West*, Vol. 12, No. 3, Whole No. 47 (Spring 1976) reprinted from Preface to *The Lead Steer* by Jack M. Potter (1936).

Dullenty, Jim. "Elzy Lay's Outlaw Career Ended in Prison." *Newsletter*, NOLA, Vol. 2, No. 4 (Spring 1977).

Eckhardt, Charles Frederick. "The Last Gasp of the Wild Bunch: Ben Kilpatrick at Baxter's Curve, March 13, 1912." *Hidden History*, San Antonio, Tex., University of Texas, Institute of Texan Cultures, 2001.

Edwards, Harold L. "Pat Garrett and the Las Cruces Bank Robbery." *True West*, Vol. 45, No. 2, Whole No. 358 (February 1998).

Ernst, Donna B. "Unraveling Two Outlaws Named Carver." *Journal*, WOLA, Vol. VI, No. 3 (Fall 1997).

———. "The Real Tom Capehart." *Journal*, WOLA, Vol. IX, No. 2 (Summer 2000).

———. "A Deadly Year for St. Johns Lawmen." *Quarterly*, NOLA, Vol. 25, No. 1 (January–March 2001).

———. "George S. Nixon, More Than One Run-in with Outlaws." *Journal*, WOLA, Vol. X, No. 2 (Summer 2001).

———. "Before the Wild Bunch Struck a Bank in Winnemucca, Nov., They Hit a Store in Three Creek, Idaho." *Wild West* (December 2001).

Farmer, Harold. "The 'Old Timer' of Verde Valley." *Pioneer West* (November 1967).

Hoover, H.A. "The Gentle Train Robber." *New Mexico* (January 1956).

Holt, Roy D. "The End of Will Carver." *True West*, Vol. 15, No. 4, Whole No. 99 (June 1972).

Hornung, Chuck. "They Called Him 'Stuttering Bob': Robert W. Lewis, New Mexico Lawman." *Quarterly*, NOLA, Vol. XXII, No. 4 (October 1998).

Hovey, Walter. (Dorothy Sturges, ed.) "Black Jack Ketchum Tried to Give Me a Break!" *True West*, Vol. 19, No. 1, Whole No. 110 (April 1972).

Huff, J. Wesley. "Malpais Mystery." *New Mexico* (April 1947).

Hunter, J. Marvin . "Black Jack Ketchum and his Gang." *Frontier Times*, Vol. 16, No. 7 (misprinted as No. 6) (April 1939).

———. "The Way of the Transgressor." *Frontier Times*, Vol. 19, No. 3 (December 1941).

———. "George Scarborough, Peace Officer." *Frontier Times*, Vol. 24, No. 9 (June 1947).

———. "Jim Ketchum's Last Stand." *Frontier Times*, Vol. 24, No. 12 (September 1947).

Joyce, W.H. "Hold Up of Southern Pacific Express No. 20—Lozier, Texas." *Main Lines* (May–June 1967).

Kennedy, Bruce W. "Two Faces of Death." *True West*, Vol. 49, No. 11, Whole No. 390 (November 2000).

Kildare, Maurice (Gladwell Richardson). "The Willcox Double Robbery." *Real West* (June 1968).

———. "Who Killed Rogers and Wingfield?" *Real West* (July 1968).

Kindred, Wayne. "The Hunt for the Great Northern Train Robbers." *Quarterly*, NOLA, Vol. XXV, No. 1 (January–March 2000).

Lamb, F. Bruce. "Shootout at Turkey Creek." *Santa Fe New Mexican*, Supplement, March 5, 1978.

Livingston, Carl B. "Hunting Down the Black Jack Gang." *Wide World* (August, September, October 1930; rep. March, April, May 1955).

Lyon, Fern. "Butch Cassidy and the Sundance Kid." *New Mexico*, Vol. 50, Nos. 11-12 (November and December 1972).

Maddox, Holmes. "George Scarborough." *Frontier Times*, Vol. 24, No. 9 (June 1947), reprinted from *The Cattleman*.

Martin, R.I. "A Lively Day in Belle Fourche." *True West*, Vol. 9, No. 4, Whole No. 50 (April 1962).

Mayhall, Mildred P. "George McJunkin's Pile of Bones." *Old West*, Vol. 10, No. 2, Whole No. 38 (Winter 1973).

Meadows, Anne, and Buck Daniel. "Showdown at San Vicente." *True West*, Vol. 40, No. 2, Whole No. 298 (February 1993).

Merwin, Nelle. "The Great Willcox Train Robbery." *Golden West*, Vol. 2, No. 2 (January 1966)

McBryde, Carolyn Bullion. "The Thorny Rose." *True West*, Vol. 38, No. 4, Whole No. 276 (April 1992).

McGaw, Bill. "'Sundance Kid' Taught Alma Youth to Shoot with Right Hand." *The Southwesterner* (January 1962).

Nolen, Oran Warder. "Noah H. Rose—Frontier Camera." *Old West*, Vol. 4, No. 3, Whole No. 15 (Spring 1968).

North, Dick. "When the Tiger of the Wild Bunch Broke Out of the Knoxville Jail!" *Frontier Times*, Vol. 49, No. 5, New Series No. 97 (September 1975).

O'Dell, Roy. "Bank Robbery at Cody, Wyoming: A Who Done It (sic)?" English Westerners' *Tally Sheet*, Vol. 42, No. 2 (Summer 1996).

Parsons, Chuck. "The Fate of Several Texas Outlaws in the Indian Territory." *Okolha*, Vol. 1, No. 4 (Winter 2004).

Potter, Colonel Jack. "Riding with Black Jack." *Sheriff and Police Journal*, Taos, N.M. (May 1941), reprint of chapter in Potter's *Lead Steer and other Stories*, q.v.

Rasch, Phillip J. "Finis for 'Red' Weaver." *English Westerners' Brand Book* (January 1956).

———. "Death Comes to St. Johns." *Quarterly* NOLA (Autumn 1982), reprinted in *Desperadoes of New Mexico*, same publisher, 1999.

Rickards, Colin. "There Were All Sorts of Gunfighters." *Old West*, Vol. 6, No. 1, Whole No. 21 (Fall 1969).

Romero, Trancito (as told to R.C. Valdez). "I Saw Black Jack Hanged." *True West*, Vol. 6, No. 1, Whole No. 29 (October 1958).

Schoenberger, Dale T. "The Tall Texan." *True West*, Vol. 38, No. 4, Whole No. 276 (April 1992)

Secrest, Clark. "'Black Jack Died Game': The Bandit Career of Thomas E. Ketchum." *Colorado Heritage* (Autumn 2000).

Sturgis, Richard W. "I Trailed Black Jack Ketchum." *True West*, Vol. 10, No. 6, Whole No. 58 (August 1963).

Sullivan, Jerry M. "Heist in a West Texas Sandstorm." *True West*, Vol. 21, No. 2, Whole No. 126 (December 1973).

'Tana Mac. "The Long Long Trail." *Frontier Times*, Vol. 35, No. 2, New Series No. 14 (Spring 1961).

Tanner, Karen Holliday, and John D., Jr. "The Great Grant's Robbery." *True West*, Vol. 45, No. 8, Whole No. 377 (September 1999).

———. "Shoot-out at Parker's Well." *True West*, Vol. 46, No. 9, Whole No. 388 (August 2000)

———. "Rewards and Justice Did Not Mix: The Logan, New Mexico, Train Robbery." *Journal* Wild West History Association, Vol. 1, No. 1 (February 2008).

———. "A Tale of Two Photographs." *Journal* WWHA, Vol. 1, No. 4. (August 2008).

Thompson, Albert W. "'Black Jack', the Texas Outlaw." *Frontier Times*, Vol. 3, No. 8 (May 1926), reprinted from Clayton, N.M., *News*.

Titsworth, B.D. "Hole-in-the-Wall Gang." *True West*, Vol. 4, Nos. 2 & 3, Whole Nos. 18 & 19 (December 1956 and February 1957); reprinted in *The Best of True West* (annual), Vol. 2, No. 1 (1978).

Townsend, E.E. "The Robbery of the Valentine Store." *Voice of the Mexican Border* (December 1933).

Weatherby, Chris. "From No Account to Plain Mean." *Old West*, Vol. 10, No. 4, Whole No. 40 (Summer 1974).

White, Marjorie. "Death Pass in the Peloncillos." *Frontier Times*, Vol. 10, No. 4, New Series, No. 42 (July 1966).

Williams, Clayton W. "That Topographical Ghost—Horsehead Crossing." *Old West*, Vol. 11, No. 2, Whole No. 42 (Winter 1974).

Williams, Gary. "New Facts about Kid Curry—Last of The Wild Bunch." *The West*, Vol. 1, No. 1 (March 1964).

MISCELLANEOUS SOURCES

The Army List (Quarterly), December 1877; September 1882–December 1883; April 1901–July 1902 inclusive. The War Office, London.

Basil D. Arthur Scrapbooks, Nos. 3 & 4. A collection of newspaper cuttings, not always dated or identified, but apparently from the *San Angelo Standard* and *Standard-Times* through to the 1940s. Angelo State University, San Angelo, West Texas Collection.

Fort Jordan Stockade, Clayton, New Mexico: *The Black Jack Story*. This attractive little souvenir booklet contains some information given by Fructuoso Garcia, son of the sheriff who was in charge of the execution of Tom Ketchum.

"Ketchum Family History." The product of more than thirty years of research by Berry Spradley, whose mother, Wallene Spradley, was the daughter of Sam Ketchum's only son, William Berry Ketchum. This is perhaps the most important single source of information of all those consulted.

James Landon Lay and Descendants: "Family History Report." Compiled by John D. Tanner, Jr.; copy to author, August 2001.

Lloyds Register of British and Foreign Shipping from 1st July 1899 to 30th June 1900: Vol.1—Steamers. London, Lloyds, 1900.

Lloyds Weekly Shipping Index. Vol. XLII (6 July 1900–18 January 1901); Vol. XLIII (25 January–24 May 1901). London, Lloyds, 1901.

Joe[l] Tom Meador Research Files. Meador, who died in his early forties with his work incomplete, left copious genealogical and general notes on many Southwest Texas pioneer families. The files consulted related to the Atkinses, Bazes, Bullions, Bylers, Ryans, and Upshaws. Angelo State University, San Angelo, West Texas Collection.

Murdoch, Harvey. "Elzy Lay." Address at 9th Annual WOLA Convention, Buffalo, Wyoming, July 22, 1999; transcribed by John D. Tanner, Jr. (Murdoch is the grandson of Lay and his first wife, née Maude Davis.).

Pinkerton's National Detective Agency: File on Tom Ketchum. A slender collection of press cuttings, the most useful being a letter from W.H. Reno dated September 12, 1899, published in the following month's issue of *The Chicago Detective*. For the rest, the file includes a newspaper reprint of Jack Potter's article "Riding with Black Jack" and half a dozen short items on the deaths of Sam and Tom Ketchum. The agency was not asked to investigate any of the Ketchums' crimes; hence the absence of original documents. This material, sparse as it is, appears to have been almost the sole source of information on the Ketchums drawn on by James Horan for his *Desperate Men* and later writings. Library of Congress, Washington, D.C., Manuscript Division: Box 90, Folder 6.

Reno, Lawrence R. "My Grandfather and the "Black Jack" Ketchum Gang." Address at 10th Annual WOLA Convention, El Paso, Texas, July 22, 2000; transcribed by John D. Tanner, Jr. (Larry Reno was the grandson of William H. Reno, who spent most of a lifetime in law enforcement.)

San Simon Cattle and Canal Company: *List of Known Employees*. Transcribed by Willola Elliott.

Sonora, Texas: Annotated street plan of Sonora, as it was circa 1901. Sketched for author by Jo-Ann Palmer, Secretary of the Sutton County Historical Society.

INDEX

References to geographical locations have been included only when the relevant passage contributes to the narrative or to an understanding of it. All references to the endnotes have been excluded, with the exception of a few of the more significant or discursive, since the annotation is in general complementary and subordinate to the text to which it relates.

Blair, James Knox, 268
Blanton, James, 348
"Bob" (indictee), 33, 142
Bochat, Will, 76, 77
Bodry, George, 254
Boer War (South African War), 339
Bogan, William, 180
Bose, John C., 36
Bonito, Severiano, 110
Borque, Atanacio, 63
Borrego, Antonio, 195, 341
Bowie, Ariz., 104, 108, 112, 121, 199
Bowman, George D., 249, 250
Boyd, John, 157, 160, 221
"Brady" (bank robber). *See* "Hood, Bob"
Brady, Tex., 281, 328
Brewery Gulch saloon (Bisbee), 68
Briant, Elijah S., 281, 285, 288–92, 294, 330
Bridge Junction, Ark., 330, 331
Bridger, Mont., 322
Brock, Henry, 264–65
"Bronco Bill." *See* Walters, William
Brooks, James, 250, 251
Brooks, Lizzie (née Weaver), 250
Brown, J. Frazer, 18
Brown, Rube, 150
Brown, W.K., 73, 75
Brown's Hole (Brown's Park), 9, 28, 146, 148, 272–74
Buchanan, R.P., 141
Bucket of Blood saloon, (Pearce, Ariz.), 68
Buenos Aires, Argentina, 275–77, 281, 334
Bull Springs, Mexico, 269, 325
Bullion, Daniel B., 44, 47, 102, 390n.1
Bullion, Fereby (née Byler, later Scott), 44, 373 n.18
Bullion, J. Henry, 44
Bullion, Laura, 44, 46–48, 50, 51–55, 141, 293, 294, 317, 319–21, 327, 330, 332, 333, 339, 345
Bullion, Mary Frances (known as Fannie Lee) (later Hanks), 44, 50, 53, 146, 317, 327, 333, 374n.19
Bunker, William B., 239–43, 298, 301
Burgersdorp, Cape Colony, South Africa, 337, 338
Burk's Creek, Tex., 30, 75, 78, 79, 83
"Burleson's store" (Knickerbocker, Tex.), 50. *See also* Hardin, Thomas R.

Burns, Ore., 50
Burns, James, 76, 136
Burns, Walter Noble, 352
Burrow, Reuben Houston and gang, 33
Bursum, Holm Olaf, 195, 234, 324
Bush Valley (now Alpine), Ariz., 94
Butte, Mont., 251, 252
Byler, Annie Weldy, 14, 15, 44, 50, 51, 60
Byler, Elliott Rucker, 44, 293, 317, 319
Byler, Fereby, 44. *See also* Bullion, Fereby
Byler, Jacob A. (Jake), 44, 59, 60, 293, 333, 373n.18
Byler, Lucinda (later Lambert), 44, 46, 50, 294, 317
Byler, Mary, 44
Byler, Samantha, 44
Byler, Serena, 44, 47, 317
Byler, Stacy, 44
Byler, Viana Elliott (later Carver), 44, 46, 47, 293

CA Bar ranch, 34
Cackley, Ed, 85
Calvert, Mary, 327
Cambridge, England, 16
Cameron, William H., 158
Camp, W.W., 145
Camp Verde, Ariz., 156–60, 205, 218, 252, 307
Campbell, Brook, 73; Robert, 162, 183
Cantrell, John D., 202–204
Cape Colony Volunteers, 336
Capehart, Thomas, introduced, 9–10; as recalled by Axford, 68; as portrayed by French, 68, 200, 247, 258; arrested in Tex Canyon, 113–15 (in Hovey's account, 121); in custody, 116; indicted in federal court, 118; tried at Silver City and acquitted, 119–22; rearrested and taken to Las Cruces, 123, 124; again acquitted, 124–27; released, 127; decides on outlawry, 127–28; believed guilty by Haley, innocent by others, 131; joins WS, 152; and "G.W. Franks" controversy, 188; putative role in Folsom getaway plans, 200, and at Chimney Wells, 205; resumes contact with Carver, 235; joins Cassidy and Weaver, 247; distant connection with Las Cruces bank robbery, 250; French

declines to see Berry, but converses with
Shield, 218–19; forearm amputated, 220;
attempts to trick Stewart and Sloan,
234–35; federal charges delayed, 236;
Otero declines to extradite, 236–37; taken
to Las Vegas, pleads guilty to federal
indictment, 237; sentence deferred, 238;
byplay with bystanders, 238; tried in
Clayton on territorial charge, 238–43;
sentenced to death, and appeals, 243–44,
297, 298–99; Culley on his demeanor,
244; appeal rejected and execution date
reset, 299; Ben Clark and other visitors,
299–30; returned to Clayton for execution, 301–2; disputes about gallows drop,
302; "the bogus respite," 302–3; spurns
spiritual advice, 303, 304; visited by
Thompson, the Guyers, etc., 303; his
"strange request," 304; pre-execution
photos and statement, 304–8; beheaded
by noose, 309–11; Berry refuses corpse,
312; conflicting explanations for decapitation, 312–13; his no-hanging promise
fulfilled, 314; comments of *Raton Range*,
315; body removed to new cemetery,
342–43; commemorative marker added,
343; valedictory verdict, 343; myth of
"Mexican" murder, 344–47; mistakenly
accused of killing Legg, 348–49.
*(Note: The subjects of all subsequent
entries under this surname are identified
by their relationship to the above, unless
stated to the contrary.)*
Ketchum, Alice Doty (niece), 327
Ketchum, Barsha Green (niece), 327
Ketchum, Barsha Ola (née Shields) (sister-
in-law), 31, 50, 327
Ketchum, Chester Van Buren (uncle), 17
Ketchum, Edward (great-grandfather), 17
Ketchum, Elizabeth (cousin), 17, 18
Ketchum, Elizabeth (sister), 17, 18, 19, mar-
ries John Wesley Smith 26
Ketchum, George (born in Mexico, appar-
ently unrelated), 25–26
Ketchum, George W. (cousin), 17, 18
Ketchum, Green Berry Sr., (father), 16, 17,
19
Ketchum, Green Berry, Jr., (Berry, brother),
appearance and characteristics, 29, 32,

328; gang's banker, 13–14, 134, 181; birth
and education, 17, 18, 19; as head of
household, 18, 21; misses 1880 Census,
20; calls Sam and Tom "wild", 22; quarrels with Tom, 22–23, 27, 30, 31, 32, 42;
buys land from Sam and moves to Tom
Green County, 25, 40; settlement with
Sam and Tom, 27; thrives as trader and
stockman, 31–32, 41, 53, 134, 147; head
bitten by horse, 29; marries Barsha Ola
Shields, 31; at San Angelo Fair, 35; a joke
on Tom, 38; joins Democratic club, 38;
threatens Powers, 56; foreknowledge of
Lozier robbery? 75, 301; ranch as gang's
rendezvous and hideout, 78, 82, 134, 146;
arranges Sam's burial in Santa Fe, 195,
198; at Midland carnival, 215, 218; learns
of Tom's capture, 215; Tom's disparagement and refusal to see him, 217, 218,
301, 306, 312; declines Tom's corpse, 312;
Loomis's leg-pull, 314; hunts for Folsom
plunder, 325; later prosperity, local reputation, and last years, 13, 327–28; potential witness for Ben Kilpatrick, 330;
rumored implication in Baxter Curve
robbery scheme, 331–32
Ketchum, Gresella (wife of George, both
born in Mexico), 25–26
Ketchum, Henry (son of Nicholas), 22, mar-
ries Clara Louise Shields 31
Ketchum, Jacob (great-uncle), 16
Ketchum, James (uncle), 16, 17, 18
Ketchum, John N. (uncle) 17, 18
Ketchum, Laura (niece), 22
Ketchum, Lavinia (aunt, marries Reuben
Smith), 19
Ketchum, Louisa J., née Greenlee (sister-in-
law), 22
Ketchum, Margaret (aunt), 17
Ketchum, Mary Ellen (aunt), 17, 18
Ketchum, Mary Reasor (great-grand-
mother), 16
Ketchum, Nancy Blake (sister, marries Bige
Duncan), 17, 21, 41, 42, 134, 328
Ketchum, Nicholas (apparently no relation),
21–22
Ketchum, Nora Blake (niece), 327
Ketchum, Peter Reasor, Sr. (grandfather), 16
Ketchum, Peter R. Jr. (uncle), 17, 18

tion of the fight, 233; takes Tom to
Clayton for trial, 239, 242; believed by
French to suspect him, 247; accuses
Atkins, 253; takes Tom to Clayton for
execution, 301–2; is cursed by him, 303,
307; an uneasy night, 304; interviewed
after execution, 312, 348; sends piece of
rope to Howe, 313; why so often inter-
viewed, 348; wrongly says gang killed
Legg, 348; affirms Carver as "Franks,"
352–53; contact with A. Thompson (but
not Livingston?), 383–84n.41; and
reward poster, 404n.56
Rhode, Print, 250
Rhodes, Eugene Manlove, 70, 82
Richards, Joe, 90, 91, 116
Richland Creek, Tex., 17, 20
Richland Springs, Tex., 19, 21, 23, 25
Rimington, Michael Frederick, 335
Rincon, N.M., 170, 190, 223, 292
Rio Grande City, Tex., 33, 43
Rio Penasco, 204
Rio Salada, N.M., 93
Riverside, Wyo, 276
Robbers' Roost, Utah, 269, 272
Robbins, Joseph E., 210, 242
Roberts, James, 93
Roberts, Mr. and Mrs. Edward J., 120
Rockey (Rocky) Creek, Tex., 40, 287
Rodgers, Emma, 105
"Ro[d]gers, Annie." See Moore, Delia
Rogan, James C., 17
Rogers, James, 409n.23
Rogers, Oliver, 409n.23
Rogers, R.M. "Mack," 156–57, 159–60, 221,
408, 409
Rogers, William, 183
Rollins, Jack, 149
Romero, Secundino, 129
Room Forty-four, 96
Roosa, John, 86
Roosevelt, Theodore, 341
Rose, Jim, 273
Rose, Joe, 273, 320
Rose, William, 158
Rosmead Junction, Cape Colony, South
Africa, 336
Roswell, N.M., 25, 32, 34, 64, 98, 148, 154,
202, 216, 218, 347

Roup, Steve, 234
Rowell, Lawrence F., 148–49
Rucker district, Ariz., 116
Runyon, Charles, 51, 75; Silas B., "Dick,"
58–59, 252
Russell (conductor), 106
Rutledge, J.T. "Tol," 26
"Ryan, Jim." See Parker, Robert Leroy
Ryan, Mark, 146
Ryan, Meritt, 75
Ryan, Virgil, 75
Ryan, Virginia (later Mrs. M.P. Baze), 42
Ryburn, John, 35

76 ranch, N.M., 67
7D ranch, Tex., 7, 11, 143–44
7HL ranch, 34
S Cross ranch, 34
Saguache Creek, Colo., 322
St. John, Charles E., 105, 118, 124; Daisey,
105
St. Johns, Ariz., 258–59, 266, 268–70
St. Paul (ship), 254
Salado Creek, N.M., 93
Salt Lake City, Utah, 147, 280, 323
Samuels station, Tex., 71
San Angelo, Tex., 5, 13, 28. 29, 35, 38, 40, 42,
57, 59, 72, 79, 138–39, 170, 198, 219,
252–54, 282, 294, 314. 319, 328, 336, 340
San Antonio, Tex., 17, 45, 48, 49, 76, 77–78,
80, 81, 93, 135, 251, 278, 279, 280, 281
San Francisco, Calif., 137, 160, 334
San Francisco (Frisco), N.M., 93, 249, 297,
325. See also Upper San Francisco Plaza,
N.M.
San Francisco River, N.M., 93
San Miguel Co., N.M., 60, 62, 66
San Rafael Hospital (Trinidad, Colo.), 211,
213, 215
San Saba Co., Tex., 4, 13, 17, 19–22, 25, 26,
28, 31, 32, 35, 40, 53, 102, 144, 146, 153,
267, 319, 323, 328, (Stock Association),
24
San Saba River, Tex., 17, 25, 30
San Simon, Ariz., 95, 102, 108, 112, 114, 115,
260, 264, 266, 268
San Simon Cattle Co., 95, 102
San Simon Valley, Ariz., 106, 112, 120
San Vicente, Bolivia, 334